The St. Martin's Guide to Public Speaking

The St. Martin's Guide to Public Speaking

Joseph S. Tuman
San Francisco State University

Douglas M. Fraleigh
California State University–Fresno

Bedford / St. Martin's
Boston ◆ New York

We dedicate this work to our families.

Joe: *To my children, Helen and Nathaniel, who grew magically during the five years in which this project was realized, and to my wife, Kirsten, for all her love and support.*

Doug: *To Nancy, who contributed excellent ideas and students, and to Douglas and Whitney, who were interested and supportive.*

For Bedford/St. Martin's

Developmental Editor: Simon Glick
Senior Production Editor: Michael Weber
Senior Production Supervisor: Joe Ford
Marketing Manager: Richard Cadman
Art Director: Lucy Krikorian
Text Design: Claire Seng-Niemoeller
Graphics: Burmar
Photo Research: Robin Raffer
Cover Design: Donna Lee Dennison
Cover Photos: Corbis. Printed by permission of the Norman Rockwell Family Agency. © 1943 by the Norman Rockwell Family Agency; © Bettman Corbis; © Eyewire by Getty Images
Composition: Monotype Composition Company, Inc.
Printing and Binding: R. R. Donnelley & Sons Company

President: Joan E. Feinberg
Publisher for History and Communication: Patricia Rossi
Director of Marketing: Karen R. Melton
Director of Editing, Design, and Production: Marcia Cohen
Managing Editor: Erica T. Appel

Library of Congress Control Number: 2002103115

Manufactured in the United States of America.

8   7   6   5   4   3
f   e   d   c   b   a

For information, write: Bedford/St. Martin's, 75 Arlington Street, Boston, MA 02116   (617-399-4000)

ISBN   0-312-17072-6 (book)
       0-312-25833-X (CD)
       0-312-40458-1 (book/CD)

Acknowledgments and copyrights appear at the back of the book on page 535, which constitutes an extension of the copyright page.

Brief Contents

Preface

As longtime instructors, we have observed many students who struggle in public speaking courses. Even if they do reasonably well on multiple-choice tests that gauge their understanding of public speaking concepts, these students seem unable to deliver good speeches. After twenty years of teaching and countless conversations with instructors and students, we came to the perhaps obvious conclusion that the best way to teach public speaking is not only to teach students the *principles* but also to provide them with a practical way to apply those principles *in practice*. For years, we searched for a textbook that would help us do this but never found one. We were forced to supplement the textbook we were using with our own instruction for applying the text's contents to the actual process of speech making.

And then we stumbled across a textbook that changed everything. Written for composition students, *The St. Martin's Guide to Writing* exemplified the link between principles and practice that we had been emphasizing in our public speaking courses. We were delighted by its self-contained writing guides, which distilled the writing process into discrete skills and strategies and then helped students apply them to the business of developing, drafting, and revising papers. It occurred to us that a similar approach to principles and practices would benefit public speaking students as well. Why not use the framework of this *writing* text as a model for a new *public speaking* text? We set out to write a book that would emphasize the process of speech preparation while showing how to link principles with practice: *The St. Martin's Guide to Public Speaking*.

So how exactly does *The St. Martin's Guide to Pubic Speaking* work? First, we offer students clear explanations of public speaking principles and practical advice for developing their speeches. Then we go one step further by giving students a useful framework for speech making that takes them from invention to delivery, at every step of the process helping them apply the key skills they have learned. When students begin to think of public speaking as a craft consisting of a set of learnable skills, they see that giving speeches is like other tasks they perform every day. Their speech apprehension diminishes, their skills improve quickly and dramatically, and their confidence soars. We have found that with the preparation and practice steps outlined in this book, most students can become good public speakers.

Features

● *Speech Guides*

The second part of the book contains, for us, its most exciting innovation. In it, unique Speech Guides walk students through the speech-making process for each of the most commonly assigned speech types: informative (Chapter 14), persuasive (Chapter 15), special occasion (Chapter 16), and impromptu (Chapter 17).

Each Speech Guide offers a self-contained framework for working through the process of speech making from start to finish.

Marginal references to the free CD-ROM encourage students to access the unique guide pedagogy in an interactive format.

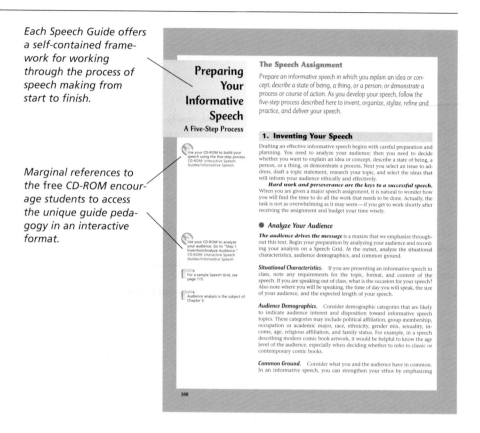

Preparing Your Informative Speech
A Five-Step Process

Use your CD-ROM to build your speech using the five-step process. CD-ROM: Interactive Speech Guides/Informative Speech

Use your CD-ROM to analyze your audience. Go to "Step 1 Invention/Analyze Audience." CD-ROM: Interactive Speech Guides/Informative Speech

For a sample Speech Grid, see page 115.

Audience analysis is the subject of Chapter 5.

The Speech Assignment

Prepare an informative speech in which you *explain* an idea or concept; *describe* a state of being, a thing, or a person; or *demonstrate* a process or course of action. As you develop your speech, follow the five-step process described here to invent, organize, stylize, refine and practice, and deliver your speech.

1. Inventing Your Speech

Drafting an effective informative speech begins with careful preparation and planning. You need to analyze your audience; then you need to decide whether you want to explain an idea or concept, describe a state of being, a person, or a thing, or demonstrate a process. Next you select an issue to address, draft a topic statement, research your topic, and select the ideas that will inform your audience ethically and effectively.

Hard work and perseverance are the keys to a successful speech. When you are given a major speech assignment, it is natural to wonder how you will find the time to do all the work that needs to be done. Actually, the task is not as overwhelming as it may seem—if you get to work shortly after receiving the assignment and budget your time wisely.

● *Analyze Your Audience*

The audience drives the message is a maxim that we emphasize throughout this text. Begin your preparation by analyzing your audience and recording your analysis on a Speech Grid. At the outset, analyze the situational characteristics, audience demographics, and common ground.

Situational Characteristics. If you are presenting an informative speech in class, note any requirements for the topic, format, and content of the speech. If you are speaking out of class, what is the occasion for your speech? Also note where you will be speaking, the time of day you will speak, the size of your audience, and the expected length of your speech.

Audience Demographics. Consider demographic categories that are likely to indicate audience interest and disposition toward informative speech topics. These categories may include political affiliation, group membership, occupation or academic major, race, ethnicity, gender mix, sexuality, income, age, religious affiliation, and family status. For example, in a speech describing modern comic book artwork, it would be helpful to know the age level of the audience, especially when deciding whether to refer to classic or contemporary comic books.

Common Ground. Consider what you and the audience have in common. In an informative speech, you can strengthen your ethos by emphasizing

388

Each of these chapters offers a self-contained framework for working through the process of speech making from start to finish. These chapters begin with speech models—student and professional—accompanied by analyses of how the speakers used the principles covered in the first part of the book. Then the Speech Guides in each chapter help students implement the principles of effective speech preparation by leading them through the five steps of crafting their own speeches—invention, organization, development, refinement and practice, and delivery. The advice in each guide is tailored to each of the speech types. We ask students to consider their speech purpose, audience analysis, and ethical principles and then to use critical thinking skills to make good decisions about how to prepare and deliver their message.

We have provided briefer versions of these guides in other parts of the book where they will be of the most help: A Quick-Start Speech Guide on the inside front cover provides students with a helpful road map for preparing and delivering a typical "first week of class" speech; and a Basic Speech Guide in Chapter 2 provides a brief but thorough overview of the speech-making process to help students develop and deliver an effective speech before there has been time to cover all the key public speaking concepts in class.

The book emphasizes that speech making is a manageable *process* that can be tackled a little bit at a time. We have found that this step-by-step approach reduces students' intimidation and procrastination to ensure that they prepare early and well.

● *Speech Grids*

Rather than simply telling students that audience considerations are important, *The St. Martin's Guide to Public Speaking* demonstrates that crafting an effective speech depends on considering the audience at every step of the process. To emphasize this point, we have developed an innovative tool: *Speech Grids* that *show* students how audience considerations inform every choice they will make. Take a look, for example, at pages 137–38, 220–21, and 521–25. These *Speech Grids* are an extraordinarily useful tool that grew

Speech Grid: *Driving with cell phones*
Topic: *Cell phones and driving*
Specific purpose: *To persuade my audience to use cell phones safely while driving.*
Thesis: *Audience members should use cell phones safely when driving.*

AUDIENCE ANALYSIS	SPEECH MESSAGE
Situational Characteristics • *8 min. speech* • *25–30 in audience* • *small classroom* • *limited a-v equip.*	**ETHOS** • *I have used a cell phone in a friend's car; it was distracting.* • *I had a friend who was hurt in a cell phone distraction-related accident.* • *I have researched the topic in the library, online, and talked to friends who use cell phones while driving.*
Demographics **Age:** *17 (5); 18 (17); 19 (4); 20 (1); 22 (1)* **Ethnicity:** *African-American (2); Hmong (2); white (9); Latino/a (6); Portuguese (2); Pacific Islander, Mexican, German, Japanese, Swedish, Greek (1 each); did not say (1)* **Major:** *Undeclared (9); Liberal Studies (5); Chem, Bus, Crim (2 each); Child Devel, Engl, Bio, Premed, Journalism, Ag Bus, Econ, Comm (1 each)*	**PATHOS** • *Cell phones make users feel comfortable in unfamiliar places.* • *Photo of car involved in fatal accident.* • *Examples of cell phone–related accidents. (Source 6 — fatal accident — no source quals? Source 8 — head injury)* • *Narrative of troubles of friend who was in accident.* • *Lawyer notes that cell phone records will make litigation against driver easier. (Source 9)*
Common Ground *I, like most of class (20 students), do not own a cell phone.*	**LOGOS — Problem** • *85% of cell phone owners use in car sometimes; 27% use in half of trips. (Source 1)* • *Cell phone usage high; 40% growth rate. (Source 2)* • *Inattention increases accident risk. (Source 5 — STUDY plus Dept. of Transportation stat that inattention is a factor in 50% of accidents)* • *Studies show accident risk. (Source 5 — cites 3 good studies!)* • *10% of crashes caused by cell phone use. (Source 8 — politician quote, no study)* • *You can be cited if cell phone use causes bad driving. (Source 11)* • *Better, definitive data on cell phone risks needed. (Source 1)*
Prior Exposure • *Few (7 students) had heard about the issue of cell phones and driving; it had not been major topic in the local media.* • *Most students (20) do not own a cell phone.* • *Most who own a cell phone (6 of 8) use their phone in their car, primarily in one car.* • *Most (24 of 28) think that drunk drivers cause more accidents than cell phone users.*	**LOGOS — Cause** • *Wireless industry lobby opposes anti–cell phone laws. (Source 5)* • *People like the convenience of car phones, save time in busy world. (Sources 1, 2)* • *Communities don't want to be anti-business or anti-tech. (Source 4)* **LOGOS — Solution** • *Many states, nations considering laws against use. (Sources 5, 9)* • *Visual aid idea — video showing safe use tips.* • *Tips for safe use. (Sources 7, 12 — AAA and insurance co. tips)* • *Technology to make use as safe as possible. (Source 1)*
Audience Disposition • *Most (20 of 28) support a law banning cell phone use while driving.* • *People who do not own a cell phone are more likely to support such a law (18 of 20). Cell phone owners are opposed (2 of 8).*	• *Hands-free phones costly, may cause more accidents. (Sources 1, 4)* • *Ideas — pull over to use phone; only use when urgent; don't use to chat or make routine appointments.* • *Possible disadvantage: unfair to single out one distraction. (Source 4)* • *Cell phones help in emergency situations. (Sources 1, 4)*

Sources
See p. 176.

See p. 176.

Speech Grids help students consider the audience at every stage of the process. On the left, students answer questions about audience and context; on the right, they consider the speech message.

out of our many years of classroom experience. Each grid divides the work of speech making into two parts: On the left of the grid students ask and answer question about their audience and context; on the right, they consider topic, thesis, structure, and style. The choices students make on the right are informed by the answers they've given on the left. We have found that students deliver better speeches when they use one of these grids to prepare, so examples are carried throughout the text: Chapters 5 through 12 show the evolution of a single grid through all five steps of the speech-making process; and Appendix A offers full Speech Grids for the guides to informative, persuasive, and special occasion speaking.

● *Extensive Coverage of Principles*

The thirteen foundation chapters that comprise Part One explain the public speaking process in depth and treat all the topics and concepts traditionally assigned in an introductory speech course. Chapters 1 and 2 offer a general introduction to public speaking. Chapters 3 through 12 cover the essential skills and concepts of public speaking—including ethics, listening, audience analysis, topic selection, research, organization, message development, language, delivery, and the use of audiovisual aids. Chapter 13 shows students how the skills and concepts of the first twelve chapters can be applied to situations in other courses, on the job, or in the community.

Audience-Driven Approach.   Audience analysis and adaptation is the keystone of speech development and delivery. Accordingly, we emphasize it at every stage of the speech-making process. We introduce audience considerations in Chapters 1 and 2 and define public speaking as a transaction between speaker and audience. Later, the Speech Grids, in particular, reinforce the essential fact that the audience drives the message.

Emphasis on the Benefits of Public Speaking.   We want students to understand that public speaking skills are important and useful both in and out of the classroom. Chapter 1 begins by showing how public speaking is a must-have skill for college and beyond; Chapter 13 shows students how to use their skills once they leave the confines of the classroom and offers guidance on speaking in the community and on the job.

Abundance of Student and Professional Speeches.   Throughout the book we have tried to provide more practical examples than any other public speaking text. Twelve full-text speeches and more than fifty excerpts are drawn from a diverse body of sources including speech classrooms, the workplace, special occasions, and public addresses.

Comprehensive Coverage of Technology.   Chapter 7's discussion of how to research and evaluate the credibility of electronic sources combined with Chapter 12's advice on how to use the latest technologies to create effective visual aids and make sense of presentation software and equipment ensures that students can take full advantage of twenty-first century resources.

Robust Treatment of Ethics. We introduce ethics in Chapter 1 as a fundamental concept in effective public speaking, and Chapter 3 is devoted entirely to the subject. But we have tried to raise the topic in every instance where it could be an issue. In discussing audience analysis, for example, we caution students against inventing or exaggerating personal experience to build rapport, and ethical considerations are a fundamental consideration in the Speech Guides. In discussing listening, we offer unique guidance on becoming an ethical audience member. No other book offers such a thorough and thoughtful treatment of honesty.

Focus on Critical Thinking. Every teacher of public speaking wants students to think critically; we show them how. Chapter 4 presents practical advice for thinking critically and for processing information and questions on-the-spot. It also offers unique coverage of ethical listening. In addition to emphasizing the importance of critical thinking to successful speech making throughout the book, we follow every sample speech with an in-depth analysis that shows students how to assess the speeches of others and apply what they have learned to their own work.

Relevant Integration of Theory. Although we focus on the "how tos" of preparing a speech, all our advice is grounded in theory. The five-step preparation and delivery process that serves as the foundation of every Speech Guide is modeled on the classical canons of rhetoric. We consistently include references to literature that underlies the public speaking principles. An "In Theory" box in each of the first twelve chapters highlights a related area of research. These remind students of the significant classical and contemporary scholarship underlying the speech preparation process.

Apparatus That Benefits Learning. All the features in the *St. Martin's Guide to Public Speaking* have been designed to help students navigate the text, to reinforce topics, and to provide guidance for the process of developing and delivering speeches. Opening *objectives, vignettes,* and *maxims* drive home the central message of each chapter. *Theory boxes* in the first twelve chapters highlight recent findings in communication theory within the context of classical rhetoric. Marginal *tip boxes* throughout the text highlight important considerations of particular help to students. And end-of-chapter *summaries* and *checklists* provide an active review and application of chapter concepts.

● The St. Martin's Guide to Public Speaking: Interactive Guides and Models CD-ROM

Bedford/St. Martin's has worked with us to create a state-of-the-art companion CD-ROM that delivers the book's unique pedagogy in an interactive format. Because we know how important speech models are for students, the CD-ROM includes five full student speeches plus more than forty excerpts from professionals and students, each supported by commentary and analysis. Unlike video banks that provide students with an undifferentiated list of

Video Theater

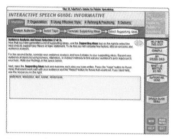

Interactive Speech Guide

examples, this unique *Video Theater* offers commentary and analysis of speeches included in the text and allows students to call up video while they're working on their speeches—*showing* rather than *telling* about the process. In addition, four *Interactive Speech Guides* extend Part Two's innovative approach by replicating the process of developing a speech, and a *Visual Presentation Tutorial* helps students integrate visual aids into their speeches and use Microsoft PowerPoint. Most important, the CD-ROM is *fully integrated* with the text. We have put thumbnail icons in the book's margins to show students exactly where on the CD they can find the electronic resources that will reinforce and extend what they learn. For more information, see the inside back cover of this text.

Resources For Students and Instructors

Resources for Students

Student Workbook

Chrys Egan, *Salisbury University;* ISBN 0-312-25829-1
This valuable workbook provides guidance for preparing informative, persuasive, and special occasion speeches and provides students with the opportunity to practice critical skills covered in the main text. It includes exercises, evaluation forms, blank speech grids, and help with organizing and outlining speeches.

Media Career Guide: Preparing for Jobs in the 21st Century, Third Edition

James Seguin, *Robert Morris College;* ISBN 0-312-39556-6
Practical and student-friendly, this up-to-date guide includes a comprehensive directory of media jobs, practical tips, and career guidance for students considering a major in communication studies and mass media.

Untangling the Web: A Guide to Mass Communication on the Web, Third Edition

Deborah Greh, *St. John's University;* ISBN 0-312-39557-4
This guide offers practical advice for novices and experts on accessing information from the Internet, conducting searches, and evaluating and citing sources.

Research and Documentation in the Electronic Age, Third Edition

Diana Hacker, *Prince George's Community College;* 0-312-25862-3
This handy booklet covers everything students need for college research assignments at the library and on the Internet, including advice for finding and evaluating Internet sources.

Resources for Instructors

Instructor's Resource Manual

Chrys Egan, *Salisbury University;* ISBN 0-312-25832-1
This comprehensive manual is a valuable resource for new and experienced instructors alike. It includes full-text speeches and analysis, plus additional

assignments, activities, exercises, advice, and ideas for teaching from the book and CD-ROM.

Testing Program
Chrys Egan, *Salisbury University*
Computerized Test Bank ISBN 0-312-25827-5;
Print Test Bank ISBN 0-312-25828-3
The St. Martin's Guide to Public Speaking offers a complete testing program, available in print and for Windows and Macintosh environments. Each chapter includes multiple-choice, true false, and fill-in-the-blank exercises as well as essay questions. Sample midterm and final examinations are also included.

Companion Web Site at <www.bedfordstmartins.com/stmartinsspeak>
Visit our site that offers guided exercises and quizzes, Web-based research activities, printable sample speech outlines, annotated research links, Power-Point slides for instructors, and much more.

PowerPoint Presentations
Available at <www.bedfordstmartins.com/stmartinsspeak>, these slides provide support for the key concepts in each chapter. They allow instructors to make classroom presentations with greater visual impact. Instructors can customize them to fit their own needs.

Blackboard and WebCT E-Packs
Blackboard ISBN 0-312-40277-5; WebCT ISBN 0-312-40275-9
New e-packs offer instructors the power of online course management along with *The St. Martin's Guide to Public Speaking*'s superior pedagogical content. Visit <www.bedfordstmartins.com/stmartinsspeak>, <www.blackboard.com>, or <www.webct.com> for more information.

The Bedford/St. Martin's Video Library
A wide selection of contemporary and historical videos focuses on public speeches and media-related issues. Qualified instructors are eligible to select videos from the resource library upon adoption of the text.

Acknowledgments

A great many people contributed much to the creation of this book, and we would like to express our gratitude here. Many teachers and coaches played a significant role in our development as public speakers from a young age. They include Jack Heald, Rogierre Wilcox, Mike Dues, John Brydon, Barbara O'Connor, Jeff Ruch, and David Wagner. Without their involvement and encouragement, it is unlikely we would have been attracted to this field in the first place. We would also like to acknowledge and thank David Green for his insights about audience analysis and his original thoughts about a speech grid, and Fred Stripp for his early contributions on delivery mechanics.

We also owe a tremendous debt of gratitude to the people who devoted their time and creativity to the details, design, and wordsmithing of this project. We thank Patricia Rossi for shepherding the project and providing ongoing support: Jennifer Bartlett for her overall editing and many hours spent coordinating the diverse efforts that went into this work; Joanne Tinsley for her excellent developmental editing; Simon Glick for his technical virtuosity in developing the CD-ROM; Michael Weber for supervising the editing and production of the manuscript; Patricia Herbst for her fine copyediting; Roberta Sobotka for her superb proofreading; our colleague and friend Professor Joseph Corcoran for writing content for the CD-ROM; and Suzanne Phelps Weir, Nancy Perry, and Michael Gillespie for their involvement with the manuscript in its early form. We thank Bedford/St. Martin's presidents Charles Christensen and Joan Feinberg for supporting this project and sharing their experience and expertise in textbook publication. We would also like to acknowledge Chrys Egan for her excellent work on the Instructor's Manual, Student Workbook, and Testing Program. We appreciate the efforts of Editorial Assistant Jessica Stockton, Editorial Intern Lisa Schlein, Photo Researcher Robin Raffer, Art Directors Lucy Krikorian and Donna Dennison, Managing Editor Erica Appel, Senior Production Supervisor Joe Ford, New Media Director Denise Wydra, and Vice President of Electronic Media Reid Sherline, each of whom played an important role in the production of this textbook. For their help in developing the student videos and CD-ROM, we are grateful to Lisa Pedicini; Midge Goldberg and everyone at A/T Media Services; John Philip and Tammie Meem; David Mogolov; and Roger Cook of the Educational Video Group. Equally significant have been the contributions of Kazuko Nashita and Donna Smith for word processing and clerical assistance.

We are very appreciative of our students who contributed to this textbook. Afua Danso, Amanda J. List, Chadwick Meyer, Enrique Morales, Lillian Gentz, and Anna Martinez contributed their time and creative energy to the production of speeches for the text and the CD-ROM. Nur Bernard, Merry Cox, Austin Ellsworth, Christian Fattorusso, Whitney Fraleigh, Brian Gamble, Rachel Harding, Ginger Huang, Sean Mackiewitz, Delphine Suter, and Mark Zemel also contributed to the CD-ROM. Robin McGehee shared her speech for use as our sample full text and extemporaneous outline in Chapter 8. We also thank all the students who shared excerpts from their speeches for use as examples, including Erica Contreras, Olivia Echeverria-Bis, Beu Her, Eric Johnson, Hyun-Jung Kim, and Liz Willey.

Many of the ideas for this textbook came from our experience teaching public speaking over the past twenty years. We thank the people who gave us the opportunity to teach and (later in our careers) the opportunity to include writing as a part of our professional life. They include Bill Southworth, Francie Tidey, Barbara Ore, Pam Stepp, Ralph Thompson, Roy Colle, and the communication faculties at California State University–Fresno and San Francisco State University, who supported our efforts to become tenure-track, and ultimately tenured, professors.

In addition, we wish to acknowledge the major contributions of the reviewers who provided encouragement and constructive suggestions throughout the development of this textbook. These reviewers include Todd Allen, Geneva College; Mike Bauer, Ball State University; Sandra Berkowitz, University of Maine; Elizabeth Berry, California State University–Northridge; Dacia Charlesworth, Southeast Missouri State University; Dominic Chavez, Texas A & M University; Crystal Coel, Murray State University; Marion

Courvillion, Mississippi State University; William Davidson, University of Wisconsin-Stevens Point; Michele Dolfin, Front Range Community College; George Fleck, Borough of Manhattan Community College; Karen Fontenot, Southeastern Louisiana University; Gwen Fuller-Stewart, Miami Dade Community College–North; William Fusfield, University of Pittsburgh; Kelby Halane, Clemson University; Christopher Harlos, North Carolina State University; Sandy Kamp, South Suburban College; Kara Laskowski, Juniata College; Bruce Loebs, Idaho State University; Libby McGlone, Columbus State Community College; Michael Murray, University of Missouri–St. Louis; Kay Neal, University of Wisconsin–Oshkosh; Rolland C. Petrello, Moorpark College; Karla Scott, St. Louis University; Kirt Shineman, Glendale Community College; June H. Smith, Angelo State University; Bill Snyder, Valencia Community College; Stella Steagall, El Paso Community College; Linda Loomis Steck, Indiana University at South Bend; Roxanne Sutherland, Clark College; Robert Terrill, Indiana University; Belinda Collings Thomson, Brescia University; Tom Veenendall, Montclair State University; Debra Vinik, Bronx Community College; Molly Meijer Wertheimer, Pennsylvania State University–Hazleton Campus; and Melinda Womack, Santiago Community College.

Special thanks to those who reviewed the book at multiple stages of revision and those who class tested chapters, including Mike Applin, Southeastern Lousiana University; Melissa Beall, University of Northern Iowa; Angela Gibson, Shelton Community College; Beverly Hendricks, California State University–San Bernardino; David Kosloski, Clark College; Elizabeth Patrick, Olivet Nazarene University; Charla Markham Shaw, University of Texas at Arlington; Mary Kay Switzer, California Polytechnic University–Pomona; David Walker, Middle Tennessee State University; Lena Hegi Welch, Tevecca Nazarene University; and Jeffrey A. Wells, Olivet Nazarene University.

This textbook is one byproduct of a friendship that began over twenty-five years ago at the 1977 Governor's Cup Speech and Debate Tournament in Sacramento, California. Although the project has required countless hours of hard work and perseverance, it has been a pleasure to work collaboratively to create this, our second textbook, together.

Contents

PART ONE

The Process of Public Speaking 1

1

Introducing Public Speaking 2

2

The Process of Developing a Speech 32

Interactive Guides and Models CD-ROM

Video Resources

Full Student Speeches

Informative Speech: Amanda J. List, *Gender-Based Responses in Sports Chatrooms*

Persuasive Speech: Anna Martinez, *"Extra Credit" You Can Live Without*

Persuasive Speech: Enrique Morales, *Without Liberty and Justice for All*

Special Occasion Speech: Lillian Gentz, *My Hero, Marilyn Hamilton*

Impromptu Speech: Frederick Garvin, *Should Possession of Marijuana Be Decriminalized?*

Speech Excerpts

Excerpt Number	Subject	Excerpt Number	Subject
1.1	Great Public Speeches (John F. Kennedy)	8.3	Using Transitions
1.2	Great Public Speeches (Barbara Jordan)	8.4	Using Signposts (Franklin D. Roosevelt)
1.3	Great Public Speeches (George W. Bush)	8.5	Using an Internal Summary
1.4	Speaking to a Diverse Audience (Jesse Jackson)	8.6	Using Humor in the Introduction (Nelson Mandela)
2.1	Appealing to Ethos (Elizabeth Dole)	8.7	Presenting a Memorable Clincher in the Conclusion
2.2	Appealing to Logos (Fidel Castro)	9.1	Incorporating a Definition (Dalai Lama)
2.3	Appealing to Pathos (Lou Gehrig)	9.2	Including the Audience in the Solution
2.4	Appealing to Pathos (Richard Nixon)	10.1	Do Not Overuse Technical Language
3.1	Making an Ethical Appeal to Pathos (Christopher Reeve)	10.2	Using Vivid Language (Heather Lamm)
5.1	Crafting Audience-Centered Messages (Barbara Bush)	11.1	Do Not Apologize for Speaking Errors
5.2	Using the Speech Grid for Audience Analysis	11.2	Making Good Eye Contact (Ronald Reagan)
5.3	Asking a Rhetorical Question	11.3	Using Effective Gestures (Colin Powell)
6.1	Narrowing a Topic	12.1	Using an Object as a Visual Aid
7.1	Supporting a Claim with a Personal Narrative	12.2	Using a Photograph as a Visual Aid
7.2	Using Statistical Evidence (Sarah Brady)	12.3	Using PowerPoint as a Visual Aid
7.3	Citing Experts Properly	12.4	Do Not Create Visual Aids While Speaking
8.1	Presenting a Complete Introduction	17.1	Bridging an Impromptu Speech Topic
8.2	Advocating a Value Judgement (Elizabeth Glaser)	17.2	Audience Analysis in an Impromptu Speech

PART ONE

The Process of Public Speaking

1 Introducing Public Speaking

OBJECTIVES

After reading Chapter 1, you should understand:

- The relevance of public speaking to your education, career, and community life.

- The deep, historical tradition of public speaking.

- The dynamic, evolving components of public speaking.

- The common tendency to feel anxiety about public speaking, and how to minimize that apprehension and use it in your favor.

Imagine it is the first day of a new semester, and students who arrived early for their public speaking class are getting acquainted. Public speaking is a graduation requirement at their college, drawing students from every department on campus. For most of the students this will be their first speech class in high school or college. They have a range of beliefs and attitudes about public speaking similar to those of the students we have taught for the past twenty years. Their conversation could go something like this:

> "I put this course off until my last semester," began Jabari. "My friends in the engineering department all waited until they were about to graduate, too."
>
> Brooke replied, "Me, too. I think it's a genetic thing. Some of us are born to speak in public, but I'm not."
>
> "I don't think it's destiny," Jefferson responded. "I worked in sales for three years before coming back to school. My company sent me to a seminar on public speaking last year, and my sales presentations improved a lot. I'm not a natural public speaker, so I think a speech course might help me in my career."
>
> Ciara joined in the conversation. "That's fine for you. But I'm an education major, and I work as a substitute teacher. How will this class help me teach second grade?"
>
> "No lie," added Chas. "I'm going into accounting, and I don't have time for a course in public speaking. I am 'speech-giving challenged'—that's one reason my career choice is to be an accountant."
>
> Mei-Xing, in her first semester of college, planned to major in drama. She was enthusiastic about public speaking. Not shy about contradicting her new classmates, she responded, "Hey. This class won't be so bad. I was nervous before my first play in seventh grade, but once I got out there on stage, it felt great. I was valedictorian at my high school and gave the graduation speech. That was fun."

Oh no, the other students thought. An eager freshman. One of those "born speakers" that Brooke had mentioned. Class valedictorian. There goes the curve!

This diversity of student opinions is not unusual. Public speaking can be a challenge. A survey reported by Whitworth and Cochran found that the number-one fear of Americans is speaking in public.[1] Why should an experience that can be this frightening be the focus of a required course? Is a course in public speaking relevant only to students planning a career in politics, law, or broadcasting? Can a person who does not feel born to be a speaker master public speaking skills?

The Benefits of a Public Speaking Class

In this chapter we address the questions raised above. If we were to reduce this chapter to a single sentiment, it would be this: ***Public speaking is "right" for you.*** What we mean by this statement is that you will learn important skills in your public speaking class, skills that will help you in your classrooms, careers, and communities of the twenty-first century. For example, improved public speaking skills will help you as a parent addressing the school board, as an employee requesting that your coworkers volunteer for a charitable cause, as you attempt to persuade the judge that your parking ticket should be voided, and as a student who is required to give an oral presentation in class. Furthermore, you will see that anyone is capable of becoming a better speaker, even a person like Brooke, who did not believe she was born to speak in public.

● *How Public Speaking Benefits You as a Student*

Oral presentations and reports are assigned in a wide variety of courses, from history to computer science to women's studies. Students with public speaking skills present their reports more effectively than those with a limited background in presenting speeches. Compare the organizing and speaking skills of the students in any of your classes that require oral presentations: you will find that well-drafted and well-delivered presentations make a better impression on the instructor and the class. The experience you gain in researching, organizing, and drafting speeches will also strengthen your performance on written assignments.

Public speaking skills also enhance your ability to participate in campus activities. If you belong to a club, team, organization, sorority, or fraternity, you may want to speak out at a group meeting or represent your group before the student senate or other campus organization. When you know how to present and deliver a speech, you are more likely to achieve your goal.

● *How Public Speaking Benefits You in Your Career*

The importance of public speaking in some careers is obvious. Students interested in politics, law, public relations, and broadcasting will be active in public speaking throughout their careers. What about people such as Chas, who plan a career in accounting? Why is a speech course relevant for them?

Whatever your career aspirations, speaking skills are an asset. According to a National Association of Colleges and Employers Job Outlook Survey, "Above all, employers expect candidates to be able to communicate. Oral communication skills ranked first in essential skills for the third year in a row."[2] Employers view strong communication skills as "an asset that adds value to their businesses."[3] Jean Gatz, a professional speaker and former employment counselor, notes that verbal skills "are essential in every work environment."[4] She also notes that knowing how to listen, another skill taught in public speaking courses, is "equally important."[5] Employees agree that communication skills are important. In the survey "Making the Grade? What American Workers Think Should Be Done to Improve Education," 87 percent of the 1,014 U.S. adult workers surveyed rated communication skills as being very important for performing their jobs.[6]

In the twenty-first century, new careers are growing rapidly in the service sector of the economy, where communication with customers and colleagues is a must. No matter what your career choice is, it would be short-sighted to assume that you will not use public speaking in any field you enter after graduation. Consider these examples:

- Richard, a police officer, was sent to break up a loud party. When he arrived, several attendees were on the brink of fighting one another, and others were yelling insults at him. Another officer might have needed to use force or take some of the belligerent partygoers to jail. By calmly talking to the crowd, Richard was able to diffuse the tension and convince the partygoers to go home. He used his public speaking and conflict resolution training to diffuse a potentially dangerous situation.

- Lina was completing her residency at a major hospital. Her job required daily communication with patients and doctors on a one-on-one basis, not public speaking. Then, during a tight budgetary year, the residents at the hospital found their patient loads and work hours increasing, to the point that Lina became active in a movement to unionize the residents and bargain for improved working conditions. When negotiations broke down, there was talk of a strike. The idea of health care professionals striking received negative publicity in the media and condemnation among community leaders. As an intern active in the pro-union movement, who understood what working conditions were like "in the trenches," Lina was asked to explain the necessity of a strike at a press conference. Lina made the union's case persuasively and professionally, earning a favorable response from the local media. Negotiations resumed, and an agreement was reached without the necessity of a strike.

It is easy to imagine how the students we mentioned at the beginning of this chapter would need public speaking skills in their careers. Jabari could find himself explaining an engineering innovation he developed to a group of investors. Ciara may find herself defending a promising new mathematics curriculum to a room full of skeptical parents who would be more comfortable if their children were taught in a traditional way. As an accountant, Chas might be asked to make a presentation to the local chamber of commerce explaining tax law changes. The need to speak well could arise in any of their careers, and the same opportunity may present itself to you.

How Public Speaking Benefits You in Your Community

Beyond work or school, you may wear many different hats in your community. For example, you may be active in organizations such as service associations, athletic leagues, clubs, religious groups, and political committees. Parents may find themselves taking on leadership roles in their children's schools, sports, clubs, and other activities. In all these roles, public speaking skills can help you.

You may already be active in political activities, like Katie, Mandeep, and Sherri, three students you will read about in Chapter 7. They went before their city council to protest the shooting of crows that roosted on a local courthouse. Others may decide to be politically active later in life. For example, after the tragic murder of his eighteen-year-old daughter, Kimber, photographer Mike Reynolds became a leader in the victims' rights movement. Reynolds spearheaded the passage of legislation imposing greater punishment on criminals, such as the "Three strikes and you're out" initiative, which mandates lengthy sentences or life imprisonment for offenders who commit a third serious crime.

To have an impact on your community, at times you will need to speak out. Whether you actively seek to lead or not, you may be encouraged to

To have an impact on your community, at times you will need to speak out. This concerned citizen in Austin, Texas, rallies to support public schools.

take leadership roles. Or, as a group member, you may have a point you want to share. However you decide to be involved in your community, the skills you learn in a public speaking class help you to be heard and to earn the respect of the groups and organizations in which you participate. You will be able to analyze your audience, research the issue, prepare a well-organized message, and present it with confidence. By being an effective listener who is sensitive to the concerns of others, as well as an ethical communicator (consider how often the public is disappointed by people in positions of power who lack ethics), you will gain respect, and people will listen to you when you speak. Those are the skills of public speaking, skills that you will learn during this term and use to your benefit in college, in your career, and in your community.

To orient you to the study of public speaking, we turn to three additional topics in this chapter. First, we discuss briefly the historical tradition of public speaking. Next, we consider several contemporary developments that greatly influence public speaking today. Finally, we review some techniques that you can use to reduce your anxiety about public speaking.

Can you become a better public speaker at the end of this course? The answer is a definite "yes!" You do not need to be a "born" speaker. Instead, willingness to try and to learn are the attributes you really need to succeed as a speaker.

Public Speaking Is a Great Tradition

When you study public speaking and put your speech skills into practice, you will be participating in a long and grand tradition. For centuries, people have studied the art and practice of public speaking and used public address to make an impact on their world.

In the Greek city-state of Athens in the fifth century B.C.E., all adult male citizens had a right to speak out in the assembly and vote on proposals. Sometimes six thousand citizens attended these meetings.[7] A century later, the Greek scholar Aristotle wrote *Rhetoric,* a systematic analysis of the art and practice of public speaking. Many of Aristotle's ideas influence the study of public speaking today. In first-century B.C.E. Rome, senators vehemently debated the issues of the day. Cicero, a Roman politician, was a renowned orator and a prolific writer on rhetoric, the craft of public speaking. Another noteworthy Roman rhetorician, Quintilian, emphasized the ideal of an ethical orator—a good person speaking well.

You will study Aristotle's time-tested concepts of *ethos, pathos,* and *logos* in Chapter 2.

Classical canons, or elements, of rhetoric inform contemporary speech preparation (see p. 37).

The tradition of public speaking was not limited to Greece and Rome. From the time of K'ung-Fu-Tze (Confucius) in the fifth century B.C.E. until the end of the third century B.C.E., China experienced an intellectual climate that rivaled that of ancient Greece.[8] Scholars traveling among the states in China advocated a variety of systems of political and economic philosophy. In fifteenth-century western Africa, traveling storytellers recited parables and humorous stories; in northeastern Africa, Islamic scholars went on lecture tours and spoke to large crowds.[9] On feast days in one African kingdom (near present-day Mali), it was traditional for a bard to dress in a bird's-head mask and deliver a speech encouraging the king to live up to the high standards of his predecessors.[10] Oratory was highly valued by Native Americans, too; indeed, oratorical ability was often deemed a more important leadership quality than bravery in battle.[11]

The tradition of public speaking flourished in colonial America as well. During the Great Awakening of the 1730s and 1740s, preachers sought to revive religious zeal, which had been waning in the colonies. George Whitefield traveled through the colonies and drew large crowds for his dynamic open-air sermons.[12] He preached in fields because churches were not large enough to accommodate the listeners.[13] Jonathan Edwards's well-known 1741 sermon "Sinners in the Hands of an Angry God" caused worshipers in Enfield, Massachusetts, to shriek and moan as Edwards described "the God that holds you over the pit of hell, much as one holds a spider."[14] Fervent preaching was not limited to men, as over one hundred evangelical women preached from the time of the Great Awakening to the early nineteenth century.[15]

As dissatisfaction with British rule grew later in the eighteenth century, public address turned to political topics. Patrick Henry, well known for his passionate oratory, concluded before the Virginia House of Burgesses in 1765 that if changes were not made, King George III could lose his head like other tyrants. Colonists began gathering in churches, schools, town squares, and taverns to express their dissatisfaction with the British.[16] In December 1773, about five thousand colonists tried to crowd into Boston's Old South Church to hear Samuel Adams and others denounce the British tea tax.[17] Passionate oratory against the tax was a prelude to the Boston Tea Party, in which colonists dressed as Mohawks boarded three ships in Boston Harbor and threw their cargoes of tea overboard.

After the Revolutionary War was won, public speech and debate had a major influence on the Constitution and the Bill of Rights. The drafters discussed the contents extensively, and there was spirited debate in the individual states regarding the merits of ratifying each document. The Constitution requires the president to deliver an annual State of the Union address, which remains a significant and highly publicized speech today. George Washington gave a presidential "farewell address" (in his case, it was actually a letter), warning Americans against international entanglements.[18] Later presidents have used a farewell address to offer perspectives and insights gained from their public service, such as Dwight Eisenhower's 1961 admonition to guard against the influence of the "military-industrial complex."[19]

In the nineteenth century, public speaking was a hallmark of American society. Public address provided Americans with the opportunity to consider political issues and to expand their knowledge and be entertained. In many parts of the country, the lyceum movement (named for the garden in Athens where Aristotle taught his students)[20] was popular. In an era without *Survivor*, MTV, *South Park*, or the World Wrestling Federation, lyceum lectures were a popular form of education and entertainment. About thirteen thousand people attended such lectures at the Lowell Institute in Boston during the winter of 1837–1838. Topics covered at the Salem, Massachusetts, lyceum lectures the next year included the honey bee, the life of Muhammad, the sun, and the legal rights of women.[21] Political debates were also very well attended. Among the most famous debates were those between Abraham Lincoln and Stephen Douglas, opponents for a U.S. Senate seat

View an excerpt from John F. Kennedy's "Ich Bin Ein Berliner."
CD-ROM: Video Theater, Excerpt 1.1

Public speaking enabled American colonists to voice their dissatisfaction with British rule. Here Patrick Henry addresses the Virginia House of Delegates.

from Illinois in 1858. Over fifteen thousand people were present for one of the debates in Freeport, Illinois, a town of only five thousand people.[22]

The antislavery movement gave rise to many opportunities for public address. One of the most effective antislavery speakers was Frederick Douglass, a former slave who moved audiences with his discussion of life under slavery. Women were active in the American Anti-Slavery Society, holding offices and delivering public lectures. Angelina Grimké was an eloquent orator who drew audience members into her presentations with descriptions of abuses she had witnessed while growing up in South Carolina. Other women who became leaders in the women's rights movement, such as Elizabeth Cady Stanton, Susan B. Anthony, and Lucy Stone, were also active in the society.[23] Despite vehement opposition by some segments of society, women's participation in public speaking expanded. Historian Phoebe Hanaford estimated that by 1876, more than thirty women had achieved national recognition for their public speaking.[24]

View an excerpt from Barbara Jordan's address to the Democratic National Convention.
CD-ROM: Video Theater, Excerpt 1.2

In the twentieth century, public address remained an important part of the American landscape. After World War I, President Woodrow Wilson traveled through the United States to speak in favor of the League of Nations. Republican leaders went to the same tour stops and presented the opposite viewpoint.[25] In 1963 approximately 250,000 people gathered near the Lincoln Memorial to hear Martin Luther King Jr. tell the audience, "I have a dream."[26] In the past few years, tens of thousands of "Promise Keepers" have crowded into football stadiums to hear speakers address issues of family and religion. The Million Man (Washington, D.C., 1995) and Million Woman (Philadelphia, 1997) marches culminated in public speeches on issues such as jobs, human rights, and respect for African Americans.[27] We live in a high-technology world of e-mail, chatrooms, and videoconferences. Nevertheless, at important events and times, such as weddings, graduations, religious services, halftime of the "big" game, and the election of a new president, we want someone to say something to us. President George W. Bush did not post a message on the White House Web site to explain the U.S. reaction to the events of September 11, 2001. He went before Congress and the nation and delivered an impassioned speech.

View an excerpt from George W. Bush's address to Congress nine days after the attacks of September 11, 2001.
CD-ROM: Video Theater, Excerpt 1.3

Public Speaking Is a Dynamic Discipline

Public speaking has a long history, and many of the principles taught by ancient scholars such as Aristotle are still relevant. However, public speaking is also a dynamic, evolving discipline. Researchers continue to learn more about the process of human communication, and communication scholars attempt to incorporate societal changes and concerns into their studies and practice. In recent decades, new perspectives on the nature of communication have come to the forefront. In addition, considerations such as culture, critical thinking, and ethics have assumed a more prominent role in the speech preparation process.

● The Transaction between Speaker and Audience

A Linear Model of Communication.   Originally, communication was viewed as a linear process. Thus, during a speech, communication was perceived as a one-way flow of ideas from a speaker to the audience. The metaphor of a hypodermic needle has been used to characterize this model. A speaker "injects" the audience members with ideas, much as a doctor injects a patient. The communication is successful if the audience members' perception of the speaker's idea matches the speaker's actual idea. There are several key concepts involved in this process (see Figure 1.1).

A person with an idea to express is the **source**, and his or her idea is the **message**. The source **encodes** the message, meaning that he or she chooses *verbal* and *nonverbal symbols* to express the idea. Verbal symbols are words that the source uses to convey an idea; nonverbal symbols are means of making a point without the use of words, such as hand gestures, appearance, and facial expression.

The message is communicated through a **channel**, which is the medium of delivery. You may simply use your voice, rely on a sound amplification

source: a person with an idea to express.

message: the idea to be expressed.

encode: choosing symbols to express an idea.

channel: the medium for delivery of a message.

FIGURE 1.1   A Linear Communication Model

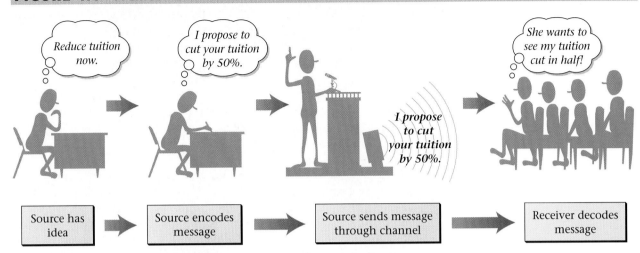

In a linear model, the ideas flow from source to receiver. The communication is successful if the receiver correctly understands the source's message.

system, or express yourself in writing. Computer-based technologies are increasingly popular channels, as people rely on e-mail, online discussion groups, and newsgroups to communicate. By this means it is possible to send and receive not only written messages, but also pictures, sounds, and other audiovisual communication.

Something that impairs the communication of a message is called **interference** or **noise**. External interference could include a power failure that causes your computer to turn off during an online chat, a loud lawnmower that disrupts a class discussion, or a beeping pager that spoils the moment during a romantic dinner. Internal interference occurs in the minds of the source or receiver. If you have difficulty carrying on a conversation because you are preoccupied with other thoughts, you are experiencing internal interference. Another example of this type of interference would be the hunger pangs of an audience member who is contemplating where to go to lunch rather than actively listening to a speech.

Messages are communicated to one or more **receivers**, those persons to whom a message is conveyed. Receivers attempt to make sense of a message by **decoding**. This means that they process the verbal and nonverbal symbols that are conveyed and they form *their own* perception of the message and its meaning. These perceptions may differ. For example, two receivers who observe a speaker wearing a backward baseball hat may decode very different messages. While one may view the hat as a symbol of disrespect for authority, another may view the hat as a symbol indicating that the speaker likes baseball. In reality, the speaker may be hiding a bad hair day rather than expressing either perceived message!

Communication as a Transaction.

Scholars no longer model communication as a one-way transmission of messages from source to receiver. Instead, communication is conceptualized as a **transaction**, an exchange in which participants continuously send and receive messages.[28] It is possible for a

interference (noise): an impairment to communicating a message.

receiver: a person that a message is communicated to.

decoding: processing a message and forming a perception of its meaning.

transaction: an exchange in which each party continuously sends and receives messages.

Middle school student Jackie Lopez sends out a message against violence in her community during a rally for the Million Mom March. What type of feedback do you think her audience responded with?

person to simultaneously be the source of one message and the receiver of another. This would be the case if you frown at a friend who is telling a bad joke that you already heard twice. It is also possible for messages to be exchanged before any participant even begins to speak. For example, a speaker may smile to show he or she is pleased to be there. Conversely, an audience member may stretch and yawn to indicate that a lengthy message would not be appreciated.

One way that a person who receives a message also fills the role of message source in a communication transaction is by providing **feedback**. A participant who shouts "Yes!" or "You go, girl!" in response to a compelling point in a speech, who looks away during a dull conversation, or who posts a scathing response after being flamed in an online chatroom, is giving feedback. Feedback is a consistent part of the communication process. It is difficult to imagine a situation where a person sends a message to people who are physically present and receives no response. Participants may respond with ideas of their own, show their disapproval through body language, or interrupt the source in the middle of a sentence. Even a person who responds to a message with a blank stare may be making a point.

Successful communication requires more than a correct perception of the source's message by the receiver. An important objective of a communication transaction is the creation of **shared meaning**. This means that the parties come to a common understanding with little confusion and few misinterpretations.[29] Rather than simply getting their own point across, people should strive to improve their own knowledge, seek understanding, and develop agreements when they communicate with others.[30]

For example, suppose you did not do well on a test because you could not sleep the night before. You told this to your instructor, Ms. Jackson, when she returned the exam, and she smiled and responded, "I understand.

feedback: a receiver's response to a source's message.

shared meaning: a common understanding between communicators.

That happened to me a few times in college, too." From a *linear* communication perspective, it would be said that the communication was probably successful: the source (you) explained why you did not do well, and the receiver (Ms. Jackson) seemed to comprehend your explanation. However, in analyzing the conversation from a *transactional* perspective, it could be said that the two of you created a deeper level of shared meaning. Suppose that you also hoped that Ms. Jackson would realize that your low score was not the result of laziness or lack of concern, while she hoped that you would realize that she did not think that you were a bad student because of one low test score. If Ms. Jackson understood that your performance was not typical and that you understood that she could empathize with your situation, then shared meaning would result from your dialogue.

Public Speaking as a Communication Transaction.   Public speaking reflects the transactional communication model we have discussed. Speakers are the primary *source* of messages because their role is to deliver the speech, with the audience acting as *receivers*. However, these functions are reversed throughout the speech as audience members convey messages to the speaker. Figure 1.2 illustrates how public speaking functions as a communication transaction.

Audience members and speakers can strive for shared meaning as they each function as sources and receivers. For example, suppose an audience member nods when the speaker says, "I need your help to fight illiteracy." The speaker must assume the role of *receiver* and *decode* the message. The member's nod may mean "I agree," or it could mean "I'm bored, move on." To better decode the message, a speaker may look for additional cues, such as a smile or a frown on the audience member's face. If the nod was meant to convey willingness to help, and the speaker responded by inviting audience members to participate in a tutoring program, shared meaning was achieved.

FIGURE 1.2   Public Speaking as a Communications Transaction

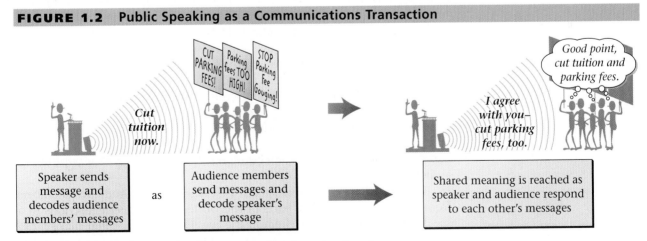

During a speech, the speaker and audience members each send and receive messages. The communication is successful if shared meaning between speaker and audience is achieved.

● *The Significance of Culture*

Consideration of the cultures represented by your audience members has become an increasingly important dimension of public speaking. When we use the term **culture**, we are referring to values, traditions, and rules for living that are passed from generation to generation.[31] Some examples of an individual's culture include religious practices, use of language, food choice, and organization of society. Culture is learned; it is not genetically transmitted to future generations.

View Jesse Jackson speaking inclusively to a diverse audience at the Democratic National Convention.
CD-ROM: Video Theater, Excerpt 1.4

A Multicultural Perspective.   The United States is a multicultural society. In the words of Arnoldo Ramos, who was born in Costa Rica and now is executive director of the Council of Latino Agencies, the United States is "a nation where everyone comes from somewhere else."[32] People came to America for many different reasons. Many Africans were brought to America against their will and forced into slavery; other immigrants came in the hope of better economic opportunities; and yet others came to escape political oppression and violence. One in ten U.S. residents were born abroad, and their birthplace is increasingly a nation in Asia or Latin America such as Mexico, the Philippines, China, or India.[33] This trend is further exemplified by a list of the ten most common surnames of home buyers in Los Angeles County: Garcia, Lee, Rodriguez, Lopez, Gonzalez, Martinez, Hernandez, Kim, Smith, and Perez.[34]

Historically, the metaphor of the melting pot was used to describe the United States. As people immigrated to this country, it was assumed that they would learn to conform to the traditions and beliefs of the Anglo-American culture. In recent years, the melting-pot metaphor has been challenged. Sociologists have questioned the value of assimilating into the dominant culture, and it has been argued that America would better be described as a salad bowl or mosaic—in other words, as a society where diverse cultures exist and are respected.[35]

Communication scholars have recognized the importance of understanding and relating to persons from diverse cultures. Myron Lustig and Jolene Koester note that it is no longer likely that your clients, customers, coworkers, or neighbors have the same values, customs, or first language as you do. Your career success and personal satisfaction will increasingly depend on how well you can communicate with persons from other cultures.[36]

In the public speaking context, cultural awareness is very important. In subsequent chapters we elaborate on cultural factors to take into account when you plan and deliver a speech. For example, the preferred method of organizing a message varies from culture to culture. Appropriate word choice may vary, depending on the cultures represented in your audience.

The presentation of your speech may also change. Audience members from cultures from various parts of the world have different reactions to a speaker who does not look them in the eye. Hand gestures that make sense to members from American cultures may be misunderstood or not understood at all by persons from other cultures. In Chapter 11, on delivery, we elaborate on these considerations.

culture: values, traditions, and rules for living passed from generation to generation.

Shiu-Chen Chiang recites the Pledge of Allegiance with over seventeen hundred new American citizens. Sociologists have questioned the value of assimilating into the dominant culture. Communication scholars have recognized the importance of understanding and relating to persons from diverse cultures.

The Audience's Worldview.   Culture is a very important determinant of each audience member's worldview, which is the lens through which each person sees the world and which significantly influences how he or she will respond to your speech. How will audience members decode your message? Will they agree with the claims you make in a speech, or will they demand further proof? Are they likely to agree or disagree with your position?

The answers to these questions will vary depending on the audience member. Culture, along with life experience, education, and other factors in an audience member's background, influence his or her worldview. As two people with lenses of different colors or magnitudes will not have the same view, audience members with different worldviews can respond to the same words quite differently.

A billboard on Interstate Highway 10 near the California-Arizona border illustrates the way that an individual's worldview influences his or her interpretation of a message. The billboard was sponsored by the California Coalition for Immigration Reform. It looked somewhat like a California state road sign but said: "Welcome to California, the illegal immigration state. Don't let this happen to your state."[37]

Mario Obledo, former California secretary of health and welfare, decoded the message as "racist, one of hatred." He viewed it as an insult to immigrants, particularly those with brown skin. Mr. Obledo's background—he is the son of an immigrant from Mexico and is a Korean War veteran with degrees in pharmacy and law—had an important influence on his worldview. He believed that the hard work of the very immigrants attacked in the billboard had helped to create prosperity in California.

How would you decode the message on the billboard? Undoubtedly some readers would agree with Mr. Obledo's interpretation, while others

Mario Obledo protested against the message on this billboard, interpreting the message as "one of hatred." What message do you perceive? How does your worldview influence your answer?

would not see the billboard as an expression of racial hatred. California Coalition chair Barbara Coe denied that the billboard was racist. She said, "I don't care what ethnicity they are, if they're here illegally, the law says they should be deported."[38] Coalition members would contend that they simply oppose persons coming to this country illegally, regardless of their ethnicity.

In response to the billboard, Mario Obledo drafted a press release warning that he would burn or deface the billboard on June 27, 1998. He decided to paint his own message on the billboard, perhaps "Welcome to the land of opportunity." Before June 27, the sign was removed by the billboard company and the California Coalition was given a refund.

To the coalition that sponsored the billboard, Obledo's threats constituted terrorism. Others might see his threats as justified acts of civil disobedience. You might have a third perspective. It all depends on your worldview!

● *The Emphasis on Critical Thinking*

College educators place an increasing value on teaching students to be effective critical thinkers. Many schools now require a course that emphasizes critical thinking skills as part of their general education requirements. These skills have an important role in speech preparation and analysis.

When you use **critical thinking**, you decide "what to believe and how to act after a careful evaluation of the evidence and reasoning in a communication."[39] This text will encourage you to use critical thinking in two ways: by evaluating your beliefs about the *topic* you have chosen in an open-minded manner and by carefully considering the *choices* you make at each stage of the speech preparation process. Critical thinking requires that you analyze your own assumptions, and the ideas of others, before you make a judgment about an issue or question.[40]

Critical Thinking about Your Topic.   In this text, we encourage you to think carefully about the information you present in your speeches and about the research materials you use to support the points you make. A speech should not be based merely on your personal opinion or on information from the first two or three sources you uncover in your research.

Before you present ideas to an audience, you should be confident that the ideas are reasonable. Suspend judgment about the main points you plan to make and consider other perspectives. For example, if you drive a car to campus, you may assume that it would be desirable to demolish an old building on campus and replace it with a parking structure. Historical preservation advocates and environmentalists are likely to have different viewpoints. Critical thinkers carefully consider the perspective of these groups and are willing to modify their opinions if other ideas make sense. After considering diverse perspectives, you will have a better idea about the best information you can present to the audience.

Another important critical thinking skill is to evaluate the truth or probable truth of a claim. Anybody can state an opinion, but not all opinions are based on careful analysis. If you are researching the environmental impact of building a new parking garage on campus, a report by a scientist who has studied the issue is more likely to be accurate than are unsupported opinions presented in an angry letter to the editor of the local newspaper.

By using critical thinking when preparing your speech, you can be more confident that you are providing your audience with useful information.

Critical Thinking at Each Stage of Speech Preparation.   In this text, we provide a step-by-step plan for developing an effective speech. Although there is a logical sequence of steps to be followed when you prepare a speech, it would be wrong to say that any book or computer software can produce a speech for you in the same way that an assembly line produces a product.

Each stage of the speech preparation process requires you to make choices. You will face questions such as these:

What would be the best topic for my speech?

How can I clearly explain a difficult concept to my audience?

Which words are most likely to convey my passion about a topic to the audience?

critical thinking: deciding on beliefs and actions after a careful evaluation of alternatives.

There are no set answers to such questions. This textbook and the accompanying software can tell you what factors to take into account, but the final choice is yours. Every audience and every speech situation is unique. You need to use critical thinking to make good decisions about how you can accomplish the purpose of your speech and how to do it in an ethical manner.

● *The Importance of Ethics*

Ethics, a set of beliefs shared by a group about what behaviors are correct or incorrect, are not a new consideration in public speaking. In the first century C.E., the Roman rhetorician Quintilian argued that parents and teachers should strive to produce "the good man speaking well." Today, to avoid the obvious sexism in this phrase, we would say "good *person* speaking well." The underlying premise is noteworthy. Communicators should be virtuous, moral, and public-spirited, as well as effective orators.[41]

During the last quarter century, there has been renewed emphasis on ethical public speaking. One obvious reason for this trend is that society has lived through so much unethical communication. The lack of trust extends beyond the usual suspects such as politicians, lawyers, and business executives. Journalists have fabricated news stories in the hopes of winning awards. Even doctors and members of the clergy do not have high credibility according to one-third or more of the adults participating in a Gallup poll (see Table 1.1).

Ethics are now an important focus in the study of communication (and in other disciplines, too). There is more to public speaking than presenting your message in a manner that will induce your audience to agree with you.

TABLE 1.1 Whom Do Americans Trust?

A 1999 Gallup survey of Americans evaluated how they would rate the honesty and ethical standards of people in different fields. There are diverse levels of trust for each profession, and at least one-fourth of Americans do not give high ratings to any group.

	LEVEL OF TRUST		
PROFESSION	Very High/High	Average	Very Low/Low
Nurses	73%	24%	2%
Medical doctors	58%	34%	7%
Clergy	56%	33%	9%
Judges	53%	35%	10%
Journalists	24%	53%	22%
Business executives	23%	59%	15%
Lawyers	13%	45%	41%
Congressmen	11%	54%	34%

Note: Percentages do not add to 100 percent because some respondents gave no opinion.

Source: Adapted from McAneny, L. (1999, November 16). Nurses displace pharmacists at the top of the expanded honesty and ethics poll. *The Gallup Organization.* Retrieved November 9, 2001 from the World Wide Web: <http://www.gallup.com/poll/releases/pr991116.asp>.

It is also imperative that you treat your audience in an ethical way. One general principle of speech ethics is to treat your audience members as you would wish to be treated if you were in the audience. In Chapter 3 we elaborate on the principles of ethical communication. Key considerations include being truthful with your audience, contributing to audience members' ability to make a well-informed decision about your topic, avoiding manipulative or fallacious reasoning, and incorporating research materials properly in your speech. We also examine the importance of an ethical audience.

Overcoming Speech Anxiety

In this section of Chapter 1 we provide an overview of speech anxiety and suggestions for minimizing its negative effects. Was Jabari, whom you read about in the opening pages of this chapter, wise to avoid a public speaking class until his final semester? Is Brooke right—are there some people, such as Mei-Xing, who seem to be naturally gifted as speakers and others who never will be able to speak well in public? Speech anxiety can be very real for all speakers, whether they are experienced speakers, natural speakers, or beginners. Despite any anxiety you may feel, this remains true: ***Public speaking is "right" for you.*** You may not be able to control whether you experience anxiety, but you can reduce anxiety and improve your ability to speak in public.

● *The Nature of Speech Anxiety*

The fear or worry that people experience when anticipating or delivering a speech is called **speech anxiety** or **stage fright**. Speech anxiety is one aspect of the broader concept of **communication apprehension**, which James McCroskey, a leading researcher in this field, defines as "an individual's level of fear or anxiety associated with either real or anticipated communication with another person or persons."[42]

Some people generally experience anxiety about communicating, regardless of the situation; this is referred to as *trait apprehension.* More people experience *state apprehension,* which means that they experience anxiety at particular times or in particular communication contexts.[43] For example, you may feel comfortable talking to a group of friends but become very nervous while talking to strangers at a party. Perhaps you feel comfortable participating in group discussions at meetings of a community organization you belong to, but you are very uncomfortable speaking up in meetings at work. When you feel anxious about situations such as these, although you do not dread all communication situations, you are experiencing state apprehension.

Public speaking is one context in which state apprehension is common. Most people are nervous before they speak, even professionals who know their subject well.[44] One often-cited study found that about three-fourths of all college students reported some fear of speaking in public.[45] Although Mei-Xing had performed before audiences many times, she felt uncertainty every time she imagined herself as the only student speaker before a crowd of four thousand people at her graduation. Typically, a moderate amount of anxiety speeds your heart rate, and you become more energized and atten-

speech anxiety (stage fright): fear or worry that people feel when anticipating or delivering a speech.

communication apprehension: fear or anxiety accompanying real or anticipated communication.

Surveys may suggest that some people fear public speaking more than they fear death. In a public speaking class, you can learn how to minimize the anxiety you feel before delivering a speech. Which of the methods described on pages 21–26 would work best for you?

TIP

If you feel a moderate amount of tension before you speak, take it as a good sign. It is not an indication that you are incapable of speaking well; instead, your body is telling you "I'm ready to go!"

tive to the task at hand. Experiencing a few "butterflies" in your stomach does not mean that you are too nervous to speak well; it just means that you are focused on your speech.

Experiencing a total lack of anxiety may be a greater threat to effective speaking. Indeed, speakers who experience no anxiety are unlikely to deliver their best speech. One former public speaking student who failed to attend a practice session with his teaching assistant left this message on her answering machine: "Sorry I missed you at the videotaping. Not to worry, my natural charm and speaking style will captivate the audience." On the day of his speech, that speaker did speak clearly and seemed very confident in front of the class. However, there was no enthusiasm in his voice, he failed to notice the signal when his speaking time ended, and his speech ran four minutes long. Because of his overconfidence, he was oblivious to the fact that he was out of time, and, more important, he lost the audience's interest in his speech.

Other speakers experience a higher level of speech anxiety. For them, the physical and mental consequences of speech anxiety affect their ability to prepare and deliver an effective speech. Instead of noticing a few butterflies fluttering in your stomach, you may experience serious discomfort. You could have symptoms of anxiety that are visible to your audience, such as trembling hands or excessive perspiration. High apprehension might impair your delivery by making your mouth dry, tightening your vocal cords, or causing you to rush through your speech.

High speech anxiety also has a mental dimension. It may cause you to repress unpleasant thoughts about an upcoming speech by postponing your preparation until the last minute, impairing your ability to prepare an effective speech. Anxiety can also reduce your ability to concentrate. High levels of apprehension result in more decision-making errors while preparing a speech and cause a greater likelihood that speakers will perceive that their speech is a failure.[46]

The experience of high anxiety is not abnormal; in fact, one study found that 15 to 20 percent of all college students suffer oral communication apprehension at a level that seriously interferes with their ability to function.[47] If you experience a high level of speech anxiety, do not blame yourself. Contemporary research provides some evidence that communication apprehension may have a genetic component,[48] much as genes can predispose some persons to be happier or more aggressive than others. This does not mean, as Brooke suggests at the beginning of this chapter, that you are born to be either a good speaker or a bad one. It does mean that if you experience high apprehension, you will need to pay particular attention to the strategies for overcoming its effects. You can determine your level of anxiety by completing the self-assessment exercise in Figure 1.3.

● *Reducing the Effects of Speech Anxiety*

Speech anxiety has the potential to interfere with your success as a speaker, but you need not let it defeat you. Speech anxiety can be managed and treated, and with determination and effort you can stop it from stopping you. In this section we consider a variety of steps you can take to minimize the negative consequences of speech anxiety. These steps are particularly important for speakers who experience a high degree of anxiety, but they will also help any student improve as a public speaker.

Get Help for Speech Anxiety.   Three treatment methods have been shown to reduce speech anxiety.[49] **Desensitization** begins with instruction in relaxation techniques. Speakers then learn how to use relaxation to relieve tension when thinking about public speaking, rather than reacting with anxiety. For example, they can discover how to relax their muscles or visualize a favorite place. In **cognitive restructuring**, speakers identify their fears about public speaking; then the instructor attempts to show why these fears are not rational. Students are provided with a more rational belief (a coping statement) to use as an alternative. For example, a speaker who fears audience rejection for saying "um" while pausing during a speech will learn that this is a small mistake that audiences will forgive. That fear should be replaced by a rational thought such as "The audience will be focused on my message. They will hardly notice it if I occasionally say 'um' during my speech."

The third treatment is **skills training**. By learning how to prepare and deliver a good speech, speakers reduce their anxiety as they gain confidence in their ability. Research confirms that "students often enroll in required speech courses with trepidation yet attribute the development of confidence and poise to their collegiate public speaking experiences."[50]

Skills training is provided in nearly every public speaking class. Assistance in desensitization or cognitive restructuring may be offered through a speech lab on your campus or in a speech class targeted to high-apprehension students. If you have high anxiety, these programs are an excellent investment of your time. Ask your instructor, consult a campus directory, or check your school or speech department Web site to determine what services are available.

Desensitization, cognitive restructuring, and skills training are three ways that you can receive assistance in reducing speech apprehension. There are also strategies that you can use on your own to reduce anxiety.

desensitization: learning to use relaxation to relieve tension when contemplating public speaking.

cognitive restructuring: learning to substitute a more rational belief for identified fears about public speaking.

skills training: reducing anxiety by learning how to prepare and deliver a good speech.

FIGURE 1.3   Measuring Your Level of Apprehension

Use the Personal Report of Communication Apprehension (PRCA-24B) to determine your level of communication apprehension.

Directions: This instrument is composed of 24 statements concerning your feelings about communication with other people. Please indicate in the space provided the degree to which each statement applies to you by marking whether you (1) Strongly Agree, (2) Agree, (3) Are Undecided, (4) Disagree, or (5) Strongly Disagree with each statement. There are no right or wrong answers. Many of the statements are similar to other statements. Do not be concerned about this. Work quickly: Just record your first impressions.

_____ 1. When talking in a small group of acquaintances, I am tense and nervous.

_____ 2. When presenting a talk to a group of strangers, I am tense and nervous.

_____ 3. When conversing with a friend, I am calm and relaxed.

_____ 4. When talking in a large meeting of acquaintances, I am calm and relaxed.

_____ 5. When presenting a talk to a group of friends, I am tense and nervous.

_____ 6. When conversing with an acquaintance, I am calm and relaxed.

_____ 7. When talking in a large meeting of strangers, I am tense and nervous.

_____ 8. When talking in a small group of strangers, I am tense and nervous.

_____ 9. When talking in a small group of friends, I am calm and relaxed.

_____ 10. When presenting a talk to a group of acquaintances, I am calm and relaxed.

_____ 11. When I am conversing with a stranger, I am calm and relaxed.

_____ 12. When talking in a large meeting of friends, I am tense and nervous.

_____ 13. When presenting a talk to a group of strangers, I am calm and relaxed.

_____ 14. When conversing with a friend, I am tense and nervous.

_____ 15. When talking in a large meeting of acquaintances, I am tense and nervous.

_____ 16. When talking in a small group of acquaintances, I am calm and relaxed.

_____ 17. When talking in a small group of strangers, I am calm and relaxed.

_____ 18. When presenting a talk to a group of friends, I am calm and relaxed.

_____ 19. When conversing with an acquaintance, I am tense and nervous.

_____ 20. When talking in a large meeting of strangers, I am calm and relaxed.

_____ 21. When presenting a talk to a group of acquaintances, I am tense and nervous.

_____ 22. When conversing with a stranger, I am tense and nervous.

_____ 23. When talking in a large meeting of friends, I am calm and relaxed.

_____ 24. When talking in a small group of friends, I am tense and nervous.

FIGURE 1.3   Measuring Your Level of Apprehension *continued*

COMPUTING YOUR SCORE

Add or subtract your scores for each item as indicated below to obtain a sub-score for each communication context:

Subscore	Scoring Formula
Group Discussion	18 + scores for items 9, 16, and 17 − scores for items 1, 8, and 24
Meetings	18 + scores for items 4, 20, and 23 − scores for items 7, 12, and 15
Interpersonal Conversation	18 + scores for items 3, 6, and 11 − scores for items 14, 19, and 22
Public Speaking	18 + scores for items 10, 13, and 18 − scores for items 2, 5, and 21

To obtain a total score for communication apprehension, add your scores for group discussion, meetings, interpersonal conversation, and public speaking.

ANALYZING YOUR SCORES

Total scores for communication apprehension range from a low of 24 to a high of 120. An average score is 72. If you score higher than 72, you are typically more apprehensive about communication than the average person. If your score is below 72, you are generally less apprehensive. Scores above 85 indicate a very high level of apprehension, and scores below 59 indicate a very low level.

On individual contexts, possible scores range from a low of 6 to a high of 30. An average score is 18. What is your score for public speaking anxiety? Most Americans score higher than 18.

Source: McCroskey, J. C. (1986). *An introduction to rhetorical communication* (5th ed.). Englewood Cliffs, NJ: Prentice-Hall.

Use Self-Help Techniques to Minimize Apprehension.

There are many steps you can take to reduce anxiety while you are preparing your speech and while you are waiting or delivering your speech.

Select a Topic You Know and Enjoy.   In Chapter 6 we elaborate on the topic selection process and provide several criteria for making that choice. Among the topics that are appropriate for your speech, select one that you know well and would enjoy speaking about. If you know your subject well, you can re-search and plan your speech more easily than with a less familiar topic, leaving more time to practice your speech. More practice helps you to be better prepared and more relaxed in front of the audience. When you deliver your speech, it will be easier to explain a familiar topic naturally, as you would in a conversation with a friend, rather than straining to remember what you wanted to say. When you select a subject you enjoy, your interest will add enthusiasm to your speaking voice, which pulls the audience into your speech.

Prepare Your Speech Early.   It is important to resist the temptation to procrastinate. Select a topic as soon as possible when you receive an assignment, and follow the steps for speech preparation described in this text. Research has found that students with high communication apprehension can reduce speech anxiety by preparing well.[51] Furthermore, researchers have found

Your instructor will usually allow a range of acceptable topics on an assignment.

Outlining is explained briefly on pages 46–50 and in detail in Chapter 8 (for a sample outline, see p. 204).

that students experience lower anxiety when they are working on their speech than they experience just after the instructor gives the assignment.[52] Promise yourself that you will get to work and stay on schedule, so that you have a completed *speech outline*—a point-by-point text of your speech points and subpoints using complete sentences or detailed phrases, structured in outline format—well before the day it will be presented. When you are apprehensive about a speech, it is easy to be critical of yourself, writing and rewriting a passage until you are satisfied. Your top priority should be the timely completion of a draft of your outline, rather than creating the perfect draft. When you complete a first outline efficiently, you will have time to improve it before your speech is to be delivered.

Drafting your speech outline early will help you in several ways. First, you eliminate one source of anxiety because you have a speech that is prepared—there is no more worry about whether you can finish your speech on time. Second, you can improve your speech. Was there a section in your draft you did not feel good about? If so, you have time to go back and fix it. You will have more time to spend on the important task of fine-tuning the introduction and conclusion, ensuring that your speech begins and ends on a strong note. You will be better able to concentrate on revisions when you do not feel the pressure of finishing the entire speech. Third, you will have more time to practice your speech. Your anxiety is more likely to get the better of you if you are trying to deliver an unfamiliar speech than if you are presenting one you know well.

Once you finish a draft of your speech, it will be easier to take advantage of help offered by other people. If your campus has a speech lab or speech tutorial center, take your speech in to get feedback and to practice your delivery. Find out when your instructor has office hours, and ask him or her to check your outline.

Speaking with your teacher might be an intimidating task because the same communication apprehension that makes it difficult to speak in public can make it difficult to talk to an authority figure. If you are reluctant to talk to your instructor, write a note or communicate through e-mail (if this technology is available for both of you). People who choose to teach public speaking usually enjoy interacting with students. It is difficult for us to help a student who waits until the last minute to ask, "What should I do my speech on?" Most instructors believe it is a pleasure to work with students who are making a real effort on an assignment.

When you receive feedback from your instructor before presenting a speech, you reduce a major source of anxiety—wondering how your speech will be evaluated.[53] If you have a problem that needs fixing, or if you are not sure what is expected on an assignment, your teacher can help you. Often we find that the students who see us are already on the right track, and a few encouraging words from the teacher are a helpful medicine for anxiety.

Take Care of Yourself.   If your mind and body are not sharp, speech anxiety will increase. A good night's sleep will do more to prepare your mind and body for a speech than will a great party or an all-night poker game. Too much sugar can make you overly hyped, as can excessive caffeine. If you do not feel much like eating a full meal on the day you are giving a speech, eat a light meal before you speak and reward yourself with a favorite meal when your speech is done.

TIP

Carefully plan your schedule so that you can take good care of yourself before you present your speech.

It is hard to get sufficient sleep and prepare a nutritious meal if you have to work six hours, study for a test, and write a ten-page paper the day before a speech is scheduled. Having too much to do in too little time adds to anyone's anxiety. Look at the syllabi for all your courses early in the semester to see when major assignments are due. Advance planning for when you will study and complete your assignments will make the days you have speeches due less hectic.

Visualize a Successful Speech.   **Visualization** involves imagining yourself in a successful situation, such as presenting your speech effectively to a supportive audience. This technique has been found to reduce the communication apprehension of public speaking students.[54] If you contemplate negative situations such as forgetting your notes, boring the audience, or having the podium fall over in the middle of your speech, anxiety can mount on top of anxiety.

Replace negative thoughts about your speech with positive images of your speech. Imagine that you are walking confidently to the front of the room. Then see yourself presenting your speech to the audience the same way that you would speak in a conversation with a friend. Visualize the audience nodding in agreement with a key point, smiling when an idea hits home, and laughing at your joke. Your speech was excellent! Imagine the audience's applause once you have finished your speech. The power of positive thinking is not just a cliché. When you replace negative thoughts about your speech with positive ones, you reduce your anxiety.

Use Relaxation Techniques.   Speech anxiety can cause your muscles to tense and can overload your mind with negative thoughts. If your friends noticed how you were feeling, they might say: "This speech is not a life-or-death situation. Chill. Relax." That is exactly what you would like to do, but few of us can relax on command when we are uptight. You can use several **relaxation strategies**.

Exercise is one effective form of relaxation before you do speech preparation tasks such as research, outlining, or practicing, and it can also relax you on the day you are scheduled to speak. Exercising reduces the stress in your body, and many people work more productively after they exercise. You can also relax wherever you are by tightening and releasing your muscles. Breathe in as you tighten a group of muscles and out as you release (you may want to progress from your neck muscles down to your feet). Finally, if these techniques do not work for you, try to budget some time for a different activity that you enjoy, whether it is reading, watching a movie (comedies are great for relaxation), listening to music, or gardening. If there is no time or opportunity for active relaxation techniques, imagine something that relaxes you. For some people, that may be sitting on the top of a mountain, for others, a sunset at the beach.

Relaxing thoughts or quiet muscle relaxation can be very helpful when you are waiting for your turn to speak. Your anxiety may heighten as the time for your speech approaches. You may be trying (unsuccessfully) to think of your speech word-for-word, or worrying about the audience's reaction to your speech. Instead of allowing negative thoughts to build up tension, try to use relaxation to reduce the tension.

Volunteer to Speak First.   Speakers experience a higher level of mental anxiety shortly before their performance than during the speech itself.[55] If

visualization: contemplating a successful presentation of your speech and favorable audience reaction.

relaxation strategies: techniques that reduce muscle tension and negative thoughts.

Comparing public speaking with dreaded tasks is not the best option for an apprehensive speaker. You can do more to relax by imagining a favorite place or activity instead. What is a thought that is relaxing to you?

you have high speech anxiety, ask to speak as early in the class or program as possible. That way there will be less time for your anxiety to build.

Never Defeat Yourself When You Are Speaking. During the course of a speech, it is easy to be your own worst critic. Focus on what you can do to deliver your message well. Do not fall into the trap of making negative judgments as you speak. Does an audience member look upset? If so, chances are that she locked her keys in the car or is worrying about her own speech, not expressing hostility to you.

Did you make a mistake? That does not make your speech a failure. Forget about it and continue on with your speech. Even if you make a major mistake, do not assume your speech is a disaster. Your classmates will be hoping you recover and finish strong, not silently snickering at your bad luck. Some speakers have encountered serious difficulties, such as delivering the wrong speech, remaining silent for two minutes while putting a jumbled pile of note cards in the right order, or watching their dog (a visual aid) have an "accident" as their speech concluded. When we have seen these situations in class, the first comment from an audience member has consistently been a supportive statement about the speaker's effort to recover from the problem.

● *The Audience and the Apprehensive Speaker*

In Chapter 4, on listening skills, you will read about the importance of being a good audience when your classmates are speaking. It is important to show this respect to all classmates, and this advice is essential when a speaker is obviously nervous.

One of the reasons for speech anxiety is the stress produced by standing up in front of a group of people, particularly if the speaker does not know most members of the group well. Apprehensive speakers worry that these unfamiliar people may dislike their speech and dislike them.

If a speaker seems very nervous when speaking, make a special effort to provide nonverbal support. An encouraging smile or an understanding nod when an anxious speaker makes a good point gives the feedback she or he needs. Many public speaking instructors ask students for feedback after speeches are presented in class. Be sure to write down what a speaker does well, so you can make a positive comment when his or her speech is discussed. Pay particular attention to the phrasing of criticism. Like any other student in a public speaking class, apprehensive students need to learn both what they are doing well and what they need to work on. Blunt criticism can easily make a student more apprehensive, but a well-phrased suggestion can make a speaker more competent and lead to greater self-confidence. The emphasis should always be on *constructive* criticism, something speakers can build on and use to improve their speech or delivery.

Can speech anxiety ever be eliminated? For most people, the answer is "no." Anxiety is a natural response, even for experienced speakers. However, there are ways to reduce apprehension and steps you can take to minimize its effects. If you experience some anxiety despite these efforts, you are just like many other people. Few speakers can avoid these feelings completely; indeed, moderate anxiety actually can help you be more focused on your speech, rather than taking a successful performance for granted.

The most important message of Chapter 1 is: ***Public speaking is "right" for you.*** On the first day of their class, Jabari, Brooke, Ciara, and Chas expressed typical concerns: What does one learn in a public speaking class? Is it relevant to my major? Is public speaking a skill that only a select number of fortunate people such as Jefferson and Mei-Xing can master? But when the term comes to an end, many public speaking students are looking forward to vacation but also are feeling better about their ability. Students become better speakers and are ready to put their skills to use. In our twenty years of teaching, we have never encountered a student who was *not* born to be a public speaker. We hope that this book can help make your study of public speaking worthwhile.

Summary

We began Chapter 1 with the reasons it is beneficial for you to study public speaking. You can use the skills and experience you gain in this class when you are assigned oral presentations in other courses. The ability to communicate well has been essential throughout history and will continue to be so in the twenty-first century. An ability to speak in public is useful in many careers, and many prospective employers are looking for college graduates with oral communication skills. Furthermore, effective public speakers can be decision makers rather than decision takers in their communities. When you participate in community organizations—whether political, recreational, educational, or religious—you can use the skills you learn in a public speaking class to have your voice heard and make a difference.

We considered the rich tradition of public speaking. For centuries, speakers from all parts of the globe have attempted to influence, inform, and entertain others. Public speaking played a vital role in the founding of the American republic, and as the twenty-first century begins, people who hope to make an impact on society continue to use public speaking to get their messages across.

Public speaking has a long history, but it is also a dynamic and evolving discipline. We provided four examples of contemporary themes:

- *Public speaking as a transaction.* Although the speaker was once conceptualized as a hypodermic needle "injecting" a message into audience members, public speaking is now recognized as a communication transaction. This means that the speaker and audience simultaneously act as sources and receivers of messages and achieve a shared meaning.

- *Public speaking in a multicultural nation.* The United States is a multicultural society. The audience you address may not share your world view. It is important to be aware of the diverse cultures represented in your audience and take those cultures into account when planning your message.

- *Public speaking and critical thinking.* Critical thinking, or making decisions after you have carefully evaluated alternative perspectives, is essential in speech preparation. You should use critical thinking to examine your opinions about the topic of your speech and also use it during the speech preparation process. Each stage of the five-step process you will learn will require you to carefully consider how you can best communicate your message to the audience.

- *Public speaking in an ethical manner.* A good speaker should be ethical as well as effective. It is important to treat your audience as you would want to be treated if you were an audience member, contributing to the ability of the audience to make a good decision rather than manipulating the members' decision.

In the last section of Chapter 1, we acknowledged that public speaking can be difficult for some people. Speech apprehension is a very real anxiety that most of us experience to some extent. Fortunately, there are a variety of methods that can reduce the effects of high speech anxiety, as shown in the following checklist of options.

Checklist

HOW SPEECH ANXIETY CAN BE REDUCED

Get Help for Speech Anxiety

____ Desensitization (p. 21)

____ Cognitive restructuring (p. 21)

____ Skills training (p. 21)

Use Self-Help Techniques to Minimize Apprehension

____ Select a topic you know and enjoy (p. 23)

____ Prepare your speech early (p. 23)

____ Take care of yourself (p. 24)

____ Visualize a successful speech (p. 25)

____ Use relaxation techniques (p. 25)

____ Volunteer to speak first (p. 25)

____ Never defeat yourself when you are speaking (p. 26)

Be a Supportive Audience Member

____ Provide nonverbal support (p. 26)

____ Provide positive feedback and helpful, constructive suggestions
(p. 27)

Key Terms and Concepts

source (p. 10)
message (p. 10)
encoding (p. 10)
channel (p. 10)
interference (noise) (p. 11)
receiver (p. 11)
decoding (p. 11)
transaction (p. 11)
feedback (p. 12)
shared meaning (p. 12)

culture (p. 14)
critical thinking (p. 17)
speech anxiety (stage fright) (p. 19)
communication apprehension (p. 19)
desensitization (p. 21)
cognitive restructuring (p. 21)
skills training (p. 21)
visualization (p. 25)
relaxation strategies (p. 25)

Source Notes

1. Whitworth, R. H., & Cochran, C. (1996). Evaluation of integrated versus unitary treatments for reducing public speaking anxiety. *Communication Education, 45,* 306–314, at 306.
2. National Association of Colleges and Employers. (1996, November 15). Employers predict better job market for new grads. *Job Web.* Retrieved July 17, 1999 from the World Wide Web: <http://www.jobweb.org/pubs/pr/pr111596.htm>.
3. Wage, K. (1998, December 7). Lack of communication becomes a hindrance in job search. *The Business Journal,* p. 35.
4. National Association of Colleges and Employers. (1997, July 8). Employers create composite of ideal employee. *Job Web.* Retrieved July 17, 1999 from the World Wide Web: <http://www.jobweb.org/pubs/pr/pr070897.htm>.
5. National Association of Colleges and Employers. (1997, July 8, p. 2).
6. Heldrich Center for Workforce Development (2000, June 14). *Are America's schools and skills making the grade?* Retrieved November 11, 2001 from the World Wide Web: <http://www.heldrich.rutgers.edu/publications/WTV/release614.000.doc>.
7. Finley, M. I. (1983). *Politics in the ancient world* (pp. 59, 73). New York: Cambridge University Press.
8. Bodde, D. (1967). *China's first unifier* (p. 181). Hong Kong: Hong Kong University Press.
9. Boahen, A. A. (1977). Kingdoms of West Africa (p. 69). In M. Bain & E. Lewis (Eds.), *From freedom to freedom.* New York: Random House.
10. Welch, G. (1977). The authors who talked (p. 39). In M. Bain & E. Lewis (Eds.), *From freedom to freedom.* New York: Random House.
11. Brooks, C., Lewis, R. W. B., & Warren, R. P. (1973). *American literature: the makers and the making* (vol. 1, p. 1179). New York: St. Martin's Press.

12. Brinkley, A. (1999). *American history: A survey* (10th ed., Vol. 1, pp. 103-104). Burr Ridge, IL: McGraw-Hill.
13. Gabler, N. (2001, January 14). A victim of the third great awakening. *Los Angeles Times,* p. M1.
14. Brooks, Lewis, & Warren (1973, p. 84).
15. Brekus, C. A. (1998). *Strangers and pilgrims: Female preaching in America, 1740–1845* (p. 3). Chapel Hill, NC: University of North Carolina Press.
16. Brinkley (1999, p. 132).
17. Lewis, P. (1973). *The grand incendiary: A biography of Samuel Adams* (p. 180). New York: Dial Press.
18. Brinkley (1999, p. 211).
19. Scott, R. L. (1990). Eisenhower's farewell: The epistemic function of argument. In R. Trapp & J. Schuetz (Eds.), *Perspectives on argumentation* (p. 155). Prospect Heights, IL: Waveland Press.
20. Bode, C. (1956). *The American lyceum: Town meeting of the mind* (p. 3). New York: Oxford University Press.
21. Bode (1956, pp. 48-49).
22. Lincoln-Douglas Debates of 1858. (2000). *Illinois in the Civil War.* Retrieved July 12, 2000 from the World Wide Web: <http://www.illinoiscivilwar.org/debates.html>.
23. DuBois, E. C. (1992). *The Elizabeth Cady Stanton–Susan B. Anthony reader* (p. 8). Boston: Northeastern University Press.
24. Zophy, A. H. (Ed.). (1990). *Handbook of American women's history* (p. 499). New York: Garland.
25. Harris, B. (2000, July 28). Texans take Bush fight on the road. *Los Angeles Times,* p. A16.
26. Ayres, A. (Ed.). (1993). *The wisdom of Martin Luther King, Jr.* New York: Penguin Books.
27. Muhammad, M. Z. (1998, February). Students are the vanguard of Million Woman March. *The Black Collegian, 28,* 10. Million Man March draws more than 1 million black men to nation's capital. (1995, October 30). *Jet, 88,* 4.
28. Berko, R. M., Wolvin, A. D., & Wolvin, D. R. (1985). *Communicating: A social and career focus* (3rd ed., p. 42). Boston: Houghton Mifflin.
29. Stewart, J. (1999). *Bridges, not walls* (7th ed., p. 16). New York: McGraw-Hill.
30. Lustig, M. W., & Koester, J. (1993). *Intercultural competence: Interpersonal communication across cultures* (p. 31). New York: HarperCollins.
31. Bodley, J. H. (1994). An anthropological perspective. *What is culture?* Retrieved July 12, 2000 from the World Wide Web: <http://www.wsu.edu:8001/vcwsh/commons/topics/culture/culture-definitions/bodley-text.html> (site last updated March 1, 1996).
32. *Hearing to receive testimony on S. 1367, S. 1617, S. 1670, S. 2020, S. 2478, and S. 2485: Before the Subcommittee on National Parks, Historic Preservation, and Recreation of the Senate Energy Committee,* 106 Cong., 2d Sess. (2000, May 11) (testimony of Arnoldo Ramos). Retrieved June 28, 2000 from the World Wide Web: <http://energy.senate.gov/hearings/national_parks/5_11Cats&Dogs/Ramos.htm>.
33. The myth of the melting pot. (1998). *Washington Post.com.* Retrieved July 12, 2000 from the World Wide Web: <http://www.washingtonpost.com/wp-srv/national/longterm/meltingpot/maps.htm>.
34. Esrey, W. T. (1998, September 23). *Remarks to the United States Hispanic Chamber of Commerce.* Retrieved June 23, 2000 from the World Wide Web: <http://www3.sprint.com/sprint/press/speeches/ushcc.html>.
35. Branigin, W. (1998, May 25). Immigrants shunning idea of assimilation. *Washington Post,* p. A1.
36. Lustig & Koester (1993, p. 11).
37. Former LULAC president receives nation's highest civilian award. *League of United Latin American Citizens.* Retrieved June 25, 1998 from the World Wide Web: <http://www.lulac.org/Issues/Releases/Obledo.html>.
    King, P. (1998, June 24). With gusto but no inferno, Obledo brought down "racist" billboard. *The Fresno Bee,* p. B1.

38. Reynolds, J. California's bizarre billboard war over immigration. *Minorities' Job Bank*. Retrieved October 27, 1999 from the World Wide Web: <http://www.minorities-jb.com/hispanic/politics/archives/billboard7.html>.

39. Bell, J. (1995). Evaluating psychological information: Sharpening your critical thinking skills. (2d ed., p. 72). Cited in J. Bell (1996, December 15), *Critical thinking as described by psychologists*. Retrieved July 14, 2000 from the World Wide Web: <http://academic.pg.cc.md.us/~wpeirce/MCCCTR/bell1.html>.

40. Morris, C. (1993). Psychology (pp. xv–xvi). Cited in J. Bell (1996, December 15). *Critical thinking as described by psychologists*. Retrieved July 14, 2000 from the World Wide Web: <http://academic.pg.cc.md.us/~wpeirce/MCCCTR/bell1.html>.

41. Bizzell, P., & Herzberg, B. (1990). *The rhetorical tradition* (p. 35). Boston: Bedford/St. Martin's.

42. McCroskey, J. C. (1986). *An introduction to rhetorical communication* (5th ed., p. 24). Englewood Cliffs, NJ: Prentice-Hall.

43. Sawyer, C. R. & Behnke, R. R. (1999). State anxiety patterns for public speaking and the behavior inhibition system. *Communication Reports, 12,* 33–41, at 33.

44. Hines, R. W. (1997, September). Addressing speech anxiety. *The Rotarian*. Retrieved June 23, 1998 from the World Wide Web: <http://www.rotary.org/publications/magazines/the_rotarian/9709/16.htm>.

45. Zimbardo, P. G. (1977). *Shyness: What it is and what to do about it* (p. 37). Reading, MA: Addison-Wesley.

46. Cronin, M. W., Grice, G. L., & Olsen, R. K., Jr. (1994). The effects of interactive video instruction in coping with speech fright. *Communication Education, 43,* 42–53, at 42.

47. McCroskey, J. C. (1977). Classroom consequences of communication apprehension. *Communication Education, 26,* 27–33, at 28.

48. Beatty, M. J., McCroskey, J. C., & Heisel, A. D. (1998). Communication apprehension as temperamental expression: A communibiological paradigm. *Communication Monographs, 65,* 197–219.

49. Allen, M., Hunter, J. E., & Donohue, W. A. (1989). Meta-analysis of self-report data on the effectiveness of public speaking anxiety treatment techniques. *Communication Education, 38,* 54–76.

50. Sawyer & Behnke (1999, p. 32).

51. Menzel, K. E., & Carrell, L. J. (1994). The relationship between preparation and performance in public speaking. *Communication Education, 43,* 17–26, at 24.

52. Behnke, R. R., & Sawyer, C. R. (1999). Milestones of anticipatory public speaking anxiety. *Communication Education, 48,* 165–172, at 171.

53. McCroskey (1986, p. 31).

54. Ayres, J. (1995). Comparing self-constructed visualization scripts with guided visualization. *Communication Reports, 8,* 193–199.

55. Sawyer & Behnke (1999, p. 34).

"Preparation and perseverance are the keys to a successful speech."

The Process of Developing a Speech

OBJECTIVES

After reading Chapter 2, you should understand:

- The importance of careful planning and preparation when you develop a speech.

- The classical canons of rhetoric and their applicability to speech preparation and delivery.

- The concepts of ethos, logos, and pathos.

- The steps involved in preparing an effective speech.

- How to apply those steps to prepare a beginning-of-the-semester speech assignment.

On August 28, 1963, tens of thousands of Americans participated in the March on Washington for Jobs and Freedom. The marchers began at the Washington Monument and proceeded to the Lincoln Memorial for an afternoon program that began with civil rights songs and hymns and culminated with speeches in support of civil rights.[1] After about three hours, the final orator stood at the lectern, with the Lincoln Memorial in the background, and addressed an audience that had grown to approximately 250,000 people.[2]

The speaker, Dr. Martin Luther King Jr., told the audience, "I have a dream." Dr. King's inspiring message about "a dream big enough to include all Americans"[3] deeply moved the audience, many of whom cheered and cried at its conclusion. The speech was covered by major television networks and newspapers and made an impression on people throughout the world. In the aftermath of the March on Washington, Congress passed civil rights legislation.

The "I Have a Dream" speech has been called "the greatest American speech since Lincoln's Gettysburg address."[4] Dr. King was a gifted public speaker; he had won an oratorical contest at age fifteen.[5] During his career he often spoke before thousands of people, and he had described his dream of freedom and equality on other occasions. If anyone could deliver an effective speech on the spur of the moment, it was an experienced and talented orator like Dr. King.

Nevertheless, Martin Luther King Jr. devoted most of the two days before the March on Washington to preparing his speech, and he stayed up all night before he spoke. It was "the most carefully written address he had ever delivered."[6] (Dr. King had the experience and talent to craft an effective

Martin Luther King Jr.'s "I Have a Dream" speech was one of the most eloquent and effective speeches of the twentieth century. The success of this speech shows the importance of careful preparation.

speech in two full days, working through the night. Less experienced speakers need to begin their preparation earlier.)

The careful consideration that Dr. King gave to his "I Have a Dream" speech exemplifies an important lesson about preparation that all public speakers need to learn: ***Preparation and perseverance are the keys to a successful speech.*** This adage expresses the essence of this chapter and of this book. We have found that students who have a well-organized plan for speech preparation, and who devote enough time to following that plan, become more effective speakers than students who rely on natural talent and confidence rather than hard work.

In Chapter 2 we examine speech preparation. The chapter begins by introducing this process. We consider the need for careful planning and then present the five classical canons of rhetoric, which are similar to the basic steps you should follow to prepare and deliver a speech. We also introduce the concepts of ethos, pathos, and logos, which you will see applied time and again during the speech preparation process throughout this text.

After introducing these important topics, we move to a key part of Chapter 2, the Basic Speech Guide. The Basic Speech Guide provides you with enough guidance to deliver a successful speech early in the term. In nearly any public speaking course, you will be presenting speeches to your classmates before you cover all the concepts explained in the textbook. As its name implies, the Basic Speech Guide is not meant to offer the last word on effective speech preparation; rather, it presents an overview of the steps involved in creating an effective speech. It is geared specifically to help you develop your first speech; comprehensive guides in Chapters 14 through 17 should be used to prepare your major speech assignments.

The Importance of Speech Preparation

Suppose that early in the semester, a class was asked to prepare five-minute speeches on the topic "Identify one artifact of your culture and explain why it is important to you." One student, Jason, selected bagpipes for his topic because his mother's side of his family came from Scotland. Jason was given a week to prepare, but he did not get started until the day before his speech was due. Then he went to the library and found a book that described the various parts of a bagpipe, an article on bagpipe history, and an encyclopedia entry on bagpipes.

When Jason got home, he sat down at his computer and began writing. First, he identified various parts of a bagpipe. Then he summarized the article on bagpipe history, dating back to the Roman Empire. Finally he included some information from the encyclopedia about Scottish bagpipes. At times, the encyclopedic information he wrote down duplicated a point he had already made, but Jason didn't notice. When he finished, it was late and he decided not to practice delivering his speech. He figured that his presentation would go well because he had just drafted it and it would be fresh in his mind.

The next day, when Jason started delivering his speech in class, the material seemed unfamiliar. As a result, he read his speech carefully, word-for-word, to the audience. He did not notice that his classmates lost interest when he began presenting material from the encyclopedia that duplicated what he had already said. He was unaware that when a speech is read to the audience by a speaker who is unaccustomed to the content, the delivery fails to generate audience enthusiasm. In order to present an effective speech, Jason needed a better plan.

● *Common Speech Preparation Problems*

Because Jason did not know how to go about preparing a speech, he experienced typical problems that students encounter when they are new to public speaking. Fortunately, careful preparation can address these problems.

The first problem is that speakers may not allocate enough time to prepare the speech. Students who wait until the last minute to get ready usually have weaker speeches than their better prepared classmates. This was true for Jason: he did not thoroughly research his subject, nor did he plan how to use his information most effectively. He allowed no time to practice delivering his speech. Even when there are only a few days to get a speech ready, it is best to get an early start and spread the preparation tasks over the available time.

A second problem results from speakers simply reporting whatever they happen to have researched. They do not consider what information might be most interesting or useful to their listeners, nor do they try to organize it in a manner that is easy to follow. This happened when Jason's encyclopedia information covered some points he had already made. Jason should have

It is important to practice your speech before presenting it in class. Check your schedule when you receive a speech assignment, and budget enough time to prepare.

selected the aspects of bagpipes that he wanted to emphasize to the audience and then presented them one at a time, using information from his research sources to support his ideas.

A third problem of preparation is revealed when a speech does not meet the objectives of an assignment. A speech that is well researched, organized, and presented, and that impresses many of the students in the class, will not be successful if it does not fulfill the purpose of the assignment. Jason erroneously included information about bagpipes that did not relate to the Scottish culture, and he completely failed to address the second part of the assignment, which asked him to explain why bagpipes were important to him.

These three problems are common for speakers in a beginning class. The good news is that you need not succumb to them; with a little hard work they can be avoided.

● *Careful Preparation Leads to Effective Speeches*

To prepare a speech successfully, you first need to know how to go about the business of preparation. Excellent speeches do not happen by accident. They are not a product of "good speech" genes, nor are they likely to be thrown together spontaneously an hour before they are presented. There are steps to follow in order to develop a first-rate speech. We introduce you to the basic steps in this chapter and elaborate on each of them later in the text.

In addition, we want to emphasize the importance of considering what is expected of you as a speaker when you plan your speeches. In classroom speeches, it is important to understand and fulfill all requirements of each assignment. Certain requirements are common in public speaking classes, and throughout this text we remind you of these typical expectations. In out-of-class speeches there is no professor giving an assignment, but you still will want to be certain that your speech fulfills the audience's expectations. In every speaking situation, there are topics and time parameters that are appropriate and others that are inappropriate. For example, a thirty-minute group presentation on the need to strengthen poultry inspection safeguards could satisfy the requirements of an oral assignment for an animal science or nutrition class. A half-hour speech, however, would be too long for most after-dinner speeches, and this topic would be particularly inappropriate if the audience had just dined on chicken enchiladas!

Speech Preparation: A Five-Step Process

The process for speech preparation that we recommend is not new. In the Basic Speech Guide that we present later in this chapter, and in the speech guides for later assignments (in Chapters 14 through 17), the steps you will learn are based on the classical canons, or elements, of rhetoric, which have been taught for more than two thousand years.

Cicero (106–43 B.C.E.), a Roman lawyer and politician, was one of history's most accomplished orators. In *De inventione* (I. 9) he described five elements essential in the preparation of any speech. Cicero referred to them as invention, arrangement, expression, memory, and delivery. These are the classical canons of rhetoric, and they continue to be important factors shaping the preparation of a speech. These canons have had a significant influence on the five steps of speech preparation that we recommend in this text: invention, organization, style, preparation, and delivery.[7]

Invention is the generation of ideas for use in your speech, including your own thoughts on the topic and ideas that you have researched. Under the topic "invention," we also include the selection of ideas that will best achieve your objectives in an ethical manner. Successful invention requires a sound understanding of your audience and an ability to apply the concepts of *ethos, logos,* and *pathos* (see In Theory box 2.1 on the next page) to develop an effective and credible speech.

Organization (arrangement) is the structuring of your ideas in a way that conveys them to the audience effectively. Most speeches (including nearly every classroom speech) have three main parts—introduction, body, and conclusion. The core of your speech is the body. The best way to arrange the ideas in the body depends on your objectives.

Style (expression) involves the selection of language that will best express your ideas to the audience. Good style includes stating your ideas clearly and understandably, making your ideas memorable, and avoiding bias in your language.

Preparation (memory), as we use the term, refers to the work you do in order to be in command of your speech when you present it to the audience.[8] The classical canon of memory originally emphasized the use of techniques both for learning a speech by heart and for selecting a mental stockpile of "the best words, phrases, and figures" taken from the best compositions, so that communicators "will always have in their memory something which they may imitate."[9] Ideas from this stockpile could be spontaneously recalled and injected when appropriate in a speech.[10] As we emphasize in Chapter 11, on delivery skills, there are few situations where a memorized, word-for-word presentation is appropriate anymore. Nevertheless, it is important to prepare

invention: generating ideas to use in your speech.

organization: organizing your ideas to convey your message effectively.

style: selecting words that best express your ideas to the audience.

preparation: in contemporary usage, planning and practicing to be in command of your speech.

INVENTION	ORGANIZATION	STYLE	PREPARATION	DELIVERY

In Theory 2.1

ETHOS, LOGOS, AND PATHOS: IMPORTANT CONCEPTS IN SPEECH PREPARATION

During the *invention* stage of speech preparation, you consider what points you might want to use to develop your topic or thesis, and you select those that will best enable you to communicate your message to the audience. Here we introduce three concepts that are very important to this process. *Ethos, logos,* and *pathos* have been recognized as essential modes of proof in speeches for twenty-five centuries. Aristotle (384–322 B.C.E.), one of history's most renowned teachers of rhetoric, philosophy, and ethics (among other subjects), explained these three "species" of proof. In his *Rhetoric,* Aristotle wrote that **ethos** refers to the credibility of the speaker, **logos** to the capability of the speaker's message to show the truth to the audience, and **pathos** to the speaker's ability to dispose the audience to feel emotion.[11]

Centuries later, appeals to ethos (credibility), logos (reason), and pathos (the emotions) continue to be recognized as important means by which speakers achieve their objective. Modern communication researchers have added to our understanding of these three vital forces. We explain them here; in later chapters we show you how to use them to develop an effective and ethical speech.

limited notes to remind you of the ideas that you intend to develop and for use when practicing the delivering of your speech.

Delivery refers to the use of your voice and body as you are presenting the speech to your audience. Strong delivery skills make a powerful impression on an audience; poor delivery skills have the opposite effect. Therefore, you need to ensure that your voice, gestures, eye contact, and movements are appropriate for the audience and the setting of your speech.

● Ethos: The Credibility of the Speaker

Aristotle wrote that *practical wisdom* and *virtue* are major components of a speaker's ethos. He also noted that speakers should exhibit *goodwill* toward the audience, meaning that speakers should want what is best for their audience, rather than what benefits themselves.[12]

For *practical wisdom* and *virtue,* contemporary scholars substitute *competence* and *trustworthiness.* If audience members perceive that a speaker is knowledgeable about the subject of his or her speech, and can be relied on to be honest and fair, they are more likely to believe what is being said.[13] Contemporary research has identified three elements of *goodwill:* understanding another person's needs and feelings, having empathy for others' views (even if the speaker does not agree), and being quick to respond to the communication of others.[14]

In sum, if you are to be a credible speaker, your audience must recognize that you know your subject well, must believe that you speak truthfully, and must believe that you care about them.

● Logos: Proving Claims to the Audience

Aristotle wrote that "persuasion occurs through the arguments when we show the truth or the apparent truth from whatever is persuasive in each case."[15] Whether you are attempting to persuade, inform, or achieve other

View Elizabeth Dole making an appeal to ethos at the Duke University Commencement.
CD-ROM: Video Theater, Excerpt 2.1

delivery: the use of your voice and body to present the speech.

ethos: the credibility of the speaker.

logos: the capability of a message to prove truth to the audience.

pathos: disposing the audience to feel emotion.

objectives, in most speeches you need to convince your audience that points you make are *likely* to be true. (We say "likely" because few claims can be proven with absolute certainty, and most decisions are based on what we believe is probably true.) You show that your claims are probably true by providing supporting reasons that are convincing to the audience.

In this text, we discuss several methods of proving claims to your audience. Formal logic offers one possible means of supporting an idea, but the term *logos* has a broader meaning. *Logos* also refers to an explanation or rationale for action, and to argument and discourse.[16]

One option for supporting a claim is through the use of information from credible sources that you have researched. If you back up your assertions with proof, and if audience members believe that the source of your proof is credible, they are likely to accept your claim.

You can also prove a point through the use of reasoning. There are several common patterns of reasoning, such as providing examples that support the claim you are making or comparing a known situation to a less familiar one.

Audiences may also judge a claim to be true because it appears to be consistent with a believable story. Brief anecdotes or more extended stories can be used to make a point to the audience. According to one major perspective on communication, humans are by their very nature storytelling beings, and people evaluate communication as they evaluate stories.[17]

Audience members will have different responses to a speech depending on the effectiveness of the speaker's appeal to emotion (pathos). When actor Michael J. Fox testified before a Senate appropriations subcommittee hearing on stem cell research, listeners probably found his words compelling because of his own experience with Parkinson's disease.

● *Pathos: Disposing the Audience to Feel Emotion*

Aristotle objected to many of the handbooks on rhetoric of his era because they focused on arousing emotions rather than using more reasoned arguments, but he recognized that humans do not base judgments on logic alone.[18] He noted that an audience will have different responses to a speech, depending on the emotion (pathos) they are led to feel.[19] In the *Rhetoric*, Aristotle analyzed a wide variety of emotions that could be aroused in an audience, including anger, calmness, friendliness, enmity, fear, confidence, shame, and pity.

Human emotions have been referred to as "the primary motivating system of all activity."[20] An audience may be influenced by one speaker but not another because one speaker was able to invoke a greater emotional response.

One example of the influential role of pathos came during public hearings on a ban on recombinant DNA research in Cambridge, Massachusetts. Opponents built a logical case for the ban, providing a detailed analysis of the safety hazards and an appeal for "the inviolability of the human germ plasm."[21] Speaking against the ban, Dr. David Nathan focused on compassion for children with cancer. He said that he had no "love of the germ plasm"; instead he was concerned about the needs of his patients. He noted that he had twenty patients with cancer and could name every one of them for the audience. Dr. Nathan indicated that he was counting on developments in DNA research to deal with his patients' problems.[22]

The outcome of the hearing was a recommendation that DNA research be permitted (with safeguards). The appeal to pathos had been effective. The board members making the recommendation, including some previously opposed to the research, were persuaded by the emotional appeal. One

View Fidel Castro making an appeal to logos at the UN Earth Summit.
CD-ROM: Video Theater, Excerpt 2.2

View Lou Gehrig making an appeal to pathos during his farewell address at Yankee Stadium.
CD-ROM: Video Theater, Excerpt 2.3

"Let's run through this once more—and, remember, you choke up at Paragraph Three and brush away the tear at Paragraph Five."

Might the decision have been different if opponents of DNA research had used narratives such as *Frankenstein* and *Jurassic Park* to support their argument, while supporters merely recited dry statistics about cancer? See page 231 on effective use of supporting materials.

Ethics is the subject of Chapter 3, and ethical considerations are covered in each speech guide in Part Two.

View Richard Nixon making an appeal to pathos during his "Checkers" speech.
CD-ROM: Video Theater, Excerpt 2.4

member indicated that she was impressed by Dr. Nathan, noting that "he was pale with the passion of the children." Another indicated that "when you start raising issues of childhood cancer, it has a very persuasive force to it."[23]

Speakers who use appeals to pathos should do so with care. Emotional appeals can make a powerful impression on an audience, but they can also be abused. A speaker might persuade certain audiences by appealing to racist beliefs—a strategy that would be repugnant even if it were effective.[24] Ethical considerations are very important when you are planning appeals to pathos.

When using appeals to pathos, be sure to keep your audience in mind. Audience members can be persuaded by an emotional appeal when it is consistent with their values. However, an emotional appeal cannot create feelings that the audience simply does not have. For example, a speech describing how a veterinarian performed surgery on an injured Labrador retriever would appeal more to an audience of dog lovers than to a group that was not interested in dogs. It is necessary to know your audience well when making an appeal to pathos.

In sum, ethos, logos, and pathos will have important influences on the audience's reaction to a speech. We tie these concepts directly into speech preparation in each of the speech guides in this text.

Preparation and perseverance are the keys to a successful speech.
To use your time wisely and ensure the best results from your hard work, you need a plan for preparing your speech.

The Basic Speech Guide has two purposes:

1. *To orient you to the process of developing a speech.* You will learn what steps to follow in order to prepare and deliver an effective speech. These five steps are modeled on the classical canons of rhetoric (see Table 2.1), and you can use them to prepare any type of speech.

2. *To guide you in the preparation of a first speech assignment.* The Basic Speech Guide provides you with information about each step to use to prepare a first speech assignment. Chapters 3 through 12 elaborate on each step of the preparation process, and the speech guides (Chapters 14 through 17) provide more comprehensive advice for following these steps on each of the major speech assignments you are likely to have later in the course. You can also use the Basic Speech Guide or the more detailed speech guides to prepare for public speaking opportunities out of class.

1. Inventing Your Speech

● Analyze Your Audience

A speech is delivered for the benefit of the audience. To make your speech worthwhile for your listeners, begin your speech planning with **audience analysis**. This means that you learn about the audience members (or make educated guesses) before selecting a topic and choosing the ideas you will use to develop that topic. After you select a topic, you will continue to use audience analysis in order to decide how best to develop that subject for your audience.

You may not have the opportunity to conduct a detailed audience analysis before an early-in-the-term classroom speech. However, you probably have had conversations with classmates and learned about their interests and backgrounds. You may also have heard them share information about themselves, particularly if your instructor had all students introduce themselves

Audience analysis is the subject of Chapter 5. Follow these steps before choosing a topic.

TABLE 2.1 The Five Steps for Speech Preparation

CANON	SPEECH GUIDE STEP
1. Invention	1. Inventing Your Speech
2. Organization (Arrangement)	2. Organizing and Outlining Your Speech
3. Style (Expression)	3. Using Effective Style in Your Speech
4. Preparation (Memory)	4. Refining and Practicing Your Speech
5. Delivery	5. Delivering Your Speech

audience analysis: considering the characteristics of your audience to understand their orientation to your speech.

or a classmate early in the course. In addition, you and your classmates will have common experiences in your public speaking class and common experiences as students at your college.

Here are some examples of questions that may be useful for analyzing your audience:

- Are there popular sports teams, activities, and traditions on campus? Unpopular experiences such as scarce parking and long waits for financial aid checks?
- Are the students in your class interested in politics? If so, what political affiliations are common?
- Are many of your classmates seniors? Freshmen? Do most students live on campus or commute?
- What are the cultures and backgrounds of your classmates? Are they similar to yours or different?

Jot down your ideas about your classmates and your common experiences. When we cover topic development in this Basic Guide, we suggest how you can use these ideas to make your speech worthwhile for the audience.

● *Select and Refine Your Topic*

Your **topic** is the subject you will address in your speech. Usually, the topic for your first speech depends on the assignment you are given. Representative assignments include informing the class about an interesting topic you studied in another course, telling the class about a pet peeve, or persuading the class that a particular problem in society is serious. Your topic must fit the requirements of the assignment.

To choose a topic, make a list of potential topics and select the best one. Use your audience analysis to make an educated guess about which topic will be most interesting to the audience. Your choice should also be familiar and interesting to you.

After selecting a topic, decide on the **specific purpose** of your speech. The specific purpose is the primary goal of your speech. Speeches have different goals, such as:

- *Informing:* increasing your audience's understanding or awareness of your subject
- *Persuading:* trying to influence your audience's beliefs or actions with respect to your subject
- *Inspiring:* touching your audience's feelings or emotions
- *Entertaining:* providing your audience with a lighthearted (but worthwhile) look at your topic

Unless a purpose is assigned, decide what is most important for audience members to understand, believe, feel, or do about your topic after they listen to your speech. That will be the specific purpose of your speech. Here are some examples of specific purposes:

Topic selection is detailed in Chapter 6.

Deciding on your specific purpose is discussed on pages 134–36.

topic: the subject you will address in your speech.

specific purpose: the primary goal of your speech.

To inform my audience about how my ethics course helped me to formulate guidelines for living

To convince my audience to consider compatibility first when choosing a roommate

To tell my audience why African-American mothers are my heroes

To entertain my audience with a lighthearted look at the late-registration process on our campus

● *Generate Ideas to Support Your Topic*

Your specific purpose is the basis for the content of your speech. The ideas you ultimately develop and the information you present must support this purpose. You generate these ideas through brainstorming and researching.

Brainstorm Supporting Ideas.   When you are **brainstorming** ideas for your speech, you list every idea that comes to mind for developing your topic. Remember that you should consider ethos, logos, and pathos. Use these guidelines to generate the maximum number of ideas:

For ethos, logos, and pathos, see pages 38–40.

1. *Write down any ideas you might be able to use to develop your topic.* During the brainstorming session, your goal is to create a diverse list of *possible* ideas for your speech, not to make a final decision about which ones you will use. That decision should not be made until you have considered your own ideas, researched your topic, and reviewed your audience analysis.

2. *Consider your interests, knowledge, and concerns about your topic.* Be certain to write down anything you might be interested in saying to explain your subject and achieve your specific purpose.

3. *Use the ideas you have as a basis for generating more ideas.* For example, if you plan to define a term or concept, ask yourself whether there are other ways you could get your audience to understand it, and whether there are other terms you should define. If you note a possible solution to a problem, ask yourself whether there are other ways the problem could be solved.

4. *Write down ideas even if you are not sure they are correct.* When you research your speech, you can check the validity of these ideas and exclude any that turn out to be unsubstantiated.

5. *Write down ideas even if they do not appear to be very strong or important.* Later, when you are selecting the ideas you will use, you can analyze their quality. At that time you can decide whether a given point should be included, needs to be strengthened, or should be rejected.

Research Your Topic.   Research is an important step when you are preparing a speech. Information from experts on your topic will strengthen the credibility of your speech. Even if your instructor requires less research for your first speech than for later assignments, research will help ensure that there are no gaps in your knowledge of the topic. You can also find answers to any questions you have about your subject.

For ethos and credibility, see page 38.

brainstorming: listing *all* possible ideas as they come to mind, withholding decisions on their merits.

Research is an important step when you are preparing a speech. This student uses the library reference shelves, one of many resources available for research.

Many resources are available for researching your speech—for example, the library, the Internet, and interviews with authorities on your topic. If you are working on a speech early in the semester (before you have read Chapter 7, on research), we recommend that you start with the resources with which you are most familiar.

Keep an accurate **bibliographic record** of each book, article, Web site, or other source that you consult and may want to use in your speech. This record should include

- Author's name
- Author's qualifications (reasons why the author is qualified to speak on your subject, such as his or her job, education, or reputation in the field)
- Name of the research source (book title; newspaper, magazine, or Web site name; and so on)
- Publication date or the date a Web site was last updated
- Page(s) on which you found the information

Record, copy, or print useful information that you find while researching. If you are taking notes, be sure to copy the author's words accurately. Keep all the information you find in one familiar place, so it will be easily accessible when you prepare your speech.

● *Choose the Best Ideas to Develop Your Topic*

Next, decide which ideas you will develop in your speech. Consider each idea that you generated while brainstorming and researching. Highlight those that appear promising, and cross off any that you decide not to use.

bibliographic record: basic information about the author and the publication or Web site for a research source.

Ethics, audience analysis, and your specific purpose are important factors to consider when you are choosing the best ideas.

Ethical Considerations in Content Selection.
Public speakers have an ethical responsibility to their audience. You owe the people who give up their time to listen to your speech an ethical presentation. It may not be possible to convince every audience of your viewpoint, or captivate each person with your information, but you should always end your speech knowing that you have been conscientious and honest.

As you prepare your first speech, a good general rule is to treat your audience as you would expect a speaker to treat you. Think of what goes through your mind when you hear a person making a sales pitch. Most people wonder whether salespeople are telling the truth or would say anything to make a sale. You do not want your audience to have a similar attitude toward you. If you have questions about the ethics of presenting any of the ideas from your brainstorming or research, cross them off your list and exclude them from your speech. Once you have excluded any idea that raises ethical concerns, it is important to determine which ideas would best communicate your message to your audience.

Audience Analysis and Content Selection.
Audience analysis is an essential consideration when you are selecting ideas. Review the audience analysis you prepared as you began to work on your speech, and add any new information discovered since then. Use this information to choose the ideas that will be best for your audience. Here are several key principles to keep in mind when you use audience analysis to adapt your speech to the audience:

- Include points that show the audience how they can use the information you are presenting.
- Include points that show the audience how they are affected by the topic you are discussing.
- Include examples that are likely to be familiar to the audience.
- Use research sources that the audience is likely to find believable.
- Consider what the audience is likely to know about your topic, so that you do not select material that is too complex or so simple that they lose interest.

On your list of potential ideas for your speech, cross out ideas that are unlikely to be effective, given your audience analysis. Highlight any ideas that you think will be particularly effective in conveying your message.

Your Speech Objective and Content Selection.
Your specific purpose is the third major factor to consider when you are selecting ideas to include in your speech. To accomplish your specific purpose, you may need to help the audience understand new material, prove facts to the audience, touch the audience's emotions, or achieve a combination of these objectives. Here are the types of information that should be a priority for selection, depending on your objectives.

To Increase Audience Understanding.   Often in your speech you will be presenting information that is familiar to you but new to many members of the audience. To increase audience understanding, select ideas that define new terms and provide descriptions of unfamiliar people, places, or objects. One of the most effective ways to introduce new information is by *comparing* that information with something familiar to the audience.

To Prove a Fact to the Audience.   If there are facts that audience members must accept before they will agree with a point you are making, you must prove those facts to their satisfaction. Use *logos* to accomplish this objective.

The proof you offer can be based on evidence or reasoning. **Evidence** is information taken from your research sources. The evidence you present should come from a person whom the audience will accept as knowledgeable and unbiased. When you use **reasoning**, you must supply a good reason that will convince the audience that the claim you are making is true. When you develop reasons, remember that the members of your audience will judge whether your "story" rings true.

To Touch the Audience's Emotions.   To inspire the audience, appeals to pathos are very important. Two methods to use are *humanizing general facts* and *developing empathy.* Use specific examples, and show the audience that real people are behind the facts and numbers you present. For example, in a speech on aiding the homeless you might provide an example of a young child in a homeless shelter who benefited from a volunteer's help. You can use empathy to touch listeners' emotions by helping them imagine how they would feel "in another person's shoes."

Once you have selected the best ideas based on your ethics, audience analysis, and speech purpose, you need to organize these ideas effectively.

2. Organizing and Outlining Your Speech

● Introduction to Organization

A speech should be *well organized.* Your ideas need to be structured in such a way that the audience can follow your message easily. To organize your speech, draft an **outline** that clearly lists the points and subpoints that you intend to make in your speech.

A speech outline has three major parts: the *introduction,* the *body,* and the *conclusion.* The **introduction** gains the audience's attention and orients the audience to your speech topic and structure. The **body** of your speech develops and supports your main points. The **conclusion** summarizes your main ideas and provides a memorable ending to your speech.

● Outline the Body of Your Speech

The body of your speech, where you develop your message, will be the longest section because it is the heart of your speech. Prepare the body first, even though the body of your speech will follow the introduction when you present your speech. You need to know the content of your speech *before* you plan the introduction or conclusion.

For logos and evaluation of claims, see page 38.

For more on outline formats, see Chapter 8.

evidence: information obtained from research sources.

reasoning: supplying good reasons why supporting materials justify a claim.

outline: a listing of the points and subpoints that convey the message of your speech.

introduction: the first part of a speech; it gains the audience's attention and orients the audience.

body: the main part of a speech, where the main points are developed and supported.

conclusion: the final part of a speech; it summarizes the main points and provides a memorable ending.

Begin outlining the body of your speech by selecting a limited number of main points and then organizing the material that supports those main points.

Select Your Main Points.   The body of a speech develops a few specific **main points**—major ideas that you plan to emphasize. It is common to have from two to five main points, although your instructor may ask you to develop a single main point in your first speech.

Review your list of ideas. Evaluate the ideas that you highlighted, and select the ones that you believe will be most interesting and useful for your audience. If an idea will take a minute or two to explain and develop, it can be a main point by itself. If you have ideas that will take less time to present, attempt to group them into categories so that two or more of these briefer ideas support one main point. Be sure to select an appropriate number of main points, given your speaking time.

Express each main point in a single sentence that states the idea you are developing. On your outline, number each main point with a Roman numeral.

Develop Your Main Points.   Main points are supported by **subpoints**. They put "meat" into your main points and enable the audience to understand why the points you are making are true. On your outline, indicate each subpoint with a capital letter, and indent each one under the main point it is intended to support.

An important principle of outlining is **subordination**. Each main point must relate to your specific purpose, and each subpoint must relate to the main point it supports. If you include supporting material under any subpoint, it must relate to that subpoint.

Proper **citation of evidence**, in your outline, is also important. When you are basing an idea on information you have researched, you must attribute that idea to the original author. Identify the author, his or her qualifications (if available), the source of your evidence (book title; name of magazine, newspaper, or Web site; and so on), the date, and the page number.

Here is an example of an outline of one main point. This example comes from the first speech assigned to students in a public speaking class that was part of the International Summer Program held in 1999 at California State University at Fresno. The students were asked to compare something from their home countries or cultures with something they observed in the United States. Hyun-Jung Kim analyzed provisions for disabled people in the United States and Korea. Notice some of the different means she uses to support her main points.

> For an example of citation of evidence in an outline, see the outline that begins below.

main points: a limited number of major ideas to be emphasized in a speech.

subpoints: ideas that support a main point.

subordination: making supporting materials relevant to the point that they are intended to support.

citation of evidence: providing bibliographic information that identifies the original source of evidence.

Body

I. I have been impressed by provisions for disabled people in the United States.
   A. The U.S. has an Americans with Disabilities Act. According to the Rocky Mountain ADA Technical Assistance Center, on their *ADA*

Use of evidence

Homepage, last updated June 10, 1999, "The ADA extends rights and responsibilities to people with disabilities that are no more and no less than those that already exist for other citizens."

B. I was glad to see provisions for disabled people on public transportation.

Use of example

1. While waiting for the bus at a shopping mall, I noticed a woman in a wheelchair and wondered how she could get on the bus. The bus came and the driver helped her on, using a special device for the wheelchair. He also helped her to use a safety belt. I marveled at this equipment and also the driver's kindness.

Use of comparison

2. In Korea, on the contrary, a disabled person could not even think about riding public transportation. When the bus arrives, everybody rushes to get on and the bus starts as soon as the last person steps on. Sometimes it is even hard for a person with no disability to get on the bus.

C. I was pleased to see how buildings are designed.

Use of examples

1. There are specially designed entrances for the disabled at most school buildings.
2. There are also special restrooms for the disabled at each building.
3. It is important to treat disabled people with respect. I would like to see these kinds of facilities built in Korea.

● *Outline the Introduction and Conclusion*

Draft the Introduction.   The introduction to a speech serves several important purposes. Every purpose is the basis for one major section of the introduction. Your instructor may require a specific combination of purposes in an introduction or have preferences for the order in which they are presented. Here we note five that are particularly important.

1. *Gain the Audience's Attention.* The audience must be focused on you and ready to listen. A frequently used technique for gaining audience attention is to begin with a brief story or anecdote, a quotation, a striking fact or statistic, or a joke. Relate the opening you choose to your audience and topic.

2. *Indicate the Thesis or Topic of Your Speech.* Once you have the attention of the audience, tell them what your speech is about—in a single sentence.

3. *Connect with Your Audience.* When audience members hear your topic, they may wonder, "What's in it for me?" In one or two sentences, summarize why audience members should listen to your speech. What does the topic have to offer them? Is there information they need to know? Information they can use themselves or share with loved ones?

For ethos and credibility, see page 38.

4. *Establish Your Credibility.* Your credibility, or ethos, influences the audience response to your speech. To establish with the audience that you are a believable source of information, describe any special expertise, experience, or education relating to your topic.

5. *Preview Your Main Points.* A preview of main points helps the audience follow your speech. It is similar to a road map in that it helps the audience understand where you will be going in your speech. In a preview, you tell the audience only the title or concept of each main point (in no more than one sentence per point). The development of these points takes place in the body of your speech.

Each component of your introduction should be brief so that most of your speech time is reserved for the body. Media law student Travis was assigned a speech to "discuss a subject that you learned in another college course." He selected copyright law, a topic he covered in his media law class. His introduction contained the following points:

Introduction

I. Imagine that you watch a new song by your favorite group on MTV. You want to hear it again, so you get on the Internet and try to use a service such as Napster and download it. But instead of this great new tune, you get the message, "this site is currently unavailable." That is what might happen if Napster loses a copyright infringement lawsuit.   *Attention-getter*

II. Today, I would like to introduce the topic of copyright infringement and explain how it may affect your ability to access music online.   *Indicate topic*

III. During our introduction speeches, all the students indicated that they listen to one or more types of music. Copyright law affects your ability to access that music.   *Connect with the audience*

IV. We studied copyright law in my media law course, and I also researched the Napster issue to prepare for this assignment.   *Credibility*

V. The topics that I will cover are the main purposes of copyright law, how the law applies in the Napster lawsuit, and how that case might affect your ability to access music.[1]   *Preview*

Draft the Conclusion.   In your conclusion, summarize what you have said, and leave the audience with a memorable impression of your speech. There are two main parts to a conclusion: a summary of what you said and an ending that we refer to as a **clincher**. The clincher is a closing sentence or paragraph that will leave your audience with a memory of your speech. A clincher may be related to the introduction (for example, supplying the happy ending to a story you began in the attention-getter). Or a clincher may consist of a statement or quotation that characterizes what your speech has been about.

Public speaking student Beu Her gave a speech introducing his classmate Liz Willey. In the introduction, he had noted that because of her love of cats, her friends sometimes call her the "Black Cat." Here is how Beu concluded his speech:

[1]After Travis presented his speech, the Ninth Circuit U.S. Court of Appeals held that Napster was liable for copyright infringement. Napster went offline in July 2001, although the company hoped to be back in business in 2002.

Sources: Gross, R. (2001, February 26). Ninth Circuit Napster ruling requires P2P developers ensure no one misuses their system. *Electronic Frontier Foundation.* Retrieved November 11, 2001 from the World Wide Web: http://www.eff.org/Intellectual_property/P2P/Napster/20010226_rgross_nap_essay.html>. Harris, R. (2001, October 30). New Napster delayed until next year. *Associated Press News Report.*

clincher: a closing that leaves the audience with a memory of the speech.

Conclusion

Summary

I. Today, we learned that Liz Willey is a dedicated biology student. She grew up in a Catholic family but now believes in Taoism and Buddhism. Liz is a vegetarian who loves pets, muscle cars, and all sorts of music.

Clincher

II. So if you ever see a woman driving a Camaro with her system up, playing the music of Steve Vai while eating a peanut butter sandwich . . . it is probably Liz, the Black Cat.

● Incorporate Transitions

Once your introduction, body, and conclusion are finished, connect the parts of your speech. You accomplish this through the use of transitions. A **transition** is a sentence that tells the audience that you are moving from one major idea to another. Transitions are helpful in the following places:

1. Between the introduction and the first main point
2. Between each main point
3. Between the final main point and the conclusion

Here is how Eric Johnson used transitions in his speech of introduction for classmate Erica Contreras:

- " . . . First, let's talk about Erica's athletic talents. . . ." *(transition from introduction to main point I)*
- " . . . There is more to Erica than athleticism. Let's consider her studious nature. . . ." *(transition from main point I to main point II)*
- " . . . Of course, there are other priorities in life besides studying, and she is very family oriented. . . ." *(transition between main points II and III)*
- " . . . Today, I hope you have found Erica to be as interesting a person as I have. . . ." *(transition from the body of the speech to the conclusion)*

3. Using Effective Style

Effective style is discussed in Chapter 10.

Good word choice can do much to make a speech memorable and interesting. Inappropriate word choice can confuse your audience and harm your credibility as a speaker. Here are some guidelines to remember when you are preparing your first outline:

- *Use words the audience will understand.* You cannot communicate if the audience does not know the meaning of your words.
- *Use precise terms to express an idea.* Select words that convey the specific meaning you intend, rather than more general terms.
- *Use language that makes your speech come alive.* You will have the greatest effect on your audience if your words help listeners to see and feel your

transition: a sentence that indicates that you are moving from one major idea to another.

ideas. Dr. King's word choice in the "I Have a Dream" speech was a major reason why the speech was so effective. The statement "I have a dream" conveyed a message of hope in a way that plain language such as "I think things will get better" never could.

- *Simplify your sentences.* Speeches differ from printed works because audience members cannot reread part of a speech if they become confused. When speaking, emphasize statements that express a single thought.

- *Avoid bias in your language.* You will lose credibility if your words stereotype or demean people. Avoid gender stereotypes, and do not use *man* or *he* when referring to situations and professions in which both men and women are likely to participate. Use the noun or phrase preferred by a particular ethnic group when referring to that group.

4. Refining and Practicing Your Speech

● Review Your Outline from a Critical Perspective

It is natural to feel a certain relief after completing your first speech outline. However, your speech will be even better if you review what you have written and make any needed corrections or changes. If possible, have a friend or family member read your outline and provide feedback. Your instructor or teaching assistant may be willing to look at it and make constructive suggestions.

Use the checklist on page 53 to ensure that no information is left out.

● Prepare for Extemporaneous Delivery

Extemporaneous speaking is an alternative to relying on a complete manuscript that is read or memorized word-for-word. When using **extemporaneous delivery**, a speaker relies on condensed notes, referring to them only when necessary. These limited notes are often written on note cards or printed on a small number of pages in a large font. For classroom speeches, check which form of notes your instructor prefers.

Extemporaneous delivery is the best type of delivery for most public speeches. When you speak extemporaneously, your notes include main points, the titles of major subpoints, and direct quotations. You explain and develop the subpoints in your own words, as you would in a conversation.

Your notes remind you of the main ideas. If you lose your place, you can refer to them to refresh your memory. Your style will seem more natural if you explain your ideas to the audience as you would in a conversation, rather than reading them from a script.

In sum, to prepare for extemporaneous delivery, practice delivering your speech with the complete outline first. As the content becomes familiar, practice developing the subpoints in your own words, referring to your outline only if you cannot think of what to say. After practicing several times, condense your notes.

TIP

Instructors have different policies for the length and format of speech notes. Be sure to check for what is expected.

extemporaneous delivery: a speech presented with limited notes that the speaker uses only to refresh his or her memory.

This is an extemporaneous presentation from limited notes. Prepare similar notes for your speech. Look at your audience while explaining your ideas in your own words. Use your notes only to refresh your memory.

5. Delivering Your Speech

● *Mitigate Communication Apprehension*

For tips for reducing speech anxiety, see pages 21–26.

It is normal to be nervous, particularly before you deliver your first speech. In Chapter 1 we presented several techniques for reducing apprehension. If you are extremely nervous about speaking in front of your classmates, check to see whether any professional assistance is available on your campus.

Effective preparation is one good method for reducing speech apprehension. If you follow the steps recommended in this chapter and take your instructor's advice, you will be well on your way to presenting a good speech. Use the checklist at the end of this chapter to remind yourself to include all the "right stuff."

● *Deliver Your Speech Well*

We present detailed advice on delivery in Chapter 11. But in the meantime what should you emphasize for your first speech? We have several recommendations, and your instructor may add some delivery practices for you to emphasize from the outset.

1. *Project your voice.* Speak loudly enough that your audience can easily hear what you are saying.
2. *Do not speak too fast.* Many speakers tend to rush through a speech, particularly if they are nervous. Speak at a rate that enables you to pronounce the words clearly and allows the audience to follow your speech.
3. *Convey interest in your topic.* People prefer not to listen to a speech delivered in a monotone. If you maintain energy and variety in your speaking voice, you will build audience enthusiasm for your speech.

4. *Maintain eye contact.* When delivering your speech, look at your audience. Make eye contact with a specific audience member for at least several seconds, and then change your focus to someone else. Be sure to make eye contact with people in all sections of the room during the course of your speech.

● Learn from Your First Speech

Recall the Chinese proverb that a thousand-mile journey starts with a single step. If your initial speaking assignment is the first step in your public speaking career, use that proverb to keep your speech in perspective. You will have more opportunities to speak in class and even more chances outside the classroom. If you can learn something from each speaking experience, you will grow as a public speaker.

Every speaker, whether a rookie or a veteran, has room for improvement in his or her public speaking abilities. Your instructor will provide feedback after the first speech, and your classmates will probably have the chance to offer suggestions, too. Listen to the ideas they present, and keep a record of any that you consider helpful for your next speech. Be sure to save any written comments from your instructor because these will remind you what he or she wants you to emphasize the next time you present a speech.

Summary

Preparation and perseverance are the keys to a successful speech. The most successful speeches in history, such as Dr. Martin Luther King Jr.'s "I Have a Dream" speech, are usually the result of careful thought and planning. Both beginning and more experienced speakers should remember this lesson.

In Chapter 2 we introduced the process of effective speech preparation. Use the checklist below to ensure that you effectively use the material you learned in this chapter to prepare your first speech. *Each instructor is also likely to have his or her own unique requirements for every speech assignment. Be sure to add your teacher's requirements to this preparation checklist.*

The five major steps on the checklist are similar to the classical canons of rhetoric (p. 37), and they can be followed to prepare all your speeches. In Chapters 3 through 13 we will elaborate on how you follow these steps to craft the best speech possible.

Checklist

INVENTING YOUR SPEECH

Analyze Your Audience

____ Learn about your audience (p. 41)

____ List facts and educated guesses about your audience (p. 42)

Select and Refine Your Topic

____ Select the best topic, considering your audience, your knowledge and experience, and the speech assignment (p. 42)

____ Determine your specific purpose (pp. 42–43)

Generate Ideas to Support Your Topic

____ Generate ideas through brainstorming and research (pp. 43–44)

Choose the Best Ideas to Develop Your Topic

____ Select the best ideas for your speech, based on ethics, audience analysis, and your objectives (pp. 44–46)

ORGANIZING AND OUTLINING YOUR SPEECH

Outline the Body of Your Speech

____ Select main points (p. 47)

____ Develop subpoints to support main points (p. 47)

____ Cite evidence properly in your outline (p. 47)

Outline the Introduction and Conclusion

____ Gain audience attention, indicate thesis or topic, connect with audience, establish credibility, and preview main points (pp. 48–49)

____ Summarize main points and draft a clincher (pp. 49–50)

Incorporate Transitions

____ Use transitions to connect main points and major sections of the speech (p. 50)

USING EFFECTIVE STYLE

____ Review the language used in your outline to ensure that you are using words the audience understands, precise terms to express an idea, words that make your speech come alive, simplified sentences, and bias-free language (pp. 50–51)

REFINING AND PRACTICING YOUR SPEECH

____ Review your outline from a critical perspective (p. 51)

____ Plan and practice extemporaneous delivery (p. 51)

DELIVERING YOUR SPEECH

____ Take steps to minimize speech apprehension (p. 51)

____ Check tips for delivery (pp. 52–53)

Key Terms and Concepts

invention (p. 37)
organization (p. 37)

style (p. 37)
preparation (p. 37)

Source Notes

1. Davis, L. G. (1973). *I have a dream . . . The life and times of Martin Luther King, Jr.* Westport, CT: Greenwood Press.
2. Ayres, A. (Ed.). (1993). *The wisdom of Martin Luther King, Jr.* New York: Penguin Books.
3. Davis (1973, p. 137).
4. Ayres (1993, p. 63).
5. Miller, K. D., & Lewis, E. M. (1996, p. 151). Touchstones, authorities, and Marian Anderson: The making of "I have a dream." In B. Ward and T. Badger (Eds.), *The making of Martin Luther King and the civil rights movement*. New York: New York University Press.
6. Ayres (1993, pp. 62–63).
7. Cicero. (1960). *De inventione* (H. M. Hubbell, Trans.). London: Heinemann.
8. Wilson. J. F., & Arnold, C. C. (1974). *Public speaking as a liberal art* (3rd ed., p. 337). Boston: Allyn and Bacon.
9. Bizzell, P., & Herzberg, B. (1990). *The rhetorical tradition* (pp. 32, 310). Boston: Bedford/St. Martin's.
10. Bizzell & Herzberg (1990, p. 310).
11. Aristotle. (1991). *On rhetoric* (G. A. Kennedy, Trans., p. 1356a). New York: Oxford University Press.
12. Aristotle (1991, p. 1378a).
13. Reinard, J. C. (1991). *Foundations of argument* (pp. 353–354). Dubuque, IA: W. C. Brown.
14. McCroskey, J. C., & Teven, J. J. (1999). Goodwill: A reexamination of the construct and its measurement. *Communication Monographs, 66*(1), 90–103, at 92.
15. Aristotle (1991, p. 1356a).
16. Johnstone, C. L. (1980). An Aristotelian trilogy: Ethics, rhetoric, politics, and the search for moral truth. *Philosophy and Rhetoric, 13*(1), 1–24, at 18.
17. Fisher, W. R. (1987). *Human communication as narration: Toward a philosophy of reason, value, and action.* Columbia: University of South Carolina Press.
18. Kennedy, G. A. (1991). Introduction (p. 39, n. 45). In Aristotle, *On rhetoric* (G. A. Kennedy, Trans.). New York: Oxford University Press.
19. Aristotle (1991, p. 1356a).
20. Callahan, S. (1988). The role of emotion in ethical decisionmaking. *Hastings Center Report 18*(3), 9–14, at 9.
21. Waddell, C. (1990). The role of *pathos* in the decision-making process: A study in the rhetoric of science policy. *Quarterly Journal of Speech, 76*(4), 381–400, at 386.
22. Waddell (1990, pp. 386–387).
23. Waddell (1990, p. 387).
24. McGee, B. R. (1998). Rehabilitating emotion: The troublesome case of the Ku Klux Klan. *Argumentation and Advocacy, 34*(4), 173–188.

"Always consider the ethical implications of a speech as you develop, draft, and deliver it."

3

Speech Ethics

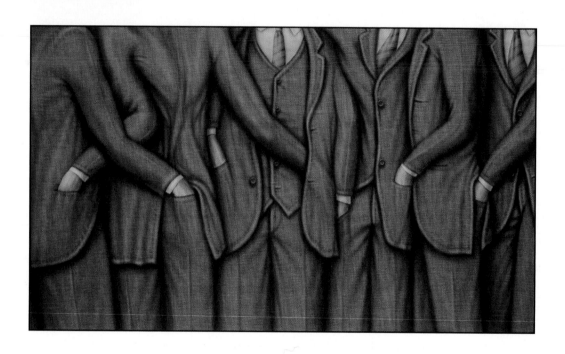

OBJECTIVES

After reading Chapter 3, you should understand:

- The importance of ethics in communication and public speaking.

- The distinction between situational and absolute ethics.

- The relationship between ethics and truthful communication.

- The ethical dilemmas posed by stealing the work of others.

- The ethical implications of reasoning and evidence.

- Guidelines for the ethical audience.

Suppose that John, a recent college graduate (and former speech student), is now working for an insurance company in the Midwest as an assistant to the benefits manager. John is efficient and friendly. One day when his boss is out of town on business, John is asked to speak for his boss at a department meeting. John presents several recommendations that could lower his department's operating costs and increase productivity. In so doing, John continually refers to these ideas as "mine" and as ideas "I have developed," although he borrowed from other people nearly all of the ideas he advocates.

After John's presentation, the department adopts his recommendations. As noted before, these recommendations will help the department, but they are not John's ideas.

Should John have acknowledged the originator of the ideas he presented? Or does his decision not to do so really not matter because the outcome was beneficial to the department?

Before you answer, let's add another wrinkle. Suppose that John personally benefits from this presentation—that because of it he receives a bonus or a promotion. Would that outcome affect your answer about his use of ideas that were not his own?

These questions raise the issue of *ethical responsibility in communication*—in this case, on the part of the speaker. A dictionary definition of *ethics* refers to the discipline dealing with good and evil and moral duty. *Ethics* is a term that many people use but few use in the same way, to mean the same thing. In this text, when we consider **ethics**, we are referring to a set of beliefs shared by a group about what behaviors are correct and what behaviors are incorrect. In that sense, ethics is really about how people should act toward one another. Have we been truthful? Have we treated others fairly? If we were to reduce the main message of this chapter to a single idea, it would

ethics: a set of shared beliefs about what behaviors are correct and what behaviors are incorrect.

be this: ***Always consider the ethical implications of a speech as you develop, draft, and deliver it.***

In this chapter we examine ethical behavior in public speaking, focusing on the different ethical concerns you may confront in the preparation or delivery of your speech. These include being truthful to your audience, crediting sources you use in your speech, carefully presenting your reasoning and evidence, and avoiding personal attacks and hate speech. Because ethical dilemmas can also confront audience members, we also consider the "ethical audience," examining such issues as being courteous and open-minded, listening and thinking critically, and holding speakers accountable for their words.

Ethical Behavior in Public Speaking

In nearly all facets of life, we may face ethical choices. In public speaking, ethics can be a factor in the development, writing, and delivery of a speech. It can also apply to the way audience members respond to a speech or speaker.

How do some people respond to the ethical choices they face? Some prefer to adopt a code of beliefs they will always use. We call this **ethical absolutism**, and it means what it says: The same ethical belief system must always be employed, regardless of the situation. Others employ an ethical belief system that they apply more selectively. These individuals believe in what is called **situational ethics**, meaning that ethical beliefs about the right behavior may vary, depending on the situation. In a public speaking context, most people believe that lying is wrong, a violation of ethics (not to mention, in some contexts, a violation of the law). But these same individuals might think nothing of intentionally exaggerating their qualifications or background in a presentation related to a job interview—particularly if they believe that "everybody does it and gets away with it." Would you agree with this?

Ethics can also vary from one culture to another. This is to say that some ethical standards are culturally relative. In some cultures knowledge is considered to be collectively owned. In cultures with a strong oral tradition, stories are passed from generation to generation and are shared as general cultural knowledge. In such cultures, working together or paraphrasing without attribution is not tantamount to cheating or unethical practice. In this book, however, our discussion reflects a Western cultural perspective, although we recognize that there may be other cultural views and beliefs about these subjects.

As you approach the following section on ethics, ask yourself: Do *I* have a set of beliefs regarding my behavior toward others? Do I have a code of ethics? Do I follow my code of ethics always and absolutely or only in certain situations? How do I apply it to my communication transactions, and particularly to public speaking? To help you answer these questions, we turn to some of the significant ethical issues you may face in communication, including practicing truthful communication, crediting the work of others, following rules of sound reasoning and avoiding fallacies, and never using hate speech.

View Christopher Reeve making an ethical appeal to pathos at the Democratic National Convention. CD-ROM: Video Theater, Excerpt 3.1

ethical absolutism: the belief that a single ethical system is appropriate in every situation.

situational ethics: ethical beliefs that vary from one situation or culture to another.

Practicing Truthful Communication

The first application of ethics in public speaking is quite basic: Tell your audience the truth. How do you feel when you find out someone has not been truthful with you? Most people resent it. Audience members who discover they have been lied to will seldom do or believe what the speaker has asked of them. Moreover, people remember when they have been lied to. A speaker who is known to have lied before will have a difficult time convincing an audience of his or her credibility in a speech.

That being said, it must also be stressed that the term *truth* is fairly subjective and eludes precise definition. It may be easier to describe what is meant by truth for the purpose of public speaking by describing what is *not* truth in public speaking.

Lying, completely withholding the truth, is the most obvious form of distorting the truth. With a lie, a speaker intends to deceive an audience. People often lie because they fear what listeners or an audience would do if they knew the truth. For example, a student named Martin once fabricated an identity for himself as an expert on the subject matter of his speech. Calling himself a public school teacher with ten years of experience as a kindergarten teacher, he addressed the subject of bilingual education in elementary school. Martin, however, had never been a teacher, but he feared how the audience would react to his ideas if they were aware of his lack of experience. Ironically, the audience might have accepted his ideas in any event. By lying, Martin placed himself in a precarious position if and when the audience learned of his deception.

Half-truths occur when a speaker reveals part of the truth but mixes it with a lie. In effect, a half-truth is the same as an outright lie: the audience is deceived. Consider, for example, Elisabeth, the division manager in a small company. In a presentation to her management committee, she admits that her division was not profitable in the past quarter and suggests that the reason for this underperformance was a slowdown in the economy, causing fewer people to buy her division's products. The first part of Elisabeth's explanation (about the economic slowdown) was truthful, but the rest (connecting the slowdown to the division's lack of profitability) was a lie. The real reason for her division's lack of profitability is that Elisabeth spent too much money settling costly lawsuits arising from her mismanagement.

False inference results when an audience reaches a conclusion that the speaker knows to be false. The speaker intentionally drops clues and cues designed to make the audience believe a falsehood. For example, in a presentation called "UFOs, Extraterrestrials, and the Supernatural," Jim, a student, described a series of unconnected events that occurred in a tiny midwestern town: an increase in the number of babies with birth defects, a slight increase in the rate of kidnapping, and a rapid increase in the amount of farmland seized by the government. Although Jim did not say there was a government conspiracy to conceal the presence of aliens and UFOs or a plot to cross-breed aliens and humans, he clearly intended the audience to draw this inference from his presentation of the "facts." In reality, the increase in babies with birth defects was an increase of one: from six to seven. The increase in kidnapping was actually a statewide statistic, believed to be due to a change in the laws about divorce and child custody. And the government

lying: deceiving by completely withholding the truth.

half-truths: statements that deceive by revealing part but not all of the truth.

false inference: an inaccurate conclusion that an audience reaches when a speaker provides misleading clues and cues.

had seized or forced the sale of land in some areas—but only for the construction of a highway bypass. Jim had arranged his facts so that the audience would infer that the government was trying to conceal the presence of space aliens.

Taking evidence out of context is another source of false inference. The speaker restates someone's words but does not explain to the audience the situation or context in which those words were originally expressed. The speaker selectively uses someone else's words to support his or her purpose.

In a speech about the dispute over whether electrical power lines in neighborhoods can be linked to higher-than-normal rates of cancer, Russell, a student speaker, quoted an epidemiologist and implied that the epidemiologist saw no connection between power lines and cancer. What Russell did not explain was that the expert's statement—"[T]here is no observable link between the presence of power lines and cancer in the area"—came from this longer statement:

> . . . My opponents have argued *there is no observable link between the presence of these power lines and cancer in the area*. But surely, they are wrong. While I cannot definitively say that one causes the other, there is still a connection of some kind, meriting further study. . . .

Russell tried to defend his use of this statement by arguing that he accurately quoted the expert's testimony. In point of fact, those were the expert's words, but Russell ignored their context and allowed his audience to infer a different conclusion from the one the expert had reached. By taking evidence out of context, Russell distorted the expert's words and misled the audience.

Omission, also a source of false inference, misleads the audience not by what is said but rather by what is left unsaid. Philosophers have long argued about whether keeping silent about something is lying—and is unethical behavior.

If silence about a topic will mislead an audience, and if you are aware of the likelihood of this deception but withhold information anyway, you have intentionally misled the audience. Lying, half-truths, false inferences, and taking evidence out of context are—unlike omission—all *active* efforts by the speaker to mislead. Nevertheless, the purpose of omission is to mislead or deceive, making omission similar to lying and the other means of deception.

A speaker who fails to practice truthful communication is inhibiting rather than enhancing audience members' ability to make good decisions. This type of speaker views audience members as consumers of information and takes a cynical *caveat emptor* approach: "Let the buyer (listener) beware."

Of course, some people lie, but most of us hope for and expect the truth—especially when listening to speeches. For this reason, deliberate acts of deception and silent omissions achieve the same effect: deception of the audience (see In Theory box 3.1).

In a student presentation about on-campus drug use, Jill was asked by a member of her audience (during a question-and-answer period) about the extent of the drug problem in her dormitory during the past year. Jill had forcefully argued that the university's zero-tolerance of student pot smokers was too harsh. When asked this question about her dormitory, however, Jill merely smiled and moved on to another question. To observers, her

President Bill Clinton provides an excellent example of how half-truths can affect the perception of a person's ethics. Here he apologizes to the country for not being completely honest in his statements about his relationship with Monica Lewinsky.

omission: failing to mention something and misleading the audience not by what is said but by what is left unsaid.

| **INVENTION** | **ORGANIZATION** | **STYLE** | **PREPARATION** | **DELIVERY** |

In Theory 3.1

THE TRUTH BIAS

In Chapter 2 we introduced the canons of rhetoric, one of which is *style*, the selection of language to best express your ideas. It is critical that the words you choose enhance your ethos as an honest speaker. Do most audience members automatically recognize a lie or other forms of deception in a public speaking situation? Not necessarily. Research indicates that 57 percent of the time most people cannot detect when they are being lied to.[1]

How many times have you witnessed a speech by a government official caught up in a controversy, by a public person accused of wrongdoing, or even by a classmate claiming experience or expertise? Do you automatically assume that someone is telling you the truth? Although political scandals and sensational trials involving celebrities may have raised the level of skepticism many of us experience when listening to politicians, lawyers, press agents, and the like, we typically do not experience the same skepticism when we are listening to ordinary people in public speaking situations. One reason for the difficulty in detecting a speaker's lie or deception is that no one verbal or nonverbal behavior infallibly distinguishes a lie or other deception from truth-telling.[2] Moreover, people often rely (erroneously, as it turns out) on their bias for truth-telling.[3] This so-called truth bias means that most people are inclined to judge messages as true.[4]

The strong presumption of truthfulness suggests that deception in speech making goes undetected half of the time. Of course, this begs the question of whether you should lie because you might get away with it. The strong bias for truth-telling should be an indicator to you that most people in this society want and expect honesty in communication.

---

silence suggested that there was no drug problem in her dormitory. In point of fact, her dorm had the worst record of on-campus drug abuse. Later, Jill defended her silence as appropriate because she had not lied about drug use problems in her dorm. Most of her classmates, however, said that her silence implied that there was no drug use problem. Her omission had misled the audience.

Never lie, never tell half-truths, never produce false inferences, never use evidence out of context, and never omit pertinent information. If you fear the truth may weaken your argument, then you need to do more thinking and researching about your topic. There are at least two sides to every issue, as well as multiple solutions and answers and different points of view to consider. If you fear what your audience may think if they know the truth, consider the opposite: what will people think if you lie to them and they know or find out about your deception? In most situations, the audience's reaction to a lie will be worse than their reaction to an unwelcome truth.

Furthermore, if you do not tell the truth, you may contribute to the making of a poorly informed decision by the audience. Always remember your obligation, as noted in our discussion of ethics in Chapter 1, to enhance the audience's ability to make a fair and rational decision.

> **TIP**
>
> *To be an ethical speaker, our advice is simple and practical: Always tell the truth in your speeches.*

Crediting the Work of Others

When you research a topic, you are likely to find interesting ideas and facts that you may want to use in your presentation. Should you write them into your speech?

If you doubt the consequences of lifting only a few words from a source without crediting them, consider the example of Senator Joseph Biden. In his quest for the Democratic nomination for the presidency in 1988, Biden used words that were not his own, taken from others' speeches. The media caught on, and a once-leading contender was out of the race.

TIP

Most colleges and universities have clear and strict rules about plagiarism. Any student guilty of plagiarism is likely to face serious legal consequences that will affect his or her success as a student.

For more on plagiarism, see page 173.

plagiarism: using someone else's words as if they were your own.

Suppose you find an article or perhaps the text of another speech on "your" subject. Maybe you like the way the article or speech is worded. Would there be any problem if you wrote the article into your speech? Would there be a problem if you took only a portion of the article or speech? (The answer to those two questions is "yes.") Suppose you paraphrased what you had read. Could you use your paraphrasing without citing the original source? (The answer is "no.")

Using another person's ideas or words as if they were your own is **plagiarism**, and it is always unethical. If you plagiarize, you mislead the audience because you are misrepresenting the source of the material you use. If you plagiarize, you treat others unfairly because you are stealing their words or ideas. That is exactly what John did in the example given at the beginning of this chapter. By suggesting the ideas in his speech were his own, he misled the audience and unfairly profited from the experience.

Plagiarism is a particularly vexing problem for students of speech classes, who must (by requirement) research presentations as part of their assignments. Even well-meaning students are often confused as to what constitutes plagiarism. To help you understand, we will examine two situations in which plagiarism can occur: quoting from a source and paraphrasing the work of others.

● *Quoting from a Source*

A student named Stefan gave an informative speech called "The History of Stop Signs." He had gotten his inspiration for the topic from a newspaper article that he spotted in his mother's recycling pile when he was home from school one weekend. He thought the topic was unusual enough to make a great speech, and he immediately told his instructor that he wanted to use it.

When trying to research the speech, Stefan could find nothing beyond the newspaper article. As his speech day approached, he began to panic. In desperation, Stefan reasoned that no one in class would have seen the article, because it was in a small local paper. He took the article and used all of it, nearly verbatim, as his speech.

It turned out that the article was a reprint of a story that first appeared in a large national newspaper, and, coincidentally, Stefan's instructor had read it. Stefan's actions amounted to stealing, earning him an F in the class and triggering his school's disciplinary rules (automatic suspension).

What Stefan did is a clear example of plagiarism. But suppose he had taken only one-third or one-half or only a few lines of the article and represented the text as his own? Would that still be plagiarism? The answer is an unequivocal "yes." Whether Stefan used five pages, one page, or only one sentence, his actions would amount to stealing the words and ideas of the original writer. Whether you steal only one or two eggs or the whole dozen is of little consequence to the shop owner; in either case, you stole the eggs.

Plagiarism is particularly common when students research a speech topic by looking for background material on the Internet. The temptation to lift and use text from a Web site or Web page can be overwhelming. But doing so without attribution is stealing.

Most of the direct quotations that you use in a public speech will be short—a line or two or at most a paragraph. To avoid plagiarizing, you must attribute the quote to its source. How should you cite the source? Your instructor is likely to provide specific rules, and we strongly advise you to check with him or her before researching your speech.

Had Stefan relied on occasional quotes from the article, he could have attributed his borrowings in the following way:

> As Robert Smith wrote in the July 22nd issue of the *Sun County Times* (at page 44), "the history of the stop sign can be traced back to the old social controls imposed by early governments on pedestrian traffic."

The first part of this sentence is the attribution. Notice that the page number is mentioned. We recommend including it to be complete, although at times mentioning the author, source, and publication date may be enough.

For more on citation form, see pages 171–72 and Appendix B.

● *Paraphrasing the Work of Others*

Suppose Stefan had not lifted the text of the original but instead had used **paraphrasing**—restating the ideas of the author in his own words. Would that have been plagiarism?

This is where the rules about plagiarism become slightly murky. If you are using your words but not necessarily your own ideas, are you really stealing? In class, instructors do not expect you to be an authority on every topic on which you will speak; you *will* have to research your topics. You may be wondering: "How can it be plagiarism if I'm paraphrasing the words or ideas of another? After all, these *are* my words!"

For more on topic research, see Chapter 7.

Most students struggle with this question regularly in college. The answer comes in two parts. The first involves *what* and *how much* you are saying in your own words. Stefan could have rewritten the newspaper article about stop signs, putting everything in his own words but still using the structure and ideas or content of the original. Had he done so, his actions still would have been plagiarism because he would have taken the ideas and structure created by another person and represented them as his own. The difference between that and using the author's original words without attribution is only one of degree. Stefan would have added nothing to the original article, and he would have been trying to fool the audience into thinking that they were hearing his ideas and his method of arranging them.

Second is the matter of attribution. When you fail to acknowledge the original source, whether you are paraphrasing or directly quoting, you are being unfair to the original author and deceiving your audience. If Stefan paraphrased all or even part of the article without attribution, he would be guilty of plagiarism.

ESL	Paraphrasing

Paraphrasing can present a particular challenge for ESL students and other non-native speakers of English who hail from cultures with a strong oral, storytelling tradition. Acknowledgment of original sources may seem unnecessary to individuals from such cultures, where information is believed to be collectively owned and is passed in story form from generation to generation. Audiences steeped in Western culture may be unaware of the underlying reasons why some speakers do not credit the original source of paraphrased or quoted material. For this reason, always be careful to properly attribute your sources.

paraphrasing: restating the words of someone else in your own words.

How can you avoid plagiaristic paraphrasing? When you are creating a speech, do not paraphrase sections of someone else's words or ideas unless you give a full citation for the original source. Stefan, for example, should mention the author and source before presenting the information he is using:

> According to Robert Smith, writing in the July 22 issue of the *Sun County Times,* on page 44, more and more municipalities are replacing stop signs with traffic lights because they believe the lights will be more effective at preventing accidents. Smith suggests that communities that have made this change are seeing promising results.

The first part of the first sentence contains the full attribution. By providing it, Stefan ensures that the audience is fully aware of the original source of his words and ideas, and he treats the original author fairly.

Using Sound Reasoning and Evidence

Ethical problems also arise when a speaker intentionally misuses models of logic to deceive an audience. Although there are many models of logic, we focus on three that are commonly misused in speech class assignments, usually in persuasive presentations.

● Example Reasoning

A speaker who intentionally makes a generalization about all members of a group that is based on limited information about only part of that group commits a fallacy in **example reasoning**.

A student suggested in a speech that all apples grown in a certain county in northern Washington should be destroyed or at least boycotted because they had been found to contain residue of a toxic pesticide. Although she generalized about all apples grown in that county, the information she based her statement on applied only to three Washington Red apples taken from one farm.

There *was* a health risk; the speaker was correct about the need for caution. But she had knowingly over generalized about an entire crop of apples. As we explain in Chapter 9, this faulty reasoning is an fallacy, and it is frequently the product of sloppy or inadequate research. Before making such a broad generalization, this speaker should have done more research to see whether other varieties of apples or whether Washington Red apples on other farms also showed traces of the pesticide.

● Post Hoc (After the Fact) Fallacy

A **post hoc fallacy** occurs when a speaker knowingly attributes the cause of something to something else merely because one thing occurred after the other (the Latin phrase *post hoc* means "after this"). The speaker argues that "something happened after the fact, therefore because of the fact."

In a speech about famous murders, a student described the killing of a famous man by his ex-wife. The student suggested that if the woman had

For more on post hoc fallacies, see page 241.

example reasoning: a generalization about all members of a group that is based on limited information about only part of that group.

post hoc fallacy: falsely attributing the cause of something merely because one thing occurred after the other.

| INVENTION | ORGANIZATION | STYLE | PREPARATION | DELIVERY |

In Theory 3.2

PERSONAL ATTACKS AND HATE SPEECH

The canon of rhetoric pertaining to *style* stresses the importance of using language that avoids bias. In modern times, we think about bias in the context of bigotry and prejudice. Insults or epithets that attack an individual on the basis of certain immutable characteristics—such as race, ethnicity, gender, national origin, sexuality, religion, or age—are known

as *hate speech.*[5] Hate speech tends to dehumanize the individuals it targets, undermining their self-esteem and feelings of self-worth.[6] It can also bring out the prejudice and bigotry in an audience, directing their feelings toward an individual or group of people who share the same characteristics. Hate speech serves no constructive purpose, and we strongly advise against its use in class presentations. For more on the need to avoid biased language, see pages 277–79.

been drinking before the murder, "it could be argued that drinking caused the ex-wife to commit the murder, because alcohol is known to be a cause of criminal behavior." If this reasoning had been used in combination with other evidence (such as a weapon with the ex-wife's fingerprints), there would have been no problem. But because no other evidence was offered, the speaker misled the audience. By itself, the ex-wife's consumption of alcohol was proof of nothing.

● *Personal Attacks*

Some speakers try to advance a point or argument with personal attacks against their opponent. Such an attack is known as an **ad hominem attack**, (in Latin, *ad hominem* means "to the man").

In a student body campaign speech, one student referred to his opponent as "a racist," "a goody two-shoes," "a fascist," and "a radical-right religious nut," hoping to appeal to his audience's biases against outspoken Christians on campus. The opponent was an outspoken Christian Baptist, but there was no evidence that he was a racist, a fascist, or a radical-right religious nut. The speaker employed those words intentionally to deflect attention from himself and persuade the audience to reject the other candidate. Unless there is evidence to support the claims and the claims are relevant, this tactic is unethical. Deliberately launching an ad hominem attack is unfair to the person on the receiving end and misleads the audience. A variation of the ad hominem attack is an attack that expresses bigotry and prejudice. (See In Theory box 3.2.)

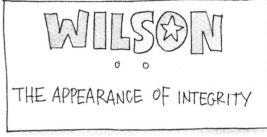

ad hominem attack: an attack on an opponent's character.

The Ethical Audience

Thus far we have discussed ethical issues in communication from the perspective of the speaker. Are ethics a concern only for the public speaker, or do audience members bear some responsibilities here as well? In this section we consider ethics and the audience. Among the qualities that characterize what we term the **ethical audience** are courtesy, open-mindedness, critical thinking, and willingness to hold the speaker accountable.

● *Be Courteous*

The first component of ethical behavior for an audience is fundamental: show the speaker the courtesy that you expect and hope to receive when it is your turn to speak. Focus your attention on the speaker; do not continue activities or conversations that may distract you or the speaker during the speech. Before the speaker begins, put away newspapers, books, class assignments, and any other material you may have been reading. Terminate all conversations with other classmates, whether in oral or written form (passing notes is an annoying distraction). Also turn off pagers and cell phones.

● *Be Open-Minded*

An ethical audience member keeps an open mind about speakers and topics. Even if you had a bad experience with or you strongly dislike a speaker, you should not automatically ignore the message in his or her speech. The same is true of whatever topic the speaker may address. Even if you have definite views about the topic (for example, you have a strong opinion about

ethical audience: an audience that shows courtesy, open-mindedness, and critical thinking and demands speaker accountability.

Every presentation creates an opportunity for the ethical audience.

whether to pass new gun control laws), do not judge the topic without listening to the speech. You might hear something that changes your mind— or at least broadens your perspective.

● *Listen and Think Critically*

As you take in the speech, attempt to be an interactive listener. We describe interactive listening in detail in Chapter 4. Here we can summarize by suggesting that your listening be focused on what the speaker is really trying to communicate. Ignore distractions, and give the speaker your full attention. Think critically about what is being said. Does it make sense to you? Are you communicating that you are listening? It is your responsibility to truly consider what is being said and to ask questions where and if appropriate.

● *Hold the Speaker Accountable*

The only thing worse than prejudging a speaker or topic is mindlessly accepting everything that is offered. Not only is it your responsibility to listen—even to subjects you disagree with or disapprove of—but it also is your responsibility to hold the speaker accountable for his or her words. Don't be afraid to impose that accountability. Let speakers know, after their speeches are finished, that you expect them to defend their words and own their message.

To accomplish this, listen with an open mind to any public speech— even something you disagree with. If you still disagree at the end of the speech (or when the time for questions or comments arises), ask questions that allow the speaker to explain or defend his or her ideas. If your instructor encourages your comments, explain your reaction to the speech.

When you insist on accountability, do not personally attack, insult, or threaten the speaker. If you are confrontational in your feedback, the likely consequence is that you will not have a meaningful exchange of information and you will undermine your effort to hold the speaker accountable. You will be in a better position if your comments are politely worded and courteously delivered.

It is also important that your comments or questions be *constructive*— meaning that they add to the discussion of the subject—not *destructive*— meaning that they take away from, alter, or diminish the discussion of the subject. These comments were made by a student audience member in a basic speech course:

> I can't believe what I heard. Suggesting that people who do not carpool don't care about air pollution is the dumbest idea I have ever heard!

True, the student was holding the speaker accountable for his words. But the intensity of emotion in the statement, coupled with the word "dumbest," caused the speaker to miss the larger point the audience member was trying to make. Instead, the speaker felt attacked and was effectively silenced. This kind of criticism is destructive. How might you word it constructively?

Look for comments that enhance a discussion of the speech subject and help the speaker think about ways to make the speech better—for example:

> Perhaps I misunderstood what you were saying. Were you suggesting that anyone who fails to carpool doesn't care about air pollution? In my experience there are lots of reasons people do not carpool. Sometimes, riders aren't available. Also, some of us who drive enjoy privacy. Did you consider those possibilities, too?

In this comment, the audience member is still holding the speaker accountable for his statement, but without attacking the speaker or tearing down what was said. The question politely asks whether the speaker has considered all the possible reasons people do not carpool. Notice as well that the audience member gives the speaker an opportunity to clarify and respond to the question—and add to the discussion—without becoming defensive or feeling silenced. This kind of ethical audience behavior fosters understanding of the speech in a way that benefits both the speaker and the audience.

Summary

This chapter focused on the ethical issues facing us in public speaking—both as speakers and as audience members. Ethics refers to shared beliefs about what behaviors are appropriate, especially in terms of treating others truthfully and fairly. Some people apply ethics only in certain situations, but we believe you will be better off with a consistent code of ethics in public speaking.

The checklist indicates how you can use the material from this chapter to prepare for your speech.

Checklist

PRACTICING TRUTHFUL COMMUNICATION

____ Always be truthful in your speech (p. 59)

____ Do not tell half-truths in your speech (p. 59)

____ Do not encourage false inference in your speech (p. 59)

____ Avoid presenting evidence taken out of context (p. 60)

____ Do not use omission to mislead your audience (p. 60)

____ Follow the best practice, and always tell the truth in your public speaking (p. 61)

CREDITING THE WORK OF OTHERS

____ Take credit for your own work but not for the work of others (plagiarism) (p. 62)

____ Use source attribution when quoting directly from a source (p. 63)

____ Use source attribution when paraphrasing a source (p. 63)

_____ Mention the author, the title of the source, and the publication date when citing a source (p. 64)

USING SOUND REASONING AND EVIDENCE

_____ Avoid overgeneralizing and committing the fallacy of example reasoning (p. 64)

_____ Avoid assigning a false cause through the post hoc fallacy (p. 64)

_____ Do not engage in ad hominem attacks (p. 65)

_____ Do not engage in hate speech (p. 65)

THE ETHICAL AUDIENCE

_____ Be courteous to the speaker (p. 66)

_____ Be open-minded about the speaker and topic (p. 66)

_____ Listen and think critically (p. 67)

_____ Hold the speaker accountable (p. 67)

_____ Offer constructive criticism instead of destructive comments (p. 67)

Key Terms and Concepts

ethics (p. 57)
ethical absolutism (p. 58)
situational ethics (p. 58)
lying (p. 59)
half-truths (p. 59)
false inference (p. 59)
omission (p. 60)

plagiarism (p. 62)
paraphrasing (p. 63)
example reasoning (p. 64)
post hoc fallacy (p. 64)
ad hominem attack (p. 65)
ethical audience (p. 66)

Source Notes

1. Kraut, R. (1980). Humans as lie detectors. *Journal of Communication, 30,* 209–216.
2. Burgoon, J. D., Buller, D. B., & Woodall, W. G. (1989). *Nonverbal behavior: The unspoken dialogue.* New York: Harper and Row.
3. Zuckerman, M., Koestner, R., Colella, M. J., & Alton, A. O. (1980). Anchoring in the detection of deception and leakage. *Journal of Personality and Social Psychology, 47,* 301–311.
4. Levine, T. R., Park, H. S., & McCornak, S. A. (1999). Accuracy in detecting truth and lies: Documenting the "veracity effect." *Communication Monographs, 66,* 125–144.
5. Fraleigh, D., & Tuman, J. (1997). *Freedom of speech in the marketplace of ideas* (pp. 168–193). New York: St. Martin's Press.
6. Delgado, R. (1993). Words that wound: A tort action for racial insults, epithets, and name calling. In *Words that wound* (p. 91). Boulder, Co: Westview Press.

"Listening is vital to the public speaking process."

4 Listening Skills and Public Speaking

OBJECTIVES

After reading Chapter 4, you should understand:

- The impact of listening on the processing and retention of the speech message.

- Why communicating that you are listening is important.

- Causes of ineffective listening by both the speaker and the audience.

- Three components of interactive listening.

- Speaker-oriented techniques to enhance audience listening.

- Audience-oriented techniques to enhance listening and speech evaluation.

The importance of listening by members of the audience should be obvious. Less obvious, perhaps, but no less important is the listening a speaker must do. You listen to people you interview when you plan and research your speech. You listen to audience members as you learn about audience analysis. You also listen to audience members during question-and-answer periods and when you receive feedback about your speech from your instructor and other audience members. Effective listening is critical to your success as a speaker.

Alicia, a second-year student at a northeastern community college, learned this lesson the hard way. She had been assigned a persuasive speech for her basic speech course. As she prepared her speech, she decided to persuade her audience to adopt a strict, 100 percent vegetarian diet. To learn more about the dietary habits and preferences of her classroom audience, Alicia used personal interviews. So far so good. But when she reviewed her notes of the interviews she had conducted with five of her classmates, she saw a familiar pattern: in the spaces for answers to her questions, she had written few if any comments from her classmates. When Alicia reflected on the interviews, she recalled that they had gone well; her classmates seemed to like her. There had been much to talk about, but there hadn't been much for her to write down. On reflection, Alicia concluded that her classmates had not been a responsive bunch. The truth of the matter, as you will see, was quite different.

Alicia went ahead with her speech as planned, but she received an unenthusiastic response from most of her classmates when she recommended the switch to a vegetarian diet. When her instructor later offered a critique of the speech, he asked her whether she had considered the views of her audience before drafting it.

Alicia replied that she had interviewed several classmates. At that point, first one and then several of her interview subjects chimed in, observing that Alicia's habit in the interview had been to talk and talk and talk but seldom to listen. One recalled that she asked him a question but then seemed to answer for him before he could reply. Another noted that as he was quietly considering his answer to a question, Alicia filled his silence with more questions. Two others noted that Alicia seemed happy to discuss her own dietary concerns but was not particularly interested in listening to theirs.

Alicia had made a less-than-favorable impression on each of her interviewees. Worse, she lacked a solid sense of what her audience members thought, the absence of which left her without direction in her speech.

Some researchers have found that many listeners miss 100 percent of the feeling or content of oral messages because hearing is not the same as listening.[1] *Hearing* is about receiving messages; *listening* is about paying attention to and thinking about what is being said. All too often, people hear messages superficially, failing to listen for the deepest meanings in what people say.[2] Understanding the distinction between hearing and listening is critical if you hope to improve your listening skills, especially in the public speaking process.

If we were to reduce the message of this chapter to a single statement, it would be this: ***Listening is vital to the public speaking process.*** As Alicia's case demonstrates, listening can be critical to the success of a speech. Her story is not uncommon—many people are less than effective at listening. The result is that they miss many vital messages from others.[3] In addition, they communicate that they are *not* listening. Both of these realities can impair the communication experience. Of course, it doesn't have to be this way. Effective listening skills can be learned, but as with any communication skill, learning them requires discipline and practice. As you will see, when used effectively, listening skills increase not only what you understand but how much of a message you retain. Best of all, they project a favorable message: you are listening.

In this chapter we examine the important role of listening in public speaking. We look first at the impact of listening; then we examine some causes of ineffective listening behaviors. We continue with a look at solutions for effective listening and conclude with advice you can use to enhance interactive listening as both a speaker and an audience member.

How Listening Impacts the Public Speaking Process

Listening skills can have an impact before and after a public speaking experience. Strong listening skills are called for during the research phase and during the presentation of the speech. Equally important, if individuals are to recall what was said, effective listening is necessary.

In this section we consider the impact of listening on the public speaking experience by examining how it affects *processing* (actively thinking about what is said) and *retention* (remembering what we have heard). Let's consider each of these in turn.

● *Processing the Message*

Processing is actively thinking about, considering, and weighing a message. Processing occurs during a speech when the speaker pauses to give the audience a chance to digest what has been said.

Jeff, a salesperson for a computer software company, was frustrated when, after two meetings, the president of a local company still appeared to have concerns about the cost of Jeff's software. Jeff was exasperated because he had addressed the "cost" issue in both presentations. He had shown the cost-saving benefits of his software—benefits that vastly outweighed the expense to the client. He was certain he had effectively shown why a failure to change ultimately would cost the company even more. During both meetings Jeff assumed that the president heard and understood his message. Confident his cost figures had been accepted, Jeff spent a lot of time on other issues. The president, however, had "listened" but had not really heard Jeff's message. The president's failure to process Jeff's message cost Jeff the sale and cost the prospective client an opportunity to reduce business costs by purchasing new software.

> **TIP**
>
> *Remember this: If you process the message, you will be able to ask questions that might enhance your understanding of what has been said.*

● *Retaining What You Have Heard*

Listening also impacts **retention**, the ability to remember what is heard. Consider, for a moment, your own listening behavior as a student in class. How much of a lecture do you retain if you have not really been paying attention? How good is your memory in such a situation if you have not been taking notes? How good is your retention even if you did take notes but weren't really paying attention? How accurate are your notes in such a situation? The answers to these questions depend on how you listen. If you listen ineffectively, you will retain very little.

Early research on memory retention in oral communication situations found that listeners recalled very little of the content of oral messages they had listened to.[4] These early studies suggested that what audience members retain may vary anywhere from 25 percent of the message content[5] to as little as 10 percent.[6] They further suggested that this poor showing of memory could be charted and predicted in any speech situation.[7] Researchers believed that this low rate of message retention was true for all audience members. Subsequent research has shown that this is not the case.

In a later study of the listening patterns of bank employees in a variety of situations over a ten-year period, one of the authors of this textbook found that poor memory retention of a speech was directly related to audience inattentiveness during the speech message.[8] Like earlier research, this study found that individuals with poor listening habits remembered only a fraction (25 percent or less) of what had been said to them in formal presentations, and what they remembered was sometimes inaccurate as to the content of the speech or confused with something else in the listener's mind. Among poor listeners, the inability to remember accurately what had been said worsened over a short period of only three to six hours from the time of the original communication.

The data from this study also revealed a recurring pattern of attentiveness in people who did not listen well. At the beginning of a presentation,

processing: actively thinking about what is being said.

retention: remembering what was said.

FIGURE 4.1 Measuring Attentiveness

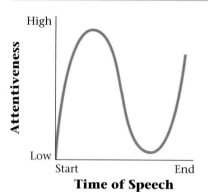

Individuals who do not listen well show a characteristic pattern of attentiveness: their level of attention is low at the beginning of a speech, then quickly climbs and falls, rebounding only at the end of the speech.

TIP

The important point for speakers is this: Be aware of when the periods of greater audience attentiveness occur during a speech, and be sure to make key points clearly and forcefully at those times, when the audience is most likely to be paying attention.

audience members paid little attention. As the speakers continued, these listeners' levels of attention quickly climbed and then fell to a very low level, only to rebound near the end of the speech (see Figure 4.1). With a pattern of listening as sporadic as this, these listeners were neither attending to the whole message nor were they processing it. No wonder, then, that they were retaining little. We have more to say below about the causes of such poor listening behavior.

Causes of Ineffective Listening

In this section we look at several behaviors that cause ineffective listening, and we consider when they are most likely to occur in the public speaking process. First, we examine ineffective listening behaviors that often plague the speaker as interviewer/researcher. Second, we look at ineffective listening behaviors that often impede the speaker's interactions with the audience. Third, we switch to an audience perspective and consider ineffective listening behaviors typically found among audience members. Although we make these distinctions for instructional purposes, remember that ineffective listening can transcend categories and that any listener can fall prey to these behaviors.

● Ineffective Listening during Interviews

For more on encoding and decoding a message for a specific audience, see pages 10–11.

You will be called on to gather data and ideas for any prepared speech you do. You also will need to engage in audience analysis. In both cases you may need to interview either experts (for research about the speech) or audience members (for audience analysis). Good interviewing skills call for innovative questions and probing skills; they also require good listening skills. Without these, speakers can fall back on behaviors that impede listening, including *unprocessed note taking, nonlistening,* and *nervous listening.*

Good interviewing for speech research requires effective listening skills.

Some students experience difficulty with interviewing, particularly if they rely on **unprocessed note taking**—that is, they take notes indiscriminately, without thinking about what has been said. There is nothing wrong with taking notes; doing so is an important part of conducting research and audience analysis. People who practice unprocessed note taking, however, listen *only* to take notes. In effect, the words they hear enter their ears and just as quickly exit their pens or pencils onto a piece of paper. What's missing is any processing of what was said in between the listening and the writing of the notes. Unless they can refer to their notes, people who listen like this are hard-pressed to recall anything that was said to them. Worse, because they only focus on note taking instead of also considering or processing what they have heard, they seldom interact with the person speaking and miss opportunities to ask questions or comment on what they have heard. They thus seldom retain much of what was said. During the research phase, unprocessed note taking may result in a failure to ask helpful follow-up questions in interviews.

Other students experience difficulty while researching a speech because of **nonlistening**. This behavior is exactly what the term implies: these individuals do not listen to what is being said. For the most part, these researchers are more interested in what they have to say and less interested (or completely uninterested) in anything the interviewee has to offer. Nonlistening can occur in interviews when the researchers are particularly fond of the questions they have created and happy to comment on each and every one of them before the subject can respond. This was Alicia's problem and explains why she heard nothing but her own answers to her questions about her classmates' dietary preferences.

TIP

Does this mean you should never take notes when listening to an interviewee as you research a speech? No. Taking notes is important. But to listen effectively, you must do more than take notes. You must also consider what has been said and be willing to ask questions or make comments.

---

unprocessed note taking: taking notes while listening to a speech but without thinking about what has been said.

nonlistening: failure to listen because the listener is not interested in what is being said.

For more on conducting an
interview, see pages 167–70.

Finally, some students may experience difficulty in listening during an interview because they are nervous. These interviewers are perfectly willing to process a message—and to actually listen. The problem for such individuals arises when interviewees are slow to respond to a question—perhaps wanting to weigh their answers and carefully choose their words. An interviewer who exhibits **nervous listening** is likely to misinterpret this pause as a stonewalling silence, a refusal to answer. The mistake that nervous listeners make is to talk through the interviewee's silence. They end the silence with more questions or maybe even comments. As a result, the subject is never really given a chance to answer, and the interviewer's research is incomplete.

● *Ineffective Listening during Audience Interactions*

Speakers must listen carefully when they interact with audience members during question-and-answer periods. Speakers can get themselves into trouble during such interactions—and lose their credibility—by showing *argumentative, agenda-driven,* or *interruptive* listening behaviors.

Speakers who feel conflict with the audience may exhibit **argumentative listening**: they listen but are focusing on how they will rebut what they hear. They listen to only as much as they need to hear in order to argue in response. Argumentative listening can easily afflict public speakers who may feel some nervousness and perceive questions as personal attacks. Again the result is that the speaker hears only a portion of what has been said.

Public speakers who are very focused on the details of their presentation may demonstrate **agenda-driven listening**. As they listen to questions from the audience, they are thinking about what to say next in their own speech. Typically they examine their notes while the question is being asked, and often their response is brief and, worse, not on point as they transition back to their own agenda, jump-starting the speech. An audience that sees and hears a speaker who is not listening to questions is likely to doubt the speaker's credibility.

Another type of ineffective listening during a question-and-answer period is evident when speakers repeatedly interrupt audience members who are trying to ask questions. The speaker may interrupt by trying to anticipate the question and express it for the audience member or, worse, by beginning an answer before the question is complete. Such **interruptive listening** is problematic for two reasons. First, the speaker does not hear everything that is being asked and said and thus may not really understand the question or comment. Second, the speaker is being arrogant and rude to the audience. The result of interruptive listening is decreased understanding on the part of the speaker and some well-founded hostility among audience members.

● *Ineffective Listening within the Audience*

Any of the ineffective listening behaviors exhibited by speakers might also be exhibited by audience members listening to a speech. In our experience, however, two other ineffective behaviors are more common within audiences: *defeated listening* and *superficial listening*.

nervous listening: ineffective listening that causes a listener to misinterpret and talk through a speaker's silence.

argumentative listening: listening to only as much as the listener needs to hear in order to argue in response.

agenda-driven listening: half-listening to audience questions while focusing on what to say next in the presentation.

interruptive listening: listening in anticipation of a speaker's point and interrupting with comments or questions.

Defeated listening occurs when an audience member feels that the subject matter or the delivery of the speech is too difficult to follow. The audience member literally stops trying to follow what is being said. Defeated listening can happen when presentations deal with technical subject matter. If speakers create speeches that are beyond the understanding of their audience, their words are likely to create a number of defeated listeners in the audience. Defeated listening can also occur when a speech is disorganized or when presenters speak too quickly or too softly, or use visual aids that make it difficult for the audience to follow the speech (for example, the visual aids are not visible to the entire audience). When speakers make the audience work too hard to keep up, eventually some audience members give up.

Superficial listening occurs when audience members are distracted by other things during the speech and only act as if they are listening. The distraction may be anything from an outside noise to a visual aid that was not removed after its use. There is also a risk of superficial listening when a speaker distributes handouts. As audience members scan the handout, they typically give only half of their attention to the speaker. Superficial listening also occurs when audience members are reading or working on books, notes, letters, and other items while listening to the speech.

In each of those scenarios, the listener hears only part of what has been said, creating a number of problems. First, superficial listeners may miss the main message of the speech altogether. Second, superficial listeners by listening to only part of the speech may confuse the message of the speaker. Third, superficial listeners often telegraph their listening behavior to the speaker either through inattentive nonverbal communication (such as lack of eye contact) or perhaps through the poor quality of their interactions with the speaker. After the speech, superficial listeners may not interact with questions or comments, or their questions and comments may indicate that they weren't paying attention. The net effect of superficial listening for the speaker is likely to be frustration, disappointment, and perhaps resentment.

Becoming a More Effective Listener

Ineffective listening is a common problem, but it can be readily overcome. In this section we consider how listeners—either as speakers doing research or as audience members—can improve their listening skills through *interactive listening*. We also consider what speakers can do to encourage audience members to listen fully.

● *Interactive Listening*

Ineffective listening is not likely to occur when listeners feel some connection with the words they are hearing. This connection is achieved when they are interested in the subject matter, when they process (consider) what they are hearing, and when they communicate this interest back to the source of the message. Some scholars call this type of listening "active listening," but we believe that term ignores the interactive nature of this listening behavior. We prefer to call it **interactive listening**, because this type of

defeated listening: giving up on listening because the speech is too difficult to follow.

superficial listening: paying scant attention because of distractions but acting as if one is listening.

interactive listening: type of listening that requires reciprocal communication between speaker and listener.

Listeners need to feel connected to the words they are hearing. When listeners are interested in the subject matter, process what they are hearing, and communicate that interest back to the source of the message, they are engaging in interactive listening.

listening requires reciprocal communication, or interaction—between speaker and listener and between listener and speaker. Listening in this way creates a two-way connection between individuals: the listener is also a communicator, and the speaker is also a listener. Interactive listening requires the listener to filter out distractions, focus on what has just been said, and communicate that she or he is paying attention.

Filter Out Distractions.   An interactive listener must learn to filter out anything that could serve as a distraction from what is being said. Suppose that you are conducting interview research. You must focus on the answer to the question you just asked, rather than looking ahead to other questions. You must not become distracted by the silence of an interviewee and keep talking to fill the void. Instead, pause for several seconds, allowing the interviewee to collect his or her thoughts. Suppose that an audience member asks you a question in the middle of your speech. You must focus on what the audience member is asking, rather than looking ahead to the rest of the speech. If you are an audience member, filtering out also means not reading, working on, or thinking about other materials when you are listening to a presentation.

Focus on What Has Just Been Said.   In addition to filtering out anything that may distract you, you must focus on what is being said. You must listen without interrupting and then process the message. Processing requires you to think about what has been said. What do you think is being said? How does it make you feel? Do you agree or disagree with what you're hearing? Do you have questions? Comments? A different point of view?

Communicate That You Are Listening.   The first two steps of interactive listening—filtering and focusing—assist you in hearing what is being said. The third step involves making the other person understand (and feel good about the fact) that you are listening. What does the way in which you listen indicate about you? What does it suggest about what you think of the person who is speaking? A speaker sees nonlistening audience members and perceives discourtesy, boredom, or lack of interest. Nonlistening can make the speaker angry or nervous. It can affect the rate of delivery (speaking too fast) and distract the speaker from his or her presentation.

Communicating that you are listening is accomplished through a combination of nonverbal and verbal cues. Look at the other person both when he or she is speaking and when you are responding. Indicate nonverbally—perhaps with a smile or nod of your head—that you are willing to listen.

When the opportunity presents itself, verbally communicate that you are listening. During the question-and-answer session, ask questions that are relevant and thoughtful. If you are not sure you understood the speaker's message, paraphrase what you think he or she said, and invite the speaker's comment before continuing with your question. This brief summary before the question indicates that you were listening and allows the speaker to correct your perception if you misunderstood the message. Asking a thoughtful question communicates more than just the question; it also communicates that you listened to and processed what the other person said.

Interactive listening results when you really do make an effort to listen and focus on what is being said—thus processing and retaining the message—and to communicate that you are listening, making the other person feel good about communicating with you.

● Maximizing Audience Listening

In spite of your best efforts, you may encounter situations in which the audience does not effectively listen—sometimes because of the situation, sometimes because of something you're doing as a speaker. Here are some suggestions about what you can do as a speaker to help the audience listen to and remember your message.

Anticipate Ineffective Listening Behavior in Your Audience.   You can employ audience analysis not only to tailor your message to your audience but also to prevent ineffective listening. This can be accomplished in several ways. Here are four methods.

First, consider the time of day to anticipate what audience members' levels of attention and energy might be. If you are speaking to a class that meets on Monday mornings at 8:30 A.M., you can anticipate that audience members may have a limited attention span because they are tired from the weekend and not yet focused on the new week.

Second, think about how long audience members will be exposed to your speech, and decide whether the length of your speech might eventually discourage good listening. At 8:30 on a Monday morning, a long speech with no audience interaction is likely to encourage poor listening. A short speech with time allotted for a question-and-answer session might more effectively induce audience members to pay attention and listen.

For more on nonverbal messages and encoding, see pages 10–13.

For more on eye contact and communicating that you are listening, see pages 298–300.

TIP

As a speaker, don't allow the fact that the audience appears not to be listening to make you nervous or angry or distract you from your speech. Instead, view nonlistening as a reminder to establish eye contact with audience members, or perhaps begin a question-and-answer period to stimulate audience attention and listening.

For more on audience-centered messages, see pages 90–91.

| INVENTION | ORGANIZATION | STYLE | PREPARATION | DELIVERY |

In Theory 4.1

HOW AUDIENCE DIFFERENCES CAN AFFECT LISTENING

In Chapter 2 we introduced you to the five canons of rhetoric, which include both *invention* (the generation of ideas for your speech) and *delivery* (the use of your voice and body as you present your speech to your audience). These two canons are implicated when we consider how audience differences—especially as they relate to ethnicity and age—can affect listening.

In one study of listening and culture, Americans were seen as belonging to an individual-centered culture in which listeners tended to pay close attention to the expression of feelings by the speaker.[9] Israelis, in contrast, were seen to set aside personal regard and focus their listening attention on the accuracy of the information gathered.

Some understanding of the cultural influences that affect the ways audience members listen might cause a speaker to approach the canon of invention differently, especially in terms of which ideas to present to different groups. For example, ideas and facts that related to feelings would be of more interest to and promote better listening by an American audience, while facts with demonstrable accuracy would be of greater interest to an Israeli audience.

The same study also demonstrated that cultural differences also have implications for the style of delivery. Germans were seen as listeners likely to interrupt and pepper a speaker with questions and comments. Knowing this ahead of time might encourage a speaker to plan for question-and-answer sessions—and to avoid communicating a sense of frustration when being interrupted.

The canon of delivery is also influenced by how age differences in the audience affect listening behavior. For example, a study[10] of listening among people from age 17 to age 92 found that listeners up to the age of 40 needed only minor increases in decibel (volume) level to listen comfortably to a presentation. Between ages 40 and 60, however, the volume or loudness of the presentation needed to be increased substantially, and it increased still more after age 60. Consideration of age differences, therefore, might affect speech delivery (volume) to promote effective listening.

Third, consider the background of the members of your audience. How much do they already know about your subject? If it is too technical, they may become defeated listeners. If they are new to your topic, you will need to explain unfamiliar terms. Also consider how the cultural background of your audience may influence listening behavior (see In Theory box 4.1).

Fourth, consider whether members of your audience are likely to be argumentative listeners, and adapt your message accordingly. Remember that argumentative listeners tend to listen to only as much of your presentation as they want to argue about. For them, you might do well to initially acknowledge any dispute and then repeatedly press your main message.

Tailor Your Delivery to Encourage Effective Listening. Sometimes people in your audience will exhibit ineffective listening (mostly defeated listening) because of your delivery. For this reason it is important for you to pay attention to factors that affect delivery, such as volume, fluency, projection, rate, and pausing. Speaking too quietly may inhibit listening, as may poor fluency, rapid-fire delivery, or excessive pausing.

The same is true of eye contact and gestures. Failing to look at the audience, turning your back to the audience as you adjust a visual aid, and obtrusive gestures can all distract the audience and discourage listening.

For more on speaking volume, fluency, rate, and pausing, see pages 290–97.

Use Audiovisual Aids Strategically to Encourage Effective Listening.   This suggestion refers primarily to your ability to control audience interaction with any audiovisual aid (the use of audiovisual aids is discussed in detail in Chapter 12). When trying to encourage effective listening, remember these two simple rules: First, audiovisual aids can be used to capture audience attention, and spacing them throughout a speech can maintain interest. Second, don't present an audiovisual aid until you're ready for the audience to see or hear it; and when you're finished with it, put it away. If you fail to control interaction, the audience may become distracted (looking at an audiovisual aid too soon or too late) and listen superficially.

Front-Load Your Main Message, and Use Repetition to Enhance Listening. Recall from Figure 4.1 that listeners tend to pay the most attention immediately after the beginning of a speech. This suggests that a listener is most likely to retain your main message if you front-load it. Figure 4.1 indicates that audience attentiveness rises again near the end of the speech, so repeating the main message near the conclusion will provide another opportunity for listeners to retain what you are saying.

Effective Listening and Critiquing As an Audience Member

Thus far we have considered the importance of listening to, understanding, and processing what is said. For an audience member, listening can also be crucial to whatever **speech critique**—written or oral feedback offered after a speech—your teacher may require you to present. Critiques are a key component of public speaking classes. They afford speakers a chance to immediately learn from their speech experience. They also give audience members an opportunity to work with the material covered in lectures (and in this book) and hone important critical thinking skills throughout the term.

To assist you, we provide two speech evaluation and feedback forms. The short form (Figure 4.2), especially useful before you have gotten farther into this textbook, provides general categories for evaluation and feedback. The long form (Figure 4.3) will be more appropriate after you have read more of this text; it is quite detailed. Note that these forms are only two of numerous options available for critiquing. They are intended as a starting place for your thoughts about critiquing a speech.

Whatever evaluation format you use, audience feedback can be a valuable learning tool for all, especially if you adhere to the following guidelines.

● *Be an Interactive Listener*

When you listen in anticipation of a critique, you become another teacher in the course. You really need to know what the speaker said in order to critique it effectively.

TIP

Use either of the speech evaluation and feedback forms to assess your own speech after you have spoken to an audience.

For a printable version of the long speech evaluation form, go to "Step 5 Delivery/Learn from Your Speech."
CD-ROM: Interactive Speech Guides

speech critique: written or oral feedback offered after a speech.

FIGURE 4.2 Speech Evaluation and Feedback — Short Form

Speech Topic
Was the speech topic made clear to you?

_____

_____

Audience Analysis
Was the speech tailored to the audience?

_____

_____

Speech Delivery
Did the speaker demonstrate an effective delivery?

_____

_____

FIGURE 4.3 Speech Evaluation and Feedback — Long Form

Speech Topic
Was the speech topic made clear to you?

_____

_____

Was the topic appropriate for the speech assignment?

_____

_____

Was the topic adequately developed in the speech?

_____

_____

Audience Analysis
Was the speech tailored to the audience?

_____

_____

Did the speaker interact with the audience?

_____

_____

(continued)

FIGURE 4.3   Speech Evaluation and Feedback — Long Form
(continued)

Did the speaker make use of the audience's prior exposure to the topic?

_____

_____

Organization of the Speech
Was the main idea (thesis) of the speech clear to you?

_____

_____

Did the speaker give a preview of the organization?

_____

_____

Were the supporting points of the speech clear and easy to follow?

_____

_____

Could you follow the structure of the speech?

_____

_____

Did the speaker have an effective conclusion?

_____

_____

Speech Delivery
Did the speaker demonstrate an effective delivery in terms of fluency, voice
volume, speed, pronunciation, and articulation?

_____

_____

Did the speaker demonstrate an effective delivery in terms of eye contact,
gestures, and movement?

_____

_____

Did the speaker appear nervous or uncomfortable?

_____

_____

(continued)

FIGURE 4.3   Speech Evaluation and Feedback — Long Form
(continued)

Speech and Language
Did the speaker use language effectively?

_____

_____

Speech and Audiovisual Aids
Did the speaker use audiovisual aids?

_____

_____

If so, were these aids accessible to all in the audience?

_____

_____

Did the aids help you understand the speech?

_____

_____

Speech Ethics
Did the speaker have any problems with truthful communication (lying, omission, false inference, half-truths, or taking evidence out of context) in the speech?

_____

_____

Overall Assessment
What is one thing you liked about the speech?

_____

_____

What is one thing you would change in the speech?

_____

_____

_____

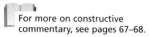
For more on constructive
commentary, see pages 67–68.

constructive criticism: helpful
feedback that the speaker can use to
strengthen the next speech.

● *Use Your Listening Skills to Offer Constructive Criticism*

Constructive criticism is feedback the speaker can build upon. To be constructive, you have to understand what the speaker is trying to accomplish with the speech. You'll want to listen for and remember the main objectives of the type of speech being presented and listen to see how well the speaker accomplishes them.

● *Take Notes on the Message and Delivery*

Jot down your comments about each speaker's delivery and message as soon as you hear and observe the presentation. If you wait until all speakers are finished, recalling the details of any single delivery may be hard. Think about the speaker's delivery skills. What did you like? What worked well? What could this speaker improve upon?

● *Note Specific Examples to Support Feedback*

A comment such as "good eye contact" or "work on organization" will not help the speaker. Support general comments with specific examples, such as "You made eye contact with every section of the room," or "You had a good preview, but your organization could have been better if you had transitions between main points."

● *Be an Ethical Audience Member*

Be courteous. Treat the speaker with the courtesy that you hope and expect to receive when it is your turn to speak. Listen with an open mind. Do not prejudge a speaker or a topic. Think critically about what was said, and be willing to hold the speaker accountable for his or her words. That last point is important for the critique. If you are offended by or disagree with something in the speech, tell the speaker. Do so with courtesy, and avoid an ad hominem attack. Explain why you are offended or disagree, and give examples if possible. Doing this will help the speaker understand your point of view—and build on the experience for the next speech.

> **TIP**
>
> *When offering constructive criticism to speakers, try not to think of what you're saying as criticism in the negative sense. Rather, think of it as objective, fair, and honest feedback. Offer it in the way you would like to receive feedback when you speak.*

For more on ad hominem attacks and ethical behavior, see pages 65–68.

Summary

Listening is of vital importance to creating, delivering, and observing a public speech. Listening is critical because of the impact it can have on one's ability to process a message, to retain that message, and to communicate interactively. In this chapter we examined the many ways that ineffective listening negatively affects public speaking, as well as solutions and suggestions for promoting effective listening in both you and your audience.

The checklist shows how you can use material from this chapter to improve your own listening skills, both as a speaker and as an audience member, and help audience members be effective listeners when you speak.

Checklist

ENGAGE IN INTERACTIVE LISTENING

____ Filter out distractions (p. 78)

____ Focus on what has just been said (p. 78)

____ Communicate that you are listening (p. 79)

AS A SPEAKER, MAXIMIZE AUDIENCE LISTENING

____ Anticipate ineffective listening behavior in your audience (p. 79)

____ Tailor your delivery to encourage effective listening (p. 80)

____ Use audiovisual aids strategically to encourage effective listening (p. 81)

____ Front-load your main message, and use repetition to enhance listening (p. 81)

AS AN AUDIENCE MEMBER, LISTEN MORE EFFECTIVELY

____ Listen interactively (p. 81)

____ Use your listening skills to offer constructive criticism (p. 84)

____ Take notes on the message and delivery (p. 85)

____ Note specific examples to support feedback (p. 85)

____ Be an ethical audience member (p. 85)

Key Terms and Concepts

processing (p. 73)
retention (p. 73)
unprocessed notetaking (p. 75)
nonlistening (p. 75)
nervous listening (p. 76)
argumentative listening (p. 76)
agenda-driven listening (p. 76)

interruptive listening (p. 76)
defeated listening (p. 77)
superficial listening (p. 77)
interactive listening (p. 77)
speech critique (p. 81)
constructive criticism (p. 84)

Source Notes

1. Stewart, J. (1986). *Bridges, not walls* (4th ed., p. 181). New York: Random House.
2. Bolton, R. (1979). Listening is more than merely hearing. Cited in Stewart (1986, p. 159).
3. Clark, A. (1989). Communication confidence and listening competence: An investigation of the relationships of willingness to communicate, communication apprehension, and receiver apprehension to comprehension of content and emotional meaning in spoken messages. *Communication Education, 38,* 237–248, at 238.
4. Stafford, L., & Daly, J. (1984). Conversational memory: The effects of recall mode and memory expectancies on remembrances of natural conversations. *Human Communication Research, 10,* 379–402.
   Keenan, J., MacWhinney, B., & Mayhew, D. (1977). Pragmatics in memory: A study of natural conversations. *Journal of Verbal Learning and Verbal Behavior, 16,* 549–560.
   Kintsch, W., & Bates, E. (1977). Recognition memory for statements from a classroom lecture. *Journal of Experimental Psychology: Human Learning and Memory, 3,* 150–159.
5. Benoit, S., & Jones, G. (1986). Listening: It can be taught. *Journal of Education for Business, 63,* 229–232.

6. Stafford & Daly (1984, p. 379).

7. For example, business communications consultant David Green initially suggested that audience retention levels rose and fell at different points in a speech. One of his many contributions to communications consulting was to graphically illustrate this with what he called a "retention curve."

8. Study by TCC Consulting (San Francisco, CA), undertaken between 1987 and 1997.

9. Kiewitz, C., Weaver, J., Brosius, H., & Weimann, G. (1997). Cultural differences in listening style preferences: A comparison of young adults in Germany, Israel and the United States. *International Journal of Public Opinion Research, 9*(3), 233–247 at 233.

10. Coren, S. (1994). Most comfortable listening level as a function of age. *Ergonomics, 37*(7), 1269–1281, at 1269.

"The audience drives the message."

5 Audience Analysis

After reading Chapter 5, you should understand:

- Why and how your audience is relevant to the creation of your speech message.

- The importance of analyzing your audience before and during your speech.

- Characteristics of your audience to consider before you speak, including situational characteristics, demographics, common ground, prior exposure, and disposition.

- Techniques you can use to learn more about your audience.

Julie's job was to sell managed funds to investors. Recently she met with the treasurer of a large municipal water district that had $25 million, raised from a bond measure, to be used for construction of a new dam. Construction was not set to begin for one year, and the treasurer wanted to invest the money until it was needed. Julie was given an opportunity to bid for his business, so she went to the district office to make a formal presentation.

The presentation did not go well. In spite of her youth (she was fresh out of college), Julie made an extremely good living from her sales commissions. On this day, she dressed as usual in a designer suit, drove to the district headquarters, and—as fate would have it—parked her expensive car right in front of the treasurer's office window. The treasurer was a simple man, easily old enough to be Julie's grandfather. He lived on a public employee's salary. He wore button-down shirts with clip-on ties and polyester pants. His office was simple and spartan, reflecting his attitude about spending money.

From the moment Julie parked her car and marched into the treasurer's office, the day was lost. When Julie recommended that the treasurer take an "aggressive" approach to investing the water district's money—meaning that he accept some risk in order to (perhaps) reap high returns, he winced. When she repeatedly addressed him as "Bernie" even though he had introduced himself as "Mr. Harrison," he looked increasingly uncomfortable. What Julie had hoped would be a twenty-minute presentation to "Bernie," followed by a presentation to the board of directors, ended up being a ten-minute talk. In the end, the gist of the treasurer's response was "Don't call us, we'll call you."

Later, with her supervisor, Julie considered what went wrong. She realized that she had known very little about "Bernie" prior to their meeting. She had obtained no personal information about him or about investments that might appear safe to a manager of public money. Worse yet, when she saw that her presentation was not going well, she made no effort to adjust her message. Instead, she did what many inexperienced speakers do in similar situations: she delivered her message in the way she was accustomed to. But "Bernie" wasn't listening, and consequently "Bernie" wasn't buying.

Julie's experience shows how important it is to analyze your audience both before and during your presentation. Indeed, if we were to reduce this chapter to one sentence, it would be this: *The audience drives the message.* This means that the effectiveness of a speech depends on the speaker's knowledge of the audience and how he or she crafts the speech message to the audience.

In this chapter we take you through the process of **audience analysis**, highlighting facts about your audience that are important to know and explaining methods you can use to obtain these facts. In later chapters we consider in detail how to use this information to adapt to your audience and prepare an effective message.

Audience-Centered Messages

We have all experienced generic speeches—"canned" presentations that had been delivered countless times in precisely the same way. This type of presentation can occur when the speaker considers his or her message too important to compromise with any consideration of the audience. When someone just "mails in" the speech, regardless of the audience, listeners react with boredom, irritation, and lack of attention.

In contrast, a number of benefits result when it is obvious that a speaker has taken audience members into consideration and tailored the message to them. First, audience members are typically more interested and attentive. Second, they better relate to the speaker because they realize that the speaker has made an effort to understand them. Third, they better relate to the message because it has been targeted at their needs, interests, and values; the speech is attuned to their interests and not likely to raise issues that are irrelevant to them. The result is simple: The speaker is more likely to be successful with the message. Had Julie taken these facts to heart, she would have had a better chance of getting the account.

Most of us intuitively practice audience analysis and adaptation in our daily interactions with people. Suppose you wanted to request an extension for a late assignment. What would you say to a professor who interacted easily with students and had granted such a request to your friend last semester? How would your message be different if the professor were very formal, distant from students, and known to be unsympathetic to excuses? Clearly, knowing the teacher's attitudes toward extensions or her previous interactions with students would shape the way you approached her. Or suppose you were given two concert tickets and wanted to invite someone to join you. If you were asking an old friend, you would simply pick up the phone and invite him. But if you wanted to invite someone you had just met in class and hoped to get to know better, you would spend more time crafting a message in the hopes that you might receive an affirmative reply. We all individualize our messages in ordinary conversation, and it is equally important that we adapt our messages to our audiences in public speaking.

View Barbara Bush crafting an audience-centered message at the Republican National Convention. CD-ROM: Video Theater, Excerpt 5.1

audience analysis: considering the characteristics of your audience to better understand their orientation to your speech.

To understand your audience before you develop your speech, you need to obtain various kinds of information about your audience. We have organized this information into five categories: *situational characteristics, demographics, common ground, prior exposure,* and *audience disposition,* each of which we consider in this chapter. Throughout the chapter, we refer to a Speech Grid (see Figure 5.1) that you can use to organize the information you collect for audience analysis. As you progress through this book and beyond this course, you can use the Speech Grid to guide you through the audience analysis in each particular situation for which you are developing a speech. It is important that you address the "audience analysis" column of the grid before you attempt to outline or write the speech itself. Remember, an effective speech is one in which ***the audience drives the message***.

FIGURE 5.1   Speech Grid

Topic:
Specific purpose:
Thesis or topic statement:

AUDIENCE ANALYSIS	SPEECH MESSAGE
Situational Characteristics	
Audience Size	
How many will be in the audience?	
Time	
• *How long will my audience be exposed to my message?*	
• *At what time of day/week will my audience be exposed to my message?*	In later chapters, you will compose your speech message here.
Location	
• *Where will my audience be listening to my speech?*	
• *Is audiovisual equipment available for me to use?*	
Audience Mobility	
Will my audience be mobile or stationary?	
Demographics	
Relevant characteristics could include age, gender, race and ethnicity, religious orientation, and other factors (e.g., student major, educational background, political affiliation).	
Common Ground	
Do I have anything in common with my audience?	
Prior Exposure	
• *Has my audience been exposed to this speech message before?*	
• *What was the result of the prior exposure?*	
• *If the message failed, why was it unsuccessful?*	
Audience Disposition	
Is my audience hostile, sympathetic, or neutral?	

Use your CD-ROM to analyze your audience. Go to "Step 1 Invention/Analyze Audience." **CD-ROM: Interactive Speech Guides**

Determining Situational Characteristics

Situational characteristics are factors in a particular speaking setting that you can observe or find out about before you give your speech. They include *audience size, time, location* or *forum,* and *audience mobility.*

● *Size of the Audience*

When conducting an audience analysis for a speech, it is important that you determine **audience size**—that is, how many people will be present when you give your speech. In a classroom setting, the size of your audience should be obvious. In the real world beyond school, you will need to ask the person who invites you to speak how many people will be in the audience. Will there be a group of seven to ten people? twenty-five to thirty? three hundred? a thousand? Would a difference in any of these numbers affect what you do in your speech?

To answer that last question, consider the recent example of Jeanine, a marketing representative for a software manufacturer in California's Silicon Valley. Her product, revolutionary at the time, enabled computer users to quickly create visual aids that could be used in business presentations. Jeanine's company asked her to visit ten cities across the country and give what she referred to as a "dog and pony show," a presentation in which she would speak about and demonstrate her product. Her audiences would range from three hundred to five hundred prospective buyers, all invited guests of her company, seated in large hotel ballrooms.

When the day arrived for her first presentation, Jeanine realized that something was very different. In past presentations, she had spoken about her product before boards or committees of five to seven people. She found that with the larger group, answering questions from the audience was almost impossible. She had a limited time to speak, and if she allowed everyone to ask a question, as she did when addressing a small group, she would never get through her presentation. That, in turn, led to another realization: if she couldn't hold a lengthy question-and-answer session, she would have to *assume some of the more obvious questions* and incorporate them into the presentation. Here we see how a simple characteristic of the audience already starts to influence how the message is derived.

Jeanine also realized that in this larger group, there would be more variance in audience members' knowledge and experience with computers. Although all listeners would have purchasing authority, not all would have technical backgrounds or much familiarity with using computers. Jeanine therefore had to decide which questions she should assume and incorporate. After some thought, she settled on an approach that teachers in large classrooms often take. They "teach to the middle"—that is, they don't construct a lecture only for those few students who are ahead of the rest of the class, and they don't slow everything down for those few who are falling behind. Because of the size of her group, Jeanine decided to do the same—teach to the middle—so her speech content became more general, rather than detailed, as she revised her presentation to include as many people as possible.

In summary, then, *size matters when it comes to audiences and speech presentations.* The smaller the group size, the greater is the opportunity for interaction through techniques such as question-and-answer periods. In

situational characteristics: characteristics of the speech setting, including audience size, time, location, and audience mobility.

audience size: the number of people in the audience.

such settings, speakers can be far more detailed and specific about the message, because they can target their message based on the needs of a small group. Conversely, the larger the audience, the smaller is the opportunity for interaction, and the greater is the need for anticipated questions and a more general message.

● *Time*

Another important consideration in audience analysis is time, both *presentation time* and the audience's *body clock.*

It's usually easy to determine **presentation time**—how long your audience will be exposed to your message. How long do you have to speak: thirty seconds? five minutes? twenty minutes? an hour? as long as you wish? The answer can be critical to how your speech is received, because audience members' attentiveness typically depends on their expectations about how long the speech will be.

Just as the size of the audience can affect what you do in your speech, so, too, can any time limitations that the audience mentally places on your delivery. If the audience is expecting a brief address but you deliver a long speech, many audience members will focus on the fact that your speech is too long. They will be tempted to think about when you will end rather than about the content of your ideas. Furthermore, when you take your time and provide lots of detail, you may ramble on, going off on tangents and never emphasizing your main point. You may demonstrate much knowledge on a general subject but do little to convey a specific message or answer a particular question. Delivering a long speech may seem desirable because it gives you more opportunity to develop your ideas, but it requires more effort to stay focused on a central or main point.

Some people consider a short speech risky because it does not afford an opportunity to cover all the issues. There is some validity to this concern. To be effective in a thirty-second speech is in many ways more difficult than in a ten-minute speech. When there is less time, you have to make difficult decisions about what to leave in. Remember, though, that some of the most powerful persuasive messages—television ads—are only fifteen to thirty seconds long, yet they convey a wide range of information to audiences and greatly influence behavior. A short time allotment for your speech presents you with the same opportunity and the same challenge.

In sum, the longer the time period allotted for your speech, the greater is the potential for you to cover a wide range of topics, but also greater is the risk that your speech will become unfocused and unclear. The shorter the allotted time, the greater is the need for you to be a good editor, carefully reducing your message to something quickly digested by your audience.

Presentation time, however, is only one aspect of the "time" factor in audience analysis. Also important is what we call the audience members' **body clock**. Body clock, also known as **chronemics**, refers to a description of where the audience is in their week, or day, as they listen to your speech. Are they listening to your speech early in the morning, just after lunch, or at the end of the day? Is it a Monday or Friday? Is a speech delivered at 8:30 on a Monday morning likely to elicit the same reaction as one delivered on Wednesday at 2:00 P.M.? What about 4:00 P.M. on Friday? If you can choose when you will speak, is one time or day necessarily better than another?

presentation time: the amount of time allotted for a presentation.

body clock: a description of where the audience members are in their day or week (e.g., Monday morning, still tired from the weekend) as they listen to your speech.

chronemics: the study of time as it relates to human communication.

| INVENTION | ORGANIZATION | STYLE | PREPARATION | DELIVERY |

In Theory 5.1

ASSESSING THE AUDIENCE BY THINKING ABOUT TIME

In Chapter 2 we described the canons of rhetoric, one of which is *invention,* the generation of ideas that can be used in your speech. Successful invention requires adequate analysis of the audience, right down to an evaluation of the body clock of audience members. The study of time as it relates to human communication is known as chronemics.[1] This can refer to a concept of time as biological,[2] physiological,[3] and psychological.[4] Thinking about how time affects your audience will give you additional insight into the ways they may receive your speech. As has been observed, "Time gives form and structure to our lives."[5]

Most teachers are painfully aware of how hard it is to motivate a class that meets at 8:00 on a Monday morning. Many students have difficulty paying attention at that time because they are still mentally rooted in the weekend just past and are not yet coming to terms with the activities and work of the upcoming week. There are similar distractions for people close to mealtime, at the end of the day, or at the end of the week.

Is it impossible to speak effectively to people at such times? Clearly not. If you are locked into an undesirable speaking time, you can make adjustments in your speech. To draw your audience's attention to you, you might include more humor or anecdotal references, making your speech lighter in content and tone and more entertaining. Or, with your teacher's approval, you might open by asking direct questions of some audience members to heighten their attentiveness. Or you might accept the limits of a body-clock attention deficit and adjust the length of your speech.

On one occasion, one of the authors of this book was asked to give a presentation to a group of lawyers on a Tuesday at approximately 3:00 P.M. The speech (detailing some negotiation strategies) was supposed to last twenty-five minutes and was part of an all-day conference. As the day went on, the schedule lagged, and the negotiations speech could not begin until 4:30 P.M. Out of politeness (and contractual obligation—they had already paid!), the lawyers were willing to give the speaker the full twenty-five minutes. But they were obviously very tired, and it was likely that their attention span would be minimal. Consequently, it seemed advantageous to reduce the message on strategies to five minutes of simple tips, followed by a question-and-answer period. The lawyers became invigorated with a shorter presentation, and as a result they actively participated in the questions.

As you can see, *presentation time* and *body clock* are interrelated factors. One influences the other. In the real world, none of these audience characteristics operates within a vacuum. For example, in the case of the lawyers, if the *audience size* had been five hundred, a twenty-minute question-and-answer period open to all might not have worked because there would have been too many people asking questions and too little time to provide answers. Late in the day, facing a large audience with a limited attention span, a speaker is well advised to shorten the speech and simplify the main message, anticipating questions that might be asked and incorporating them into the speech.

● *Location*

In audience analysis it is important to determine **location**, also known as **forum**—the place where the audience will be listening to your speech. Will the audience be in a classroom? an auditorium? a meeting room? a conference room? indoors? outdoors? Does location matter? If you have a choice, what location should you choose?

The answer to the last two questions is well demonstrated with the following true story. Joe, a high school junior, was running for student body president. Each candidate was required to deliver a campaign speech at an afternoon rally. The location of the rally was the recently completed high school quad, a plaza built approximately eight feet below the level of four surrounding brick buildings—a design that produced some rather spectacular acoustics when sound from within the plaza projected against any of the surrounding buildings. Joe was the first speaker. To add volume and project his voice above the din of the crowd, he spoke into a microphone, not realizing that his voice was already naturally amplified by the surrounding buildings. Using the microphone made him too loud for that forum, and students groaned and grimaced in response to a presentation that was literally painful to hear.

All locations offer challenges and opportunities. Joe's mistake was his failure to consider ahead of time what that location might mean for his speech and his audience. Speaking loud enough in an outdoor setting can be very difficult—hence the need for a microphone. Any location with surrounding walls presents possibilities for amplifying the voice by natural projection. The key is to consider what the forum offers. Check to see what the space looks like. How will your voice carry in the room? Stand where you will be speaking, and imagine yourself delivering the speech. Stand where the audience will be, and do the same. Can you address everyone in this forum equally? Will everyone be able to see and hear you?

As you consider the audience in a particular forum, be guided by this question: Is your forum appropriate for the speech you plan to give? Did you ever have to make a presentation in class only to discover that the setting was not appropriate for the speech you planned to give? Perhaps the room could not accommodate your visual aids—there was no poster board, or no tacks, or no tape, or no chalk. To avoid finding yourself in a location where the lack of support for audiovisual aids places limitations on how you deliver your speech, always check the location in advance and adjust your speech or delivery accordingly.

To further illustrate the importance of assessing the location, we offer another example. Marilyn, a product development specialist for a company manufacturing copy machines, was asked to give a speech to fifty people in a hotel conference room. Her voice was loud enough, and she was eager to interact with the audience by walking around the room while she spoke, without using a microphone. Unfortunately, at the time of her presentation, a loud and festive Bar Mitzvah was under way in the ballroom next door. The two rooms shared a ventilation system, and while Marilyn was speaking, noise and music from the celebration next door seeped into her room, preventing listeners in the back rows from hearing her speech.

For more on speaking volume and projection, see pages 290–93.

TIP

When planning your speech, visit your speaking location ahead of time.

location (forum): the place where the audience will listen to the speech.

In the cases of both Marilyn and Joe, failure to assess the forum in advance of the presentation led to problems. If Joe had known about the plaza's acoustics, he might have planned his speech differently—perhaps coming out from behind the podium, ignoring the microphone, and getting closer to his audience. Marilyn would have been better served in another location—or by asking her audience to move closer to the center of the room. And anyone who has ever had to speak in a forum without the necessary materials for visual aids knows the wisdom of preparing an alternative plan (such as visual aids that can be held up by hand). In every speaking situation, the last thing you want to do is to learn about the forum *after* you've begun your presentation.

● *Mobility of the Audience*

Another important factor in audience analysis is to determine **audience mobility**, the ability of the audience to move into and out of a speech location at will. Knowing in advance about an audience's mobility—and the likely propensity of individuals to arrive late and leave early—might affect how you craft and deliver your message.

Consider an easy example of a stationary audience: the college classroom—perhaps your speech class. Teachers enjoy the benefit of a fixed audience, secure in the knowledge that college students have paid to be where they are and feel compelled to stay until the class is finished (particularly if attendance is a grading criterion). Every student has probably had a class in which the teacher's lectures left something to be desired. Sometimes what accounts for this lackluster performance is the knowledge that the audience (the students) must be there. How different might your classes be if students could enter and exit almost at will? Would teachers lecture in the same way? Not if they wanted to keep class attendance high. The importance of preparing a message that held the audience's attention would increase.

Salespeople who routinely demonstrate their wares at conventions or county fairs understand this. In the small, cramped booths of an exhibition hall, you will find everyone from local political candidates to encyclopedia sellers. Perhaps the most fascinating vendors at such events are the ones who occupy the prized "intersection" booths, so-called because of their position at the intersection of connecting aisles. For these vendors, more than for most speakers, the speech presentation is greatly influenced by the amount and nature of pedestrian traffic. The audience is entirely mobile, in between mouthfuls of cotton candy or corndogs, and usually in a mood to look and not buy. These vendors craft their messages so as to stop this traffic, often interactively involving the audience in the product presentation itself. One such vendor was selling a special knife for chopping fruit and vegetables. He purposely selected bright and colorful fruit and arranged pre-chopped pieces in humorous patterns (one plate of watermelon cubes was arranged to look like a hound dog) to attract attention. Because he knew his audience was mobile, he purposely made his speech interactive, stopping some passersby and encouraging them to "play" with the knife and the fruit. Soon, others gathered to watch. Sound silly? That same vendor often persuaded hundreds of people to purchase his knives in a single day—at a tidy profit.

audience mobility: the ability of an audience to move into and out of a speech location at will.

A professional salesperson uses different delivery skills and audience interaction to attract an otherwise mobile audience.

What did he do that was so different from what other vendors were doing? Because his audience was mobile, he knew he had to attract their attention and then offer something interactive to sustain that attention. In other words, the vendor was successful because he recognized that ***the audience drives the message.***

Incorporating Demographics

The second category of information for audience analysis is **demographics**, characteristics such as age, gender, race and ethnicity, religious orientation, educational background, and political affiliation. Information about these characteristics will help you know your audience and anticipate their attitudes and beliefs concerning your topic.

Demographic research often is used for marketing purposes. Advertisers attempt to discover who would most closely identify with or wish to purchase specific products. Demographic information influences advertisers' marketing messages. For example, much of the television programming on Saturday mornings features cartoon characters. The programs themselves might tell you something about the audience the sponsors think is watching, but a better way to identify the audience is to look at advertising. On a typical Saturday morning, you will see advertising for sugary cereals, sweet desserts, fast food, and, most particularly, toys. The pairing of those advertisements with cartoon programs gives you a pretty fair idea of who the sponsor assumes is watching: children. Everything in the thirty-second spots (choice of actors, colors, language, visuals, memorable tag-lines) is

demographics: audience characteristics such as age, gender mix, race, ethnicity, religious orientation, educational background, and political affiliation.

For more on truth-telling and speech, see pages 59–61.

calculated to appeal to the target audience. We may question the ethics of advertisements that stimulate the desire of unsuspecting children for unhealthy foods, but there is no denying that these ads are very effective.

In this section we examine age, gender, and other significant demographic characteristics that you should consider in order to make your speech effective.

● Age

Age is an important factor affecting how audience members respond to your message. Would age be a consideration for a speech explaining the necessity of regular savings for retirement? Of course it would. The same message would not be appropriate for both an audience of recent college graduates and an audience of aging baby boomers.

Naturally, when the audience is large, age may be difficult to pinpoint with certainty. That is why you will want to make your best estimate—perhaps estimating a range of ages. For a speech on retirement savings, let's assume that your audience members are adult workers at a factory in Michigan and that most of these workers are in their thirties. Will their age affect their response to your message? It certainly will. Many people in their thirties probably have not focused on retirement issues yet and may just be developing an awareness of the need to save. Their response will likely differ from that of workers in their early twenties (very low awareness of the need to save for retirement) or workers in their late forties (heightened awareness).

● Gender

You might want to know whether women will outnumber men in your audience, or vice versa. The **gender makeup** of the audience—*mixed* (male and female) or *single gender* (all female or all male)—is likely to affect reactions to your speech. Some stories, examples, or illustrations might resonate better with one gender grouping than with another.

In recent years, people who sell automobiles realized that more and more women were buying cars and that sales pitches traditionally aimed at men did not work so well with women. Minh, who worked as a car salesman while in school, noted that different approaches were needed to sell Volvo station wagons to women and to men. Features such as a turbo-charged engine, performance tires, and special detailing appealed to men. Many working women and mothers were more interested in features related to safety, reliability, reasonable cost, and overall quality. The same broad message was aimed at both men and women: Please buy this wonderful car. But when selling to women, Minh emphasized a safer chassis and construction, and when selling to men, he touted greater horsepower and torque for speed and power. In mixed-gender situations, it is critical to consider how both men and women might react to your speech.

age: how old members of your audience are.

gender makeup: the proportion of males and females in the audience.

race: recognizable features and distinct traits transmissible by descent and shared by members of a particular group.

● Race and Ethnicity

Is the **race** of individuals or groups in your audience likely to affect their reaction to your speech? We want to caution you that race does *not* automatically explain or predict a person's position on an issue or reaction to your message. For example, not every American of white European descent feels the same way about affirmative action, and neither does every African American.

Nevertheless, the racial makeup of your audience may be an important consideration if you are developing a speech on affirmative action. Race can be a powerful factor in conditioning an audience's reaction to a topic, particularly in the United States, where racial issues are sensitive and affect people throughout their lives.

Ethnicity, cultural background—usually associated with shared religion, national origin, and language—is another important demographic. A student named Gunther learned about ethnic differences the hard way. Designated by his student government to speak to several student clubs seeking student government recognition, Gunther met with the Middle Eastern Society Club on campus and spoke before an audience that he had been told would consist of students from Iraq who had fled to the United States soon after the Gulf War began. He politely addressed them all as "Iraquis" or "students from Iraq" but later learned that his audience was made up of Assyrians who had been living in Iraq. Although Assyria no longer exists, millions of people identify themselves as Assyrians. They speak the same language, practice the same religion (Christian Church of the East), and have their own distinctive traditions and customs. Most members of Gunther's audience realized that his mislabeling of them was unintentional, but many still took offense at being categorized as an ethnic group with which they did not identify, and one that had afforded them little protection or status as a religious minority in Iraq. The misidentification became a source of distraction for some, causing them to miss parts of Gunther's presentation.

As we said above, race and ethnicity do not automatically explain or predict an audience member's orientation to an issue or speech, but both can play an important role in shaping that orientation by providing a context for filtering that issue or message. For that reason, making sure that you consider these demographic characteristics in your audience analysis is very important.

● *Religious Orientation*

Religious beliefs, often associated with ethnicity, can be an independent demographic characteristic. The degree to which **religious orientation** is a critical factor in an audience member's life determines the extent to which religion affects an individual's reaction to your speech. Within the United States, there are many different religious groups—Christians, Jews, Muslims, Buddhists, Hindus, Baha'is, to name just a few. And within some of the large religious groups there are numerous subdivisions with separate positions and beliefs. For example, Anglicans and Roman Catholics share common elements in their celebration of the Eucharist, but they are widely divided over allegiance to the papacy and over specific issues such as admitting women to the priesthood. Likewise, Muslims do not agree about every issue, and Reform Jews and Orthodox Jews certainly part ways with one another on some issues. Of course, like any other demographic characteristic, religious orientation does not necessarily preordain (pardon the pun) an audience's reaction. But it can exert great influence.

ethnicity: cultural background.

religious orientation: religious beliefs.

Pope John Paul II displays his understanding of the religious background of his audience in a speech in Jerusalem. What topics might require you to take into consideration the religious beliefs of your audience?

To understand this idea, consider the example of Pope John Paul II's address to the state of Israel at the Yad Vashem Holocaust Memorial in Jerusalem in March 2000.[6] The pope touched on an enormously sensitive issue for Jews who felt that his predecessors had been at least indifferent to Jewish suffering in the Holocaust. Mindful of the fact that the religious orientation of his audience would very strongly influence their feelings about the subject matter of his speech, Pope John Paul repeatedly made use of Old Testament passages to describe suffering and awareness of human evil, and he firmly condemned any act of hatred, any persecution, and all displays of anti-Semitism directed at Jews by Christians at any time and at any place. Why did the pope make this last point about Christian anti-Semitism when speaking about the Holocaust? Surely no responsible individual equates Nazi treachery with Christianity. For many Jews, however, the historical context for anti-Semitism extends back to a period called the Inquisition, in which Jews suffered at the hands of the Catholic Church. Understandably, the memory of the Church's role in the Inquisition might influence the degree to which any Jew found Pope John Paul, leader of the Church, credible on the issue of the Holocaust. Analyzing his audience gave the pope insight about the sensitivities of his audience and provided guidance for constructing his speech.

● *Educational Background*

Education can influence an audience's reception and reaction to your speech—if for no other reason than a well-educated audience may already have been exposed to facts you otherwise might have explained in your speech. We should caution here that by **educational background** we do not mean the amount of formal schooling your audience has had; rather, we mean the extent to which your audience is already informed or educated about your topic or related topics. Knowing about this type of "prior exposure" will help you decide the degree to which you will have to provide background information and explain some of the facts in your speech.

Roy, a civil engineer working for a regional planning commission, often made oral presentations to the commission, making recommendations about zoning variances that would allow or disallow construction or development. The commission would vote on his recommendations. The seven members of the commission, however, were not zoning experts; they were laypeople from the community, elected to three-year terms. Regional election rules did not allow them to serve more than one term. Unlike Roy, they had no particular education or training in regional planning.

Roy quickly discovered that, to be effective, he should never presume the commission's knowledge of or familiarity with any technical issues or terminology. Adapting to his situation, he kept his speeches simple, explaining or avoiding technical terms and, when possible, comparing the issues to be resolved by upcoming votes with past situations the commission had already handled. Obviously, his approach would have been different if the commission members had been people with education in planning or people who had served multiple terms.

Understanding the educational background of the audience will give you valuable insight into their ability to digest and comprehend technical, involved, or complex information. The audience's educational background has clear implications for your use of audiovisual aids. An audience not well informed about your topic might benefit from audiovisual aids designed to explain the subject matter. The audience's educational background also has implications for the way you organize the speech in order to help listeners understand what is being said, and the way you deliver the speech. An audience relatively new to your subject might benefit from a slow rate of delivery that gives them an opportunity to absorb and process the information.

For more on the use of audiovisual aids to simplify complex messages, see pages 325–31.

For more on organization and audience comprehension, see pages 180–81.

For more on the rate of delivery, see pages 292–93.

● *Political Affiliation*

In some respects, **political affiliation**—political beliefs and positions—is the most difficult of the demographic characteristics to pin down. Traditional political labels —"liberal" and "conservative," "Democrat" and "Republican"—do not yield definitions. "Conservative," for example, may refer to *fiscal* conservatism (belief in the need for a balanced budget and no tax increases), to *law and order* conservatism (a stronger criminal justice system), or even to *foreign policy* conservatism (a stronger defense and increased military readiness). And not all members of your audience who call themselves "conservative" necessarily fall into all three of these categories. That lack of precision extends as well to Democrats and Republicans. Party membership

educational background: the extent to which your audience is educated or informed about your topic.

political affiliation: the political beliefs and positions of your audience.

does not guarantee that someone will vote in a certain way or exhibit a certain behavior. Labels, therefore, will be less useful to you than an understanding of your audience's views on specific political issues. Nevertheless, knowing the political orientation of your audience can help you to understand their perspective about certain issues or individuals (leaders and candidates).

● *Using Demographics Wisely*

We are not suggesting that you gather demographic information so that you can manipulate your audience. But it is important that as a speaker you understand and use this information to help get your message across. Each audience is different, and identifying some characteristics or behavior patterns shared by many members of a given audience can give you insights into how they think and what their response to your message might be. You can then incorporate these insights into the development of your speech to frame your message for the audience.

Jackie, a thirty-two-year-old student in a speech class, was asked by a public agency to give a speech about safe-sex practices—first to an audience of teenage youths in a facility for runaways and then to an audience of middle-income working parents at a school meeting. The basic message was to be the same for both presentations: safe-sex practices decrease the likelihood of unwanted pregnancy and sexually transmitted disease.

Jackie quickly determined that she needed to craft the message in very different ways for each audience. The teenagers, all runaways, were already suspicious of authority figures—especially those who were significantly older than they and wanted to lecture them on social behavior. Jackie thus decided to make no references in her speech to the teens to anything that might call attention to the difference between her age and theirs. She was also careful not to lecture and instead invited them to share their experiences, creating an atmosphere in which they felt more like her peers. In addition, mindful that her young audience had already been exposed to threats and intimidation (which had prompted some of them to run away in the first place), she avoided scare tactics.

In her speech to the parents, however, Jackie wanted to build trust right away. A mother herself, she made pointed references to raising her own daughter and talked about the "difficulties of parenthood." Because she knew that some parents didn't want to believe that pregnancy or disease could ever be a problem for their children, Jackie used recent health department statistics detailing the transmission rate of deadly diseases among sexually active youths.

The message (safe sex) was the same for both groups, but Jackie's crafting of that message reflected her awareness of demographic differences she had identified in the groups ahead of time.

Establishing Common Ground

A third category of audience analysis is **common ground**—beliefs, values, and experiences that audience members and the speaker have in common. Is there anything similar in your backgrounds or experiences that might prompt an audience member to look at you and say, "You and I are alike in

common ground: beliefs, values, and experiences shared by the audience and speaker.

Candidates attempt to establish common ground nonverbally.

some ways, and I might think the way you do about this"? Common ground can have many bases—a common experience or similar background, mutual interests or preferences.

A student named Jay gave a presentation in which he tried to persuade the members of his speech class that using mass transit was vastly preferable to driving an automobile. The school Jay attended had a large number of commuting students, and like many in his audience, Jay had spent his first year of college as a commuter—driving to the campus every day, always caught up in traffic, never able to find parking. When making his arguments for mass transit, Jay referred to this experience because he knew that many of his listeners also encountered those problems daily.

Sometimes common ground must be described, as Jay did in the previous example. In other instances, the existence of common ground can be communicated nonverbally. For example, a candidate for public office who makes a presentation to an audience that consists of individuals who share some characteristic or interest is likely to don a hat or cap that signals his or her commonality with the audience—a cap with a union label on the brim for a union audience, a military-style hat with insignia for veterans' groups, or a cowboy hat for an audience in Texas, or a sport cap (like a baseball cap) with the insignia of a local college or professional team.

Of course, putting on a hat does not necessarily mean that common ground actually exists. A baseball cap does not make a speaker a baseball fan any more than a cowboy hat makes one a cowboy. Speakers should signal the existence of common ground honestly and responsibly and reinforce the nonverbal message in their speech message.

View a student using the Speech Grid for audience analysis while establishing common ground.
CD-ROM: Video Theater, Excerpt 5.2

For more on truthfulness, lying, half-truths, and false inference, see pages 59–61.

Identifying Prior Exposure

The next category of audience analysis pertains to **prior exposure**, the extent to which the audience has already been exposed to your message. Why study prior exposure? Awareness of prior knowledge and of the audience's likely response to what you plan to say will help you decide whether to repeat a familiar message or craft something new. Answering the three questions listed below will help you pin down what prior exposure there is and how to take advantage of it.

View a student asking a rhetorical question, prompting the audience to consider prior exposure.
CD-ROM: Video Theater, Excerpt 5.3

● *Has My Audience Been Exposed to This Message Before?*

If the answer to this question is "no," you are in uncharted territory, the audience will not have a preconceived notion about your message, and you will need to explain the issues and concepts in basic terms. If the answer is "yes" (meaning the audience has been exposed to this message), you need to move on to the next question.

● *What Was the Result of the Audience's Prior Exposure?*

Surprisingly, many people fail to take into account the result of prior exposure. If the goal of an earlier speech was persuasion, was the audience persuaded? Did audience members adopt the desired action or belief? If the speech was supposed to be informative, were audience members interested in the subject? Did they understand the information?

If the answer is that the message was effective and the speech achieved its desired goals, then the objective in your speech will be to reinforce the message the audience heard previously, add new information, and/or motivate audience members to take action.

If the answer is that the message was not effective and the speech achieved nothing, then you know what approach you need to avoid. If you were to repeat the unsuccessful approach used previously, and nothing in the audience environment had changed, your speech would likely yield the same negative result. Consequently, when the answer to our second question is "nothing," you need to move on to the third question.

● *If the Message Failed Before, Why Was It Unsuccessful?*

During the planning of your speech, it is important to assess what went wrong when the audience encountered the message before. Learn from past mistakes (your own and those of others), and unless your audience environment has changed, adjust your message accordingly.

Presidential campaigns provide examples of messages that continue to be successful and messages that need to be changed. In both 1992 and 1996, speeches by the Republican presidential candidates—President George Bush in 1992 and Senator Bob Dole in 1996—emphasized essentially the same message: less government, lower taxes, and a strong military defense. In both election years, however, voters seemed more interested in political messages emphasizing economic growth, jobs, and prosperity. An assessment of the prior exposure of the voting public from 1992 should have told

prior exposure: the extent to which an audience has already been exposed to a subject.

Senator Dole that he needed a new message in 1996, but Dole relied on the same message, to his detriment. By 2000, Republican candidate Governor George W. Bush, son of the former president, had a different core message and sought to attract independent-minded voters to the Republican side with descriptions of what he called "compassionate conservatism." He still stressed points about a smaller government and lower taxes, but he also emphasized an expanded role for the federal government in enhancing public education, while offering younger voters alternatives for retirement savings and social security. In short, in 2000, George W. Bush realized that the public's prior exposure to the traditional, well-worn Republican message would guarantee an election defeat and that a change was required.

Similarly, in 1992 and 1996 Bill Clinton successfully altered earlier Democrat Party messages, taking a decidedly more centrist approach to attract voters to his cause. In 1992 he emphasized the need for economic focus, in 1996 his success at promoting economic growth. His speeches in both elections strongly featured the domestic economy.

By the year 2000, little had changed to increase voters' concern about the economic outlook, and the prior-exposure analysis used by President Clinton should have told Vice President Al Gore, who hoped to succeed Clinton, to emphasize the same message. Gore's speeches, however, gave equal weight to other issues besides economic growth and never really trumpeted the success of the Clinton/Gore administration in enhancing the domestic economy. The election results, on that basis, were predictable. Al Gore failed by not staying with a message that probably would have worked again. George W. Bush succeeded by altering an old familiar message.

Identifying Audience Disposition

The fifth and final category of audience analysis involves the disposition of the audience. In most situations, audiences can be segmented into one of three groups: *hostile, sympathetic,* and *neutral.* Understanding which group your audience (or the majority of your audience) fits into can give you some insight into how your audience might react to your message.

A **hostile audience** is an audience that is opposed either to the message or to the speaker personally. Consequently, a hostile audience is reluctant from the start to accept a speech. In contrast, a **sympathetic audience** already holds the speaker in high personal esteem or agrees with the message to such a degree that it is predisposed to respond favorably to a speech.

A **neutral audience** is an audience that does not have strong negative or strong positive opinions about the speaker or the message. An audience may be neutral because its members are apathetic and not interested in the speaker or the speaker's ideas. Or audience members may be very interested in hearing the speaker but undecided about the speaker's subject.

Why is it important to analyze audience disposition? First, if you are to face a uniformly *hostile* audience, you probably will be wasting your time and energy if you simply repeat a message that works well with a sympathetic audience. Does this mean that you shouldn't bother addressing a truly hostile audience? No. Every speech offers a new opportunity. We merely suggest that in such situations you should modify your objectives. Be realistic

hostile audience: an audience already in opposition to a speech topic or to a speaker personally.

sympathetic audience: an audience already favorably inclined toward a speech topic or toward a speaker personally.

neutral audience: an undecided audience.

Al Gore speaks to a sympathetic audience. If he was addressing a hostile audience, he would need to establish common ground and consider audience members' reservations about his viewpoint.

about what you can accomplish. For example, although it may be impossible to convince members of a hostile audience to do something they don't want to do, it is certainly possible to convince them to at least reevaluate their opposition to what you propose or to you personally.

Second, if you are to address a truly *sympathetic* audience, you will be wasting your time if you expend significant rhetorical resources trying to do too much. If members of an audience are uniformly sympathetic, they won't need much encouragement from you. In such a situation, your speech should be a motivational presentation—preaching, as it were, to the converted. Rather than simply asking audience members to agree with you, you can encourage them to be more actively involved in the issue or activity you are discussing.

Third, a *neutral* audience comes to your speech with no particular predisposition about you or your message. It is important to know about such an audience in advance, as well as the reason for its neutral status. Does the audience's neutrality result from apathy, disinterest, or the lack of firm conviction about you or the issue you are addressing? Critical to members of a neutral audience is the fact that they *can* be moved one way or the other. In such a situation, and in light of the other results of your audience analysis, your speech should address their apathy, disinterest, or lack of conviction, informing, motivating, and persuading them.

Keep in mind this caveat about audience disposition: your audience is unlikely to fit neatly into one dispositional group. Within most audiences, you are likely to observe elements of all three groups at the same time. In such situations, you will want your remarks to reflect the proportion of each group (hostile, sympathetic, and neutral) in the audience, as well as the significance of each group to the outcome of your speech. Suppose that you are

"Good luck with your lecture, Eric—they're loaded for white male."

facing an audience in which most people are neutral, a small percentage are hostile or sympathetic, and the hostile people are very vocal. What will you do? You may want to expend only enough rhetorical resources to silence the hostile, just enough to motivate the sympathetic, and the vast balance to reach the neutral. Your strategy will change, depending on the mix of hostility, sympathy, and neutrality evident in your audience.

Techniques for Conducting Audience Analysis

Thus far we have described the types of information you need to effectively analyze your audience and craft your message. In this section we explain three techniques you can use to obtain that information for audience analysis: surveying, interviewing, and observing.

● *Surveying Your Audience*

A **survey** is a set of written questions that you ask your audience to answer in advance of your speech. Surveys are helpful when you are doing an audience analysis because you directly ask people who will be listening to your speech for the information you need. If the audience is small—let's say thirty or less—you will want to survey everyone. If it is larger, you may want to survey a smaller number, a representative sample of all people in the audience.

Megan, a student in a speech class, wanted to give an informative speech on dental anesthetics. Her goal was to provide the audience (her

> **TIP**
>
> *When preparing a presentation for your class, don't be reluctant to talk to and survey other students to get a good understanding of their background and their orientation to your speech.*

survey: a set of written questions answered by audience members in advance of a speech.

classmates) with facts that they did not already know, so that they would be able to make more-informed decisions when they went to the dentist. Megan learned about her audience by surveying her classmates before she outlined her speech. Figure 5.2 shows the questions she asked.

As Megan's survey illustrates, there are three general types of questions that you may want to ask: *fixed-response, scaled,* and *open-ended* questions.

Fixed-response questions give respondents a set of two or more answers and ask them to check the response(s) that apply. You may want a simple yes-or-no reply, or you may want to give respondents several choices.

Megan would not want to give the same speech to an audience of individuals who had rarely experienced dental anesthesia (or any type of dental care) as she would give to an audience in which many members were familiar with the current options for patients. Hence, she began her survey with four fixed-response questions. The answers would tell her something about the audience's experience and intentions in seeking out dental care. This information would help her uncover useful demographic information (such as whether this audience has experience with dental care) and possibly would uncover common ground (perhaps Megan and her classmates have had similar reasons for visiting a dentist).

FIGURE 5.2   Megan's Dental Survey

1. Have you ever been a patient at a dentist's office?

    yes _____   no _____

2. In the past, why have you decided to go to the dentist?
    (circle as many as necessary)

    a. regular checkup
    b. specific procedure (e.g., teeth cleaning)
    c. specific problem (e.g., cracked filling)

3. Have you ever been given an anesthetic at a dentist's office?

    yes _____   no _____

4. Have you ever been given the following anesthetics?
    (circle as many as necessary)

    a. a Novocain injection
    b. laughing gas
    c. a general anesthetic (one that put you to sleep)
    d. a gel or spray

5. When you are going to have dental treatment, how important is it to you that you experience no pain?
       Please answer on a scale of 1 to 10, with "1" representing "not important at all" and "10" representing "very important."

    1   2   3   4   5   6   7   8   9   10
    (unimportant)   (somewhat important)   (very important)

6. Describe any problems you may have had during recent visits to the dentist (e.g., pain, discomfort, etc.).

    _____

---

fixed-response questions:
questions that ask the respondent to choose among two or more possible answers.

Scaled questions give respondents a set of fixed responses and measure the intensity of their feelings about their answers. The scale is sometimes numerical, such as the scale ranging from 1 to 10 in question 5 of Megan's survey. Other times, the scale consists of a range of verbal options, such as "strongly agree," "agree," "neutral," "disagree," "strongly disagree."

Knowing the intensity of audience members' beliefs can be very helpful, shedding light on their prior exposure to your topic and their disposition. In question 5 Megan sought to discover the extent to which pain influenced her classmates' attitudes about visiting the dentist. Classmates who were very frightened by the prospect of pain probably would be predisposed to follow her suggestions for alleviating pain.

Open-ended questions allow respondents to write any answer of their choosing. In question 6 of Megan's survey, respondents are asked to describe any problems they have had with dentists.

Open-ended questions may offer the best way to find the information you need about your audience. You may not be able to anticipate all the responses the audience could give to a fixed-response question. Megan wanted to explain in her speech how the proper choice of anesthetic could reduce many of the problems people have when visiting the dentist. She could not anticipate every problem, so she asked an open-ended question.

Another benefit of open-ended questions is that they ask respondents to communicate in their own words. Fixed-response questions put words in respondents' mouths by requiring them to pick one of the options even if none of the options accurately describes their views. Megan wanted to research the diversity of problems her audience had encountered when visiting the dentist, and her open-ended question allowed each person to state an individual answer.

Through the use of fixed-response, scaled, and open-ended questions, you can create a questionnaire to learn about your audience. If it is not practical for you to distribute a questionnaire to the people who will be in your audience, you may want to try an interview instead.

● *Interviewing Your Audience*

You may want to conduct an **interview** with one or more of the people who will be in your audience. Interviewing offers several advantages. One is that it gives you an opportunity to interact with people. During a face-to-face conversation, you might learn relevant facts that you would not know to ask about in a survey. Also, an interview gives at least some members of your audience a chance to meet you before you speak. This "ice breaker" function can be especially helpful if you won't know most of the people you will be addressing. Finally, when it may not be feasible to distribute surveys to your entire audience, interviewing a few members will provide you with useful information. Interview as many people as time permits. The nature of this interaction will limit how much you can do.

Choose interviewees carefully. It would be easiest to talk to audience members you already know. And if the group has a leader, you might be inclined to interview him or her. But members of your audience may have diverse backgrounds and interests, in which case you should try to interview a range of audience members.

scaled questions: fixed-response questions that measure the intensity of respondents' feelings about their answers.

open-ended questions: questions that allow respondents to give any answer of their choosing.

interview: a face-to-face conversation for gathering information about your audience.

The experience of Jan, the president of a university communication department's student professional society, illustrates the importance of carefully considering whom to interview. One of Jan's professors invited her to come to class and give a speech to recruit new members for the society. Jan had a friend in that class, and the friend told Jan that he would be interested in learning about opportunities to network with communications professionals. The society sponsored several social events to bring members in contact with alumni working in communication-related fields, so Jan focused on these events when she addressed the class. At the end of the presentation, few students took the club brochures Jan distributed, and none ever went to one of the club meetings. The problem was that the class she addressed was a general education course, and many of the students were not majoring or minoring in communication and they were not interested in networking with communications professionals.

Had Jan talked not only to her friend but to other members of the class—or to the professor, also in her audience—she would have learned that many members of her audience had very limited public speaking experience. Knowing this, Jan could have focused her speech on the professional society's tutoring program, and she might have enticed more students to join.

Interviews and surveys are two effective methods of obtaining information about your audience. But you may not always have the chance to communicate with any audience member before you speak. If this is the case, you can use observation to learn about your audience.

● Observing Your Audience

It is important to learn whatever you can about your audience, even if you cannot communicate with them directly. Observation should begin in advance of your speech and continue as you arrive at your speech location and give your speech.

Indirect Analysis before Your Speech.   You may be able to find out information about your audience without conducting surveys or interviews. We call this strategy **indirect audience analysis**. Begin by considering the context of your speech. Why is the audience going to be there? If your talk is to occur during a class, you have a captive audience. This speaks to the audience mobility question on the Speech Grid (see Figure 5.1).

Your status as a student provides you and your audience with obvious common ground, and you know that audience members have at least some background in the academic discipline of the course. If you were a member of the College Republicans and were asked to participate in a debate at the College Democrats' club, you would likely find a hostile audience. Those attending would be there voluntarily and could leave at any time. Politics would be a major interest to your audience, and the fact that both you and your audience participate in political clubs on campus would give you some common ground.

You may be able to obtain literature about members of your audience. If they belong to an organization, they may possess pamphlets or brochures that they distribute. Or newspaper or magazine articles or even books may have been written about them.

indirect audience analysis:
gathering information about your audience from sources other than surveys and interviews.

One of the authors of this book can recall his impression at meeting Senator Robert Kennedy shortly before his untimely and tragic death in 1968. Kennedy was seeking the Democratic nomination for the presidency and was in California, attempting to gather support. While on a whistle-stop tour of California's San Joaquin Valley, in the town of Turlock, Kennedy spoke from the back of the train, standing beside the author's mother and father. Kennedy began his speech with a reference to the fact he had been on the train for hours, during which time he had been served "leftover turkey pot pie" for breakfast and "turkey and swiss on dark bread" for lunch. And, he said, his wife had already informed him that he would be eating "turkey and mashed potatoes" for dinner. The afternoon crowd roared with delight at all the humorous references to turkeys, which by no small coincidence were part of the area's primary industry. When later the author asked his father how Kennedy knew about the small town's turkey and poultry industry, the father replied that in the local newspaper Kennedy had seen an advertisement with headlines screaming "Turkeys from Turlock!" for upcoming holiday dinners. Still on the train, he had asked for an explanation of the ad and then quickly changed his speech for the Turlock crowd.

Analysis at Your Speech Location.   When you arrive to do your presentation, you can analyze your audience. The cars in the parking lot (and the inevitable bumper stickers) may give you insight into your listeners' tastes and interests. You can determine demographic variables such as gender, age, and ethnicity by looking at your audience. Consider whether what you see matches up with what you assumed while preparing your speech. Some listeners may have signs, banners, or even T-shirts that express their feelings on the issue you are discussing. People may wear buttons or pins symbolizing their views on certain issues. If classical music is being played, you may have different expectations than you would have if the audience is listening to acid rock, rap, or country music.

Analysis during Your Speech.   The audience analysis process does not stop when it is time for you to begin your speech. Regardless of whether you were able to interview or survey audience members ahead of time or could not begin your analysis until you arrived at the site of your speech, you should update your analysis and adaptation as the speech progresses.

In Chapter 1 we noted that communication is a transaction between you and the people you address. While you are delivering your message, your audience will also be sending messages to you. You can maximize your effectiveness by adapting to these messages.

Do audience members seem bored? If so, you probably will want to put more energy and enthusiasm into the delivery of your speech. Does their body language suggest they are opposed to your point of view? A friendly smile and a tone of voice that indicates your respect for them can help to break the ice. Do they look uncomfortable? If possible, you may want to move to a different location in the room; members of the audience will shift their focus and body positions as you move and perhaps feel more relaxed.

As you gain experience in public speaking, you may be able to do on-the-spot audience analysis and make refinements that will make your message more effective. You may want to provide more explanation of a point if the audience seems confused. You may want to incorporate humor if the audience seems tense or restless. If you are delivering a persuasive speech, you may even want to revise your expectations for the audience, based on the feedback you are receiving.

Suppose you had planned to advocate that your classmates boycott the school cafeteria until a better variety of food was served, but as the speech progresses, you get the impression that the audience is not concerned about this issue. You may decide to ask audience members to sign a petition instead. Suppose you are speaking in favor of students carpooling to school, and the audience seems enthused. You might want to expand your speech to add a plan for meeting after class to organize car pools.

A good example of this speech revision technique was offered by Ed, one of four college students debating national defense policy before a local service club. The issue was whether the United States should construct a "Star Wars" defense program in space. Earlier in the week, Ed had prepared his speech, covering the reasons he felt Star Wars was a bad idea. Upon arrival at the club meeting, Ed noticed a "4 Way Test" banner on the wall. The test listed four questions that should be asked whenever a new idea was proposed. While the club members and the other students were eating their barbecue luncheon, Ed reorganized his speech. He used the club's own "4 Way Test" to question the Star Wars plan, and he explained why it would fail all four parts of the test.

From the moment Ed announced that he would be using a "4 Way Test," he had audience members in the palm of his hand, regardless of their opinions on the issue prior to the speech. Ed's speech was a rousing success because he acted on the maxim ***The audience drives the message.***

Summary

In this chapter we focused on the importance of audience analysis in crafting your speech message. We considered five categories for analysis: situational characteristics, demographics, common ground, prior exposure, and disposition of the audience. We examined how the information for these categories can be derived from the use of surveys, interviews, and observation. Audience analysis should take place not only before the speech but also during the presentation.

The checklist shows how you can use the material from this chapter to prepare for your speech.

Checklist

CONSIDER CHARACTERISTICS OF THE SITUATION

____ What is the size of the audience? (p. 92)

____ What is the presentation time for your speech? (p. 93)

____ Where are your audience members in their body clock? (p. 93)

____ What is the location of the speech? (p. 95)

____ Are audiovisual aids available for your audience? (p. 95)

____ Is your audience stationary or mobile? (p. 96)

INCORPORATE DEMOGRAPHICS

____ What is the age of audience members? (p. 98)

____ What is the gender makeup of your audience? (p. 98)

____ What is the racial and ethnic makeup of your audience? (p. 98)

____ What is the religious orientation of your audience? (p. 99)

____ What is the educational background of your audience with respect to your topic? (p. 101)

____ What is the political affiliation of your audience? (p. 101)

ESTABLISH COMMON GROUND

____ Do you have common ground with your audience? (p. 102)

____ Do you need to verbalize your common ground? (p. 103)

____ Will your audience perceive your common ground if you never say anything about it? (p. 103)

ANALYZE PRIOR EXPOSURE

____ Has the audience been exposed to the speech message before? (p. 104)

____ What was the result of the prior exposure? (p. 104)

____ If the message was unsuccessful, why so? (p. 104)

UNDERSTAND THE DISPOSITION OF THE AUDIENCE

____ Do you have a hostile audience? (p. 105)

____ Do you have a sympathetic audience? (p. 105)

____ Do you have a neutral audience? (p. 105)

GATHER INFORMATION FROM AUDIENCE MEMBERS BY SURVEYING OR INTERVIEWING

____ Consider using fixed-response questions (p. 108)

____ Consider using scaled questions (p. 109)

____ Consider using open-ended questions (p. 109)

____ Consider interviewing individual audience members (p. 109)

OBSERVE YOUR AUDIENCE TO GATHER MORE INFORMATION

____ Use indirect analysis before the speech (p. 110)

____ Analyze the audience at the speech location (p. 111)

____ Analyze the audience during the speech (p. 111)

Key Terms and Concepts

audience analysis (p. 90)
situational characteristics (p. 92)
audience size (p. 92)
presentation time (p. 93)
body clock (p. 93)
chronemics (p. 93)
location (forum) (p. 95)
audience mobility (p. 96)
demographics (p. 97)
age (p. 98)
gender makeup (p. 98)
race (p. 98)
ethnicity (p. 99)
religious orientation (p. 99)

educational background (p. 101)
political affiliation (p. 101)
common ground (p. 102)
prior exposure (p. 104)
hostile audience (p. 105)
sympathetic audience (p. 105)
neutral audience (p. 105)
survey (p. 107)
fixed-response questions (p. 108)
scaled questions (p. 109)
open-ended questions (p. 109)
interview (p. 109)
indirect audience analysis (p. 110)

Speech Grid Application

The Evolution of a Speech Grid

Speech Grid Applications, showing the evolution of a Speech Grid, are included near the end of Chapters 5 through 12. They illustrate how one student, Samantha, uses a grid to prepare a speech.

At the beginning of the speech preparation process, Samantha records on the left side of her grid the information she already has about her audience. This includes information about the classroom where she will speak and basic demographic information from a general survey that her classmates completed. If Samantha did not have such survey results, she could insert educated guesses about her audience. These would be based on conversations with her classmates and on information she learned from watching and listening to them in class.

Samantha has not yet selected a topic, so the areas for her topic—specific purpose, and thesis or topic statement—are blank. Her preliminary audience analysis will be one of the factors she will take into account when selecting her topic. (Chapter 6 covers topic selection and shows how to use the grid in that process.)

After Samantha selects a topic, she will survey her audience and obtain additional information about common ground, prior exposure, and audience disposition. She will insert this information in the appropriate sections on the left side of her grid. Then she will begin to research and develop her own ideas that she might use in her speech. She will enter these on the right side of her grid. As we cover the speech preparation steps in later chapters, the Speech Grid Application will show how Samantha adds material to her grid and uses the grid to plan her speech.

Speech Grid: _____

Topic: _____

Specific purpose: _____

Thesis: _____

AUDIENCE ANALYSIS	SPEECH MESSAGE
Situational Characteristics • *8 min. speech* • *25–30 in audience* • *small classroom* • *limited a-v equip.* **Demographics** **Age:** *17 (5); 18 (17); 19 (4); 20 (1); 22 (1)* **Ethnicity:** *African-American (2); Hmong (2); white (9); Latino/a (6); Portuguese (2); Pacific Islander, Mexican, German, Japanese, Swedish, Greek (1 each); did not say (1)* **Major:** *Undeclared (9); Liberal Studies (5); Chem, Bus, Crim (2 each); Child Devel, Engl, Bio, Premed, Journalism, Ag Bus, Econ, Comm, (1 each)* **Common Ground** **Prior Exposure** **Audience Disposition**	In later chapters, you will compose your speech message here.

Source Notes

1. Bruneau, T. (1977). The study of time in human interaction. *Communication, 6,* 1–30.
2. This concerns time as it relates to biochemical codings that relate internal clocks, biochemical rhythms, and the influence and regulation of internal clocks and rhythms on human behavior.
3. Time that involves the physics of human behavior, especially human sensory experience.
4. Human time experienced at the level of memory, anticipation, modes of thinking, and processing, and—most significant for our purposes—levels of consciousness.
5. Cohen, J. (1970). *Homo psychologicus* (p. 106). London: Allen and Unwin.
6. The official Vatican text of the pope's speech was reprinted in the *New York Times,* March 23, 2000, at p. A1.

6

Topic Selection

OBJECTIVES

After reading Chapter 6, you should understand:

● The importance of carefully considering your speech topic.

● Processes you can use to generate possible speech topics.

● Criteria for selecting the best topic, based on your audience analysis, your knowledge and interests, and the speech context.

● The steps to take to narrow and refine the topic you select.

Annette's first major assignment in her public speaking class was an informative speech. The assignment required students to explain an object, concept, or process. The **topic**, or subject to be addressed, needed to be unique (not one that the instructor had heard in class many times) and researchable.

Annette's initial response to the assignment was typical: "I can't think of any good topics." Nevertheless, she began making a list of subjects she might want to discuss. "Roommates," "dream analysis," and "how to give blood" were three that she considered. However, a quick trip to the library revealed that there was not much information on roommates that could be researched. And, when she checked with her instructor, he told her that "dream analysis" and "how to give blood" were frequently used topics and therefore not acceptable choices. Her teacher suggested that she consider something interesting that she had learned in another class.

Of the subjects Annette had studied, which might interest her classmates? Her audience analysis revealed that many members were freshmen who had recently graduated from high school. Annette was a math major, but she was one of few students with an interest in math or science. In economics, she had enjoyed learning about capitalism and socialism, but she thought those concepts would be too complex for an eight-minute speech.

Then Annette had an inspiration. She remembered learning about the right to a jury trial in a government course. Annette had been called for jury duty the previous summer, and she had served as a juror in a burglary case. Because of their age, it was likely that few of her classmates had ever been on a jury, yet they were likely to be called in the future. Before serving, Annette had had no idea of what jury duty would be like, and she had faced the task with considerable trepidation. Having been through the experience, she could ensure that her classmates would not be in the dark. Furthermore, this was a subject that could be researched. She could look up what citizens' rights and responsibilities are when they are assigned jury duty. She could

For a definition of informative speaking, see page 126.

topic: the subject you will address in your speech.

research her college's policy regarding students called for jury duty. Would their absences be excused? Would they be expected to keep up with their coursework while serving on a jury? She proposed this topic to her instructor, and he said, "Great! This is an important civic responsibility that students should learn more about."

As Annette's experience shows, even if you are unsure what subject to speak about at the outset, you can find a good topic if you put your mind to it. In this chapter, we examine how to select a subject area for your topic, narrow your topic to fit the available time, and determine your purpose given your audience analysis and any requirements for your speech. If we were to reduce this chapter to a single sentence, it would be this: ***Your topic focuses the message.*** We say this because once you have followed the process of topic selection described in this chapter, the topic you have selected and refined will govern the content of your speech.

Use your CD-ROM to develop, select, and narrow your topic. Go to "Step 2 Invention/Select Topic." CD-ROM: Interactive Speech Guides

Developing a Set of Potential Topics

Possible speech topics are as varied as human experience. Your topic could be lighthearted or serious, address ancient history or current events, or relate to professional interests or a recreational activity. Here are some of the topics used by students over the past few years:

airplane "black boxes"	hydrogen-powered cars
backpacking	my dog Max
Cleopatra	my mom the hero
cloning	sharks
earthquake survival	school prayer
Ecuador	standardized tests
encryption	Timbuktu University
food irradiation	Venus
Great Wall of China	wilderness preservation
history of toilets	zebras

To select the best topic for your speech, begin by developing a diverse set of possibilities. You can do this by using a number of strategies: *brainstorming, word association, mind mapping,* and *researching* (see Figure 6.1).

● *Brainstorm Topics*

For more on brainstorming, see page 43.

Begin the topic selection process by **brainstorming** potential topic areas for your speech. Remember that when you brainstorm, you list every idea you can think of, without assessing the merits of the ideas. Your initial goal is to generate a large number of possible subjects. While brainstorming, consider your interests and talents, experiences you have had, issues you care about, organizations you belong to, people you admire, events you find significant, places you have been, and lessons about life you have found important (see Figure 6.2). Think about favorites in each of these categories.

brainstorming: listing all possible ideas as they come to mind, withholding decisions on their merits.

FIGURE 6.1   Strategies for Generating Topic Choices

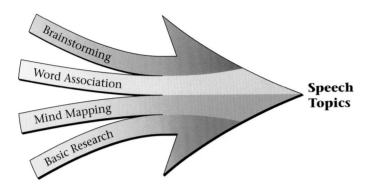

For example, what is your favorite use of spare time? What is the most interesting course you have ever taken? What is the best organization you have ever belonged to? Write down each favorite, and others that are close to the top. Your list will begin to grow.

● *Use Word Association*

Another technique for generating topics is **word association**. When using this method, begin by listing one potential topic (as you do when brainstorming), and then write whatever comes to mind when you think about that idea. The second idea may suggest a third topic, and so on. Write each thought that comes to mind to the right of the previous topic (see Figure 6.3). If you use word association on every idea for a topic that you generated while brainstorming, your set of options will grow.

FIGURE 6.2   Helpful Categories for Brainstorming

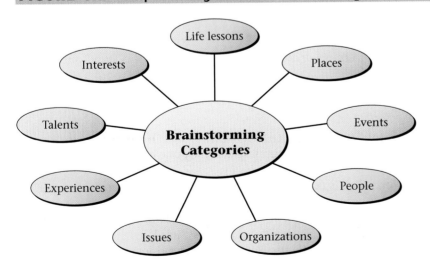

word association: listing the ideas that come to mind when you mention a specific word or phrase.

FIGURE 6.3 Word Association

To develop a variety of topics, write down whatever idea each word or phrase suggests.

- **my football coach** → football practice → team meetings → success comes when preparation meets opportunity
- **animal rights** → fake fur → counterfeit money → counterfeit software
- **outdoors** → backpacking → backpacking on the Appalachian Trail
- **our college** → campus parking problems → bicycling to school → carpooling
- **Chinese food** → China → travel to China → what to do before visiting China

---

TIP

When making an initial topic list, don't waste time evaluating the merits of each possibility. Your initial goal is to list a wide variety of topics. Later you will decide which topics have potential for your speech assignment.

One reason for listing every potential topic while using word association is that even a clearly inappropriate topic may be the basis for finding a more appropriate one. Mike's experience when he was assigned to deliver a speech on "a tip for college success" provides an example of why topics should not be rejected at this stage. While brainstorming, Mike thought of his football coach, an unlikely topic for this assignment. He associated the coach's name with the coach's favorite saying: "Success comes when preparation meets opportunity." That quotation formed the basis for an excellent speech about study habits.

● Use Mind Mapping

Mind mapping (sometimes called *cognitive mapping*) is an alternative to brainstorming and word association. Those two techniques produce lists in a linear format. When doing **mind mapping**, you write down a word or phrase. Then around that word or phrase you write other ideas that relate to it.[1] Figure 6.4 shows some mind maps.

Here are some recommendations for mapping:

- Use images in addition to words.
- Start from the center of the page and work outward.
- Print rather than write in script.
- Use colors to indicate associations and to make ideas stand out.
- Use arrows or other visual aids to show links between different ideas.
- Don't get stuck on one concept. If you run out of ideas, move on to a new theme.
- Jot ideas down anywhere, as they occur, wherever they fit.
- Be creative. Make mind mapping an enjoyable experience.[2]

Mind mapping is considered advantageous because it enables better use of your brain's potential than do brainstorming and word associations.[3] The brain does not keep track of information in neat lines,[4] nor does a mind map. The use of colors, pictures, and symbols stimulates the right half of the brain, and such images are also kept in your mind longer, enabling you to create more associations.[5] Thus you can generate more topic ideas.

mind mapping: writing down a word or phrase and then creatively surrounding that word or phrase with ideas that come to mind when you think of it.

FIGURE 6.4   Using Mind Mapping to Generate Topics

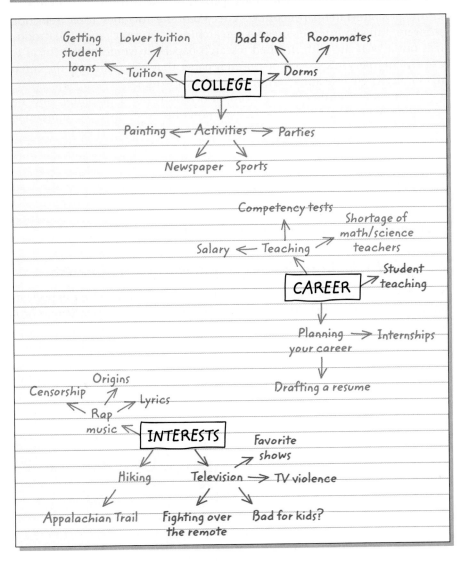

Mapping can be a very effective method for coming up with possible topics, generating ideas to develop a topic, and even taking notes in class. For more details on mind mapping, search for "mind mapping" on the Internet, or consult books on this technique, such as *The Mind Map Book.*[6]

● *Research for Topics*

To discover more potential topics, you can use some simple research techniques. You may be reminded of ideas for topics by scanning the table of contents of magazines you find interesting or by looking at subject-based indexes on the Internet. General news magazines are good resources for topic ideas because they include current events and articles on science, famous people, and the arts. You may want to go to the library and scan recent issues.

Internet subject indexes are discussed on pages 159–62.

There is software on the Internet that can help you search for possible topics. One example is the "Idea Directory," which can be found at <http://www.researchpaper.com>.[7] This Web site includes topic selection software, links to Internet sites for researching your topic, and a chatroom. It is not a Web site with finished research papers. It would be unethical to use another person's speech or research paper that you found on the Internet or anywhere else and claim it as your own work.

After brainstorming, using word association, mind mapping, and researching, you should have a variety of potential topics (we recommend at least twenty) and be ready to choose the best one for your speech.

To review ethical responsibilities for proper attribution, see pages 61–64.

Selecting the Best Topic

When you choose a topic, the decision should be based on your audience, your interests and knowledge, and the context of your speech.

● *Consider Audience Members' Knowledge and Interests*

Your speech should be worthwhile for the audience. When you expect an audience to give up their time to listen to your speech, it is up to you to provide a message that they will find interesting and important.

Before you can select a topic for your audience, it is important to learn about the people you will be addressing. Conduct a preliminary audience analysis (see Chapter 5), and record this information on your Speech Grid.

Would the preservation of wild horses and burros be a good speech topic? Only if your audience finds the subject interesting or worthwhile. What would a speaker want to learn about the audience before selecting this topic?

When choosing a topic, use what you know or can infer about audience members' interests and experiences. The topic you select should satisfy one or more of these questions:

See the sample grid on page 137 for an example of how audience analysis is used to select a topic.

- Is the topic likely to interest your audience?
- Is the topic likely to be one that audience members need to know about (for their own benefit or for the benefit of society)?
- Is the topic likely to inspire, entertain, or emotionally move your audience?

If your topic is unlikely to accomplish any of those objectives, ask yourself how a speech on that topic would benefit the audience. If no benefits are apparent, avoid that topic (unless it is assigned to you).

● *Consider Your Own Knowledge and Interests*

There are several benefits to selecting a topic that is familiar to you. You will be a more fluent and enthusiastic speaker if your subject is familiar. Also, audience members will be more likely to believe the claims you make if they know of your experience in the subject area you are addressing. Furthermore, because you already know about your topic, you can target your research on finding specific information that will strengthen your speech. You will not need to spend time looking up general background facts.

It is also helpful to select a topic that interests you. This is particularly important if you are asked to choose from a set of unfamiliar topics for a course assignment. It takes time to develop a good speech. If you are not interested in your topic, it will be difficult to maintain the energy required to research, organize, and practice your speech.

In addition, it is difficult to get an audience enthused about your speech if the topic is boring to you. One of our students captivated his audience with a speech on Legos (although the members of the class had not played with toys for years) because his enthusiasm for the subject was so evident. Conversely, a student who appeared totally disinterested in the topic of job interviews did not have a successful speech even though his topic was highly relevant to a college audience.

One student learned about the importance of selecting an interesting and familiar topic the hard way. She selected "child care" and in her speech compared day care centers to in-home day care providers. She did not have children herself and lacked firsthand experience with any type of day care. She researched her subject but knew less about it than did several classmates whose children were in day care. The cost figures she cited were national averages, which were quite different from the costs in the community where she attended college. She made some obvious mistakes, for example, assuming that in-home providers would not have any educational background in child development. When it was time for questions from the audience, several times she had to defer to other members of the class who had more experience with child care than she did.

When discussing topics for the next round of speeches, this speaker candidly noted that another member of the class should have spoken on child care, and she (a business major) wisely decided to advocate student invest-ment in individual retirement accounts. Her knowledge and interest in that topic resulted in an excellent speech.

● *Consider the Context of Your Speech*

For more on situational characteristics, see pp. 92–97.

The context of your speech is another consideration in topic selection. The **context** is the occasion, surrounding environment, and situation in which the speech will occur. These factors often make one topic choice better than another.

The occasion may call for a particular topic or type of topic. If you are speaking at a retirement dinner or memorial service, the person being com-memorated will be the focus of your speech. If you are addressing a meeting about neighborhood safety in your community, you will be expected to focus on safety and not on other local issues. If you are asked to speak at an awards banquet for a campus organization to which you belong, the audi-ence will expect an upbeat speech on a topic related to that organization. A speech on more serious ideas, such as the need for changes in higher educa-tion, would be better saved for a more formal occasion.

Situational characteristics such as audience size, audience mobility, and the time and location of your speech should also influence your topic selec-tion. If you know that there will be many distractions where you are speak-ing, select a topic that is particularly likely to hold the audience's attention. If you would need to play an audiotape to present one potential topic, but you know you will be speaking at a location where it would be difficult for the audience to hear the tape, choose a different topic.

Finally, there may be requirements that dictate a specific topic or type of topic. In the classroom or on the job, you may be assigned a particular subject. Your history teacher may assign an oral report on ancient China, or your employer may ask you to prepare a sales presentation on a new prod-uct. The nature of an assignment may influence your topic choice as well. In most classroom assignments you will be expected to include references to research, and for these speeches you need a topic that can be satisfactorily researched. A humorous speech about your experiences as a food server, hor-ror stories about your ex-roommates, or a demonstration of how you make your favorite fruit salad will not fit this type of assignment.

Your instructor may also require you to present a specific type of speech— for example, one that addresses a controversial issue or presents an interesting concept that you learned in a college course. The topic of political extremists speaking on campus would fit the former assignment; a speech on the dis-covery of the planet Pluto would fit the latter. When there are requirements for your speech, you must select a topic that meets those requirements.

● *Be Timely in Selecting Your Topic*

One more point is critical to topic selection and the entire speech prepara-tion process: select a topic and stay with it. If you believe you need to re-search or investigate a few potential topics before making a final choice, do that task and select *one* topic as quickly as possible.

context: the occasion, surrounding environment, and situation in which the speech occurs.

| INVENTION | ORGANIZATION | STYLE | PREPARATION | DELIVERY |

In Theory 6.1

STAYING WITH YOUR TOPIC CHOICE

Topic selection is a key part of the *invention* stage of speech preparation. Research from a variety of perspectives supports the advice to select a topic early and stick with it.

An analysis of over one thousand speech diaries written by students in college speech classes revealed one consistent difference between good speakers and weak ones: the topic selection process. The more successful speakers carefully considered their topic choice but chose a topic promptly and then stayed with it, putting their time into preparation. Less successful speakers spent days attempting to choose an acceptable topic.[8]

One benefit from selecting a topic early and beginning your preparation is a reduction in speech anxiety. Recall from Chapter 1 that you can reduce the apprehension you experience after receiving a speech assignment by beginning to work on the speech. You can also reduce speech anxiety by preparing well, but you cannot prepare until you have settled on a topic. (For a discussion of how early speech preparation can reduce anxiety, see p. 23.)

Another benefit is additional time for preparation. Every hour that you spend agonizing over topic selection is an hour that you cannot spend preparing the content of your speech or practicing your delivery. Researchers have estimated that "anywhere from 46% to 95% of college students regularly procrastinate on academic assignments."[9] Other studies have found misconceptions among college students who procrastinate, including a tendency to overestimate the time left to perform a task and underestimate the time needed to finish a task.[10] This means that if you delay speech preparation, you could easily discover that there is not sufficient time remaining to prepare and practice well. Conversely, a significant relationship between methodical, disciplined study and academic performance has been found.[11]

The point is clear: soon after receiving a speech assignment, brainstorm and evaluate potential topics. But once you have done that, select the optimal topic and do not waver. Use your time to prepare the best speech you can.

You jeopardize your ability to prepare a good speech if you spend too much time selecting a speech topic and have too little time to work on the topic you have chosen (See In Theory box 6.1). Avoid wavering between two or more choices, working on one topic and then becoming discouraged and trying another. Once you have carefully considered a topic choice, you are better off focusing your time and energy into planning the best speech possible on that topic, rather than worrying about your topic choice or losing all the time you invested in your first topic by starting over on a second. If you begin to work on a topic and then run into trouble while preparing your speech, it is better to approach the topic from a different angle instead of rejecting the topic wholesale.

For an example of shifting to another angle on your topic, see page 112.

Refining Your Topic

Once you have selected a topic, decide how you will develop it. There are two major considerations when you refine your topic: the effect you want your speech to have and the narrowing of your topic to achieve that effect.

● *Decide on the Rhetorical Purpose of Your Speech*

When you prepare a speech, you should have at least one objective in mind. What do you hope your speech will do for the audience? Is your goal to inspire the audience to take action? to agree with you that a certain belief is right or wrong? to become better informed? to feel angry or amused? to experience some combination of these effects? The intended effect constitutes your **rhetorical purpose**.

Four Typical Rhetorical Purposes.   Amber was allowed to select the topic of her choice for the first assignment in her public speaking class. She selected her major, theater arts, and considered a variety of options for developing this topic:

- She could tell her audience (the class) about the courses taken by a student majoring in theater arts.
- She could try to convince her audience to attend the play that the department was about to present.
- She could amuse her audience with stories about actors and actresses who forgot their lines.
- She could tell an inspiring story about a student in the department who overcame great obstacles to earn the lead in a major production.

Each option would result in a speech that related to theater arts on campus in some way, but the rhetorical purpose of each would be different—to inform, to persuade, to entertain, or inspire. Each would be likely to have a different effect on the audience members. Let's look briefly at each of those four purposes, which are typical purposes of the speeches that are assigned in public speaking classes and also of the speeches that you may be asked to deliver outside the classroom (they are not the only possible rhetorical purposes, however).

One purpose of a speech can be *to inform the audience*. When your purpose is **informative**, the message is educational, and the objective is to increase the audience's understanding or awareness of your subject. If Amber decides to tell her audience about the courses offered by the theater arts department, her message will be informative. The intended effect of her speech will be to increase audience understanding of what students majoring in theater arts study.

Another purpose of a speech can be *to persuade the audience*. You may want to do more than deepen your audience's understanding of a topic. You may take a position on an issue in order to encourage your audience to consider or adopt a new position or belief, to strengthen an existing position or belief, or to take action after listening to your speech. When you have these goals, your rhetorical purpose is **persuasive**.

Amber's second speech idea, encouraging class members to attend a play, would yield a persuasive message. In this speech, she would do more than provide the audience with information about the theater arts program. She would try to persuade them to take action by giving up their time and money to attend a performance.

rhetorical purpose: the audience reaction you intend to achieve with your speech.

informative purpose: an intent to increase audience members' understanding or awareness.

persuasive purpose: an intent to influence audience members' beliefs or actions.

For many topics, a speech could have any of the four rhetorical purposes. Take this steak dinner, for example. A man giving an informative speech could discuss the nutritional value of a meal like this and explain how to measure the nutritional value of other meals. If the rhetorical purpose was persuasive, the speaker could attempt to convince the audience to consider an alternative, vegetarian diet. If the purpose was entertainment, the speaker could share his recollections of his experiences as a waiter, including the time he stumbled and dropped an expensive steak dinner in the lap of the customer who had ordered it. Finally, if the speaker wanted to inspire his audience, he could tell how he overcame seemingly insurmountable obstacles to achieve his lifelong ambition of becoming a chef.

A third purpose of a speech can be *to entertain the audience*. There are contexts in which it is especially appropriate for the audience to enjoy your speech, much as they might enjoy a good novel or movie. The "roast" of a best friend or an after-dinner speech are two examples. Although you may make some serious points, your main purpose is not to deepen listeners' understanding of your subject or to motivate the audience to take any action. When your purpose is **entertainment**, your objective is to get the audience smiling or laughing as a result of your presentation.

Amber's third possible topic, accounts of performers who forgot their lines, would have this effect. Just as people find shows about "bloopers" in sports or movies entertaining, an audience would enjoy anecdotes about actors and actresses forgetting their speeches on stage.

A fourth purpose is *to inspire the audience*. You may want your speech to touch your audience's emotions. You hope your audience will feel empathy, respect, warmth, or sadness because of your speech. When your primary

entertainment purpose: an intent to provide audience members with a lighthearted perspective on your topic.

purpose is **inspirational**, you are not necessarily trying to move the audience to take direct action as a result of their feelings; rather, you want listeners to experience an emotion.

Radio and television commentators and newspaper columnists often report human interest stories, such as an anecdote about a lottery winner who gave the money to a worthy cause. Listeners or readers generally do not respond by making their own donations to charity, but their faith in humanity may be strengthened. Amber's fourth topic possibility, how a student overcame tremendous odds to earn the lead in a play, would yield a speech with an inspirational purpose.

Assigned Rhetorical Purposes and Topic Selection.

In some contexts, the rhetorical purpose may be a given. Your assignment may be to present an informative speech in class, or you may be asked to persuade your city council to expand bus routes. When your purpose is assigned, add "appropriateness for your purpose" as a criterion for topic selection. Some topics, such as "odd habits of television personalities," would be unlikely to fit a persuasive speech assignment well, and topics such as "violence in the schools" are not likely to be appropriate for an after-dinner speech.

Multiple Rhetorical Purposes.

Public speaking assignments often emphasize one purpose, such as "Prepare an *informative* speech" or "*Persuade* the audience to adopt your viewpoint on a controversial social issue." But speeches need not always have a single rhetorical purpose. In some contexts, you may have multiple purposes. For example, if you worked for a nonprofit organization, you might give a speech to community leaders to *inform* them about your organization and *persuade* them to volunteer their time.

Furthermore, speeches in or out of the classroom may have more than one effect. For example, an informative speech explaining how exercise reduces stress may persuade audience members to exercise more. An entertaining speech about "drivers' excuses for traffic violations" may inform audience members that the police have already heard most of the excuses that motorists give and persuade listeners to be safer drivers.

● *Narrow Your Topic*

In addition to selecting a rhetorical purpose, you will select the elements of your topic on which you will focus. Ordinarily it is best to focus on a very limited aspect of your topic: ideas that you can develop in the available time and ideas that will best accomplish your rhetorical purpose.

Speakers encounter difficulty when they attempt to cover a topic that is too broad. Many student speeches about sports, for example, are problematic because they attempt to cover too much material. An overly ambitious speaker typically selects one sport for a topic (for example, tennis, field hockey, or lacrosse) and attempts in eight or ten minutes to cover the equipment used in that sport, the rules of the game, techniques for playing well, and maybe even the sport's history. But think about it! In ten minutes, could you explain the rules of your favorite sport or game to a friend who had never played? Would your friend understand the rules well enough to play? No, he or she would not learn and remember all the rules, unless the

---

The informative and persuasive Speech Guides (in Chapters 14 and 15) cover speeches where the rhetorical purpose is given. The impromptu and special occasion speeches (in Chapters 16 and 17) may have different purposes, depending on the topic or context.

View a student explaining how she narrowed her topic.
CD-ROM: Video Theater, Excerpt 6.1

inspirational purpose: an intent to touch audience members' emotions.

game was very simple. If you could not satisfactorily explain the rules in ten minutes, you obviously could not add in strategy or equipment, among other things.

Despite the impossibility of covering a broad topic well, many new speakers try to do just that. Their speeches end up being an overwhelming mix of too much information and not enough explanation.

One of the best sports speeches we have heard narrowed the topic of tennis down to an informative presentation about four interesting tennis personalities. The points the speaker covered, such as the classic 1973 "Battle of the Sexes" match between Billie Jean King and Bobby Riggs, could be explained in a manner that was interesting and relevant. Even audience members who were not tennis fans or had not been born when that match took place had a favorable response to the speech.

Figure 6.5 presents several guidelines to follow when you are narrowing your focus to a specific aspect of your topic. When you make this choice, as you did when choosing a topic, consider your audience, your own interests and expertise, and the speaking situation. Also think about your rhetorical purpose and the available speech time.

Select an Aspect That Is Appropriate to Your Audience.   A speech should be given for the benefit of the audience members. When you are deciding how to narrow your topic, be certain that the aspect you select will be interesting or important to your audience. See the Speech Grid Application on page 137 for an example of how to use audience analysis to narrow a topic.

Kendra, who wanted to speak about figure skating, successfully narrowed her topic. She surveyed her class and found out that few people were interested in a speech about how to skate, the topic she had planned to emphasize. However, most of the class intended to watch the Winter Olympics, so Kendra revised her plans and spoke to her classmates about how they could score the skating events while watching at home and could make their own decisions about who should win the competition. Because this was information the audience could use, and wanted to use, Kendra's speech was very well received.

TIP

Narrow the focus of your speech so you do not overwhelm audience members with information and so you have time to effectively explain the points that are most important to make.

FIGURE 6.5   Narrowing Your Topic: Which Aspect to Select

Your Topic:
Potential Aspects to Cover

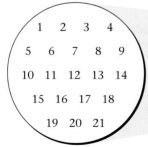

Consider:
1. Your audience
2. Your interests and expertise
3. Situational characteristics
4. Your rhetorical purpose
5. Available time

Your Narrowed Topic:
Aspects You Will Cover

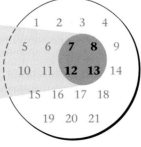

When narrowing your topic, consider the cultures represented in your audience. Kendra's speech on ice skating or the previously mentioned speech on tennis personalities would be particularly interesting if the speaker included examples of athletes from cultures represented in the audience. If your audience members are members of cultures that place a uniquely high value on family relationships, hard work, or religious observance, a main point that related to one of those topics would be effective.

Even when your topic is assigned, you can still narrow the topic appropriately for your audience. If you were required to speak on the cloning of sheep, a discussion of the techniques used to clone a sheep could be very interesting to biology or agriculture majors. However, the audience in a general education speech course might be interested in a less technical aspect of the subject—perhaps a discussion of the ethical concerns surrounding the cloning of sheep or the effect that cloning might have on the quality of meat and wool.

Select an Aspect That Fits Your Experience and Expertise. Your special expertise or unique perspectives about an aspect of your subject area can provide a basis for narrowing your topic. One example of a unique perspective is provided by Natasha, a student who had grown up in the former Soviet Union before moving to the United States. Natasha had been active in dance since she was a young child in the Soviet Union. This experience gave her an excellent angle for narrowing her general topic of ballet. She compared ballet training in the Soviet Union and in the United States, giving the audience a fascinating insight into Soviet philosophy and culture, in addition to informing them about ballet. Interesting information that your audience is unlikely to encounter elsewhere often provides a good focus for your message.

Select an Aspect That Is Appropriate to the Situational Characteristics of the Speech. Situational characteristics may help you determine what elements of your topic to expand on. Michelle, a student who was interested in entomology (the study of insects), chose bugs as her general topic. A speech about the uses of bugs to determine the time of death of a murder victim was rejected because the speech was to be delivered shortly after lunch and several audience members were squeamish about insects. She also decided not to develop a main point that relied on small, live bugs for a visual aid, because the speech was to be delivered in a large room. Instead, she made a wise decision to focus on interesting facts about bees. A main point about honey was perfect for after-lunch discourse, and rather than using an actual bee for a visual aid in the large room, she used her arms to simulate how a bee uses its wings.

Select an Aspect That Fits Your Rhetorical Purpose. Many parts of any general subject can be emphasized, depending on the rhetorical purpose of your speech. You should be certain that the part you have chosen will be appropriate for your purpose. A speech about cloning would be appropriate as an informative message, but if you wanted to argue that cloning humans was good or bad, that topic would be more appropriate for a persuasive speech. If you wanted to entertain the audience, you might think of humorous examples of people or things that you and the audience would rather not see cloned.

ESL | Topics and Time Limits

It is easier to deliver a speech in a second language if you select a topic that you know well. Topics about your home country or your culture may be easier for you to speak about because they are familiar. Furthermore, they can fascinate your fellow classmates. Over the years, our international students have shared information about diverse topics ranging from the customs of Ramadan to ranching in Chile.

When you select a topic area, be sure that it is not too broad. Many Americans prefer to organize their time around a predictable schedule. They may experience stress in work or business contexts where time is viewed more flexibly.[1] If the time limit for speeches is eight minutes, your instructor and most of your classmates will expect your speech to last no longer than eight minutes. For example, you obviously cannot review the entire history of a country in eight minutes, nor can you replicate a thirty-minute ceremony within that time.

Time your speech when you are practicing to be sure that it is not too long. If you find the speech takes more than the available time, narrow your topic. For example, you might discuss only a particularly important century in the history of your country, or explain the high point of a significant cultural ceremony.

[1]Hall, E. T. (1989). *Beyond culture* (p. 17). New York: Anchor Books.

Select an Aspect That Can Be Covered within Your Time Limit.   Whether you are speaking in a classroom or out in the community, it is inconsiderate to take more time than you have been allocated. Audiences will likely become frustrated and may stop listening if you exceed the allocated time.

A speech explaining the rules of soccer would take too long, but a speech discussing one specific aspect in great detail, such as how to shoot a penalty shot, would be doable and interesting.

TIP

Be careful not to over-estimate the amount of material you can cover in one speech.

Your speech will be ineffective if you speak too fast to fit all the material in or if you cover your ideas too briefly rather than explaining them well.

Speakers are more likely to overestimate, rather than underestimate, how easily an audience will follow the points they make. A speech focusing exclusively on the reasons why the dinosaurs in the movie *Jurassic Park* could not really be cloned with present technology could easily take ten minutes. This very limited segment of the general subject of cloning would provide more than enough information to explain in the available time, particularly if many audience members had a limited scientific background.

● *Draft Your Specific Purpose and Thesis or Topic Statement*

After you decide on your rhetorical purpose and narrow your topic, the next steps in topic selection are determining your specific purpose and drafting your thesis or topic statement. These ideas will guide your preparation and provide a brief, accurate description of what your speech is about.

State Your Specific Purpose.   Your **specific purpose** expresses the objective of your speech. It precisely conveys the rhetorical purpose and narrowed topic of your speech in a single sentence.

Drafting a Specific Purpose.   A well-written specific purpose statement has several characteristics. First, the specific purpose *conveys the rhetorical purpose of your speech*. Specific purpose statements commonly begin with a phrase indicating the rhetorical purpose, such as "to inform," "to persuade," or "to inspire." A specific purpose could be "to inform my audience about debate in nineteenth-century Japan" or "to persuade my audience to walk to school on Earth Day."

Second, the specific purpose *indicates how you narrowed your topic*. Compare these two potential specific purposes for Chuck's persuasive speech:

- To persuade my audience to support airline safety
- To persuade my audience to pay careful attention to the flight attendant's safety presentation when traveling by air

The second statement provides a better indication of how Chuck narrowed the focus of his speech on airline safety. His speech is not covering all aspects of airplane safety. The focus is on the flight attendant's safety message, as the second statement indicates.

Third, the specific purpose *describes your topic accurately.* Consider the example of Luke, a student who prepared an excellent speech on home schooling. Rather than attending a high school, he had been taught by his parents at home. His speech explained how students who are schooled at home can still experience typical high school activities and social events. Which topic statement describes his speech more accurately?

- To inform my audience how home-schooled students have the same educational opportunities as students attending high school
- To inform my audience how home-schooled students can participate in dances and parties, sports, and extracurricular activities during their high school years

specific purpose: the objective of your speech.

The first specific purpose was the one that Luke submitted. That statement may have characterized some other speech well, but it did not describe Luke's speech accurately. He did not intend to tell the audience about the educational opportunities of home-schooled children. His speech was about these students' opportunities to participate in activities and sports. Luke needed a purpose statement like the second one to characterize his speech accurately.

Using the Specific Purpose to Guide Your Preparation.   Your specific purpose should be written on your Speech Grid (see the sample grid on p. 138). The ideas you present in your speech should all help you to accomplish your purpose, and you should exclude ideas not relevant to your purpose. Your specific purpose is something like the sideline on a football field or tennis court. It indicates which ideas are "out of bounds," given the objective you have chosen (see Figure 6.6).

Modifying the Specific Purpose If Warranted.   Your specific purpose is a *working idea* because you may decide to revise it as you continue to prepare your speech. As you develop your ideas, research your topic, and learn more about your audience, you may opt to refine your specific purpose. A change in the way you elaborate on your topic can make your speech even stronger, but remember that *it is not advisable to change to a brand-new subject area.* As noted earlier, speakers who do not settle on a subject and work with it are likely to end up spending too much time thinking about which topic to use and not enough time preparing their speeches.

> **TIP**
>
> *Throughout the speech preparation process, it is important to keep your specific purpose in mind.*

FIGURE 6.6   **The Specific Purpose Focuses Speech Development**

Early in this chapter we discussed Annette's speech about jury duty. If her specific purpose was "to inform my audience about what to expect if called for jury duty," that purpose would dictate what ideas may be used. She should only use points that relate to her specific purpose (inside boundary) and exclude those that do not.

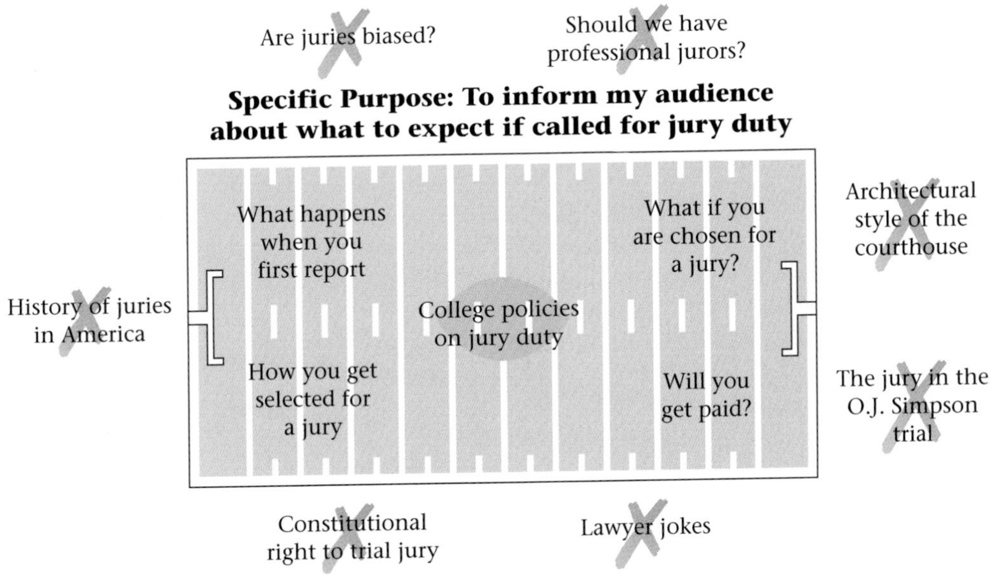

Are juries biased?   Should we have professional jurors?

Specific Purpose: To inform my audience about what to expect if called for jury duty

What happens when you first report

What if you are chosen for a jury?

Architectural style of the courthouse

History of juries in America

College policies on jury duty

How you get selected for a jury

Will you get paid?

The jury in the O.J. Simpson trial

Constitutional right to trial jury

Lawyer jokes

A good example of a modification in the focus of a speech is provided by a student whose original purpose was to persuade the audience that the United States should construct a colony in space. While researching the subject, he discovered that technical problems and political realities would prevent colonization for twenty-five years or more. This made his original purpose untenable, so he changed his objective and advocated expanded research and development to overcome barriers to space colonization. His specific purpose became "to persuade my audience that research and development of space colonization should be expanded," and he was able to support this viewpoint well.

Prepare Your Thesis or Topic Statement.   Once you have decided on a specific purpose, you should be able to express what your speech is about in a sentence. We use the terms *thesis* and *topic statement* to refer to this sentence. The term **thesis** is commonly used when a speech is persuasive; a thesis is a position you are advocating. For example, a speech arguing that birth control pills should receive the same insurance coverage as Viagra would be defending a position or thesis. When you are informing, inspiring, or entertaining an audience, you usually are not advocating a belief that you want the audience to adopt or an action you want the audience to take. We use the term **topic statement** for a single sentence that sums up the message of a speech that is not intended to persuade.

The thesis and the topic sentence convey the "bottom line" of your speech to your listeners, enabling them to understand the ultimate message that all the facts and ideas in your speech work together to support. You will indicate the thesis or topic sentence in your introduction and reiterate it in your conclusion. If audience members can remember this statement, they should be able to remember the essence of your speech.

A good thesis or topic sentence will convey your purpose and topic to the audience efficiently and accurately. Here are some guidelines to follow.

First, a good thesis or topic statement *is limited to one sentence*—it is not a paragraph and not an essay. Its function is to efficiently tell the audience what your speech is about, not to provide all the details. It should be expressed in a complete *statement* that conveys the heart of your message, not in a *question* for the audience to ponder.

Compare these two topic statements for Marjorie's speech presenting the Most Valuable Player Award to a member of the women's soccer team:

- Michelle's play on the field and leadership off the field earned her the Most Valuable Player Award.

- Michelle is our most valuable player because she was a leading scorer, scoring the winning goal in the playoffs. She was also a supportive teammate who worked hard in practice, and a role model for our own players. She also set a good example for the many youth players who came to watch our games.

The first example conveys the purpose of the speech efficiently. In one sentence, we learn that Michelle is the Most Valuable Player for two primary reasons. The second example contains too many sentences and too much information. The information about Michelle will provide excellent support

For the basics on introductions and conclusions, see pages 48–50. For more on these topics, see Chapter 8.

thesis: the position advocated in a persuasive speech.

topic statement: a single sentence that sums up the message of a speech that is not intended to persuade.

in the body of Majorie's speech. It cannot all be presented in an efficient sentence.

Second, a good topic sentence *clearly conveys what you hope the audience will know, do, or feel as a result of your speech.* The audience can better follow your message if they know what to expect.

Compare these two topic sentences that Annette could use for her informative speech about jury duty:

- Today, I plan to talk about jury duty.
- College students called for jury duty need to know campus policies and courtroom procedures for prospective jurors.

The first statement provides little information about the speech. Audience members would have no idea of the speaker's rhetorical purpose and no understanding of how the speaker planned to narrow the topic of jury duty. The second statement does much more to orient audience members. It tells them that the speaker will present an informative message about what students can expect from their university and at the courthouse if they are called for jury duty.

Third, a good topic statement *is consistent with the specific purpose.* These two statements are intended to characterize the same speech. If they are at odds with each other, when you use the specific purpose to prepare your speech, the resulting message could differ from the speech your topic sentence describes.

Suppose that Jasmine's specific purpose is "To persuade my audience to abstain from eating meat for one week" and her message provides reasons why this would be a healthy experiment. If her topic sentence is "People need to eat a balanced diet," the audience will not be ready for the vegetarian message she intends to present. Most audience members will expect a speech describing a balanced diet and explaining why eating one is a good idea. What Jasmine needs to write is a topic sentence like this: "A week-long meatless diet can show you the path to a healthier lifestyle." That would give her audience a more accurate understanding of her message.

After refining your topic statement or thesis and your specific purpose, you will be able to make appropriate choices when you select ideas from the right side of your Speech Grid for use in your speech. We elaborate on what to write on the right side of the grid in upcoming chapters.

For more on using your Speech Grid to select content, see page 256.

Summary

When preparing a speech, remember that ***your topic focuses the message.*** Once you determine the topic and purpose of your speech, they will control the content of your speech. In this chapter, we discussed the steps to take to choose a topic that will be appropriate for the audience, the occasion, and yourself. We considered how to refine your topic and draft the specific purpose and thesis or topic statements. The Speech Grid Application at the end of this chapter shows how your grid assists you in this process. Use the following checklist to review these steps as you prepare your speeches.

Checklist

DEVELOP A SET OF POTENTIAL TOPICS

____ Brainstorm topics (p. 118)

____ Use word association (p. 119)

____ Use mind mapping (p. 120)

____ Research for topics (p. 121)

SELECT THE BEST TOPIC

____ Consider audience members' knowledge and interests (p. 122)

____ Consider your own knowledge and interests (p. 123)

____ Consider the context of your speech (p. 124)

____ Be timely in selecting your topic (p. 124)

REFINE YOUR TOPIC

____ Decide on the rhetorical purpose of your speech (p. 126)

____ Narrow your topic to fit the available time and focus on the most appropriate aspects of your topic (p. 128)

____ Prepare a specific purpose statement (p. 132)

____ Formulate a thesis or topic statement (p. 134)

Key Terms and Concepts

topic (p. 117)
brainstorming (p. 118)
word association (p. 119)
mind mapping (p. 120)
context (p. 124)
rhetorical purpose (p. 126)
informative purpose (p. 126)

persuasive purpose (p. 126)
entertainment purpose (p. 127)
inspirational purpose (p. 128)
specific purpose (p. 132)
thesis (p. 134)
topic statement (p. 134)

Speech Grid Application

The Evolution of a Speech Grid

Speech Grid Applications, showing the evolution of a Speech Grid, are included near the end of Chapters 5 through 12. They illustrate how one student, Samantha, uses a grid to prepare a speech.

The grid in Chapter 5 shows information that Samantha knew about audience members before conducting a survey (see p. 107). That information is printed in red on the grid in this chapter.

Samantha adds information to her grid during the topic selection process. During this effort, she selects a topic, surveys her audience with respect to that topic, and finally narrows and refines the topic. The next two sections explain her topic selection and refinement decisions. The information that Samantha adds to her grid is printed in black.

Pre-Survey Preparation.   For her topic, Samantha selects cell phones. She bases this choice on two factors: (1) she has noticed several of her classmates carrying cell phones to school, and (2) she already has some demographic information about her fellow students. Twenty-seven of 28 students are in the 18–21 age group. Samantha figures that people in this age group are likely to be familiar with new technology and to consider buying a cell phone in the future.

Samantha decides to narrow her topic to "driving while using a cell phone." She is troubled by a recent news report about the accident risks created by such behavior. A speech targeted at reducing these risks will be timely and provide her audience with important information. On her grid, she writes "cell phones and driving" for her speech topic.

Post-Survey Preparation.   Samantha surveys her class to determine the audience's prior exposure and disposition toward her topic. She gathers the following information, which she adds to the left side of her grid:

- 8 out of 28 students currently own a cell phone. Another 12 students think it is "likely" or "highly likely" that they will own one within three years.
- 7 students have heard about the issue of cell phones and driving.
- 6 of 8 cell phone owners use their phone in the car. Each cell phone owner has one car as his or her primary auto transportation.
- 24 of 28 students believe that drunk drivers cause more accidents than do cell phone users.
- 20 of 28 students would support a law banning cell phone use while driving. Only 2 of the 8 cell phone owners would favor such a ban; 18 of the 20 non–cell phone owners would support it.

Samantha opposes the use of cell phones while driving. These survey results show that she and a majority of her audience are on common ground, but that several audience members are likely to be hostile to the majority view. Therefore, instead of advocating a ban in her speech, she decides to focus on cell phone safety while driving. She writes that down on her grid in the "specific purpose" and "thesis" sections.

Speech Grid: *Driving with cell phones*
Topic: *Cell phones and driving*
Specific purpose: *To persuade my audience to use cell phones safely while driving.*
Thesis: *Audience members should use cell phones safely when driving.*

AUDIENCE ANALYSIS	SPEECH MESSAGE
Situational Characteristics • *8 min. speech* • *25–30 in audience* • *small classroom* • *limited a-v equip.* **Demographics** **Age:** *17 (5); 18 (17); 19 (4); 20 (1); 22 (1)* **Ethnicity:** *African-American (2); Hmong (2); white (9); Latino/a (6); Portuguese (2); Pacific Islander, Mexican, German, Japanese, Swedish, Greek (1 each); did not say (1)* **Major:** *Undeclared (9); Liberal Studies (5); Chem, Bus, Crim (2 each); Child Devel, Engl, Bio, Premed, Journalism, Ag Bus, Econ, Comm (1 each)* **Common Ground** *I, like most of class, (20 students) do not own a cell phone.* **Prior Exposure** • *Few (7 students) had heard about the issue of cell phones and driving; it had not been major topic in the local media.* • *Most students (20) do not own a cell phone.* • *Most who own a cell phone (6 of 8) use their phone in their car, primarily in one car.* • *Most (24 of 28) think that drunk drivers cause more accidents than cell phone users.* **Audience Disposition** • *Most (20 of 28) support a law banning cell phone use while driving.* • *People who do not own a cell phone are more likely to support such a law (18 of 20). Cell phone owners are opposed (2 of 8).*	In later chapters, you will compose your speech message here.

Source Notes

1. Mind Mapping FAQ. (1996, October 26). Retrieved December 3, 1999 from the World Wide Web: <http://www.ozemail.com.au/~caveman/Creative/Mindmap/mindmapfaq.html>.
2. Russell, P. *How to mind map.* Retrieved December 3, 1999 from the World Wide Web: <http://www.peterussell.com/MindMaps/HowTo.html>.
3. Boyley, S. (1999, October 31). *Mind mapping.* Retrieved December 3, 1999 from the World Wide Web: <http://www.nlpmind.com/doc/nlpmind-1381.htm>.
4. Russell, P. *Advantages of mind maps.* Retrieved January 13, 2000 from the World Wide Web: <http://www.peterussell.com/Mindmaps/Advantages.html>.
5. Jetter, M. (1999, November 28). The mind map method. *The Mind Manager.* Retrieved April 28, 2000 from the World Wide Web: <http://www.pbconnect.se/MindMan/dokument/Mindmapmethod.htm>.
6. Buzan, T., & Buzan, B. (1996). *The mind map book: How to use radiant thinking to maximize your brain's untapped potential.* New York: Plume Books.
7. Infonautics Corporation. (1996). *Researchpaper.com.* Retrieved December 3, 1999 from the World Wide Web: <http://www.researchpaper.com>.
8. Wilson, J. F., & Arnold, C. C. (1974). *Public speaking as a liberal art* (3rd ed., pp. 70–71). Boston: Allyn and Bacon.
9. Janssen, T., & Carton, J. S. (1999, December). The effects of locus of control and task difficulty on procrastination. *Journal of Genetic Psychology, 160,* 436.
10. Ferrari, J. R., Johnson, J. L., & McCown, W. G. (1995). *Procrastination and task avoidance: Theory, research, and treatment* (p. 197). New York: Plenum Press.
11. Rau, W., & Durand, A. (2000, January). The academic ethic and college grades: Does hard work help students to "make the grade"? *Sociology of Education, 73,* 20.

"It is not a fact until you prove it to the audience."

7 Research and Evidence

OBJECTIVES

After reading Chapter 7, you should understand:

● The importance of researching your speech and the benefits of using evidence in your speech.

● Major types of evidence to use in a speech.

● Criteria for determining the credibility of evidence.

● Categories of information resources to consult when researching your speech and how best to find information from each resource.

● The process of Internet research and the advantages and disadvantages of using this information network.

● How to cite evidence in your speech.

Katie, Mandeep, and Sherri were appalled to learn that the police in their town were shooting the crows that regularly gathered on top of the local courthouse. They called the police department to protest and were told that the practice was necessary because the crows were annoying and the droppings they left on the sidewalk were creating a health risk. The police claimed that other tactics for eradicating the birds were too expensive.

These three students became active opponents of the practice of shooting crows. After gathering signatures on petitions and presenting them to city officials, they were invited to speak at a city council meeting. They were informed that the police chief would be there to present his side of the issue.

Katie and her friends needed to be prepared to answer the claims of the police chief. Were the crows truly creating a health hazard? Had any other towns or cities plagued by crows found alternatives to shooting? How effective and expensive were any alternatives? Katie, Mandeep, and Sherri needed to find the answers to these questions; otherwise, the city council probably would accept the police chief's justification and allow the shooting to continue.

This example of Katie and her friends illustrates the fact that speakers usually need to obtain information before they deliver a speech. They may need to learn background information on their topic, to obtain information that can be used in their speech, or both. In this chapter you will study how to accomplish both of these tasks when you prepare a speech. You will study how to research a speech and also how to use research as evidence in your speech. By **research**, we mean the investigation of what other people have

research: investigation of what other people have said about your topic.

said or written about your topic. We use the term **source** (or research sources) to refer to the people or publications from which you obtain information. By **evidence**, we mean the information from these sources that you actually use in your speech to support your ideas. Quotations from experts, examples, and statistics are typical forms of evidence that you will use. Representative examples of evidence in speeches and speech outlines can be found on page 205 in Chapter 14.

We begin Chapter 7 with a brief discussion of the importance of research and evidence when you prepare a speech. Then we introduce the primary types of evidence you should use in your speech, and we discuss what makes an evidence source credible. We also cover the process of researching a speech, with an emphasis on major categories of research materials to consult when preparing your speech—libraries, the Internet, and interviews. Finally, we consider how best to present evidence in your speech.

The Importance of Research and Evidence

- "I'm from Missouri, the 'Show Me' State."
- "The proof is in the pudding."
- "Show me the money!"

Those three statements reflect the premise of this chapter: ***It is not a fact until you prove it to the audience.*** Often proof or evidence beyond the speaker's assertion is required.

Research and evidence are important building blocks in preparing an effective speech. As you research your topic, you acquire a broad base of information to use when planning your speech. Evidence makes the points you are developing in your speech more believable to audience members. The opinion of the speaker is usually not the strongest proof that a point is true. In the classroom, especially, speaking assignments typically require students to address issues or topics that other persons know more about because of their education or expertise.

When you use evidence from sources that the audience finds credible, you increase the probability that your claims will be believed.[1] If audience members are uncertain about a point you are making (or think that you are wrong), evidence can convince them to accept that point. If they accept that the source of your evidence is trustworthy and better informed than they are, they are more likely to agree with your claim even if they would not accept your opinion alone.

In addition, when you cite evidence from sources that you have researched, you strengthen your credibility as a speaker.[2] Audience members consider you better prepared because you have taken the time to research. They are more likely to believe that you know what you are talking about, because they can tell you have investigated your subject.

Finally, research enables you to give a more ethical presentation because you can be confident that the claims you make are accurate. As we noted in Chapter 3, ethical speakers do not assert facts of which they are unsure. For example, it would be unethical for Katie, Mandeep, and Sherri to tell their

source: persons or publications from which you obtain information.

evidence: information from research sources used to support your claims.

audience that the crows are not a health risk unless they had carefully investigated the issue and found this to be the case.

As you prepare your speech, remember: ***It is not a fact until you prove it to your audience.*** When you invest time in researching your speech, the reward comes when you have credible evidence to convince your audience that the claims you make are true.

Types of Evidence

What should you be looking for when you research your speech? In general, you may use any information that helps to achieve your specific purpose. However, several categories of information are typically used to support ideas in a speech. These include *examples, testimony, narratives, facts,* and *statistics.* In this section we describe each of these categories and provide examples of how you can use them in a speech.

● *Examples*

Examples are samples or instances that you use to support a general claim. In everyday conversation, you often use examples to back up a claim. If you claim that parking is difficult on your campus because Monday you could not find a spot and on Tuesday your roommate had to drive around for fifteen minutes to find a space, you are using examples to support the general claim that parking is difficult.

Sometimes you will use one or more *short examples* to illustrate a point in your speech. Katie, Mandeep, and Sherri could use one or more of these short examples to show that many cultures have negative stereotypes about crows:

> Franklin Coombs, author of *The Crows,* published in 1978, wrote:
> *In the French tradition...bad priests became ravens and bad nuns became crows.*

> Suthon Sukphisit, a writer for the *Bangkok Post,* noted an example of negativity in "Post Tips," July 7, 1997:
> *In Thailand, the degrading word "ee" precedes the name of a despised person, and it is traditional to refer to the "kaa" (the Thai word for crow) as "ee-kaa."*

> Paul Lamble, a freelance writer, noted how the English language is used to denigrate crows in the *Missouri Conservationist,* January 1997:
> *The expression "to eat crow" means to do something disagreeable, to "crow" is to brag obnoxiously, and wrinkles around the eyes are called "crow's feet."*

Katie and her friends could also use a short example to illustrate how humans and crows can coexist and share:

> Nile Thompson of Dushuyay Research, in the *American Indian Culture and Research Journal,* Fall 1992, indicated:
> *The Twana Native American society observed crow flocks to locate patches of ripe blackberries. Another type of berry was not eaten by the Twana because it was considered to be "crow food."*

examples: samples or instances that you use to support a general claim.

Extended examples also can be used to illustrate a point. An extended example provides details about the instance being used, giving the audience a deeper and richer picture of the point being made. It also can be used to develop an appeal to pathos. Katie, Mandeep, and Sherri could use this extended example:

> In the November–December 1992 issue of *The North American Review*, nature writer Lance Kinseth showed how a once-plentiful species could be exterminated:
>> *In 1876 a breeding colony of passenger pigeons covered a 28 by 4 square mile area. John James Audubon reported streams of passenger pigeons that exceeded one billion birds, darkening the sky in a passing front. By 1904 the last bird was shot. A peaceful, seasonal glory, extinct. Now...hunting references encourage excessive crow kills as a public service. Large winter roosts have been sprayed, poisoned and bombed with shrapnel grenades, killing as many as 100,000 crows. We still do not simply overlook but intentionally hate.*

● Testimony

Testimony consists of statements or claims made by other people that you use to support your claim. One common form of testimony is *expert testimony*, which is information provided by a person who is informed on the topic and respected in his or her field. Katie, Mandeep, and Sherri could use authorities to argue that shooting crows would be futile:

> Dr. Kevin McGowan, curator of the Cornell Museum of Vertebrates, noted on the Web page *Frequently Asked Questions about Crows*, last updated January 3, 2000:
>> *Crow society is filled with excess crows that are waiting for an opportunity to breed (the helpless staying home and helping their parents raise young). If you kill some territory holders off, you just create a breeding opportunity for the crows waiting in the wings.*

You also may want to use *lay testimony* to support a point. Lay testimony comes from ordinary people who are not regarded as experts on your topic. This type of evidence is less convincing on a point that requires specialized knowledge, but it can be effective if the topic is one that an ordinary person is qualified to speak on, particularly when he or she expresses the point in language that the audience can relate to.

Here is an example of lay testimony from an artist who offered his opinion on why crows are special birds:

testimony: statements by other people that support a point you are making.

> According to Tony Angell, in the book *Ravens, Crows, Magpies, and Jays*, published in 1978:
>> *To some degree, perhaps greater than most of us would admit, we find this intelligent family of birds [crows] most attractive because they are not too unlike ourselves....They squabble within their families and wage battles with those clans that would impinge upon their home ground....Like us, they seem to have fleeting moments of joy when the mate is won, the game is played, the belly is full, and the sun shines on our backs.*

● Narratives

A **narrative** is an anecdote or a story that supports a point in your speech. Recall from Chapter 2 that humans are storytelling beings who may evaluate almost any speaker's message as if it were a story. A narrative may best get an idea across to your audience because the point is expressed in a story-like form.

To support the claim that there are better alternatives than shooting crows, Katie and her friends could use this narrative about crows that roosted on the domes of the Kremlin, in Moscow, Russia:

> According to Jeffery Boswall, former British Broadcasting Natural History Television producer, in *Discover* magazine, March 1987:
>
> *Muscovites are fond of the crows. They feed them. It wasn't going to contribute to the contentment of the people for government officials to be seen shooting their crows. Besides, it wouldn't solve the problem, because new crows would soon arrive to fill any vacancies on the domes.*
>
> *The keepers of the Kremlin turned to Alexander Sorokin of the Research Institute for Nature Conservation. Sorokin relied on bioacoustics, the study of wildlife sounds.*
>
> *He knew the meaning of several calls in the crows' vocabulary. From the roof of the Kremlin, loudspeakers sent out the crow call that means "I've been caught by a falcon, please mob until it lets me go." A falcon was then released and it attacked. When the crows discovered that a falcon was attacking them, rather than straddling a hapless crow on a ledge, they could not understand what was happening and they left. The routine is repeated twice a week and for all practical purposes, the Kremlin is crowless.*

View a student supporting a claim with a personal narrative.
CD-ROM: Video Theater, Excerpt 7.1

● Facts

Facts are statements that are generally accepted as true or can easily be proved true to a reasonable person. They do not involve controversial ideas. If you looked up the information in a variety of sources, you would be likely to find the same answer. In a speech, you use factual evidence to prove a point with which the audience may be unfamiliar.

Katie, Mandeep, and Sherri may want to prove that there are affordable alternatives to shooting crows. They could use factual evidence such as this:

> According to *U.C. Davis News*, February 14, 1997:
>
> *An audiotape with the distressed "caw"-ry of the American crow has been released through the U.C. Division of Agriculture and Natural Resources. The audiotape costs $10.50 plus shipping and handling, and requires no specialized equipment or federal, state, or local permits.*

View Sarah Brady supporting a claim with statistical evidence at the Democratic National Convention.
CD-ROM: Video Theater, Excerpt 7.2

● Statistics

Statistics are information presented in numerical form. They can be used to quantify points that you are making in your speech. If Katie and her friends wanted to prove that crows are beneficial for pest control, they could use this statistic:

narrative: an anecdote or story that supports a point in your speech.

facts: statements that are accepted as true or can be proved true to a reasonable person.

statistics: information presented in numerical form.

According to Tony Angell in the book *Ravens, Crows, Magpies, and Jays,* published in 1978:

> *One biologist (Madison, 1976) found that a single family of crows consumed more than* forty thousand *grubs, caterpillars, army worms, and other insects in a single nesting season.*

To recap this section, when you research evidence to use in your speech, look for examples, testimony, facts, narratives, and statistics. However, if audience members are to accept the evidence that you have researched, they need to accept the reliability of your sources, but not all sources are created equal. The next section addresses the question of what makes a source credible.

The Credibility of Research Sources

Most people can remember a few of the participants and commentators from the O.J. Simpson trial that they found not credible. Greta Van Susteran was an exception. After the trial, Cable News Network gave Van Susteran her own legal program, Burden of Proof (co-hosted with Roger Cossack). When you plan your speeches, be sure to use sources that your audience will find credible.

expertise: the knowledge necessary to offer reliable facts or opinions.

objectivity: being free of any bias that would prevent an impartial judgment.

If Katie, Mandeep, and Sherri used evidence from a radical animal liberation group to support the claim that crows and humans have equal rights, skeptics on the city council would be likely to exclaim, "Consider the source!" This remark reflects the fact that people's opinions about a source often influence whether they decide to believe the information.

What makes a source of evidence credible? If you expect your evidence to be believed, you need to use your critical thinking skills to evaluate the credibility of the evidence sources you research and use in your speech. When you evaluate credibility, three important considerations are the *expertise, objectivity,* and *recency* of your sources.

● Expertise

Your sources will be more credible if they have **expertise** in the subject you are speaking about. This means they have the knowledge necessary to offer reliable facts or opinions about the topic they are discussing. Indicators of expertise are the education, experience, and reputation of a source in his or her field. For example, a doctor or a nutrition professor would be a good source of information on the question of whether eating red meat is healthy. A person who lived in Thailand for ten years would be a better source for an informative speech about that nation than someone who has only read travel brochures about the country. When you evaluate credibility, be certain that your source is speaking in his or her area of expertise. A Supreme Court justice is an expert in the field of law but would not be an expert on the question of the scientific benefits that could result from sending astronauts to Mars.

● Objectivity

Another important consideration is the **objectivity** of a source. Objective sources are people who do not have a bias that would impair their ability to make an impartial judgment on the issue you are considering. A biased source is not credible. Have you ever heard a salesperson make comments such as these?

- "My brother bought a chair just like that one, and he loves it."

- "You look great in those pants."
- "You better buy it now, because prices are going up next week."

You are likely to be skeptical of the truth of these claims. Salespeople are paid to make sales, and it is reasonable to suspect that much of what they say is calculated to get you to buy their product.

Avoid the use of biased sources wherever possible. If the information you rely on is taken from a source who has a bias, you cannot be sure that you have met your ethical duties to research and to present truthful facts to the audience. Furthermore, if you use biased evidence, audience members are unlikely to accept the point you are trying to prove.[3]

Reluctant testimony is evidence from a person with an interest in an issue that contradicts what that person would be expected to say. If the police chief told Katie, Mandeep, and Sherri that there was no good reason to shoot crows, or if an animal rights activist said that the killing was justified, each opinion would be an example of reluctant testimony. Reluctant testimony is likely to be more persuasive than biased testimony, but unbiased testimony is typically even more convincing.[4]

● Recency

Another important factor when determining the credibility of research sources is **recency**—the age or timeliness of evidence. As a general rule, recent evidence is more persuasive than older evidence. Change is a constant factor in many aspects of life. Consider these examples:

- *Computer technology.* At the beginning of the 1990s, the average person did not know what the Internet was. By the year 2000, an estimated 155 million English speakers and 147 million non-English speakers were using the Internet.[5]
- *Economic conditions.* At the beginning of the 1990s, many U.S. commentators predicted that the Japanese economy soon would surpass that of the United States. Later in the decade, after the U.S. economy rebounded, Japanese economist Yasuhiko Shibate noted that "the American age is back."[6]
- *The physical environment.* Ten years ago, you may have loved the pristine wilderness of the national park you visited. Today, you may find that a road now brings hundreds of cars to the previously remote lake where you camped.
- *Advances in research.* Ten years ago, the medical community had few answers in the fight against AIDS. Now researchers know that certain combinations of drugs can substantially improve the immune system's ability to defend itself, and the question of a cure has become "when rather than if."[7]

Because ongoing change is a reality, the more recent your evidence is, the more likely it is to be accurate. If you have a choice between two *reliable* sources, one written three months ago, and the other written several years ago, select the more recent evidence.

TIP

Use evidence from sources that your audience will find objective. If you must use evidence from a source whom the audience may find biased, explain why the analysis that the source provides is reasonable.

View a student citing experts properly.
CD-ROM: Video Theater, Excerpt 7.3

reluctant testimony: evidence stating the opposite of what would be expected, given a source's stake in the issue.

recency: the age or timeliness of evidence.

Although recency is an important criterion for evaluating evidence, do not reject all evidence that is not current. Some evidence is considered "classic" and endures to this day. For example, the teachings of K'ung-Fu-Tze (Confucius) are ancient but nevertheless command more respect than the precepts of many contemporary philosophers. The ideas of Machiavelli are still pertinent to the subject of international relations even though they are almost five hundred years old. To decide whether evidence is outdated, ask the following question: Has the claim made by my source become doubtful or false because of changing circumstances since the claim was made?

In the past two sections, we considered what types of information to look for when you are researching a topic and how to determine whether the sources you research are credible. We turn now to how to research evidence.

What Makes a Good Researcher?

Good researchers develop a strategy for finding and keeping track of the information they need. Gaining experience, they improve on that strategy throughout their lifetime, particularly as new technologies change the nature of research. What follows is a five-step research process that you can follow if you are new to researching or incorporate into your own strategy if you are a veteran researcher.

● 1. Inventory Your Research Needs

To decide what research you need, consider the subject you are researching, the type of speech you are giving, and your audience analysis. For classroom speeches, also find out whether your instructor has any research requirements. Determine whether you need to get more general information on your subject first, or whether you are ready to research specific aspects of your topic. Make a list of the subject matter you need to research and the questions you need to answer before preparing your speech.

● 2. Discover Sources of Information on Your Topic

TIP

Check the Library of Congress Subject Headings, a reference work available in many libraries, for different headings used to categorize a subject.

Develop a list of potential sources by researching library indexes (increasingly available online), searching on the Internet, and considering people to interview. When you do library or Internet research, look under a variety of subject headings or key words that relate to your topic. It is highly unlikely that no information on your topic exists. Consider synonyms for the subject you are researching, along with broader or narrower terms for your topic area.

Keep a list of potential sources you find in indexes, and record the bibliographic information for any source you might be interested in researching. This information includes:

Name of author

Title of the author's work

Title of the publication containing the author's work when the work is in a newspaper, magazine, or anthology

Date and volume number of the publication

Page number(s) where the work is printed

Record similar information from Internet sources that you research, including the "address," or URL (see p. 158). Also keep track of information that would help you contact potential interviewees.

3. Prioritize Your Sources

You will learn the most about your topic and manage your time most efficiently if you prioritize your sources and check the ones you think will be most helpful first. When prioritizing, ask yourself what type of information you need in order to get started. You may need general or specific information, depending on your familiarity with the subject and on whether you have decided on a working topic statement or thesis. If you have already narrowed your topic, focus on sources that pertain to the portion of the topic that you will be addressing. Also consider which sources are likely to be the most credible and the recency of the information.

For more on the working thesis or topic statement, see page 134.

4. Research Your Sources Systematically

Once you have a list of prioritized sources, it is time to settle in and read them. To help you stay organized while researching, we offer the following guidelines:

- *Keep a record of each source that you read.* As you check each source on your list, jot down brief notes to keep track of which sources you have read. Identify promising sources with an asterisk or some other symbol, and put a brief comment such as "irrelevant" or "supports other side" next to sources that are not helpful.

- *Obtain a copy of sources or parts of sources that you may use.* Obtain a copy of any information you find that you may want to include in your speech. Some students take notes on index cards; others prefer checking publications out of the library, photocopying relevant pages, or downloading computer files onto a disk they can take home. To avoid losing any information, have a *specific location* (such as a folder) where you place all the information you research.

- *Use your Speech Grid to organize your evidence.* Your Speech Grid provides an easy method for keeping track of the evidence you obtain from researching. Each time you find useful information in a source, record the point that is made on your Speech Grid. You can see examples of information recorded on a grid in the Speech Grid Application at the end of this chapter. On your grid, write down the source number and the point that the evidence supports. On your grid, you may also wish to make notes about the evidence you insert. For example, you might want to summarize the content of the evidence, indicate the author's credentials, or note that the evidence is particularly strong. This information will help you select the best evidence from your grid when you are ready to draft your speech.

● 5. Identify Gaps in Your Research and Find the Needed Information

After noting on your grid the evidence you might use in your speech, you may discover that you need to do more research before drafting a speech. For example, you may find that the evidence supporting a claim is weak, or that you have no evidence to support a key point. If this is the case, check your list of sources to see whether any of them may provide the information you need. You might remember reading information that did not seem useful at the time but does seem helpful now that you know more about your topic.

You might also consult different indexes from the ones you already tried and investigate other sources of information. Finally, you can always ask for help finding the information you need. You may get help from a professor on campus, a librarian, an expert on the subject in your community, or from an online discussion group that focuses on your subject area.

Major Information Resources for Researching Your Speech

The five-step process described above for researching your speech can be followed whether you are using the library, the Internet, interviews, or a combination of these options. In this section we elaborate on each of these information resources.

● Library Research

If Katie, Mandeep, and Sherri want to research the subject of crows in the library, they can turn to several different types of information sources: periodicals, newspapers, abstracts, books, and government documents. They can consult a variety of directories to find out what information is available in those sources. As you will see, each type of source has particular strengths, which will be a consideration when you are deciding which sources are best for your speech. Table 7.1 describes steps you can take to maximize the usefulness of your library time.

Periodicals.   Not only magazines written for the general public (such as *Ms.* and *Sports Illustrated*) but also scholarly or technical publications (such as the *American Journal of Public Health* and *Chemical and Engineering News*) are **periodicals**—publications that appear at regular intervals of more than one day. Citations for articles in periodicals are contained in both general and specialized indexes. General indexes cover a wide variety of disciplines. Specialized indexes focus on one discipline, such as business, education, or medicine. Table 7.2 lists general and specialized indexes that are available in many college libraries.

General Periodical Indexes.   Many periodical indexes are now computer-based indexes. These databases can be used to find citations and, increasingly, the texts of articles. The *Readers' Guide to Periodical Literature* is one

periodicals: magazines, journals, and other publications that appear at regular intervals of more than one day (e.g., weekly or monthly).

TABLE 7.1   Getting the Most Out of Your Library

When you are researching in the library, be sure to ask for help when you need it, use available technology, and check your sources efficiently.

ADVICE	BENEFIT
1. **Ask for Help.** *The most important advice to follow may be this: "If you do not know, ask."*	Professional librarians spend each workday in the library and are very familiar with the library's indexes, publications, and technology. They are experienced at helping students research a wide variety of topics. You do not want to spend your scarce time wandering around the library trying to find a particular journal or experimenting with an index you are not sure how to use. When professionals are being paid to make your research easier, take advantage of their expertise. College libraries may have librarians who specialize in particular courses or departments. See whether your library staff includes a specialist who can help you.
2. **Use the Technology.** *To make the best use of your research time, take advantage of the diverse technology available in most libraries.*	A rapidly increasing number of sources are indexed online, and the sources themselves are often accessible with the click of a mouse. Libraries are adding this technology to get more information to you and to get it to you faster. Find out which computer databases your library has, and learn how to use them. Attend special classes and workshops on these databases if they are offered, or pick up handouts that teach you about online research.
3. **Use Each Source Once.** *Try to work with each possible evidence source only once.*	This suggestion is akin to advice given by time management experts who tell clients to "look at each piece of mail only once." If you discover a helpful source, take notes, get a copy of the information you need, or check that source out before you leave the library. Your research will get bogged down if you read material that looks promising but leave it in the library to be retrieved later. It will cost you time to go back to the library and reread that source, and you take the chance that the source will not be available when you return.

TABLE 7.2   Examples of Periodical Indexes

GENERAL INDEXES	SPECIALIZED INDEXES
Academic Index (InfoTrac)	*Applied Science and Technology Index*
Ethnic News Watch	*Art Index*
LEXIS-NEXIS Academic Universe	*Bibliography of Agriculture* (available online as AGRICOLA)
Readers' Guide to Periodical Literature	*Biological and Agricultural Index*
	Cumulative Index to Nursing and Allied Health
	Current Index to Journals in Education
	General Science Index
	Humanities Index
	Index to Legal Periodicals
	MEDLINE (medical journals)
	Music Index
	Philosopher's Index
	PsychINFO
	Social Sciences Index

At the library, you are surrounded by thousands of volumes of reference materials and have databases and indexes to guide you through those texts. Searching databases and indexes minimizes time and maximizes information.

general index that many people are familiar with. However, other general indexes contain a higher percentage of references that will be appropriate for a college audience. For example, the *Academic Index* (a part of the *InfoTrac* database that is available on CD-ROM) covers fifteen hundred journals on a wide variety of subjects from 1980 to the present. About one-third of the articles indexed are directly available as you use this database. The *LEXIS-NEXIS Academic Universe* contains citations and news articles from a wide variety of newspapers and magazines. It also contains information from the fields of government, business, and medicine. The *Ethnic News Watch* indexes journals and newspapers from a wide variety of ethnic communities. The *LEXIS-NEXIS Academic Universe* and *Ethnic News Watch* are **full text databases**, meaning that the complete text of each article is provided in addition to the citation.

An InfoTrac search of the *Academic Index* provided several articles about crows that Katie, Mandeep, and Sherri could use. Here is the citation for an article about methods of bird control that do not involve shooting. It was found under the subject heading "bird pests":

SOURCE   : Technology Review, July 1993, v. 96, p. 20
TITLE   : High-Tech Scarecrows (Bird-control devices for airports)
AUTHOR   : Colum Lynch

full text database: a resource providing a citation and the full text of the article cited.

This citation provides the needed bibliographic information. The researchers should copy the journal, date, volume (v.), starting page number, article title, and author for their records. Then they would determine whether the library carries the journal *Technology Review,* and if it does, where volume 96 of this publication is kept. Next, Katie, Mandeep, and Sherri could read the article to find information for their presentation.

We recommend the use of computerized indexes rather than bound indexes whenever possible. In addition to the basic information on the article, computer databases often provide an abstract of the article (a summary of its contents) or even allow you to access the article itself. You may be able to print citations or articles obtained from online databases, save them on your own disk, or e-mail them to your own computer, saving yourself time in the research process. Another advantage to online indexes is that they often contain citations to more than one type of source. You can conveniently discover sources pertaining to your topic from journals, newspapers, and other sources listed in the same index.

Specialized Periodical Indexes.   Some periodical indexes focus on specific subject areas. These indexes are increasingly available online. If your library has a specialized index relating to your topic, be sure to include it in your research. Specialized indexes cover many more journals that relate to your topic than a general index does.

After you check periodical indexes and obtain a list of articles to research, find out whether your library carries the periodicals you need, and if so, where they are located. Each library has its own system for finding out this information and a different way of organizing its periodicals. Do not be surprised if some periodicals are on open shelves, others on microfilm, and others behind a checkout desk.

If your library does not have the periodicals you need, and they are not available online, you still may be able to locate them. One option is to see whether the article you need can be obtained by your library through *interlibrary loan.* Another is to check with other libraries in your area and see whether they have the sources you need. These options may take some time, which is another reason for beginning your research early.

Newspapers.   Newspapers are another good source for research. Your library may have an index for your local newspaper or for newspapers from large cities in your region. Major newspapers such as the *New York Times,* the *Washington Post,* and the *Christian Science Monitor* have their own indexes. The *National Newspaper Index* (another component of the *InfoTrac* system) compiles citations for articles in those three newspapers, along with the *Los Angeles Times* and *Wall Street Journal. Newspaper Abstracts on Disc* allows you to search by subject for abstracts of articles in major U.S. newspapers. *LEXIS-NEXIS* is an excellent source of current news and information, including newspaper articles, wire service reports, journals, and other sources. This resource includes references to many regional newspapers in addition to major national newspapers. *Editorials on File* reprints sets of editorials taking different perspectives on current issues. A wide variety of newspapers across the United States and Canada are included in this resource.

Your library is likely to have the major national newspapers (and leading local or regional ones) on microfilm. Research on microfilm can be cumbersome and slow, so you will be better off if you can find a computer database that enables you to access directly the text of articles.

Abstracts.   **Abstracts** are indexes that provide summaries of articles or documents along with the bibliographical data. Your library may have abstracts of journal articles, books, newspaper articles, scholarly papers, or other sources. Typically, abstract research begins in a subject index that provides entries on a particular subject. Each entry has a number that indicates where to find the abstract for that source. You then look up the abstract in a separate volume or section.

The following entry is taken from the 1996 *Environmental Abstracts Annual* (p. 229) under the subject heading "birds:"

Keeping Birds Away, *Solid Waste Technol,* Nov–Dec 95, v9, n6, p. 38
96-01794

This entry gives the bibliographic information necessary to look up the article "Keeping Birds Away" in the journal *Solid Waste Technology.* In addition, in bold type the citation indicates the abstract number. The number **96** indicates the year, and **01794** is the abstract number. The researchers could look in *Environmental Abstracts* for 1996, under abstract number 01794, and find the following summary of the article. The summary would enable them to decide whether to research the article:

96-01794   **Keeping Birds Away**, *Solid Waste Technol,* Nov–Dec 95, v9, n6, p38 (2) journal article.

Birds are attracted to landfills in large numbers. These legions of scavenging birds can pose serious safety problems if the landfill is situated in the vicinity of an airport. The bird-control techniques used by the operators of the Hidden Valley Landfill (Puyallup, WA) are detailed....The bird-control system at the landfill site consists of a set of six wooden poles rising 20–30 feet above the working surface of the landfill. Fence wire is then strung between the poles, thus creating a wire grid. The wire used to form the grid should be visible but somewhat difficult to see. Apparently, the birds do not like to fly where they cannot maneuver with absolute confidence. Other products available for bird control are discussed. (2 photos)

Abstracts are helpful when you research because you can learn about the contents of relevant documents or articles before you retrieve them. This knowledge makes you a more effective researcher because you can focus your time on locating and retrieving the sources that look most useful and save yourself the trouble of finding sources that you are not likely to use.

Abstracts are available on a variety of subjects. Representative collections of abstracts include *Chemical Abstracts, Environmental Abstracts, ERIC* (Educational Resources Information Center), *Historical Abstracts, Psychological Abstracts, Social Work Abstracts, Sociofile* (covering sociology and related social science fields), and *Women's Studies Abstracts.*

Books.   Books are indexed in an **online catalog** in most college and university libraries. These computer-based systems have replaced the traditional card catalogs, enabling you to be more efficient and get more information about the books in your library.

Typically an online catalog gives you several options, such as searching for all the books on a particular subject, books by a given author, and books by title (or all titles including the words you select). You generally will want

abstract: an index that provides summaries of articles or documents in addition to the citation.

online catalog: a computer-based index of library materials.

to start searching by subject. If you have prepared a good list of potential subject headings, you can search those headings and find the books your library has on your topic.

A computer-based search of a subject area will yield a list of books on your topic. You can often use a mouse to click on those individual books in which you are interested, obtaining their location in the library and the bibliographic information. For example, Katie, Mandeep, and Sherri would find the following information in the library online catalog under the subject heading "birds—behavior":

AUTHOR	: Kilham, Lawrence
TITLE	: The American crow and the common raven/by Lawrence Kilham; illus. by Joan Waltermire
IMPRINT	: College Station: Texas A&M University Press, c1989

LIBRARY	COLLECTION/CALL NUMBER	STATUS
Stack	QL 696 P2367 K55 1989	In Library

This citation in the online catalog contains the bibliographic information (author, title, publisher, date) about this book on crows. In addition, it shows in what part of the library the book can be found (the library stacks), gives the call number to tell where the book is located on the shelves, and also indicates that the book is now in the library. If the book were checked out, the citation would give that information instead, along with the date it is due.

Some online catalogs contain citations to books and journals in more than one library (such as all the colleges in a state system). In this case, you would know where you might be able to order the book through interlibrary loan.

Government Documents.   Government documents provide helpful information about many of the subjects covered by governmental laws and regulations. Federal documents are most commonly found in the library, and your library will probably have some documents published by your state and local governments also. Resources for locating federal government documents include the following:

- *Monthly Catalog of U.S. Government Publications.* This catalog provides citations to federal publications, congressional hearings, and congressional committee reports. Many of these reports provide detailed information on foreign and domestic policy issues. Congressional hearings are typically held before major federal legislation is adopted, and experts on both sides of the issue often testify. Because the number of government documents available varies greatly from library to library, you need to begin your research early. If the document you need is unavailable, it may take a few weeks to order it from the government or request it on interlibrary loan. This index is now available online as *GPO on a Silver Platter.*

- *Congressional Quarterly Weekly Report.* These reports are available in most libraries. An index indicates the pages where specific topics or bills pending before Congress are covered. You can then look up the information in the applicable weekly reports. The reports contain timely information about the status of legislation being considered by the federal government, and also a more detailed discussion of key bills and issues. These discussions often include the viewpoints of leading supporters and opponents of pending legislation.

- *Congressional Record Index.* The *Congressional Record* provides a transcript of the proceedings in the House and Senate each day. Senators and representatives often insert newspaper editorials, statements by experts in the field, and other information into the record as well. The index enables you to find the text of bills that have been introduced in Congress, debates and other information on particular issues or bills, and speeches on the floor of the House and Senate by the members of Congress.

● *Internet Research*

If you have access to the **Internet**, a global network of computers, your research options are greatly expanded. This vast and rapidly expanding resource serves many purposes that aid you in speech preparation. You can find information on diverse speech topics; however, you need to evaluate carefully the credibility of Internet sources before using evidence from them in your speech.

Katie, Mandeep, and Sherri could use the Internet to investigate their topic in a variety of ways. They could research online for information from government documents, scientific reports, and wildlife protection organizations. They could also transmit questions to manufacturers of bird control technologies in London or discover which techniques are used in Moscow. The Internet—and one of its major components, the **World Wide Web**— can be a valuable resource for speech preparation because it provides access to all of these sources and more.

The Internet and World Wide Web: An Overview. Any person with a computer and basic supporting technology can access the Internet and send or receive messages by means of a computer. The World Wide Web, a component of the Internet, consists of computers that rely on the **hypertext transfer protocol (http)** to convey information to one another. This protocol enables your computer to receive text, graphics, video, and sound from another computer regardless of the format the information is stored in.

Information on the World Wide Web is often compiled through the use of **Web sites**. A Web site is similar to a book, magazine, newspaper, pamphlet, videotape, or other compilation of information. It is created by a person (you could create one yourself) and stored on one or more computers, which are often referred to as **servers**. For example, universities create Web sites for prospective students, companies provide Web sites for customers who want to learn more about their products, governments develop Web sites for information and documents, and community organizations maintain Web sites to inform people about upcoming events.

Web sites usually have a **home page**, the first page you see when you access a site on your computer. The home page serves the purpose of both a book cover and an index. It often includes pictures or colorful graphics that

Internet: a global network of computers.

World Wide Web: the component of the Internet consisting of computers that rely on http (see below).

hypertext transfer protocol (http): a process that enables one computer to receive materials from another computer regardless of the format the materials are stored in.

Web site: a compilation of information that is available on the World Wide Web.

server: a computer that stores information available on the Internet.

home page: the first page of a Web site.

catch the viewer's eye. The home page also indicates what information is available at that Web site (see Figure 7.1).

A Web site contains **links** to other Web pages. These links may be to other pages created by the author of the Web site (internal links) or to pages created by others (external links). Following a link is the computer network equivalent of turning to a different chapter in a book or using fast-forward to move to the next song on a tape or CD. A link is usually indicated by text that appears in a different color from the print on the page and is underlined. It may be indicated by an *icon,* which is a picture symbolizing what the link contains. When you want to investigate a link, you use your mouse to click on that link. The Web page that is linked may be stored on the same computer as the home page, or it may be stored on a computer five thousand miles away. For example, the home page of a travel agency in Miami, Florida, could contain a link to the agency's price list for fishing trips in Alaska (an internal link) or a link to the Web site of a fishing guide on Nunivak Island in Alaska (an external link).

FIGURE 7.1   **Example of a Home Page**

The home page of the American Society of Crows and Ravens includes links to several other Web sites. These links are highlighted by the use of blue ink and underlining. To access each of these sites, you simply click on it with your mouse. Which link do you think would be most helpful for Katie, Mandeep, and Sherri?

link: a connection from one Web page or site to another.

When you begin your research on the World Wide Web, your problem will not be "there is nothing about my topic on the Web." The contents of the Web dwarf the number of traditional publications available in any library. As of September 2000, the size of the Web was estimated to be a billion pages, with growth of a million pages per day.[8] Your challenges will be navigating this vast resource to find the information you need and ensuring that the source of the information is credible.

Getting Around on the Web. Each Web page has its own **uniform resource locator (URL)**, or Internet address. A Web site maintained by a company that specializes in nonlethal bird control solutions has the following URL:

<http://www.birdbarrier.com>

The first part of the address (*http*) directs the host computer to send the information to your computer by using the hypertext transfer protocol. The second part (*www*) indicates that this site is on the World Wide Web. The final portion of the URL (*birdbarrier.com*) is the actual address for this site.

If you click on your computer's Internet icon, you will get a page containing a place to enter the Internet address you are looking for. You must input the address correctly. Unlike a mail carrier, who can be forgiving if you make a slight error in a person's name or street address, a computer will not access an electronic address if you make any errors. If you make a small error—if you type "birdba**r**ier" instead of "birdba**rr**ier"—you will get a message saying that the computer cannot retrieve the document.

The software that enables you to access Web sites, move from one site to another, and "save" useful sites is called a **browser**. The typical browser allows you to click on an icon or on words to utilize several helpful functions:

go to (address)—opens a Web site when you have entered its URL.

back—enables you to move from one Web page back to the previous Web page you were looking at, for example, back to a home page after you checked a link.

forward—enables you to return to a site you moved back from.

print—prints the page you are on.

bookmark (favorite place)—enables you to "save" a Web page for future reference. The **bookmark** is a very important function because during research, you may find several Web sites containing material that you may want to use in your speech. *Once you leave a site, it may be difficult to remember how you found that site, and it is cumbersome to write down every URL and enter it again to research a site further.* The bookmark or favorite place function will store the URL of that site and keep a record of the titles of all the sites you bookmark. When you want to

uniform resource locator (URL): the Internet address of a Web page.

browser: software that enables you to access Web sites and move from one site to another.

bookmark: a function enabling you to save a link to a Web page for future reference.

find a site again, you simply open your list of favorite places and click on the title of the one you want to access.

Using Search Engines to Find Web Sites on Your Topic

How Search Engines Work.   Internet **search engines** can be used to find Web sites that apply to your topic. Search engine programs (sometimes called "spiders") visit Web pages and index what they find. The index created contains every Web page that the spider has found. When you use a search engine, you enter one or more key words or questions (on some search engines) that describe your topic. For example, Katie and her friends could enter a key word or two about crows or ask "Where can we find information on crows?" In either case, search engine software screens all the Web pages that have been indexed to find pages containing the best matches for the key words that were entered.[9] You are given a list of Web sites containing your key words, and you also may be given information about their contents. With the click of a mouse, you can select and examine any document on the list.

It is not unusual for thousands of Web sites to contain all of your key words, but the search engines rank the sites by *relevance,* based on factors such as how frequently your key words are used and whether they are used in the title or appear near the top of a Web page.[10] It is best to start with the first ten or twenty sites obtained when you research because they are most likely to satisfy your needs.

Selecting Search Engines.   Some of the most popular search engines, along with their URLs and some features of each engine, are listed in Table 7.3. This list will undoubtedly change as new engines are added, changed, or combined, but it provides a good starting point.

Table 7.3 also provides the URLs for several **metasearch engines**. These engines consult several search engines to find Web sites that contain your key words. Their use will give you access to more of the documents available on the Web. According to a study by Lawrence and Giles, the most commonly used search engines index only about 16 percent of the documents available to the public on the average, often with limited overlap.[11] If you are researching a difficult-to-find topic, a metasearch engine is more likely to find useful Web sites. However, when using a metasearch engine, you need to use a simple search request that will be understood by all of the search engines that the metasearch engine checks. For complex searches that can't be reduced to a simple search request, metasearch engines may be less helpful.[12]

By one estimate, there are more than a thousand search engines in existence.[13] Which search engine is best for you? We recommend that you try several (including metasearch engines) to learn the search process and see which unique features of the different engines you prefer. Once you have a basic understanding of search engines, you can read comparisons of their features. Search engine reviews often highlight key features of different search tools and provide updates as more features become available.[14] These are helpful once you become familiar with Internet searches. Because search engines upgrade their features often and new online services continue to be established, periodically check for reviews if you use the Internet for research.

search engine: a program that searches the Internet for Web pages containing the terms that you specify.

metasearch engine: a program that checks several search engines for your key terms.

TABLE 7.3   Popular Search and Metasearch Engines

SEARCH ENGINES

Search Engine	Features
• AltaVista <www.altavista.com>	Indexes a large number of Web pages; fast and comprehensive.
• Excite <www.excite.com>	Broad-based Web searches; also provides non-Web reference material.
• FAST Search <www.alltheweb.com>	Endeavors to index the entire Web; the first search engine to index 200 million Web pages.
• Go (Infoseek) <www.go.com>	Search procedure provides excellent results for broad, general searches.
• Google <www.google.com>	Matches up Web pages based on key words; first Web pages listed are those that other pages link to the most.
• HotBot <www.hotbot.com>	Searches large number of Web pages; users can search for features, e.g., images or video clips.
• Northern Light <www.northernlight.com>	Large number of sites indexed; organizes search results by topic.
• Yahoo! <www.yahoo.com>	Uses a search engine to supplement its own human-compiled directory.

METASEARCH ENGINES

Metasearch Engine	Features
• Dogpile <www.dogpile.com>	Sends your search to engines, directories, and specialized search sites.
• Inference Find <www.infind.com>	Uses major search services; groups results by subject.
• MetaCrawler <www.metacrawler.com>	Allows customized and power searches on multiple search engines.
• Metafind <www.metafind.com>	Searches several major engines and organizes the results.
• ProFusion <www.profusion.com>	Allows customized searches, broken link detection.
• SavvySearch <www.savvysearch.com>	Customizable; covers a wide variety of general and specialty sites.
• SurfWax.com <www.surfwax.com>	Helps you focus search words; provides page summaries.

Sources: Greh, D. (2000). *Untangling the web: A guide to mass communication on the web* (2nd ed.). Boston: Bedford/St. Martin's; Sullivan, D. (1999). The major search engines. *Search Engine Watch* [online]. <http://www.searchenginewatch.com/links/Major_Search_Engines/The/Major_Search_Engines> (site visited October 4, 1999); Sullivan, D. (2000). Major metacrawlers. *Search Engine Watch* [online]. <http://www.searchenginewatch.com/links/Metacrawlers/Major_Metacrawlers> (site visited February 7, 2000).

You can look for reviews in computer-oriented periodicals. Also, Web sites such as *Search Engine Watch* provide information about search engines and advice about how to use them. *Search Engine Watch* can be found at <http://www.searchenginewatch.com>.

The Internet can provide you with enormous amounts of information, if you know where to look. Search engines can help you navigate, but be sure your final source will be credible to your audience.

Using Search Engines.   When you use a search engine, your selection of key words is very important. The spider that is combing the search engine index on your behalf will only return sites that contain the exact words you specified. Therefore, you should prepare a list of synonyms and try several sets of search terms in order to ensure that you are not missing useful Web sites. In addition, it is helpful to use several words that describe your topic in order to narrow it as much as possible. For example, the descriptor "crows birds pests" will give Katie and her friends more useful Web sites for their research than will the single word "crows." The latter is likely to turn up more information on the rock group Counting Crows or the Crow tribe than on their subject.

Many search engines enable you to click on an *advanced search* link, which will provide commands you can use to make your search more precise. Table 7.4 describes several common techniques that can improve your chances of finding information on your topic. Each search engine offers different features, so it is advisable to check the *advanced search* function of the specific engine you are using.

Using Web Directories to Find Sites on Your Topic.   You can do research on the Internet by accessing **Web directories** that can lead you to helpful sites. These directories are similar to traditional library indexes. Human editors compile them, reviewing Web sites and indexing them into subject categories and subcategories. You begin with a category that appears to be relevant to your research, and you follow links to the subcategory that seems most likely to contain useful information. You can then link to those sites directly from the index. Yahoo! and many other Internet search services attempt to provide both a directory and a search engine to help you find sites.

Web directory: a human-created, subject-based index to Internet resources.

TABLE 7.4   Helpful Search Engine Commands

COMMAND	PURPOSE
+ (plus)	Ensures that the Web pages found have all the words entered. For example, a search for "+crows +eradication" would turn up only sites containing both words.
– (minus)	Ensures that the Web pages found do not have one or more words entered. For example, "crows – counting – Sheryl" would exclude sites for Counting Crows or Sheryl Crow.
* (asterisk)	The asterisk is often called a wildcard. When inserted at the end of a word or word fragment, it returns more sites that may relate to your topic. For example, "crow*" would search for any word beginning with *c-r-o-w,* including *crow* and *crows.* It also would display less promising links to sites containing words such as *crowing.*
"phrase"	When quotation marks are placed around a phrase, the search engine looks for pages that contain the entire phrase. Thus "crow eradication technology" would turn up only sites containing the entire phrase, rather than sites containing the words *crow, eradication,* and *technology* at different places.
Boolean operators	Boolean operators are terms such as *and* (e.g., "crows AND eradication AND technology"), *or* (e.g., "eradication OR control"), *not* (e.g., "crows NOT counting"), and *near* (e.g., "crows NEAR disease") that you can use to narrow your search or exclude words that produce irrelevant documents.

There are advantages and disadvantages to relying on directories when researching. A Web directory is beneficial because it is created by human editors who can read a document, judge the appropriate category to place it in, and evaluate the document's quality. A computer program searching for key words lacks the brain power to analyze a document's context or quality. However, search engines have the advantage of machine power. They can cover more Web sites than a human being could possibly cover in the same time,[15] providing you with more Web sites that may relate to your topic. *Because search engines and directories have different strengths, it is advisable to use both in your research.* Table 7.5 provides URLs for some directories you may want to use in your research.

Advantages and Disadvantages of Internet Research.

Researching the Internet can be analogous to sending an untrained dog out to retrieve the morning paper. He may come back with the newspaper, or he may end up getting hit by a car or eating the neighbor's chickens. There are pitfalls and benefits to relying on this vast information resource, and it is important to understand them if you are going to conduct Internet research wisely.

Benefits of Internet Research. One benefit of the Internet is its convenience. Without leaving your desk, you can access information on nearly any topic. If your campus library is plagued by long lines and cumbersome procedures for accessing materials, Internet research can be more efficient. The Internet can be particularly helpful if you are working at home and need one piece of information or the answer to one question.

TABLE 7.5   Web Directories

DIRECTORY	FEATURES
• Ask Jeeves <www.askjeeves.com>	You ask a question; the service tries to find pages that answer your question.
• LookSmart <www.looksmart.com>	Human-compiled directory. Other search services supplement their findings with LookSmart.
• Lycos <www.lycos.com>	Gets listings from the Open Directory Project (below) and also uses a spider to search the Web.
• Open Directory <www.dmoz.org>	Relies on volunteer editors to review and classify Web sites.
• Refdesk <www.refdesk.com>	Links to news, reference tools, Web editions of magazines and newspapers. Includes "Ask the Experts" feature.
• NBCi <nbci.msnbc.com/nbci.asp>	Directory begun in 1997, backed by NBC.
• Yahoo! <www.yahoo.com>	Large and popular human-compiled directory with over 1 million sites listed.

Source: Sullivan, D. (1999). The major search engines. *Search Engine Watch* [online]. <http://www .searchenginewatch.com/links/Major_Search_Engines/The/Major_Search_Engines> (site visited October 4, 1999).

Another benefit is the speed with which information is placed on the Internet. A news report, a new research finding, or an interesting addition to an organization's Web page can be instantly available to a worldwide audience. The delays associated with printing traditional written evidence are avoided.

A third benefit is the volume of information available. Recall that the size of the World Wide Web is estimated to be a billion pages, with a rapid growth rate.[16] The smaller the collection of research material at your own library, the more difficult it is to obtain sufficient, high-quality evidence on your topic. With *careful* searching, you have a chance to find Internet evidence that simply does not exist in your own library.

The convenience of Internet use and the diversity of topics that can be researched make this resource very popular with college students. However, Internet research should not be the only type of research you conduct, because there are also problems with Internet research.

Disadvantages of Internet Research.   One disadvantage is that you are unlikely to find all the best sources for your topic on the World Wide Web. Despite the vastness of the Web, most of the world's knowledge is still contained in printed works.[17] For example, many books and journal articles are copyrighted, meaning they are unlikely to be available on the Internet or are accessible only if you pay a fee. Authorities in many fields publish their works in books and scholarly journals, and often you will need to obtain these materials at a traditional library. (If your college library offers remote access, you may be able to access library indexes on your personal computer. The library may also have some articles or other library resources available through remote access.)

A second disadvantage is that the credibility of Internet evidence is low in some cases and uncertain in others. Weak sources will hurt your credibility and reduce the effectiveness of your evidence (see In Theory box 7.1).

INVENTION	ORGANIZATION	STYLE	PREPARATION	DELIVERY

In Theory 7.1

THE IMPORTANCE OF CREDIBLE INTERNET SOURCES

An important aspect of *invention* is researching your speech and considering what evidence to include in your presentation. This process requires critical thinking about any evidence you find on the Internet and, possibly, further investigation into the sources of that evidence.

When assessing the credibility of Internet evidence, use the same criteria that you use to evaluate any other source. Two essential standards for credibility are whether your sources are *qualified* and *objective*. (For more on expertise and objectivity, see p. 146.) Research confirms the importance of evidence that meets these criteria. Luchok and McCroskey (1978) found that evidence from good sources was perceived to be of higher quality than evidence from poor sources. The use of a low-quality source also had a negative impact on the *communicator's* credibility.[18] Fleshler, Ilardo, and Demoretcky (1974) compared evidence from sources whose names, positions, and affiliations were stated, with evidence ascribed to a general source (such as "a study was done"). The researchers concluded that the use of more concrete documentation resulted in "significantly more positive evaluations of the message and the speaker."[19] Finally, evidence from biased sources (sources who argue in favor of their own interests) is not likely to be perceived as valid. Such communicators are regarded as insincere (Eagly, Wood, & Chaiken, 1978; Pastore & Horowitz, 1955).[20]

Based on these research findings, three factors are particularly important when you are considering the use of Internet evidence.

1. Know the *expertise* of your Internet sources. Books, magazine articles, and news reports are scrutinized by editors before publication. Scholarly books and journal articles are subject to review by experts in the field (peer review) before they are published. Some online sources (such as scholarly electronic journals) follow this process, but it is not required.

Anyone with sufficient computer skills can place information onto the Internet; there is no guarantee the information has been subjected to any independent fact-checking or review. Therefore, it is important to identify the author of any document you find on the Internet and determine his or her qualifications before using that source as evidence in a speech (see p. 165 for some tips on finding more information about Internet sources). If you cannot determine the source of an Internet document, do not use it.

2. Consider the *objectivity* of your Internet sources. The motive of Internet sources must be taken into account. Much information has been placed on the World Wide Web by companies that are trying to sell you their products. For example, information about crow eradication technology that has been placed on the Web by a manufacturer of that technology is likely to be colored by the manufacturer's economic self-interest. In addition, many extremist groups have Web sites, and the information on those sites is dubious because of ideological bias. Web page sponsors can use just about any name they wish. They may mask their bias with a neutral-sounding title, such as "The Official Facts about Animal Rights."

Before using Internet research in your speech, be sure to consider the source. For some suggestions about investigating and analyzing Internet sources, see page 165. Be confident that the source you are using does not have a bias that makes its objectivity suspect.

3. Indicate in your speech the *authorship* of Internet evidence. A mistake that many students make is presenting the URL as if it were the source of their Internet evidence. A student who found a relevant capital punishment Web site with the Yahoo! search engine might erroneously refer to the source as "yahoo.com" or "www.deathpenalty.com," providing no information about the actual author and his or her credentials. A reference to a search engine is akin to the "a study found" source citation that researchers have found to be ineffective. In your speech, be sure to provide a full citation to Internet evidence, as you would to any other source. (For the correct format for citing Internet evidence, see p. 172.)

Furthermore, you cannot fulfill your ethical duty to research carefully when you do not know whether the facts you are presenting come from reliable sources.

Investigating the Source of a Web Site.   In Theory box 7.1 discussed the importance of knowing the objectivity and expertise of Internet sources. You can learn more about these sources by investigating the sponsoring organization and analyzing the URL suffix.

For more on the ethical duty to research carefully, see page 61.

Investigate the Sponsoring Organization or Author.   When the expertise and objectivity of an Internet source are not apparent, you will need to do some investigation to gain the information you need. If there is no author of an Internet document, try to determine what organization sponsored the Web site where you found the document and assess the credibility of that organization. If this information is not available on the Web site you are researching, you need to do some detective work. Look for links from that Web site to other sites about the sponsoring organization. You can also do an Internet search, using the organization's name as the search term(s).[21] If there is an author but no qualifications are provided, you can use search engines to learn more about the author.

What information might provide insight about a Web site sponsor? Robert Berkman, a faculty member of the graduate media-studies program at the New School University, who conducts workshops on searching the Internet, suggests that you look for the purpose of the organization. This can give you insight into the organization's objectivity or bias. Also see whether any directors or board members of the organization are listed. If they are, use the Internet to check their other affiliations. Determine whether any political or economic interest may compromise their objectivity.[22]

Consider the examples of two URLs taken from possible sources of evidence on the topic of racial profiling (law enforcement use of race as a basis for traffic stops or arrests). The first is <www.stats.org>. If you go to that address and follow the "About STATS" link, you can discover that the site sponsors are the Statistical Assessment Service. They refer to themselves as a nonpartisan, nonprofit research organization, and their advisory board includes faculty members from universities such as Harvard, Penn, and UC Berkeley. You also can follow links to newspaper articles about STATS. Those articles indicate that the organization receives more funding from conservative than from liberal foundations but also has received contributions from La Raza and the U.S. Commission on Civil Rights.

The second URL pertaining to racial profiling is <www.racialprofile.com>. If you go to that address, you find a Web site created by DATAssociates, a management consulting service, as a marketing tool. One of the services DATAssociates offers is targeted to police departments, to help them deal with perceptions of racial profiling. You would expect this company to have expertise in the area of racial profiling, because that is a significant focus of the services it advertises. However, DATAssociates, like any other business, might not be objective about the need for its services. It is in the company's economic interests to emphasize the risks of racial profiling as much as possible (building up the need for DATAssociates' expertise) and to persuade police departments that using the company's services will effectively minimize those risks.

From these two examples, you can see that a URL alone tells you little about the author of Internet evidence. Indeed, there would be nothing to stop the friends of a convicted felon from creating a <profilingvictim.com> site in an effort to gain contributions for their pal.

TIP

Before using Internet evidence, determine who the author is and evaluate his or her credibility.

To decode a URL, see page 158.

Analyze the URL Suffix. You can analyze a URL to make inferences about the credibility of an Internet source.[23] Each URL has a suffix such as "gov" or "edu" that tells what kind of site it is. You should not make blanket assumptions about any given suffix, but the suffix does offer clues to help you evaluate the credibility of Internet sources.

Information included in a government site ("gov") is likely to come from a source with some expertise on the topic. Government agencies hire persons with experience and knowledge in their field, and they have access to a wide variety of information. However, objectivity is problematic. Government agencies are unlikely to criticize their own programs, and they may selectively choose information that casts their efforts (or those of their political allies) in the best possible light.

Educational institutions ("edu") are likely to include information from professors and researchers who know their subject well and have less financial bias than other sources (unless they have a consulting contract with a particular company or agency, in which case they are unlikely to want to make their client look bad). However, you need to be careful that you are not using the Web page of an undergraduate student at that college.

A commercial site ("com") is likely to be selling you something, either through a direct advertisement or by presenting favorable information about their products. The DATAssociates Web site at <www.racialprofile.com> is an example of this type of site. When the author has an economic self-interest, objectivity is more suspect. However, a site with the "com" suffix may belong to a credible source who has simply purchased space on a local Internet service provider that is identified by a commercial suffix.

Nonprofit organizations often have the "org" suffix on their Internet addresses. If you are going to use evidence from an organization, it is important to know something about the expertise and objectivity of that group. For example, the American Society of Crows and Ravens is sympathetic toward crows, but a farmers' or hunters' organization is likely to believe strongly that human needs take precedence over animal rights. Katie, Mandeep, and Sherri would need to consider whether the ideology of each group was likely to compromise its objectivity. You should also be aware that commercial sites were recently given the option to select the suffix "org" instead of "com" when registering their sites, making it even more important to determine exactly who a site sponsor is.[24]

Other Internet addresses end with the suffix "net," for network. This could mean that a computer network company is hosting its own Web page, in which case you should consider the credibility of the company with respect to the topic of your speech. The "net" suffix may also indicate that a person has purchased space on a computer, in which case his or her credibility should be determined.

Additional Internet Resources.

In addition to searching on the World Wide Web, you can make other uses of the Internet when researching your speech. Electronic mail, **e-mail**, enables you to correspond with another person by computer much as you would through traditional (snail) mail, except it lets you send and receive messages instantaneously rather than waiting for the mail carrier. You use e-mail addresses to send and receive messages.

e-mail: communication sent from one person to another by computer.

When you need a question answered by an expert in your subject, e-mail can be a more effective means than a telephone call or letter. People who are too busy to be interrupted by the phone or to write a letter can respond to an e-mail efficiently and at their convenience. At many colleges you can find the e-mail address of an instructor about as easily as you can find his or her office telephone number. If you wish to contact an expert who is not located on your campus, directories of e-mail addresses are becoming increasingly common. Your Internet provider may maintain a directory of addresses, and Web sites may include e-mail addresses or other links that enable you to send a message to the author. Show the same courtesy to a person you contact online that you would show to someone you interview in person (see p. 169).

Persons with common interests can participate in **discussion groups** that communicate through e-mail. When you join one of these groups, you *post* (send) messages to the group's e-mail address. Your message can be read by any member of the group, and you can read messages posted by other group members. It is also possible to **backchannel** (have a private exchange with) a group member to communicate on subjects of common interest.

When researching your speech, you can post questions about the subject or about your research needs, and you can easily get ideas from people located throughout the United States and in other countries, too. You also can keep track of what issues are timely and important to other people who are interested in your topic, which may give you ideas for your speech. You ordinarily would not use information from a discussion group as evidence because the message is not the equivalent of a published source. You cannot be certain who the author is, and a listener could not easily verify the evidence you cite. Nevertheless, such a group can be a good source of ideas or background information.

To locate a discussion group, check with your Internet provider to see whether they provide access to discussion groups. You may also find the e-mail addresses of discussion groups through a search engine.

Interview Research

Libraries and Internet sites are two of the most common research sources, but an interview can also be an excellent speech preparation resource. Interview research lets you talk to your source about whatever questions or issues are most important to you; you are not limited to whatever your source has written. The information you gain from an interview can be used as evidence in your speech, just like information from any other source. When you would like to learn about your topic through an interview, here are some guidelines to follow.

Preparing for Interview Research. The first step in any research effort is to *determine your research needs*. Decide what information could best be obtained through an interview. Are there any questions you are having a hard time answering by researching written sources? Is there any individual who would add credibility to your speech?

discussion groups: online communities of persons who post and respond to messages on topics of mutual interest.

backchannel: to have a private exchange with a member of a discussion group.

Check with your instructor to see when it is acceptable to use a friend, classmate, or yourself as an evidence source for an assignment.

Once you know what you would like to get out of an interview, *decide on whom to interview*. The person you talk to should be an expert on the subject; on most topics, a relative or a roommate would not be the best source of evidence. If there is a department on your campus with expertise in your subject, ask the department chair or another knowledgeable person which professor would be best to interview.

You also may obtain information from off-campus sources such as a political official, a government agency, or a local business leader. An officer in a community group or club with an interest in your topic can be another valuable resource. There are organizations that work in the political arena (such as the National Rifle Association's Institute for Legislative Action or Citizens for Handgun Control) and groups that focus on hobbies and interests (such as the Basenji Club of America or the Low Rider Club). You can consult a phone directory or the Internet to look for groups or organizations that have expertise in your topic area.

It is best to start with a leader or high-ranking person when requesting an interview. Do not assume that this person will be unwilling to talk to you. Many of these leaders are "people persons" who enjoy talking about their careers or interests, and they will make time to help students. Katie and her friends were pleasantly surprised when the police chief agreed to be interviewed, and their session was very informative even though they were speaking against the police crow eradication efforts. If the person you want to interview is too busy, he or she may ask another qualified person to do the interview or may give you a lead about another potential subject.

Setting Up Your Interview.

When you contact the person you would like to interview, identify yourself, explain that you are preparing a speech (briefly describe your topic), and describe (in general terms) what you hope to learn from the interview. Be direct and to the point when you are making your request, and then be prepared to answer any questions the interviewee may have.

Your interview subject may want to confirm that you are truly a student preparing a speech. One of our students was researching the topic of burning military draft cards, a form of protest during the Vietnam War. When this student called the local army recruiting center for information, the commanding officer was convinced that the caller really intended to burn his own draft registration card and was reluctant to provide any help. An interviewee may also want more specific information about you or may just want to become comfortable talking to you before agreeing to be interviewed. If you can go in person to request the interview, your chances of a positive response increase. It is easier to tell a person "no" on the telephone.

Be flexible when requesting an interview. A busy person may only have thirty minutes open in a typical week and you will need to accommodate that schedule.

Planning the Interview.

Once you know whom you will be interviewing, decide what you need to learn *from that person*. Focus on questions that he or she is in a unique position to answer. Katie, Mandeep, and Sherri would have different sets of questions for the police chief, for an animal rights activist, and for a representative of a company that sells nonlethal crow eradication devices.

There are questions that are effective in an interview, and questions that you should avoid because they create a barrier to effective communication. Ask *focused questions* if you need specific information. Ask *open-ended questions* if you want the interviewee to elaborate or provide examples. Open-ended questions should clearly indicate the type of information you are looking for, so your subject does not spend time going into detail about information you do not really need. It is also acceptable to ask the interviewee a *candid question* on a topic that he or she may prefer to avoid, but you should phrase it professionally. There are other types of questions that should be avoided. For example, do not include questions that use loaded language or ask confrontational questions that may make interview subjects needlessly uncomfortable. If you are too hostile, you may cause an interviewee to feel threatened and begin providing guarded answers. For examples of each of these types of questions, see Table 7.6.

Conducting the Interview.   Be on time for your interview. It is inconsiderate to keep a person waiting, particularly someone who is making the time

TABLE 7.6   Sample Interview Questions to Ask (or Avoid)

TYPE OF QUESTION	EXAMPLES
Questions calling for specific information	1. "How long has the police force used shooting as a crow eradication strategy?" 2. "How many police officers work on crow eradication during a typical night?"
Open-ended questions—directed	1. "Why does your department believe that shooting is the best eradication strategy for crows?" 2. "What would your department do if the city council voted to ban the shooting of crows?"
Open-ended questions—not focused on the interview topic (to be avoided)	1. "What are your biggest challenges as chief of police?" 2. "How is police work in a small town different than it would be in a large city?"
Follow-up questions	1. "Have you asked other cities how they deal with problem crows?" [Subject says "yes."] "Have you tried any of the alternatives to shooting that other towns use?" 2. "Do you know how much it would cost to scare crows away by broadcasting crow distress signals?" [Subject says "no."] "If the cost were reasonable, would you be willing to try distress signals?"
Candid questions, professionally phrased	1. "How do the officers assigned to eradication feel about shooting these birds?" 2. "Are there higher crime-prevention priorities for our police force than shooting the crows?"
Hostile, unprofessional questions (to be avoided)	1. "Does your department continue shooting the crows because the police have fun using these innocent birds for target practice?" 2. "Don't you think it is wrong to have the police taking the time to blast harmless crows when there are violent crimes your force has not solved?"

to talk to you. Also, dress professionally unless the occasion warrants different attire (for example, if your interview is taking place on a farm). When you arrive, greet your interviewee and introduce yourself if the two of you have not already met.

There are several considerations to keep in mind during the interview:

- Begin with friendly questions that will be easy to answer. It is important to establish rapport with the person you are interviewing before you move on to more difficult questions. However, if the interviewee has a limited amount of time, move on to your most important questions quickly.

- Keep the interview focused on the topics you need to have addressed. If the interviewee digresses to points that do not relate to your subject, politely steer the discussion back to the topic.

For more on eye contact, see pages 53 and 298.

- Maintain eye contact with your interview subject. Occasionally you may need to look down to remind yourself of questions you want to ask or to make some notes. Nevertheless, you should make the interview process as conversational as possible.

- You may deviate from your planned questions if new ideas come up during the course of your interview. Ask follow-up questions if you need clarification of an answer or would like more information.

For tips on effective listening, see pages 77–79.

- Listen carefully so that you hear the answers that your interview subject is actually giving, rather than answers you are expecting or hoping for. It is helpful to paraphrase a key answer back to the person you are questioning to be certain that you understood what was said.

- You may tape an interview only with your subject's permission. Taping an interview secretly would be a serious breach of ethics. You should refrain from taping if the interviewee is likely to be inhibited from speaking candidly while being recorded.

After the Interview Is Over. Immediately check your notes, and be certain that you wrote down all the answers you may want to use in your speech. If you did not get everything in your notes, write down the interviewee's complete answers while the interview is still fresh in your mind. If you cannot remember an answer for sure, recheck with the interviewee rather than putting down your best guess. If you are going to be using material from your interview in your speech, double-check with your interviewee to be certain you are quoting or paraphrasing accurately. Whether you are using the information in your speech or not, be sure to send a thank you note to the person you interviewed.

The Format for Presenting Evidence in Speeches

After you have researched your topic and found strong evidence to back up the points you want to make in your speech, you will want to be certain that your audience understands when you are using evidence. A number of guidelines pertain here.

● *Present Evidence in Claim-Source-Support Order*

When you are going to use evidence in a speech, it is best to tell the audience what point you will make and then present your evidence. For example, in an informative or commemorative speech about Cammi Granato, captain of the gold medal–winning U.S. Women's Hockey Team, you could use evidence to show how she got her start in hockey. It would be presented as shown here:

Cammi Granato honed her skills playing hockey with her brothers in the basement of their home.	**The Claim**
Ken Campbell, senior editor for *The Hockey News,* wrote this about the family competitions in *American Hockey Magazine,* December 1997:	**The Source**
The Granato kids painted lines on the floor, set up nets and played two on two, Tony and Cammi against Donnie and Robbie. "Those games got pretty intense," Tony [her brother] recalls. "But Cammi hung right in there and she never backed down. She was one of the most tenacious kids I've ever seen."	**The Support**

Remember that when you present evidence, you must attribute the information to the author and quote or paraphrase the author's statement accurately.

It is very important to cite the source of a unit of evidence *immediately before* you present that evidence in your speech. Why is it not acceptable

For more on attribution, see page 61. For ethical guidelines on quoting or paraphrasing accurately, see pages 62–63.

ESL	**Citing Your Sources**

Understanding how to cite the sources you have researched for your speech is very important. In American universities, this is not just a principle of successful speaking, it is also an ethical responsibility.

Speakers (and writers) are expected to give credit for ideas that they borrow from others. A failure to credit the author can be viewed as dishonesty.[1] If you cite the source each time you use another person's idea, audience members will know which ideas you are borrowing and which are your own.

In Western cultures, proper citation of evidence also strengthens the points that you are making. When you support your claims, preferably you will use evidence provided by unbiased experts.[2] The use of a proper citation format also reflects on your professionalism.[3]

When you prepare your speech remember to cite the source properly each time you use information that you have researched. The citation format can be reviewed above on this page.

[1]Teays, W. (1996). *Second thoughts: Critical thinking from a multicultural perspective* (p. 300). Mountain View, CA: Mayfield.

[2]Lustig, M., & Koester, J. (1993). *Intercultural competence: Interpersonal communication across cultures* (p. 228). New York: HarperCollins.

[3]Teays, p. 300.

to list all of your research sources together at the beginning or end of your speech? The reason is simple: doing so would make your evidence less credible.[25] The audience would not know which claims in your speech are backed by evidence and which are not. Nor would they know which source is the basis for any particular claim. If audience members have doubts about a point you are making, you can best answer those doubts if they understand what source you are using to support that particular claim.

Evidence is also more effective when you present the source just before you provide the text of the evidence, rather than stating evidence and then identifying its source. When you present the source first, you cue audience members to listen for evidence: they know that you are about to back up your claim with evidence. If you present evidence first and then indicate the source, audience members may be confused because they will not know at what point you began to cite evidence, even if you later indicate the source.

● *Document Internet Sources*

In your speech, cite evidence from online sources as you would cite sources of traditional printed evidence. Present the author, his or her qualifications, the title of the source, and the date. Also note that the source was accessed online. You need not mention the URL in your speech (it is likely to be long and difficult for the audience to follow), but you should have this information available in case any audience members request it.

The date of Internet sources can be problematic. If you are using a specific document from the Web and it is dated, present that date. If you are researching a Web site that is periodically updated, and the date of the page you are using is not given, use the date the site was last updated. This information is usually noted on the first or last Web page. If you can find no date, indicate the date you researched that page.

Here is how Katie, Mandeep, and Sherri could present information about potential benefits of crows that they researched online:

> According to Paul Lamble, a Kansas City freelance writer, in *Missouri Conservationist,* January 1997, accessed online:
> Given the diversity of their diets, crows don't depend on the farmer's grain and can even be considered beneficial because they consume so many pest insects.

Whether you are citing evidence from the Internet or evidence from traditional sources, the sequence is the same. When you use a claim-source-support sequence, the audience will easily digest the evidence you are presenting.

Summary

Research and evidence are important building blocks for constructing a successful speech. Research is the process of learning what other people have said or written about your topic. Evidence is the end product of your research. You use information from your research sources (evidence) to support the claims you make in your speech.

The importance of research and evidence can be summarized in one sentence: ***It is not a fact until you prove it to the audience.*** Evidence is necessary in most speeches because speakers are not experts in every subject that they discuss and an audience is unlikely to be convinced by a speaker's assertions alone. When you use evidence from sources that the audience accepts as credible to prove your claims, you increase the likelihood that the audience will believe your claims. Furthermore, your own credibility as a speaker is strengthened because the use of evidence indicates that you have taken the time to research your topic and prepare for the speech.

The checklist shows how you can use the material from this chapter to research your speech and present the evidence you discover effectively.

Checklist

KNOW WHAT TO LOOK FOR

_____ Types of evidence (p. 143)

_____ Credible evidence sources (p. 146)

FOLLOW AN ORGANIZED RESEARCH PROCESS

_____ Inventory your research needs (p. 148)

_____ Discover sources of information on your topic (p. 148)

_____ Prioritize and read your sources (p. 149)

_____ Research your sources systematically (p. 149)

_____ Identify gaps in your research, and find needed information (p. 150)

RESEARCH A VARIETY OF INFORMATION RESOURCES

Library Research

_____ Apply general principles of library research (p. 151)

_____ Research periodicals (p. 150)

_____ Research newspapers (p. 153)

_____ Research abstracts (p. 154)

_____ Research books (p. 154)

_____ Research government documents (p. 155)

Internet Research

_____ Understand how to get around on the Web (p. 158)

_____ Use search engines to find Web sites (p. 159)

_____ Use directories to find Web sites (p. 161)

_____ Be aware of the drawbacks of relying only on Internet research (p. 163)

_____ Evaluate the credibility of Internet evidence (p. 164)

_____ Use other Internet resources (p. 166)

Interview Research

____ Prepare for interview research (p. 167)

____ Set up your interview (p. 168)

____ Plan the interview (p. 168)

____ Conduct the interview (p. 169)

____ Follow up after the interview (p. 170)

PRESENTING EVIDENCE IN YOUR SPEECH

____ Present evidence in claim-source-support order (p. 171)

____ Document Internet sources properly (p. 172)

Key Terms and Concepts

research (p. 141)
source (p. 142)
evidence (p. 142)
examples (p. 143)
testimony (p. 144)
narrative (p. 145)
facts (p. 145)
statistics (p. 145)
expertise (p. 146)
objectivity (p. 146)
reluctant testimony (p. 147)
recency (p. 147)
periodicals (p. 150)
full text database (p. 152)
abstract (p. 154)
online catalog (p. 154)
Internet (p. 156)

World Wide Web (p. 156)
hypertext transfer protocol (http) (p. 156)
Web site (p. 156)
server (p. 156)
home page (p. 157)
link (p. 157)
uniform resource locator (URL) (p. 158)
browser (p. 158)
bookmark (p. 158)
search engine (p. 159)
metasearch engine (p. 159)
Web directory (p. 161)
e-mail (p. 166)
discussion groups (p. 167)
backchannel (p. 167)

Speech Grid Application

The Evolution of a Speech Grid

Speech Grid Applications, showing the evolution of a Speech Grid, are included near the end of Chapters 5 through 12. They illustrate how one student, Samantha, uses a grid to prepare a speech.

In this chapter we see how Samantha's grid looks after she researches her topic. Samantha summarizes evidence under the headings "Ethos," "Pathos," and "Logos." At the end of the grid, she lists full citations for her evidence and numbers each citation. The list includes citations for all her research sources, even those she does not intend to use. If she later decides that a particular source is relevant, she will be able to locate that source easily. On the grid itself, she refers to her sources by number. She also makes notes to indicate particularly strong evidence and potential weaknesses.

Although Samantha supports greater efforts to promote safe cell phone use while driving, she notes evidence against her thesis. She will need to take opposing views into account when planning her message.

Speech Grid: Driving with cell phones
Topic: Cell phones and driving
Specific purpose: To persuade my audience to use cell phones safely while driving.
Thesis: Audience members should use cell phones safely when driving.

AUDIENCE ANALYSIS	SPEECH MESSAGE
Situational Characteristics • 8 min. speech • 25–30 in audience • small classroom • limited a-v equip. **Demographics** **Age:** 17 (5); 18 (17); 19 (4); 20 (1); 22 (1) **Ethnicity:** African-American (2); Hmong (2); white (9); Latino/a (6); Portuguese (2); Pacific Islander, Mexican, German, Japanese, Swedish, Greek (1 each); did not say (1) **Major:** Undeclared (9); Liberal Studies (5); Chem, Bus, Crim (2 each); Child Devel, Engl, Bio, Premed, Journalism, Ag Bus, Econ, Comm (1 each) **Common Ground** I, like most of class (20 students), do not own a cell phone.	**ETHOS** • I have researched the topic in the library, online, and talked to friends who use cell phones while driving. • I talked to a friend who was hurt in a cell phone–related accident. She said that the driver's call was not important and that her injuries were painful and caused her to miss work and school for a week. **PATHOS** • Photo of car involved in fatal accident. • Narrative of troubles of friend who was in accident. • Examples of cell phone–related accidents. (Source 6 — fatal accident — no source quals? Source 8 — head injury) • Lawyer notes that cell phone records will make litigation against driver easier. (Source 9) **LOGOS** • Technology to make use as safe as possible. (Source 1) • Hands-free phones costly, may cause <u>more</u> accidents. (Sources 1, 4) • People like the convenience of car phones, save time in busy world. (Sources 1, 2) • Better, definitive data on cell phone risks needed. (Source 1)

(continued)

Speech Grid, continued

AUDIENCE ANALYSIS	SPEECH MESSAGE
Prior Exposure • Few (7 students) had heard about the issue of cell phones and driving; it had not been major topic in the local media. • Most students (20) do not own a cell phone. • Most who own a cell phone (6 of 8) use their phone in their car, primarily in one car. • Most (24 of 28) think that drunk drivers cause more accidents than cell phone users. **Audience Disposition** • Most (20 of 28) support a law banning cell phone use while driving. • People who do not own a cell phone are more likely to support such a law (18 of 20). Cell phone owners are opposed (2 of 8).	• 85% of cell phone owners use in car sometimes; 27% use in half of trips. (Source 1) • Cell phones help in emergency situations. (Sources 1, 4) • Cell phone usage high; 40% growth rate. (Source 2) • Possible disadvantage: unfair to single out one distraction. (Source 4) • Communities don't want to be anti-business or anti-tech. (Source 4) • Inattention increases accident risk. (Source 5 — STUDY plus Dept. of Transportation stat that inattention is a factor in 50% of accidents) • Studies show accident risk. (Source 5 — cites 3 good studies!) • Wireless industry lobby opposes anti-cell phone laws. (Source 5) • Many states, nations considering laws against use. (Sources 5, 9) • Tips for safe use. (Sources 7, 12 — AAA and insurance co. tips) • 10% of crashes caused by cell phone use. (Source 8 — politician quote, no study) • You can be cited if cell phone use causes bad driving. (Source 11)

Sources
1. National Highway Traffic Safety Administration. (1999, November 2). *An investigation of the safety implications of wireless communication in vehicles.*
2. PRNewswire. (2000, June 12). *Delphi communications technologies keep drivers in touch and at ease.*
3. Neergaard, L. (2000, June 12). *FDA to oversee cell phone safety.*
4. PRNewswire. (2000, May 31). *Questions raised about proposal to restrict cell-phone usage while driving.*
5. Hall, A. (2000, May 26). Just how dangerous is a cell phone behind the wheel. *Business Week Online.*
6. Yarsky, R. (1999, May 19). *Cellular phone usage.* Retrieved June 20, 2000 from the World Wide Web: <http://riskmail.lsu.edu/archive/may99/00000475.htm>.
7. Bresnahan, J. (1998, April 3). *Cell phones may increase accidents.* Retrieved June 20, 2000 from the World Wide Web: <http://2cns.jrn.msu.edu/articles/ss98/040398/phones.html>.
8. Gerwig, A. (1999, April 2). Lawmakers: Cell phones causing auto accidents. *North Hills News Record.* Retrieved June 20, 2000 from the World Wide Web: <http://triblive.com/news/newsrec/0402hcel.html>.
9. Cell phones in cars—more accidents on highways? (1999). *Voiceoftheinjured.com.* Retrieved June 20, 2000 from the World Wide Web: <http://voiceoftheinjured.com/a-aa-cell-phones-accidents-injuries.html>.
10. Evans, B. (1999). Realtors are high risks for cell phone car accidents. *Realty Times.* Retrieved June 20, 2000 from the World Wide Web: <http://realtytimes.com/rtnews/rtapages/19990708_cellphones.htm>.
11. 2plus, Inc. (1998). *Cell phones: Are they a safety hazard?* Retrieved June 20, 2000 from the World Wide Web: <http://www.commutersregister.com/ct/articles/9807/cover.htm>.
12. Jacobson, J. (1997). Do cellular phones cause more vehicle accidents? *Safety Meeting Outline 97-0702.* Retrieved June 20, 2000 from the World Wide Web: <http://www.eig.com/smos/smo97072.htm>.

Source Notes

1. Rieke, R. D., & Sillars, M. O. (1993). *Argumentation and critical decision making* (3rd ed., p. 177). New York: HarperCollins.
2. Reinard, J. C. (1991). *Foundations of argument* (p. 113). Dubuque, IA: Wm. C. Brown.
3. Pastore, N., & Horowitz, M. W. (1955). The influence of attributed motive on the acceptance of a statement. *Journal of Abnormal and Social Psychology, 51,* 331–332.

4. McCroskey, J. C. (1986). *An introduction to rhetorical communication* (5th ed., p. 166). Englewood Cliffs, NJ: Prentice-Hall.

5. Global Reach. (2000, March 31). *Global Internet Statistics (by Language)*. Retrieved June 1, 2000 from the World Wide Web: <http://www.glreach.com/globstats/index.php3>.

6. Kirkland, R. (1997, June 9). America in the world: Still on top, with no challenger. *Fortune, 135,* 86.

7. Groopman, J. (1996, August 12). Chasing the cure: Vancouver's AIDS promise. *The New Republic, 215,* 14.

8. Zetter, K., & McCracken, H. (2000, September). How to stop searching and start finding. *PC World, 18,* 129–143 at 130.

9. Sullivan, D. How search engines work. *Search Engine Watch* [online]. <http://www.searchenginewatch.com/webmasters/work.html> (site visited October 4, 1999).

10. Sullivan, D. How search engines rank web pages. *Search Engine Watch* [online]. <http://www.searchenginewatch.com/webmasters/rank.html> (site visited October 4, 1999).

11. Lawrence, S., & Giles, C. L. (1999). Accessibility of information on the web. *Nature, 400,* 107–109.

12. Berkman, R. (2000, January 21). Searching for the right search engine. *The Chronicle of Higher Education, 46,* B6.

13. Crowley, B. (1999, August). Search engines losing ground on the Internet. *Hydrocarbon Processing, 78,* 23.

14. Greenberg, I., & Garber, L. (1999, August). Searching for new search technologies. *Computer, 32,* 4.
    Quible, Z. (1999, September). Guiding students in finding information on the web. *Business Communication Quarterly, 62,* 57.

15. Tanaka, J. (1999, September 27). The perfect search: The web is growing by millions of pages every year. *Newsweek, 134,* 71.

16. Zetter & McCracken (2000, p. 130).

17. Berkman, R. (2000, July 28). Internet searching is not always what it seems. *Chronicle of Higher Education, 46,* B9.

18. Luchok, J., & McCroskey, J. C. (1978). The effect of quality of evidence on attitude change and source credibility. *Southern Speech Communication Journal, 43,* 371–383, at 381–382.

19. Fleshler, H., Ilardo, J., & Demoretcky, J. (1974, Summer). The influence of field dependence, speaker credibility set, and message documentation on evaluations of speaker and message credibility. *Southern Speech Communication Journal, 39,* 389–402, at 400.

20. Eagly, A. H., Wood, W., & Chaiken, S. (1978). Causal inferences about communicators and their effect on opinion change. *Journal of Personality and Social Psychology, 36,* 424–435, at 425.
    Pastore & Horowitz (1955).

21. Berkman (2000, p. B9).

22. Berkman (2000, p. B9).

23. The authors thank Joe Corcoran, speech instructor at Santa Rosa Junior College and Webmaster of the Northern California Forensics Association Web site, for his contribution to this section.

24. Berkman (2000, p. B9).

25. Reinard (1991, p. 106).

"Good organization makes the message clear."

8 Organizing and Outlining

After reading Chapter 8, you should understand:

- The importance of having a well-organized speech.

- The purpose of a detailed speech outline and the process of preparing one.

- The organization of a speech in a linear format, with main points and supporting material, an introduction, and a conclusion.

- The use of connecting words and signposts in an outline to highlight your organization.

- The organization of a speech in nonlinear formats and contexts in which nonlinear formats may be effective.

- The purpose of an extemporaneous speaking outline and the process of preparing one.

Leann began a speech by telling her classmates, "My name is Leann, and my speech is about magazines targeted at women and teenage girls." Then Leann showed the audience several magazine advertisements featuring extremely thin models. One of the ads was for cosmetics, and when she displayed it, she used evidence to show how the testing of cosmetics harms animals. She also discussed how these ads depressed her when she was a teenager, because it was impossible to look like the models no matter how little she ate.

Next, in magazines targeted to women, Leann identified titles of articles that she found inane, including "What His Kitchen Tells You about Him" and "Which Spice Girl Are You?" She contrasted these articles with two serious features from financial magazines targeted to men and women. These articles described potential investments for children's college education, including a Roth individual retirement account. Because many in the class did not know what a Roth account was, she spent about a minute explaining its features. After comparing the two types of magazines, Leann reasoned that the articles in magazines targeted only at women dealt with more trivial issues than did the articles in magazines intended for both genders.

Leann closed with her strongest point. She presented research from several well-qualified sources addressing the "beauty myth." She had evidence establishing that ads with unrealistically slender models are a cause of anorexia and bulimia and may undermine the self-esteem of teenage girls. She concluded by presenting research from medical experts detailing how audience members could help friends who were anorexic, and she implored the class to use this advice if they had a friend who needed help. Finally, she said, "That's it," and sat down.

Leann was disappointed by the audience members' and instructor's responses to her speech. She had researched her topic thoroughly and thought she had delivered her message effectively. However, post-speech comments focused on how difficult it was to follow her message. After a beginning that failed to capture the audience's attention or give any indication of the main ideas she would be presenting, she had abruptly jumped into the core of her speech. As Leann digressed from her announced topic, audience members became more confused. She had indicated that her topic was magazines targeted to women, yet she devoted considerable time to other issues, such as cosmetic testing on animals and the Roth individual retirement account. Her appeal to offer help if audience members' friends were afflicted with anorexia was sincerely delivered, but she never did discuss what should be done about *magazines* that contribute to the problem. Rather than tying all her ideas together at the end, she abruptly finished and sat down.

Leann's speech was not effective because she was *disorganized*. Because the audience could not follow her speech, they were unable to benefit from the well-researched information she had presented. Her experience demonstrates the importance of good organization to the presentation of a successful speech.

The manner in which a presentation is organized makes a difference in how effective audiences find a speaker and his or her message. In this chapter we explain how to prepare an **organized speech**. When we say a speech is well organized, we mean that the ideas presented in it are *arranged* and *emphasized* in a manner that makes it easy for the audience to comprehend the message.

Many of your speeches will be organized in outline form. An **outline** is your plan for what you intend to say. It contains the text of your speech in complete sentences or detailed phrases. Usually, main ideas are noted with Roman numerals, and supporting ideas are noted with capital letters, which are indented. You can use an outline to work with the wording of your speech as you prepare, when you begin practicing your delivery, and as the basis for the short extemporaneous outline that you should use when you deliver your speech. See page 204 for a sample linear outline and page 215 for an extemporaneous outline.

For more on extemporaneous delivery from limited notes, see pages 51 and 289.

We begin our coverage of speech organization with an explanation of the reasons why good organization enhances the effectiveness of a speech. We describe a linear organization for the body, introduction, and conclusion of your speech, and consider alternatives to the linear format. Finally, we discuss how to prepare a brief extemporaneous outline to refer to when you deliver your speech.

organized speech: a speech in which ideas are arranged and emphasized to maximize audience understanding.

outline: a written text in which Roman numerals, capital letters, and Arabic numbers structure the ideas. Provides a clearly arranged plan for your speech.

The Importance of Good Organization

If we had to condense the main idea of this chapter to a single sentence, it would be this: *Good organization makes the message clear.* Without a planned organizational format, your speech can easily become a confusing collection of thoughts that your audience will struggle to follow. Good organization helps your audience understand your message, enhances your credibility, and improves your ability to deliver your speech well.

When your speech is clearly structured, audience members better comprehend your message.[1] They know what the main points are because these ideas stand out and cue them to listen for the supporting information that follows. When your message is organized, audience members can be active listeners and effectively process your information because they know what to expect. When your speech is disorganized, even audience members who are paying attention will need to devote their mental energy to ascertaining the thesis of your speech, or to figuring out what point you are trying to make, instead of focusing on your message. Recall your own efforts to take notes in class when a lecture was disorganized. You probably became frustrated by the need to spend time structuring your notes so they would make sense when you read them later. And while you were concentrating on that task, you could not direct your attention to the concepts being presented.

Good organization is particularly important in oral communication. Readers can go back and read information again if they are confused by a book, magazine, or Web page. A listener does not have this option when a speech is being presented. Therefore, you need to help audience members follow your ideas as they are hearing them.

When your speech is well organized, your credibility may be enhanced. Effective organization is a sign that you have taken time to prepare. When audience members notice good organization, it enhances their perception of you as a competent speaker. When you seem prepared and competent, these traits can make audience members more favorably disposed toward you and toward your message. When your speech is disorganized, the audience will perceive you as a less credible speaker.[2] And that perception will undermine the effectiveness of your speech.

Finally, when your speech is well organized, it facilitates good delivery. You know exactly which point you are discussing and what to cover next. This means you do not need to concentrate simultaneously on deciding what to say and trying to present your message effectively. When you understand how to organize a speech, your delivery is more fluent,[3] and you are able to maintain eye contact with your audience rather than reading your notes. If you know where you are in your speech, and where you are going next, speaking with confidence and without hesitation is easier. You experience less speech anxiety because you are well prepared.

For more on how careful preparation can reduce speech anxiety, see page 23.

In summary, when your speech is well organized, your audience will be more likely to listen to the speech and understand what you are saying. Your credibility and delivery will be strengthened, and you will not frustrate or distract audience members who are expecting a clearly organized message.

Outlining Your Speech: Linear Organization

Speeches may be organized in a *linear* or a *nonlinear* format. Nonlinear formats are discussed later in this chapter. The linear format is most commonly used in classroom speeches and in many other public speaking contexts in Western cultures. By **linear organization**, we mean a speech in which the thesis or topic sentence is presented early and the bulk of the speech develops **main points** that directly relate to the thesis or topic sentence.

linear organization: a speech structure in which a series of main ideas clearly relate to and support a thesis or topic sentence.

main points: a limited number of major ideas to be emphasized in a speech.

The outline of a speech with a linear organization consists of three parts: the *introduction, body,* and *conclusion.* The **introduction** motivates the audience to listen to your speech, reveals your topic (and thesis if you are taking a position), establishes your ethos, and previews your main points. The **body** is the main part of the speech. It offers support for the main points you are using to develop your topic or defend your thesis. It is here that you spend most of your speaking time, developing and supporting your main points. The **conclusion** wraps up the speech and leaves a lasting impression in listeners' minds. Organizing words and phrases inserted at key places in your speech emphasize the main points, help the audience keep track of supporting ideas, and link one part of the speech to the next.

We now take you through the stages of outlining a speech. You may want to look at the completed sample outline on page 204, or at one of the outlines on your CD-ROM, so you can visualize what the finished product looks like.

● *Outlining the Body of Your Speech*

Begin your outline by drafting the body of your speech. This is the part in which you explain and develop the ideas that support your topic or thesis. The body is the heart of your speech; the introduction and conclusion are subordinate to it. Although the introduction comes first when you deliver your speech, you need to know what the body of your speech will say before you can draft the introduction. Place "Body" in large, bold letters at the start of this section of your outline.

Draft the Main Points.   The body of your speech should center on a limited number of major ideas that you will develop. Each main point should be stated in one sentence. On your outline, note main points with Roman numerals. Each one supports your topic or thesis, and each should be an idea that is necessary or very important to your speech. Consider the following advice when drafting your main points.

Speeches Need to Focus on Main Points.   Your speech should be centered on specific main points, rather than providing a set of randomly ordered ideas about your topic. Even a five-minute speech will contain fifty or more sentences, and the audience cannot remember every detail.

When you emphasize a few main points, you indicate which ideas are most important to remember. Audience members can then focus on these major concepts. You highlight what you hope to prove or demonstrate through your supporting materials, helping listeners to make sense out of the details in your speech. You also break your speech into smaller parts for your audience. Rather than forcing listeners to process your speech as one long message, you allow your audience to focus on several shorter messages, one at a time.

Select an Appropriate Number of Main Points.   Review the ideas on your Speech Grid to identify potential main points. A single idea that you develop in detail could be a main point, as could a combination of several ideas that fit together to support a point (see Figure 8.1).

introduction: the beginning of a speech, which gains audience attention and orients the members.

body: the main part of a speech, where the main points are developed and supported.

conclusion: the final part of a speech; it summarizes main ideas and provides a memorable ending.

FIGURE 8.1 Organizing Ideas into Main Points

In a speech, ideas are typically organized into between two to five main points.
Ideas from the Speech Grid (left) get organized into categories (right). If each
idea is on a note card, it is easy to move ideas into potential categories.

A speech should ordinarily have from two to five main points. Three seems to be the most common number, but there is no hard-and-fast rule. If you want to make more than five points, you probably will be giving the audience too many main ideas to remember. Also, you are unlikely to have enough speaking time to develop six or more points. If you need to reduce the number of main points, consider these suggestions:

- See whether any of your main points are related. Are there two or more points that you can combine into a single broader category?
- Review your audience analysis. Can you exclude any points because they will be less effective with your audience?
- Evaluate which points are most important to developing your topic or thesis. Can you exclude one or more points that are not essential?

If you have only one main point, that point becomes the topic or thesis of your speech. Organize the information you plan to use to support that point into two to five key ideas, which become your main points.

Word the Main Points Carefully. Each main point must be a sentence that characterizes the supporting material accurately. You are giving the audience the "bottom line" when you indicate a main point. Consider what you intend to say when developing that idea, and ensure that your wording reflects your intent.

Main points should use vivid and descriptive language to generate interest. Effective word choice builds audience interest. Consider the following sets of main points for speeches on penguins, gun control, and a valued coworker. Notice that the second set uses more descriptive and precise language than the first set:

Mundane First Set
- Here is where penguins live.
- Guns are harmful.
- Frank did a good job at our company.

Descriptive Second Set
- Penguins live in the cold and remote environment of Antarctica.
- Handguns cause tragic accidental and intentional injuries.
- Frank made "Weddings to Go" receptions renowned throughout our community.

Main points should be worded to help the audience visualize the structure of your speech. One way to accomplish this goal is through the use of parallel sentence structure for each main point. For example, if your first main point begins with the subject and verb, subsequent main points should do the same. Another way to highlight main ideas is by using the subject of your speech in each sentence. When all main points have similar structure and wording, they stand out and help communicate to your audience that a new main idea is about to be developed. Consider the following sets of main points for an informative speech about raccoons. The sentences in the first set lack parallel structure. The sentences in the second set are parallel in form and will help the audience realize that each is a main point.

Nonparallel First Set

- Few animals can match the intellect of the raccoon.
- These masked marvels are very resourceful in maintaining a balanced diet.
- You might decide to sponsor one of these rascals at our local zoo.

Parallel Second Set

- Raccoons are one of nature's most intelligent species.
- Raccoons are naturally gifted dietitians.
- Raccoons are available for sponsorship at our zoo, if you wish to become a "parent."

When you know what your main points are going to be, and you have carefully considered their wording, you are ready to develop each point.

Structure the Main Points.   Various patterns are used to organize speeches. In this section we introduce several that are commonly used. You should select the pattern that best enables you to present your ideas to the audience. We elaborate on the selection of an optimal pattern for each genre of speech in Chapters 14 to 17.

Temporal Pattern.   In a **temporal pattern**, you present the information in a time sequence, from beginning to end. Each main point covers a particular point in time or period of time. If you are discussing a subject that follows a sequence, such as a historical event or a process, this pattern will help the audience keep track of the sequence. A speech discussing the decline and rebound of bald eagles in the lower forty-eight states could use a temporal pattern:

I. In 1963, the bald eagle had nearly disappeared from the lower forty-eight states.
II. In 1972, the pesticide DDT was banned in the United States.
III. During the past quarter century, governments and individual citizens took steps to protect eagles.
IV. By 1995, the bald eagle had made a remarkable comeback.

Spatial Pattern.   In a **spatial pattern**, each main point represents a physical part or a geographical section of the topic. This approach is effective when you have a subject that can be broken down into specific parts or locations. You take the audience from one part to the next, much as a museum guide takes a group from exhibit to exhibit, or as an anatomy professor might lecture about the parts of the human skeleton from head to toe. A speaker could use a spatial approach to discuss prehistoric cultures:

I. Early Europeans adapted to the Ice Age and competed with fellow carnivores for prey.

Use your CD-ROM to select an organizational pattern and structure your main points. Go to "Step 2 Organization/Body." CD-ROM: Interactive Speech Guides

temporal pattern: a speech structure in which main points are organized in a time sequence from beginning to end.

spatial pattern: a speech structure in which each main point covers a physical or geographic part of the topic.

II. Prehistoric people in Thailand lived in dense forests.
III. Australian Aborigines were the world's first known food processors.

Causal Pattern. If your speech is explaining a cause-and-effect relationship, a **causal pattern** will help the audience understand the link between cause and effect. There are two ways to organize main points when you use this pattern. First, if there are several major causes of the situation or phenomenon you are discussing, each main point covers one of the causes. Second, if there is a chain of events between cause and effect, each main point becomes one link in the chain from cause to effect. To explain why e-commerce has grown significantly, a speaker might use this chain of causation:

I. Internet usage grew rapidly in the 1990s.
II. Businesses took advantage of this new channel of communication by marketing products online.
III. Consumers have increasingly chosen to shop online because of the convenience.

Comparison Pattern. A **comparison pattern** organizes the speech around major similarities and differences between two events, objects, or situations. Each main point discusses an important similarity or difference. This pattern can help the audience learn about a new subject by comparing it to a subject with which they are familiar. A speaker might compare newly discovered planets outside our solar system with the planets in our own system as follows:

I. The orbits of planets outside our solar system are often different from our planets' paths.
II. In composition and size, planets outside our solar system are often similar to Jupiter.
III. Many planets outside our solar system have moons, as our planets do.
IV. Some planets outside our solar system are in a "habitable zone," as Earth is.

Problem-Cause-Solution Pattern. A **problem-cause-solution pattern** can be used if you are asking the audience to support a new governmental policy or to take action. The first main point argues that one or more problems exist. The second main point covers the cause(s) of the problem. The third main point develops your proposed solution, which mitigates or eliminates the cause(s). A problem-cause-solution format could be effective in a speech advocating expanded use of solar energy. Here is an example of the main points that could be advocated in a problem-cause-solution pattern:

I. Fossil fuel energy sources hurt our environment and our pocketbooks.
II. Current energy policies encourage fossil fuel usage.
III. Expanded tax credits for solar technology would promote clean, inexpensive energy.

Criteria-Application Pattern. A **criteria-application pattern** advocates standards for making a value judgment and then applies those stan-

causal pattern: a speech structure in which main points explain a cause-and-effect relationship.

comparison pattern: a speech structure in which each main point analyzes similarities or differences among two or more subjects.

problem-cause-solution pattern: a speech structure in which the first main point argues that a problem exists, the second indicates its cause, and the third provides a plan to remedy the problem.

criteria-application pattern: a speech structure in which the main points advocate standards for making a value judgment and apply those standards to the topic.

dards to the subject in question. A **value judgment** attaches an evaluation or label (such as *good, bad, moral,* or *immoral*) to a subject. For example, you might argue that abortion is immoral (or moral) or that bicycles offer a better (or less practical) means of transportation than cars.

This pattern accommodates two main points. The first advocates the **criteria** that should be used to make the value judgment. Criteria are standards by which the judgment is made. After the criteria have been established, the second main point is the *application* of the criteria to the subject of your speech.

One type of speech where the criteria-application pattern works well is the "hero" speech (which explains why a person is a hero in his or her community or culture). To use this pattern, the speaker first advocates criteria for heroism. Then the speaker shows why a specific person deserves to be considered a hero, based on those criteria. Here is how Jeanine used this approach in a speech about her cousin Kyle:

I. If a person overcomes serious hardship while maintaining an optimistic attitude, he or she is a hero.
II. My six-year-old cousin Kyle is a hero to me because he has maintained a positive outlook on life despite his parents' marital troubles and his father's cancer.

Categorical Pattern. If the main points you select do not fit any of the patterns mentioned thus far, another option is a **categorical pattern**. In this pattern, each main point explains a different aspect (category) of your topic. When you use this pattern, each main point should emphasize one of the most important features of your topic that you want the audience to understand. All of your main points must support the specific purpose of your speech. For example, Jodie was presenting an after-dinner speech on the environmental consequences of holiday shopping. She used a categorical pattern as follows:

I. Tons of garbage are generated by wrapping paper, envelopes, and packaging materials.
II. Thousands of barrels of gasoline pollute the air as we drive to the homes of friends and relatives who will make us feel guilty if we do not bring a present.
III. Volumes of nonbiodegradable plastics will end up in landfills once kids get bored with the toys they are given.
IV. Seriously, I hope you will remember to do your part to protect the environment during the holiday season.

Support the Main Points. Each main point on your outline must be developed with supporting material. Supporting material enables the audience to understand the points you are making and provides reasons why your points are true. As we explain in Chapter 9, you use a variety of information to develop main points, including examples, evidence, explanations, and visual aids.

When you outline your speech, organize your supporting information into **subpoints**, ideas that explain, elaborate on, or prove a main idea. They

View Elizabeth Glaser advocating a value judgment at the Democratic National Convention. CD-ROM: Video Theater, Excerpt 8.1

For more on entertainment as a rhetorical purpose, see page 127.

value judgment: an evaluation or label (such as *good* or *bad*) applied to the topic of a speech.

criteria: standards for making a value judgment.

categorical pattern: a speech structure in which each main point covers a different aspect of the topic.

subpoint: an idea that supports a main point.

are indicated by capital letters and are indented on your speech outline. If you develop a subpoint with two or more different ideas, each of these ideas is a **sub-subpoint**. They are indicated by Arabic numbers and are placed beneath the subpoint they support and are indented to the right. Typically, the number of subpoints and sub-subpoints ranges from two to four. The structure of your outline will look like this:

I. Main point one
   A. Subpoint one
      1. Sub-subpoint one
      2. Sub-subpoint two
   B. Subpoint two
      1. Sub-subpoint one
      2. Sub-subpoint two
      3. Sub-subpoint three
II. Main point two

When you organize your supporting materials into subpoints and sub-subpoints, keep in mind these guidelines.

Supporting Materials Must Relate to the Point You Are Making. **Subordination** is a key concept in outlining. Subpoints must relate to the main point they are supposed to support, and sub-subpoints must relate to the subpoint they are supposed to support.

Compare the materials supporting each main point in this outline of an informative speech on filmmaking in India:

I. Culture plays an important role in Indian filmmaking.
   A. Indian movie makers developed a style of their own by the 1950s, based on the teachings of *Natya Shastra (Science of Theater)*, a 1,000-year-old Hindu book. Entertainment was to embody nine essences: love, hate, sorrow, disgust, joy, compassion, pity, pride, and courage.[4]
   B. In the Indian culture, women are expected to be closely tied to their families. Thus female stars are often chaperoned by their mothers, who sit at the edge of the set.[5]
II. There are differences between Indian-made films and films made in the United States.
   A. In India, films need not follow the linear, scripted story line that is popular in Western movies. Of any 100 films made in India, about three will have scripts prepared in advance, according to screenwriter Anjum Rajabali.[6]
   B. Many Indian films do not address serious social issues. Director Shyam Bengal notes that mass cinema "is nothing more than a series of continuing sensations. New pictures are made to imitate whatever was most successful previously in order to mop up the largest audience."[7]

Notice that both subpoints for main point I pertain to the subject of that main point, the role of culture in Indian filmmaking. Then notice that only

Use your CD-ROM to draft materials to support your main points. Go to "Step 1 Invention/Generate Supporting Ideas." CD-ROM: Interactive Speech Guides

sub-subpoint: an idea that supports a subpoint.

subordination: making each unit of supporting information relevant to the main point or subpoint that it is intended to support.

one of the subpoints for main point II pertains to the subject of that main point. Subpoint B is not relevant to the idea that it is supposed to be supporting. It does not provide a reason why U.S.-made and Indian-made films are different. Indeed, you can probably think of many American-made films with little intellectual content.

How can you tell whether your supporting materials relate to the point they are supposed to be making? One good test is to complete the following sentence for each of your supporting points:

"This supports the point I am making because _____."

If you cannot come up with a logical way to complete this sentence, chances are good that the supporting idea is not relevant.

What can you do if you have supporting material that is important to include in your speech but it does not pertain to the main point or subpoint that you are developing? To include such information, find a different place in your speech where the information will fit, rewrite the main point to encompass the additional information, or develop that information into an additional main point. One of those techniques, rewriting a main point, was used to make both subpoints relevant in the following example, taken from a speech on carpooling. In the first example, subpoint B does not fit the subject of main point I. In the second example, the main point was rewritten (indicated by italics) to include the ideas in subpoint B.

First Example

I. Carpooling to school helps the environment.
   A. When fewer cars are driven to campus, pollution is reduced.
   B. When students carpool, they spend less money on gas and parking.

Second Example

I. Carpooling to school helps the environment *and your pocketbook.*
   A. When fewer cars are driven to campus, pollution is reduced.
   B. When students carpool, they spend less money on gas and parking.

Outlines Should Not Contain Single Subpoints or Sub-subpoints.   A traditional rule of outlining is that if you have one subordinate point, you must have a second. An outline with a single sub-subpoint would look like this:

   A. Belize is an interesting country to visit.
      1. The Howler Monkey Sanctuary is fascinating.

If you have only one supporting idea for a point you are making, fold it into the point itself. In the preceding example, you could combine the main point and subpoint as follows:

   A. The Howler Monkey Sanctuary in Belize is fascinating to visit.

If you do not want to merge a point and the supporting information, another option is to include a second item of support. In the preceding example, you could discuss another interesting place to visit in Belize. That place would be the basis of a second sub-subpoint:

A. Belize is an interesting country to visit.
   1. You can see humans and primates living in harmony at the Howler Monkey Sanctuary.
   2. You may find signs of the Americas' largest cat, the jaguar, at the Cockscomb Basin Sanctuary.

The Speech Guide chapters of this text give you ideas for choosing the best supporting materials for different types of speeches. Be sure that you understand what type of information is best to include, given the purpose of your speech.

Once your main points and supporting material are outlined, you are ready to insert organizing language that will make the structure of your speech as easy as possible for audience members to understand.

Insert Organizing Words and Sentences. As the author of your speech, you know what your main points are, when you are moving from one idea to another, and what part of the speech you are delivering at any point in time. However, without assistance from you, your audience will have difficulty keeping track of your organization. To see how difficult this task can be, watch a speech with two or three classmates. Separately, try to outline the speaker's main points. Unless the speech is very well organized, chances are good that you and your classmates' perceptions of the main points will differ.

To make the structure of your speech easy for audience members to follow, you must insert organizing words and sentences after you draft the content. The primary types of organizing language are *transitions, signposts,* and *internal previews and summaries.*

Transitions. A **transition** is a sentence that indicates you are moving from one part of your speech to the next. Transitions usually include an indication that you have completed one idea and an indication that you will be presenting a new idea. Here are some examples of transitions:

- Now that you have learned about wildlife sanctuaries in Belize, let me describe Mayan archaeological sites you can visit.
- The beaches of Belize are very beautiful, but wait until you discover the scenery in the rain forest.
- After a day of experiencing the countryside of Belize, you will be ready to sample the local cuisine at dinner.

Transitions are sentences that you insert into your speech outline. They are not a substitute for main points or for other parts of your speech. On your outline, you can indicate a transition by placing it in brackets:

[*Transition:* The food and scenery in Belize may be a new adventure, but you will find the language very familiar.]

View a student using transitions.
CD-ROM: Video Theater,
Excerpt 8.2

transition: a sentence indicating movement from one part of a speech to the next.

There are several places in your speech where it is important to provide a transition—for example, between the introduction and the body, between each main point, and between the final main point and the conclusion. You may want to insert additional transitions between major subpoints. Such extra transitions can be particularly helpful if you have a long subpoint and want to make sure that the audience knows when you are moving to the next subpoint.

Signposts.   **Signposts** are words or phrases within sentences that help the audience understand a speech's structure. Signposts in a speech serve the same function as their counterparts on a road. Highway signs inform drivers of direction and how the roads are organized; speech signposts inform audiences about the direction and organization of a speech.

You can use signposts to show you are at a specific place in your speech (for example, "to preview my main ideas," or "my third main point is," or "in summary"). You can also use signposts to help the audience realize the structure of your subpoints. For example, in a persuasive speech advocating educational reform, you might have a main point on the causes of poor student performance. You could write your subpoints with signposts as follows:

- *One cause* of educational failure is inadequate funding of public schools.
- *Another cause* is educators' low expectations for students.
- *An additional cause* of our schools' failure is that athletics receive higher priority than academics.

This type of signposting highlights each cause and makes it easier for the audience to understand and remember your analysis of the causes of inadequate student performances. Table 8.1 presents some examples of typical signposts.

Internal Previews and Internal Summaries.   You may have a main point that is supported by several different ideas or requires considerable detail to develop. To help the audience follow your explanation of this point, you may want to use an **internal preview**, a short listing of the ideas that will follow. Or to help the audience remember what you have just said, you might use an **internal summary**, a quick review of what you said on a main point.

In an informative speech on taking tests, suppose that one main point covers test preparation. You might begin that main point with an internal preview. On your outline, you would indicate the preview as follows:

II. Test preparation requires good planning and healthy living.
    [*Internal preview:* The four steps for test preparation that I will cover are: plan your study time in advance, follow your study schedule, get a good night's sleep, and eat a healthy breakfast.]
    A. Successful test taking requires advance planning.
    . . .

An internal summary is inserted in your outline at the end of a main point. In a persuasive speech on campaign finance reform, you might summarize a main point on proposed solutions as follows on page 193:

View Franklin D. Roosevelt using signposts during a "Fireside Chat." CD-ROM: Video Theater, Excerpt 8.3

View a student using an internal summary. CD-ROM: Video Theater, Excerpt 8.4

signpost: a word or phrase that helps the audience understand a speech's structure.

internal preview: a brief indication of ideas that will be presented in the next point.

internal summary: a brief review of ideas presented in a point just covered.

TABLE 8.1 Examples of Commonly Used Signposts

Here are examples of signposts (in italics) that you can use to help the audience follow the structure of your speeches. When preparing a speech, insert similar signposts.

To Indicate Your Speech Topic or Thesis

- *This afternoon, I hope to convince you that* [thesis].
- [Topic] *is what I will discuss today.*

To Indicate Credibility

- *My experience with* [topic] *includes* . . .
- *I am familiar with* [topic] *because* . . .

To Indicate That You Are Previewing Your Main Points

- Today, *I will stress the following contentions* . . .
- *There are three major reasons I will offer* to support my thesis . . .

To Indicate That You Are Making a Transition

- So *let's begin by considering* . . .
- *Now that you know* [main point *I*], *we can consider why* [main point *II*].

To Help the Audience Understand the Order and Structure of Points You Are Presenting

- *First* is the impact of . . . *Second* is the result of . . . *Third* is the outcome of . . .
- *One cause of* _____ *is* _____ . . . . *Another cause of* _____ *is* _____ . . . . *A further cause of* _____ *is* _____.

To Indicate the Importance of an Idea

- *If you only remember one idea,* it is _____.
- *The most troublesome consequence of* _____ is _____.

To Indicate That You Are Referring to a Research Source

- *According to* the *Washington Post National Weekly Edition,* October 13, 1997, "_____."
- In the periodical *Nature Watch,* in March of last year, ecologist Cheyenne Montez *reported,* "_____."

To Indicate That You Are Going to Present Supporting Material

- Why should you visit _____? *Let me show you* three fascinating reasons.
- I am opposed to _____. *Let me explain* the changes that I believe are needed.

To Indicate That You Are Ready to Conclude

- *In conclusion,* _____.
- *I hope you have seen* _____.

You should not begin a speech with a bald-faced lie. There are many effective ways to start. Choose the one that best gains audience attention.

[*Internal summary:* To review my proposed solutions: First, the government should require that all federal elections be publicly funded and establish a nonpartisan agency to enforce finance laws. Second, you, too, can be part of the solution by refusing to vote for candidates who accept large contributions.]

Once you have prepared the body of your speech and incorporated the appropriate organizing language, you are ready to draft the introduction.

● *Outlining Your Introduction*

Once you know what you will say in the body of your speech, you can prepare an effective introduction. The introduction supports your speech by preparing the audience to listen to your message. A good introduction accomplishes many purposes: it gains the audience's attention and interest, orients the audience to the purpose and structure of your speech, establishes your ethos, and connects your topic with the audience. All this and yet the introduction should not consume much more than one minute of a five-to-ten-minute speech!

You need to plan a beginning that is both efficient and effective. Place "Introduction" in large, bold letters at the start of your outline. Each of the five major components of your introduction (covered, in order, next) should be indicated with a Roman numeral (or a capital letter if your instructor prefers) on your outline.

Gain the Audience's Attention.   Begin with an **attention-getter**, content intended to gain audience members' interest. An audience is not ordinarily required to pay attention to a speech. Audience members are human, and when you stand up to speak, their interest may be focused elsewhere—contemplating their own problems or being distracted by a person or object in the room. The audience needs to be concentrating on you and your message if your message is to have an effect.

View a student presenting a complete introduction.
CD-ROM: Video Theater, Excerpt 8.5

attention-getter: content intended to gain the audience's interest at the start of a speech.

You can employ many strategies to gain the attention of your listeners. We discuss several of these options and provide examples of attention-getters in Figure 8.2.

Tell a Story or Anecdote That Relates to Your Topic.   People are often fascinated by stories. A convincing or interesting anecdote that embodies an important point of your speech *and can be presented in the available time* can make an effective beginning. The story should relate to your topic and seem believable. You lose credibility if audience members perceive that your story or anecdote is not realistic, so do not make up a story unless you disclose that it is a hypothetical example.

To review the ethical duty to be truthful, see page 59.

Begin with a Striking or Thought-Provoking Statement.   A significant fact or idea pertaining to your topic immediately pulls the audience into your speech. You may present a statistic showing the importance of your topic, or you may introduce the topic or thesis of your speech in a memorable way. The audience is more likely to be pulled into your speech if the information is new or if you use compelling language or examples. An idea that sounds like the "same old information" the audience has already heard will have less of an effect.

Build Up Suspense or Curiosity before Revealing Your Topic.   You may want to begin your speech in general terms, building audience suspense before you indicate the topic. For example, you might say you will address one of the biggest problems of the new century or will present one of the most exotic vacation spots in the world. Audience members' curiosity will be aroused, and they will listen attentively to satisfy their curiosity.

Establish Common Ground with Your Audience.   You may wish to begin by referring to important similarities between you and the audience. Audience members find persons who are more like themselves to be more credible speakers, and this type of introduction can also serve as an ice-breaker. However, for this type of introduction to be effective, the audience must perceive that there truly is common ground. Your credibility will nosedive if the audience believes you are falsely appealing to a shared interest or experience.

View Nelson Mandela incorporate humor while accepting the Congressional Gold Medal.
CD-ROM: Video Theater, Excerpt 8.6

Compliment the Audience.   Most people appreciate compliments. If you admire certain qualities of your audience members, sharing those feelings can be a good beginning. If your audience members belong to a specific group, or have some common positive trait (such as giving their time to serve the community), you can highlight those qualities to begin your speech. It is important that your compliments be heart-felt. If they seem insincere or contrived, your ethos will suffer.

TIP

If you begin on a humorous note, the joke should relate to the topic of your speech, and it should not be offensive to audience members.

Use Humor.   Most people enjoy a funny joke or amusing story. Humor can break the ice in a tense situation and cause both the speaker and the audience to relax.

Ask the Audience a Question.   A question can be an attention-gaining beginning because it calls for an active response by the audience. However, ask a question only if you are likely to get what you would consider a favorable

Rosie O'Donnell spoke at the Million Mom March in Washington, D.C., in 2000. Do you think mothers seeing her speak against guns perceived greater common ground with her because she, too, is a mother, or with politicians who speak out against guns? What if the politician did not have children?

answer. On the one hand, it would be a deflating experience to ask "Who wants to learn about the fascinating sport of curling?" and have no audience members indicate any interest. On the other hand, if you ask "What do you want to know about Winter Olympic sports?" you may get far more responses than you can incorporate into the available time. To be safe, you may wish to start your speech with a *rhetorical question,* a question you expect the audience to think of an answer to, without stating a response. An example of a rhetorical question is "What sport comes to mind when you think about the Winter Olympics?" This type of question invites the audience to consider your point but does not ask for an active response.

Begin with a Quotation.   A stimulating quotation that is relevant to your topic can be an effective beginning to a speech, especially if the quotation is from a person the audience likes and respects. Generally avoid a quotation from someone whom the audience does not find credible.

Use Your Audience Analysis to Choose the Most Effective Attention-Getter. The audience is the key factor to consider when selecting an attention-getter. For example, if your audience's *disposition* is unfavorable, you may want to begin by establishing common ground. If you need to build your audience's *interest* in your speech, an anecdote or suspense-building attention-getter can be effective. If audience members are likely to be tired because of the *time* of your speech, a good joke or a striking statement can pull them into your speech. For every speech, use critical thinking to determine which attention-getter will best spark interest.

For more on critical thinking, see page 17.

FIGURE 8.2   **Attention-Getting Techniques in Public Speeches**

Here are seven examples of introductions used by public speakers to capture the audience's attention. Which techniques are they using? Identify the techniques in the spaces provided; then check your answers against those provided at the end of the figure.

1. Vaclav Havel, beginning his address upon assuming the presidency of Czechoslovakia on New Year's Day, 1990.

My dear fellow citizens, for forty years on this day you heard from my predecessors the same thing in a number of variations: how our country is flourishing, how many millions of tons of steel we produce, how happy we all are, how we trust our government, and what bright prospects lie ahead of us. I assume you did not propose me for this office so that I, too, should lie to you.[1]

Technique(s): _____

2. Jane Alexander, chair of the National Endowment for the Arts, addressing the Economic Club of Detroit on the importance of investment in the arts in 1995.

As I prepared for this trip, I was reminded of an arts exhibition that I saw at Union Station in Washington, D.C., last year. A group of arts students took used Yugos—you remember those little cars from Yugoslavia—and had a fun time in the name of art. There was a Yugo turned on its fender and made into a giant cigarette lighter, there was a Yugo made into an accordion, and one painted in bright colors as a police car with a coin slot—25 cents a ride in the kiddy car. It's doubtful you'd see such a transformation of an American car. You know how to make serious cars here in Detroit.[2]

Technique(s): _____

3. Sojourner Truth, a former slave who became active in the antislavery and women's rights movements, addressing a women's convention in New York City in 1853. Her audience included many hecklers as well as supporters.

Is it not good for me to come and draw forth a spirit, to see what kind of spirit people are of? I am a citizen of the State of New York. I was born in the State of New York; and now I am a good citizen of this state. I was born here, and I can tell you I feel at home here.[3]

Technique(s): _____

4. Norm Bertasavage, member of the Branch Township Planning Commission, addressing a 1996 veterans' Memorial Day celebration in Llewellyn, Pennsylvania:

Thank you Commander Farrell, my fellow veterans, Honored Guest, ladies and gentlemen. I would like to begin this address by giving you a mathematical equation to take with you when you leave here today. That equation is $E = MC^3$. No, that is not an error, the one that says $E = MC^2$ is for geniuses. This one is for the rest of us....

It is an equation for effective government. The M stands for maturity because only people of maturity, no matter what their age, are needed for effective government. The three C's stand for Concern, Commitment, and Compassion.[4]

Technique(s): _____

5. Nancy Dickey, M.D., chair of the American Medical Association, addressing a professional development conference for women in 1996.

Good morning. How many of you had one of these dolls when you were growing up? Or if you have children—I know you recognize this bright pink package from Mattel.

But this particular toy is special, because she...is Dr. Barbie. And if I had room up here, I suppose I could also show you Air Force Pilot Barbie, Business Suit Barbie, Broker Barbie and...Ken.

Indicate the Topic or Thesis of Your Speech.   Once you have the attention of your audience members, tell them what you will be discussing. (See Figure 8.3 for an example of a newspaper headline that does both.) At this point, the primary question in listeners' minds is "What will this speech be about?" If they have to spend too much time pondering this question, you may lose their interest.

For examples of a topic sentence and a thesis, see pages 134–35.

We use the terms *topic statement* and *thesis* for this second part of your introduction because you have a thesis for a persuasive speech and a topic statement for other types of speeches. When you draft your outline, the thesis or topic statement is the second main part of the introduction section.

Present your topic statement or thesis in one sentence. It should be clearly signposted so that the audience has no doubts that you are indicating the topic and purpose of your speech. To see the uncertainty that a vague thesis or topic statement can cause, compare the following three alternatives:

FIGURE 8.2   Attention-Getting Techniques in Public Speeches *(continued)*

Now I'm not sure all of those dolls really exist—but they do make a point—That even in the merchandise-driven world of Mattel, what a woman chooses to be when she grows up—is a decision that is formed while she is growing up.[5]

Technique(s): _____

6. Anwar el-Sadat, president of Egypt, addressing the Israeli Knesset in 1970, ten days after he said he "would go to the ends of the earth" to pursue peace.

I come to you today on solid ground to shape a new life and to establish peace. We all love this land, the land of God; we all, Moslems, Christians, and Jews, all worship God. Under God. God's teachings and commandments are love, sincerity, security, and peace.[6]

Technique(s): _____

7. Myles Brand, president of Indiana University, delivering a speech on trends in higher education to the Economic Club of Indianapolis in 1997.

As the president of one of the largest universities in the country, I'm accustomed to reading reports by the dozen. But a recent one on developments in the labor force really caught my attention. It said that in California's Silicon Valley, software companies are adding 50,000 jobs a year at salaries that set a nation high average of about $70,000. And the North Carolina Biotechnology Center predicts that the state's biotech payrolls will climb as much as 100,000 during the next 20 years.

These figures may sound familiar; they come from *Time* magazine's January 20th cover story entitled, "Where the Jobs Are." Must reading for everyone in business and education.[7]

Technique(s): _____

Answers

1. striking statement
2. anecdote, complimenting the audience
3. common ground
4. building curiosity
5. asking a question, thought-provoking statement
6. common ground
7. thought-provoking statement

Source Notes:

[1] Havel, V. (1992). Playwright-dissident Vaclav Havel assumes the presidency of Czechoslovakia. In W. Safire (Ed.), *Lend me your ears: Great speeches in history* (pp. 629–634). New York: Norton.

[2] Alexander, J. (1996, January 15). Our investment in culture. *Vital Speeches, 62,* 210.

[3] Lipscomb, D. (1995). Sojourner Truth: A practical public discourse. In A. Lunsford (Ed.), *Reclaiming rhetorica: Women in the rhetorical tradition* (pp. 227–245). Pittsburgh: University of Pittsburgh Press.

[4] Bertasavage, N. (1996, August). War without end. *Vital Speeches, 62,* 632.

[5] Dickey, N. (1996, July 15). Our sisters' sickness, our sisters' satchels. *Vital Speeches, 62,* 582.

[6] Sadat, A. (1992). Egypt's president Anwar el-Sadat travels to Jerusalem to address Israel's Knesset. In W. Safire (Ed.), *Lend me your ears: Great speeches in history* (pp. 849–852). New York: Norton.

[7] Brand, M. (1997, April 15). Some major trends in higher education. *Vital Speeches, 63,* 402–405.

Attention-Getter

I. The tallest mountain in North America. Grizzly bears eating berries just ten feet from the road. Clean, fresh air that you will not find in "the lower 48."

Possible Topic or Thesis Statements

Option 1

II. All these features can be found in a pristine wilderness environment.

Option 2

II. You can find all these features in Denali National Park, Alaska, and *today I would like to tell you about the natural wonders of Denali.*

Option 3

II. You can find all these features in Denali National Park, Alaska, and *I hope to convince you to try a vacation in Denali.*

Option 1 does not clearly indicate the focus of the speech. Audience members will not know that the subject is Denali National Park, nor will they understand whether the speaker simply intends to describe a given

FIGURE 8.3

The Answer Is on the Tip of Many Tongues

We should be working to preserve the native languages of our immigrants

By Geoffrey Nunberg

PALO ALTO, Calif.

FBI director Robert Mueller exposed one of the most glaring deficiencies in our intelligence capabilities when he made a public appeal for translators of Arabic, Farsi and Pashto, which some people took as the occasion to criticize foreign-language programs in American schools and universities. If the war on terrorism awakens some students and school administrators to the importance of language study, so much the better. But it would be a mistake to lay responsibility for our lack of strategic language resources chiefly with schools or universities—or to believe they are in a position to rectify the problem.

We need instead to take advantage of the resources that the promise of America has brought to our shores—children who are growing up speaking those languages in cities across the country, from Alexandria, Va., and Brooklyn to San Francisco. The Census Bureau estimates that 40,000 Afghans are living in America, the majority of them ethnic Pashtuns, and others put the figures several times higher.

Our lack of linguistic expertise is not a new problem—nor one that will go away soon. The FBI has acknowledged that it could have had warnings of the 1993 World Trade Center bombing from intercepted tapes and notebooks in Arabic if it had had the resources to translate them; similarly, the United States could have known ahead of time about the 1998 nuclear tests in India and Pakistan if it had been able to translate information in its possession.

Foreign-language study in the United States is not suffering from nearly such a dramatic decline as some have suggested. True, the proportion of college students studying languages has dropped over recent decades, but that's largely because most of the growth in college enrollment has been in new programs that tend to give the traditional liberal arts curriculum less emphasis than older schools do. At elite universities, in fact, enrollment in language courses is up. At Stanford, it has increased 20 percent in the past decade.

What's more, a 1997 study by the Center for Applied Linguistics in Washington showed that the number of both public and private high schools offering foreign languages had held steady since 1987, and that the number of elementary schools offering languages had increased from 22 to 31 percent. Even more impressively, there has been a 50 percent increase in the number of elementary schools offering intensive or immersion programs aimed at developing true fluency in foreign languages. That is a sign that Americans are finally starting to learn what Europeans have known for a long time—that language mastery has to come early in life. But whether in Europe or America, the fact remains that most children learn

much use in screening intercepted phone calls between suspected terrorists.

What was really sad about the FBI's appeal for Arabic and Pashto translators is that, of all countries, the United States is not short of speakers of those languages, both in the form of recent immigrants and, more importantly, their bilingual children, who satisfy the citizenship and residency requirements that national security demands of its language experts.

In fact, given the broad linguistic backgrounds of American immigrants (the Department of Education estimates that more than 100 languages are spoken by students in the Fairfax County,

The English-only movement has encouraged the belief that assimilation necessarily involves giving up a foreign tongue. It leaves us in an odd position: We encourage the children of immigrants to become monolingual, then lament when there's no one available to translate the very languages these students grew up speaking.

OVER THE PAST CENTURY, AMERICA'S ATTITUDE toward foreign-language learning has changed several times. At the turn of the 20th century, more than 6 percent of American school-children were receiving most or all of their primary education in

An Arabic class at the Clara Mohammed School in Washington, D.C.

FILE PHOTO BY RICK BOWMER—THE WASHINGTON POST

This headline from the Washington Post *illustrates the first two components of an introduction: the attention-getter and the topic. The headline arouses the reader's curiosity, and the subhead indicates the main point of the article in one sentence.*

place, persuade them to take a vacation there, or discuss a general theme such as environmental protection.

Options 2 and 3 do more to orient the audience. Option 2 makes the topic apparent. The speech will be an informative message about the wonders of Denali. The focus will not be on visiting Denali; the audience will learn about the park without leaving their seats. Option 3, appropriate for a persuasive message, indicates that the speaker hopes to convince the audience to visit Denali.

Connect with the Audience. The audience needs to be interested in your speech; otherwise, they are unlikely to listen actively. If your topic might seem irrelevant or unimportant, you need to convince listeners that your message is worth their attention. A colleague of ours, Dr. Gail Sorenson, referred to this concept as "WIIFM" (whiff-em). By this she meant that audience members wonder "What's in it for me?"

TIP

When you outline your introduction, be sure that the second part clearly indicates the topic to your audience.

The third part of your introduction should therefore relate your subject to the audience's needs, interests, or feelings. In one sentence or a short paragraph, highlight why the audience should be interested in your speech. These ideas are not to be developed in detail during the introduction; you will do so in the body of the speech.

Here are some examples of how speakers can connect with the audience in the introduction:

Connecting with the audience conveys good will, an important part of ethos (see p. 38).

- Driving while intoxicated is not just a problem on somebody else's campus. According to the campus police chief, driving-while-intoxicated cases involving our students have increased by 45 percent since 1995.

- Many of you have probably not lost sleep over the potential deficit in our state's budget. It did not make my "Top Ten Worries" list either. But when I read that the governor proposed a 20 percent tuition increase as one means of making up the shortfall, I realized that it was time to worry.

- Today, I would like to present the history of the war between the United States and Mexico from a Mexican perspective, to provide you with an alternative to the romanticized version that many of you were taught in your high school history class.

- My survey showed that 87 percent of this class is tired of jokes about politicians and their interns. So today, let's take an entertaining look at the art of asking for a date.

Establish Your Credibility.   Once you have the audience's attention and listeners know what your speech is about, demonstrate that you are an appropriate person to deliver the message. Although you will include evidence from other sources in your speech, you also will present your own ideas and opinions. Why should the audience believe you? In the fourth component of your introduction, you can answer that question by indicating why you are a credible source of information about your topic.

How does a speaker demonstrate credibility, thereby strengthening his or her ethos? Many of the same characteristics that make an evidence source credible, such as experience, education, and research in the subject area of your speech, also make a speaker credible. Audience members also need to believe that they can trust you and that you have their best interests at heart.

To demonstrate credibility, you can explain how you have gained knowledge about the subject of your speech. Use only one or two sentences, and emphasize your most relevant credentials (the audience does not need your résumé or life history!). Your word choice should not indicate a feeling of superiority; if you have strong qualifications, it is appropriate to err on the side of modesty.

An appropriate demonstration of credibility was provided by Alexandra in her introduction to an informative speech about judging competitive ice skating. Having won nearly one hundred awards during her skating career, including a third-place finish at the National Junior Olympics, she was well qualified to speak on this subject. She had been certified to judge competitions and had been a judge at several prestigious events in her home state. She knew much more about her subject than any person in the audience.

Alexandra established her credibility in a clear but modest way:

> I have been active in the sport of ice skating since I was six years old, and won my fair share of events. I still love skating, so after retiring from competition, I became certified as a judge and have judged at many competitions during the past two years.

Alexandra's audience had no doubt that she was a good source of information on the sport of ice skating. She effectively summarized her experience without providing excessive detail about specific awards and specific competitions, which would have meant little to the audience.

There is one more important consideration when you are establishing your credibility. If you have any reason to be biased about the subject of your speech, you should disclose your bias to the audience. Your credibility as a speaker will be severely damaged if the audience discovers that you are not an objective source of information. The audience, however, will respect a person who is honest enough to reveal any biases, and your honesty will enhance their ability to make an informed decision about your message.

After demonstrating your credibility, you are ready for the final component of your introduction, the preview.

Preview the Main Points of Your Speech. The **preview** is a brief statement of the main points you will be developing to support your topic or thesis. The preview lets the audience know how your speech will be organized. Audience members will be cued for what main ideas to listen for and remember. They will find it easier to follow your speech if they know how you plan to approach the topic.

Consider how previews help you when you are a listener. In class, it is helpful if your professor indicates what will be happening on a particular day. If you are told, "Today I will finish lecturing on the War of 1812, go over your next assignment, and give you time to work in your groups," you know what to expect and can then give your attention to the lecture. You do not need to wonder (worry?) about whether directions on the next assignment will be forthcoming. A preview in your speech helps the audience in the same way.

Your preview is the final part of the introduction section of your outline. It should be brief, no more than a few sentences long. At this point in your speech, you are indicating the structure of your speech, not developing your ideas. You could simply note the main points in one sentence each or mention them all in one sentence.

When you refer to a single main point in your preview, avoid the use of *and* and other connecting words. In the preview of a speech introduction, a speaker might say, "I will cover Jason's high school coursework and his activities." The use of *and* makes it difficult to determine whether there is a single main point (high school) or two different ones (coursework and activities). If these concepts are subpoints for a single main point, it would be better to say, "I will cover Jason's high school years" in your preview of this main point.

To help the audience understand that you are previewing, it is also important to signpost in this part of your speech; otherwise, the audience may not realize that your main points are being previewed.

For more on the ethical duties to disclose bias and promote informed decision making, see pages 58 and 147.

preview: a brief statement of the main points to be developed in the body of a speech.

Consider the following two previews that could be used in a speech on judging ice skating.

Preview 1

V. The rules of judging, the ways you can judge, and the many controversies over Olympic judges are all interesting aspects of judging competitive skating.

Preview 2

V. Today, *three major topics* about judging competitive skating will be covered: *first,* we'll look at rules for judging the event, *followed by* tips you can use to score the performances yourself, and, *finally,* controversies in the judging at previous Olympics.

Both previews offer information about the main points to be developed. Preview one, however, is less explicit. The points are mentioned, but the audience is not alerted to listen for a preview of main points because there is no signpost. At best, the sentence hints that a preview may have been given. Preview two signals the speech structure clearly: the speaker uses the signpost "three major topics" to show that the main points of the speech are forthcoming. The speaker also uses the signposts "first," "followed by," and "finally" to make it easy for the audience to understand exactly what the main points will be.

In summary, the main components of a speech introduction are the attention-getter, topic or thesis statement, connection with the audience, credibility statement, and preview of main points. Remember that it is important to include a transition before you begin the first main point of your speech. Fitting all this information into one minute or so can be a challenge. The effort is worth your time, however, because audience members will be prepared to listen to your speech. Once your introduction is prepared, complete the speech by drafting your conclusion.

Recall: your entire introduction should generally last about one minute (see p. 193).

● *Outlining Your Conclusion*

The purpose of the conclusion of a speech is to wrap up the message developed in the body and leave an impression of the speech in audience members' minds. The conclusion is not the place to develop new ideas about the topic. Instead, the purpose is to summarize the main points and provide a memorable ending. Generally, try to conclude in one minute or less. Few sins of a speaker are worse than saying "In conclusion" and then continuing to speak for several more minutes. When you indicate that you are concluding, the audience expects that the speech is coming to an end. No matter how well written the end of your speech is, it will not achieve its objective if it is delivered to a frustrated audience who thought that the speech would be over minutes ago.

Provide a Transition to Your Conclusion.   After presenting your final main point, insert a transition that underscores that you are finished with the body and ready to wrap up your presentation. Your transition should use signposting to make it clear that you are finishing. A persuasive speech on

THE WIZARD OF ID   **Brant parker and Johnny hart**

When you say "In conclusion," you need to conclude. Your audience will be expecting you to wrap up your speech.

To review signposts, see page 200.
To review previews, see page 191.

donating blood might have this transition (signposts noted in italics): "I hope *you have been convinced* that volunteer donors are literally the lifeblood of our community's hospitals. *In conclusion,* please keep this in mind...."

After inserting a transition to the conclusion in your outline, place the word "Conclusion" in large, bold letters at the start of this section of your outline.

Summarize Your Main Points.

The first part of your conclusion is a **summary**, a brief review of your main points. The summary is similar to the preview of main points in the introduction. A summary may be one compound sentence that reviews all of your main points and restates your topic or thesis, or you may restate the topic and main points using complete sentences for each. In either case, your goal is to remind the audience of your main ideas one last time. An effective summary increases the likelihood that audience members will remember your message because it helps them put your speech together in their own minds. For an example of a summary, see the "conclusion" section of the sample outline on page 207.

Be sure that your summary includes each main point. Avoid the mistake of reiterating a few favorite subpoints from the body of your speech; instead, focus on main points. Remember that two reasons for having main points are (1) to break the speech down into manageable sections for audience members to process and (2) to help the audience understand the structure of the speech. Your main points will seem less important if the summary does not focus on them.

> **TIP**
>
> *When you draft your outline, check the summary to be sure that each main point is clearly included.*

Finish with a Memorable Clincher.

The final thought you present should indicate the "bottom line" of your speech—that is, what you most want the audience to do or remember. This ending, or **clincher**, needs to leave a lasting impression of the speech in the minds of your listeners. After your speech ends, audience members will have countless demands on their time and attention. If your speech is to be memorable, the clincher must be carefully considered and effectively worded.

The clincher—the second item in the conclusion section of your outline—should take up no more than thirty seconds in a typical five-to-ten-

summary: a brief review of the main points that were covered in the body of a speech.

clincher: an ending intended to leave a lasting impression of a speech.

minute speech. There are several types of clinchers you can use to end your speech.

Tie Your Ending to Your Introduction.   If you begin your speech with an anecdote or example, it is often possible to extend that example to reinforce your message when you conclude your speech. A persuasive speech asking audience members to serve as volunteer tutors began with the story of Hector, a twelve-year-old at risk of dropping out of school because he had fallen behind his classmates. The clincher used the story of Hector effectively:

> Remember Hector, the boy who was on the verge of dropping out in sixth grade. A student at this university named Ana became his tutor and role model. Today Hector has a B average in high school and has applied to several colleges. There are many more Hectors in our local schools, and your help as a tutor will make sure that there is a happy ending to their stories as well.

View a student presenting a memorable clincher in a conclusion.
CD-ROM: Video Theater, Excerpt 8.7

End with a Striking Sentence or Phrase.   There may be a single sentence or phrase that effectively sums up your speech. Advertisers often use simple slogans because they are easy to remember. For example, a product is referred to as "The one," or a candidate is said to possess "the right stuff for the job." We do not recommend that a speaker end with a trivial phrase or a catchy tune, but often a speaker can craft memorable language that does relate to the speech.

One example is the conclusion of Kathy's informative speech about the mental health benefits of running. She ended with this clincher:

> So I hope you will remember that running is not just good for your body, but it is also great for your mind.

Here is another example. Shaeng's speech about Hmong history effectively concluded with a theme that had been evident in each main point:

> The name Hmong means "free." And no matter what continent we are living on, that is what we will always be—a free people.

Conclude with an Emotional Message.   When a speaker touches your feelings, that message will have more impact than cold hard facts alone. Often, an emotional thought makes a speech memorable. This type of ending is particularly effective in a persuasive or commemorative speech. Gus concluded a tribute to a pet in this way:

> My mind flooded with memories: finding him as a tiny kit and nursing him to health with my own hands. He became my best friend. I let him go lovingly, with the same arms that held him fast as a baby. Good-bye my friend—I'll never forget you.

End with a Story or Anecdote.   A story that exemplifies the message of your speech can be an effective conclusion that your audience will remember. The story or anecdote must be credible. The following story of Albert Einstein was an effective clincher in a speech advocating greater efforts to raise students' self-esteem and prevent them from dropping out:

Over one hundred years ago, there was a boy who was considered "backward" by his teachers. They said the boy was mentally slow and adrift forever in his foolish dreams. His father said that when he asked the headmaster what profession his son should adopt, he was told, "It doesn't matter, he'll never make a success of anything."[8]

Who was that hopeless student? Believe it or not, his name was Albert Einstein. We must never give up on the mind of a child. Educators must convince every student that he or she is valued and capable of learning. Not a single dropout should be acceptable.

Use your audience analysis and specific purpose to choose the clincher that will make your speech memorable. For example, if you began your speech with an anecdote that is highly relevant to the audience, it would be effective to tie that beginning to your conclusion. If you have a quotation from a person who is highly regarded by your audience, that would make an effective ending. If you want the audience to take action, an emotional message might inspire them to act. If you want the audience to remember a particular theme from your speech, a striking sentence that captures that theme will work well.

If you follow the steps recommended in this chapter (see p. 217 for a checklist), you will have a complete outline of your speech once the conclusion is drafted (your instructor may require you to append a bibliography to your outline). You can use this outline as you practice your delivery and become more familiar with your message. If you use a word processor to draft your outline, save that file so you can make later corrections and revisions easily. Your outline also will be the basis for the shorter extemporaneous outline (described later in this chapter) that you will use when speaking.

When you are drafting an outline, it is often helpful to have an example to refer to. In the next section we present an annotated sample outline. The CD-ROM includes software that you can use to customize a template for outlining the speeches you prepare.

A Sample Linear Speech Outline

Robin McGehee of William Carey College represented Mississippi in the 1996 Interstate Oratorical Competition. Her speech, "A Deadly Mistake," advocated steps that should be taken to reduce prescription drug errors. What follows is an outline of Robin's speech, accompanied by annotations that highlight the concepts of organizing and outlining discussed in this chapter.

Your instructor may require a "specific purpose" statement. The speech itself begins with main point I of the introduction.

A Deadly Mistake

Specific Purpose: To persuade my audience that prescription drug errors are a serious health threat in the United States, requiring their own efforts to reduce the problem, accompanied by new governmental policies.

Introduction

Robin begins with an anecdote to gain the audience's attention.

I. On July 15, 1994, Megan McClave was admitted for tonsillectomy surgery as an outpatient. Four days later, Megan was dead. As stated in the May 1995 issue of *Ladies' Home Journal,* her death was not caused by the surgeon or the nurse. This academically gifted girl died because a pharmacist with nearly thirty years of experience made a deadly mistake. He filled a prescription for the painkiller Demerol with a bottle of Roxanol, describing it to Megan's father as a generic substitute. The prescription label read: "Dispense two to three teaspoons every four hours as needed." In reality, Roxanol is a brand name for morphine and is supposed to be dispensed in tiny drops, typically to critically ill patients. Megan followed the directions on the label, eventually swallowing enough morphine to shut down her respiratory system. Everyone makes mistakes, right? Perhaps. But this was a deadly mistake that could have been avoided.

II. Today, I hope to convince you, as consumers, to personally act to reduce prescription drug errors, and to support government policies that reduce these errors.

III. After my library and interview research revealed that Megan's tragedy was only the tip of the iceberg, I became determined to convince my audiences that they, too, are at risk, but that they can act to avoid these deadly mistakes.

IV. Today, let's consider the consequences of drug errors, some of the causes of these errors, and finally, address some urgent and immediate solutions to this lethal dilemma.

[*Transition:* Let's start by analyzing how serious the problem of prescription drug errors is.]

Body

I. The consequences of prescription drug errors can lead healthy patients to become dead patients.

   A. Megan's case is not rare. The December 1994 issue of *Prevention Magazine* notes that currently "about 10% of all hospital admissions are due to problems with medications."

   B. *USA Today* reported on October 3, 1995, that prescription drug–related problems cost an estimated $75.6 billion in medical bills each year.

   C. Deaths are an even more tragic cost.

      1. It is estimated in the December 21, 1994, *Journal of the American Medical Association* that "180,000 people die each year, partly as a result of prescription drug errors, the equivalent of three jumbo-jet crashes every two days."

      2. The November 23, 1992, issue of *Drug Topics* provides an example of needless loss: "an elderly woman was given a prescription for acetazolamide to treat her glaucoma. What she received from the pharmacist was hypoglycemic acetohexamide. As a result, she lapsed into a coma and died 12 days later."

[*Transition:* Drug errors are causing needless death and suffering. Why do these deadly mistakes continue?]

II. The causes of prescription drug errors are many.

   A. One cause is a lack of reporting requirements.

      1. In the United States, only one state, North Carolina, requires that deaths due to prescription errors be reported. What that

The source of the anecdote is included.

Credibility and connecting with the audience are included in main point III of the introduction.

The signpost "Today, let's consider" cues the audience to a preview of the speech.

Transition from the introduction to the body.

Sources are cited when research material is used to support a point.

Subpoints and sub-subpoints are indented and relate to the point they support.

The three main points have parallel wording—the _____ (consequences, causes, and solutions) of prescription drug errors.

means is that if you or I needed a prescription filled while at this tournament [the Interstate Oratorical Contest], and the local pharmacist filled the prescription wrong, causing a death, there would not have to be a report to indicate that the death was caused by a pharmacist's mistake.

2. The lack of reporting means that many mistakes are kept secret. According to an interview with an attorney involved in litigation against Eckerd Corporation, in the January 23, 1995, issue of *Drug Topics, confidential* Eckerd documents showed there were "almost 10,000 reported misfilled prescriptions over five years in its stores in Louisiana, Oklahoma, and Texas."

3. When drug errors are not reported, we receive no explanation of why or how a pharmacist could confuse Demerol with the deadly Roxanol. The pharmacist remains licensed to practice and is able to make more mistakes in the future. There is no explanation of how this problem could have been prevented. We cannot save Megan and the many other patients who die each year unless we learn from pharmacist mistakes and implement precautionary measures.

The terms "One," "Another," and "Additional" signpost each subpoint on the cause of the problem.

B. Another cause is the trust we place in medical care professionals.
1. Persons in the health care professions are among the most trusted individuals in our society.
2. The question is whether we, the patients, have come to trust these human beings too much. Pharmacists, like other workers, can get tired on the job. The job may become routine, they may be distracted, or they may assume that someone else is taking care of the job.
3. *Drug Topics* magazine, November 23, 1992, reported an example of what can happen when we simply assume that our prescription is correct: "A prescription of methotrexate with confusing dosage instructions was filled by a pharmacist. Although he had doubt, the pharmacist did not phone the physician or ask the patient why she was taking the powerful chemotherapy drug prescribed. He assumed she had cancer. She took the drug daily. The error was discovered by another pharmacist when she returned for a refill, but it was too late. Three days later, she died."

C. Additional causes of drug errors exist. They include pharmacist confusion of drugs with similar names, doctors' handwriting that is difficult to read, patients who have no patience with the drug-dispensing process, and shorthanded pharmacies plagued by interruptions and distractions while dispensing prescriptions.

The transition links main point II to main point III.

[*Transition:* We have seen that there are many causes of drug errors, but are there solutions that will save the lives of people who just want to feel better? The answer is yes.]

III. The solutions to prescription drug errors depend on both individual and government efforts.

A. First, drug errors should be reported.

The words "First," "Second," "Third," and "Fourth" signpost the four components of the solution.

1. We, as customers of the health care profession and citizens of the United States, should ask our congressional representatives to pass the Safe Medications Bill of 1995.

2. This bill will improve public health and safety by creating a clear and uniform reporting system for deaths that occur while prescribing, administering, or dispensing drugs. Needless tragedies would be reported and future accidents avoided.

3. According to the June 22, 1995, *Congressional Record,* Representatives Coyne, Lewis, and Stark reintroduced this bill, but the bill does not have enough public support.

4. In a phone conversation with Representative Coyne, I learned that if more public support can be shown, he will guarantee that our voices will be heard. After this speech, I will pass out a ready-to-sign petition. With your signature added, we can send that voice that is desperately needed to Washington.

B. Second, drug errors should be investigated and acted on.

1. We cannot expect a problem to go away if we do not help or reprimand the person who is the cause.

2. If a police officer wrongly shoots a person, that officer is suspended until a formal investigation is conducted. Why should it be different if a pharmacist's negligence takes the life of an innocent patient?

3. Even if the pharmacist is not at fault, there should be an investigation to determine how the problem could be prevented in the future.

C. Third, drugs that can be lethal should be labeled with a fluorescent color. The color would warn the pharmacist to be certain that the drug is dispensed correctly and that patients are counseled in its proper use.

D. Fourth and finally, I will distribute a wallet-sized card provided by the American Pharmacy Association. The card features reminders of action you can take to reduce the risk of drug error. These actions include:

1. Write down the name, dose, and purpose of the drug when it is prescribed;

2. introduce yourself to the pharmacist;

3. read the prescription label carefully to be certain that you have received the proper drug; and

4. ask the pharmacist any questions you have, and get a phone number you can call if you have questions later.

5. Use this card as a quick reference when having a prescription filled, and it may save your life or the life of a loved one.

[*Transition:* In conclusion, I hope that you have become more aware of the prescription drug error problem in the United States.]

Conclusion

I. Today, we have discussed the deadly consequences of drug errors, focused on some causes of these errors, and addressed immediate solutions to this lethal dilemma. The prescription errors that pharmacists are making are serious, but the bright side to this problem is that with careful steps, we can do much to reduce these deadly mistakes.

II. Remember Megan McClave and her family, and how a young life was lost because of a deadly mistake that could have been avoided. If the pharmacist had been more careful, or Megan's family had known the

Use of "have become" in transition signals that the speaker is about to wrap up her speech.

The main points of the speech are efficiently summarized.

The clincher refers to the anecdote from the introduction and leaves the audience with a challenge.

right questions to ask, this girl would be alive today. Are you going to take these questions and use them the next time you or a loved one need a prescription filled, or will you walk out the door without them? Let's not allow these needless deaths to continue.

References

Conlan, M. (1995, May). Spotlight r. ph's under critical media eye. *Drug Topics, 139,* 44-45.

Coyne, W. (1995, June 22). Extensions of remarks. *Congressional Record, 104,* E1321.

Leape, L. (1994, December 21). Error in medicine. *Journal of the American Medical Association, 272,* 1851.

McLellan, D. (1995, May). Megan won't wake up. *Ladies' Home Journal, 112,* 132.

Prescription misuse costs nation billions. (1995, October 3). *USA Today,* D4.

Vickens, C. (1992, November 23). Breaking the trust. *Drug Topics, 136,* 58-62.

Research sources are fully cited in the references section. Check with your instructor to see what format he or she prefers for citations.

Remember that you should also identify the source during your speech—not just in the references list—when you refer to material you have researched.

The organizational structure of speeches we have considered up to this point in Chapter 8, including Robin McGehee's speech, "A Deadly Mistake," has been linear. Several characteristics of the linear organization are evident in Robin's speech:

1. The thesis of Robin's speech is presented in the introduction, and her main ideas are previewed.
2. Robin has three explicit main points in this speech, all of which support her thesis.
3. The structure of Robin's speech is made apparent through signposts and transitions.
4. Robin specifically indicates the actions she hopes the audience and the government will take.

In the next section of this chapter we discuss alternatives to the linear organization and consider when you and your audience may benefit from a nonlinear format.

Alternatives to Linear Organization

We describe three patterns that can be used instead of a thesis-support linear organization. The *deferred-thesis, web,* and *narrative* patterns are commonly discussed as alternatives to the linear format in the field of public speaking. *Audience disposition* and the *cultures* represented in your audience (see In Theory box 8.1) may influence your choice of patterns.

● *Deferred-Thesis Pattern*

deferred-thesis pattern: a speech structure in which the thesis is first revealed toward the end of the speech.

In a **deferred-thesis pattern**, your main points build to the thesis, but you do not indicate that thesis until near the end of your speech.

Deferring the statement of your thesis may be the best strategy if you are speaking to a hostile audience. When you face this type of audience, giving the thesis in the introduction can be counterproductive, because audience members may react negatively when they hear it and stop listening attentively to your speech. Even if you offer a strong justification for the position you are taking, the audience may not listen actively because your thesis has turned them off. Therefore, you may wish to present your reasoning first and then state the thesis later in your speech.

For more on barriers to effective listening, see page 74.

Consider the example of Olivia Echeverria-Bis, a student whose persuasive speech asked audience members to reduce or eliminate their milk consumption. If her audience analysis revealed that many members were regular milk drinkers who initially would react negatively to this idea, she could vary from the linear pattern. If Olivia used a deferred-thesis pattern, the thesis and preview sections of her introduction would change as follows:

	Linear Organization	**Deferred-Thesis Pattern**	
Attention-getter	I. No species except humans drinks milk beyond infancy and no other species naturally drinks the milk of a different species.	I. [Same attention-getter]	
Thesis	II. Today, I hope to convince you to join with the animal kingdom and stop drinking milk.	II. Today, we will explore the issue of milk consumption by humans.	*State topic without revealing thesis*
Credibility	III. I have researched the opinions of medical professionals in the library and on the Internet.	III. [Same credibility]	
Connect with the audience	IV. On your surveys, 82 percent of the class indicated an interest in having a healthier diet.	IV. [Same words to connect with the audience]	
Preview	V. Today we will discuss the health risks of milk, the reasons that milk is unhealthy, and the advice of doctors who recommend the elimination of milk from our diets.	V. Today we will discuss how milk is produced and how production methods affect humans, and we will consider alternate dietary sources for calcium and vitamin D.	*Preview, note main points, do not reveal thesis*

If Olivia used a deferred-thesis pattern, her first two main points would be the problem and cause, just as they would be with a problem-cause-solution pattern. She would show possible health risks caused by milk consumption and then would consider the causes of these risks. Her third main

To review the problem-cause-solution pattern, see page 186.

point, however, would differ from one pattern to the other. With a linear format, the title of the main point indicates her specific objective, "We should eliminate milk from our diets." The supporting points would elaborate on this proposal. With a deferred thesis, the main point could be titled "Potential alternatives to milk in our diets." Her subpoints could build up to the thesis, which would be revealed in the last subpoint. Olivia might develop her third point this way:

A. Alternative sources for calcium and vitamin D are readily available.
B. Medical experts recommend the use of alternative sources rather than milk.
C. You should use these alternatives and eliminate milk from your diet.

● Web Pattern

When a speech is organized in a **web pattern**, each main point reflects or elaborates on a core idea.[9] At the end of each main point, the speaker briefly discusses how that point relates to the core idea. The metaphor of a web is apt because each main point links back to a core idea much as strands are woven out from the center of a web.

Figure 8.4 and the outline of the body of Olivia's speech, which follows, show how Olivia's speech on milk could be organized in a web pattern. Notice how each main point relates back to the core idea.

FIGURE 8.4   The Web Organizational Pattern

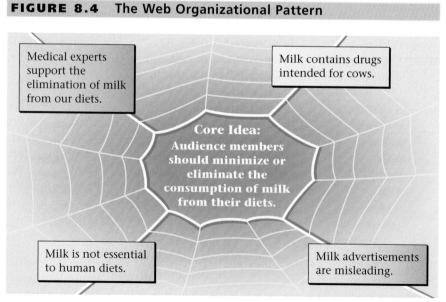

In a web organizational pattern, each of the main points relates back to the core idea of the speech.

web pattern: a speech structure in which each main point is related back to a core idea.

Outline of the Body of Olivia's Speech

Core idea: Audience members should minimize or completely completely eliminate milk from their diets.

Body

I. Milk contains drugs intended for cows.
   A. For years, cows could graze for food.
   B. Now, many cows are crowded into pens and are given growth hormones, antibiotics, and tranquilizers.
   C. Drugs administered to cows harm humans.
      1. The drugs get into the milk we buy.
      2. The drugs cause colic and intestinal bleeding in infants.
      3. The drugs cause food allergies, ear infections, juvenile diabetes, and multiple sclerosis.
   D. Because the drugs intended for cows are getting into our milk supply and causing disease, you should reduce your milk consumption.
II. Milk advertisements are misleading.
   A. The dairy industry incorrectly claims that it is natural for humans to drink cows' milk.
   B. The U.S. Department of Agriculture promotes milk consumption because it wants to reduce the government's milk surplus.
   C. You should not be fooled by pro-milk advertising. Reduce your consumption of milk.
III. Milk is not essential to human diets.
   A. There are alternative sources of calcium.
   B. There are alternative sources of Vitamin D.
   C. Because you can obtain the nutrients found in milk from sources that are not contaminated with drugs, you should reduce milk consumption.
IV. Medical experts support the elimination of milk from our diets.
   A. Many experts agree that we should stop drinking milk.
   B. Because medical experts recommend the elimination of milk from our diets, take good care of yourself and follow their advice.

● *Narrative*

A **narrative** tells a story. A speech that is a narrative does not have a traditional, explicit thesis supported by developed main points. Instead, you support your thesis with a story, using one or more characters. Your narrative may have heroes, villains, or victims. Your story should feature a plot and build to a climax that conveys the main idea of your speech to audience members. The audience should be able to determine your thesis intuitively from the story and see how the story demonstrates that the thesis is true. Typically, a high-context audience (see In Theory box 8.1) will be better able to figure out the claims of a narrative and ascertain the thesis of your speech. It is important to supply cues that help the audience decode your message.

For example, suppose you want to persuade your audience that smoking should be prohibited. Your narrative could tell the story of a close friend or relative who was a smoker and died of cancer. You would need to assume that your audience is familiar with the scientific evidence linking tobacco to various health risks and that they would understand from the context of your story that you are advocating a ban on cigarettes.

narrative: a speech organized as a story, using characters and a plot to convey the message.

INVENTION	ORGANIZATION	STYLE	PREPARATION	DELIVERY

In Theory 8.1

WHEN THE AUDIENCE PREFERS A NONLINEAR FORMAT

The linear format has been emphasized in many public speaking courses in the United States. However, scholars analyzing diverse languages have identified differences in the manner in which topics are developed in the world's cultures. The "correct" method of organizing ideas in one culture may be perceived as illogical, unclear, and even discourteous in other cultures.[10] Scholars also have identified different organizational preferences among men and women.[11] Here we consider two differences that may influence how you organize your speech.

High-Context and Low-Context Cultures. In mainstream Western culture, respect for the audience obliges a speaker to make the message so precise that the audience can follow it with little effort.[12] Such precision is not the norm in all cultures, and one reason for the difference is that some cultures are *low context* and others are *high context*. In a **low-context culture**, the message is primarily communicated through the speaker's words.[13] In a **high-context culture**, audiences obtain meaning not only from the speaker's words but also from the communication context and cultural norms.[14] In a high-context culture, a speaker may talk around a point but provide listeners with the information they need to understand what the speaker intends. It is the audience's responsibility to determine the meaning based on these clues or shared understandings of their culture. It may even be considered rude to tell the listener the specific point being made.[15]

Suppose, for example, a speaker's thesis is that audience members should ride a bicycle or walk to school. In a low-context culture, the speaker would indicate that thesis in the introduction, and the main points would provide reasons why this action is desirable. In a high-context culture, the speaker would be less likely to present a thesis. The first two points could show that the environment is at risk and explain how automobiles are a major cause of pollution, congesting the campus. A third point could indicate that individuals in the audience members' culture have a long tradition of living in harmony with nature. From this information, the audience would realize that the speaker is advocating a change from automobiles to environment-friendly transportation.

High-context cultures include the Japanese, Chinese, Korean, and Arab. German, Swiss, and Scandinavian cultures are at the opposite end of the spectrum.[16] Within the United States, Anglo-Americans (particularly men)[17] tend to fall in the low-context range, and Native Americans[18] and African Americans[19] are higher-context. Latin American cultures are also high context.[20]

If many people in your audience are members of high-context cultures, a narrative pattern or web pattern (pp. 210–11) is often an effective arrangement choice.

Digression from the Thesis or Purpose. Cultures vary in their expectation that a communicator will remain focused on the thesis or topic. In the Hindi language, a paragraph often digresses to several different thoughts rather than developing one unified thought.[21] For over two thousand years, a "bush-clearing pattern" has been used in China. According to Fan Shen, this entails "clear[ing] the surrounding bushes before attacking the real target... before touching one's main thesis, one should first state the conditions of composition: how, why, and when the piece is being composed."[22]

If you decide to include a main point that would seem "irrelevant" in a traditional thesis-support format, that decision should be based on *audience* preferences or expectations. Here are some examples of main points that audience members might expect a speaker to address before developing the main topics or thesis of a speech.

- Begin with a main point covering your experience with the subject of the speech. This approach could be appropriate if you need to elaborate on your credibility before the audience will accept the ideas you are presenting, or if the audience wonders what your connection to the topic is.

- Begin with a main point discussing why you decided to present a speech on this topic. If you have any bias on the topic, it should be disclosed.

- Begin with a main point addressing the audience's reservations about the topic or perspective you are advocating. This analysis would be important if your audience analysis indicated that audience members would not be receptive to your ideas until you addressed their concerns.

To see how the linear organization and narrative differ, compare the following abbreviated outlines on the topic of prohibiting cigarettes:

Linear Organization	**Narrative**
Introduction	**Introduction**
I. Attention-getter (Endearing story about Aunt Amanda)	Aunt Amanda was my favorite aunt. She always had time to talk to me, and although she was fifty-six when I was seventeen, she understood what it was like to be a teenager. She never attended college, but she kept telling me that I would be the first person in our family to get a degree.
II. Thesis (Cigarettes should be prohibited.)	
III. Credibility	
IV. Connect with the audience.	
V. Preview	
Body	**Body**
I. Cigarette smoking is hazardous to your health.	I. I called Aunt Amanda when I got an A on my first college essay. She tearfully told me that she had been diagnosed with lung cancer and did not have long to live.
II. Tobacco company advertising hooks new addicts.	II. Aunt Amanda had been a heavy smoker since she was my age. The models in magazine and television ads seemed so glamorous when they smoked. So my aunt started smoking, and although she tried, she could never quit.
III. The federal government should prohibit smoking.	III. Aunt Amanda got so mad at me when I was caught smoking at school. She said that if it was up to her, smoking would be outlawed like any other dangerous drug. She told me that it was not as glamorous as those ads make it seem, and that once you get started, it is impossible to stop.
Conclusion	**Conclusion**
I. Summary	I. Now my Aunt Amanda will never see me graduate from college. I miss her so much. But I will always be thankful that she encouraged me to go to college.
II. Clincher (Smoking killed my Aunt Amanda, but if we outlaw smoking, other families will be spared the loss I have felt.)	II. And I am even more thankful for her life-saving message: "Smoking kills like any other dangerous drug, and there ought to be a law against this hazardous product."

low-context culture: a culture in which the speaker's words are the primary factors in communicating and understanding a message.

high-context culture: a culture in which context and cultural norms are key factors in communicating and understanding a message.

As this discussion of alternatives to the linear format shows, there are diverse methods you can use to organize your ideas. Whether you use a linear organization or a different approach, remember: ***Good organization makes the message clear.*** Choose the method of organization that best enables your audience to understand your speech.

Preparing an Extemporaneous Outline

In most public speaking contexts, your speech will be more effective if you use *extemporaneous delivery*. Recall from Chapter 2 that this means you speak from limited notes, rather than from a word-for-word manuscript. To speak extemporaneously, you need to prepare an **extemporaneous outline**. This outline consists of limited notes to remind yourself of the key parts of your speech, and it is considerably shorter than the outline you create when preparing your speech. You prepare an extemporaneous outline after practicing your speech several times and becoming familiar with the ideas on your detailed outline. You then use it for your final practices and for delivering your speech.

● *The Form of an Extemporaneous Outline*

Speakers prepare extemporaneous outlines on note cards or on regular 8½-by-11-inch paper. Remember that the purpose of this outline is to remind yourself of the key ideas in your speech. Therefore, it should be easy for you to use it as a reference during your presentation. If you use a word processor, double-space your outline using a large font size (14 or 16 point) that will be easy to see. If you write your outline on note cards, be sure to write neatly and leave space between each line. If you cram too much information onto note cards, it will be difficult to find the points you are looking for while speaking.

Structure your extemporaneous outline much like your detailed outline. Indent subordinate points below the ideas they support, and use Roman numerals, capital letters, and numbers. This setup will help you to visualize the structure of your speech while you are presenting it. Number each note card or page of your notes.

● *The Content of an Extemporaneous Outline*

When you prepare an extemporaneous outline, your goal is to condense your speech notes but retain enough information to remind yourself of what you intend to say. Here are a few suggestions to help you decide what to write down.

Main Points and Subpoints. Write each main point in a complete sentence or a very detailed phrase. Also note subpoints in a way that will bring to mind the *idea* you want to express as you deliver your speech. Use key words or phrases that will make sense to you if you glance at them during your speech. Remember that your goal is to convey each idea (subpoint) to

---

See pages 215 and 204 to compare a sample extemporaneous outline with a complete outline.

TIP

Be sure that your notes are in the proper order before you deliver your speech.

extemporaneous outline: a brief outline that reminds a speaker of the speech structure, key ideas to be developed, presentation tips, and evidence quotations.

the audience in a conversational manner. Your goal is not to repeat the wording of your detailed outline every time you deliver your speech.

Sub-Subpoints.   You do not need to include every sub-subpoint in your extemporaneous outline. If you feel comfortable explaining a subpoint in your own words, leave the sub-subpoints out of your outline. This will make your delivery more conversational. If you have a long subpoint, you may wish to include a brief phrase as a reminder of what each sub-subpoint will be.

Evidence.   When you use evidence, you need to quote your sources accurately. Therefore, direct quotations are one type of information that you should insert word-for-word on your outline.

Difficult Words.   If you use words that are difficult to pronounce or remember, include them on your outline. For example, in Robin McGehee's sample extemporaneous outline which follows, the complex names of medications such as acetazolamide are included.

Transitions.   Include a brief reminder of each transition in your speech. These need not be word-for-word in your extemporaneous outline, but they should serve their purpose as a bridge from one idea to the next.

Reminders.   In the margin of your outline, jot down reminders to aid yourself in delivery. For example, write "Slow down" if you tend to speak too fast, "Eye contact" if you tend to look down, or "Key point" if you want to emphasize a particular idea. If you are using visual aids, include reminders such as "Cover when done." Such reminders can be circled or written in a different color from the outline itself so they stand out.

> For more on the importance of conversational delivery, see pages 289–90.

> **TIP**
>
> *Use a different color of ink for evidence, difficult words, or other ideas that you want to stand out.*

> For tips on using visual aids, see Chapter 12.

A Sample Extemporaneous Outline

Here is an extemporaneous outline of Robin McGehee's speech, "A Deadly Mistake." Compare this outline with her detailed outline (see pp. 204–208), and notice how Robin condensed the information.

Introduction
I. Megan McClave anecdote
   —experienced pharmacist gave her Roxanol (morphine), not Demerol
II. Thesis—individual and govt. action to stop deadly mistakes
III. Library and interview research. Megan was tip of iceberg. We are all at risk.
IV. Preview: consequences of drug errors, causes, solution

Transition to Main Point I
I. Drug errors are deadly.
   A. *Prevention Magazine,* Dec. 1994: "about 10% of all hospital admissions are due to problems with medications."
   B. *USA Today,* Oct. 3, 1995: prescription drug–related problems cost an estimated $75.6 billion in bills each year.

Look up

Pause

C. Tragic deaths result.
 1. *JAMA,* Dec. 21, 1994: "180,000 people die each year, partly as a result of prescription drug errors, the equivalent of three jumbo-jet crashes every two days."

Slowly

 2. *Drug Topics,* Nov. 23, 1992: "an elderly woman was given a prescription for *acetazolamide* (a set a ZOLE a mide) to treat her glaucoma. What she received from the pharmacist was hypoglycemic *acetohexamide* (a set oh HEX a mide). As a result, she lapsed into a coma and died 12 days later. "

Transition to Main Point II

II. Many causes of prescription drug errors
 A. Lack of reporting requirements
  1. Only North Carolina requires reporting.
  2. Many mistakes kept secret. According to attorney in the case against Eckerd Corporation, *Drug Topics,* Jan. 23, 1995: "almost 10,000 reported misfilled prescriptions over five years in its stores in Louisiana, Oklahoma, and Texas."
  3. No reporting, cannot learn from mistakes
 B. Too much trust in pharmacists
  1. Health care professionals very trusted
  2. But they can make human errors.
  3. *Drug Topics* magazine, Nov. 23, 1992: "A prescription of *methotrexate* (meth oh TREX ate) with confusing dosage instructions was filled by a pharmacist. Although he had doubt, the pharmacist did not phone the physician or ask the patient why she was taking the powerful chemotherapy drug prescribed. He assumed she had cancer. She took the drug daily. The error was discovered by another pharmacist when she returned for a refill, but it was too late. Three days later, she died."
 C. Other causes: drugs with similar names, bad handwriting, distractions while pharmacists are working

Transition to Main Point III

III. The solution depends on individuals and government.
 A. Report errors.
  1. Safe Medications Bill should be passed.
  2. Will create uniform reporting system
  3. *Congressional Record,* June 22, 1995: Representatives Coyne, Lewis, and Stark reintroduced this bill, but the bill does not have enough public support.
 B. Investigate and act on errors.

Look up

  1. Help or reprimand individual pharmacists.
  2. Police analogy
  3. Even if no fault, should learn how to prevent future errors
 C. Label lethal drugs with fluorescent color.
 D. Distribute wallet-sized card with reminders.

Transition to Conclusion

I. Summary: problem of prescription drug errors, causes, solutions
II. Remember Megan. Don't let it happen again.

Robin's extemporaneous outline demonstrates the key features of the outline that you should use to deliver a speech. The evidence Robin quotes is word-for-word, but her subpoints are limited to key words or phrases. She includes reminders to slow down and look at the audience, along with the phonetic spelling of difficult words. When you prepare a speech, be sure that your extemporaneous outline includes the reminders you need to refresh your memory.

Summary

Good organization makes the message clear. The main message of Chapter 8 is that organization is a vital quality of an effective speech. The ideas you want to present should be arranged and emphasized in a manner that makes your speech easy for the audience to follow. When your speech is well organized, the audience will be able to focus on your speech and understand it, and you will be perceived as a credible speaker.

A speech is organized into three main parts: introduction, body, and conclusion. In a speech with a linear organization (often used in Western cultures), the thesis or topic is made clear in the introduction, and each main point supports that thesis or topic. Signposts and transitions are used to highlight main ideas. Other cultures favor a nonlinear approach, in which case the main ideas are implicit and audience members infer them from the context of the speech and their own cultural background.

Speech organization begins with a detailed outline, a thorough plan for what you intend to say in your speech. Main ideas are indicated in Roman numerals, and supporting ideas are indented and indicated by capital letters and numbers. You use this outline as you revise and improve your speech, and you can use it until you are familiar enough with its content that you can deliver the speech extemporaneously. You then prepare a limited, extemporaneous outline to remind yourself of key ideas, which you will explain in your own words rather than relying on word-for-word memorization.

There are a variety of linear and nonlinear patterns that you can use to organize your message. Use audience analysis to determine what type of organization will be best for your audience. Regardless of the pattern you choose, it is important to plan a well-organized speech. Like good delivery, evidence, and audience adaptation, effective organization is one of the major determinants of a successful speech.

The checklist shows how you can use the material from this chapter to organize and outline your speech.

Checklist

OUTLINE THE BODY OF YOUR SPEECH

____ Draft the main points (p. 182)

____ Structure the main points in an appropriate pattern (p. 185)

____ Support the main points in outline form (p. 187)

____ Insert organizing words and sentences (p. 190)

OUTLINE THE INTRODUCTION

____ Prepare an attention-getter (p. 193)

____ Prepare a topic sentence or thesis (p. 197)

____ Connect with the audience (p. 198)

____ Establish your credibility (p. 199)

____ Preview your main points (p. 200)

OUTLINE YOUR CONCLUSION

____ Prepare a transition to your conclusion (p. 201)

____ Summarize your main points (p. 202)

____ Prepare a memorable clincher (p. 202)

CONSIDER A NONLINEAR ORGANIZATION FOR YOUR AUDIENCE

____ Deferred thesis (p. 208)

____ Web (p. 210)

____ Narrative (p. 211)

PREPARE YOUR EXTEMPORANEOUS OUTLINE

Preparing an Appropriate Outline Format

____ Use note cards or paper and a large font (p. 214)

____ Avoid crowding your notes (p. 214)

____ Number your pages or cards (p. 214)

Preparing the Content of the Outline

____ Main points and subpoints (p. 214)

____ Limited notes for supporting material (p. 215)

____ Quotations should be word-for-word (p. 215)

____ Include difficult or hard-to-pronounce words (p. 215)

____ Brief transitions (p. 215)

____ Include delivery reminders (p. 215)

Key Terms and Concepts

organized speech (p. 180)

outline (p. 180)

linear organization (p. 181)

main points (p. 181)

introduction (p. 182)

body (p. 182)

conclusion (p. 182)

temporal pattern (p. 185)

spatial pattern (p. 185)

causal pattern (p. 186)

Please turn the page for the Speech Grid Application.

Speech Grid Application

The Evolution of a Speech Grid

Speech Grid Applications, showing the evolution of a Speech Grid, are included near the end of Chapters 5 through 12. They illustrate how one student, Samantha, uses a grid to prepare a speech.

In this chapter we see how Samantha organizes the body of her speech, using the information she inserted on her grid. At this stage of speech preparation, Samantha's grid contains ideas that she has researched and ideas that she has invented. Samantha decides to organize these ideas into a problem-cause-solution pattern, so she subdivides the "Logos" section of the grid into "Problem," "Cause," and "Solution" categories. Use the software on your CD-ROM to categorize your ideas according to the main points you select when planning your speech.

Following Samantha's grid is her outline of the main points she intends to make in her speech. Notice how she took ideas from the grid and organized them. In Chapter 9 we discuss the development of subpoints and show why Samantha makes her final determination of which subpoints to use to support her main points.

Speech Grid: Driving with cell phones
Topic: Cell phones and driving
Specific purpose: To persuade my audience to use cell phones safely while driving.
Thesis: Audience members should use cell phones safely when driving.

AUDIENCE ANALYSIS	SPEECH MESSAGE
Situational Characteristics • 8 min. speech • 25–30 in audience • small classroom • limited a-v equip. **Demographics** **Age:** 17 (5); 18 (17); 19 (4); 20 (1); 22 (1) **Ethnicity:** African-American (2); Hmong (2); white (9); Latino/a (6); Portuguese (2); Pacific Islander, Mexican, German, Japanese, Swedish, Greek (1 each); did not say (1) **Major:** Undeclared (9); Liberal Studies (5); Chem, Bus, Crim (2 each); Child Devel, Engl, Bio, Premed, Journalism, Ag Bus, Econ, Comm (1 each) **Common Ground** I, like most of class (20 students), do not own a cell phone.	**ETHOS** • I have used a cell phone in a friend's car; it was distracting. • I had a friend who was hurt in a cell phone distraction-related accident. • I have researched the topic in the library, online, and talked to friends who use cell phones while driving. **PATHOS** • Cell phones make users feel comfortable in unfamiliar places. • Photo of car involved in fatal accident. • Examples of cell phone–related accidents. (Source 6 — fatal accident — no source quals? Source 8 — head injury) • Narrative of troubles of friend who was in accident. • Lawyer notes that cell phone records will make litigation against driver easier. (Source 9) **LOGOS — Problem** • 85% of cell phone owners use in car sometimes; 27% use in half of trips. (Source 1) • Cell phone usage high; 40% growth rate. (Source 2) • Inattention increases accident risk. (Source 5 — STUDY plus Dept. of Transportation stat that inattention is a factor in 50% of accidents)

(continued)

Speech Grid, continued

AUDIENCE ANALYSIS	SPEECH MESSAGE
Prior Exposure · Few (7 students) had heard about the issue of cell phones and driving; it had not been major topic in the local media. · Most students (20) do not own a cell phone. · Most who own a cell phone (6 of 8) use their phone in their car, primarily in one car. · Most (24 of 28) think that drunk drivers cause more accidents than cell phone users. **Audience Disposition** · Most (20 of 28) support a law banning cell phone use while driving. · People who do not own a cell phone are more likely to support such a law (18 of 20). Cell phone owners are opposed (2 of 8).	· Studies show accident risk. (Source 5 — cites 3 good studies!) · 10% of crashes caused by cell phone use. (Source 8 — politician quote, no study) · You can be cited if cell phone use causes bad driving. (Source 11) · Better, definitive data on cell phone risks needed. (Source 1) **LOGOS — Cause** · Wireless industry lobby opposes anti—cell phone laws. (Source 5) · People like the convenience of car phones, save time in busy world. (Sources 1, 2) · Communities don't want to be anti-business or anti-tech. (Source 4) **LOGOS — Solution** · Many states, nations considering laws against use. (Sources 5, 9) · Visual aid idea — video showing safe use tips. · Tips for safe use. (Sources 7, 12 — AAA and insurance co. tips) · Technology to make use as safe as possible. (Source 1) · Hands-free phones costly, may cause _more_ accidents. (Sources 1, 4) · Ideas — pull over to use phone; only use when urgent; don't use to chat or make routine appointments. · Possible disadvantage: unfair to single out one distraction. (Source 4) · Cell phones help in emergency situations. (Sources 1, 4)

Sources
See p. 176.

As noted on page 182, the ideas on your grid should be organized into a limited number of main points. (See Figure 8.1 for an example of how this can be done.) The following outline shows the main points that Samantha created, based on the ideas from her grid.

Outline of Main Points: Driving with Cell Phones

Body

I. Driving while gabbing is a growing problem.
   A. Cell phone usage is high and growing.
      1. 40% growth rate. (Source 2)
      2. Growth rate high among 18–25-year-old drivers. (Source 1)
   B. Cell phone usage while driving is common. (Source 1)
   C. Cell phone usage risks accidents.
      1. Inattention is a major risk factor.
         a. Source 5—factor in 50% of accidents.
         b. This risk is similar to the drinking and driving risk.
      2. Research confirms danger of driving while gabbing.
         Source 5—Volanti study found that drivers who use car phones more than 50 minutes each month had five times the chance of accidents as people who do not talk and drive. Also accidents involving drivers with cell phones are more likely to be fatal.
      3. Narrative of troubles of friend who was in an accident.

       D. Cell phone usage risks police citation. (Source 11)

  II. The driving-while-gabbing problem has several causes.

       A. Cell phone usage helps drivers manage their busy lives more efficiently.

          1. Evidence from Source 2.

          2. My friends mostly use their cell phones to make appointments and catch up with family and friends because school and work demands take up most of their time.

       B. Legislators are reluctant to act.

          1. The wireless industry lobby opposes anti–cell phone laws. (Source 5)

          2. Communities do not want to seem anti-business or anti-tech. (Source 4)

  III. Driving-while-gabbing risks should be reduced.

       A. Other nations have passed laws restricting cell phone use. (Source 9)

       B. You can act to make driving with cell phones safer.

          1. Whenever possible, pull over before making or taking a call.

          2. Only use your cell phone if it is urgent; don't use to chat or make an appointment to get your hair cut.

          3. AAA recommends that you assess traffic conditions before placing a call, and avoid complicated conversations. (Source 7)

          4. Stop talking on the phone immediately when traffic conditions become unsafe.
Source 12—Hang up without warning if necessary. You can explain later because you will still be alive.

          5. Do not assume that hands-free cell phones ensure safety. (Source 4)

       C. Safe driving does not stop beneficial cell phone uses.

          1. There may be good reasons for using car cell phones.

             a. Many of you indicated that you feel safer driving in unfamiliar places if you have a phone.

             b. Cell phones are helpful in emergency situations.

          2. The safe driving tips enable you to have a cell phone in your car and use it if you need help. However, it is not worth risking your life to have a routine conversation.

Source Notes

1. McCroskey, J. C. (1986). *An introduction to rhetorical communication* (5th ed., p. 185). Englewood Cliffs, NJ: Prentice-Hall.

2. McCroskey, J. C. (1969, March). The effects of disorganization and nonfluency on attitude change and source credibility. *Speech Monographs, 36,* 13–21.
Sharp, H., Jr., & McClung, T. (1966, June). Effect of organization on the speaker's ethos. *Speech Monographs, 33,* 182–183.

3. Greene, J. O. (1984, Fall). Speech preparation processes and verbal fluency. *Human Communication Research, 11,* 61–84, at 78.

4. Simons, L. M. (2001, January). Inside bollywood. *Smithsonian, 31,* 46–55, at 50.

5. Simons (2001, p. 55).

6. Simons (2001, p. 49).

7. Simons (2001, p. 52).

8. Clark, R. (1973). *Einstein: The life and times* (p. 26). London: Hodder and Stoughton.

9. Foss, S., & Foss, K. (1994). *Inviting transformation: Presentational speaking for a changing world* (p. 35). Prospect Heights, IL: Waveland Press.

10. Lustig, M., & Koester, J. (1993). *Intercultural competence: Interpersonal communication across cultures* (p. 221). New York: HarperCollins.

11. Annas, P., & Tenney, D. (1996). Positioning oneself: A feminist approach to argument. In B. Emmel, P. Resch, & D. Tenney (Eds.), *Argument revisited; argument redefined* (pp. 127–152, at p. 130). Thousand Oaks, CA: Sage.

12. Fox, H. (1994). *Listening to the world: Cultural issues in academic writing* (p. 114). Urbana, IL: National Council of Teachers of English.

13. Hall, E. (1981). *Beyond culture* (p. 91). New York: Anchor Books.

14. Hall (1981, p. 101).

15. Lustig & Koester (1993, pp. 219–221).

16. Porter, R., & Samovar, L. (1994). An introduction to intercultural communication. In L. Samovar & R. Porter (Eds.), *Intercultural communication: A reader* (7th ed., pp. 4–26, at p. 23). Belmont, CA: Wadsworth.

17. Annas & Tenney (1996, p. 130).

18. Hecht, M., Andersen, P., & Ribeau, S. (1989). The cultural dimensions of nonverbal communication. In M. K. Asante & W. Gudykunst (Eds.), *Handbook of international and intercultural communication* (pp. 163–185, at p. 176). Newbury Park, CA: Sage.

19. Hall (1981, p. 230).

20. Hecht, Andersen, & Ribeau (1989, p. 176).

21. Lustig & Koester (1993, p. 220).

22. Fan Shen. (1989, December). The classroom as the wider culture: Identity as a key to learning English composition. *College Composition and Communication, 40,* 459–466, at 463.

9

Developing an Effective Message

OBJECTIVES

After reading Chapter 9, you should understand:

● The importance of carefully planning your main points and subpoints in order to achieve your rhetorical purpose.

● Methods for developing subpoints that increase audience understanding of your topic.

● How to use evidence and reasoning to prove facts to your audience.

● Techniques for presenting ideas in order to motivate your audience.

● Formats for organizing main points and subpoints in a persuasive manner.

Sarah selected the topic "health maintenance organizations (HMOs)" for her informative speaking assignment. HMOs are insurance plans that cover a full range of members' medical care needs for a flat monthly payment. They differ from traditional fee-for-service plans, which require patients to pay a fee for each specific medical service they receive. The topic was a good choice, given Sarah's audience. Many were juniors or seniors who soon would be starting their careers and would need to select a health insurance plan. Several students had studied doctor-patient communication at a local HMO while doing a project for their health communication course. Others were nursing majors who one day might work for an HMO.

In the body of her speech, Sarah discussed three main points. First, she covered the history of health maintenance organizations, noting important dates and events since the 1920s. Second, she presented definitions that were important to understanding HMOs, such as co-payments, gatekeeper physicians, and utilization review. Third, she identified several of the largest HMOs in the area and described key features of each. For a visual aid, she presented a map showing the location of the main office of each HMO.

Sarah's classmates appreciated her topic selection and organization. However, their comments after the speech indicated that Sarah had not added to their understanding of the topic. Her main point on the history of HMOs consisted only of a list of dates and events, without elaboration. She did not answer questions the audience wondered about: Where was the first HMO located? Was it successful? How much per year were members charged?

Her main point on definitions did not hold the audience's attention either. Each subpoint merely defined a term. For example, *utilization review* was defined as "the HMO administrators' review of whether a medical procedure recommended by the patient's physician is necessary and whether the setting for the medical care is appropriate." Audience members unfamiliar with the term had questions. How is it determined that a medical procedure is "necessary"? What is a medical care "setting"? Furthermore, her placement of this main point (second) added to audience confusion. She used some of these terms in her first main point before she provided their definition in her second main point.

The third main point presented useful information about each HMO in the area, but it was impossible for the audience to keep track of it all. Sarah indicated that one plan offered no deductibles, a second plan required no co-payments, and a third had a very few participating doctors. Many audience members had difficulty remembering what all these terms meant, and there was little chance that they would remember each HMO's distinctive features.

The audience feedback taught Sarah an important lesson about the development of a speech. When planning future speeches, she would remember that a good topic does not ensure an effective speech. Sarah realized that she needed to develop her speech in a manner that her audience would find interesting and understandable. You should do the same when you prepare your speeches.

In Chapter 9 we provide guidelines for preparing the body of a speech. We begin by discussing the importance of developing the body of a speech effectively. Then we examine three aspects of speech development: increasing audience members' understanding of a topic, proving facts to the audience, and motivating the audience. We also present three patterns for structuring ideas in a persuasive manner. We close with a section that demonstrates how the different concepts in this chapter can fit together to create an effective speech.

The techniques you will learn in this chapter are important to the final development of your outline. You should use them when you decide which of the ideas on your Speech Grid will be most effective given your audience, and also when you shape the ideas that you have chosen from your grid (see the Speech Grid Application on p. 256).

The Importance of an Effectively Developed Message

To review rhetorical purposes, see page 126.

If we had to reduce this chapter to a single sentence, it would be this: ***The sum of the parts determines the success of the whole speech***. In other words, each subpoint of your speech helps to determine whether you will achieve your rhetorical purpose. In an excellent speech, each subpoint is selected and planned so that the audience will understand and agree with the main point it supports, and each main point is selected and planned to convince the audience about the thesis or enhance their understanding of the topic.

Consider a class period in which you felt you learned a lot about a subject, a political argument you found persuasive, or a movie that kept you enthralled for two or three hours. Chances are good that the success of each communication was achieved because the message was carefully planned. The teacher used language that you could understand, presented examples that made the concepts clear, and made the subject relevant to you. The political argument offered convincing proof of the claims made and touched your emotions in a way that you remembered when you went to the voting booth. The movie combined an interesting story with memorable characters and a believable plot. At the conclusion of each of these presentations, it was clear how all the parts fit together, and you were satisfied with the result. Your speech should have the same effect on your audience.

To achieve this effect, you must develop your main points and subpoints in a way that accomplishes your rhetorical purpose. The points you present need to build audience members' interest and understanding of your topic, convince listeners that facts are true, appeal to their emotions, and motivate audience members when appropriate. Some of these objectives are more important than others in any particular type of speech—for example, explanation may be especially important in an informative speech, and motivation will be especially important in a persuasive speech. Nevertheless, objectives should not be categorized as appropriate for informative, persuasive, or inspiring speeches *only*. There are likely to be times in any type of speech when each of these objectives needs to be accomplished.

To explain the process of developing your speech, we use the examples of Sarah's persuasive speech on the topic of HMOs, which opened this chapter, and Gabe's informative speech on cyberterrorism, which we describe in the next section.

Increasing Audience Understanding

The audience must actively listen and understand your message for a speech to be effective. When your rhetorical purpose is to inform the audience, this will be the primary objective of your speech. Even if you have a different rhetorical purpose—for example, to persuade—you are likely to introduce new concepts in your speech that need to be explained.

To increase audience understanding, the subpoints you use must be based on your audience analysis. If you have chosen your topic well, it will be familiar to you and less familiar to your audience. Thus you need to develop your topic to help audience members gain an understanding of the new material you are presenting. The ideas you discuss should come to life in your listeners' minds. There are several strategies you can use to enable your audience to learn about your topic.

Gabe, for example, was preparing an informative speech on cyberterrorism. His audience analysis indicated that most classmates assumed that the topic had something to do with computers and terrorism, but beyond that, they knew little about the subject. How could Gabe develop his points to ensure that his speech would be interesting and educational to the audience? To do this, he might turn to techniques such as *definition, illustration with examples, explanation, description,* and *comparison.*

View the Dalai Lama incorporating a definition in his "Spirituality in Today's World." CD-ROM: Video Theater, Excerpt 9.1

expert definition: a definition from a credible source in the field in which the term is used.

dictionary definition: a definition from a general or specialized dictionary.

etymological definition: a definition that explains the linguistic origin of a term.

● *Definition*

When you introduce new information to audience members, you probably will be using words with which they are unfamiliar. They may need to have you clarify what the subject of your speech refers to, and it is possible that they will be unaware of terms that are commonly used in discussions of your topic. If you use these terms without defining them, audience members will be frustrated and have difficulty listening to—let alone understanding—your message.

Audience analysis is essential to the effective use of definition. Use the type of definition most likely to increase audience understanding of a term. Your options include *expert, dictionary, etymological, functional,* and *comparative* definitions.

Expert Definitions.

An **expert definition** is taken from a person or organization that is a credible source of information on the topic being defined. To determine who is an expert, use the same criteria for credibility that you would use for any other evidence source (experience and background in the topic area and objectivity).

Here is an example of a definition of *terrorism* from an expert source that Gabe could use in his speech:

> According to Mark Pollitt of the FBI Laboratory, the U.S. Department of State defines terrorism as "premeditated, politically motivated violence perpetrated against noncombatant targets by subnational groups or clandestine agents.[1]

Dictionary Definitions.

A **dictionary definition** provides the meaning of a term that appears in a dictionary. You might use a general dictionary such as *Merriam-Webster's Collegiate Dictionary* to define a term. Or you might use a specialized dictionary from the field of your topic to obtain a more precise definition for your speech.

Gabe could use a specialized dictionary for the field of computers as a source of this definition of cyberterrorism:

> According to the *Computer Currents High Tech Dictionary, cyberterrorism* is "a terrorist attack on, or by means of, computer systems."[2]

Etymological Definitions.

An **etymological definition** explains the linguistic origin of a term. This type of definition is appropriate if the origin is interesting or will help the audience to understand the term you are defining. Otherwise, etymological definitions should be used sparingly. Gabe's audience might find this explanation of the origin of the word *cyber* interesting:

> According to the *Tech Encyclopedia,* 1999, *cyber* is a prefix attached to everyday words to add a computer, electronic, or online connotation. It is taken from the term *cybernetics,* which was coined by a preeminent mathematician, Norbert Wiener. Cybernetics is the comparison of human and machine processes, often focused on machines that imitate human behavior.[3]

Functional Definitions.   A **functional definition** explains how something is used or what it does. For example, Gabe could define *cyberterrorism countermeasures* as actions that can be taken to reduce or eliminate the effects of a cyberterrorist attack, such as strengthening the security of information technology systems or having contingency plans and emergency response teams in place.

Comparative Definitions.   A **comparative definition** explains how the term you are defining is similar to or different from an object or concept with which audience members are familiar. If they can relate a new term to something they already understand, their understanding will increase.

If Gabe's classmates are familiar with the use of weapons in traditional terrorist attacks, he could use a comparative definition to highlight the essential features of cyberterrorism:

> Mass destruction warfare utilizes chemical, biological, radiological, and nuclear weaponry, whereas cyberterrorism utilizes information technology devices to inflict mass disruption of an opponent's critical information technology infrastructure.[4]

● Illustration with Examples

Examples are specific instances you use to illustrate a point in your speech. Examples provide an effective way of supporting a point because they help the audience understand its meaning and relevance. Suppose Gabe said, "There are many dangers posed by cyberterrorism." Audience members are likely to wonder what type of actions cyberterrorists could take and how serious these incidents might be. Gabe could use examples such as these to give the audience a better perspective on cyberterrorism:

- *The Tamil Tigers, opponents of the Sri Lankan government, bombarded the government's embassies with e-mail, causing their Internet systems to crash.*[5]

- *In a simulation at a cyberterrorism conference, terrorists hacked into the IRS audit system and sent out millions of audit notices and tax-due notices, and also jammed the phone, fax, and e-mail lines into the IRS so that irate citizens got busy signals. The result was a grassroots rebellion and the resignation of a senator.*[6]

- *In 1998, a team of National Security Agency computer specialists posed as hackers for North Korea. They penetrated and could have shut down the command and control structure of the U.S. Pacific Command, which is in charge of 100,000 U.S. troops that would be activated in wars with North Korea or China.*[7]

When you present a new concept to the audience, it is helpful to include both examples and *nonexamples,* which are instances that can be mistaken for true examples. This strategy helps audience members understand the essential features of a concept and differentiate features that are not essential.[8] Gabe could use these pairs of examples and nonexamples in his speech:

functional definition: a definition that explains how a term is used or what something does.

comparative definition: a definition that explains how a term is similar to or different from a familiar object or concept.

examples: specific instances that illustrate a point in your speech.

- Criminals who hack into IRS computers and multiply every taxpayers' refund by ten, with the goal of bankrupting the U.S. government, are cyberterrorists. Conversely, criminals who access IRS computers in order to delete their own tax liability are not cyberterrorists because their motive is personal (saving money), not political (destroying the government).

- An anti-American paramilitary group that bombs a key military computer facility is engaged in cyberterrorism. If that same group uses the Internet to research chemical weapons manufacture, with the intent of using these weapons against American civilians, they are not engaging in cyberterrorism because they are neither attacking computer systems nor attacking by means of a computer system.

Explanation

An **explanation** helps your audience understand how something happens, why something happens, or what something is. In developing a point, you may need to explain the steps in a process from beginning to end. Other times you will want to explain how one event or circumstance leads to a particular result (a cause-and-effect relationship) or why an event occurs or is important. Gabe could explain why "time is of the essence" when a cyberterrorist attack takes place:

> On the information warfare battlefield what might have transpired in weeks on the ground is compressed into minutes. Programs that probe for unauthorized modems or passwords that allow access to a system operate faster than humans can think.... Once the battle has begun, it lasts only as long as it takes the telecommunications link to deliver a program that acts as an electronic file shredder. The best defense is to get the bad guys first.[9]

To be effective, an explanation should be presented in a manner that the audience can follow. If members of Gabe's audience are familiar with the speed of computer operations, they will understand why time is critical when cyberterrorists attack. If they are not very familiar with computers, Gabe might ask the audience to recall how fast their personal computers can delete a file, or he might present a statistic about how many operations a computer can do in one second.

Description

Description is the use of clear and vivid language to help your audience visualize the person, object, place, or phenomenon you are describing. A good description paints a picture in audience members' minds. Descriptive language highlights noteworthy features that audience members will understand and find memorable.

Consider these two options that Gabe could use to help the audience form a mental image of cyberterrorism:

Option One

Armed men enter codes into computers. Then cities go black because power grids collapse, jets collide, and chemical plants release toxic clouds. This is information warfare.

For more on descriptive language, see page 275.

explanation: an analysis of how or why something happens or why something is true.

description: the use of clear and vivid language to help the audience visualize what you are discussing.

Descriptive language makes the object you are describing come to life for the audience. How would you describe this graffiti? Consider the size, shape, colors, and materials used. How does graffiti craft an effective message?

Option Two

Armed men hastily key secret codes into computers. Seconds later cities go black as power grids collapse. Tourist-filled jumbo jets collide in midair. Chemical plants release clouds of toxic gas. It has all the makings of a Hollywood blockbuster, the title is information warfare.[10]

The first option tells what happens in a cyberterrorism scenario, but the language is matter-of-fact. The second option uses descriptive language — "hastily key secret codes," "seconds later cities go black," and "tourist-filled jumbo jets collide in midair" — that helps audience members to visualize terrorist incidents. Listeners can imagine how fast these events would unfold and how disastrous they would be. Descriptive language paints a dramatic picture of what would happen if cyberterrorists were successful.

● *Illustration by Analogy*

An **analogy** is a comparison based on similarities between two phenomena that are otherwise different. It helps audience members relate new information to more familiar information. Gabe might illustrate the effect of cyberterrorism by comparing it to the Y2K problem, which the audience is likely to be familiar with:

The results of cyberterrorist attacks would be similar to the feared results of the Y2K problem: removal of bank records, disabling of computer programs, and failure of defense communications or electric power distribution. The main difference is that Y2K problems were unintended whereas cyberterrorists intentionally disable computer systems.

analogy: a comparison based on similarities between two phenomena that are otherwise different.

For more on the importance of demonstrating goodwill towards audience members, see page 38.

When you prepare a speech assignment, one effective source of comparisons is information that you learned from the speeches of your classmates. You *know* that the audience has recently been presented with that information, and it demonstrates your goodwill to show that you learned things from your classmates' speeches. Also consider the cultures represented in your audience when preparing analogies. Traditions and examples from a variety of cultures make your speech more appealing to diverse segments of the audience. For example, a speaker might compare fasting during a hunger strike to fasting traditions for Yom Kippur, Lent, and Ramadan.

When your topic is a complex idea, it is particularly helpful to select an analogy that explains more than one point in your speech. By continuing to use the same familiar object of comparison, you strengthen audience members' ability to use their existing knowledge to understand new information.[11] For example, an explanation of human vision could use a camera as the object of comparison, comparing the parts of an eye to the parts of a camera.[12]

Proving Facts to Your Audience

Proof is an important element of many points you make in a speech. The audience is unlikely to accept all your claims. Recall the adage from Chapter 7: **It is not a fact until you prove it to the audience**. If the audience disagrees with a fact you assert, or doubts its truth, you need to support the assertion. Sarah, for example, may discover that audience members do not believe that they are likely to have a problem with an HMO. Gabe's audience may wonder how terrorists could gain access to vital computer systems. The premises underlying these points are important to the success of their speeches, so it is important for Sarah and Gabe to prove to the satisfaction of their respective audiences that they are true.

In this section we consider how speakers can use evidence and reasoning to prove the claims they make in a speech.

● *Use of Evidence*

For complete evidence citations, see pages 170–72.

When your audience analysis indicates that audience members may not simply take your word about the truth or accuracy of a claim you are making, you need proof. Begin by checking your Speech Grid. You may already have found the evidence you need to convince your audience that what you are asserting in your speech is true. If not, use the research strategies discussed in Chapter 7 to find credible evidence. After completing your research, present it in a manner that you think your audience will find convincing. There are several principles to follow to use evidence effectively.

Identify Your Sources and Their Qualifications. Identify the name, position, and affiliation of an evidence source before presenting his or her message. Do not use vague references such as "studies show" or "the newspaper said." Concrete documentation results in a more favorable evaluation of your message and strengthens your credibility.[13] To ensure the credibility of your sources, use persons who are unbiased.[14]

Match the Claim and the Evidence.   Carefully word your claim so that it accurately reflects what your evidence proves. When you use evidence that is not directly related to the point you are making, you are less likely to convince audience members of the point you are making, and your credibility will be damaged.[15]

Select Precise Evidence.   Use evidence that presents specific dates, places, numbers, and other facts. For example, it would be better to use evidence indicating that "only 35% of college students who score in the bottom half of entrance examinations will graduate in four years" than evidence stating that "it appears that few students who rank low in the entering class will make it through college." Evidence presenting specific facts is more persuasive than less-specific evidence—and it strengthens your credibility.[16]

Include Vivid Evidence.   Audiences are more likely to be persuaded by vivid evidence, such as concrete details about a particular person. For example, assume Sarah wants to make the point that HMOs try to avoid paying for emergency medical care. To support that claim, she could include evidence documenting the plight of Karen, a twenty-eight-year-old woman who was out of town on business in upstate New York and lost consciousness at her hotel. The hotel manager called an ambulance, which took her to the nearest hospital. Karen's HMO tried to deny the claim, first insisting that the situation had not been an emergency and then claiming to have "lost" her bill.[17]

Speakers must keep ethics in mind when selecting vivid evidence. Vivid evidence can be persuasive even if it does not depict a typical case. For example, a detailed description of the history of one person who had been on welfare for sixteen years was found to have a greater influence on an audience's perceptions of welfare recipients than statewide statistics showing that 90 percent of welfare recipients are off the rolls within four years.[18] The use of evidence that depicts an atypical situation would constitute a half-truth, unless the audience is told that the situation described is not the norm.

> For more on ethics and half-truths, see page 59.

Use Evidence That Is New to Audience Members.   Use your audience analysis to determine what evidence on your grid is likely to be new to your listeners. If they are already familiar with your evidence, it probably has already achieved any effect that is possible. Evidence that is new to the audience is more likely to have an impact on listeners' attitudes and perceptions of your credibility.[19]

● *Principles of Evidence Use: An Application*

Now we can consider how Sarah might better use evidence to support her claims about HMOs. She needs to convince audience members that they are at risk of receiving lower-quality health care from an HMO unless they take action. Her audience analysis reveals that some audience members have been to HMOs (for example, as part of a class project) but are not sure whether they will ever enroll in an HMO and are not aware of any issues related to HMO economics or the medical care received by HMO members. Here are examples of evidence that Sarah could use to support the links in her argument with effective proof.

a. Document That Audience Members Are Likely to Rely on an HMO to Cover Their Medical Care Costs

This evidence is new to audience members; they do not know how many Americans are enrolled in HMOs.

Use precise statistics and facts.

When you graduate and get a job, there is a high probability that an HMO will be your insurer.

Dr. Charles Bertrand, an expert witness in medical malpractice cases, quantified this fact in *Consumers' Research Magazine,* October 1998, "At present, around 160 million Americans are enrolled in HMOs or other types of managed health-care plans."[20] Increasingly, these plans are investor owned, meaning that their primary objective is to earn profits. According to a July 13, 1999, press release from Physicians for a National Health Program, "between 1985 and 1998, the proportion of HMO members enrolled in investor-owned plans increased from 26% to 62%."[21]

b. Prove That Many HMO Plans Restrict Needed Services

Use high-credibility *sources, e.g., a Harvard professor. Always cite the source* before *presenting evidence.*

HMO plans contain provisions that limit medical services, even when your doctor recommends them.

According to Robert Blendon, professor of health policy and management at the Harvard School of Public Health, in *U.S. News & World Report,* October 13, 1997, "All these [managed care] plans have within them the phrase 'medically necessary and appropriate care.' Nobody told people that what that meant was their doctor might want to do something and the plan wouldn't permit it."[22]

Use of "smart bomb" and "land mines" makes this evidence vivid. Follow up with statistics showing these situations are typical.

In *Consumers' Research Magazine,* December 1997, M. Stanton Evans explains that "while promising a vast array of benefits for everyday procedures, the HMO regime sets out to limit the big-ticket items." Evans cites congressional testimony that "the smart bomb of cost containment...is medical necessities denials.... [E]ven if a plan has a clear benefit package and has all the other perks, like free eye exams or free screening tests for cancer...the member's physician will never be the final authority. This might go unnoticed for simple needs, like a regular office visit or a bout of the flu, but...when something unexpected or expensive happens...land mines start exploding everywhere" (ellipses in the original).[23]

These limitations are resulting in a denial of physician-recommended services. According to a Kaiser Family Foundation survey of doctors and nurses reported in a July 28, 1999, A.P. Press Release, "87% of doctors said their patients had experienced some type of denial of coverage over the last two years. Most common, 79%, was trouble getting approval for a drug they wanted to prescribe. 69% said they had trouble getting a diagnostic test approved; 60%, a hospital stay; 52%, referral to a specialist; and 38% for mental health or substance abuse referrals."[24]

c. Show That Denial of Needed Care Harms HMO Members

Evidence about a specific person adds vividness, humanizes numerical evidence.

HMO restrictions on health services are decreasing the quality of care.

An article by Robert Howe in *Time* magazine, February 1, 1999, reports the case of David Goodrich, who was diagnosed with stomach cancer. The doctors in David's health plan stated that they did not have the expertise to treat his rare form of cancer, leiomyosarcoma, and they referred him to specialists outside the plan. His insurance company challenged his use of out-of-plan doctors and experimental treatments that specialists urged. Within four months, the cancer spread to his liver. He continued to battle his insurer for two years, but his fate was sealed and he died at age 44.[25]

David Goodrich's case is not an isolated example. In the May 21, 1998, *New England Journal of Medicine,* Robert Kuttner writes that "a study by Ware and colleagues found that chronically ill elderly and poor patients in three cities had worse clinical outcomes in HMOs than in fee-for-service plans."[26] These problems are particularly acute in for-profit HMOs. According to Dr. Steffie Woolhandler, Associate Professor of Medicine at Harvard, in the previously cited Physicians for a National Health Program press release, July 13, 1999, "investor owned HMOs pay more attention to their profits than to their patients. Mammography rates in investor-owned plans are 8% lower. If all American women were enrolled in for-profit HMOs instead of non-profits, 5,925 would die from breast cancer."[27]

Evidence from high-credibility sources shows that David Goodrich's case is not atypical.

● Use of Reasoning

Another way to support claims that you make in your speech is through the use of reasoning. We emphasize **inductive reasoning**, in which you take facts that audience members accept as true (or that you can prove) and argue that those facts justify the claim you are making. You ask the audience to make an *inductive leap* and agree that the facts establish your claim.

People commonly use inductive reasoning in their communications, whether they are aware of it or not. You have undoubtedly heard your friends and family members make statements such as these:

- "You liked the movie *Jurassic Park,* so you will love *Godzilla.*"
- "You spend every weekend sitting on the couch eating junk food and watching football. No wonder you're overweight and out of shape."
- "The service at the Beef and Brew Tavern is terrible. We ate there three times, and each time our servers got the order wrong."
- "This must be a boring class. The guy in the back row has a box of No-Doz."

Each of these four statements includes a fact that is offered in support of a claim:

Claim	Supporting Fact
1. You will love *Godzilla.*	1. You liked *Jurassic Park.*
2. Inactivity and over-consumption of junk food cause people to be in poor shape.	2. You snack while watching football every weekend, and you are overweight and out of shape.
3. The service at the Beef and Brew is terrible	3. We ate there three times, and each time the service was poor.
4. This class is boring.	4. A person in the back row has a box of No-Doz.

In each of these examples, the communicator uses inductive reasoning. A claim is made and supporting facts are offered. Do you agree that the supporting facts justify the claim in each of these examples?

inductive reasoning: basing a general conclusion on particular facts or instances.

To use reasoning effectively in your speech, you need to ensure that the audience agrees that the facts you present support your claim. Gabe and Sarah could use four types of inductive reasoning to support claims in their speeches.

Inductive Generalization.

When you use **inductive generalization** (also known as **example reasoning**), you present specific instances that support the general claim you are making. Your goal is to persuade the audience to accept your claim, based on these instances. The audience must be persuaded that your examples supply sufficient proof of your general claim.

If Sarah wanted to claim that HMOs have denied needed medical care to their members, she could use examples to support an inductive generalization, as follows:

> HMOs may limit needed medical care in the name of making money. In the book *Health against Wealth: HMOs and the Breakdown of Medical Trust*, 1996, *Wall Street Journal* health care writer George Anders discussed the case of Lamona and James Adams's six-month-old son. At 3:30 A.M., he had a temperature of 104 degrees. Lamona called her HMO's hot line. Although several hospitals were closer, she was instructed to drive the baby to a hospital 42 miles away in northern Atlanta. Why? Lamona's plan had contracted to send most of its pediatric cases to the north Atlanta hospital in return for a significant discount. Young James III had a bacterial infection that could have become lethal in hours. After the long drive in the rain, both of his hands and feet had to be amputated because all the blood cells and tissue in his extremities had died.[28]
>
> The Adamses' troubles are not unique. In their October 13, 1997, *U.S. News & World Report* article "Are HMOs the Right Prescription?" Susan Brink and Nancy Shute report that a California mother died because her HMO delayed a referral to a specialist. Furthermore, in Texas, the Department of Insurance fined an HMO $1 million for "unacceptable disregard for the quality of care," including the refusal to pay for emergency care for a patient in diabetic shock.[29]

For an inductive generalization to be reliable, the examples you select must be *significant* and *representative*. To have **significant examples**, you must offer enough instances to persuade your audience that the examples are common occurrences.

It is difficult to present a large number of examples in the time available for a speech. For example, Sarah planned to use three examples (James Adams III, a California mother, and a Texas HMO) to make a generalization about the millions of decisions HMOs make each year. But three examples are a minuscule percentage of the total number of decisions made by HMOs each year. When speakers draw a general conclusion from a small number of examples, they risk committing a logical fallacy known as the **hasty generalization fallacy**.

How, then, could Sarah provide sufficient examples? She cannot simply add examples to her speech. Nielsen Media Research surveys five thousand families in order to estimate how many people are watching a given television program nationwide.[30] That's not possible for Sarah. Instead, she could attempt to make her examples *rhetorically significant*.[31] This means that her examples achieve the rhetorical purpose of persuading the audience.

inductive generalization (example reasoning): presenting specific instances that support the claim you are making.

significant examples: a sufficient number of examples to convince the audience your general claim is true.

hasty generalization fallacy: the fallacy that results when a general conclusion is based on an insufficient number of examples.

Recall from Chapter 1 that audiences do not come into a speech as blank slates. They interpret a message in light of their experiences and what they heard or read from other people. If Sarah's examples are consistent with audience members' perceptions of how businesses such as insurance companies operate, listeners will be likely to accept her claim. Conversely, if many in the audience have been treated well by insurance companies and have had no difficulty in obtaining medical care, the examples will be less convincing.

In addition to marshaling significant examples, you must provide **representative examples**. This means that the audience must perceive that the instances you have chosen are typical of the class they represent. Members of Sarah's audience could wonder whether her examples describe typical HMO behavior or whether the behavior she discusses is the result of a few "bad apples." To make her examples representative, Sarah mentions HMOs that operate in three different states and enroll individuals of different ages and with different medical conditions. Her claim will be more convincing with diverse examples than it would be if she based her claim on a single HMO or a single medical procedure. When you use example reasoning, you should take similar care to select varied instances. Keep in mind, too, that from an ethical perspective, it is important for your examples to be typical (see p. 64).

Comparison Reasoning.   When you use **comparison reasoning**, you argue that two instances are similar and that what is known to be true of one instance is likely to be true of the other. If you argue that Philosophy 122 is a hard course because Philosophy 121 was a hard course, you are using comparison reasoning. People who argue that the prohibition of marijuana will never be successful because the prohibition of alcohol failed are also using this type of reasoning.

An argument relying on comparison reasoning has three parts. Part 1 is a claim that is known to be true. Part 2 makes the comparison: you argue that the subject of the known claim is very similar to the subject of your claim. Part 3 is the conclusion: you argue that because the two claims are similar, what is true of one claim is true of the other. The claims about Philosophy 122 and the prohibition of marijuana could be structured in this way:

Philosophy Courses Comparison

I. Philosophy 122 is a hard course. *(the claim you intend to prove)*
   A. Philosophy 121 is a hard course. *(part 1, the claim known to be true)*
   B. Philosophy 121 and Philosophy 122 are similar courses. They have the same instructor, they have similar homework assignments, and all tests are two-hour essay exams. *(part 2, comparing the subjects of the two claims)*
   C. Because the two courses are similar, Philosophy 122 must also be a hard course. *(part 3, the conclusion)*

Marijuana and Alcohol Prohibition Comparison

I. The prohibition of marijuana cannot be successful. *(the claim you are making)*

TIP

It is essential to analyze your audience to determine whether your examples will be rhetorically significant.

representative examples: examples that are typical of the class they represent.

comparison reasoning: claiming that because two instances are similar, what is true of one is true of the other.

A. The prohibition of alcohol was a failure. *(part 1, the known fact)*

B. The prohibition of marijuana will fail for the same reasons that the prohibition of alcohol failed: Both can be used in private, where consumption is hard to detect. Laws regulating the use of both have been disobeyed on a wide scale. *(part 2, comparing the subjects of the two claims)*

C. Because of similarities in the use of marijuana and alcohol, marijuana prohibition is destined to fail just as alcohol prohibition failed. *(part 3, the conclusion)*

The effectiveness of comparison reasoning depends on two factors. First, does the audience accept the "known" facts? The philosophy course example assumes that the audience agrees that Philosophy 121 is difficult. If audience members had heard that Philosophy 121 was easy, you would need to prove to them that this was not the case. Second, the audience must agree that the two situations are comparable. In the prohibition example, the reasoning would fail if the audience did not believe that marijuana use and alcohol use were comparable.

Gabe could use comparison reasoning to show that cyberterrorists could damage U.S. information systems. He could compare terrorists to computer hackers who have already penetrated computer systems, as follows:

Gabe's claim

Terrorists will be able to get into computer systems. According to *The Futurist,* March–April 1997, one official from the U.S. intelligence community has boasted that "with $1 billion and 20 capable hackers, he could shut down America." [Walter] Laqueur [of the Center for Strategic and International Studies] "points to the well-publicized examples in recent years of teenage hackers penetrating highly secret systems in every field."[32]

Part 1, facts that Gabe can prove

According to Jane's Information Group, in a September 21, 1999, document *Cyberwarfare: Fact or Fiction,* "Cyberwarfare involves a different set of training requirements [than training in nuclear and biological weapons] that is also more readily available. Thus, training in computer science is now widely prevalent among terrorist groups."[33]

Part 2, showing that terrorists are now well versed in computers, as hackers are

Part 3, the conclusion

Because U.S. hackers can penetrate information systems and cause damage, and terrorists can and are receiving similar training in computer systems, the risk of terrorist abuse of such systems is high.

Gabe could successfully prove his claim by comparison reasoning if the audience agreed that U.S. hackers can penetrate computer systems and that terrorists can obtain the same type of training and experience in computers as hackers have. Notice how Gabe uses evidence to support his claim that terrorists are becoming well versed in computer science; he does this because the computer literacy of terrorists may be unknown to the audience. Some members may even find it counterintuitive that organizations with a propensity to use violence would also be interested in computer training.

Causal Reasoning.   When you use **causal reasoning**, you argue that one occurrence causes another because one is a logical result of the other. Cause-and-effect relationships often need to be established when you are building a case. If you want to convince your audience to watch less television, you will probably need to show that television causes harmful effects. If you ad-

causal reasoning: claiming that one occurrence causes another because one is a logical result of the other.

Is this picture a good piece of evidence to back up the claim that cars cause air pollution? What could you use to supplement the picture to make it even more convincing to your audience?

vocate military-style boot camps for juvenile criminals, your speech will be more convincing if you show how this type of punishment will bring a reduction in crime.

Audience analysis is important when you use causal reasoning. If your reasoning is consistent with the audience's worldview, it is likely to be convincing. For example, audience members who watch little television because they feel that most shows are worthless would be likely to accept any reasonable evidence or argument showing that television is harmful. But audience members who enjoy watching many hours of television each week and do not perceive that they are being harmed will be skeptical of your message. You will need convincing proof from evidence sources they find credible if you want them to consider your point of view.

When using causal reasoning, be careful to avoid committing the **post hoc fallacy**. This fallacy takes its name from the Latin phrase *post hoc ergo propter hoc,* meaning "after this, therefore because of this." The fallacy occurs when you assume that because one event preceded another event, the first event must have caused the second one. For example, if you showed that one county established a juvenile boot camp and the crime rate in that county declined by 15 percent the next year, you might be tempted to argue that the establishment of the boot camp caused the decline. However, this cause-and-effect relationship is not certain. Other factors such as an improving economy in the area may have worked to reduce crime. Your argument would be much stronger if you could show that a neighboring county that did not have a boot camp but did experience economic growth saw no similar reduction in crime.

For the effect of audience members' worldviews, see page 15.

post hoc fallacy: the fallacy that results from assuming that one event caused a second one simply because the first one preceded the second.

Causal reasoning would be essential for Sarah in her persuasive speech on health maintenance organizations. A key point in her speech is that the economic structure of profit-making HMOs encourages decisions to deny medical care. Sarah could present her causal argument as follows:

> The structure of health maintenance organizations can *cause* a denial of needed care. How are HMOs structured economically? In the December 1997 issue of *Consumers' Research Magazine,* M. Stanton Evans writes that HMOs "undertake to provide for people's medical needs for a fixed amount of money, then manage the care we receive to stay within the limits."[34]
>
> How does this structure cause a denial of needed care? Consider this example. Suppose all your neighbors pay you an annual fee. In return, you agree to find and hire housekeepers when you think their houses need cleaning. The fewer times you decide their houses need cleaning, the more of their fee you get to pocket. You might let their houses get pretty messy. The same incentive is true for HMOs. "In simplest terms," as Mr. Evans puts it, "the HMO can make more money by doing less."[35]
>
> How can they decline to pay for needed care? In *U.S. News & World Report,* October 13, 1997, Robert Blendon, professor of health policy and management at the Harvard School of Public Health, notes that all managed care plans "have within them the phrase 'medically necessary and appropriate care.' Nobody told people that what that meant was their doctor might want to do something and the plan wouldn't permit it."[36] Professor Ralph Greco of the Robert Wood Johnson Medical School, in *The Lancet,* April 1998, wrote that under managed care, "medical judgment had been replaced by algorithms based on cost and efficiency.... Chemotherapy for cancers was given only when there was unequivocal proof that a cure was likely—often hard to prove during an individual's life. Even simple conditions, such as hernias and breast lumps, were covered only if it could be proven that not to treat them would have negative consequences."[37]

In this example, Sarah's causal argument is carefully developed. She begins with the cause, documenting that HMOs receive a fixed amount of money per patient regardless of how many medical services a patient uses. Next, Sarah discusses the effect. She begins with a hypothetical example, asking the audience what they would do if they ran a house-cleaning business that was structured like an HMO. This example alone is likely to convince sympathetic audience members. They will quickly accept Sarah's point of view if they have had difficulties obtaining medical care, or if they believe that HMOs are out to make money like any other business.

Other audience members, however, may be skeptical. Some may have had no difficulty in obtaining medical care themselves or doubt that anyone in the medical field would let sick people suffer in order to make money. To convince these listeners, Sarah reinforces her point that HMOs might refuse to cover medical care even when a doctor concludes that it is necessary. By quoting two experts, professors at leading universities, Sarah maximizes the likelihood that all audience members will accept her point of view.

sign reasoning: claiming that a fact is true because indirect indicators suggest that it is true.

Sign Reasoning.

When you use **sign reasoning**, you claim that a fact is true because indirect indicators suggest that it is true. Here are three examples. A prosecutor may argue that the defendant is guilty because fingerprints were found on the murder weapon. You might conclude that it is raining because several of your classmates are carrying wet umbrellas. You may decide that a restaurant is "smoke free" because there are no ashtrays on the tables. In each example, indirect indicators are *signs* that the fact is true.

Sign reasoning relies on *indirect* proof of a fact. If you are new to the study of reasoning, differentiating indirect proof from other types of support can be a challenge. The table that follows shows how the same fact may be proved indirectly, through sign reasoning, or directly, through different types of support:

Claim	Direct Proof	Indirect Signs
It is raining outside.	You look outside and see rain. *(personal observation)*	Several students in the classroom are carrying wet umbrellas.
A lot of students signed up for Astronomy 7.	The professor says the class is full, and there is a long waiting list. *(testimony)*	The textbook for Astronomy 7 was sold out in the bookstore on the first day of the term.
Students have fun in Physics 111.	Six students in Physics 111 told me it is a fun class. *(reasoning to a general conclusion from direct examples)*	When you walk by the Physics 111 class, the room is full and students are smiling.

Sign reasoning is most effective if there are several consistent signs of the fact you are claiming, and few inconsistent signs. Consider the claim that graduation rates are down. If the number of students signing up for interviews for full-time employment is down, that could be a sign that the number of students who are graduating is declining. If you also had evidence that sales of graduation announcements in the bookstore have declined, your reasoning would be strengthened. However, if the facts also reveal that your college has hired more workers to process graduation applications, or that more chairs are being set up in the auditorium where graduation is to be held, these signs would make your claim less likely. Perhaps the decline in job interviews on campus really indicates that more graduates are applying for jobs online as use of the Internet expands, rather than that the number of graduates is declining.

Gabe could use sign reasoning to support the claim that the risk of cyberterrorism is increasing:

There are several indicators that the probability of cyberterrorism is increasing. Raisuke Miyawaki, senior adviser to Japan's Commission on Critical Infrastructure Protection, presented a speech on June 29, 1999, indicating that "Japan's National Police Agency has just created Japan's first 'cyberpolice' division. [The agency] opened an office in Tokyo that will serve as a high-tech cybercrime investigative and analysis center."[38] In the United States, a January 7, 2000, CBS News story indicated that President Clinton will "ask Congress for $91 million to battle computer terrorism."[39] On September 21, 1999, Joshua Sinai reported in *Cyberwarfare: Fact or Fiction* that "training in computer science is now widely prevalent among terrorist groups."[40]

This support constitutes sign reasoning because the evidence provides indirect signs that the probability of cyberterrorism is increasing. Gabe is arguing that if both the United States and Japan are allocating resources to fight cyberterrorism, and if members of terrorist groups are becoming educated in computer science, chances are good that the risk is growing. Even though he has no direct evidence (for example, captured documents outlining terrorist plans to increase cyberattacks or testimony from a law enforcement source who infiltrated a terrorist group), he can use these indirect signs to support his point.

Reasoning and Ethics.   Suppose a speaker knows of weaknesses in his or her own reasoning. For example, suppose a speaker wants audience members to protest higher parking fees on campus by parking without a permit for one day. The speaker claims that the campus police will not issue parking tickets because a similar protest occurred at a nearby college and nobody was ticketed. This argument may sound persuasive, but it would be less persuasive if listeners knew what the speaker knows: the police chief of the nearby college agreed that fees were too high, whereas their own campus police chief is opposed to the protest.

If you were the speaker, you might feel it is advantageous to use the argument because it will help convince the audience to participate in the protest. But if you were an audience member and trusted the speaker's reasoning, would you like to see this argument used on you? How would you feel if you participated in the protest and found a $20 parking ticket waiting on your car?

Communicators have an ethical duty not to withhold relevant information from the audience. Without knowing the position of their own campus police chief, the audience cannot make an informed decision about whether to participate in the protest.

If you know your reasoning is faulty, it is not ethical to use it in a speech even if it may be persuasive. When covering each type of reasoning in this chapter, we include a discussion of how to evaluate its strength. If you know your reasoning is weak, look for better ways to prove your argument or soften the claim you are making. For instance, if you have several examples that support a point but you are aware of counterexamples, you should say that your examples show what can happen *sometimes,* rather than claiming that they prove a consistent pattern.

Although relying on faulty reasoning may seem expedient, an ethical persuader will not use this strategy on the audience. The concept of the *universal audience* (see In Theory box 9.1) provides a framework speakers can use to consider the ethical implications of their message.

To review ethics and truthfulness and informed decision making, see Chapter 3.

| INVENTION | ORGANIZATION | STYLE | PREPARATION | DELIVERY |

In Theory 9.1

ETHICAL PERSUASION AND THE UNIVERSAL AUDIENCE

In Chapter 9 we emphasize the importance of developing a message that is both persuasive and ethical. Speakers should not use unethical arguments, such as arguments based on fallacies or faulty reasoning, even if those arguments may persuade a given audience. Such arguments do not contribute to the audience's ability to make an informed decision.

The arguments you select depend on your target audience. Belgian scholars Chaim Perelman and Lucy Olbrechts-Tyteca made a distinction, based on the target audience, between *persuasive* arguments and *convincing* arguments. Persuasive argumentation "only claims validity for a particular audience"; convincing argumentation "presumes to gain the adherence of every rational being."[41] The Belgian scholars referred to an audience persuaded by convincing argumentation as the **universal audience**, consisting of all competent adult persons.[42]

Perelman and Olbrechts-Tyteca were focusing on a universal audience for philosophical discourse, but other theorists have extended the concept. Communicators can focus on a universal audience as the target audience. When inventing a message that appeals to a universal audience, communicators do not limit their analysis to arguments that seem convincing to themselves or to a particular social group. Instead, they develop a message that the broader society will consider reasonable.[43] This theory of universality, in the words of James Crosswhite, "tries to establish the possibility of reasoning—where people must imagine new ways of being audiences for one another's reasoning (more universal ways)."[44]

Adaptation to the universal audience would serve as a check on unethical messages. Christopher

Tindale notes that "the universal audience, as a representation of reasonableness in the context, cannot value effectiveness over reasonableness. In this way manipulation is ruled out."[45] For example, a speaker might be able to persuade a particular audience that the preponderance of information on the Internet is worthless by proving that one specific Web site contains no useful material. A universal audience, however, would reject this argument as unreasonable because it is based on a hasty generalization fallacy. (For the hasty generalization fallacy, see p. 263). Another speaker might persuade a particular audience that China will be a military aggressor during the next decade by appealing to that audience's prejudices. Universal audience members, however, would set aside their own prejudices and not be convinced.[46] (To review the importance of avoiding prejudicial language, see p. 276.)

Allen Scult argued that communicators should seek the adherence of both the particular audience and the universal audience:

> Validation of your argument lies in securing the adherence of both, i.e., your construct of the universal audience and the actual audience you are addressing. . . . The universal audience conceived as the community of minds competent to judge your argument keeps you from submitting to the temptation to persuade the particular audience you are addressing at any cost.[47]

During the invention process, use your critical thinking skills to evaluate the ideas on your Speech Grid from two perspectives: those of your target audience and those of the universal audience. If you select points that would be effective with both audiences, you can be an ethical and convincing persuader.

Developing Subpoints to Motivate Your Audience

You may not be able to achieve your rhetorical purpose with sound evidence and reasoning alone. Good arguments, by themselves, are not always persuasive. For example, at some point, you probably have engaged in some fun or impulsive activity instead of studying for a test. You recognized the fact

universal audience: a hypothetical audience consisting of every rational person.

that studying was necessary, because you needed more time to learn the material, you needed to do well on the exam to succeed in the course, and your career plans depend on a successful academic record. Nevertheless, despite the logic of the case for studying, you decided to take the night off and enjoy life.

Just as a sound set of facts alone may not be enough to persuade you to study, a list of good reasons may not be sufficient to convince your audience. Logical reasons and evidence are very important elements of persuasion, but you need to present them in a way that touches your audience's feelings. If you want your audience to take action or to change long-held attitudes, your speech needs to inspire your audience in a way that will have lasting impact. In this section we discuss how to arrange and present facts in order to motivate your audience.

Strategies that you use to motivate your audience should not be based on deceit or manipulation. The information that you present should be true to the best of your knowledge. Your intention is to arrange factual information in a convincing manner, not to distort the truth. In addition, you should not manipulate the audience by presenting arguments you know to be fallacious even though they may be persuasive. You should foster your audience's ability to make a rational decision about the thesis of your speech. You can do this through a number of strategies, five of which we now consider.

● *Emotional Appeals*

An **emotional appeal** relies on pathos to motivate the audience. In Chapter 2 we emphasized the effectiveness of this type of appeal. Humans are more likely to respond to your message when their feelings have been touched. Sarah might use the following evidence to illustrate the importance of being able to select the doctor who is most effective, rather than the one who is most economical:

> Trey McPherson was born with half of his heart shrunken and nearly useless, a condition that causes most children to die in infancy.
> Fortunately, Trey was not one of these victims, because he was treated by a leading pediatric heart surgeon. After two surgeries, Trey's parents were able to experience the joy of seeing their ten-month-old son climb out of his crib at the hospital. Except for a bandage on his tiny chest, it was difficult to tell that Trey had recently experienced open-heart surgery.
> Unfortunately, many babies are not as fortunate as Trey. Although this skillful surgeon's patients have far-above-average survival rates, many pediatric cardiologists in the New York area find their "favorite surgeon is frequently off limits because of price if a child belongs to an HMO."[48]

Sarah could appeal to a variety of emotions with this example. It helps the audience understand, in human terms, what it means to be able to select the best cardiologist available rather than the one who is most economical. She could make her audience *angry* because an infant with a serious heart condition could be denied the best available medical care on economic grounds. Sarah could discuss the *injustice* of a system that attempts to require parents to accept lower-quality care for their children. She could get her audience to *empathize* by imagining how they would feel if a loved one with

emotional appeal: an appeal that invokes pathos to motivate audience members.

Individuals and organizations often appeal to your emotions with pictures of people or animals who might benefit from your actions. Why might this picture be more convincing and effective than a statement if someone was trying to persuade you that cows in factories are treated like machines? Why might this strategy backfire?

a serious disease was forced to settle for inferior medical care. Sarah could also focus on positive emotions such as the *joy* that Trey's family felt when the child recovered from surgery so well.

It is important to remember that you are unlikely to have time to include a significant number of emotional appeals in a typical speech, particularly if the appeals are based on extended examples. When you do present an emotional appeal, also provide evidence that gives audience members an accurate picture of how often the conditions or cases you cite occur.

● *Appeals to Fear*

A **fear appeal**, an argument that arouses fear in the minds of audience members, can be a powerful motivator.[49] To be effective, the appeal should demonstrate a serious threat to listeners' well-being.[50] To be an ethical persuader, it is imperative that you base your fear appeal on accurate information. Do not exaggerate to make your appeal more persuasive.

For example, if Gabe found evidence to indicate that cyberterrorists could disrupt air traffic control systems or electric power grids, he could use these facts as the basis of a fear appeal. However, it would be unethical of him to exaggerate the facts he researched and use a fear appeal, such as "Cyberterrorists could gain control of all American computer systems," that cannot be supported by evidence.

fear appeal: an appeal that arouses fear in audience members' minds.

A fear appeal is more likely to succeed if audience members perceive that they are capable of remedying the problem.[51] If they are presented with a frightening situation and they feel that they are unable to take the recommended actions (or they believe that the recommendations will not reduce the threat), they are more likely to ignore or repress the message.[52] Furthermore, an appeal based on an immediate problem will be more persuasive than an appeal warning about harm in the future.[53]

Sarah could use a fear appeal in her speech, based on her examples of patients who were denied needed care. First, she would need to prove that many audience members are likely to have health insurance coverage through an HMO and to be confronted with a serious medical problem at some time. Second, it would be important to focus on problems the audience would experience soon, rather than in the distant future. Thus, if the average age of an audience member was twenty-two, Sarah should focus on childbirth and children's health issues rather than on medical conditions that people experience later in life. Third, she would need to show audience members that they can remedy the problem. She could prove that some HMOs provide patients and doctors with a wide choice of specialists, allow patients to go to high-quality hospitals, and have an unbiased appeals process if care is denied. By telling her audience what to look for when signing up with a health maintenance organization, she could give listeners a means of reducing the fears she had established.

● *Cost-Benefit Arguments*

A **cost-benefit argument** is straightforward. You attempt to convince your audience that the benefits of accepting your proposition outweigh the costs. This strategy can be very effective because you are asking audience members to do what is in their own best interest. To be effective, a cost-benefit argument depends on reliable audience analysis. You need to know which costs and benefits audience members perceive to be important, or you need to be able to convince them that the costs and benefits you are discussing are very important.

In her speech, Sarah could use a cost-benefit approach to convince her audience to do some research before selecting an HMO. She could show how relatively easy it is to compare HMOs—for example, by checking to see whether an HMO is accredited by the National Committee for Quality Assurance or by comparing the rankings put out by consumer organizations.[54]

Sarah could argue that the *costs* of health plan research are small. It takes only an hour or two of audience members' time (at their convenience) and involves little, if any, expense. Sarah could then point to *benefits* that outweigh the small investment of time. She could document the high probability that each audience member will face a major illness at some time, and she could demonstrate that some HMOs offer significantly more options than their competitors.

When using a cost-benefit approach, pay close attention to *audience members'* perceptions. We often hear speeches encouraging classmates to volunteer for worthy causes such as donating blood or tutoring underprivileged children. Even though the speakers tell their audience that the rewards they experience will be worth their time, the audience fails to act. If listen-

cost-benefit argument: advocacy contending that the benefits of your thesis outweigh the costs.

ers are able to visualize themselves experiencing a reward, this strategy is more likely to succeed. It is also more persuasive when the speaker can show the audience how to minimize the cost. Here is how Leslie adapted a cost-benefit appeal to her audience:

> I hope you can spare some time to help the young children in our community. You do not need to drive downtown to help out. Students can volunteer to read to children at the Day Care Center in our library at story hour each day. The next time you are using the library in the afternoon, walk past the center and see what a good time the kids and your classmates are having. Share a story from your culture or a book you loved as a child. If you find you enjoy volunteering, you can even sign up for a community service course for academic credit.

● Foot-in-the-Door and Door-in-the-Face Strategies

The next strategies pertain to the order in which you mention proposed actions. With a **foot-in-the-door strategy**, you begin with a small request with which most of the audience is likely to comply. You follow that request with a greater request that you hope the audience will agree to. The second request is the primary objective of your speech. With a **door-in-the-face strategy**, you take the opposite approach. You begin with a substantial request with which the audience is not likely to comply. You follow that request with a more moderate proposal that you believe the audience will agree to. The second proposal is your primary objective.

The foot-in-the-door and door-in-the-face strategies have been found to be effective when the persuader is making a *prosocial* request.[55] This means that the proposal provides a benefit for society, rather than a benefit that primarily serves the persuader. A request that audience members contribute time or money to a charitable organization would be prosocial; a request that audience members buy the persuader's product or service would not be.

Furthermore, for the door-in-the-face strategy to be effective, the initial request should not be unbelievably large. Otherwise, you may lose credibility as audience members wonder "What kind of fool does this person take me for?"[56] Thus, if your goal is to ask the audience to volunteer a Saturday afternoon to help build a playground for neighborhood children, you will not first ask listeners to donate a year of their lives serving overseas in the Peace Corps.

If Gabe wanted to use the foot-in-the-door strategy, his first subpoint might request members of the audience to sign a petition urging the federal government to take steps to protect vital computer networks from cyberterrorism. The audience would be likely to see the logic in this step and comply. Gabe's next subpoint would be a request to support a tax increase to fund government countermeasures against cyberterrorists. Once listeners had decided that it was worthwhile to sign a petition, Gabe would be hoping that they would be more receptive to the more substantial request to pay higher taxes in order to reduce the effectiveness of cyberterrorism.

Kim's speech, delivered in class on the day a Gay and Lesbian Pride rally was being held on campus, used the door-in-the-face technique effectively:

foot-in-the-door strategy:
advocacy that begins with a small request and follows up with a greater request that is the speaker's primary objective.

door-in-the-face strategy:
advocacy that begins with a substantial request (likely to be rejected) and follows up with a more moderate request that is the speaker's primary objective.

If you agree with me that prejudice against any group of people is wrong, I hope you will voice your feelings at the noontime rally in front of the student union.

I am also giving you a pink triangle. In Nazi concentration camps, the triangle was used to signify what they considered sexual deviance, including homosexuality. Now it has been reclaimed by the Gay Rights movement as a symbol of empowerment.

Even if you cannot attend the rally, please keep this triangle in your backpack as a reminder. Gay men and lesbians deserve to be judged on their character, not their sexual orientation. When you see this triangle in your backpack, remember—any time you make a stereotypical comment or laugh at an anti-gay joke, or use "gay" as a derisive adjective, you may unknowingly be putting down your best friend, your favorite instructor, your brother, or your sister.

Organizing Main Points and Subpoints to Persuade Your Audience

In Chapter 8 we explored several options for organizing the main points of your speech so that your audience can comprehend and follow your message. Now we discuss three methods of organization that may make your message understandable and also more persuasive: a *two-sided argument,* a *motivated-sequence format,* and a *comparative-advantage format.* These patterns can be inserted in your outline as main points or subpoints.

● *Two-Sided Arguments*

In a **two-sided argument**, you initiate points that prove your thesis, but you also acknowledge and respond to arguments against your thesis. Your goal is to demonstrate why these counterarguments should not defeat your position.

If an opposing issue is very significant, you may commit an entire main point to rebutting it. For example, if Sarah proposed that independent boards of physicians should review HMO decisions not to pay for treatment, she could respond to possible criticisms of her proposal. One reason why HMOs have become popular is that health care costs rose much faster than the rate of inflation in the 1970s and 1980s. Some doctors were perceived to be ordering unnecessary tests and treatments, knowing that insurance companies probably would pay for whatever they ordered. After she developed and explained the benefits of her solution, Sarah could discuss these reservations in her next main point. (She also would need to incorporate evidence and reasoning to back up these points in her outline.)

. . .

An argument against her thesis

two-sided argument: a message acknowledging and responding to arguments against the thesis.

III. Independent review boards will not cause a return to skyrocketing medical costs.
   A. HMOs expanded rapidly as a response to inflation in medical care costs and the fear that doctors were performing unnecessary tests and procedures.

[*Transition:* a reduction in costs and an increase in efficiency have been important benefits of HMOs, but these would not be compromised by my proposal.]

    B. Independent review boards will not lead to wasteful medical expenses. Board physicians will be independent, rather than working for the patient or the HMO. Therefore they would be likely to approve only treatments that are medically justified.

A rebuttal to the argument against her thesis

If Sarah wanted to include two-sided analysis that did not require a full main point, she could devote a subpoint to achieving this purpose. For example, she might structure a main point as shown here (in her speech and outline, she would support these subpoints with evidence and reasoning):

...

III. The benefits of independent review of HMO decisions outweigh the costs.

    A. Independent review boards will improve the quality of patient care.

    B. Independent review boards will not cause a significant increase in health care costs.

An argument supporting Sarah's thesis

A subpoint rebutting a main argument against Sarah's thesis.

A two-sided argument can be effective in persuading your audience. It changes audience members' attitudes in the direction of your thesis and also can strengthen your credibility.[57] If your audience analysis indicates that members of your audience have concerns about your proposal, they are unlikely to be persuaded unless you address their concerns. In addition, an ethical persuader enhances audience members' ability to make good decisions, rather than manipulating the audience. By acknowledging and responding to potential reservations to your thesis, you give the audience more complete information for decision making.

TIP

During the invention process, analyze which arguments against your position may be convincing to audience members, and respond to those viewpoints in a two-sided argument.

● *Motivated-Sequence Format*

If the thesis of your speech centers on action you hope the audience will take, a **motivated-sequence format** offers an effective means of structuring your main points. Developed by Alan Monroe over sixty years ago,[58] this organizational pattern continues to be popular. You probably have encountered it in television commercials and other advertisements. A motivated sequence aims to establish five main points:

1. *Attention.* You begin by getting the audience's attention and creating a desire to hear your message.

2. *Need.* Once audience members are prepared to listen, you convince them that there is a need for your proposal. If you intend to motivate them to act, the need(s) you identify must be significant and relevant to them.

3. *Satisfaction.* Your next main point develops your proposed solution and explains how it will remedy (satisfy) the need you have identified. This main point is no different from the solution in a problem-solution format.

To review techniques for gaining audience attention, see page 193.

motivated-sequence format: an organizational pattern structure to inspire audience action.

4. *Visualization.* On this main point, you create a mental picture for audience members so they can imagine how your proposal will make them better off personally or will benefit society. Some ways to help the audience visualize include providing examples describing where your proposal has succeeded, presenting anecdotes about individuals who have benefited from plans such as yours, and making "before and after" comparisons showing conditions with and without your plan.

5. *Action.* Your final main point indicates what action you want audience members to take. How are they to actively participate in the solution? For example, you may ask the audience to make a lifestyle change, to participate in the democratic process to achieve social change, or to volunteer in the community.

This arrangement of points can be effective because it is psychologically satisfying to the audience. You begin by raising concern about a need, then show that your proposal can satisfy that concern. By asking audience members to visualize how the proposal will improve their lives or their communities, you focus their thinking on the benefits of your solution.

If the thesis of Sarah's persuasive speech was that audience members should learn how to obtain the medical treatment they need from their HMO, she could develop the following ideas in each main point. In her outline and speech, Sarah would select some of the techniques we discussed in this chapter to support and develop these main points:

I. *Attention.* If you or a loved one were threatened by a serious illness, you would want the best treatment possible. Imagine how angry and frightened you would feel if your doctor recommended an expensive but promising treatment for a serious illness and your insurance company refused to pay for it.

II. *Need.* At some point in your life, it is almost certain that you or a loved one will suffer a serious illness. The health insurance company you rely on to cover the treatment will probably be an HMO or some other managed care provider. This company may deny the medical care that offers the best hope because of cost. You need to know what to do if care is denied.

III. *Satisfaction.* You do not need to take "no" for an answer. By enlisting your doctor as an ally, becoming aware of your rights, and understanding how to secure your rights, you can ensure that you or a loved one can obtain the best care possible.

Now you can buy your ticket on-line with up-to-the-minute information on flights, schedules and bookings   IBERIA

Imagine that you have a product to sell online. What could you put on a banner to capture audience attention? How would you follow up with the remainder of a motivated sequence?

IV. *Visualization.* In John Grisham's novel *The Rainmaker,* Donny Ray Black dies because he is denied potentially life-saving treatment for leukemia by a profiteering insurance company. Imagine how you would feel if this happened to you or a loved one. Fortunately, this fictional scenario need not be reality for you. Modern medicine often works miracles, and if you know how to insist on your rights, you can obtain the best treatment possible.

V. *Action.* Now is the time to be prepared. If you are selecting an HMO, read the fine print of each contract carefully to determine which organization gives you the fairest appeal process if care is denied. I will provide the address of a Web site you can research to learn what your rights are under state law. Information is power, and it may save your life.

It is also possible to incorporate a motivated-sequence format into the basic outline structure explained in Chapter 8. Start with an attention-getter, and then expand the *attention* step to include the other components of a speech introduction. Follow that with a transition to the body of your speech, where the main points will be the *need, satisfaction, visualization,* and *action* steps of the motivated sequence. Finally, provide a transition to your conclusion, and end with a summary of main points and a clincher. If you are going to use a motivated-sequence format, check with your instructor to see whether he or she would prefer for you to use the traditional outline form (with a complete introduction and conclusion) or just the five components of the sequence (attention, need, satisfaction, visualization, and action).

To review the components of an introduction, see page 193; transitions, page 190; conclusions, page 201.

● *Comparative-Advantage Format*

When you use a **comparative-advantage format**, you discuss reasons why the solution you propose is more advantageous than the current system. This structure highlights the advantages of your proposal. It provides an alternative to a problem-solution pattern when your speech does not address a glaring crisis but nevertheless would be better than existing policies. A proposal that the federal government stop minting pennies or that a local high school change its dress code are two examples of plans that may be beneficial even if they do not reduce any monumental problems in society.

To review the problem-cause-solution pattern, see page 186.

When using a comparative-advantage pattern, the first main point on your outline explains your solution, and each subsequent main point explains one advantage of that solution in comparison with the present system. The subpoints for each advantage should include proof that the plan will gain the advantage and show how the advantage is significant.

If Sarah's thesis was that people should take advantage of preventive medicine offered by HMOs, her main points could be structured as follows. In her outline, Sarah would include evidence and reasoning to support her claims.

comparative-advantage format: an organizational pattern that highlights the advantages of your proposal in comparison with the current system.

I. *Solution.* You should enroll in an HMO that offers diverse preventive medicine options.

A. Definition of preventive medicine

B. How to determine which preventive medicine services, such as early detection of health problems, nutrition counseling, exercise classes, and smoking cessation programs, are offered by an HMO.

II. *Advantage.* The proposed solution limits the effects of serious diseases.

The plan gains the advantage.

A. When serious medical conditions are discovered in their early stages, treatment is more likely to be successful.

The advantage is significant.

B. Serious medical conditions become more life threatening and costly to treat if they are not detected early.

III. *Advantage.* The proposed solution ensures better nutrition.

The plan gains the advantage.

A. HMO nutrition counseling causes patients to eat healthier diets.

The advantage is significant.

B. Good nutrition is important to physical and mental health.

IV. *Advantage.* The proposed solution ensures healthier lifestyles.

The plan gains the advantage.

A. HMOs have effective programs to help patients cease unhealthy behaviors such as smoking and alcohol abuse.

The advantage is significant.

B. Curtailing these behaviors will improve patients' health.

Pulling It All Together: Aiding Understanding, Proving Facts, and Motivating Your Audience

You usually will develop your main points by using some of the techniques discussed in this chapter. From your Speech Grid, select the ideas that meet the criteria for effective use of the techniques you are using, or add more effective ideas through invention and research.

Sarah should use a combination of techniques to support her main points. At some places, she will need to help her audience understand new information. Other times, she will need to prove facts. She will also want to motivate her audience to act, so that listeners are not victims of penny-pinching policies by an HMO.

To review critical thinking, see page 17.

Sarah will need to use critical thinking to identify the points that will best accomplish her rhetorical purpose. She will not have enough speaking time to use every technique discussed in this chapter or to use all the evidence and reasoning pertaining to HMOs that we have presented. As you will need to do when you prepare a speech, Sarah should consider her audience analysis and select the ideas that best get her message across to the listeners. Here is one example of the ideas Sarah could select to support her main points. Notice how several techniques presented in this chapter are used.

I. HMOs have denied needed care.

Example and emotional appeal

A. An HMO required six-month-old James Adams III to travel forty-two miles to an emergency room, and the delay resulted in the amputation of his hands and feet.

Two-sided argument

B. Some persons contend that these examples are infrequent, caused by a few bad apples. In reality, denial of needed care is common.

1. According to a Kaiser Family Foundation survey, in a July 28, 1999, AP Press Release, "87% of doctors said their patients had

experienced some type of denial of coverage over the last two years. Most common, 79%, was trouble getting approval for a drug they wanted to prescribe. 69% said they had trouble getting a diagnostic test approved; 60%, a hospital stay...."

2. Dr. Steffie Woolhandler, Associate Professor of Medicine at Harvard, in a July 13, 1999, Physicians for a National Health Program press release, notes that "investor owned HMOs pay more attention to their profits than to their patients. Mammography rates in investor-owned plans are 8% lower. If all American women were enrolled in for-profit HMOs instead of non-profits, 5,925 would die from breast cancer." *Evidence and fear appeal*

II. The economic structure of profit-making HMOs leads to denial of care.

A. HMOs base doctor payments on *capitation,* meaning that they get a flat rate per patient, regardless of how healthy or sick each person is. Hospitals face a similar payment system. *Definition*

B. Under a system of capitation, health care providers can often make the most money by giving less care. *Causal reasoning*

III. You should select your HMO carefully.

A. Selecting a health insurance company is a major decision much like buying a house. *Comparison*

B. If you had a life-threatening illness, imagine how you would feel if a treatment your doctor recommended was denied by some accountant on economic grounds. *Fear appeal*

C. You can find a good HMO if you do your homework.

1. According to Daphna Gregg in the April 1996 *Harvard Health Letter,* consumers can order a copy of all health plans the National Committee for Quality Assurance has assessed, along with their accreditation status and a summary of their findings for individual plans. *Evidence*

2. A significant number of high-quality HMOs are available. A *U.S. News & World Report* survey was published on October 23, 1997, and used data from the National Committee for Quality Assurance. HMOs received a composite score based on factors such as prevention, physician and member turnover and satisfaction, access to care, and accreditation. Of the 37 top-scoring HMOs, 33 were nonprofit plans. *Evidence; show audience members that they can take steps to reduce the fear*

Summary

An effective message must be carefully crafted. Good speeches are not merely a set of paragraphs that pertain to a topic area; they are carefully planned messages. Your subpoints should develop your main points in a manner that achieves your rhetorical purpose. Remember: **The sum of the parts determines the success of the whole**. Carefully consider each part of your speech to ensure that the finished product is successful.

In Chapter 9 we focused on three major objectives you are likely to have in a speech: increasing audience understanding, proving facts to the audience, and motivating or inspiring the audience. We also presented three formats that enable you to organize main points and subpoints in a persuasive manner. The following checklist should serve as a reminder of major options you have for accomplishing each of these objectives.

Checklist

INCREASING AUDIENCE UNDERSTANDING

____ Define key terms (p. 228)

____ Use examples (p. 229)

____ Provide explanations (p. 230)

____ Present descriptions (p. 230)

____ Offer analogies (p. 231)

PROVING FACTS TO YOUR AUDIENCE

Use Evidence Effectively

____ Identify your sources and their qualifications (p. 232)

____ Match the claim and evidence (p. 233)

____ Select precise evidence (p. 233)

____ Include vivid evidence (p. 233)

____ Use evidence that is new to audience members (p. 233)

Use Reasoning Effectively

____ Inductive generalization (p. 236)

____ Comparison reasoning (p. 237)

____ Causal reasoning (p. 238)

____ Sign reasoning (p. 240)

____ Adhere to ethical considerations (p. 242)

DEVELOPING SUBPOINTS TO MOTIVATE YOUR AUDIENCE

____ Emotional appeals (p. 244)

____ Fear appeals (p. 245)

____ Cost-benefit arguments (p. 246)

____ Foot-in-the-door and door-in-the-face strategies (p. 247)

ORGANIZING MAIN POINTS AND SUBPOINTS TO PERSUADE YOUR AUDIENCE

____ Two-sided arguments (p. 248)

____ Motivated-sequence format (p. 249)

____ Comparative-advantage format (p. 251)

Key Terms and Concepts

expert definition (p. 228)
dictionary definition (p. 228)
etymological definition (p. 228)
functional definition (p. 229)
comparative definition (p. 229)
examples (p. 229)
explanation (p. 230)
description (p. 230)
analogy (p. 231)
inductive reasoning (p. 235)
inductive generalization
   (example reasoning) (p. 236)
significant examples (p. 236)
hasty generalization fallacy
   (p. 236)

representative examples (p. 237)
comparison reasoning (p. 237)
causal reasoning (p. 238)
post hoc fallacy (p. 239)
sign reasoning (p. 240)
universal audience (p. 243)
emotional appeal (p. 244)
fear appeal (p. 245)
cost-benefit argument (p. 246)
foot-in-the-door strategy (p. 247)
door-in-the-face strategy (p. 247)
two-sided argument (p. 248)
motivated-sequence format (p. 249)
comparative-advantage format
   (p. 251)

Please turn the page for the Speech Grid Application.

Speech Grid Application

The Evolution of a Speech Grid

Speech Grid Applications, showing the evolution of a Speech Grid, are included near the end of Chapters 5 through 12. They illustrate how one student, Samantha, uses a grid to prepare a speech.

In this section, you will learn how Samantha used her Speech Grid to select some ideas for use in her speech and reject others. Margin notes indicate why she made these choices in order to adapt the speech to her audience, using the principles discussed in this chapter.

In Chapter 8, you saw how Samantha organized ideas from her grid into three main points for the body of her speech. That organizational structure is reprinted at the end of her grid for your reference.

Speech Grid: Driving with cell phones
Topic: Cell phones and driving
Specific purpose: To persuade my audience to use cell phones safely while driving.
Thesis: Audience members should use cell phones safely when driving.

AUDIENCE ANALYSIS	SPEECH MESSAGE
Situational Characteristics • 8 min. speech • 25–30 in audience • small classroom • limited a-v equip. **Demographics** **Age:** 17 (5); 18 (17); 19 (4); 20 (1); 22 (1) **Ethnicity:** African-American (2); Hmong (2); white (9); Latino/a (6); Portuguese (2); Pacific Islander, Mexican, German, Japanese, Swedish, Greek (1 each); did not say (1) **Major:** Undeclared (9); Liberal Studies (5); Chem, Bus, Crim (2 each); Child Devel, Engl, Bio, Premed, Journalism, Ag Bus, Econ, Comm (1 each) **Common Ground** I, like most of class (20 students), do not own a cell phone. **Prior Exposure** • Few (7 students) had heard about the issue of cell phones and driving; it had not been major topic in the local media.	**ETHOS** • I have used a cell phone in a friend's car; it was distracting. • I had a friend who was hurt in a cell phone distraction–related accident. • I have researched the topic in the library, online, and talked to friends who use cell phones while driving. **PATHOS** • Cell phones make users feel comfortable in unfamiliar places. • ~~Photo of car involved in fatal accident.~~ • ~~Examples of cell phone–related accidents. (Source 6 — fatal accident — no source quals? Source 8 — head injury)~~ • Narrative of troubles of friend who was in accident. • ~~Lawyer notes that cell phone records will make litigation against driver easier. (Source 9)~~ **LOGOS — Problem** • 85% of cell phone owners use in car sometimes; 27% use in half of trips. (Source 1) • Cell phone usage high; 40% growth rate. (Source 2)

Specific example for ***vividness.*** *Use with studies on IC.*

Use ***two-sided*** *message in solution. Audience sees this cell phone benefit.*

Reject—photo is too small for whole class to see.

Reject—one source is weak, other example is vague.

Reject—risk too remote to persuade audience.

Show ***relevance to audience.*** *Twenty do not use cell phones now; show likely future use.*

(continued)

Speech Grid, continued

AUDIENCE ANALYSIS	SPEECH MESSAGE	
• Most students (20) do not own a cell phone. • Most who own a cell phone (6 of 8) use their phone in their car, primarily in one car. • Most (24 of 28) think that drunk drivers cause more accidents than cell phone users. **Audience Disposition** • Most (20 of 28) support a law banning cell phone use while driving. • People who do not own a cell phone are more likely to support such a law (18 of 20). Cell phone owners are opposed (2 of 8).	• Inattention increases accident risk. (Source 5 — STUDY plus Dept. of Transportation stat that inattention is a factor in 50% of accidents) • Studies show accident risk. (Source 5 — cites 3 good studies!) • ~~10% of crashes caused by cell phone use. (Source 8 — politician quote, no study)~~ • You can be cited if cell phone use causes bad driving. (Source 11) • Better, definitive data on cell phone risks needed. (Source 1) LOGOS — Cause • Wireless industry lobby opposes anti-cell phone laws. (Source 5) • People like the convenience of car phones, save time in busy world. (Sources 1, 2) • Communities don't want to be anti-business or anti-tech. (Source 4) LOGOS — Solution • Many states, nations considering laws against use. (Sources 5, 9) • Visual aid idea — video showing safe use tips. • Tips for safe use. (Sources 7, 12 — AAA and insurance co. tips) • Technology to make use as safe as possible. (Source 1) • Hands-free phones costly, may cause <u>more</u> accidents. (Sources 1, 4) • Ideas — pull over to use phone; only use when urgent; don't use to chat or make routine appointments. • Possible disadvantage: unfair to single out one distraction. (Source 4) • Cell phones help in emergency situations. (Sources 1, 4)	*Important—24 of 28 classmates believe cell phone use is not risky like DUI. Use **comparison**.* *Reject because more **credible** sources available.* *Considered **ethics** here; decided there was sufficient evidence to be confident that cell phone use is risky.* *This cause important, relates best to **young** audience (demographics).* ***Door-in-the-face.** Follow with more moderate solutions.* *No a-v equipment available.* *Important to emphasize what audience should do to drive safer with cell phones.* *Good point. Use **two-sided message**.*

Sources
See p. 176.

Outline of Main Points: Driving with Cell Phones

Body

I. Driving while gabbing is a growing problem.
   A. Cell phone usage is high and growing.
      1. 40% growth rate. (Source 2)
      2. Growth rate high among 18–25-year-old drivers. (Source 1)
   B. Cell phone usage while driving is common. (Source 1)
   C. Cell phone usage risks accidents.

      1. Inattention is a major risk factor.
        a. Source 5—factor in 50% of accidents.
        b. This risk is similar to the drinking and driving risk.
      2. Research confirms danger of driving while gabbing.
        Source 5—Volanti study found that drivers who use car phones more than 50 minutes each month had five times the chance of accidents as people who do not talk and drive. Also accidents involving drivers with cell phones are more likely to be fatal.
      3. Narrative of troubles of friend who was in an accident.
    D. Cell phone usage risks police citation. (Source 11)
  II. The driving-while-gabbing problem has several causes.
    A. Cell phone usage helps drivers manage their busy lives more efficiently.
      1. Evidence from Source 2.
      2. My friends mostly use their cell phones to make appointments and catch up with family and friends because school and work demands take up most of their time.
    B. Legislators are reluctant to act.
      1. The wireless industry lobby opposes anti–cell phone laws. (Source 5)
      2. Communities do not want to seem anti-business or anti-tech. (Source 4)
  III. Driving-while-gabbing risks should be reduced.
    A. Other nations have passed laws restricting cell phone use. (Source 9)
    B. You can act to make driving with cell phones safer.
      1. Whenever possible, pull over before making or taking a call.
      2. Only use your cell phone if it is urgent; don't use to chat or make an appointment to get your hair cut.
      3. AAA recommends that you assess traffic conditions before placing a call, and avoid complicated conversations. (Source 7)
      4. Stop talking on the phone immediately when traffic conditions become unsafe.
        Source 12—Hang up without warning if necessary. You can explain later because you will still be alive.
      5. Do not assume that hands-free cell phones ensure safety. (Source 4)
    C. Safe driving does not stop beneficial cell phone uses.
      1. There may be good reasons for using car cell phones.
        a. Many of you indicated that you feel safer driving in unfamiliar places if you have a phone.
        b. Cell phones are helpful in emergency situations.
      2. The safe driving tips enable you to have a cell phone in your car and use it if you need help. However, it is not worth risking your life to have a routine conversation.

Source Notes

1. Pollitt, M. M. *Cyberterrorism: Fact or fancy?* Retrieved January 8, 2000 from the World Wide Web: <http://www.cs.georgetown.edu/~denning/infosec/pollitt.html>.
2. CCI Computer. *High tech dictionary.* Retrieved March 17, 2000 from the World Wide Web: <http://www.currents.net/resources/dictionary/definition.phtml>.

3. CMPnet. (1999). *Tech Encyclopedia*. Retrieved March 17, 2000 from the World Wide Web: <http://www.techweb.com/encyclopedia/defineterm.cgi>.

4. Sinai, J. (1999, September 21). *Cyberwarfare: Fact or fiction?* Retrieved January 8, 2000 from the World Wide Web: <http://jir.janes.com/sample/jir0499.html>.

5. Thom, G. (1999, July 24). *Web of fear: Cyber terror may be the price we pay for the growth of the Internet*. Retrieved January 8, 2000 from the World Wide Web: <http://www.infowar.com/class_3/99/class3_080299a_j.shtml>.

6. Hess, P. (1999, November 30). *Industry, feds play at cyberterror*. Retrieved January 8, 2000 from the World Wide Web: <http://www.infowar.com/class_3/99/class3_113099a_j.shtml>.

7. Maier, T. (1999, April 5). Is U.S. ready for cyberwarfare? *Insight on the News, 15,* 18.

8. Rowan, K. E. (1995, July). A new pedagogy for explanatory public speaking: Why arrangement should not substitute for invention. *Communication Education, 44,* 236–250.

9. Wilson, J. (1999, March). Information warfare. *Popular Mechanics, 176,* 58.

10. Wilson (1999, p. 58).

11. Rowan (1995, p. 245).

12. Rowan (1995, p. 45).

13. Fleshler, H., Ilardo, J., & Demoretcky, J. (1974, Summer). The influence of field dependence, speaker credibility set, and message documentation on evaluations of speaker and message credibility. *Southern Speech Communication Journal, 34,* 389–402, at 400.

14. McCroskey, J. C. (1969, April). A summary of experimental research on the effects of evidence in persuasive communication. *Quarterly Journal of Speech, 55,* 169–176, at 172.

15. McCroskey, J. C. (1986). *An introduction to rhetorical communication* (5th ed., p. 167). Englewood Cliffs, NJ: Prentice-Hall.

16. Kline, J. A. (1969, December). Interaction of evidence and readers' intelligence on the effects of short messages. *Quarterly Journal of Speech, 55,* 407–413, at 413.

17. Morgan, P. (1997, April). Can this medical plan be saved? How to make your HMO work for you. *Prevention, 49,* 96.

18. Hamill, R., Wilson, T., & Nisbett, R. (1980). Insensitivity to sample bias: Generalizing from atypical cases. *Journal of Personality and Social Psychology, 39,* 578–589.

19. McCroskey (1969, p. 175).

20. Bertrand, C. (1998, October). HMOs and medical malpractice. *Consumers' Research Magazine, 81,* 10.

21. Physicians for a National Health Program. (1999, July 13). *Quality of care lower in for-profit HMOs than in non-profits*. Retrieved April 5, 2000 from the World Wide Web: <http://www.pnhp.org/PRESS799.html>.

22. Physicians for a National Health Program (1999).

23. Evans, M. S. (1997, December). If you're in an HMO, here's why. *Consumers' Research Magazine, 80,* 10.

24. Meckler, L. (1999, July 28). Surveys show frustration with HMOs. A.P. Press Release.

25. Howe, R. F. (1999, February 1). The people vs. HMOs. *Time, 153,* 46.

26. Kuttner, R. (1998, May 21). Must good HMOs go bad? *New England Journal of Medicine, 338,* 1558–1563, at 1559.

27. Physicians for a National Health Program (1999).

28. Anders, G. (1996). *Health against Wealth: HMOs and the Breakdown of Medical Trust*. Boston: Houghton Mifflin.

29. Brink, S., & Shute, N. (1997, October 13). Are HMOs the right prescription? *U.S. News & World Report, 123,* 60.

30. Nielsen Media Research. What TV ratings really mean. Retrieved June 5, 1998 from the World Wide Web: <http://www.nielsenmedia.com/wtrrm.shtml>.

31. Berube, D. (1984). Debating hasty generalization. *CEDA* [Cross Examination Debate Association] *Yearbook, 1984.*

32. World Future Society. (1997, March–April). Terrorism via the Internet. *The Futurist, 31,* 64.

33. Sinai (1999, p. 5).

34. Evans (1997, p. 10).
35. Evans (1997).
36. Brink & Shute (1997).
37. Greco, R. (1998, April 4). The oasis. *The Lancet, 351,* 1052–1053.
38. Miyawaki, R. (1999, June 29). The fight against cyberterrorism: A Japanese view. *Center for Strategic and International Studies.* Retrieved January 8, 2000 from the World Wide Web: <http://www.csis.org/html/sp990629Miyawaki.html>.
39. CBS. (2000, January 7). Clinton seeks cyberdefense. *CBS News.* Retrieved January 7, 2000 from the World Wide Web: <http://www.cbs.com/now/story/0,1597,147103-311,00.shtml>.
40. Sinai (1999, p. 5).
41. Perelman, C., & Olbrechts-Tyteca, L. (1969). *The new rhetoric: A treatise on argumentation* (p. 28) (J. Wilkinson and P. Weaver, Trans.). Notre Dame, IN: University of Notre Dame Press.
42. Perelman & Olbrechts-Tyteca (1969, p. 30).
43. Crosswhite, J. (1995). Is there an audience for this argument? Fallacies, theories, and relativisms. *Philosophy and Rhetoric, 28,* 134–145, at 141.
44. Crosswhite (1995).
45. Tindale, C. W. (1999). *Acts of arguing: A rhetorical model of argument* (p. 117). Albany: State University of New York Press.
46. Tindale (1999, p. 118).
47. Scult, A. (1989). Perelman's universal audience: One perspective. In R. Dearin (Ed.), *The new rhetoric of Chaim Perelman: Statement and response* (pp. 153–162, at p. 159). New York: University Press of America.
48. Anders (1996, pp. 108–109).
49. Witte, K., & Morrison, K. (2000, Winter). Examining the influence of trait anxiety/repression-sensitization on individuals' reactions to fear appeals. *Western Journal of Communication, 64,* 1–27, at 1.
50. Mongeau, P. A. (1998). Another look at fear-arousing persuasive appeals. In M. Allen & R. W. Preiss (Eds.), *Persuasion: Advances through meta-analysis* (pp. 53–68, at p. 66). Cresskill, NJ: Hampton Press.
51. Mongeau (1998).
52. Witte & Morrison (2000, pp. 2–3).
53. Mongeau (1998, p. 66).
54. Brink & Shute (1997, p. 60).
55. Dillard, J. P., Hunter, J. E., & Burgoon, M. (1984, Summer). Sequential-request persuasive strategies. *Human Communication Research, 10,* 461–488, at 484.
56. Dillard et al. (1984).
57. Allen, M. (1998). Comparing the persuasive effectiveness: one- and two-sided message. In M. Allen & R. W. Preiss (Eds.), *Persuasion: Advances through meta-analysis* (pp. 87–98, at p. 96). Cresskill, NJ: Hampton Press.
58. Monroe, A. (1935). *Principles and types of speech.* (New York: Scott, Foresman).

10 Language and Speech

OBJECTIVES

After reading Chapter 10, you should understand:

- The significance of language and word choice.

- How to express your speech message clearly.

- Techniques you can use to express ideas creatively.

- The importance of choosing language that avoids bias and the perception of bias.

Can you recall a speech that moved or affected you in some way—whether it was something you heard long ago or more recently? Perhaps you were moved by the sincerity of the speaker or by the position she took, or perhaps you simply liked the subject matter. Chances are good that if the speech was memorable to you, one reason was specific words or expressions that the speaker used.

Recall that in Chapter 2, we discussed Martin Luther King Jr.'s "I Have a Dream" speech. The statement "I have a dream" was the title later given to the speech because it was an especially memorable expression in a speech rich with powerful language. Dr. King dreamed of a time and place free from prejudice and discrimination, and his dream inspired a country. Nearly forty years after his death, people are still moved by his words—and especially by his stirring "I have a dream." If Dr. King had calmly stated, "I hope that" instead of "I have a dream" as a frame for his speech, the impact of his message would have been very different.

In 1999, U.S. senator Dianne Feinstein offered her views about the United States' bombing campaign in Yugoslavia. Especially mindful of the accidental damage done by a NATO bomb to the Chinese Embassy in Belgrade, Feinstein said: "I don't believe you can win wars by tossing bombs around like popcorn."[1] The senator intended to convey her displeasure with and criticism of the NATO campaign, but what she said was more noteworthy because of the humorous confusion it created. Let's ignore for the moment her comparison of bombs to popcorn. The larger problem with her remark was that people who heard her speech did not hear her message that bombing should not be done indiscriminately. Instead, they speculated about whether people actually "toss" popcorn about. Her comparison didn't ring true, so her message didn't come across. When a speaker is not careful about word choice, the audience may remember not the intended message but the confusing or ambiguous language in which it was expressed.

For more on using comparisons effectively, see page 275.

That was a lesson learned by Marvin, a student giving an informative speech about law enforcement techniques in large cities. Marvin was a civilian volunteer with the local police department, and his ambition was to become a homicide investigator. In his speech he repeatedly referred to "policemen," and he discussed "handling perps," "running informants," and what he characterized as "problems of law enforcement in certain communities that don't want to help the police but feel justified demanding more perfection out of policemen."

Students in Marvin's audience had mixed reactions to his speech. Many found him credible because of his volunteer experience and his wide vocabulary of police terms and slang. Others found some of his slang impenetrable. Some women in the audience were put off by his use of "policemen," instead of the gender-neutral term *police officers.* Some listeners found the phrase "certain communities" insensitive and the word "perfection" laughable because of recent episodes of excessive police violence. Clearly, Marvin failed to get his message across to many in his audience.

If we were to reduce the message of this chapter to a single sentence, it would be this: ***Choose your words carefully.*** Words often have an impact beyond their grammatical function within a sentence. Sometimes they are imbued with multiple meanings, not simply their literal meaning. Occasionally they stand out and remain in the listener's mind. Used carefully, words convey precise meaning or paint a picture or provide context for the audience. Used carelessly, they add little to the message and may obscure it.

In an average speech there may be hundreds or thousands of words. Do they all matter? The answer is "yes." Language and word choice are extremely important—both for the positive effects they can have on the message and for the negative and often unintended effects they also can have.

We begin this chapter with a discussion of the significance of language and word choice. Then we offer suggestions to help you present your message clearly, express your ideas creatively, and avoid bias in language.

The Significance of Language and Word Choice

Words do not exist within a vacuum, apart from their use in the real world. Words derive their power and significance from their meaning. Can you remember the first time someone at school said something unkind to you—no doubt hurting your feelings? Later, a teacher or your parents might have repeated the cliché about "sticks and stones," but probably you still felt bad. What's more, you likely knew why you felt that way. Contrary to what your parent or teacher said, the unkind statements were not "just words." They had power—the power to hurt.

Words can hurt, but they also can be positive and affirming. Words can lift an audience, inspire listeners, change their thinking, or perhaps motivate them to action. The power of language and the importance of word choice derive from two different kinds of meaning that words convey: *denotative* and *connotative* meaning.

● *Denotative Meaning*

The **denotative meaning** of a word is its precise and exact dictionary definition. A speaker who chooses words that she or he believes will precisely and unambiguously convey the speech message has good reason to believe that there will be no doubt about what the speaker means. Of course, this belief rests on the assumption that everyone in the audience is fully informed about the denotative meaning of the speaker's words.

That assumption is pretty safe for words with only one meaning. But many words and phrases have several meanings. A dictionary often shows multiple uses of, and multiple meanings for, words. Let's consider the word *register*. It is both a noun and a verb. As a noun, *register* has nine different meanings. Here are three of them: (1) a record of items or details (as in "He entered his personal information in the medical *register*."), (2) a range of the human voice or of a musical instrument (as in "The *register* of Harold's voice was limited."), (3) a heating regulator or opening for hot air in a structure (as in "He opened the *register,* letting more heat into the room."). As a verb, *register* has five different meanings. One is "to convey an impression" (as in, "Her comment did not *register* with me until later.").

You probably wouldn't want to confuse the various meanings of register—for example, substituting *register* meaning "the range of a voice," for *register* meaning "a hot-air opening"—unless you were trying to suggest that a particular singer was full of hot air! Which of these meanings would the audience necessarily attach to the word used in a speech? Denotative meaning is also interpreted according to the context in which the word is used as well as by the audience's ability to associate a given meaning with a certain word.

For more on the audience's ability to understand word choice, see the demographics discussion on page 97.

Be careful with your word choice, because many words have multiple meanings. For example, you can pitch a baseball, but you can also pitch an idea. Make sure your usage makes clear to your audience what meaning you intend.

denotative meaning: the precise and exact dictionary meaning of a word.

● Connotative Meaning

The **connotative meaning** of a word is an association implied by the word in addition to its literal, denotative meaning. Speakers rely on connotation to appeal to listeners' emotions or intense feelings. For example, Western diplomats decried the repression of ethnic Albanians living in Kosovo as "ethnic cleansing." The term had a powerful connotative meaning for millions of people familiar with the Holocaust in World War II and evoked strong feelings of support for the Kosovo Albanians. Would world reaction—let alone reaction by the surrounding European countries—have been so strong if this repression had been called simply "a political tragedy" or "an unfortunate action by the government in Belgrade"? Perhaps not.

Your ability to take advantage of the connotative meanings of words will depend on your assessment of your audience—their experience and their feelings about certain subjects and words. On the one hand, words with powerful connotative meanings can make a powerful impression on your audience. For example, a student named Lois once complained: "Modern filmmakers in Hollywood are not artists. They are simply technicians who prostitute their talents, making films aimed at people who will watch their movies two or three times at the Cineplex!" When Lois used the verb *prostitute,* she accessed the emotional association that most people have with this word, and she made her point more forcefully than she might have made it if she had only said that Hollywood filmmakers "sell out for the money." Most students in the audience clearly understood the connotative meaning.

On the other hand, it is important to be sure that the connotation is appropriate for the speech. For example, a student named Albert made this statement in an impromptu speech about a school district's refusal to lower the student/teacher ratio for class size in elementary schools: "That kind of decision really demonstrates some bigotry by the school board!" The word *bigotry* actually refers to the state of mind of a person who is intolerantly devoted to his or her personal opinions or prejudices. The connotative meaning of this word, however, often brings to mind racial prejudice, and, indeed, many students in Albert's class had been victims of racial prejudice. Albert did not intend a racial connotation, but students inferred from Albert's use of *bigotry* that issues of race were behind the school board's decision. If you were Albert, how might you have stated this?

● Spoken Language and the Audience

Words in general do have impact in terms of their denotative and connotative meanings. With respect to *spoken* language in particular, word choice has additional significance in two very important ways for the audience listening to your speech. First and foremost, word choice is critical to ensuring that your audience fully understands your specific speech message. Vague or abstract language and speech passages filled with impenetrable jargon or verbal clutter can keep the audience from grasping your main point. Careful attention to language and word choice, therefore, helps the audience to follow your speech message.

Second, your word choice is a reflection on you as a speaker. In earlier chapters we introduced the concept of a speaker's *ethos,* or personal credi-

For more on connotative meaning and the audience's prior exposure to the speech message, see page 105.

For more on spoken language and the speaker's ethos, see page 38.

connotative meaning: the implied meaning of a word.

bility, and we discussed the ways this can influence an audience's perception of a speech message. On occasion, a speaker with strong ethos can make up for a weak or potentially controversial speech message. Language and word choice help the audience to understand your ethos, because the words you choose and the ways you phrase them say something about you.

A student speaker named Gillian gave an informative presentation about armor plating used during the Ottoman Empire. She showed photographs depicting the armor worn by soldiers and their horses and was careful to use the correct terminology in a way that the audience would understand. At one point she discussed a "gilded copper chanfrein," which she quickly explained was "forehead armor for the horse—like the helmet a soldier might wear." Her use of the technical terminology enabled the audience to see her as credible in the sense of being authoritative, and her ability to explain by analogy helped her to make the message accessible without condescending to the audience.

It should be obvious to you that your choice of words makes a difference. There are many ways to express an idea. The words you choose can greatly influence whether your message is listened to, understood, and accepted and acted on. How do you know which words or expressions will be most effective with your audience? In the rest of this chapter we examine three criteria to consider when choosing the words to use in a speech: clarity, creativity, and appropriateness.

Presenting Your Message Clearly

Perhaps most important of all, the message of your speech must be expressed clearly. After a speech, you may have heard someone say about the speaker, "I don't know what he said, but he sure sounded good!" Such a statement is a polite way of saying, "I have no idea what he was talking about!" To ensure that your message will be clear, your language must be understandable, concrete, proper, and concise.

● *Use Understandable Language*

To present your ideas successfully, you must be sure that your audience knows what your words mean. Unfamiliar terms can cause listeners to lose interest once they decide it will take too much mental energy to make sense of what you are saying.

Understandable language refers to words that are *recognizable* to the audience—words that all in the audience will understand. Would you expect a class of first-year college students to know and use legal terminology? Some students might know a few terms from a previous class, popular novels, television programs, or the occasional legal thriller movie. A smaller number might be working their way through school as paralegals or legal assistants. It is more than likely, however, that obscure legal terms—such as *in personum jurisdiction*—will not be understood by everyone in the audience. In contrast, a technical term such as *jurisdiction* probably would be understood by the entire audience because it is in common use by most people.

For more on using language that the audience will understand, see page 101.

To review demographics, life experience, and common ground, see pages 97–104.

Audience analysis is the key to using recognizable language. The educational background of audience members can suggest their general vocabulary level. In addition, demographic information and assumptions about audience members' life experiences and common ground can inform your decisions about what language the audience will understand.

Recall the speech delivered by Marvin, who looked forward to a career in law enforcement, and look at Figure 10.1 to see a portion of Marvin's Speech Grid. Marvin would have been better served to think through the implications of the demographic section of his audience analysis and consider what they might mean for his word choice. The demographic section of his grid should have clued him to the need to avoid language that could be interpreted as sexist ("policeman" instead of *officer*) and expressions that specific groups of listeners might find offensive (such as ominous references to "certain communities").

In addition, no one in Marvin's audience had any technical knowledge about law enforcement. Thus Marvin should have been careful to avoid **jargon**—specialized or technical words or phrases familiar to people in a specific field or group. When he discussed "handling perps," he was using jargon. The word *perps* is slang for *perpetrators*—individuals who are suspected of committing a crime. *Perpetrator* itself is a technical term. If the audience understands the term, the choice of words is fine; but if the audience does not know the term, the choice of words becomes a barrier to under-

FIGURE 10.1 **Marvin's Audience Analysis**

Situational Characteristics
- 5–7 minute speech length.
- 26 audience members (25 students and one teacher).
- Large classroom; videotape player and monitor available.

Demographics
- Of the 26 audience members, 20 are female.
- Majority of students have lived in large metropolitan area all of their lives.
- At least six students grew up in relative poverty.
- Most of the audience members are fairly liberal on most political issues, but conservative on law-and-order issues.
- Most have no real experience with the police.

Common Ground
- All but one audience member are students.
- All of us live in the city.

Prior Exposure
Limited to what they have heard from their parents, or more likely seen in the news or in films.

jargon: specialized or technical words or phrases familiar to people in a specific field or group.

standing. Look at Figure 10.1. Do you think it is likely everyone in Marvin's audience knew what *perps* means?

Jargon also includes abbreviations, acronyms, and other expressions. People in the field of information technology, for example, use a lot of jargon. The abbreviation *f2f* refers to *face-to-face* communication—real-world interaction between two or more people, as opposed to electronic communication online. The term *snail mail* refers to correspondence delivered by the postal system and is intended as a dig at the relative slowness of that system in comparison with the speed of e-mail. Such expressions are recognizable to anyone conversant with computer technology and the Internet; but to someone with no knowledge or experience in that area, deciphering those terms would be like trying to understand a foreign language.

View a student incorrectly using overly technical language.
CD-ROM: Video Theater, Excerpt 10.1

Should you always avoid jargon? No. But you must remember these two simple rules:

1. *If you can say something in plain and simple language, do so.* Unless you see a pressing reason to use jargon (for example, you are certain that everyone in your audience will understand the terms you want to use, and you want to impress the audience with your command of the terms), use simple words. Very rarely do speakers lose favor with an audience for using words that everyone could understand!

2. *If you want to use jargon, explain it first so that everyone in the audience will understand what is being said.* Speakers occasionally try to impress an audience with their vocabulary. But listeners who don't understand what is said or use those words themselves will be unlikely to follow the speech message and may feel the speaker is showing off or, worse, being condescending.

To illustrate that latter point, consider the following passage from the beginning of a speech by a student named Jackson, in explanation of a study he conducted:

> I intended to employ an ethnographic research design in analyzing the data collected in order to remain consistent with the dominant pedagogy and epistemological assumptions embedded in the theoretical view of economic theory as noted above and used in the analysis process. This would help to illuminate the relationship between research, theory and pedagogical praxis, while admittedly problematizing the dominant epistemological presumptions in most previous studies.

Attempting to be eloquent, Jackson risks sounding pedantic or self-important. Should you always avoid words and phrases such as *problematizing, praxis,* and *dominant epistemological presumptions*? No. Jackson's vocabulary might be appropriate for his audience—university professors attending an economics seminar.

Always use your audience analysis when considering whether your word choice will be appropriate for your audience. Obviously, Jackson's explanation probably would be inappropriate for a general audience—who might indeed think Jackson was showing off his vocabulary. The rule should always be: Use language that is familiar to the audience. More often than not, simple words are the best choice.

Use Concrete Words

When you think about what words to use to convey a certain message, also consider whether those words are abstract or specific. *Abstract words* can be confusing and ambiguous for the audience. *Concrete words* are specific and suggest exactly what you mean. Consider these three sentences, which range from abstract to concrete:

> This past week, Jane arrived in a vehicle.   *(abstract)*
> Four days ago, Jane arrived in a car.   *(less abstract)*
> Last Tuesday at noon, Jane arrived in a blue Toyota.   *(concrete)*

Only the third sentence tells exactly how and when Jane arrived. If this information is relevant to the presentation, the third sentence certainly conveys more information than the first or second sentences.

Likewise, in the next set of examples, see how the speaker used what he thought was descriptive language to express his feelings about a job proposal:

> The proposal seemed *a little lean* to me.

What exactly did the speaker mean: that the proposal lacked weight? was thin? was not fat? A second effort produced less abstract language:

> The proposal *did not have enough details*.

Although this was an improvement, a listener still would not know what details the speaker was referring to. The third effort produced a concrete statement:

> The proposal did not have enough details *about the signing bonus*.

In your speeches, consider how specific you are being. Are your words vague? Is there more than one way to interpret what you are saying? Is the audience receiving the information you wish to share?

Use Words Properly

The audience's understanding of your message will improve if you use words that express precisely the point you want to convey. Inaccurate word choice confuses the audience or undermines your credibility if the audience doesn't know what you are trying to say but does know that you used a word incorrectly. For example, in a speech forecasting a long period of low general economic activity accompanied by widespread unemployment, a speaker referred to this situation as a "recession," although she was describing the characteristics of a full-blown economic depression—far worse and more damaging than a recession. Misuse of *recession* led to confusion and raised questions about the speaker's credibility.

On occasion, the failure to use the proper words produces unintended humorous results—often at the speaker's expense. A student once referred to the activities of "grunge rockers," whom he accused of "various kinds of immortal behavior." The audience laughed, assuming that he probably meant immoral behavior.

Even the president of the United States is not immune from making an occasional lapse in word choice. In his final State of the Union address, President Bill Clinton referred to the desire of his vice president, Al Gore, to make more "liberal" communities. The word the president wanted to use was *livable*. You can well imagine the reception this misstatement received in the Republican-controlled Congress.

The foregoing examples illustrate the need for precise word choice and definition. President Clinton knew the precise word but was unable to avoid using the wrong word (most likely because the two words sounded alike—although some of his critics joked that his lapse was a Freudian slip). In the cases of each student, however, the failure to use words properly most likely resulted from ignorance about their meaning.

> **TIP**
>
> *If you aren't sure you know the meaning of a certain word, look it up in the dictionary to be sure you are using it properly.*

● Use Concise Language

An audience listening to your speech must grasp your ideas as they are presented. Audience members cannot reread or rehear a page of your speech to gain a better understanding of what you are trying to say. For this reason, most of your sentences should express a single thought. Although long sentences linking different ideas may be understandable when they are read, listeners may have difficulty following them in a speech.

As a rule of thumb, use the fewest words necessary to express an idea. As you outline your speech, consider whether you can make the same point in fewer words. Occasionally you may want to add words or phrases because they bring color, eloquence, wit, or humor to your speech. But in every case, be certain you have a good reason to insert those extra words; if you do not, word economy is preferable.

We refer to unnecessary words in a speech as **verbal clutter** because they are more than is necessary for the presentation and make it hard for the audience to follow what is being said. Clutter often occurs when many words are used where one word would suffice. Here are some examples; the clutter appears in italics:

> "The death penalty cannot deter crime *for the reason that* murderers do not think about the consequences of their actions."

> "*Regardless of the fact that* you do not agree with the government's position, you cannot dispute the FCC's ruling."

> "If we are *to make contact* with our bargaining opponents, we have to find a mutually acceptable schedule."

Those sentences are easily revised to eliminate clutter. Notice the effect of the concise underlined words:

verbal clutter: unnecessary words in a speech; they make it hard for the audience to follow what is said.

> "The death penalty cannot deter crime <u>because</u> murderers do not think about the consequences of their actions."

> "<u>Although</u> you do not agree with the government's position, you cannot dispute the FCC's ruling."

> "If we are to <u>meet</u> with our bargaining opponents, we have to find a mutually acceptable schedule."

In each sentence, verbal clutter disappeared when a single-word alternative replaced a wordy phrase. As a rule, you should check your speech outline for places where one word can replace an unnecessarily lengthy phrase.

Expressing Your Ideas Creatively

At the beginning of this chapter we noted that words have considerable power to move an audience, especially when used in creative ways. In this section we consider how speakers achieve this effect through the use of repetition, hypothetical examples, personal examples, vivid language, and metaphors and similes.

● *Use Repetition*

Occasionally you will want to emphasize a certain point in your speech. A valuable tool for drawing the audience's attention (and memory) to something is the thoughtful use of repetition. For example, you may wish to repeat a point, right after making it the first time:

> At the end of the battle, every soldier was killed. Every soldier.

This use of repetition draws listeners' attention to the central point of your statement. In the preceding example, the speaker wished to emphasize that every soldier *on both sides* died. This type of repetition can be dramatic and should be used judiciously. If you repeat nearly everything you have said, the audience will think you are emphasizing everything and will wonder what is really important in your speech. Worse, you will seem melodramatic. Used selectively, however, repeating what you've just said can be very effective.

Another way to use repetition is to come back to a point not right away but later in the speech. You are repeating yourself, but the distance separating the initial statement from the repeated one lets the repetition come across like a gentle reminder. You can see this technique in the following passage from a student named Allyson in her informative speech about trekking across Russia:

> When most people think about mountains in Russia, if they know anything, they think about the Urals. These are old mountains, stretching some 1,200 miles, from north to south. The mountains themselves are covered with taigas—large forests that blanket the area. As I mentioned before, these 1,200 miles are an impressive sight, with all sorts of wildlife, including wolves, bears, and many different game birds.

Allyson repeats the distance, north to south, of the Urals because she wants the audience to remember this information later, when she discusses the difficulties and challenges of backpacking there.

Finally, you may want to repeat a point—but to do so in different words. *Rewording* is a good idea when you say something that may be difficult for everyone in the audience to understand and remember. Rewording allows the audience to more easily grasp what you mean. Here is an example:

> According to the engineering report, the shuttle booster rockets had systems failure with the cooling system, not to mention serious problems with the outer hatch doors and the manually operated crane; that is to say, there were at least three mechanical problems we know of with this last shuttle mission.

In this instance, rewording makes the list of problems easier to remember. Rewording works particularly well in those parts of your speech where you enumerate a list or make a technical statement that might be difficult for the audience to follow.

● Use Hypothetical Examples

Technical, complicated messages provide an opportunity to use **hypothetical examples**—imagined examples or scenarios that you describe to illustrate the point you are trying to make. These work particularly well when you are trying to demonstrate a complicated point. An audience often can follow a complicated point if you first present a hypothetical example.

Assume that you wanted to inform your audience about the legal test for defamation of character. A student named Blake gave a speech on this subject, introducing it with a hypothetical example:

> Suppose a news station decided to send a camera crew and reporter along with a paramedic team to record their average day. Say that this team was later called out to an accident on the interstate and pulled a badly hurt individual from a burning wreck of a car. Now suppose the camera crew taped the whole rescue, and the reporter talked to the victim when she was sedated with painkillers. Under the influence of painkillers, the victim said many foolish things, including some unkind words about her employer. Would the television station be justified in broadcasting the whole story—including everything the victim said to the reporter? What would the victim's rights be here, if any?

Hypothetical examples work best with topics that may be too difficult to understand unless audience members can see them in operation *and* think and process them in their own minds. This technique encourages the audience to interact with the speaker and the subject matter of the speech.

● Use Personal Examples

Illustrating a concept with examples may be especially effective when the examples are real and personal to the speaker or the audience. You may decide to illustrate the point you making with a personal anecdote. Adam, a sophomore in a speech class, did this in an informative speech about phobias:

hypothetical example: an imagined example or scenario intended to illustrate a specific point.

Phobias come in many different forms—and most, if not all, can be cured with therapy and/or medication. I know this, because I've lived with one of these myself. Although you would not know it to look at me today, I once had a horrible fear of flying. Just the thought of getting near a big jet used to give me the shakes. Sweaty palms. The works. It was a real problem. But a half year of therapy—which included taking some flights with someone I really trusted—cured me of the fear.

Adam illustrates one type of phobia in a way that gives him credibility (he can speak from experience) but avoids making light of his subject and running the risk of offending anyone in the audience with similar fears. Personal examples are excellent for building speaker credibility, and they are a particularly effective way to do so without making anyone in the audience feel as though the speaker is examining or making light of his or her life.

For more on a speaker's personal examples and common ground with the audience, see page 102.

The same is true for examples that may be more common to the audience. In this instance, the speaker, searching for common ground, may want to use an example familiar to the audience. In a speech on credit card debt, a freshman student named Jackie said:

You really have to be careful about these credit cards. You get on somebody's mailing list right after you're out of high school and into college. Suddenly your mailbox is filled with offers of free credit cards. And they don't have a service charge for the first three months. You can get credit up to five thousand dollars. Just a minimum payment each month. Hasn't that happened to most of you in this room? It happened to me, too. And we all know how fast that credit card debt can pile up!

Jackie used an example with which the audience could immediately identify.

● *Use Vivid Language to Create Imagery*

Vivid language grabs the attention of your audience with words and phrases that are meaningful and colorful rather than ordinary. By *vivid*, we mean full of life or vigor and able to appeal to all our senses—touch, hearing, taste, smell, and sight. The following examples from an autobiographical presentation in a speech class illustrate the difference between ordinary and vivid word choice. Here Jamie is describing what it was like to live with his family as a young child:

View Heather Lamm using vivid language at the Reform Party National Convention.
CD-ROM: Video Theater, Excerpt 10.2

I remember those mornings at home only too well. Mom would call us if we overslept. She was downstairs making breakfast, every morning at eight o'clock sharp. My brothers and I would fight to be the first into the bathroom.

Although this passage is fairly descriptive, consider the second version with more vivid word choice:

vivid language: words and phrases that are colorful, full of life and vigor; the kind of language that appeals to the senses.

Mornings were memorable in my house. It was always cold in the room I shared with my brothers. With no curtains on our windows, light would stream in, poking us in the eyes before Mom ever called us down for breakfast. The smell of bacon wafting upstairs did the rest. Routinely we shoved one another, forming a line outside the bathroom, knowing Mom would demand to know if we had washed up before coming to the table.

The second version conveys the same basic information as the first but paints a more textured picture of the scene, with stronger **imagery** for the audience. The speaker's graphic and descriptive language gives the audience a mental impression (or image) of the concepts and ideas he is trying to convey. We can feel the cold air, see the bright light, smell the bacon, and hear Mom's voice. Vivid language brings the second version to life and makes it memorable.

When you think about what you want to say to the audience, ask yourself whether you are using words that are descriptive and image-rich. Imagery can add life and color to your speech and help the audience to see what you are trying to communicate. That being said, however, remember that vivid language is most effective when used sparingly.

Senator Dianne Feinstein's humorous gaffe—comparing dropping bombs to throwing popcorn—overshadowed the importance of her message. What can you do to ensure that a similar problem will not arise when you try to use imagery and creative language in your speeches?

● *Use Similes and Metaphors*

Similes and metaphors suggest similarities between objects that are not alike. A **simile** makes an explicit comparison. A **metaphor** makes an implicit one. Similes contain the words *like* or *as*. Here are three examples; the similes appear in italics:

- His mind works *like an adding machine.*
- After bumping her head, she fell *like a tree.*
- The baby's crying was *as sweet as music* to his ears.

Metaphors compare objects that are not alike by identifying one object with the other; the comparisons, however, are not meant to be taken literally. Here are three examples; the metaphors appear in italics:

- My willpower is *my shield against temptation.*
- Her life was *a journey along a path filled with obstacles.*
- Technology is *the engine driving this economic boom.*

When you use similes and metaphors, you need to be aware of the problems they can create. The comparison has to work.

Senator Feinstein's attempt at simile ("I don't believe you can win wars by tossing bombs around like popcorn.") doesn't work. She would have made her point far more effectively if she had said, "I don't believe you can win wars by tossing bombs around like baseballs," or "I don't believe you can win wars by scattering bombs around like so much loose change." In these rewordings, the compared items are dissimilar, but the comparison makes sense.

Likewise, avoid mixing comparisons—that is, using more than one metaphor or simile at a time. Otherwise, you might produce some unintentionally funny statements. Here are two examples. The first contains mixed metaphors; the second, mixed similes:

imagery: graphic and descriptive language that creates a mental impression (or image) of what is said.

simile: an explicit comparison of things that are not alike.

metaphor: an implicit comparison of things that are not alike.

Outlawing the possession of marijuana paraphernalia was exactly the bullet the House of Representatives needed to cook the new drug bill and drive it over to the Senate.

The new father danced like a butterfly, bouncing off the delivery room walls and giggling like a young baby with gas.

In the first, an act of legislation is compared to a bullet, and the bullet is then said to cook and drive! In the second, a new parent is compared to a butterfly that dances and bounces (so far so good) but also giggles like a baby with gas.

When used properly, metaphors and similes can help the audience understand and experience one idea through reference to another.[2] Metaphors can also allow people to experience a new idea "in terms that resonate with their past experience, but also to reveal these experiences vividly to others."[3]

Similes and metaphors are very effective tools for creatively making comparisons in your speech. Just remember to look for comparisons that make sense and to avoid mixing them.

Choosing Appropriate Language

Your word choice should not reflect bias against other cultures or individuals. When speakers use **biased language**—word choice that suggests prejudice or preconceptions—they lose credibility with the audience. Judgments based on the race, ethnicity, gender, sexuality, religion, or mental or physical ability of groups or individuals are to be avoided. Audience members who believe a speaker is attacking members of their culture or group are unlikely to take the speaker's ideas seriously—or even to listen attentively to the speech. Even if a particular group is not represented in the audience, avoid any semblance of biased language. In the rest of this section we present some principles you can use to keep biased language out of your speech.

● *Avoid Negative Stereotypes*

Negative stereotypes are negative generalizations about characteristics that members of a group are powerless to change, such as race, ethnicity, or gender, and about characteristics that may be central to a person's identity, such as religious beliefs (see In Theory box 10.1). Negative stereotypes rest on the false assumption that characteristics that may be shared by some in the group are true of all members of the group.

Avoiding stereotypes does not require you to be "politically correct." The question posed by the term *political correctness* is a source of concern—and friction—in American society. To be politically correct is supposedly to hold ideas and use language that reflect a politically liberal perspective. Conservatives often complain about having political correctness imposed on them if they are criticized for not espousing a certain political position or for making a reference or using a label unacceptable to those on the political left. For example, positions that are not environmentally friendly are deemed politically incorrect, as is the use of terms such as "black American"

biased language: word choice that reflects prejudice or preconceptions about other cultures and individuals.

negative stereotype: a negative generalization about a group of people, suggesting that characteristics that may be shared by some in the group are true of all in the group.

| INVENTION | ORGANIZATION | STYLE | PREPARATION | DELIVERY |

In Theory 10.1

LABELS, STEREOTYPES, AND IDENTITY

In Chapter 2 we introduced the canons of rhetoric, one of which is *style,* the selection of language to best express your ideas. Language and word choice affect a speaker's credibility and sometimes have a negative impact on the audience.

What's in a name? What's in a label? Does it really matter what you call people? On occasion you may hear a speech in which the speaker makes what she or he thinks is an offhand remark or a humorous reference, but you know that what you are hearing is biased language—specifically, a label. Examples include comments about "Asian drivers" or "Latin lovers" or the "mentally retarded," or a remark suggesting that a losing male boxer fought "like a girl." If such remarks aren't intended as insults, how important are they? Ask yourself how you would feel if you were a member of the group being referred to.

In their own fashion, labels impose an identity on the group they reference. Labels may affect our sense of our own identity and the identity of others in negative ways.[4] Labels not only reinforce stereotypes but undermine self-esteem and produce a negative self-image. Even commonly used, seemingly innocent labels have this effect. For example, if people are always referring to you as "wheelchair bound," how long do you think it will take you to think of yourself as bound and limited?

(instead of "African American") and "girl" or "gal" (instead of "woman" when referring to an adult woman). Those who complain about political correctness view it as a form of liberal censorship.

Those who are accused of promoting political correctness respond that the term itself is the creation of the political right. They observe that there is no singular perspective from the left (or from the right) about what ideas are "correct" and there certainly is no group or mind-set that regulates and censors supposedly politically incorrect ideas or language. Moreover, they point out, the term *political correctness* itself is a label and effectively marginalizes liberal viewpoints in the same way that race and gender-based labels marginalize racial groups and women.

Unless you are assigned a specific point of view about a particular topic, you should advocate the viewpoint you believe. Regardless of your position, you must support your position with credible evidence and logical reasoning; otherwise, you are likely to be perceived as prejudiced. A speaker who tackled a controversial issue such as affirmative action and asserted, "We all know that affirmative action programs give jobs to unqualified women and minorities," would be suspected of bias by any audience members who disagreed.

For more on the use of evidence and logical reasoning in your speech message, see pages 232–42.

Stereotyping also can come into play when speakers make claims that go beyond the facts that their evidence proves. Suppose a speaker offers only a few examples of unqualified persons who received jobs because of affirmative action, but insists that those examples are proof that everyone who benefits from affirmative action is unqualified. The speaker would be making a claim without proof and would be perpetuating a negative stereotype.

For more on stereotyping and inductive reasoning, see pages 235–37.

Some topics are loaded with potential for controversy and often with potential for bias. Here, in particular, a speaker needs to be careful to emphasize arguments that do not rely on stereotypes. For example, an argument against affirmative action could focus on the claim that race or gender should play no role in hiring decisions. A speaker could advocate stronger remedies for any individual who is discriminated against. By arguing against giving a person a job because of ethnicity or gender, and also against denying a job because of racism or sexism, the speaker can better get his or her message across to a diverse audience.

● *Use Gender-Neutral References*

Experts in grammar openly advocated the use of the generic *he* as early as 1553,[5] and by 1850, this preference was legally supported (*he* was said to stand for *he* and *she*).[6] By the 1970s, however, modern linguists were openly questioning the generic use of masculine pronouns, because it tended to reinforce gender-based stereotypes. Today, students learn how to avoid both masculine and feminine pronouns when referring to jobs and management positions—such as chief executive officer (CEO), nurse, or high school principal—that can be held by men or women. If you say, "A CEO must keep his meeting organized," or "A good nurse is considerate of her patients," audience members may think that you are unaware of the existence of female CEOs and male nurses. To avoid gender stereotyping with pronouns, use plural forms, such as "Good *presidents* keep *their* meetings organized." Or, if a singular pronoun is appropriate in your speech, alternate the use of *she* and *he* from paragraph to paragraph or from example to example. Another technique you can use is to mention both pronouns—"she or he" and "his or her"—if your sentences will still flow smoothly.

Be careful about how you refer to gender in your speech. Not every police officer is a policeman, and not every businessperson is a businessman. Assuming characteristics such as gender can create a division between you and members of your audience.

Speaker bias may also be assumed if you use gender-specific nouns or noun phrases, such as *poetess, chairman, congressman,* and *cleaning lady*. Use **gender-neutral terms**—words that do not suggest any reference to gender—such as *poet, chair, congressional representative,* and *cleaner*. A speaker might believe that gender-specific terms are acceptable if his or her intent is not sexist. A speaker might say: "I am saying fire*man* because most firefighters are male, but I have no problem with a qualified woman being a fireman." The problem with this approach is the speaker's failure to recognize that a speech must be *audience centered*. If audience members take offense at terms such as *fireman,* the speaker loses credibility. A better way to indicate support for qualified women or men filling a role is to use a gender-neutral term.

Use Appropriate References to Ethnic Groups

You should use the noun or phrase preferred by a particular ethnic group when referring to that group. For example, *African American* is commonly preferred to *black* or *Afro-American*. It is a sign of courtesy and respect to use the name a group has chosen for itself. Sometimes, more than one name is commonly used—for example, *Latino/Latina* and *Chicano/Chicana*. If you are uncertain about which term to use, ask friends or classmates who are members of that group which name is preferable.

When ethnicity is relevant to your audience, be certain that you are referring to ethnic groups appropriately. Not all people from Laos are Hmong. A visiting professor from Nigeria is not an African American, and people from Puerto Rico or Spain are not Mexican Americans. When a word comes from a language that uses different masculine and feminine forms, you also need to pay attention to gender. For example, author Ana Castillo is a Chican**a**, not a Chican**o**. Your attentiveness to this distinction during your audience analysis will pay real dividends in your speech.

For more on ethnicity and demographics, see page 98.

Avoid Unnecessary References to Ethnicity, Gender, Sexuality, or Religion

When a person's ethnicity, religion, sexuality, or gender is not relevant to a point you are making, do not mention it in your speech. If you say "the *Chinese American* judge," "the *Jewish* baseball player," "the *male* first-grade teacher," or "the *lesbian* CEO," audience members may believe that you find it unusual for a judge to be Chinese American, a baseball player to be Jewish, a man to be a first-grade teacher, or a lesbian to run a company. You should mention these characteristics only if they are central to the point you are trying to make. An informative speech about baseball great Jackie Robinson would probably need to refer to his racial heritage. It is relevant to note that as an African American, he was subjected to many forms of racism and that he broke the "color barrier" and joined the Brooklyn Dodgers in 1947. In a speech about "underdog teams" in sports, however, you might note that Warren Moon quarterbacked the University of Washington to an improbable Rose Bowl victory in 1978. In such a context, Moon's racial background would be irrelevant.

gender-neutral terms: words that do not refer to an individual's gender.

Summary

Language and word choice are vitally important to your speech presentation because of their ability to convey precise meaning and to create vivid imagery for the audience. Many successful speeches have been enhanced by the words that the speaker used to express her or his thoughts and ideas. Whether you are a beginning or an experienced speaker, carefully consider the language and words you choose to convey your message.

In this chapter we differentiated between the denotative and connotative meaning of words. We also explored a number of techniques and concepts for using language effectively. The checklist shows how you can use the material learned from this chapter to refine the language in your speeches.

Checklist

LANGUAGE AND WORD CHOICE

____ Be aware of the significance and potential power of the words you choose (p. 264)

____ Understand the difference between *denotative* and *connotative* meanings (pp. 265–66)

____ Consider the impact that spoken language has on your audience (p. 266)

PRESENT YOUR MESSAGE CLEARLY

____ Use understandable language (p. 267)

____ Use concrete words (p. 270)

____ Use words properly (p. 270)

____ Use concise language (p. 271)

EXPRESS YOUR IDEAS CREATIVELY

____ Use repetition (p. 272)

____ Use hypothetical examples (p. 273)

____ Use personal examples (p. 273)

____ Use vivid language to create imagery (p. 274)

____ Use similes and metaphors (p. 275)

CHOOSE YOUR LANGUAGE APPROPRIATELY

____ Avoid negative stereotypes (p. 276)

____ Use gender-neutral references (p. 278)

____ Use appropriate references to ethnic groups (p. 279)

____ Avoid unnecessary references to ethnicity, gender, or religion (p. 279)

Key Terms and Concepts

denotative meaning (p. 265)

connotative meaning (p. 266)

jargon (p. 268)

verbal clutter (p. 271)

hypothetical examples (p. 273)

vivid language (p. 274)

imagery (p. 275)

simile (p. 275)

metaphor (p. 275)

biased language (p. 276)

negative stereotype (p. 276)

gender-neutral terms (p. 279)

Please turn the page for the
Speech Grid Application.

Speech Grid Application

Evolution of a Speech Grid

Speech Grid Applications, showing the evolution of a Speech Grid, are included near the end of Chapters 5 through 12. They illustrate how one student, Samantha, uses a grid to prepare a speech.

Samantha takes some of the material from each side of her grid and uses that information to make decisions on style. In this chapter we see only excerpts from Samantha's grid. For the complete grid and outline of her main points, see the Speech Grid Application in Chapter 9.

When you prepare your speeches, determine how you can use style to best convey to your audience the ideas you have selected from your grid.

AUDIENCE ANALYSIS	SPEECH MESSAGE
Demographics **Age:** 17 (5); 18 (17); 19 (4); 20 (1); 22 (1) **Ethnicity:** African-American (2); Hmong (2); white (9); Latino/a (6); Portuguese (2); Pacific Islander, Mexican, German, Japanese, Swedish, Greek (1 each); did not say (1) **Major:** Undeclared (9); Liberal Studies (5); Chem, Bus, Crim (2 each); Child Devel, Engl, Bio, Premed, Journalism, Ag Bus, Econ, Comm (1 each) **Common Ground** I, like most of class (20 students), do not own a cell phone. **Prior Exposure** • Few (7 students) had heard about the issue of cell phones and driving; it had not been major topic in the local media. • Most students (20) do not own a cell phone.	• Driving while gabbing is a growing problem. (Main point I) • The growth rate in cell phone use is high among 18–25-year-old drivers. (Main point IA2) • The risk of accidents due to cell phone usage is similar to the drinking and driving risk. (Main point IC1b) • Narrative of troubles of friend who was in an accident. (Main point IC3) • The wireless industry lobby opposes anti–cell phone laws. Communities do not want to seem anti-business or anti-tech. (Main point IIB1) • Many of you indicated that you feel safer driving in an unfamiliar place if you have a phone. (Main point IIIC1a)

Samantha's Style Considerations

GRID LANGUAGE	REVISED WORD CHOICE	
• Driving while gabbing is a growing problem.	• Driving while dialing is a growing problem.	*Change "gabbing" to "dialing." Demographics suggests students*

(continued)

Samantha's Style Considerations, continued

GRID LANGUAGE	REVISED WORD CHOICE	
• The growth rate in cell phone use is high among 18–25-year-old drivers.	• Although I am confident that my classmates are excellent drivers, my evidence indicates that people in our age group are particularly likely to become cell phone owners in the next few years.	*rarely use the term "gabbing." Maintain the phrase "driving while dialing" in each main point because it is more creative than "using a cell phone when you are driving" and it allows for repetition.*
• The risk of accidents due to cell phone usage is similar to the risk of drinking and driving.	• Driving while dialing is the driving-while-intoxicated problem of the twenty-first century. As far as the accident risk goes, it is like pounding down a beer when you are behind the wheel.	*Be sure not to stereotype young drivers as unsafe drivers.*
• Narrative of troubles of friend who was in an accident.	• My friend Stan was an innocent victim of a distracted driver. He began crossing a nearby street when the green "go" sign for pedestrians flashed. After taking several steps, Stan heard an approaching car. Before he could react, that car struck him squarely on the side, throwing him in the air and breaking his leg. The driver had not seen Stan or the red light because he was busy placing an order with a stockbroker on his cell phone.	*More vivid language. Use the simile "pounding down a beer."* *Use vivid language and a personal example.*
• The wireless industry lobby opposes anti–cell phone laws. Communities do not want to seem anti-business or anti-tech.	• The wireless industry, those companies making cell phones and other devices that transmit voices and data without a wire or other connection, is opposed to laws that would restrict cell phone use. Furthermore, state and local government leaders do not want to appear hostile to business or new technology.	*Most audience members do not own cell phones, nor are most in a business- or technology-oriented major (use of demographic). The "wireless industry" may not be a recognizable word. Change "anti-tech" to "hostile to new technology" to avoid jargon.*
• Many of you indicated that you feel safer driving in unfamiliar places if you have a phone.	• On your surveys, many of you indicated that you feel safer driving in an unfamiliar place if you have a phone. For example, if one of you had a job delivering pizzas in a neighborhood you do not know well, it would be helpful to have a phone available — if trouble arose.	*Use a hypothetical example to illustrate a point.*

Source Notes

1. Lochead, C. (1999, May 11). Feinstein condemns bombing of embassy. *San Francisco Chronicle,* p. A13.
2. Lakoff, G., & Johnson, M. (1980, p. 5). *Metaphors we live by.* Chicago: University of Chicago Press.
3. Jorgensen-Earp, C. R., & Staton, A. Q. (1993). Student metaphors for the college freshman experience. *Communication Education, 42,* 123–141, at 125.
4. Larkey, L. K., Hecht, M. L., & Martin, J. N. (1993). What's in a name? African American ethnic identity terms and self determination. *Journal of Language and Social Psychology, 12,* 302–317.
   Gething, L. (1992). *Person to person: A guide for professionals working with people with disabilities* (2nd ed.). New York: Powell's.
5. Stringer, J. L., & Hopper, R. (1998). Generic *he* in conversation? *Quarterly Journal of Speech, 84,* 209–221.
6. Cameron, D. (1985, p. 68). *Feminism and linguistic theory.* New York: St. Martin's Press.

"How you say something is often as important as what you say."

11

Delivery Skills

OBJECTIVES

After reading Chapter 11, you should understand:

● The advantages and disadvantages of three modes of speech delivery.

● Different aspects of nonverbal communication and how to use them effectively.

● How to match your delivery skills with your audience analysis.

● The ethical implications of skillful speech delivery.

Helen, a student in a college-level marine biology class, just completed an oral presentation of her report on the white whale (beluga). As an experienced writer, she had concentrated on structuring her presentation. In only ten minutes she was able to comment on a beluga's physical characteristics, relationship to other whales, diet, mating habits, birth and care of young calves, and migration patterns. She had prepared the speech in outline form and delivered it using a series of five-by-seven-inch cards. She even had prepared visual aids—enlarged copies of photos showing belugas at different stages of life.

Helen received a B– from her instructor. She was surprised because she had worked hard on her report and she felt it was detailed and thorough. She expected an A– or better. When she asked about the grade, her instructor asked her to look at a videotape recording of her speech. The instructor taped every student presentation, so student speakers could see what he had seen.

The tape proved enlightening. While watching herself (a nerve-wracking but useful exercise), Helen noticed several things about her speech. She found it hard to hear her own voice because she had spoken very quietly. She noticed that she seemed to be speaking very fast—possibly because she had so much to cover in ten minutes. Maybe, she thought, she had too much to cover in this span of time.

Turning down the sound for a moment, she watched to see what she looked like when speaking. Again, the video was instructive. She had been overly preoccupied with her note cards. Throughout the speech she repeatedly looked at them, turning them over nervously in her hands. She seldom looked at the camera, which was located in the center of the audience. Worse, she had turned away from the audience several times to point out something in her photos of the whales. When she did so, she turned her back completely to the audience and appeared to be speaking to the photo.

By viewing the videotape, Helen learned some valuable lessons about the importance of delivery in a public speaking situation. If the teacher had given her a second chance, and if you had been advising her for her next speech, what might you have suggested about her delivery techniques? What aspects of her delivery (based on the descriptions above) would you have changed? How—and why?

The Importance of Good Delivery

If we had to sum up this chapter into one easily remembered statement, it would be this: ***How you say something is often as important as what you say.*** We note this here because it is also the case that all members of the audience—in spite of your best efforts to tailor your message to them—will not necessarily listen to everything in your speech. Listeners can be easily distracted by something you are doing and may fixate on that distraction to such an extent that they miss what you are saying. In short, they focus not on what you are saying but on how you are saying it.

To be sure, part of this inattentiveness is laziness and perhaps discourtesy on the audience's part. Equally, however, part of it is the speaker's fault and responsibility as well. A well-prepared and well-delivered speech is capable of dramatically impacting an audience. Think about it for a moment: in your lifetime, how many speeches or presentations have you witnessed—inside the classroom or out? Of these, how many would you say were truly outstanding? If you can think of any, ask yourself why you found them outstanding.

The chances are good that the speaker had done his or her audience analysis and honed a message that spoke to you. But the chances are equally good that the speaker was also very accomplished at speech delivery. The combination of an audience-driven, well-prepared presentation along with superior delivery produced a memorable speech.

Speech making is not only about audience analysis and adequate preparation. Delivery skills and mechanics are important as well—because of the way most people listen and because of the way you can control an audience's attention and memory by the way you deliver the message.

In this chapter we discuss speech delivery, focusing on modes of delivery, as well as on delivery skills. We also evaluate delivery skills in the context of audience analysis (again referring to the Speech Grid) and the ethical implications of a polished delivery.

Modes of Delivery

An important consideration in the delivery of a speech is the manner in which you want to speak, or your *mode of delivery*. What mode is right for you? To answer that question, let's consider the three modes of delivery available to you: reading from a script, memorization from a script, and speaking from an outline.

For more on ineffective listening by the audience, see page 74.

Use your CD-ROM to view examples of effective and ineffective delivery. Choose one of the full student speeches in the Video Theater.
CD-ROM: Video Theater, Full Speeches

In a classroom speech and in many out-of-class speech contexts, you will enjoy improved delivery if you speak from an outline. Considering the advantages and disadvantages of each mode of delivery will indicate why this is true.

● *Reading from a Script*

This mode is exactly what it sounds like: you deliver your speech by reading from a script. The script contains everything you want to say, and if you use this mode of delivery, you do not deviate from the script or ad-lib at all. You may have seen this mode employed in press conferences. A spokesperson (such as a lawyer for a professional athlete accused of wrongdoing) approaches the microphone to "make a statement" and reads from a carefully prepared script. Perhaps the statement is intended to explain the client's position or story or perhaps to make a persuasive argument against law enforcement officials for abuse of prosecution.

Delivery from a script is rarely appropriate in a classroom setting, but it may be necessary in other contexts. A script is particularly useful in assisting you to control how the speech message goes out and is received by the audience. If the message is prepared in advance and real thought went into crafting it for the audience, sticking with the script and not deviating from any of the words lets you control what you say and what you want people to hear. The latter point is the reason a lawyer might read a prepared statement. The lawyer wants to make sure that only her words are heard and reported in the news—no deviations and no surprises. She wants to control what is said and does not want her words to be used later against her or her client.

Using note cards when delivering a speech helps to keep you on track. But do not put too much information on your cards. They should act as an outline, not a script. You don't want to be reciting your speech. Your audience should think that you believe in what you are saying.

Should you, too, read from a script? Ordinarily not. There are compelling disadvantages to using this delivery mode. To begin with, often when you read a speech, you place a barrier of some kind between you and the audience. In this case, the barrier is the physical script itself. It becomes a prop—and something that you can hide behind as you read. Like other props, it can hurt your chances for eye contact with the audience, and as we discuss later in the chapter, diminished eye contact can undermine your effectiveness as a speaker.

When you read to the audience, the act of reading usually affects your tone of voice (we also discuss tone later in the chapter). You do not sound as though you are speaking. Listeners can always tell when someone is reading to them. Did any of your teachers ever read their lecture notes to the class? How did you and your classmates react? Most students eventually tune out the teacher and stop paying attention. One student once described his reaction to this delivery mode in this way: "After a while, I got bored with the whole thing. And to tell you the truth, I almost found it insulting. If all he wanted to do was read to us...well, he could have just given us the notes, and we could have read the notes for ourselves." In other contexts you will find similar reactions; some audience members will describe this mode as "condescending."

For those reasons, unless you are in an extreme situation calling for a very controlled and measured message with no deviations from the script, it is best to avoid this mode of delivery.

● *Memorization from a Script*

Memorization requires that you learn your script word-for-word. You deliver it without looking at any text, notes, or outline. You are like actors on stage or screen who memorize their dialog from a script and deliver the words in performance.

There are benefits to memorizing a speech rather than reading a script to your audience. When speaking from memory, you don't place a barrier between yourself and the audience. There is no paper to hold up, separating you from your listeners. You can maintain eye contact with the audience throughout the speech. And if you need to be careful about controlling your message, you can accomplish that goal by memorizing and carefully repeating what was written.

Of course, there are enough disadvantages to this mode of delivery to argue against its use in most speaking situations. First, memorization can affect your tone of voice in delivery, although the effect is different from that of the monotone delivery of reading. Rather, here what you often find is a delivery that comes across as slick and prepackaged or "canned." This effect results from the attempt to recite something from memory, as opposed to expressing it spontaneously and in the words of the moment. Although "slick" might work with an audience, a speaker has to be careful that "slick" does not become "canned," which is another way audiences sometimes describe memorized speeches. The term is not flattering. To call a speech "canned" is to infer it was prepared in advance and always is delivered in exactly the same way, regardless of the audience. In a sense, this kind of speech becomes more a performance and less a speech.

Second is the fact that memorization itself is very challenging—especially if you are trying to memorize more than a few sentences. Indeed, this points to the real weakness in this mode of delivery: people who speak from memory are typically wedded to the text they memorized. This means that the whole speech process stops if the speaker forgets as much as a single word or sentence. Many speakers attempting this mode experience "speaker's block": when they forget a word or line in the script, they are unable to continue with the speech until (if ever) they remember the word or line and consequently their place in the speech.

Is this mode right for you? It is unlikely that memorization will result in effective delivery. Few speakers have the capacity to memorize a large volume of information and recite it in a manner that does not sound canned. Because most people must invest too much time in order to memorize, and because few speakers have an effective delivery when presenting a memorized speech, we recommend the next option.

● *Speaking from an Outline*

Using this mode, you deliver your speech by referring to an outline that you prepared in advance. As indicated in Chapter 8, you initially prepare a full-sentence outline, which serves as a game plan for what you intend to say in your speech. Once you are familiar with your speech, you may condense your outline onto note cards. Your note cards indicate the main points, with brief reminders of the subpoints and other supporting material you will use to develop those points.

To review the creation of full-sentence outlines, see page 181.

The guiding rule for using this mode of delivery is that speakers should be able to glance at the outline and instantly be reminded of whatever they need to remember. The outline should not be a full reproduction of the text—and it should be clear, easy to read, and readily comprehensible.

You can speak from an outline in either of two ways. The most common way is to speak *extemporaneously,* meaning that you write out the outline ahead of time, learn the material in the outline, and speak spontaneously in your presentation with the outline available for reference. In different situations, however, you suddenly may be called upon to speak and have no time to prepare a written outline, as is the case in an *impromptu* speech. However, even in this kind of spontaneous speaking situation, you will be speaking with an outline—though perhaps only an outline that you keep in mind and refer to while you speak, as you would refer to a physical outline in an extemporaneous situation.

For more on speaking without preparation, see Chapter 17.

Speaking from an outline offers numerous advantages because this mode lets you avoid the disadvantages of reading from or memorizing a script. When you speak from an outline, you minimize any barrier between you and the audience. You will be glancing at the outline for only a few seconds (just long enough to spur your memory), as opposed to holding it before you and reading it to the audience. You don't have to worry about forgetting your place because the outline is at hand to remind you. The outline provides a measure of security without being cumbersome or distracting to you or the audience.

Also, speaking from an outline is desirable because it forces you to speak in your own voice. Remember the last time you could not wait to tell a friend or relative about something of interest (such as a favorite book or a sporting event you observed). You intended to discuss certain aspects of that subject, but you did not write out what you would say in advance. You simply explained the ideas in your own words at the time you had the conversation. When you can give a speech in your own voice, your delivery is *conversational*. Your speech is more effective because you are talking *with* the audience, as in an ordinary conversation, rather than reading a speech *at* the audience.

Speaking from an outline gives you a conversational style because you aren't reading and you aren't reciting. Instead, you take the general outline and deliver the speech in your own words. The words you choose may be different if you give the same speech more than once, although the main message (whatever is in the outline) will stay the same. You speak in a natural-sounding voice and are able to adapt your presentation to whatever speaking situation and audience you find. The latter point is important. It means that this mode of delivery gives you greater flexibility than the others—and it is this flexibility that allows you to adapt to the needs of a specific audience.

For all these reasons, we strongly advocate speaking from an outline, although we recognize that some situations may call for the other modes. We turn next to the mechanics or skills of speech delivery.

Nonverbal Communication and Delivery Skills

How you say something is often as significant as what you say. Recall that speech anxiety often impacts delivery, communicating the speaker's nervousness to the audience. Controlling and mastering delivery skills makes you a better speaker and thus helps you control and overcome anxiety. It is generally agreed that practice and preparation can lessen the anxiety you feel about speaking.[1] Practicing your speech with attention to and awareness of specific delivery skills can greatly decrease your anxiety.

At the beginning of this chapter we distinguished *what* you say from *how* you say it. The former depends on **verbal communication**—the words expressing the message in your speech. What you say is of course influenced by what you assume about your audience, what research and evidence (if any) you may intend to offer, and what message you intend to convey.

By contrast, speech delivery depends on **nonverbal communication**—how you communicate your speech message, both with your voice and with your body. As you will see, many factors can affect nonverbal communication. These are best categorized by distinguishing how you speak the words from how you use your body to communicate in a public speaking situation.

For tips on overcoming speech anxiety, see page 21.

verbal communication: communication that results from words.

nonverbal communication: communication that results from factors other than words, such as speaking skills and body language.

● *How You Speak*

In this section we are really considering the speaker's voice: what are some different aspects of vocal delivery, and how do they impact the speech? Among those that we discuss are volume, tone, rate of delivery, projection, articulation, pronunciation, and pausing.

Volume.   One of the problems that Helen detected when she watched the video of her speech about white whales was that she was not speaking loudly enough. (Her inability to be loud enough is a subset of what we call volume.) In technical terms, **volume** refers to the intensity of sound. In simpler terms, it refers to being loud or quiet. How loud a speaker are you? When you speak, can the audience hear you? Volume presents interesting challenges. Some people are not lough enough; others may be too loud.

Jason, a student in a speech class, was attempting an informative speech. During his presentation, he noticed that many listeners in the front row seemed to be scraping their desks on the floor as they backed away from him. If he had paid more attention, he might have noted that many listeners in close proximity to him were leaning back in their chairs, away from him. Jason's audience was trying to put some distance between themselves and the speaker because Jason was speaking too loudly. Perhaps you know people who speak too loudly, or perhaps you do so yourself. Some people tend to speak in loud voices in conversation, in small groups, and even over the telephone. More often than not, they, like Jason, don't realize how loud they are. Frequently they come from a background (such as being a member of a large family in which each child fights for attention) that encouraged loudness. Excessive volume, however, may damage a speaker's relationship with the audience because it drives listeners away.

Excessive volume was not Helen's problem. She spoke so quiely that some members of her audience, including her instructor, could not hear her. Lack of volume negatively impacted the audience's ability to hear and understand Helen's speech.

To review how the speaker influences the manner in which the audience listens, see pages 79–81.

When you begin preparing your delivery, think about your volume level. How loud is your natural speaking voice? If you aren't sure, ask some friends or relatives to give you an assessment. Then consider the audience to whom you will be speaking in your assigned presentation for class. Think as well about the forum. How loud or quiet do you need to be in your presentation? For you and every other speaker, the answer to that question will be a bit different—and much of the answer turns on what your volume level is in your normal speaking environment. In the end, the guiding rule is this: Given your audience and forum, be loud enough to be heard by everyone in the audience but not so loud that you irritate or drive away the listeners who are physically closest to you.

Tone of Voice.   **Tone of voice** (also known as *tonality*) comes from *pitch*— the highs and lows in your voice. Do you have a high-pitched voice? A low-pitched voice? Are you able to mix high and low tones and achieve some tonal variety? This ability is important for your speech because tonal variety adds color and warmth to one's voice. The absence of tonal variety can make for a bland or boring speech presentation. Audience members are likely to lose interest in a presentation if the tone of the speaker's voice never varies. That constant drone of a monotone voice is about as interesting to listen to as a straight white line stretching to infinity is to watch.

volume: the loudness or quietness of your voice.

tone of voice: the highs and lows in your voice; the pitch of your voice.

Without question, you want to avoid speaking in monotone in your delivery. But how much tonal variety is necessary to make your voice interesting and enticing? Again, this will vary depending on the individual. Follow this guiding rule: Use enough tonal variety to add color or warmth to your speech but not so much variety that you sound like a young boy whose voice is constantly cracking while he goes through puberty. As you practice a speech, try dropping your voice in some places or raising the pitch in others for variety or to emphasize certain words. If you are unclear how you use tone and pitch in a speech, ask someone to listen to you practice and give you feedback.

In addition, you can manipulate your tone by using pitch for *inflection,* which means that you change your pitch (raise or lower it) to emphasize certain words or expressions. Doing this is akin to typing something in boldface. Like boldface type, changes in inflection draw attention to words or expressions you want the audience to notice and remember. Varying your tone of voice can be very effective in your presentation.

Rate of Delivery. The speed with which you speak is your **rate of delivery**. How quickly or slowly do you speak when giving a speech? Do you usually speak that quickly or slowly? Consider the example of Lou, formerly a student at Harvard University, who spoke at a very slow rate.

Lou was asked to give an oral presentation in his seminar on music theory. After speaking for a while, he noticed that many of the students and the teacher seemed inattentive. He also became aware that those who were paying attention seemed to interrupt a great deal—not with questions about content but with questions about his *next* point.

Later, when Lou thought about the reaction of the audience, it occurred to him that although some had seemed bored with his presentation, others had been impatient and tried to move him along. He realized that his overly slow rate of delivery was negatively affecting his audience's reaction to his speech. In simple terms, he had to speak at a faster clip.

This situation is typical for people with a very slow rate of delivery. You might think that speaking slowly forces the audience to pay attention to the speaker, but the opposite is more often true. A speaker with a slow rate of delivery is likely to encounter a less-than-interested audience or a potentially impatient audience bordering on hostility. Do you fall into the "slow speaker" category? Do people tend to finish your sentences for you when you speak, either in ordinary conversation or in presentations? Although the tendency to finish your statements may appear rude, it is also a sign that listeners get tired of waiting for you and want you to move along. In essence, you are forcing the audience to work and pay attention; finishing your words for you is listeners' way of cueing you to speed up.

The opposite is true for people who speak at a very fast rate. Most people who speak quickly tend not to articulate clearly. They run their words together, particularly at the ends of sentences. The result is that listeners have a difficult time following what is being said, not because they aren't interested or have become impatient but because they cannot understand the words. Even a clearly articulated speech is difficult to follow if the rate of delivery is too fast. The audience cannot process and understand your message when you race through a speech. For this reason we recommend that speakers shorten the content of a speech if it exceeds the time limit, rather than speaking excessively fast to fit the entire speech in.

Is there a perfect rate of delivery? For every speaker the answer to this question is different. There is no perfect rate of delivery for which every

rate of delivery: the speed with which you speak.

ESL | Delivery Tips

For ESL students, we have these additional suggestions:

- *If you are a non-native ESL student with low confidence in your English abilities, you may find yourself moving cautiously through your speech, working on pronunciation and articulation. Your pronunciation and artic-ulation need to be as good as you can make them, but guard against slow-ing your speech rate down to concentrate on them. Practice your speech and ask someone to listen; ask the listener to focus on your rate of delivery.*

- *If you are a native or a non-native ESL student whose primary language is usually delivered at a much faster pace than that typical for spoken English, you may find yourself transferring the rate from your primary language to English speech. If excessive speed is hurting your pronunciation and articulation, try writing verbal cues to yourself on your speech notes or outline, reminding you to slow down.*

- *If you are a native or non-native ESL student, feeling nervous about speaking and nervous about your English, you may find that the anxiety increases your rate of delivery. ESL students who work with and practice transition lines from signposting (e.g., "This brings me to my next point...") often feel more comfortable. Transition lines are easy to practice, and familiarity with them can reassure you, slowing your rate before you move to the next part of the speech.*

speaker should strive. The guiding rule to follow is this: Be fast enough to keep your presentation lively and interesting but not so fast that you be-come inarticulate. Ask a friend or relative to listen to you and give you some feedback about your rate of delivery.

Projection.   Have you ever observed someone singing without a micro-phone and wondered how that person could be heard by people near and far? Or maybe you've watched actors in live theater speak their lines quietly yet be heard by everyone in the auditorium. Or perhaps you've listened to preachers, priests, or rabbis speaking without the benefit of electronic en-hancement of their voices. What do these people have in common? Cer-tainly they were mindful of the volume of their voices, but they were paying attention to something else as well. What the singer and speakers did to reach everyone in their respective audiences was use **projection**. Each one was able to "boom" his or her voice across a speaking area.

To project your voice, you use the air you exhale from your lungs as a conduit for the sound of your voice. The air carries the sounds you produce. In essence, projection is all about the business of breathing. To project your voice, follow these guiding rules: First, maintain good posture, whether you are seated or standing. Sit or stand up straight, with your shoulders back and your head at a neutral position. Second, when you breathe, do so deeply. Ex-hale from your diaphragm, pushing your breath away from you.

> **TIP**
>
> *When you know how to project, you can direct your voice to different areas of the speaking forum without necessarily adjusting your volume. It is best, however, to fine-tune projection and volume to capitalize on the situation and hold the at-tention of the audience.*

projection: the ability of a speaker to "boom" his or her voice across a forum; it is accomplished by using exhaled air as a conduit for the sound of the voice.

Correct posture helps you to maintain proper breathing.

View a student incorrectly apologizing for a speaking error.
CD-ROM: Video Theater, Excerpt 11.1

Articulation. **Articulation** refers to the crispness and clarity with which you speak. Like each of the other delivery skills discussed so far, good articulation is an easy victim of speech anxiety. When you are nervous, your ability to articulate your words can suffer. When you speak, are your vowel sounds clear and distinct? What about consonants—particularly those at the ends of sentences? If a word has more than one syllable, are you articulating that fact, or do multisyllabic words sound like one very long syllable? Table 11.1 provides some examples of inarticulation; see how many you recognize.

As noted above, articulation problems can occur if nervousness increases a speaker's rate of delivery. Articulation problems also can result from laziness or inattentiveness. In either case, the audience may not be able to understand what the speaker is saying. To ensure that your articulation does not confound your audience, follow this guiding rule: When you speak, clearly and distinctly articulate all the sounds of words in your speech—all vowels and consonants, as well as all syllables. Do not round off the ends of words or lower your voice at the ends of sentences.

Pronunciation. You must be able to say the words in your speech correctly, pronouncing them as they are pronounced in common usage. It is important not to confuse articulation (clarity and crispness) with **pronunciation**, saying words correctly. Like articulation, pronunciation can be

articulation: clarity and crispness of spoken words.

pronunciation: saying words correctly.

TABLE 11.1 Articulation

INARTICULATE STATEMENT	ARTICULATE STATEMENT
Ged outta ere.	Get out of here.
Tha soun good ta me.	That sounds good to me.
Heze oundin presdential.	He's sounding presidential.
Whadaayawan?	What do you want?
The dogz bing noddy.	The dog is being naughty.

affected by nervousness or caused by laziness or ignorance. Pronunciation errors can call your credibility into question and may make it difficult if not impossible for your audience to understand you.

Many people have problems with pronunciation. Elizabeth, a banking professional who provided trust services, related this story.

> In my job, I was required to work with lawyers, because they drew up the trust agreements for their clients. I worked with lawyers, but I was no lawyer myself. Sometimes they can be a little arrogant about their position, thinking that if you didn't go to law school, you shouldn't be working in a law-related field. I worked hard to earn their respect. But I noticed that when I used some legal terms or words with them, they occasionally would look at each other and smile. Like they were sharing a private joke. One such word was *testator*. That's the person who creates a testament like a trust—or maybe a will. Whenever I used that word, I always said "tes-ta-tor," as if it rhymed with "matador." And the lawyers would smirk—but nobody ever corrected me. Some time later—much later, to my chagrin— I learned that the word should actually be pronounced "tes-tay-ter."

Elizabeth's story is instructive. It is worth noting that she used correct legal terminology, including the word *trust* (a legal document that creates a right of property for someone—called a beneficiary—to be administered by a trust administrator). She used the correct word when she spoke to her audience of lawyers, and her articulation was fine as she said "tes-ta-tor." Her problem was mispronunciation. The lawyers could understand what she was saying, but her faulty pronunciation undermined her credibility with them and reinforced their notion that a non-lawyer should not be working in a law-related field. Why do you think not one of the lawyers ever corrected her mistake?

The pronunciation of people's names and place-names can also be problematic. A student named Gabriel diminished his credibility with his class by pronouncing the last name of labor organizer César Chávez "shah-vez" instead of "cha-vez." Twenty of the thirty students in Gabriel's class were Latino.

ESL | Substitution Sounds

There are some considerations for non-native ESL students: Non-native ESL speakers might substitute sounds from their primary language for the sounds made by native English speakers. Some of this substitution is inevitable and is not necessarily detrimental to your speech. Keep in mind, however, that sound substitution may make your English sound accented to native English speakers.

Substitution (especially vowel substitution) does become a problem when it actually changes the words and thus the meaning of a sentence. For example, when "fit" comes out sounding like "feet," or "kiss" becomes "keys," or "fat" becomes "fought," the audience may think you are saying something other than what you mean.

Again, practice, especially in front of a native English speaker, will be very helpful. Ask your listener to keep a list of the words you mispronounce. Review the list, and practice each word until you feel comfortable saying it.

Do you have problems with the pronunciation of any words? Like Elizabeth, you may be unaware of mistakes that you have been making for a long time. How can you be sure your pronunciation is correct? The guiding rule is simple: If you are unsure of the pronunciation of a word, find out how to say it before using it in your speech. There are many ways to do this. You can ask classmates or coworkers how a word is pronounced. This strategy is especially effective if the people you ask will be in your audience. Better still, you can refer to your dictionary. Every good dictionary provides phonetic pronunciations. Make a practice of checking the dictionary and using the phonetic pronunciation.

Articulation and Pronunciation: Audience Analysis. The rules about articulation and pronunciation presume that your audience does not articulate or pronounce the words in ways you are doing in your speech. The rules presume that someone in the audience will know the difference. That being said, we should offer a cautionary note: Words and language can evolve. They can also reflect the people who use them and the area in which they are used.

The latter point refers to *dialect,* the term for categorizing how words are articulated and pronounced—and even which words are used—as designated by geography (where do people live?) or grouping (who are the people in the group?). Sometimes, not because of nervousness, ignorance, or laziness, people use a geographic or ethnic dialect that results in articulation or pronunciation problems for the audience.

A speaker from Cambridge, Massachusetts, might declare: "I have to go pak my cah." The speaker's regional dialect causes him (and many others in New England) to make a soft "r" sound, so that "park" and "car" sound like "pak" and "cah." If the speaker has an audience that shares his dialect, there is no problem. But any person in the audience who does not use this dialect may not understand what is being said.

Should you try to steer clear of all traces of geographic or ethnic dialect? No. But you should consider your audience. If you speak in a dialect, analyze your audience, determine whether they will understand you, and make any adaptations necessary. As you would do with jargon, follow this guiding rule: If you are less than 100 percent certain that everyone in the audience will understand your dialect, try using words and pronunciations that everyone will readily understand.

For more on jargon and audience understanding, see page 268.

Pausing. Nervousness or anxiety can affect your use (or lack thereof) of **pausing**, or leaving gaps between words in a speech. When you speak, do you pause? If you do, how often do you pause? after every word? after every sentence? rarely? If you do pause, do you fill those gaps with silence or with something else?

Knowing how to pause with silence is an important delivery skill. When done effectively, pausing can afford you some important advantages as a speaker. First, it can allow you to collect your thoughts on a subject. By pausing before continuing, you can regroup and think about what you want to say next. This can reinforce the seriousness of your speech, because you seem to be choosing your words carefully. Second, pausing can allow you to be more dramatic. If you make a statement and then pause for the audience

pausing: leaving gaps between spoken words.

to consider and weigh your words, the statement comes across with slightly more urgency, as if there is a reason for concern.

These advantages presume that you are judicious in your use of pausing, engaging in it every so often, as opposed to after every sentence. It also presumes that you are pausing with silence, not with words or unintelligible sounds.

A speaker who pauses excessively—for example, after every sentence—runs the risk of misleading the audience. Think about it: If you pause excessively, what are you saying to the audience? that you constantly must collect your thoughts before continuing? that every word or sentence is dramatic? that every word or sentence is important? At some point in this kind of delivery, collecting your thoughts becomes perceived as you not knowing what you want to say. Drama becomes melodrama—and the audience begins to take you less seriously.

The same is true if you pause with words or pause with sounds. We refer to these as **verbal pausing** and **verbal tics**. Verbal pausing occurs when you use words in place of silence to fill your pause. It is common at the ends of sentences, where speakers add words that are not required by any rules of grammar to complete a sentence. Here are some examples of verbal pausing:

And . . . you know, the library was closed *. . . you know.* But I had to study somewhere, *you know.*

But . . . I didn't get to study there, *and . . . but, . . .* I had to go somewhere *. . . but . . . and . . .* I tried the dorm reading room.

And . . . like, it was so quiet there. *And, like,* I said to myself, *like* it is so quiet here.

Verbal tics are sounds (not words) used instead of silence to fill a pause. Here is an example:

Um . . . the purpose of my speech *. . . um, ah,* is *. . . ah . . .* to *. . . um, ah,* make you see how *. . . um . . .* dangerous this action *. . . ah . . .* really *. . . um . . .* is.

We mention these not to make light of them. Everyone uses verbal pausing or verbal tics at some point. They become problematic when done to excess. Any form of pausing can become a habit that the audience eventually will focus and fixate on. When that happens, the audience misses what your speech is all about.

Should you try not to pause in your speech? No. Remember that there are good reasons to pause (to collect your words, to suggest importance and drama). The guiding rule is this: Be judicious in your use of pausing, and pause with silence, not with verbal pausing or tics.

● *How You Communicate with Your Body*

Many people regard this aspect of nonverbal communication as simple body language, but it is much more than that. In this section we discuss eye contact, gestures, physical movement, proxemics, and personal appearance.

verbal pausing: the use of words instead of silence to fill a pause.

verbal tics: sounds (not words) used instead of silence to fill a pause.

For more about how audiences decode messages, see page 11.

Whether speakers realize it or not, audiences rely on speakers' nonverbal signals to decode speech messages.

Eye Contact. At the beginning of this chapter we described Helen's speech about whales, noting that while watching a video of herself speaking, Helen observed that she had looked more at her notes or visual aids than at her audience. Helen's problem is not uncommon — especially when the speaker is already nervous or overburdened with notes and visual aids. In such situations, **eye contact** — looking into the eyes of the audience and compelling audience members to look back — may become a casualty. Helen realized that lack of eye contact can create serious problems for a speaker — because of what the speaker will not observe about the audience and because of the nonverbal message the audience receives about the speaker.

What are the benefits of eye contact? Why is it important? First, from the perspective of a speaker, eye contact is important because it allows the speaker to gauge the audience's interest in the speech. If you are looking at the audience (instead of at your notes, visual aids, the ceiling, the floor — or anywhere else except at the audience), you can see how interested listeners are in you or your speech. You can register whether they seem fascinated, curious, indifferent, troubled, or irritated. If you aren't looking at your audience, you see none of these things, and you cannot adapt to your audience's feedback.

To review in-speech audience analysis, see page 111.

Second, eye contact is critical because it helps the speaker to interact with the audience. When you establish eye contact and register interest, you may see whether people understand what you are saying or have comments or questions. In some situations, you may be able to stop and take questions from the audience. If the audience is too large for questions, when you observe that listeners don't seem to understand something you've said, you can go back over it — in effect assuming their questions and providing answers. If you aren't looking at the audience, you can't do this.

Third, eye contact allows the speaker to compel an audience's attention. Father Paul, a wise Episcopalian priest, once confided about his sermonizing techniques: "When I look at my congregation, I make them look at me. And it is harder not to listen to me precisely because of that." When you and the audience establish eye contact, it is difficult for audience members to look away or mentally drift away from the speech.

From the perspective of the audience, eye contact is important for another reason: In Western culture, eye contact by the speaker is commonly perceived to be an indicator of the credibility — especially the truthfulness — of the speaker. An old saying suggests that "the eyes are the windows of the soul" — meaning that our eyes can betray what we really are or think. Related to this adage is the notion that a person's eyes reveal whether the individual is telling the truth and that a speaker who does not make eye contact with the audience probably isn't. Today, we know that notion is false. Many people can look directly into the eyes of audience members and tell falsehoods. (Indeed, many of them are elected officials!) And often a speaker's failure to establish eye contact with the audience is due to other causes, such as lack of familiarity with the subject and the need to refresh his or her memory from notes or, perhaps, nervousness. Regardless, the true

eye contact: visual contact with the eyes of another person.

ESL | **Eye Contact**

Eye contact may be problematic for non-native ESL students. In some cultures, direct eye contact is considered offensive or disrespectful, and averted eye contact is preferred. Our discussion of eye contact is not intended to call into question other cultures' traditions of communication. Our aim is to describe the techniques that work best in this English-speaking culture, in which eye contact is very important. If establishing eye contact is difficult for you, try these suggestions:

- *During your first few class presentations, try panning from one object to another. Begin by looking at the wall behind the students to your right; and then sweep left, past all the students in the audience, and look at the wall behind the students to your left. Sweeping between objects but still panning past people is better than not looking in the direction of your audience at all.*

- *As the quarter or semester progresses, begin to sweep between people, allowing yourself to become less uncomfortable with eye contact.*

- *If your comfort level remains low, make your teacher aware of the cultural reasons for your discomfort, and consider whatever options he or she might suggest.*

---

cause may be irrelevant. As long as people continue to believe that the eyes reveal the soul, they will perceive lack of eye contact as the sign of a lack of truthfulness. Secondarily, they may also perceive a lack of confidence or preparedness. Thus, a wise speaker establishes eye contact because it communicates honesty, expertise, and confidence.

It is one thing, of course, to say that eye contact is important and another to know how to use eye contact in a speaking situation. What you should do depends on the size of your audience. The guiding rule for a small audience is to establish and sustain direct eye contact with each person. Sustained eye contact allows you to truly interact with each person in the group. When the audience is large, it may be inconvenient or impossible to establish direct and lengthy eye contact with each audience member. Thus the guiding rule for a large audience is to use the technique called **panning**, which at least allows you to see each audience member.

Panning works in this way. Think of your body as a tripod and your head as a movie camera sitting atop the tripod. To "film" everyone in the group, the "camera" slowly sweeps from one side to the other in a wide panoramic shot, picking up everyone in the audience. When you use this technique, you won't spend a great deal of time with any single individual, but gradually, slowly, you will look at all audience members—or at least look in their direction.

When you are panning your audience, you should pause and establish **extended eye contact** before you change direction. Your delivery will be distracting if your head constantly turns from one side of the audience toward the other. To make extended eye contact, look at someone in the

View *Ronald Reagan making good eye contact while speaking at Moscow State University.* CD-ROM: Video Theater, Excerpt 11.2

panning: visually sweeping across an audience to establish eye contact briefly.

extended eye contact: looking at a member of the audience while you speak two to three sentences, before you resume panning.

audience as you deliver two or three sentences; then move your focus to someone else and make extended eye contact with him or her. Panning in this way offers some advantages. You suggest eye contact and thus boost your credibility. Also, you are able to see reactions across your entire audience, gauge interest, and possibly interact and compel attention.

Gestures. When people think about body language and nonverbal communication, they usually think about **gestures**—especially hand gestures. Many successful speakers use their hands to emphasize a point, pantomime or demonstrate something, or call attention to something. Sometimes, people with powerful gestures are perceived as powerful speakers. Gestures can add flair to a speaker's delivery.

Are gestures necessary for all speakers? Should you draw from an inventory of gestures to make yourself a more effective speaker? The answer to both questions is "no." Gestures can be very advantageous. But the truth is, they are often done without great awareness by the speaker. They are effective because they are natural. The teaching of public speaking once included instruction in the use of gestures for specific situations. Today, the use of canned gestures is discouraged. Gestures can detract from your speech if they appear rehearsed. Deliberate nonverbal behavior often appears insincere to the audience.[2] It is better to use your own natural gestures when delivering a speech.

To use gestures effectively, keep some guidelines in mind. First, not all audience members will interpret gestures in the same way. Look at Figure 11.1. When you see each of the gestures shown in the figure, what meaning do you take away? What does a fist mean to you? What does a shaking fist mean? How about a pointing finger or an open hand?

Not everyone sees the same thing in an open hand or a shaking fist. Some may see the fist as signaling violence, others as a show of force, others as a sign of anger, and still others as a show of determination. No single gesture that you use will be interpreted in a uniform way by the audience. Different people will see different things.[3]

Another consideration is that gestures may communicate a nonverbal message that is not consistent with the verbal message of your speech. Former president George Bush used the same gestures in nearly every presentation. The gestures—alternating a jabbing fist with a thrusting open-palmed hand—probably were intended to communicate toughness and strength, and they worked well in speeches calling for strength—for example, in a

View Colin Powell using effective gestures at the Republican National Convention.
CD-ROM: Video Theater, Excerpt 11.3

gestures: movements of the hands and arms to emphasize or demonstrate something.

FIGURE 11.1 Gestures

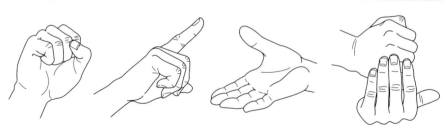

presentation urging popular support for the Gulf War or a speech urging Congress to get tough on crime. Those gestures, however, seemed inappropriate in speeches or passages of speeches in which the president wanted to communicate a more tender side or sympathy—as he often did when speaking lovingly and warmly about family or expressing sympathy for the victims of some natural disaster. Remember the Bush example, and be careful to avoid gestures that contradict your verbal speech message.

Also, avoid distracting gestures. If you use a gesture repeatedly, the audience will take notice and perhaps become distracted by it. This problem often afflicts speakers who don't know what to do with their hands while speaking. Some put their hands in their pockets. Some play with keys or change in their pockets. Some continually adjust jewelry—a watch, ring, or necklace. If a pen or pencil or pointing device is handy, some play with that. The result is the same: the gesture can distract audience members to the point that they begin to focus more on the gesture than on the speech.

Do these concerns mean that you should not use gestures? No. Your gestures will probably be those that you normally use in conversational speech. And gestures offer some real advantages. The guiding rules for this nonverbal form of communication are these: Use gestures deliberately to emphasize or illustrate points in your speech. Remain aware that not all audience members will interpret gestures in the same way. Your gestures should communicate a message that is consistent with your verbal speech message. Your gestures should not distract the audience.

President George Bush frequently gestured when he spoke. People often remembered his out-of-sync gestures instead of the message of his speech.

Physical Movement.   Some speakers do not move around at all while speaking. Perhaps they are nervous, or perhaps they feel locked into place standing behind a podium. At the other extreme are speakers who move a great deal—from side to side or back and forth—in front of the audience. We sometimes call the first group "tree trunks," because they seem rooted in place, and the second group "pacers," because of their inability to stay still for long.

Ask yourself this question as you think about **physical movement**: are you a tree trunk, a pacer, or something in between? Both extremes create problems for speakers. If you never move doing your speech, you risk boring your audience. If your vocal delivery is engaging and your topic is of great interest, or if you are deemed an authority on your subject and you are appearing before a captive audience (not unlike a teacher addressing an "audience" of students), then it may not matter if you stand still for your entire presentation. But even a teacher facing a captive audience of students can be boring as a speaker. The absence of movement tends to make the delivery stagnant and forces the audience to work harder to stay engaged.

Some physical movement by the speaker is welcome because it brings energy to the delivery and because audiences associate such movement with transitions from one point to another. Most experienced speakers move—either back and forth or side to side—to visually emphasize transitions. Besides making for a stagnant delivery, the absence of movement suggests that there are no transitions between ideas—that instead of consisting of several paragraphs presenting different ideas, the speech is like one giant, neverending paragraph. And just as a text like that would be difficult to read, so is

physical movement: the extent to which the speaker moves around during the speech.

Movement is important when you're making a speech. Don't remain in one position, but do be careful about how much you move around. Instead of being a "tree trunk" or a "pacer," incorporate movement to enliven your presentation.

a speech like that difficult to listen to. Occasional movement also allows members of the audience to adjust their positions and become more comfortable.

A speaker who paces repeatedly, however, creates problems because he or she communicates an unintended message. Audiences often perceive excessive movement as visually distracting and somewhat confusing—the message seems to be that the speaker is in a constant state of transition. Again, the audience has to work too hard to follow, and many will stop trying.

How much movement, if any, is right for you? The guiding rule is this: Move as much as necessary to invigorate your speech (even if you must come out from behind the podium) but not so much that you distract or confuse the audience.

Proxemics. A topic related to movement is **proxemics**—the speaker's use of space and distance, relative to the audience. How close should you be to the audience when speaking? How far away? Is there a perfect distance for every speech? Equally important is the question of audience analysis and culture (see In Theory box 11.1).

There is no simple, single formula for determining whether a speaker should be close to or distant from an audience; a number of factors come into play. How large is the forum? How much distance separates the audience from the speaker owing to the design of the forum? Is the speaker free to move around while he or she speaks?

proxemics: the speaker's use of space and distance, relative to the audience.

| INVENTION | ORGANIZATION | STYLE | PREPARATION | DELIVERY |

In Theory 11.1

SPACE AND PUBLIC SPEAKING

In Chapter 2 we introduced the canons of rhetoric, one of which is *delivery,* the vocal and nonverbal presentation of the speech message. Your relative closeness to, or distance from, an audience has implications for the way your speech is received. Anthropologist Edward T. Hall was the first to label this use of physical space *proxemics,*[4] and he later suggested there are four distances people in North America might use to define the nature of relationships—including the relationship between speaker and audience.[5] They are (1) *intimate distance* (ranging from a physical touching to a distance of six to eighteen inches), (2) *personal distance* (ranging from one and a half to four feet), (3) *social distance* (ranging from four to twelve feet), and (4) *public distance* (ranging from twelve to twenty-four or more feet). Intimate distance suggests intimacy; personal distance suggests a personal but not necessarily intimate relationship; social distance connotes social relationships (such as a formal business relationship); and public distance communicates a public relationship (the type of relationship you have with any stranger in public).

In the United States, *intimate* distance between individuals allows touching and may make people who are not ordinarily intimate with each other uncomfortable. This close distance also makes direct eye contact uncomfortable. Public speeches are unlikely at this distance.

Personal distance—sometimes called *personal space*—may allow touching (such as a handshake or placing a hand on someone's shoulder) but only with arms extended. Intimacy may still be a factor, but control of personal space is critical, and invasion of that space by another individual is inappropriate

or even threatening. Of course, context is also critical. Small forums and small audiences may necessitate presentations from as close as four feet—perhaps from across a meeting room table. But even in that situation, the table serves as a physical barrier reinforcing each individual's sense of personal space.

Social distance as described by Hall opens up the gap between speaker and audience and makes eye contact essential, not to mention all the other nonverbal means of communication that enhance an audience member's ability to understand what is being said. Public speaking at distances up to twelve feet (such as a speech in your classroom) is relatively common.

Public distance also underscores the need for delivery mechanics by a speaker and increases the formality of a presentation while decreasing opportunities for intimacy between speaker and audience.

Later research on proxemics has confirmed a strong association between closeness and intimacy, liking and attraction,[6] as well as immediacy-nonimmediacy of the speech message.[7]

Culture has a tremendous impact on proxemics, and Hall himself was quick to admit that his four categories of distance were drawn only from observations and interviews with white, middle-class, healthy adults, mainly natives of the northeastern seaboard of the United States. People from other cultures may have ideas about physical closeness or distance that are different from Americans'. Individuals from some European and Middle Eastern cultures, for example, may prefer greater physical closeness than do Americans in their interactions. Others—for example, people from Asian cultures—may prefer more distance for respecting relationships.[8]

In a large forum with great distance separating the speaker and the audience, it may be advisable for the speaker to try to narrow the gap, thereby helping audience members to see the speaker and possibly enhancing their ability to hear him or her as well. Moving toward a person when communicating is an act of intimacy. It suggests that something personal may be communicated. This is just as true of public speaking as it is of personal conversations.

Of course, closeness is not always welcome in interpersonal situations. Sometimes, people feel that their personal space is being violated or threatened when someone gets too close. That same feeling of unease may occur in an audience situation if the speaker moves too close to one or more audience members. This is especially likely to occur in a small forum, in which little space separates the speaker from the audience. Coming too close to an individual in that situation may produce discomfort unless the speaker is already acquainted with the audience member and knows there will be no problem.

People from some cultural backgrounds may consider physical closeness offensive or invasive. Audience analysis can alert you to potential problems.

How close to your audience should you be? The guiding rule is simple: Analyze your audience, the size and setup of your forum, and your ability to move around the forum, and move close enough to the audience to interact and allow them to see and hear you, close enough to suggest (if appropriate) intimacy, but not so close that you violate any audience member's sense of private space.

Personal Appearance.   This category of nonverbal communication is often overlooked by speakers already nervous about their delivery skills. By **personal appearance**, we mean the way you physically appear to an audience and what impressions audience members take away from their observations of you. Personal appearance pertains to everything from clothing, jewelry, hairstyle, choice of colors, and presence of eyeglasses, to grooming and hygiene.

Your appearance is important for two reasons. First, people in an audience often form their initial impression of you *before* you say anything — just by looking at you. Their first impression is informed entirely by what they see. Second, studies show that this initial impression based on appearance can be long lasting and very significant.[9] A speaker who makes a negative first impression with an audience because of his or her appearance will need to expend much time and effort to win the audience's trust and regain credibility. Thus, before you go to speak before an audience, spend some time considering your appearance.

How do you appear? What will the audience see? Many people wonder whether any rule governs appearance — perhaps a list of acceptable practices for clothing, grooming, colors, jewelry, and so on. But the only guiding rule you should follow is to do what is appropriate for the audience you are addressing. If you are giving a speech to raise money for a charity and your audience consists of Fortune 500 company executives, do not show up for your speech wearing the latest fashionably baggy jeans, an oversized T-shirt, and tennis shoes. Ask yourself what is appropriate for the audience.

For more on developing a Speech Grid, see page 115.

personal appearance: how a speaker physically appears to the audience and what impressions audience members take away from their observations.

Delivery Skills and Audience Analysis

In this section we address the issue of how the audience should factor into your thinking about delivery skills. Return to your Speech Grid and look at the left side, focusing on "situational characteristics." A characteristic such as audience size is clearly relevant to your thinking about all aspects of your

FIGURE 11.2   Delivery Skills: A Diagnostic Checkup

Now that you have read about the different factors affecting speech delivery, give your delivery skills a diagnostic checkup. Answer the following questions, and be honest about what kind of speaker you are. After completing the exercise, review it to identify your strengths and weaknesses. Then give a blank copy to a friend or classmate and ask that person to evaluate you. Compare the rankings. Do you see yourself as others see you? What are your strengths? What do you need to improve?

Speech Delivery Skills Diagnostic
Rank yourself (or the person who has given you this diagnostic) from 1 to 5, with 1 being the lowest value and 5 being the highest value.

1. Your/this individual's speaking skills
    a. volume   1 2 3 4 5
    b. tone of voice   1 2 3 4 5
    c. rate of delivery   1 2 3 4 5
    d. projection   1 2 3 4 5
    e. articulation   1 2 3 4 5
    f. pronunciation   1 2 3 4 5
    g. pausing   1 2 3 4 5
2. Your/this individual's other nonverbal communication skills
    a. eye contact   1 2 3 4 5
    b. gestures   1 2 3 4 5
    c. movement   1 2 3 4 5
    d. proxemics   1 2 3 4 5
    e. personal appearance   1 2 3 4 5
3. According to this diagnostic, your/this speaker's communication strengths are in these areas:

4. According to this diagnostic, your/this speaker's communication weaknesses are in these areas:

delivery. When you face a large audience, you may have to adjust your volume, projection, and rate of delivery. When you face a small audience, you may need to pay particular attention to nonverbal factors such as physical movement and proxemics.

A characteristic such as speech time is also relevant, especially as it relates to the body clock of the audience. Consider where listeners are in their day or week and how that affects their ability to listen and pay attention to you. You may need to articulate special words carefully for a tired audience. Or you may need to be especially vigilant about eye contact. Anything you can do to make your speech more colorful—from adjusting your tone (and avoiding monotone delivery) to using expressive gestures and movement—may be important for maintaining the audience's level of interest.

Knowledge of "demographics" and "common ground" will give you valuable insights into nonverbal factors such as your personal appearance. Grooming and dressing in a manner that is appropriate for your audience depend on information about the background of that audience (demographics). Your credibility may be enhanced if some aspect of your personal appearance visually indicates common ground with the audience.

To review ways to establish common ground, see page 102.

In all these ways, the audience drives and shapes your message.

Polished Delivery and Truthfulness: Ethical Implications

Our aim in presenting the topics discussed in this chapter is to help you become a more polished public speaker. Being "more polished" means that you can communicate effectively with your audience and, because of your delivery skills, your audience is likely to find you credible. You will accomplish all this while at the same time controlling and concealing your speech anxiety.

We would be remiss if we did not observe that being more polished also presents you with an ethical issue. Although you can use many of the strategies described in other sections of this text to build your credibility with the audience, that same audience will be inclined to find you credible simply because of your excellent delivery skills. Don't you find yourself tending to trust people who are good speakers? Don't they sound or appear believable? Aren't you inclined to feel they are telling the truth? Are you as likely to believe or trust a poor speaker?

Delivery skills empower you to reach an audience and increase the likelihood that the audience will believe and trust you. The skills are tools, and although they have no intrinsic ethical value, they certainly create the possibility for ethical dilemmas. Being perceived as a believable or trustworthy speaker does not really make you believable or trustworthy. It most certainly does not transform whatever you are saying into "truth." It only allows you to imply truthfulness to the audience.

To review speech ethics and truth-telling, see page 59.

You are well advised, therefore, to consider what you say and to whom. These delivery skills, if mastered, can give you an advantage over the audience. Consider the impact of your delivery, and aim for a responsible use of these skills. Delivery should never be used as a substitute for the message of your speech, lulling your audience into believing that what you have to say is truthful or significant to their lives simply because of how you say it.

Summary

This chapter focused on delivery skills. It evaluated three modes of delivery. It examined factors affecting how you speak and nonverbal factors affecting communication. The chapter discussed the application of delivery skills to particular audiences and ethical questions these skills can raise. The checklist shows how you can use the material from this chapter as you prepare for your speech.

Checklist

MODES OF DELIVERY

____ Read from a script if you need to control your speech message and how it is received (p. 287)

____ Memorize a script and deliver the message verbatim only if you are capable of memorizing large quantities of text and can avoid a delivery that sounds "canned" or "slick" (p. 288)

____ Deliver your speech extemporaneously from an outline (p. 289)

THINKING ABOUT HOW YOU SPEAK

____ Consider the volume of your voice (p. 291)

____ Consider your tone of voice (p. 291)

____ Think about your rate of delivery (p. 292)

____ Try projecting your voice (p. 293)

____ Concentrate on how you articulate your words (p. 294)

____ Concentrate on your pronunciation of words (p. 294)

____ Think about how audience analysis affects your articulation and pronunciation (p. 296)

____ Think about your use of pausing in a speech (p. 296)

THINKING ABOUT HOW YOU COMMUNICATE WITH YOUR BODY

____ Remember to make eye contact with your audience (p. 298)

____ Consider your use of gestures while speaking (p. 300)

____ Consider how much and where you want to use physical movement while speaking (p. 301)

____ Think about proxemics, and how close to or far from your audience you want to be (p. 302)

____ Consider your personal appearance and do what is appropriate for the audience and setting (p. 304)

DELIVERY SKILLS AND AUDIENCE ANALYSIS

____ Consider characteristics of the speaking situation—such as the size of your audience—when deciding about volume, projection, rate of delivery, physical movement, proxemics, and personal appearance (p. 305)

____ Think about the audience's body clock (p. 306)

____ Consider audience demographics and common ground when analyzing your personal appearance (p. 306)

ETHICAL IMPLICATIONS OF DELIVERY SKILLS

____ Remember that a polished delivery may make you sound credible but does not increase the truthfulness or accuracy of your message (p. 306)

Key Terms and Concepts

verbal communication (p. 290)

nonverbal communication (p. 290)

volume (p. 291)

tone of voice (p. 291)

rate of delivery (p. 292)

projection (p. 293)

articulation (p. 294)

pronunciation (p. 294)

pausing (p. 296)

verbal pausing (p. 297)

verbal tics (p. 297)

eye contact (p. 298)

panning (p. 299)

extended eye contact (p. 299)

gestures (p. 300)

physical movement (p. 301)

proxemics (p. 302)

personal appearance (p. 304)

Speech Grid Application

The Evolution of a Speech Grid

Speech Grid Applications, showing the evolution of a Speech Grid, are included near the end of Chapters 5 through 12. They illustrate how one student, Samantha, uses a grid to prepare a speech.

Samantha has taken some material from each side of her grid and used that information to make decisions on style. Here we show only excerpts from Samantha's grid. For a complete grid and outline of her main points, see page 256.

When you prepare your speeches, look at the information on your grid (particularly the situational characteristics) and determine how you can use it to optimize the delivery of your speech.

AUDIENCE ANALYSIS	SPEECH MESSAGE
Situational Characteristics • *8 min. speech* • *25–30 in audience* • *small classroom* • *limited a-v equip.* **Delivery Strategies** *Using the information noted on your Speech Grid about your audience, you can make decisions about your delivery.* 1. Practice to ensure that you can deliver the speech in eight minutes at an appropriate rate of delivery. If the speech is too long, omit some material. Do not speak so fast that audience members can't understand you. 2. Consider where audience members will be sitting when you are speaking. Be sure to make eye contact with them (three or four seconds per person). 3. The room is small, so the speech should easily be heard by all. Be sure your volume level is not too loud.	In later chapters, you will compose your speech message here.

(continued)

Speech Grid, continued

AUDIENCE ANALYSIS	SPEECH MESSAGE
4. Check the pronunciation of any unfamiliar word or name.	
5. When practicing, note which points are easy to explain without notes, and look for trouble spots. Prepare an extemporaneous outline that helps at difficult points in the speech. Make quotations word-for-word on the outline.	

Source Notes

1. Menzel, K., & Carrell, L. (1994). The relationship between preparation and performance in public speaking. *Communication Education, 43,* 19–26.
2. Manusov, V. (1991). Perceiving nonverbal messages: Effects of immediacy and encoded intent on receiver judgments. *Western Journal of Speech Communication, 55,* 235–253, at 236.
3. Burgoon, J. K., & LePoire, B. A. (1999). Nonverbal cues and interpersonal judgments: Participant and observer perceptions of intimacy, dominance, composure and formality. *Communication Monographs, 66,* 105–124, at 107.
4. Hall, E. T. (1963). System for the notation of proxemic behavior. *American Anthropologist, 65,* 1003–1026.
5. Hall, E. T. (1966). *The hidden dimensions.* New York: Doubleday.
6. Patterson, M. L. (1968). Spatial factors in social interactions. *Human Relations, 21,* 351–361.
7. Burgoon, J. K., Buller, D., Hale, J., & deTurck, M. (1984). Relational messages associated with nonverbal behaviors. *Human Communication Research, 10*(3), 351–378.
8. Hall, E. T., & Hall, M. R. (1987). *Hidden differences: Doing business with the Japanese.* New York: Doubleday.
9. Smith, L. J., & Malandro, L. (1990). Personal appearance factors which influence perceptions of credibility and approachability of men and women. In J. A. Devito & M. L. Hecht (Eds.), *The nonverbal communication reader* (p. 163). Prospect Heights, IL: Waveland Press.

12 Audiovisual Aids

After reading Chapter 12, you should understand:

- What an audiovisual aid is and how to find or create one.

- How audience analysis helps you select and create audiovisual aids.

- The significant advantages of audiovisual aids.

- Guidelines to follow to use audiovisual aids effectively.

- The ethical implications of the use of audiovisual aids.

Phil, a student in a college-level speech class, had been assigned an informative speech on a topic of his choosing. He wanted to speak about Harley-Davidson motorcycles, particularly his Harley. His goal was to inform his audience about the chief differences in quality between American-made Harley-Davidson motorcycles and foreign competitors; he also wanted to present this information in a manner that conveyed his personal enthusiasm for this particular motorcycle. After thinking about his audience, however, it occurred to Phil that he might not be able to achieve these goals with words alone, given the fact that no one else in the class was a motorcycle enthusiast. In Phil's opinion, the Harley was distinctively different from other bikes, but to appreciate the difference, the audience might have to actually see a Harley and listen to its engine running.

Phil's speech class met inside a large building, on the first floor. Although Phil, a freshman, was new to the school, he was certain that people did not bring motorcycles into the classroom. How, he wondered, would he let the class see his Harley? What options did he have, short of picking another topic?

Phil's dilemma—you will see how he resolved it later in this chapter—is the classic dilemma faced by all public speakers. At times, seeing or hearing something mentioned in a speech will help an audience understand what the speech is really about. These materials—called *audiovisual aids*—support what is being said verbally and give the audience an opportunity to see or hear information that fosters comprehension.

Of course, merely suggesting that an audiovisual aid gives an audience something to see or hear does not really explain what this device is. What precisely is an audiovisual aid? Does one have to provide both audio and visual assistance? Where do you find such things? How do you make them? How do you know whether the aid you're considering is right for your audience? In this chapter we answer these and other questions as we explain how to use audiovisual aids in your speeches.

Seeing (and Hearing) Is Believing

If we were to reduce the message of this chapter to a simple statement, it would be that sometimes seeing is believing and occasionally seeing is understanding. People often have difficulty understanding even slightly complicated topics and this difficulty increases if there are several points to consider or the speech is more than a few minutes long. That is true regardless of the speech topic—be it concept, idea, or process.

Consider your own experience. How did you learn math concepts? Did your teacher merely lecture about algebra or geometry and expect you to understand how to solve complex problems after hearing an oral explanation? Or did your teacher illustrate the problems and concepts on the chalkboard —with as many examples as possible—hoping that after seeing a visual representation of a concept, you might better understand it?

If you studied a language other than English, such as French or German, did your teacher merely lecture to you in English? Or did your teacher model the language for you, demonstrating pronunciation and accent? Perhaps he or she played a tape for you to listen to as well, before requiring you to try to speak the language.

In both cases, your teachers were using audio or visual aids grounded in their awareness that your understanding and retention of concepts would be dramatically enhanced if you could see or hear an example of what they were trying to explain. Speech communication experts have long argued that verbal facts and concepts are more likely to be learned if they are accompanied by visual cues.[1] More than four decades ago, studies documented as much as 55 percent increased learning by the audience in presentations accompanied by audiovisual aids.[2]

An **audiovisual aid** is anything (in addition to your speech) that the members of your audience can see or hear that helps them understand and remember your speech topic. An audiovisual aid is first and foremost a device that is *relevant to the speech topic*. Something that fails to meet this basic requirement may be audio or visual but it is no aid to understanding.

Types of Audiovisual Aids

An audiovisual aid can provide both audio and visual assistance at the same time (as in a video recording showing an exotic bird singing), audio assistance only (as in an audiocassette recording of a voice), or visual assistance only (as in a picture of a man on a surfboard). Traditional aids include actual objects, video and audio recordings, drawings, photographs, charts, and graphs. Computer and information technology has considerably expanded the range of possibilities available to speakers. In the remainder of this section we consider examples of each.

● *The Speaker as Audiovisual Aid*

The speaker sometimes becomes a visual aid, particularly if the topic calls for an explanation of something that requires modeling. For example, in an informative assignment, a student named Zoya spoke about her passion: rock

audiovisual aid: anything that audience members can see or hear (in addition to your speech) that helps them understand and remember your speech topic.

climbing. The speech covered the basics of climbing, as well as information about getting instruction and the best places for beginners to climb. Zoya also discussed equipment—including clothing. To provide a visual aid, she wore the clothes and special shoes she used for climbing, along with belts and clips for her equipment. For this part of her speech, Zoya became her own visual aid.

A speaker can become a visual aid as Zoya did, by wearing clothing related to some aspect of the speech topic. A speaker can also achieve this effect by demonstrating some aspect of the topic. Tinisha, a college sophomore in a public speaking class, prepared an informative speech about three styles of African dance. She orally described each one and then carefully demonstrated it. Tinisha's physical movement allowed her to become a visual aid for the subject matter of her speech.

● *Physical Objects as Visual Aids*

Any physical object can be a visual aid—from something as simple as a collection of rocks and minerals for a speech about geology to complex physical models of the molecular structure of the virus that causes AIDS. Sometimes the objects are things the audience can observe only from a distance because they are so large or unwieldy. A student named Alan gave an informative speech about the "physics of bowling." He explained everything about bowling, including the science behind drilled holes for grips, how the rotation and angle of the bowler's arm affect the force and momentum of the ball and its impact on the pins. To demonstrate, Alan used three balls, all with different kinds of holes. He displayed them on a table that he had modified, raising the legs on one side so that the balls would roll to the

View a student using an object as a visual aid.
CD-ROM: Video Theater, Excerpt 12.1

The use of visual aids can enhance your audience's understanding. For example, the proper angles at which to roll a bowling ball to knock down all ten pins are more easily shown than described.

other side and into the willing hands of an assistant, demonstrating Alan's point about the trajectory of the balls.

In other situations, a speaker may want to give audience members closer access to a visual aid, perhaps letting them handle or smell or taste it. A student named Mindy gave a persuasive speech on the legalization of marijuana, arguing that hemp is used in many kinds of products. To emphasize her point, Mindy produced a section of rope and other examples of commercial uses of hemp, and she passed them around the audience. She invited listeners to hold the rope and test its strength by pulling it taut.

● Assistants as Audiovisual Aids

Occasionally the speaker prefers the role of speaker and narrator to the role of demonstrator or model. When a demonstration might cut into speech time or decrease speaker/audience interaction, the speaker may ask someone else to demonstrate or model whatever is referred to in the speech. For example, in classes on first aid techniques for treatment of accident victims, Red Cross teachers sometimes ask an assistant to role-play the victim of a car accident, fire, or natural disaster, and then they demonstrate treatments (such as immobilizing, splinting, and bandaging) on the assistant while the class watches. In this particular example, both the teacher (who models the techniques) and the assistant (who receives the practice treatment) are visual aids.

In other situations, the speaker may stand to one side and deliver the speech while the assistant demonstrates or models. Phil's dilemma was quickly resolved when Claire, his wife, agreed to park the family Harley outside the classroom windows. Phil opened the windows and invited the audience to stand near him. Outside, Claire pointed to various parts of the motorcycle as he mentioned them. Members of the audience had to shift

Assistants can do things as simple as holding an object for you (as shown here) or they can be used to illustrate complicated things that would be difficult for the speaker to do while speaking.

their gaze from Phil (standing inside the classroom) to Claire (standing like Vanna White outside), but they saw enough to understand what he was saying, and he was able to communicate his passion for the Harley (not to mention his wife's love for him).

● *Maps, Charts, Graphs, Drawings, and Photographs as Visual Aids*

Occasionally, what the audience needs to see is not a modeling or demonstration of something but a clear explanation or illustration. When a topic is complex, a visual aid may be called for to help the audience understand what is being said. In these situations, you may wish to employ visual aids such as maps, charts, graphs, drawings, or photographs to simplify a message.

A **map** is a visual representation of geography—containing as much or as little detail and explanation as you wish. In most speech situations, less detail will help the audience more than a lot of detail. Notice that in the map shown in Figure 12.1, the speaker used red highlighting to show the route followed. This use of color made a simple message easy to follow.

A **chart** is any graphic representation that summarizes information and ideas. Charts illustrate and explain information or ideas in a way that is readily understandable and clear. Figure 12.2, on the next page, shows three types of charts: *verbal, pie,* and *flow* charts.

FIGURE 12.1   Sample Visual Aid: Maps

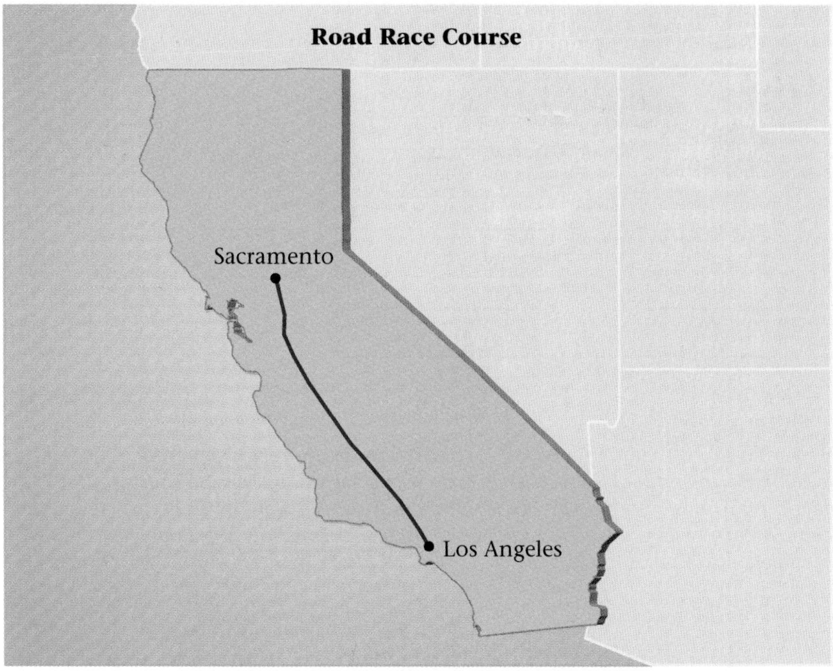

Road Race Course

Sacramento

Los Angeles

When you are describing trips or distances traveled, a map can help you communicate a sense of space to the audience.

map: a visual representation of geography.

chart: any graphic representation that summarizes information and ideas.

FIGURE 12.2 Sample Visual Aids: Charts

Travel Tips
- Making reservations
- Travel and money
- Language and culture

a. verbal chart

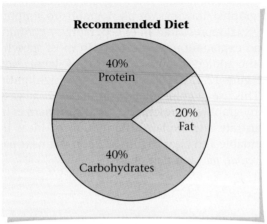

Recommended Diet

40%
Protein

20%
Fat

40%
Carbohydrates

b. pie chart

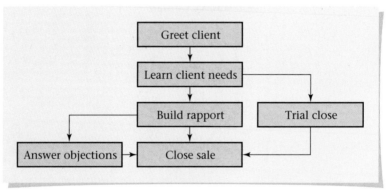

c. flow chart

a) In a verbal chart, the goals are clarity, conciseness, and directness. Verbal charts summarize and highlight what the speaker is saying. b) This pie chart displays proportions of calorie intake for athletes in such a way that it is easy to see how each category compares with the others. c) This flow chart depicts steps a salesperson takes to close a sale.

verbal chart: a chart in which words are deliberately arranged to summarize or highlight ideas.

pie chart: a circular chart that resembles a sliced pie and is used to display proportions or percentages in relation to one another.

A **verbal chart** uses words arranged in a certain format to explain ideas, concepts, or general information. A **pie chart** resembles a sliced pie. This type of chart is often used to display proportions and percentages in relation to one another. A **flow chart** demonstrates the flow or direction of information, processes, and ideas. Flow charts can be used to show the chronology of events, the steps in a process, or the evolution of an idea.

A **graph** is usually employed to show a quantitative relationship. Figure 12.3 shows two types of graph: **line** and **bar graphs**.

FIGURE 12.3   Sample Visual Aids: Graphs

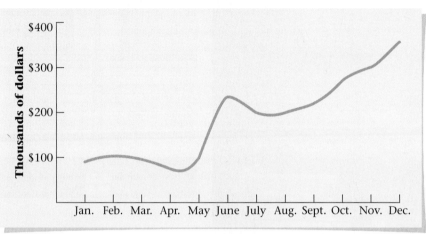

a. line graph

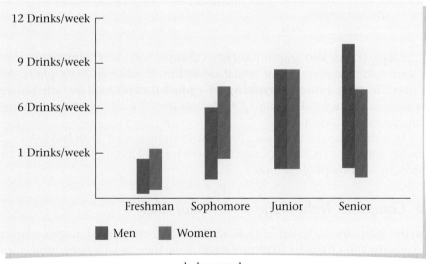

b. bar graph

a) This line graph shows sales volume over twelve months for a large retail electronics store. The revenue generated by sales (in gross dollars) is plotted on the vertical axis. Months of the year are plotted on the horizontal axis. The relationship between the two shows the sales manager when sales activity rose and fell in the previous year. b) The bar graph is from a student presentation in a speech about undergraduate on-campus alcohol consumption at a particular college in 2002. The lengths of the vertical bars indicate the proportions of men and women in each class who had one or more alcoholic drinks per week.

flow chart: a graphic depiction of the flow or direction of information, processes, or ideas.

graph: a diagram illustrating a quantitative relationship.

line graph: a graph showing the linear relationship between data plotted on the horizontal axis and data plotted on the vertical axis.

bar graph: a graph consisting of parallel bars of varying lengths; the lengths of the bars are proportionate to the quantities being compared.

FIGURE 12.4   Sample Visual Aids: Drawings and Photographs

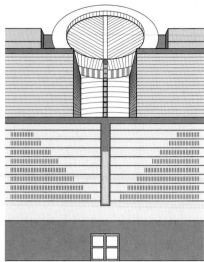

Photographs give exact details of persons or objects in the context of their surroundings. In contrast, a drawing can emphasize and simplify specific features and exclude surroundings.

Maps, charts, and graphs illustrate concepts and ideas. Sometimes what is called for, however, is an actual depiction of what is being orally described. In such a case, a **drawing** or a **photograph** may be called upon to serve as a visual aid. Figure 12.4 presents one of each depicting the same thing: a new museum.

In a drawing, the artist decides what to show and what to leave out. Of course, computer technology, described next, now lets you achieve the same effect by altering photographs.

● *Computer Technology and Visual Aids*

In the past, many visual aids were displayed on printed pages, marker boards, or flip charts or were projected from slide or overhead projectors. Computer technology has revolutionized the use of visual aids. Software programs let you create traditional tables, charts, and graphs, and many let you create illustrations, scan real photographs, and use digitally recorded pictures from digital cameras. This technology opens new avenues for creating and delivering audiovisual aids to your audience.

Once created, tables, charts, and graphs can be printed in black and white or, if you have a color printer, in vibrant colors. The most commonly known and used form of this software is Microsoft PowerPoint, a discussion of which follows in In Theory box 12.1.

View a student using a photograph as a visual aid. CD-ROM: Video Theater, Excerpt 12.2

drawing: a hand-rendered or computer-generated depiction of what is being orally described in a speech.

photograph: a film or digital image of what is being orally described in a speech.

| INVENTION | ORGANIZATION | STYLE | PREPARATION | DELIVERY |

In Theory 12.1

USING MICROSOFT POWERPOINT FOR YOUR AUDIOVISUAL AIDS

In Chapter 2 we introduced the canons of rhetoric, one of which is *style,* the selection of language and other appropriate symbols to express your ideas. Audiovisual aids contain both words and symbols and can be critical to the success of your speech. Numerous products and services exist today to assist in the creation of audiovisual aids. Although hardly the first software product to offer help with producing audiovisual aids with a computer,[3] Microsoft PowerPoint software is the most popular audiovisual aid software on the market today. Most new computers sold with pre-bundled software come with PowerPoint already installed. In earlier years, it might have been the case that only students in advanced, upper-division public speaking classes would be using PowerPoint to assist them in a presentation, but recently it has become commonplace for students in all classes—especially the basic speech course—to use this product. The latest versions of PowerPoint not only enable student users to create the traditional talking-point slides, but now also create possibilities for three-dimensional artwork and the incorporation of music into presentations.[4]

In our experience two issues tend to create challenges for students giving presentations with PowerPoint. One is the timed sequencing of slides. Later versions of this software allow speakers to preset a cadence for their slide displays so that images appear on the larger screen at whatever intervals of time (such as thirty seconds) are desired. The speaker presets the timing, and the software projects the slides at the chosen interval. The speaker does not have to return to the computer keyboard and manually click to display each slide. The use of this feature requires the speaker to be disciplined when speaking about each slide and saying what-

ever needs to be said within the chosen interval. The time limit might work in a formal, short presentation, but in classroom presentations delivered extemporaneously it often causes problems. The automatic timer often moves ahead to the next slide while the speaker is in midsentence, upsetting the speaker and prompting her or him to accelerate the rate of delivery to catch up. Timed sequencing may be best reserved for short presentations delivered from a scripted text.

The other challenge posed by PowerPoint arises when the speaker decides not to use the automatic timing feature and instead opts to change slides manually. There are three ways to do this: (1) the speaker stands beside the computer (usually a laptop set on a cart beside the projection device) and clicks to the next slide; (2) a classmate does so; (3) the speaker operates a remote control device (pointed at the computer projection unit) to advance to the next slide.

The first option is probably the least attractive, because the speaker will be facing the same direction as the audience and speaking to the screen. The lack of eye contact with the audience lessens the effectiveness of the presentation.

The second option—a classmate advances the slides—works well if the assistant is aware of the speaker's timing. In advance of the presentation, the speaker needs to discuss with the assistant the timing of slides and perhaps practice to work out any problems.

The third option—a remote control device—is highly desirable because it lets the speaker face the audience while the slide show appears on a screen behind him or her. Of course, this option is possible only if the projection unit has a remote control device—and if this device has batteries that work. If your unit has such a device, be sure to check it out *before* you speak.

This same technology allows you to print tables, charts, and graphs as black-and-white or color slides for display by a slide projector, or as plastic transparencies for display by an overhead projector. Of course, you also can display them on the original computer screen. Or you can transfer them to a larger monitor or directly download them to a special projection device that shows the image against a wall or screen (see Figure 12.5 on p. 322).

View a student using PowerPoint as a visual aid.
CD-ROM: Video Theater, Excerpt 12.3

FIGURE 12.5   Computer Technology

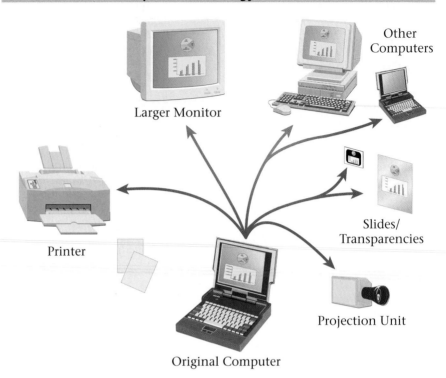

Larger Monitor

Other Computers

Printer

Slides/ Transparencies

Original Computer

Projection Unit

Modern computer technology allows you to project and share visual aids in a variety of ways for any audience.

The same technology creates identical possibilities for artwork or photographs—with a variety of increasingly spectacular special effects. Figure 12.6 shows photographic images created with a digital camera that have been altered with a software program to create slightly different representations.

Increasingly affordable video and digital video cameras allow whole video clips to be downloaded and edited with the use of similar software, or directly from the digital video camera itself. Some software allows you to

FIGURE 12.6   Using Software to Alter Photographic Visual Aids

Visual aids and photo software allow for creative manipulations of the same visual aid image.

manipulate the video in similar ways; other software also allows for selection of individual still photographs from the video. Also, regular video cameras can record on VHS tape and play back on regular monitors or TVs.

Photographs and artwork can be displayed like other visual aids (see Figure 12.5). Video can be played back on the original computer, transferred to other computers, converted back to tape and played back on video recorders, or recorded onto CD-ROM diskettes or DVDs (digital video diskettes) for later playback.

Computer technology opens almost unlimited possibilities. The days of marker boards and flip charts may be numbered.

● *Technology and Audio Aids*

For aids that are more audio than visual, you may want to consider several options. For example, you may want to use standard audiocassette tape for playback of voices, because it can easily be edited. But if your audio aid features music, you may wish to use a compact disk or a phonograph record, because the sound quality is always superior on them.

Some presentations may benefit from multiple audio aids. In one classroom informative presentation, a student named Leanna spoke about the history and development of jazz. In her speech, she used actual instruments—a tenor saxophone and an electronic keyboard—as audio and visual aids. She displayed them and demonstrated a few riffs on each. She later played a phonograph recording of a rare Charlie Parker selection (using an old record player), a tape recording of an Art Tatum selection (using a boom box), and a CD recording of a live performance by modernist Sadao Watanabe (also using the boom box, which played both CDs and audiotapes).

So far we have discussed the creation and display of an ever-growing list of possible audiovisual aids. What audiovisual aids, if any, are best for your presentation, and what should guide your selection?

Audience Analysis and the Selection of Audiovisual Aids

Because an audiovisual aid is part of the speech message you are sharing with your audience, the audience analysis considerations that guide the creation and development of your speech should drive the selection of your audiovisual aids. All audience analysis considerations are relevant, but three merit special attention: forum, demographics, and prior exposure.

To review audience analysis and the development of a speech, see Chapter 5.

● *Forum*

First, consider the *forum* when thinking about audiovisual aids. Where will the audience be exposed to your speech? Is the forum equipped to handle audiovisual aids? Are there some poster boards, flip charts, marker boards, or chalkboards? Are outlets available for slide or overhead projectors, video playback units and TV monitors, or computers and computer projector

To review forum and audience analysis, see page 95.

devices? If you are using an audiovisual aid online from another source, is a modem available? Assuming the capacity is there, will everyone in the audience have equal access to the audiovisual aid? Will everyone be able to see or hear it?

● *Demographics*

To review demographics and audience analysis, see page 97.

Next, consider audience *demographics*. The background and experience of audience members can easily predispose or predetermine their orientation to a particular visual or audio message. Are you using imagery in your visuals that is appropriate for your audience? Does the imagery appeal to something in the life experience of the audience? For example, in a speech about recycling for an audience of thirteen-year-old eighth graders at an urban public middle school, would you use the same kinds of visual aids that you might use for an audience of middle-aged farmers and ranchers who live in the rural Midwest? Probably not.

The choice of images for the thirteen-year-olds would be very much driven by their age, as well as their location. Visual aids in bright colors might draw the attention of an otherwise distracted and bored teenage audience, coupled perhaps with pictures of other young people—perhaps role models from the school—practicing recycling. Or the audiovisual aids might include a video presentation by a popular music group or well-known athletic figure showing how easily recycling can be accomplished. Would those same visual aids work with the older farmer/rancher audience? No. In many places, people from urban areas simply dump trash in the countryside, sometimes on working farmland. Farmers and ranchers might respond better to imagery suggestive of protecting farmland from the pollution of the big city. As an exercise, consider which of the images, if any, you would keep for the farmers and ranchers and what you would create and display differently.

● *Prior Exposure*

To review prior exposure and audience analysis, see page 104.

Information about the demographic characteristics of an audience can tell you much about members' *prior exposure* to your message—and about the best audiovisual aids for your presentation. Prior exposure to certain audiovisual aids may positively or negatively precondition an audience's reaction to the aid and the speech message.

A student named Jenny gave a persuasive speech in opposition to abortion. She gave the speech for her speech class, before an audience from a major metropolitan area. More than half of the class were women, and Jenny knew from interviewing them that many labeled themselves prochoice and would find visual aids depicting dead fetuses (often shown in the media by anti-abortion protesters) to be highly offensive. Armed with this knowledge, Jenny tried a different approach to make her argument that all life has value. She showed many pictures of healthy babies and the children they grew to be. She didn't change the minds of her listeners, but her speech was well received.

As suggested before, you will want to ask yourself:

1. *Has my audience been exposed to this audiovisual aid before?* If the answer is "no," no more prior-exposure analysis is necessary. If the answer is "yes," proceed to the next question.

2. *What was the result of this prior exposure?* Was the audience moved to do as the speaker intended? Was the audience informed or persuaded? If the answer is "yes," then (unless something has changed for the audience) you probably don't need to do any more prior-exposure analysis because if the aid was effective once, chances are good that it will work again. If the answer is "no," then proceed to the final question.

3. *Why was the prior exposure ineffective?* You want to avoid repeating mistakes.

Advantages Offered by Audiovisual Aids

When created and displayed properly, audiovisual aids offer several important advantages.

● *Audiovisual aids can make a dull or boring presentation more interesting.*

How often have you attended a slightly dull or clearly boring speech or lecture? Perhaps you've witnessed a speaker whose speech abilities leave a lot to be desired. Or perhaps a speech was dull because the subject matter was dull. In such situations, a colorful, bright, attractive audiovisual aid can help spruce up the speech, adding life to the presentation. Be creative when you design audiovisuals for your presentation. Look for powerful and distinct images that focus the message without distracting the audience.[5]

Conceptual ideas can confuse an audience. Make abstract ideas concrete by illustrating them with more than words.

● *Audiovisual aids can simplify a complex speech message.*

In situations where your message is either *technical, complicated* (perhaps it has many components, the sum of which is difficult for the audience to grasp), or *convoluted* (perhaps it derives from many different stories or analogies, as from a history that is difficult to assimilate), an audiovisual aid can rescue your presentation. It does so by taking a rather complex message and helping the audience to understand what you are saying by displaying it visually. Teachers often use audiovisual aids in class lectures to explain difficult concepts. They believe that if students can see as well as hear about a complex subject, they will have a better chance of understanding what's being communicated.[6]

● *Audiovisual aids build audience retention of the speech message.*

To review ineffective listening skills, see page 74.

When you hear a speech, you are likely to recall only some of it—often because of inadequacies in the speech or because of inefficiencies in your own listening behavior. Audiovisual aids help to counteract some memory problems. Many individuals find the visual message—often shorter, more immediate, and less complex than the verbal message—easier to retain and later recall.

Rules for Preparing Audiovisual Aids

Use your CD-ROM to view a full tutorial on designing visual aids and using Microsoft PowerPoint to create visual presentations. CD-ROM: Visual Presentation Tutorial

When preparing audiovisual aids for your presentation, follow these rules:

● *1. Be sure that the audiovisual aid supports your point.*

Is your point something that can be communicated visually? If an audio demonstration is called for, can it be achieved easily? What are the possible audiovisual applications? Can you use yourself or others, objects, maps, graphs, charts, tables, drawings, photographs, or video? List all the possibilities.

● *2. Consider your audience analysis when deciding what audiovisual aids you will use.*

Your analysis of the forum, prior exposure, and demographics of the audience can greatly assist you in selecting audiovisual aids that are appropriate for those who will witness your presentation. Ask yourself this question: Of all the possible aids for this speech, which aid or combination of aids will work best with this particular audience?

● *3. Make sure your audio aid is loud and clear.*

Be certain you can reproduce the sound in a way that is loud enough and clear enough to be heard by everyone in the audience. A recording must be clear, devoid of background distortion or static, and capable of being amplified adequately for everyone to hear. A video recording should have adequate sound qualities for the audience to hear and understand what is played or said.

● 4. Make sure your visual aid is large enough to be seen.

Be certain you create a visual aid large enough to be seen by everyone in the audience. All speech class instructors can tell you stories of students who tried to give speeches using visual aids—such as a wallet-size photograph of the Grand Canyon in a speech about travel opportunities—that were less than effective because they were too small. Remember this simple guideline: The larger the audience is, or the greater the distance the audience is from the visual aid, the larger the aid must appear.

● 5. Make sure your visual aid is legible and easily understood.

Be certain the individual parts of a visual message are legible and easily understood. Numbers, letters, words, sentences, and so on should be clear and easily distinguished. This is sometimes a matter of perspective. If you're creating a chart, look at it from a distance. Is it legible and understandable? Ask a classmate, friend, roommate, or family member to look at it. Can that person read and understand everything? If not, go back to the drawing board!

● 6. Follow the rules of contrast.

If you are creating something visual, remember the **rules of contrast**. Use dark colors against a light background or light colors against a dark background (see Figure 12.7). Under no circumstances use dark on dark or light on light.

FIGURE 12.7   **Examples of Contrast in Visual Aids**

NO!

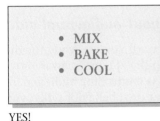

NO!

YES!   YES!

The top two visual aids are difficult to read because they ignore the rules of contrast. The bottom two visual aids observe the rules of contrast, and the contrasting colors make for better readability.

rules of contrast: when creating a visual aid, use dark colors against a light background, and use light colors against a dark background.

7. Keep the message of the audiovisual aid simple.

Be certain you are creating something that makes and keeps your speech message simple. Professional speech writers sometimes refer to this as avoiding making an audiovisual aid that is too "busy." As you work on your aid, ask yourself: Is this too busy? Have I made this more complicated than it needs to be? Is there too much information? If you aren't certain, remember this simple guideline: An audiovisual aid works best if audience members can glance at it or hear it just once and quickly understand what is being communicated. If they have to stare at it, see it more than once, or listen to it several times, it is not simple, and chances are good that it is not achieving the goal of simplifying the message.

8. Do not create the audiovisual aid while you speak.

View a student creating a visual aid while speaking, a practice to be avoided.
CD-ROM: Video Theater, Excerpt 12.4

Create the audiovisual aid in advance, and practice with it. Trying to create while you speak often leads to situations where your attention is focused on the aid and not the audience—and sometimes leads to frustration if the aid is difficult to create spontaneously.

Rules for Delivering Audiovisual Aids

After creating your audiovisual aids, you need to consider how to use them in the speech presentation. This necessity raises a number of questions for you to address: Will everyone in your audience be able to see or hear your audiovisual aid? Will audience members be distracted by aids you finished using but left out for display? When you use an audiovisual aid, where should your eye contact be? How will you balance the audiovisual aid with the speech message itself? To answer such questions and effectively display your audiovisual aids, follow these rules:

1. Make sure your audiovisual aid is accessible to everyone in your audience.

Position stereo speakers so that everyone can hear the music you're playing, or position a picture or graph front and center so that the whole audience can see it. Otherwise, some people may miss a significant part of your speech.

2. Control audience interaction with your audiovisual aid.

Do not play or show something to the audience until you are ready for the audience to hear or see it; and after finishing with the aid, put it away or remove it from the audience's consideration. Why is controlling audience interaction with an aid so important? Consider your own behavior when you are in an audience. If someone shows or plays something, aren't you likely to look or listen? Curiosity is part of human nature.

If a student speaker in your class displays all of her visual aids—for example, maps and carvings from various African countries—before her

FIGURE 12.8   Controlling Interaction before You Refer to a Visual Aid

Don't reveal a visual aid until you are ready for the audience to focus on its content.

presentation, aren't you tempted to look at them? Isn't it possible that you will still be looking at the aids when she starts to speak? Will you focus your attention on her, or might you get ahead of her speech as you look at the visual aids?

The same is likely to happen when a speaker finishes referring to an aid but does not put it away. The audience might continue to be drawn to the aid even though the speaker has finished with it. In either situation, a failure to control audience interaction with the aid can mean the audience might miss an important part of the speech.

In practice, you can control interaction in several ways. If you are using an audio recording, have the passage you want cued up ahead of time, so that you can seamlessly play it when ready. Do not play a tape or CD or record as background music to your speech because that might draw attention to the recording and away from you. If you are using a visual display,

FIGURE 12.9   Controlling Interaction after You Refer to a Visual Aid

When you are finished with a visual aid and ready to move on to a different point in your speech, remove the visual aid from the audience's sight.

consider the following techniques for controlling interaction: If you are going to tape or pin a chart to the wall, do so in advance, but tape or pin one half of the display over the other half, blocking the audience's view until you want the audience to focus on the aid (see Figure 12.8 on p. 329).

Use the same general technique when you are displaying a series of visual aids on successive sheets of a flip chart (see Figure 12.9 on p. 329). Place blank sheets of paper between all visual aids. Then, when you finish with one and flip the page, all the audience will see is a blank page, and their attention will return to you.

This technique also works with overhead transparency projections, film slide projections, and computer images. Remove the image, leaving a blank screen, or turn the equipment off.

Many students wonder whether to use handouts in a presentation. Given what we said about the need to control audience interaction, you can see that distributing handouts to the audience prior to a presentation (so that you will not have to pass them out during your speech) poses a dilemma. If you distribute the handout before the speech but do not refer to it right away, will the audience pay close attention to the speech or read the handout? In truth, some audience members will look at the handout. Does this mean you should never distribute handouts in advance of a speech? No. But it does suggest that you need to give clear instructions about the use of handouts. For example, you might pass out your visual aids facedown and tell the audience not to turn them over until you say to. As you pass the handouts along, you might explain that you do not want audience members to get ahead of you and that you want them to avoid looking at the handout until you ask them to. This strategy usually works well, although there will always be somebody in the audience who ignores your request and gets ahead of you. It is for people like this that eye contact and vocal delivery skills are critical. You want to be looking at the audience and spot those who might be getting ahead of you with the handout. If necessary, adjust your delivery by increasing your volume or moving closer to them to draw their attention back to you and away from the handout.

For tips on making eye contact, see page 298.

For tips on vocal delivery, see page 290.

For tips on physical movement, see page 301.

● 3. Do not use the visual aid as an excuse to avoid looking at your audience.

Your attention to eye contact is critical. Many inexperienced speakers look at their visual aids instead of at the audience. Obviously, you must glance at the visual aid, especially if you are referring to something on it. But if you give in to the temptation to look at the aid more than you look at the audience, you eventually may lose the audience's attention.

● 4. Remember the role that the audiovisual aid plays in your speech.

An audiovisual aid is a tool that supplements your speech; your speech is not an excuse to show or display an audiovisual aid. The speech contains your message, and you are the messenger. Speakers who misunderstand this fundamental rule about aids risk becoming superfluous as the audience focuses mostly or only on the aid.

ESL	Using Visual Aids

There are many ways to create and present audiovisual aids, and you should use whatever method feels most comfortable to you. Unless your instructor requires a specific technology, don't feel pressured to use something—for example, a videocassette recorder, an overhead projector, a computer—you aren't familiar with. If you do want to try a new technology, be sure to ask your instructor for assistance, and be certain to practice with this technology well in advance of your class speech.

If you are an ESL student and would like some assistance with the wording for flip charts, graphs, transparencies, and handouts, ask your instructor or a reliable classmate for feedback about your phrasing of bulleted points and so on. Do this before your class presentation.

Be careful to avoid reading your visual aids verbatim to your audience. This approach may lessen your speech anxiety, but it also lessens your eye contact with the audience and increases the likelihood that you will speak in a dull monotone. Practice with your visual aids. Try to paraphrase or summarize what is shown on each one, while looking at your audience.

It is not uncommon for inexperienced salespeople, for example, to rely too heavily on brochures and handouts during a presentation, mistakenly assuming that good marketing material is all that's really needed to sell a product or service. Of course, if this were true, all sales managers would fire salespeople and simply mail out brochures. But we know that for many kinds of sales presentations, a brochure (one kind of visual aid) will not work by itself. It cannot, for example, answer questions or engage in spontaneous interaction with an audience. Only a human being—a salesperson/speaker—can accomplish this. The speakers who are most effective understand this relationship between the aid and the speech and are careful never to let the aid replace the speech.

The Power of Audiovisual Aids: Ethical Implications

By making the dull more interesting and by simplifying what is complex, audiovisual aids can dramatically affect an audience's perception of a speech and enhance what individuals remember. There is great potential for the abuse of audiovisual aids, however, and you need to consider the ethical implications of your selection, creation, and display of these tools.

When you take what appears to be a dull topic and attempt to enhance its audience appeal with an audiovisual aid, do you use concepts, imagery, or words that remain true to the original message? Be careful about glamorizing or popularizing difficult topics as you translate them to a visual medium. For example, for a speech about world hunger, a student named Monica created large and colorful charts on her computer and displayed them on a large screen with a computer projection device. The colors and artwork she used were warm and communicated a mood of happiness about solutions to this complex problem. Monica herself would have been the first to admit that the solutions—involving difficult choices—were anything but warm and happy. Her charts, however, communicated just such a message, potentially misleading her audience.

Be aware that audiovisual aids can oversimplify complex messages. Consider whether your aids go too far in diluting the content and power of your message. In your desire to simplify, have you made your message simplistic, potentially trivializing the message and misleading your audience? For example, Lisa—a student in a biology class—gave a class presentation about possible solutions to pollution. She closed her speech with a visual aid—a large poster showing the word *pollution* with a large red line drawn across it and below it, in larger lettering, the slogan "Recycling—Draw the Line against Pollution!" At first glance there appeared nothing wrong with this visual aid. But Lisa's speech dealt with various types of pollution, such as air and water pollution, litter, and toxic waste, and recycling was not the solution to all of them. By leaving the audience with this particular visual aid, Lisa trivialized the issue as well as the solution.

Finally, be aware of the power of audiovisual aids. Listening to portions of a taped conversation, for example, can have a powerful impact on an audience, as can hearing selected excerpts of someone's speech or music. A photograph, chart, or table also can exert powerful influence on an audi-

Be careful that your visual aid conveys the message you intend. If you're giving a speech on one topic, your aid shouldn't focus on another. If your speech is on how factories are working to clean up air pollution, don't let your main image show them polluting the air.

ence. With the use of these tools comes a responsibility to be truthful and accurate. Have you presented a portion of a speech or conversation out of context? Have you altered (even by innocently averaging) the numbers in the study depicted in your graph to make a point in your speech? If you used software to enhance a photo and then show it without its surrounding environment, did you change the meaning of the photo?

To review speech ethics and taking facts out of context, see pages 59–61.

Because so many people are visual learners, and because simple messages (heard or seen) are more easily remembered than detailed, complicated messages, it would be easy to manipulate an audience with an audiovisual aid. Don't do it. Be responsible in your use of these tools.

Summary

This chapter focused on the use of audiovisual aids and how they can influence an audience's reception of your presentation. Audiovisual aids are tools that supplement what the speaker is saying and enhance an audience's interest in, comprehension of, and retention of a message. They can be anything from the speaker him- or herself, to an assistant, a physical object, a recording, a graph, table, chart, map, drawing, photo, or video. They can be displayed in a variety of ways—including across a computer screen.

This chapter also explored the advantages offered by audiovisual aids and several rules for preparing and using them. The checklist indicates how to use the material in this chapter to prepare for your speech.

Checklist

WHAT TYPE OF AUDIOVISUAL AID DO YOU NEED?

____ Consider whether to use yourself as an audiovisual aid (p. 314)

____ Consider using physical objects as visual aids (p. 315)

____ Consider using assistants as audiovisual aids (p. 316)

____ Consider using maps (p. 317)

____ Consider using charts (verbal, pie, flow) (p. 317)

____ Consider using graphs (line, bar) (p. 319)

____ Consider using drawings and photographs (p. 320)

____ Think about how you could use computer technology (p. 320)

____ Consider using audio technology (p. 323)

AUDIENCE ANALYSIS

____ How does the speech forum affect your choice of audiovisual aids? (p. 323)

____ What does audience demographics suggest about appropriate audiovisual aids? (p. 324)

____ How does the audience's prior exposure to the speech topic affect your creation and use of audiovisual aids? (p. 324)

____ How do you use prior-exposure analysis to select audiovisual aids? (p. 324)

ADVANTAGES OF AUDIOVISUAL AIDS

____ Use aids to make your presentation more interesting (p. 325)

____ Use aids to simplify a complex message (p. 326)

____ Use aids to build audience retention of your speech message (p. 326)

RULES FOR PREPARING AND USING AUDIOVISUAL AIDS

____ Consider whether an audiovisual aid will support your point (p. 326)

____ Consider your audience when deciding what type of aid to use (p. 326)

____ Make sure that your audio aid is loud and clear (p. 326)

____ Make sure that your visual aid is large enough to be seen (p. 327)

____ Be sure that all lettering, numbers, and symbols in your visual aid are legible and easily understood (p. 327)

____ Use contrast in your visual aid (p. 327)

____ Avoid making your aid too busy or complicated (p. 328)

____ Create your aid in advance of your speech (p. 328)

____ Make sure that your aid is accessible to everyone in your audience (p. 328)

____ Control audience interaction with your aid (p. 328)

____ Maintain eye contact with your audience while using your aid (p. 330)

____ Remember that the aid is a supplement to, and not a replacement for, the speech (p. 330)

IF YOU ARE AN ESL STUDENT

____ Work with the technology you feel most comfortable with (p. 331)

____ Practice using technology in advance (p. 331)

____ Seek out feedback on the wording of your visual aids before your speech (p. 331)

____ Try summarizing or paraphrasing (instead of reading verbatim) what is written on your visual aid, while looking at your audience (p. 331)

ETHICAL IMPLICATIONS

____ In your audiovisual aids, use concepts, words, symbols, and imagery that remain true to the original message (p. 331)

____ When using an audiovisual aid to simplify a complex point, avoid trivializing the original message (p. 331)

____ Avoid using audiovisual material out of context (p. 331)

Key Terms and Concepts

audiovisual aid (p. 314)

map (p. 317)

chart (p. 317)

verbal chart (p. 318)

pie chart (p. 318)

flow chart (p. 319)

graph (p. 319)

line graph (p. 319)

bar graph (p. 319)

drawing (p. 320)

photograph (p. 320)

rules of contrast (p. 327)

Please turn the page for the
Speech Grid Application.

Speech Grid Application

The Evolution of a Speech Grid

Speech Grid Applications, showing the evolution of a Speech Grid, are included near the end of Chapters 5 through 12. They illustrate how one student, Samantha, uses a grid to prepare a speech.

Samantha has taken some material from each side of her grid and from the outline she based on that grid, and she has used that information to make decisions about visual aids. Because some of the original ideas she noted on her grid seemed unworkable, Samantha considered other ideas from her outline about where a visual aid could be effectively used to get her message across. Here we show only excerpts from Samantha's grid and outline. For a complete grid and outline of her main points, see page 256.

When you prepare your speeches, determine which points can be effectively presented to your audience by means of visual aids, and review the situational characteristics on your grid to make good decisions about which visual aids will be workable.

Speech Grid: *Driving with cell phones*

AUDIENCE ANALYSIS	SPEECH MESSAGE
Situational Characteristics • *8 min. speech* • *25–30 in audience* • *small classroom* • *limited a-v equip.* **Demographics** **Age:** *17 (5); 18 (17); 19 (4); 20 (1); 22 (1)* **Ethnicity:** *African-American (2); Hmong (2); white (9); Latino/a (6); Portuguese (2); Pacific Islander, Mexican, German, Japanese, Swedish, Greek (1 each); did not say (1)*	*PATHOS* • *Photo of car involved in fatal accident* *LOGOS — Solution* • *Visual aid idea — video showing safe use tips*

Samantha's Visual Aid Decisions

VISUAL AID	
1. ~~Photo of car involved in fatal accident. (photo)~~	*Rejected because photo is too small for whole class to see. Do not pass photo around instead (see p. 328); it would be distracting. However, the picture would be a powerful image to reinforce the message cell phone use while driving is dangerous (see p. 325). Could use visual aid if it was possible to enlarge the picture so that the whole class could see it. Before speaking, have friend sit in the back of the room to test whether enlarged picture is visible to all.*

(continued)

Samantha's Visual Aid Decisions, continued

VISUAL AID	
~~2. Video showing safe use tips.~~	*Rejected because there was limited audiovisual equipment in the classroom. Also, the video would use up three minutes of an eight-minute speech, replacing rather than supplementing the message (p. 330).*
3. Bar chart comparing the growth rate of cell phone use by 18–25-year-olds to the overall growth rate of cell phone use.	*Use this visual aid because bar graphs help the audience comprehend numbers and percentages. Could use computer technology to create professional-looking graph (p. 320).*
4. List of the five steps involved in safe use of cell phones while driving.	*Use because five ideas are a lot to remember, and a verbal chart can help the audience keep track of the tips (p. 318). Could use the word "SAFER" as a vehicle to convey the tips:* **S***ide of the road is best* **A***ppointment-making can wait* **F***irst check driving conditions* **E***nd call NOW if necessary* **R***elying on hands-free phone risky*

Source Notes

1. Bohn, E., & Jabusch, D. (1982). The effect of four methods of instruction on the use of visual aids in speeches. *Western Journal of Speech Communication, 42*(3), 253–265.
2. Nelson, H. E., & Vandermeer, A. W. (1953). Varied sound tracks on animated film. *Speech Monographs, 20,* 261–267.
3. For example, early versions of a software program called Harvard Graphics were popular for business users but not always affordable for student users in classroom presentations.
4. Jacobs, K. (2001). A sound solution: Playing music on html presentations. Available at <www.Powerpointanswers.com>.
5. Norohona, S., & Rhodes, J. (1998, April). How to create and deliver dynamic presentations: A sourcebook. *Inc., 20,* 99.
6. Weaver, M. (1999). Make your point with effective audio visuals. *Computers in Libraries, 19,* 62.

"Apply the lessons of this book and course in your future."

13 Speaking beyond the Speech Classroom

OBJECTIVES

After reading Chapter 13, you should understand:

● How the concepts you studied this term will be useful in other classes, in the workplace, and in the community.

● How communication occurs within a small group.

● Techniques for effective public speaking to a small group, and by a small group to a larger audience.

● Factors to consider when speaking to larger audiences in other classes, in the workplace, and in the community.

Imagine that you have completed your public speaking course and are now working your way through other courses on campus. Perhaps you have a seminar on criminal justice, and you have an assignment to present your report on *Miranda* rights (the right of criminal suspects to remain silent and to legal counsel) to the other eight students in the class. Or perhaps you are studying physiology in a large lecture course, but your instructor has divided the class into small, manageable groups, each of which will be called upon at some time during the semester to explain to the entire class the results of an experiment the group conducted.

Or imagine that you have graduated from college and entered the job market to seek your fortune. Perhaps you are part of a sales and marketing team for a company selling Web design services for b2b (business-to-business) applications. Your team is often called upon to make persuasive sales presentations to established brick-and-mortar companies that wish to establish an online presence through a new Web site. You also may have to speak individually to your sales and marketing group while in an office meeting, perhaps to explain a sales report you just completed.

If you are a manager, you may need to explain a change in the rules or culture of a corporation, workplace, or nonprofit agency. How do you best explain change to employees accustomed to a certain routine?

As those scenarios suggest, many opportunities to apply the lessons of this book and course are likely to present themselves in the future. When you apply them, keep in mind two important points. The first is that some understanding of communication within groups is vital to your development as a public speaker.

The scenarios described above occur in a small-group context, either an individual speaking to a small group or a small group making a presentation to a larger audience. By **small group**, we mean a limited number of people

small group: a limited number of people gathered for a specific purpose.

339

It's likely that in the workplace you will be called upon to speak in public. The skills you've learned from this book will help in these situations.

gathered for a specific purpose. Usually the number of individuals in a small group ranges from three to fifteen (a small group is different from a *dyad*, which consists of only two individuals). Small groups are often organized to complete specific tasks. For example, a university department committee reviews a professor's bid for tenure, or a group of parents agrees to organize ride-sharing for their children on a swim team.

Speech presentations in other classes will often involve small groups, and the same can be said for life beyond school as you enter a profession or perhaps volunteer your time in a community organization or charity.[1] To that end, as we consider public speaking beyond the speech class, we begin with a general discussion of small-group communication and follow with a more focused consideration of public speaking and small groups.

The second point to remember is that the speeches you give in the workplace, in the community, or in other classes are likely to be blends of the rhetorical purposes discussed in Chapter 6. You may often have speeches that combine two or more of these purposes (informing, persuading, inspiring, or entertaining). Thus we discuss in the last section of this chapter several types of speeches you may be called upon to make, such as a speech explaining change, a speech delivering bad news, and one celebrating achievement.

For more on the different rhetorical purposes of a speech, see page 126.

Communicating in Small Groups

To some degree, the actual number of group members is important for purposes of understanding what a small group is, but more important is **group dynamics**—how group members relate to one another and view the function or purpose of the group. It is critical to the functioning of a small group that members interact with each other and that the group be working toward a goal or goals. These components of a small group probably best describe the kinds of groups you often work in for your other classes.

group dynamics: how group members relate to one another and view the function and purpose of the group.

Perhaps the instructor in one of your classes has broken down the class of thirty students into groups of five or six and assigned each group a research project, an analytical problem, or a hypothetical fact pattern. Group members are supposed to function as a team, sharing the workload, and all members are expected to contribute equally toward the research analysis or hypothetical solution.

In order for any group to work effectively, each member must exchange information and ideas openly and honestly. Suppose the teacher in a critical thinking course divides the class into five groups of six students and assigns each group the text of a speech by President George W. Bush. Each group is to analyze the speech for the use of logic, as well as the presence (if any) of fallacies of reasoning. Ideally, group members are to call or e-mail each other with their individual analyses and then work their individual ideas into one presentation they will make to the class as a whole. But what if in one group, two students don't share their analyses and instead want to make their own presentations and take individual credit for their findings? This would clearly undermine the purpose and goal of the group, resulting in an unbalanced presentation and alienating the other group members.

Equally important for effective group functioning is that the goal or objective for each group must be clearly spelled out by the instructor and understood by all group members. In a comparative literature course, an inexperienced instructor divided her class into small groups and asked the groups to "talk about" the book they had just read by author John Steinbeck. Without clearer instructions from her, or more focused objectives for group discussion, the students did talk about Steinbeck's novel *The Pearl,* but only for a short time. Before long, conversation within the groups drifted to topics ranging from movies students had seen to the quality of food in the dormitory system.

If you have ever had a similar classroom group assignment, you may have witnessed firsthand the unsatisfactory results when group members do not interact with each other effectively or when the group's purpose and objective were not comprehended by the group or clarified by the teacher. In such situations, the group functions less like a small group and more like a collection of individuals.

● *Types of Leaders*

It is tempting to divide the roles that people assume within a small group into two categories: leaders and followers. But that would be an oversimplification because there are many different types of leadership. A group member with a preexisting position of responsibility or power in an organization may be the **implied leader** in a small group within that organization. For example, the manager or director of a business unit may also sit as the chair or leader of a small-business group made up of many of her own employees as well as some from other units. In such a situation, the reality of her seniority might imply her leadership in the group.

An individual may also be a **designated leader**, either determined by the group or by some external authority creating the group. In the classroom, an instructor may designate a student as a group or team leader to eliminate the stress and time the group might expend in selecting a leader.

implied leader: a group member who has preexisting responsibility or power in an organization.

designated leader: a group member who is designated as leader by the group or by some external authority responsible for creating the group.

In some situations, a group might begin without a leader but eventually someone becomes the **emergent leader** because of the sheer force of his or her will and the strength of his or her personality. This often happens in volunteer organizations that form committees or groups to study problems or challenges. Membership in the group reflects the volunteer status of each individual. Each individual has limited time and equal status within the group and may be reluctant to lead. Eventually, however, someone emerges as leader because he or she is more assertive than other members—or is tired of sailing on a ship with no rudder!

At times, some groups function without leaders, although in these situations the responsibilities of the group are shared or the group does not function as a group at all. For example, a university faculty committee that studies issues that are related to school but fall outside the primary responsibility or expertise of group members (such as a plan for earthquake safety) might function without a leader. Everyone on the committee is busy, so all agree to share in the responsibilities of the group.

Each of the leadership roles described above has implications for public speaking within a group. The *implied* leader may be in a group with individuals who previously interacted with him or her as their division manager or department head; they may feel constrained by that preexisting authority role and may be too quick to defer to the person's authority or be overawed by the person's presence. In either case, group members might not share in the open and honest exchange of information so necessary for small-group communication; and, if the group makes a presentation to a larger audience, group members might do nothing to contradict their leader.

A *designated* leader chosen by a higher authority external to the group might also encounter difficulties. In this instance, the limiting factor for group members may be fear that contradicting or criticizing the designated leader may be interpreted as criticism of the external authority. For example, if a manager designates one employee as leader of a small group of employees, other group members may perceive that the designated leader carries the authority of the manager and believe that criticism of the leader may be interpreted as criticism of the manager. In that case, the likely result is a sort of self-censorship, known as a *chilling effect,*[2] on what other group members say within the group. In a public speaking situation, this effect limits the diversity of ideas group members share with a larger audience.

Any of the above-mentioned types of leaders face the possibility of **groupthink**,[3] the tendency of group members to accept ideas and information uncritically because of strong feelings of loyalty or single-mindedness within the group. Groupthink can develop if all group members are intimidated by the leader's authority and feel compelled to say whatever they perceive the leader wants them to say. In this case, it is not so much the self-censorship that negatively impacts communication as it is the uncritical acceptance of incomplete or half-baked ideas that emerge from the group in a presentation.

Emergent leaders also face their share of challenges in working effectively in a small group. These leaders may dominate other group members on an interpersonal basis because of the force of their personality. Other group members may be intimidated by an emergent leader's presence and allow this person to dictate to the group.

emergent leader: a group member who becomes group leader by sheer force of will and strength of personality.

groupthink: the tendency of group members to accept ideas and information uncritically because of strong feelings of loyalty or single-mindedness.

What can all leaders do to direct and lead their groups? One thing to remember is that it is critical to encourage all members to be open and honest with their ideas. Do nothing to stifle open discussion and honest exchange. Unless you (as the group leader) naively or arrogantly assume that you have all the answers (and if you do, why bother with a group?), you will benefit from all members' input and exchange of ideas. You may need to clarify how you want the group exchange to proceed. For example, you may want to announce your intentions at the beginning of the meeting, asserting that you expect all members to contribute and participate and you want no one to hold back. Tell the group you will not pull rank and assert your authority unless you observe that group members are silent or unnecessarily reluctant to make comments.

Another thing to remember if you are group leader is the importance of keeping the group on task—that is, focused on the problem or issue the group is trying to solve or work through. Often a group discussion introduces tangential issues or irrelevant side discussions. As a leader, you are responsible for keeping the group focused. Again, you may benefit from declaring your intentions at the beginning of the meeting. You may wish to tell the group that you will allow discussion only on points related to the group's primary focus. Perhaps suggest that during the actual discussion and exchange, you will temporarily give up your leadership role and become an equal group member, also free to contribute ideas. Tell the group you will resume the leader position and redirect the group if the discussion drifts off to unrelated topics.

Also, as leader, make sure that you focus on issues and not personalities. Your group will not work effectively if you focus on an individual in the group because of an annoying personality trait or interpersonal conflict. An effective leader separates the personality from the issue.

In a company-related group whose goal was to develop and recommend a workplace safety and security policy in the event of a terrorist attack, the designated leader (who was also a division manager) found that one of her group members was an employee with whom she had experienced difficulty before. He worked in the accounting department and more than once had questioned the manager's travel expenses. As a group leader, the division manager found herself ready to dismiss this employee's suggestions out of personal animosity. But after a group break, she reconsidered her position and decided to separate her personal dislike for this individual from the common sense of his suggestions to the group. Her turnaround encouraged the man, who continued to offer good recommendations.

● *Roles within a Small Group*

All members—both leaders and followers—may assume different roles within a group, depending on the group's objective or purpose.[4] **Task-oriented roles** contribute to the ability of the group to accomplish its goals. **Maintenance-oriented roles** help to maintain and strengthen efficient and effective interpersonal relations. **Self-oriented roles** accomplish little for the group and reflect the selfish ends of individual members.

Task-oriented roles take different forms in the group context. One role might be to initiate interaction by motivating a group to start working on a

task-oriented roles: roles that contribute to the ability of a group to accomplish its goals.

maintenance-oriented roles: roles that help maintain and strengthen efficient and effective interpersonal relations in a group.

self-oriented roles: roles that accomplish little for the group and are motivated by the selfish ends of individual members.

project. The role of *initiator* could be played by any group member who suggests the objective of the group and offers new ideas or proposes new solutions. Another task-oriented role involves *information gathering.* This role might require a member to offer opinions or seek out information from others. Yet another task-oriented role involves *elaborating or clarifying ideas* discussed and exchanged within the group. This role is often assumed by members with skill at commenting on the meaning or intention behind an idea or by members who are capable of providing additional information.

Maintenance-oriented roles call for different skills and functions. One maintenance role might require a group member to become a *harmonizer*— someone who decreases tension in a group, often by using humor at just the right time. This role is usually played by any group member with a healthy sense of humor and (more important) a good sense of timing.

Another maintenance role is that of *compromiser*—a member who offers a consensus-building solution that bridges a gap between rival factions. Compromisers are often group members who are well respected and seen as fair and unbiased. The latter point is critical to ensuring that a compromise or consensus solution will be agreed to by all group members.

A third maintenance role is that of *encourager.* This individual encourages and inspires other group members by offering praise or admiration for ideas and work. This role usually is best filled by a group member who is perceived not only as fair-minded but as sincere.

A fourth maintenance role is that of *gatekeeper.* The gatekeeper facilitates the exchange of information between group members who might not otherwise talk to one another. This individual is the conduit or channel through which even noncommunicative members communicate with one another. The gatekeeper must possess strong interpersonal skills of listening and conversation, as well as a strong sense of tact in knowing when to share information and when to collect information.

Unlike task-oriented and maintenance-oriented roles, self-oriented roles do not contribute to the group process in any meaningful or positive way. One such role is that of the *blocker,* someone who refuses to accept other group members' ideas or opinions. This individual is often absorbed with his or her own agenda, as well as his or her own needs. The blocker has poor interpersonal skills and contributes little or nothing to the group process.

Another self-oriented role is played by the *person who withdraws.* This individual refuses to make any contribution or participate in the group discussion. Often the person playing this role is a group member who feels out of his or her element or depth in the particular group setting. A person who feels incapable of understanding or following what is said in the group process may choose to withdraw, not necessarily physically but most definitely mentally.

The role played by someone who withdraws stands in strong contrast to another self-oriented role, that of the *dominator.* This individual frequently interrupts other group members or refuses to accept their contributions. The dominator is often argumentative for the sake of being argumentative and wants to have the last word on most subjects. Perhaps you have interacted with someone like this in a group before? Chances are, they made a very strong, very negative impression on you.

It is often a good idea for each member of a small group who is giving a presentation to have a task-oriented role.

Another self-oriented role is that of the *distracter*—a person who sends the group astray with extraneous conversation or off-topic comments. This individual is usually someone who has trouble concentrating on a topic or focusing on completion of a process.

All of those group member roles can impact public speaking in the group context. Task-oriented roles typically enhance participation and the free flow of information in a group. If you are making a presentation to a small group that practices these roles, group members will be likely to ask good questions and make constructive comments. For example, in a sales presentation to a board of directors (the board being a small group) who practiced task-oriented roles, the salesperson observed that board members asked questions about the services she was selling and that their questions complemented and built upon each other. Clearly, the board members were listening both to the questions and to the answers.

If you are a member of a small group that is making a presentation to a larger audience, task-oriented roles can help ensure that the group reaches a consensus and the presentation accurately reflects the group's sentiments. A city planning subcommittee that had explored the effects of zoning changes to allow more fast-food restaurants into the downtown area projected intense conviction in its recommendations to the city planning commission and members of the public precisely because of task-oriented roles. Having one member elaborate on and clarify the subcommittee's thoughts about how more fast-food establishments would change the character of the downtown area helped the subcommittee internally to reach consensus. That consensus was forcefully articulated to the larger audience in the final presentation.

Maintenance-oriented roles can also foster the free flow of information and ideas within a group. If you are making a presentation to a small group that uses these roles, you are likely to encounter a low-pressure, supportive audience capable of listening and asking good questions. A student making a presentation to a student council made that observation when one sympathetic council member playing the role of harmonizer rescued the presentation when the group began to ask increasingly more demanding and stressful questions of the presenter. The harmonizer relieved the tension by making a joke—but not at the presenter's expense. After the student council laughed, the questioning resumed, but in a more friendly and less intense manner.

If a small group with maintenance-oriented roles is making a presentation to a larger audience, group members are likely to work as a team, supportive of one another, and present findings or recommendations that reflect group consensus.

Groups in which members play self-oriented roles offer challenges for public speaking. If you are making a presentation to this kind of group, be prepared for any of the aforementioned role behaviors—blocking, withdrawing, dominating, or distracting—in your audience. Any of these may prevent your group audience from listening and understanding your speech message.

Most salespeople eventually encounter a small-group audience in which one member of the group wants to dominate the proceedings. Often, this person interrupts the sales presentation with irrelevant questions or pronouncements that are intended to demonstrate the group member's superior knowledge. Inexperienced salespeople may allow this self-absorbed group member to lead them away from the presentation and into a debate about the topic at hand. This seldom, if ever, makes for a strong presentation to the other group members.

If you are a member of a group afflicted with self-oriented role behavior and the group is making a presentation to a larger audience, the group's findings may appear incomplete or infighting and dissension may surface while the group presentation is being made. Your larger audience may perceive the lack of unity and consensus and wonder whether the group report reflects the opinions of all members or only the speaker's.

● *Working in a Small Group*

Members of a small group need to interact in a productive manner. Doing so, however, can be very challenging, especially in situations calling for decision making in groups with poor leadership. To be effective, group members must attempt to meet certain responsibilities.

If the group's purpose is unclear, it is critical for all group members to clarify and focus on whatever issue brought them together and what they wish to accomplish. They need to identify group goals and assignments for individual members, and they need to commit to completing both.

If some members seem less willing than others to volunteer or do work for the group, the members with the greatest self-orientation (the dominators) are likely to seize the opportunity to control the proceedings. For this reason, it is important for all members to encourage one another to participate in all aspects of the work of the group. If you observe some members who fail to participate or volunteer, ask questions of them and openly court their participation.

Because small groups (especially those whose members have other responsibilities outside the group) may often work under intense conditions or time constraints, the likelihood of interpersonal conflict or destructive arguments is great. All members thus have a responsibility to maintain a collegial atmosphere and avoid personal insults and attacks.

As work within the group proceeds, members might stray from their objectives—especially in groups with poor or no leadership. All members have a responsibility to stay focused on the group goals. Maintaining this focus requires diligence by all members, as well as willingness to avoid distractions and tangential discussions. It also requires members to be disciplined about the process of group discussion. If the group convenes for the purpose of decision making and problem solving, group members must focus on the different options available to them and on the complexity of the problem and potential solutions.

A five-step process known as **reflective thinking**[5] can help group members remain focused:

Step 1: Defining the problem

Step 2: Analyzing the problem

Step 3: Establishing criteria for solving the problem

Step 4: Generating potential solutions

Step 5: Selecting the best solution

These steps eventually lead to a group decision with consensus grounded in consideration of all sides of the problem and review of all the best solutions. A decision arrived at in that manner appears logical and is easily defensible if your group is to present your decision and solutions to a larger audience.

Sometimes members of a group want to take these steps out of sequence—for example, beginning with the solution and then working back through the steps. This approach does not demonstrate reflective thinking and is likely to lead to trouble for the group. If you begin by identifying the solution before you examine the problem, you may later find that the chosen solution does not address the problem at all. Equally, if you reverse the reflective thinking steps, you may wed yourself to one solution before adequately and completely considering all alternative solutions. For these reasons, reflective thinking requires you to begin with step 1 and take the next steps in the proper sequence.

Suppose you are on a school committee formed to develop recommendations for improving food services on campus. If your group decides to engage in reflective thinking, members would begin by identifying and defining the problem. The problem might be poor food quality or an inadequate number of food vendors on campus. Analysis of the problem might require several visits to the campus food court for observation or interviews with current food vendors as well as with students and faculty. From the interviews would come criteria for solving the problem. Students might indicate a need for larger portions, while the faculty might ask for more choices. Your group might recommend several different solutions, such as bringing in new vendors who offer more vegetarian entrees, encouraging an existing vendor to build a new salad bar, and changing the business hours of the entire food court. The group would review these options and choose the best solution.

reflective thinking: a five-step method for helping a group to stay focused on problem solving; the steps are defining the problem, analyzing the problem, establishing criteria for solving the problem, generating potential solutions, and selecting the best solution.

Public Speaking in and to Small Groups

Thus far we have considered the internal workings of small groups. Next we consider how the internal dynamics of small groups affect various strategies for public speaking and group presentations. Small-group dynamics is a factor to consider when you are speaking to a small group of which you *are not a member;* you are speaking to a small group of which you *are a member;* or, as a member of a small group, you are making a presentation to *a larger audience.* We consider each of these situations in turn.

● *Speaking to a Group as a Nonmember*

There may be occasions when you deliver a speech to an audience that is a small group with a common purpose beyond just being part of your audience. Suppose you are to appear before a state legislative committee that focuses on the environment, to express your thoughts about what the construction of new gas stations in your state may mean for highway congestion and air pollution. You are not a member of this committee and are speaking to the group as an outsider. What assumptions and strategies would you employ?

Recall the preceding discussion about roles, including leader and member, within a small group. As you consider your audience analysis for the presentation to this small group, add these questions to your consideration:

1. What is this group's specific purpose?
2. Does this group appear to have a leader? If so, does he or she share authority with other group members?
3. Does this leader appear to be a decision maker for the group, or does he or she merely facilitate group decisions democratically?
4. Do I have any common ground with the group leader or any member of the small group?

If you speak before a state legislative committee or some other government body, you will be speaking as an outsider. As an outsider, the assumptions you make and strategies you use will be different from those used by committee members addressing the committee.

Adding these questions to the questions you ordinarily would ask in your audience analysis will give you additional insight about speaking effectively to this group and its leader, in either an informative or a persuasive presentation.

The probability is much greater that the leaders or dominant members of small groups will assert themselves more forcefully than others in your audience. Leaders who occupy positions of authority—especially over decision making—may be most inclined to assert their authority with you as an outsider to the group, perhaps to demonstrate their dominance of the group itself. Such a leader may introduce you before your presentation, ask questions on behalf of the group during your presentation, and even interrupt you or move you on to a different subject altogether.

It is critical for you to have a sense about whether this leader really is the decision maker for the group or whether the group makes decisions democratically. In the former case, you may find yourself interacting almost exclusively with the leader in your speech. Ordinarily, we would not recommend doing this. But if this individual is the only audience member who will be making decisions about your request or presentation, directing most of your energies toward him or her is a sensible strategy. However, if all members of the group participate in decision making, you must be diligent about addressing everyone in the small group equally.

Whenever you speak to a group that you are not a member of, the following delivery principles are also important. Notice that they apply no differently for larger audiences but their absence can be especially damaging in a small-group context:

1. Remember that first impressions can make for lasting judgments. Dress and comport yourself appropriately for the group setting.

2. Maintain good eye contact with each member of the group. Remember to look at each individual—a task that should be easy because of the relatively small size of the audience.

3. If you are invited to sit close to the group and address members directly, do so and take advantage of the opportunity to use proximity to assist you with visual aids and handouts in a timely manner (enabling you to better control how the group interacts with the visual aids). Equally important is the fact that sitting close to the group may help you visually diminish your status as an outsider.

Dress and comport yourself appropriately for group presentations. First impressions make for lasting judgments.

● *Speaking to a Group as a Member*

In some situations you may be called upon to speak to a small group of which you are a member. For example, you may have a seat on the board of directors for a charitable nonprofit organization, and you may need to make a presentation to other board members about budgeting or policy. Again, in your audience analysis it will be useful to review roles and responsibilities within the group context. As you do so, consider the following:

- What role do *you* occupy within your small group? Are you a leader? If so, what kind: implied? designated? emergent?

- Is someone else in your group a leader? If so, what kind—implied, designated, or emergent—and what style does he or she employ?

- If you are a member but not a leader of the group, are you a harmonizer, a compromiser, or someone who encourages or gatekeeps? Do you act in a self-oriented fashion?
- Do others act self-oriented? Does anyone block, withdraw, interrupt, or distract?

If You Are the Leader. If you are presenting to a group of which you are the leader, model the behavior you expect of other group members in their communication. Be prepared to practice good listening skills, both before you speak and during any question-and-answer period. Make group members feel that they can interact with you. Don't interrupt others or dismiss their questions or comments. As you follow these practices, you may also find it easier to occasionally step away from being group leader and become just a member, as free as any other member to express thoughts and opinions. When you assume that role, the group will not feel obliged to agree with you because you are the leader and may embrace your ideas because they make sense.

You will be well served if you avoid using your implied or designated authority to persuade or manipulate others in the group. Using words or a delivery style that asserts your authority is not likely to encourage good listening in your audience but is likely to increase the possibility of groupthink or a chilling effect discouraging everyone from saying what they really think. For example, a failing dot-com business once created a committee of managers and employees to address major challenges looming in the coming fiscal quarters. The company president (a recent college graduate) was a member of the group, and he became the implied leader. The group leader made a presentation to the group in which he defended what was plainly an inadequate business plan. That inadequacy was obvious to other group members, but because the company president/implied group leader had created the plan and defended it in the meeting, no other members felt like openly criticizing the plan or discussing the problems. The result was a less-than-effective outcome for the company, which eventually lost its funding from venture capitalists and went out of business.

If You Are a Member. If you are a member of the group but not a leader, and you are called upon to present to the group, you may encounter different reactions to your speech, depending on how other members view your role in the group.

If you are seen as a *harmonizer,* people may expect only humor, satire, or sarcasm from you—which is to say, they may not take your speech message seriously. If harmonizer is your role within the group, be sure to clearly distinguish your humorous message from your serious speech message. For example, as a member of a group faced with the daunting task of cost cutting to avoid job layoffs, it may be appropriate for you to make a small joke comparing the group's task to a doctor trying to save a suicidal patient—if such humor is intended to relieve the tension of the moment and add levity to the proceedings. But the humor must be clearly distinct from the cost-cutting methods you offer in your presentation.

If you are seen as a *compromiser,* people in your group may tend to see your speech message as an attempt to avoid a position on an issue because you often advocate compromise. You may need to forcefully stress your final position in the speech. Suppose you have traditionally been a compromiser in your student workgroup on the history of science and are now presenting a recommendation to the workgroup about what should go into a final class report on Islam and science. If you usually mediated conflict between other group members and always tried to find compromise, the workgroup may assume that your recommendations are the product of collaboration between others. This assumption may not be desirable if in fact your recommendations are your own ideas. You will need to forcefully express how important you feel they are, using language that communicates your ownership and authorship of the recommendations—for example, "these are my ideas, and we haven't discussed them before. I want you to carefully consider them."

The same problem may occur if the audience perceives that your usual role is that of *encourager*. Someone who usually offers praise of others may be seen as someone who always defers to others. Again, you will need to differentiate your encouragement of others (which can be very positive) from the points you want them to consider. For example, you may want to start your presentation by acknowledging and crediting the work or ideas of others and then move to a discussion of your points—clearly labeling them for the group as such.

Finally, if you are seen as a *gatekeeper*, sharing information and encouraging the audience to move from one subject to another, recall that the audience may expect more facilitation from you—and in the speech context may expect audience interaction from and with you. Be prepared for questions and answers in your speech. For example, if you are presenting additional background material about a candidate your small-group hiring committee is considering offering a job to, anticipate the questions the committee may ask, and work the answers into your presentation. Allow time for questions, and do not let yourself become flustered if the group interrupts with questions or comments. Remember, they probably are used to dealing with you in this way.

● *Making a Group Presentation*

Suppose your group is committed to "Save the City Orchestra" and has been invited to speak before the city council to ask for more funding. How will the group make its presentation? Whether you are the leader or one of the group members, it is critical that you know how you are to participate within the group. Carefully consider the roles of all group members involved in the delivery of the speech.

A Single Speaker for the Group.   In some situations, the group leader may wish—or be called upon—to speak on behalf of the group. Or a single member other than the leader may be asked to speak for the group. If you are the speaker for your group, consider these suggestions as you prepare:

1. Make certain the group has carefully thought through all aspects of the presentation. The difference between a speech you prepare, research, and deliver yourself, and a speech that emerges from a group is that in the latter instance the group contributes substantially to the

TABLE 13.1 Methods for Encouraging Group Participation during the Invention Stage of a Presentation

SITUATION	METHOD
The group is reluctant to participate in a discussion about the invention of your speech because you are the group leader, and members appear to be deferring to your authority.	Remind the group that the oral presentation you will make reflects on the group—favorably or unfavorably. The only way to ensure members' sentiments are represented is for members to participate in creating the presentation from the very beginning.
Group members are not participating in inventing the speech message because of disinterest or because they seem happy to let you do all the work.	Draw members out with pointed questions about the subject matter. Try restating the group's objectives, paraphrasing what others have said before. Ask whether your restatement accurately captures members' views. Do the same in describing the group's challenges or the problems and attendant solutions the group is supposed to make. Inevitably, someone will object to your wording of things and correct you. Usually when that happens, other voices will follow.
Members begin offering ideas about the invention of your speech message.	Encourage group discussion by acknowledging good comments, insightful questions, and constructive criticism.

invention stage. Be sure to get input from all group members before preparing your presentation, and obtain their feedback after you outline your speech. If you experience difficulty getting other group members to participate or give you feedback during the invention stage, try using some of the methods mentioned in Table 13.1.

2. When speaking, distinguish whether you are representing your own views, the views of some members of the group, or a consensus of all group members. Be fair and accurate when summarizing other members' viewpoints.

3. Make sure that you have discussed and decided on the approach you want to take in your presentation. In a situation calling for one member of the group to speak to the larger audience, the approach will be that of a single oral report. Determine which member could best present the group's opinions. Are you the best speaker in the group? Could another member better convey the message? Does the topic require the ethos or authority of a group leader in order to be effective?

Multiple Speakers for the Group.   Some group presentations may require participation by two or more group members, perhaps even all group members. These types of presentations are most likely when groups have members with specific and differentiated expertise (for example, each member understands or is responsible for a different aspect of the topic) or a complicated topic necessitates a lengthy presentation in which the topic is divided into several subtopics. In this case, each group speaker will want to employ basic principles of public speaking and think about what is the most appropriate approach for this group presentation. There are two typical approaches. In a **symposium**, individual group members make presentations to a larger audience. In a **panel discussion**, discourse among group members is observed by a larger audience.

For a *symposium*, each group member usually stands when it is his or her turn to make a formal presentation to the larger audience. Imagine a symposium presentation by famous coaches of women's sports teams talking about recruiting female athletes. All of the coaches might make formal remarks about their experiences, what characteristics they look for in athletes, and what they have found athletes to be seeking in a women's sports program.

If you are participating in such a presentation because of your expertise or credibility, be certain to say so in your speech; not only will the audience find you more authoritative, but the group will also benefit by deriving its ethos from you. In effect, the group will be seen as more credible because you are seen as more credible. In the preceding example, every speaker should communicate his or her experience and expertise as a coach to the larger audience.

When you participate in a symposium, be respectful of other group members and their presentations. Be sure to manage your time for the presentation you give; don't speak longer than your allotted time. Make sure everyone in the group knows what will go into each presentation, and avoid repetition or unnecessary overlap of topics. Failure to discuss in advance what you'll address may leave the speaker who follows you feeling stuck because you inadvertently covered some of the points he or she was going to make.

Also remember to create interesting transitions from one speech to another. As you close your speech, think about how you will introduce the next speaker. How does that person's topic relate to yours? Make use of any connection between topics in your transition, and as a courtesy to the speaker and the audience, introduce the speaker by name.

In the symposium on recruiting female athletes, each coach would watch his or her time, and be familiar enough with the other presentations to avoid repeating or preempting comments on player recruitment, retention, and coaching that other speakers planned to address. This person would then introduce the next speaker (perhaps a basketball coach at a Big Ten school) and preview her topic.

For a *panel discussion,* group members will be seated at a table and speak as if there is a conversation going on within the group, while the audience watches and listens. In an economics class, a group of guests including professors, lawyers, and bankers might be gathered as a panel to discuss the impact of bank mergers, while the class watches and listens.

A panel discussion usually requires a *moderator*—sometimes the group leader. The moderator introduces the speakers—the *panelists*—and facilitates interaction among them. He or she may also monitor time and ask an occasional question to keep the discussion moving or direct it to other topics. In our hypothetical example, the moderator would want to be

For more on developing credibility in a speech, see page 199.

symposium: a setting in which individual presentations are made by group members to a larger audience.

panel discussion: a setting in which discourse among group members is observed by a larger audience.

especially careful in timing the presentations because lawyers and professors are notorious for speaking volumes about a topic. The panelists should listen respectfully to one another and speak in turn.

The atmosphere of a panel discussion is decidedly less formal and more casual than in a symposium. Panelists may interact with the speaker and make comments or ask questions. When you are a panelist, you should be prepared to listen and engage with your copanelists. You will be better off if you discussed how to do this in advance of the presentation, so you will know ahead of time what their questions or comments may be. The professor in our example may have considered a legal question that he knew the lawyer would ask or a regulatory question that he expected the banker to raise. Preparing some answers in advance ensures high-quality answers for the audience and helps the professor avoid looking foolish or unprepared.

Examples of Public Speaking beyond the Speech Classroom

Thus far we have examined how your participation in and with groups may affect your public speaking. Now we turn to the greater context of your public speaking beyond the classroom.

The skills you acquire in your public speaking class will prove useful in other classes, when you leave school and enter the job market, and when you participate in community work and volunteerism. In this section we briefly discuss public speaking in such settings. As you read, note how the principles of public speaking that you have been learning can be applied beyond the speech class.

● *Other Speech Contexts*

On occasion, the context or setting for a presentation may present you with challenges that do not precisely resemble what you practiced in your public speaking class or read about in this book.

A Student Group Presentation to the Whole Class.   Your first experience with public speaking or group work beyond your speech class is likely to come in another college or university class, when you are assigned to work with other students in a small group and later make a group presentation to the class as a whole. How will this work in practice?

Many teachers require every student in a group to make some kind of contribution because group presentations are usually graded. Thus the workload of your small group must be divided, and the responsibility for the presentation (unless your teacher tells you otherwise) should be evenly distributed. In most instances, all members of the group should get the same amount of speaking time during the presentation. Your instructor may require your group to make a presentation for a fixed period of time, such as twenty minutes, and then respond to questions from the audience. This requirement does not mean that the group can speak for ten minutes and use the question-and-answer session to fill the rest of the allotted time. Instead, the group presentation fills the allotted time, and group members take questions after the presentation.

Consider designating one member of the group to serve as facilitator for the group. That person would be the first speaker and then would introduce the other group members and their topics, previewing what the presentation will address.

Even though you are speaking as a member of a group, you will be addressing a larger class audience, so your individual speech will be more like the type of speech that you usually make in your public speaking class. Unlike the presentations to small groups noted above, this speech will be made to more people and therefore will require a slightly more formal delivery style (and less conversational style) than would be allowed in a small-group context. All the suggestions made in any of the Speech Guides and other chapters are important here, especially as to delivery skills. Whatever you do directly impacts not only the impression the class audience has of you but also the way audience members tend to see the group as a whole.

Make sure your group members understand the time requirements for the presentation itself, and plan the question-and-answer period (if there is to be one) well. We recommend saving the question-and-answer period for the end of all speeches by group members, to ensure that no later speaker has time taken away because questions asked of an earlier group member dragged on too long.

Finally, consider coordinating your visual aids as a group. If handouts are to be used, talk about how best to reproduce them and when to distribute them. If a slide projector, overhead projector, laptop with projection device, or other equipment is required, think through in advance how you might place all speech materials for your group on slides, on transparencies, or within a computer program like PowerPoint. Practice with this material in advance, and be sure that everyone in your class audience will be able to see it.

A Report to a Small Committee at Work.

In the workplace, most tasks and responsibilities for employees are divided among groups.[6] In corporate America, much of the decision making that goes on even at the management level is done in small groups.[7] Be prepared to participate in small groups when you leave the college or university and enter the workforce. You will have to interact in groups, and you may have to make a report within groups. Part of your job in an office might include membership on a powerful committee that oversees company compliance with government regulations affecting your business. Or it might include membership on a lesser committee formed to plan the annual company picnic. What should you consider when planning and presenting your message in such a venue?

You may be called upon to make many different types of reports in a work context. *Status reports* are informative presentations to your group concerning the status of an assignment, project, or problem you have been working on. *Findings* are informative presentations in which you summarize the results of an investigation or deliberation. *Recommendations* are reports that are persuasive to the extent that you make specific suggestions to the group about a work-related issue—usually to assist in the decision-making process.

For any type of report you are assigned, most members of the group will benefit from advance notice of your presentation—especially if the presentation is to be followed shortly by a group discussion and perhaps decision making. In the workplace, many groups choose to publish the **agenda** for a group meeting in advance and attach any reading materials necessary for advance consideration. If you find yourself preparing a workplace report to your small group, it can be helpful to distribute some materials in advance of your presentation. This will help group members digest the information in order to prepare questions, discuss the topic, and ultimately make decisions.

In many businesses, group meetings are held by **teleconference**, in which members are connected by phone lines, or **videoconference**, in which either cable, satellite, or Web transmission carries a live video feed to all members of the group. Both of these are becoming commonplace because so many large companies have gone through mergers and acquisitions and offices and staff are spread out geographically and not easily brought together in one place at one time. Teleconferences and videoconferences present specific sorts of challenges to everyone who must report to the group during a meeting.

For a teleconference, some group members may remain in their offices or cubicles and participate by means of their phone receivers or voice boxes. Alternatively, several members may gather in a conference room with one strong voice box and be connected to members in other locations by a single phone line. It is critical to remember that during a teleconference you cannot see the other people in your group unless you are with them in a conference room.

Teleconferences can be problematic. You cannot make eye contact to compel attention or determine participants' degree of attentiveness. If your presentation is lengthy, you run the risk of losing audience members as they engage in **multitasking** (working on other projects while they are listening to you) or simply become distracted by other things or other group members. Your best strategies are to distribute material in advance, allowing members to follow what you say *as you say it,* and to keep your report brief and make it interactive—inviting questions and thus compelling listeners' attention.

If you participate in a videoconference, you at least can see other group members, and they will be able to see you. But be aware that seeing them on screen is not the same as sitting across the table from them. The personal level of interaction is artificial at best, but at least you will be able to see whether they are listening and gauge how much they appear to understand or care about your topic. In this situation, too, you will benefit from advance distribution of any reading material required for the presentation, as well as from keeping your speech short and encouraging participants to ask questions.

In both teleconferences and videoconferences, you must remember that you are a member of a group—even though geography suggests otherwise—and not allow yourself to use language or a delivery style that suggests you are an outsider. Your membership in the group should give you advance credibility with other members. That credibility can help you with your report unless you say or do things on the phone or before the camera to suggest that you see yourself as an outsider (see In Theory box 13.1).

agenda: a schedule of topics to be covered or steps to be taken in an upcoming meeting.

teleconference: a group meeting in which participants are connected with each other by phones or speaker phones.

videoconference: a group meeting in which participants are connected with each other by cable, satellite, or Web transmission using video cameras and monitors.

multitasking: working on several things at once.

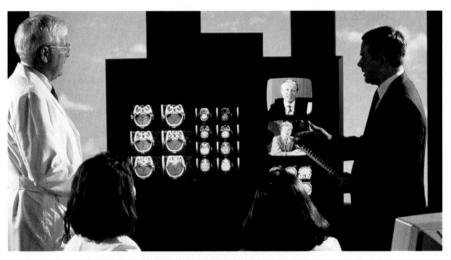

Videoconferencing allows you to see group members on a screen when they are unable to be present physically. Nevertheless, the quality of interaction suffers because participants are not face-to-face.

● *Examples of Speeches with Specific Rhetorical Purposes*

In the future you may be requested to present speeches that do not obviously fit into the categories of informative or persuasive speaking—even though their purpose is to inform or persuade (e.g., a sales speech is really a

INVENTION	ORGANIZATION	STYLE	PREPARATION	DELIVERY

In Theory 13.1

VIDEOCONFERENCING AND PRESENTATIONS

In Chapter 2 we introduced the canons of rhetoric, one of which is *delivery* of the speech message. Videoconferencing technology has obvious implications for how you deliver a message to a potentially large and geographically dispersed audience. Until recently, the technology was not in wide use for several reasons. The initial investment in videoconferencing equipment or the cost of renting such equipment was prohibitively high.[8] Also, the business climate in the United States tended to favor face-to-face meetings, because you "can't fax a handshake."[9]

Over time, however, several events conjoined to expand the use of videoconferencing—and increase the likelihood that you will experience it in your future presentations beyond the classroom. The collapse of the so-called technology boom forced businesses to reconsider the expense of traveling to face-to-face meetings. The cost of videoconferencing equipment decreased: entry-level units now cost no more than an elaborate desktop computer.[10] And the terrorist attacks of September 11, 2001, and the resulting impact on air travel prompted many businesses to embrace the technology as a less risky way of conducting meetings. Paradoxically, however, videoconferencing heightens, rather than replaces, people's desire for an eventual, face-to-face meeting.[11]

Most videoconferencing technology produces slightly delayed or lagged images of participants. Some speakers are able to enhance their delivery style by studying the slower images for signs of body language indicating attentiveness, listening, and retention of the message. This kind of spontaneous audience analysis can clue the speaker to question specific participants about the speech topic or to alter his or her volume level or rate of delivery to ensure that all participants can follow the presentation.

speech to persuade). Five of the most common of these types of speeches are explored here.

A Sales Presentation to a Small Group.

If you work in sales, you will be called upon to persuade people to buy or invest money or other resources in whatever you have to offer. Every point mentioned in the Guide to Persuasive Speaking (Chapter 15) will be of direct relevance here. It also is worth noting that in many sales situations your prospective customers may be a group of people: you will be speaking to a small group of which you are not a member. Earlier in this chapter, we discussed this type of speaking in the abstract. How does it work in practice?

Understanding how a group of prospective customers makes decisions will assist you in your presentation. Does the group as a whole make sales decisions, or does a single individual such as the group leader make the decisions? In a sales presentation to a group, focus your attention (in terms of both delivery skills such as eye contact and the use of audience analysis and adaptation) on whoever makes the decision to buy.

Consider how important audience analysis principles will be in the sales process to a small group. Especially focus on common ground, prior exposure, and selection of appeals. Do you (as an outsider and the salesperson) have anything in common with any member of the group? Do you have commonality with the group leader? If so, think about how you may want to indicate that in your presentation. Common ground has added significance in a speech to a group you are not a member of. It may bring you some of the benefits of membership by diminishing the distance between you and group members.

Has the group been exposed to this kind of sales message before—either by you or by some other sales representative? If so, how did group members react? Did they buy, did they pass, or did they reject? If they did buy, assuming nothing else has changed, you probably will want to follow a similar approach. If they passed or rejected the sales message, you will want to consider why and perhaps approach the sales call differently. For example, perhaps an earlier sales message emphasized cost savings, but the client was more concerned about quality of service.

Your ethos is likely to be important here. The group sees you as a salesperson and knows that your objective is to sell. Almost reflexively, group members believe that any salesperson is biased and lacks objectivity, and they have lower expectations of you and your knowledge than they might have of someone with specific knowledge of, or expertise in, whatever product or service you are selling. For example, one individual working as a sales representative for a pharmaceutical company found that he could be far more effective in presentations to small groups of doctors in private practice if he invoked his own past experience and expertise as a biochemist when he discussed the new drugs he was trying to persuade the doctors to prescribe for their patients. What kind of expertise do you have? What experience with the product or service can you draw upon? Expertise and experience can help the small group to see you differently and can enhance your credibility.

Finally, consider that in a sales call the element of time already discussed in the Speech Grid—both time allotted for the presentation and time of day for the audience (body clock)—may take on a dimension unique to sales

To review audience analysis and common ground, prior exposure, and selection of appeals, see Chapter 5.

work. In any sales situation, **urgency** is a key factor affecting the decision to buy the product or service. There is often a direct relationship between a perceived sense of urgency and the decision to buy: if prospective clients believe that they must decide about the sale quickly or else lose the opportunity presented by the product or service, they may be more willing to make the decision—often in your favor.

Conveying a sense of urgency may border on high-pressure tactics and raise ethical questions if you impose a time limit to unfairly manipulate a customer and generate a sale. But all we are suggesting here is that you be aware of time constraints and deadlines for decisions. If they do exist, don't be afraid to use them in a group sales call; otherwise, prospective clients may put off making a decision. The longer a decision takes, the less likely it is to resolve in your favor. Why? The reason has little to do with you specifically. During a lengthy group decision process, other variables over which you have no control may intervene (for example, sales calls by your competitors, changes in group membership, and illnesses). Your best strategy, therefore, is to communicate a sense of urgency when delivering your sales presentation to the group.

A Sales Presentation by a Sales Team.   In another common type of sales presentation, a team of salespeople, or one salesperson along with partners who offer supporting services, combine their efforts in a group presentation to a prospective client audience. All of our suggestions concerning an individual sales presentation to a small group apply to this presentation as well, as do the points made earlier in this chapter about group presentations to a larger audience. What is different and unique about a presentation by a sales team is the importance of audience analysis of the prospective client and the sharing of information by team members to the overall success of the sales presentation.

Salespeople call the audience analysis they do for a presentation "profiling the client." This type of analysis focuses on the usual points of reference, including situational characteristics, demographics, common ground, prior exposure, and audience disposition.

As a salesperson, you may be called a "BDO" (business development officer), a "new business officer," or even a "sales rep" (sales representative). In such a position, you are likely to be responsible for profiling the client or clients your sales group will meet with for a presentation. The ineffective use of this profiling information often derails group sales presentations. Problems arise when one salesperson does not share all of the profiling information with the other presenters in the group or when some information is shared but there is no discussion about what use to make of it during the presentation. One result of the failure to share information is a situation in which one salesperson has a different understanding of and different objectives for the presentation than other group members.

For example, a sales representative for a manufacturer of parts for the aerospace industry scheduled a sales meeting with purchasing agents from a regional airline. The sales representative profiled the people he would be meeting with, and the information he gathered led him to assume that the best way to persuade them to sign a contract for parts from his company was to stress the quality and integrity of his products. Because the contract was

For more on ethics and public speaking, see Chapter 3.

urgency: the sense that immediate action is necessary; a key concept in sales, used to press a customer to make a sales decision.

potentially sizable, he took his manager and one of the design engineers from his company with him to the meeting, so that all three could make a sales presentation to the purchasing agents. He did share his profiling information about the prospective clients, but he never discussed with his manager or the design engineer how to use that information strategically and what their objectives for the meeting were.

The presentation did not go well. The sales representative knew from his profile that the client was interested in the parts, but only in limited volume because of cost constraints. The manager, however, believed in selling more than parts. He wanted to sell a relationship—that is, he wanted a long-term contract. Thus, instead of emphasizing product quality and price, the manager talked about relationships and a long-term commitment. His message was plainly different from the sales representative's. The prospective clients were confused and decided to go elsewhere for their parts.

In group sales presentations, that is a common problem, but you can easily avoid it by adhering to the following suggestions:

1. After doing an audience analysis for your profile of the prospective client audience, and after developing your own sense of what the presentation should be, schedule a meeting with other group members to share that client information. Don't withhold any information from them. Their ignorance of anything pertaining to the client may lead to problems during the sales meeting or missed opportunities during the presentation.

2. Discuss roles and objectives for the sales presentation. What role will you play? If you are the person who introduces the others (who may answer questions and speak on their areas of expertise), you will be seen as the facilitator. You will talk first and slowly bring the others into the presentation. As a facilitator, you also will speak up near the end of the presentation, summarizing and (you hope) closing the sale or moving the client closer to a decision. If you are one of several presenters (but not the group leader or the facilitator), discuss with group members your area of expertise, and decide when and how you will fit into the group presentation. Each group member must share all of his or her perceptions about group objectives for the presentation. Is the goal to close the deal today? Is the objective to move the client to the next step in a long sales cycle? Make sure that all members have the same objectives.

3. During the group sales presentation, remember to adhere to the role you agreed to play in the meeting, and be very careful not to contradict or undercut other members of the group. During the presentation, be mindful that audience analysis for the client profile is an ongoing process, and be observant about details or information that may add to or change that profile.

4. Schedule a meeting with your group after the sales presentation to discuss what went on. Hold this meeting as close in time to the sales presentation as possible (if you all share a car ride back to the office, talk in the car), because your perceptions and memories will be most clear in the time just following the presentation. Go back and deconstruct the presentation. Were the assumptions about the audience cor-

rect? Was anything new learned or observed? Did all team members stay within their roles? If they did not, discuss what happened and how this might be corrected in the future. Also discuss objectives. Were they met in this presentation? Were any opportunities missed? Were group members satisfied with the results?

As part of a regular discipline, this kind of pre-, during-, and post-meeting communication will transform your sales group into a sales *team* and will improve sales.

A Presentation to Explain Change in the Workplace.

After college or university studies, you probably will find yourself in a workplace in which change is a constant fact of life: changes in business practice, changes in company policy, changes in corporate culture, changes in the laws that impact the workplace, and changes in direction or emphasis of a business. As an employee and perhaps a member of management, it may fall to you to explain what a specific change means for your workplace. What might you take from this course and this book to assist you in this endeavor?

At the outset, decide whether the purpose of this speech is informative or persuasive. Are you going to speak to people about a change that is inevitable? Or is it necessary for you to persuade employees to buy into a proposed change?

In most situations, the speech is informative. Decisions about changes in business practice, company policy, and corporate culture, and reactions to changes in the law, are usually the province of upper management. The decision for change will have been made before you deliver the speech. But that does not mean that there are no persuasion implications for your speech. While you are explaining the change to your audience, one of your goals may be to reassure workers and prevent them from sabotaging any efforts at change. The speech content is informative, but your message needs to be adapted to the audience, showing listeners that the change is in their best interest.

How will you know if explaining change is necessary and what steps will be required to do this?

First, during your audience analysis examine the existing culture of the organization. Does the company embrace change or resist change? Is the desirability of change spelled out in documents such as a company business plan? What track record is there for change? Have workers embraced it in the past?

Audience analysis is the subject of Chapter 5.

In some places, workers resist change because they are tied to their routines. Many people become comfortable with practices, customs, and behaviors that are familiar and seem effective. In such a workplace, resistance to change is likely. But one byproduct of the many business mergers and acquisitions that occurred in the past two decades is an awareness that change happens all the time. Workers may not like change, but those who have experienced it will probably accept it again.

If you determine that your workplace is resistant to change, how will you deliver your message? Presenting the change as a fait accompli may be interpreted as forcing the change on workers. This strategy may engender the resistance your speech is trying to ward off. If change is not welcome in your workplace, rethink your delivery style. Using a soft tone of voice to explain the change and express empathy may work with this audience.

Allowing time for questions and answers is critical, because individuals who resist are going to be ready with questions and comments for you. You should expect most of these questions to be self-serving and amount to complaints. That's natural. A certain period for venting of audience members' anxiety and frustration should be allowed, and the question-and-answer period will be fine for that.

You, in the role of messenger, should interpret none of the complaints or negative comments as personal attacks. Do not become defensive and lose your focus. Answer questions honestly and with empathy; acknowledge that some change may seem frustrating or difficult. Finally, be sure that you answer every question asked and that no one leaves your presentation feeling stonewalled by you or upper management.

A Speech to Deliver Bad News in an Organization. Closely related to presentations that explain change in the workplace are speeches that deliver bad news in an organizational setting. By bad news we mean information that will adversely affect, sadden, or disrupt any audience members. Bad news can include information about natural disasters, deaths, corporate takeovers, loss of benefits, and elimination of jobs. You may find yourself in a situation where you are called upon to deliver such news. What might you take from this course and this book to assist you?

You will likely be delivering a speech that is informative. As you begin your audience analysis, focus on prior exposure. Many people in your audience already have some idea about the news. Discussions at the water cooler or via organizational e-mail and chatrooms often contribute to gossip and misinformation about the bad news you are about to deliver. For example, if your news concerns the hostile takeover of your company by another, larger company, chances are very good that people were already speculating about what the takeover means for them. Rumors about elimination of jobs will be typical, and anxiety levels will be high.

In one sense, the audience's expectation of bad news makes your job less complicated. But in another sense, this prior exposure complicates your task, because the rumors are likely to be inaccurate as to the precise details of the news. Thus, you would be well served to assess the prior exposure to rumors and gossip and determine how much (if any) of it is accurate. In your speech, you may want to address the inaccuracies and explain what will really transpire. Emphasize that your objective is to be truthful and to set the record straight. Doing so helps the audience to understand how your information is different from, and more accurate than, theirs and serves to begin the process of suppressing rumors.

What mode of delivery will you use to deliver the bad news? In most situations we advocate extemporaneous delivery (speaking from an outline), but in this case you may fare better with a mix of reading a prepared statement and extemporaneous delivery from notes. Begin by reading the prepared statement exactly as it is written. This will be your insurance against audience misunderstanding or facilitation of rumors. After reading the statement, take time for questions and clarification about what it means for the audience. As you answer the questions, be sure to listen carefully and communicate that you are listening interactively. Respond with empathy for the anxiety, sadness, or distress that members of the audience are feeling.

To review audience analysis and prior exposure, see page 104.

To review delivery skills and modes of delivery, see Chapter 11.

For more on listening skills, and listening to audience questions during a presentation, see Chapter 4.

A Speech to Celebrate Achievement in a Community Nonprofit Agency.

One day, you may find yourself involved with work that benefits disadvantaged groups, local charities, or your community. Let's suppose that you are called upon to acknowledge and celebrate the achievements of an individual or a group of people in a nonprofit agency. What lessons might you take away from this course and book to assist you?

The celebration of achievement is in many respects the flip side of the delivery of bad news. Both speech intentions and occasions present extremes for the speaker and the audience, so what is true for one type of speech will in some instances be true for the other. For example, what we previously said about rumors and false speculation about bad news also applies in situations celebrating achievement. People in your audience may have been gossiping about this news (the achievement) and perhaps speculating about what it means for them. Speculation based on incomplete information and laced with inaccuracies can be problematic. As before, use the audience analysis to assess how much, if any, prior exposure there is to the message. Does the audience know what you are going to say? Beyond questions of accuracy, the audience's prior knowledge may be critical if members of the audience expect some kind of reward or special recognition for their achievement. Be prepared for that expectation, and address it in your remarks.

Also be sure to use audience analysis to help you in researching useful anecdotes about an individual whose success you are celebrating. How have individuals in the audience contributed to that success? What has the honoree meant to them?

Use specific examples in your statements of celebration. Avoid a generalization such as "Garth is hard working and self-sacrificing." Be specific: "Garth is the first person in the office and the last to leave. He often gives up weekend days—he worked last Saturday, for example—to make sure the annual reports were completed on time." Also consider whether and how you want to single out any individuals in the audience. If their contributions have in large measure brought the organization this achievement, they are deserving of recognition, and in most nonprofit settings, public recognition may be the only way of rewarding extra effort. That being said, also keep in mind that singling out some individuals for praise exposes you to the risk of leaving others out and stirring resentment among those who felt they, too, contributed to the result. Your best practice may be to say that everyone in the nonprofit group contributed to the result you are celebrating, but some individuals merit extra praise for their efforts.

Speech style is important. Be upbeat and sincere, but avoid exaggeration. The difference between "Garth is one of our most hard working, dedicated employees" and "Garth is the most significant individual in this country for raising funds to fight Alzheimer's disease" should be evident—especially if Garth is a midlevel staff member of a small community nonprofit.

Finally, when selecting your appeals for this speech, pay special attention to your own role in this agency. Are you simply the messenger chosen to celebrate the achievement? Do you represent management or an external board of trustees that oversees the activities of the nonprofit agency? Have you contributed in any way to the achievement you celebrate? If you are merely the messenger or a representative of management and oversight,

For more about audience analysis and ethos appeals, see page 199.

your ethos will be that of interested outsider for this audience. You are interested in and pleased about the results of their efforts, but you are not directly involved. Acting as though your ethos is something other than this (for example, by referring to people in the audience by their first names, even though you don't know them) will appear and ring false. In contrast, if you work for the nonprofit agency and manage some members of the audience, your ethos will be that of a leader and a knowledgeable insider. In that situation, humorous references and anecdotes that are specific to you and the audience will be appropriate and welcome. Also, acknowledging people on a first-name basis will be expected and most likely appreciated.

Summary

In this chapter we examined how you may take some of the material learned in your public speaking class and addressed in this book and apply it in other classes and in situations outside the classroom. Because much of the public speaking you may later do will involve small groups, we considered what small groups are, the roles and responsibilities of group members, how decisions are made, and what impact group communication may have on public speaking. We considered what happens when you address a small group as an outsider, and we contrasted that with a presentation you might make to a small group of which you are a member. We discussed what a group presentation to a larger audience might involve. We also considered other speaking opportunities you may have in the world beyond your speech class, including working in business or for a community nonprofit organization.

In all of these situations, we were examining the public speaking issues that we addressed in Chapters 1 through 12, but with an emphasis on how they might apply in your life beyond this course. It will always be relevant and important to maintain a working familiarity with audience analysis and the steps that go into topic selection, researching, crafting and creating a speech, the use of language, the skills of delivery, the proper application of audiovisual aids, and the impact of listening and speech ethics. Every one of these subjects has strong implications for your public speaking, not only in this class but in other classes and beyond the classroom as well. It is our hope that you will carry with you a sense of how critical these strategies and skills are and will apply them as you move beyond public speaking and the speech class.

Checklist

SMALL-GROUP LEADERS

____ Encourage all members to be open and honest with their ideas (p. 343)

____ Keep the group on task (p. 343)

____ Focus on issues, not personalities (p. 343)

USE REFLECTIVE THINKING FOR WORKING WITHIN A GROUP

____ Define the problem (p. 347)

____ Analyze the problem (p. 347)

____ Establish criteria for solving the problem (p. 347)

____ Generate potential solutions (p. 347)

____ Select the best solution (p. 347)

PLANNING YOUR SPEECH TO A GROUP AS A NONMEMBER

____ Determine the group's specific purpose (p. 348)

____ Analyze whether the group has a leader or whether authority is shared (p. 348)

____ Determine whether a leader is a decision maker or a facilitator (p. 348)

____ Look for common ground (p. 348)

SPEAKING TO A GROUP AS A NONMEMBER

____ Dress and comport yourself appropriately (p. 349)

____ Maintain good eye contact (p. 349)

____ Use physical proximity (p. 349)

SPEAKING TO A GROUP AS THE LEADER

____ Self-identify as an implied, emergent or designated leader (p. 350)

____ Use good listening skills (p. 350)

____ Encourage interaction between group members (p. 350)

____ Avoid interrupting others (p. 350)

SPEAKING TO A GROUP AS A MEMBER

____ If you are a harmonizer, separate your humorous message from your serious speech message (p. 350)

____ If you are a compromiser, forcefully stress your own final position (p. 351)

____ If you are an encourager, differentiate your encouragement of others from your serious speech message (p. 351)

____ If you are a gatekeeper, be prepared for questions, answers, and interruptions (p. 351)

MAKING A GROUP PRESENTATION: SPEAKING FOR THE GROUP BY YOURSELF

____ Get input and feedback from all group members (p. 352)

____ Distinguish your views from the views of others in the group (p. 352)

____ Be certain you are the best speaker for the group (p. 352)

MAKING A GROUP PRESENTATION IN A SYMPOSIUM

____ Express your credibility (p. 353)

____ Be respectful of other group members by watching the time limits for your speech (p. 353)

____ Avoid subject-matter overlap with other group presenters (p. 353)

MAKING A GROUP PRESENTATION IN A PANEL DISCUSSION

____ Use a moderator to introduce speakers and to facilitate discussion among panelists (p. 353)

____ Encourage panelists to listen to all speakers (p. 354)

A STUDENT GROUP PRESENTATION TO THE WHOLE CLASS

____ Evenly distribute the presentation workload to all group members (p. 354)

____ Designate a group member as moderator and facilitator (p. 355)

____ Use formal presentation delivery skills (p. 355)

____ Remember time management for each presentation (p. 355)

____ Coordinate visual aids (p. 355)

A REPORT TO A SMALL COMMITTEE AT WORK

____ Determine whether you need to make status reports, findings, or recommendations (p. 355)

____ Publish an advance agenda for your group (p. 356)

____ Avoid using language in a teleconference or videoconference that reinforces your status as outsider to the committee/group (p. 356)

A SALES PRESENTATION TO A SMALL GROUP

____ Determine how the customer makes a decision about sales (p. 358)

____ Use audience analysis when preparing your presentation (p. 358)

____ Use ethos to establish your credibility (p. 358)

____ Communicate a sense of urgency to help move the client to a decision (p. 359)

A SALES PRESENTATION BY A SALES TEAM

____ Use audience analysis to profile the client (p. 359)

____ Share audience analysis/profile information with other team members in a pre-sales meeting conference (p. 359)

____ Collectively decide on team roles and objectives before the team presentation (p. 359)

____ Avoid contradicting or undercutting other team presenters during the sales presentation (p. 360)

____ Use a post-presentation conference with other team members to analyze the presentation (p. 360)

A PRESENTATION TO EXPLAIN CHANGE IN THE WORKPLACE

____ Determine how receptive the audience is to the concept of change (p. 361)

____ Alter and soften delivery tone, and avoid being defensive if the audience is resistant to change (p. 361)

____ Communicate that change may be inevitable and beneficial (p. 361)

A SPEECH TO DELIVER BAD NEWS IN AN ORGANIZATION

____ Use prior exposure in audience analysis (p. 362)

____ Correct misinformation (p. 362)

____ Select the appropriate mode of delivery (extemporaneous or reading from a prepared statement) (p. 362)

A SPEECH TO CELEBRATE ACHIEVEMENT IN A COMMUNITY NONPROFIT AGENCY

____ Use prior exposure in audience analysis (p. 363)

____ Correct misinformation (p. 363)

____ Use audience analysis to bring out appropriate anecdotes about the audience member whose success you are celebrating (p. 363)

____ Use specific examples (p. 363)

____ Decide whether you will single out individuals for accolades or praise the entire group (p. 363)

____ Be upbeat and sincere, and avoid exaggeration (p. 363)

____ Pay attention to your role as a representative of management (p. 363)

____ Acknowledge people on a first-name basis only if you know them (p. 364)

Key Terms and Concepts

small group (p. 339)
group dynamics (p. 340)
implied leader (p. 341)
designated leader (p. 341)
emergent leader (p. 342)
groupthink (p. 342)
task-oriented roles (p. 343)
maintenance-oriented roles (p. 343)
self-oriented roles (p. 343)

reflective thinking (p. 347)
symposium (p. 353)
panel discussion (p. 353)
agenda (p. 356)
teleconference (p. 356)
videoconference (p. 356)
multitasking (p. 356)
urgency (p. 359)

Source Notes

1. Patton, B. R., & Giffin, K. (1978). *Decision-making group interaction* (2nd ed., p. 1). New York: Harper & Row.

2. Fraleigh, D. F., & Tuman, J. S. (1997). *Freedom of speech in the marketplace of ideas* (p. 25). New York: St. Martin's Press.

3. Janis, I. (1972). *Victims of groupthink.* Boston: Houghton Mifflin. The groupthink phenomenon can also occur in groups that rotate leadership and in groups in which members love each other. Any leader must take steps to guard against groupthink, either by playing devil's advocate or by occasionally asking for the opinion of a group member who the leader knows is likely to express an opinion at odds with the prevailing one.

4. Benne, K. D., & Sheats, P. (1948). Functional roles of group members. *Journal of Social Issues, 1*(4), 41–49.

5. The reflective thinking method emanates from the writings of John Dewey, an American philosopher interested in problem solving.

6. Tubbs, S. L. (1978). *A systems approach to small group communication* (p. 5). Reading, MA: Addison-Wesley.

7. Ober, S. (1995). *Contemporary business communication* (p. 498). Boston: Houghton Mifflin.

8. According to Robert Hageray, CEO of Polycom Incorporated, a Milpitas, California–based systems provider for videoconferencing, as recently as 1999 top-of-the-line corporate conferencing equipment could cost as much as $60,000.

9. Harmon, A. (2001, September 24). Remote rendezvous: Worried travelers warm up to videoconferencing. *New York Times,* p. C4.
Evangelista, B. (2001, October 1). Meetings via video. *San Francisco Chronicle: Business and Technology,* p. E1.

10. Polycom offers a basic conferencing unit costing less than 10 percent of the amount Hageray cited for top-end units in 1996.

11. James Katz, professor of communication at Rutgers University, has conducted research showing that millions of in-person meetings have been generated by people who first met using high-technology tools, including conferencing.
Katz, J., & Aspden, P. (1998). Theories, data, and potential impacts of mobile communications. *Technological Forecasting and Social Change, 57,* 133–156.
Katz, J., & Aspden, P. (1994). *Mobility and communication: Analytical trends and conceptual models.* Report for the U.S. Congress, Office of Technology Assessment, OTA N3-1640.0.

PART TWO

Guides to Public Speaking

14 Guide to Informative Speaking

Suppose you work on an airline as a flight attendant and you have been asked to give a brief presentation explaining the safety features of the aircraft as well as the procedures to follow in an emergency. How would you describe the speech you will give? Do you consider it a speech to *persuade* passengers to use their seats as floats in the event of a water landing? Does it make an *argument* for flight safety? Does it present possible alternatives for passengers, leaving them to draw their own conclusions?

In truth, the airline safety speech will do all of these things, but it is not directly persuasive, argumentative, or lacking in specific direction. Instead, it may be described as a *speech to inform* the audience—in this case, passengers—about safety, equipment, and procedures. An *informative speech* presents knowledge or information to an audience through explanation, description, or demonstration. This type of speech teaches the audience, increasing understanding, awareness, or sensitivity to the topic.

In Chapter 14 we explore the strategies and approaches called for in the creation and execution of informative speeches. We look at three informative speeches—two by college students and one by a working professional. We analyze key features of each speech and provide suggestions you can use to develop informative speeches. We also review the key features of informative speeches in general. Then we take you through a five-step process for preparing your own informative speech, incorporating the principles of public speaking developed in Part One of this text.

As you read each speech, consider how the speaker is sharing information with you. What techniques does he or she employ in approaching the audience? What do you think the speaker wants the audience to remember? Finally, is the speaker explaining, describing, or demonstrating the information in the speech?

Speeches

Chad Meyer, a sophomore in a college basic speech course, has always had an interest in marine conservation. In this class presentation he explains one particular concept aimed at protecting endangered species.

Chad Meyer's speech is available in outline format on page 506.

Translocation and Animal Instincts

BY CHAD MEYER

At a few minutes after midnight, March the 24th, 1989, a huge oil tanker ran aground on the Bligh Reef, in the icy waters of Prince William Sound. That tanker, named the *Exxon Valdez*, would eventually leak some 10.8 million gallons of its precious cargo—North Slope crude oil. The spill in the water would eventually spread over 1,500 miles of the Gulf of Alaska. In the process, some 250,000 sea birds would be killed. Add to that number some 2,800 northern sea otters, 300 harbor seals, 250 bald eagles, and 22 killer whales—and you haven't even begun to scratch at the surface of the damage done to the marine ecosystem and delicate food chain in the sound. Of course, since that time, state and federal laws have more forcefully addressed the risks of pollution and contamination associated with shipping and commerce—but the fact remains, no one causes these accidents on purpose. They're *accidents,* whether through negligence or plain bad luck. Of course, the impact on the environment is the same, regardless.

Because of this example and other threats to the environment on both land and sea, experts, government officials, and concerned individuals have long sought alternative methods to protect various species from devastating accidents like that of the *Exxon Valdez.* One method that has received much support—and even a congressional law to enforce it—involves moving the threatened species to a new location for protection. This is called *translocation.*

In this speech I would like to explain the concept of translocation—showing both how it is supposed to work and why it may ultimately fail. To do so, I will begin by explaining exactly what translocation is and then illustrate it with a contemporary example in the plight of the southern sea otter—an endangered species.

So, what exactly is "translocation"?

When the survival of a species is threatened, government protection agencies must consider many possible solutions, including laws to prohibit hunting and poaching, measures like rescue and rehabilitation—and sometimes, even extreme approaches like translocation. This approach involves the retrieval and relocation (or *trans*location) of all or a significant portion of the threatened population to another location. In this different location, it is assumed that the population will thrive—and endure.

The decision to translocate a species to a different location is a complex decision, involving sensitive environmental factors that must be balanced against certain political and economic realities.

Environmentally, this means considering the following questions. Is the target population threatened within its current habitat? Can the threat be externally controlled? Is there a viable alternative location to house this population? Does the alternate location provide all the necessities of the existing habitat? Can/would the target population thrive in this new location?

Of course, we have to temper this with *political and economic* realities. Are there advocates for the target population? Are they vocal? Can they help with money or other resources? Does the target population threaten other species in the existing habitat? Does the target population threaten human existence in the area?

Programs for translocation are common inside major urban and metropolitan areas—when wild woodland creatures are occasionally caught by professional trappers and then translocated to a more rural and wild habitat outside the city. Many of you might know what it was like to discover that a deer had gone through your trash can or perhaps a raccoon had braved an open window and ransacked your kitchen looking for food. Usually a call to the responsible law enforcement authorities will bring a trapper, who sets cages to capture and assist in translocating the animal to a forest setting.

A different example, however, may help us to see how translocation works for species *outside* city limits—outside, in point of fact, where any humans live. To see how translocation of a species is supposed to work, let us consider the case of the southern sea otter.

There are thirteen known types of otters in the world. The southern sea otter is formally known as *Enhydra lutris nereis* and is a marine mammal residing in the coastal waters of the Central and Northern Pacific Ocean. Although thought to be extinct because of hunting for its rich pelt, a small population of these otters was discovered off the California coast in 1938, and this would grow to 2,500 by the late 1970s. Federal law prohibited the hunting of these animals, but their population was still small, and so in 1987, a federal plan to translocate them to San Nicolas Island, in the Santa Barbara Channel, was created. The intent of this plan was to establish a "reserve" population of southern sea otters that might remain out of the main path of any large oil spill imperiling the California coast. It was fully expected that in addition to creating a reserve population, the translocation to San Nicolas Island would actually provide an opportunity for the southern sea otter population there to grow to over 500 by 1998. The decision to translocate met all of the above criteria for such a move. For example, *environmentally:* The southern sea otter was clearly threatened in its existing habitat from pollution by oil spills and by stress upon the fragile food chain from overfishing. According to the environmental lobby group Friends of the Sea Otter, in 2001, "Past studies have shown that sea otters are especially susceptible to oil. Once soiled, the chances of rescue and rehabilitation are slim. In the *Exxon Valdez* oil spill, greater than one thousand sea otter carcasses were collected. Wildlife veterinarians determined that up to 95% of these deaths were potentially attributable to oil."

Additionally, the southern sea otter was threatened by different kinds of fishing traps, including traps for live rockfish (similar to lobster traps), as well as gill and trammel nets.

San Nicolas Island presented a viable alternative for the southern sea otter problem. The island was federally protected and contained all of the natural resources necessary for sustaining and growing a population of this species.

Equally so, there were also *political and economic* realities to contend with. To begin with, there were and are strong, vocal environmental advocates for the southern sea otter—and while they did desire stronger measures against shipping and fishing, they were willing to support the translocation effort to San Nicolas Island.

Moreover, the possible threat of a growing southern sea otter population along the coastline might have threatened local populations of shellfish, including sea urchins and abalone.

Finally, this would in turn threaten local and smaller fisheries, whose economic vitality was tied to an abundant supply of these same shellfish.

Thus, the decision to translocate the southern sea otters was made. Under a 1986 congressional law (Public Law #99-625—the "Translocation Law"), translocation began in 1987 and continued to 1989, moving 139 southern sea otters to San Nicolas Island.

As the southern sea otter case demonstrates, however, there were and are problems with translocation. As of 1998, only 9 of the original 139 sea otters moved to the island were still known to be there. Where did the majority of this translocated population go? Andrew Johnson, program manager for sea otter research and conservation at the Monterey Bay Aquarium, interviewed May 15, 2001, thinks some of the otters may have moved on to other Channel islands and that a small number may have died. The larger amount of this population (over one hundred southern sea otters), he believes, have moved *back* to waters south of Point Conception—meaning, in effect, that in spite of a ten-year effort to protect and grow this population in another location—the sea otters have gone back to where they were before.

And this is the problem with translocation: when an animal's instincts become superior to human desire to move these animals to accommodate a number of interests, the animal's instincts will usually win out.

Translocation is a human concept, and as we have seen, it deals with complex environmental, political, and economic issues. The decisions and judgments made regarding competing interests will always be made by human beings. But as we have learned in the case of the southern sea otter—animals have their instincts, too.

Analyzing the Characteristics of Informative Speeches

Chad Meyer's speech is informative, explaining his ideas about protecting endangered species. In this speech, he is explaining a concept or idea—translocation. Meyer suggests that if we understand how the Southern Sea Otter can be threatened in its native environment, we might also understand translocation, and how it should work but why it may fail.

Using an Example to Contextualize the Topic.   Meyer's focus on the southern sea otter makes sense because translocation can be a challenging topic, complex and difficult to navigate in a single speech even for an accomplished speaker and thinker. Emphasizing the case of the southern sea otter does not dilute the topic; it gives the audience something concrete and readily identifiable to follow. In a sense, using the sea otter *contextualizes* translocation—it gives the audience a context within which to understand this method of protecting endangered species.

Main Message.   Meyer engages us with his main message—namely that translocation may fail, despite the best intentions and circumstances, if the target population follows its instincts and returns to the original habitat. Instincts cannot be controlled or artificially altered.

Organization.   Structurally, Meyer begins with a traditional device for his introduction—an anecdote that captures audience members' attention and hooks them into the speech. The *Exxon Valdez* oil spill is something that most people in his audience will be familiar with, and it allows him to get

For more on introductions and anecdotes, see page 194.

into his speech by talking about how species may be threatened by accidents resulting from human error. Meyer also reveals the purpose of his speech—to "explain the concept of translocation" by looking at a specific case study involving the southern sea otter.

Evident in the body of the speech are several organizational strategies. At one level he is using a modified *problem-cause-solution* approach. He describes the potential for environmental problems caused by oil spills and the like, and then he reviews a potential solution—translocation of the threatened species. We call his approach *modified* because he then spends the balance of the speech explaining the solution—and its problems as well. Within this structure, Meyer is also using a *categorical* approach: his internal organization is listed by categories or topics that aren't dependent on one another, other than that they explain the factors that go into a decision for translocation. You can see this approach when he lists the categories of questions for an environmental consideration, a political consideration, and an ethical consideration of his topic.

Audience Adaptation.   Notice how audience driven Meyer's speech is. He addressed a class of his fellow students, carefully using *analogies* and *examples* that he guessed they would be familiar with. For example, when he analogized translocation of sea otters to the removal of deer and raccoons from an urban area, he was assuming that most in his audience had at least indirect knowledge of the latter.

Organizational strategies are the subject of Chapter 8.

For more on the problem-cause-solution pattern, see page 186.

For more on the categorical pattern, see page 187.

● *Planning Your Informative Speech*

Although Chad Meyer appears to have no particular expertise in his topic, he compensates by citing expert sources to support the key points in his speech. He references findings by an environmental interest group, Friends of the Sea Otter. He also paraphrases a point from an expert at a nearby aquarium.

Meyer's use of expert sources helps his *credibility* in two important ways. First, it builds his credibility with his audience. In effect, Meyer derives his credibility from these sources. Second, by using an expert from the aquarium, he suggests some objectivity, since this source is a scientist and not an environmental interest group. By being objective, he helps the audience trust what he is saying. When planning your informative speech, look for expert sources that enhance your credibility and objectivity.

Meyer's speech lacks a clear *summary* in his conclusion. When preparing your own informative speeches, remember that summaries can be helpful—especially in an informative presentation. The summary should remind audience members about what they have just heard, reiterate the main points, and repeat the main message or thesis.

For more on summaries and speech structure, see page 202.

Amanda List, a college senior, gave the following speech in her technology and human communication course. In her presentation she explained the results of a study she conducted online, and then she demonstrated how she achieved her findings.

Gender-Based Responses in Sports Chatrooms

BY AMANDA J. LIST

View "Gender-Based Responses in Sports Chatrooms" by Amanda J. List.
CD-ROM: Video Theater, Full Speeches

Amanda List's speech is available in outline format on page 509. Her completed Speech Grid is on page 521.

One of the things we learned very early in this class on human communication and technology was that a very specific kind of technology, computer-mediated communication, has changed the way we communicate with one another. Earlier this semester it was suggested that computer-mediated communication, like that of the Internet, may possibly alter or evolve the way that women and men communicate with each other, as it all but eliminates face-to-face contact.

I thought that it would be interesting to test this theory, that the Internet alters the manner in which the sexes communicate with one another, in an arena (no pun intended) that interests me: professional sports. To be specific, baseball, football, and especially basketball; admittedly, hockey doesn't interest me in the slightest.

All of that having been said, today I want to demonstrate how I did a study to test whether or not the Internet truly does alter the way women and men communicate with each other on the topic of sports. I'm going to show you what I did, step-by-step, so that you can see how I reached my conclusion. First, we'll talk about how to create a working hypothesis that we can prove or disprove through experimentation. Next we'll talk about methodology: I am going to show you how you may set up a similar experiment that relates to you. For example, if one of the males in this class has an interest in knitting and has found that his maverick approach to purling is ridiculed or completely ignored by women he tries to discuss it with, he may wish to undertake a similar experiment in the Internet's undoubtedly boundless array of knitting chatrooms. By the same token, if one of the women in this room has an affinity for antique John Deere tractors, and yet has found that her method for mending a damaged chassis is overlooked despite the fact that it is completely with merit, she may wish to conduct a similar experiment in the virtual land of tractors. I'll present you with a methodology that you may put to use in your own studies. Finally, I'll show you what it is like to go online in this environment, and how to interpret the results we find.

The first step, then, is to create a working hypothesis. It has been my experience that I am treated as peculiar or odd when I discuss sports, even though I am very knowledgeable about sports. It would seem that women are not expected to know anything about a pitcher's ERA or a particular basketball player's tendency to miss the second in a one-and-one late in a game. When I make informed, relevant comments on a sports-related topic, especially in the presence of men, I am often met with the remark, "You sure do know a lot about sports, *for a woman!*" Having found this in the real world, I expected to find females treated in exactly the same manner online when discussing sports.

I have drawn upon these experiences to create the following working hypothesis: *Assuming gender is obvious, the treatment that one receives online when discussing sports-related topics will be congruous to the treatment a person encounters in face-to-face situations.*

I am now going to move on to my discussion about methodology. For the purpose of this study I created three online personas. One persona is obviously female, one is obviously male, and one is an androgynous person. The personas are very similar to each other in every respect except gender. In addition to simply creating gender-specific screen names, I also created profiles of all three personas: "Im90sGirl," "Johnny1208" and "JRG1243."

Although the screen names I chose are obviously gender specific (except for "JRG1243," which I purposely made androgynous), I also needed to create a profile for each character to support. These profiles gave information identifying me (respectively) as female, male, and unclear. For example, as my female identity, I gave my name as "Jill" in the profile, "Johnny" for the male, and "J.R." for the unclear profile.

Once I had my new identities, I was ready to foray into the world of cyber sports. I went online as all three characters at three different times of the day. The three time periods were early afternoon (1 P.M. to 5 P.M.), evening (5 P.M. to 7 P.M.), and late night (9 P.M. to midnight). I chose these three time periods in an effort to interact with a wide variety of people who would be in the chatrooms at varying times of the day.

My method for this study was to enter sports chatrooms as all three personas and make similar comments. In this manner I was able to observe the reactions of presumably the same participants in a chatroom to each of the three characters.

I went online in the early afternoon on several occasions during the study. At that particular time of the day I discovered that the overall mentality level of the participants in sports chatrooms was at about the junior high school level. The conversations taking place among the participants were banal, occasionally rude, and generally profane. At this time of the day the conversations had little, if anything, to do with sports.

When I entered the sports chatrooms in the early afternoon as Johnny, I was almost always immediately insulted. During one particular foray into America Online's "Sports Center 5" chatroom, I was quickly asked which team I liked in the NBA playoffs. I replied that I thought L.A. would definitely win the title yet again this year. I was then bombarded with messages insulting the Lakers and my "manhood."

A little later, I quickly signed on again as Jill. After many offers of cyber sex and insults (due to my rejections of those offers), I finally was asked which team I liked in the NBA playoffs. I gave the same answer as before. While I was again insulted by all the same participants who insulted me as Johnny, I was now thwarted with comments such as "Girls don't know anything about basketball" or "Dumb idiot, get out of here." When I signed on again as my androgynous persona, J.R., I was immediately questioned as to what gender I was. (I did not answer.) I gave the same answer to the question about the NBA, and while I was again insulted, none of the comments referenced my gender.

Gratefully, the level of discourse was much higher during the early evening hours, even in the same "Sports Center 5" chatroom. There were very few age/sex checks and also very few insults. I looked at several of the participants' profiles at this time of the day and discovered that their ages averaged between 20 and 40, and most were in school or were professionals.

The conversations at this time of the day were only about sports, and the participants generally stuck to the topic at hand. The participants mostly backed them up with opinions, facts, and explanations.

As Johnny, my comments and opinions were acknowledged and sometimes countered. I was invited into the conversation and began to really feel like "one of the guys."

As Johnny, I did make certain to make one comment to purposely show ignorance about sports: I confused the Sacramento Kings with the Los Angeles Kings during a discussion of the NHL. I was mildly flamed for this comment, but I was not told that I didn't belong there, nor was I asked to leave.

As Jill, during the evening hours, I was generally ignored, although I did receive a few instant messages requesting cyber sex. I was not welcomed into the conversations, and when I did interject a comment, I was either ignored or given a perfunctory response. As Jill, I was never asked for my opinion in the sports chatrooms during this time of day.

As Jill, I again made an uneducated comment, calling the Cleveland Cavaliers the "Ohio" Cavaliers. I was told to leave the sports chat area and told that women shouldn't be in those rooms.

My late-night excursions into the AOL sports chatrooms were similar in many ways to my ventures in the same rooms in the early afternoons: the banter was again inane and often had very little to do with sports.

As Johnny, I was again involved in conversations that centered around sports, but the other participants were much quicker to insult than the participants earlier in the evening.

Frankly, it was almost impossible to conduct any kind of study as a female in the chatrooms late at night: I was sent instant messages literally constantly, most of which requested cyber sex. What comments I was able to make in the AOL sports chatrooms were, again, mostly ignored. I was not asked about my opinion even after I had established that I knew a lot about the topic being discussed. On one of these occasions when I was complimented for being a knowledgeable female, I replied, "I'm a lesbian." The man who had complimented me then responded, "That explains it," and quickly left the room.

As my androgynous persona, I was asked a few times what my gender was, but I was again mostly treated like a male. I was flamed for following certain teams, but I was also asked my opinions and involved in what little conversation was going on.

From our experience today, and from the experiences I have told you about, we can draw our conclusion. I have found my hypothesis to be accurate. Online, as in face-to-face situations, women's comments and participation in sports conversation with men are neither invited nor particularly welcomed. It would appear that no matter how much a woman knows about sports, her comments are not gladly received by her male counterparts. In fact, the treatment that I received during this study as Jill was consistent among the three different time periods.

On those occasions when I made willfully ignorant comments, I was invariably flamed. As a male I was flamed for saying something stupid;

but as a female I was flamed for saying something stupid *and* for being a female.

The other interesting result of my study was that when I went online as my androgynous persona, J.R., most of the participants I encountered seemed to assume that I was a male and treated me as such.

● *Analyzing the Characteristics of Informative Speeches*

The purpose of Amanda List's speech is to inform, but, unlike Chad Meyer's speech, hers informs by demonstrating a process. She is demonstrating the process of studying Internet chatrooms to determine the validity of her hypothesis about male and female communications about professional sports. This speech succeeds as a demonstration for several reasons.

Topic Statement.   List's topic statement is very clear. Notice how she carefully and explicitly lays out what she wants to do in the study and what she expects it to show. She even labels this a speech that will "demonstrate" how to conduct such a study, so that other interested students can try to duplicate her findings.

Word Choice.   List identifies the steps in her speech to help us remember what she is doing: hypothesis, methodology, and approach. In this way she simplifies and refines the message at the same time. She also uses deliberate phrasing and direction to guide us through the presentation—like a teacher, making sure that we are with her both during and at the conclusion of every step.

Speaker Credibility.   Like Chad Meyer, Amanda List had no particular experience as a public speaker. She had no particular advance credibility with the audience as an expert or authority in her subject matter. But as a fellow student, a woman, and someone knowledgeable about sports, she did have plenty of credibility and authority for this speech.

Organization.   List's speech organization is very much chronological—and perhaps a bit categorical. It is chronological in the sense that a working hypothesis must by necessity come *before* a working methodology—and before the study itself. By taking us through her steps in this order, she is not only demonstrating what she did but also showing the audience how to duplicate her efforts and in what order. The subpoints are categorical because she lays out special categories of subtopics within her main points—for example, the different identities she creates for herself online, in the methodology portion of her speech.

● *Planning Your Informative Speech*

In this speech Amanda List informs her audience by explaining a process and technique. It might have been helpful if the audience could actually have seen what she was talking about—especially when she entered the sports chatroom. Amanda's telling us what she did informs us in one way, but actually observing her engage in the process she is describing would inform us in a very different and more meaningful way.

When you want to give an informative speech that demonstrates a process, give some real thought to the demonstration itself. Consider the *location* you're speaking in. Is it large enough to accommodate a demonstration? Could everyone see what you're doing if you demonstrated? Also consider *proxemics*. Where will you be, relative to your audience? How close will you be to your listeners? Do you plan to move around while you demonstrate?

In a demonstration speech, *audiovisual aids* can provide significant assistance. In one sense, you yourself, as the speaker, are a visual aid. But most speakers could also demonstrate by using visual or audio aids. Amanda List could have used the image of the chatroom on the projection screen and shown examples of the conversations she had.

For more on speech location and audience analysis, see page 95.

To review proxemics, see page 302.

Audiovisual aids are the subject of Chapter 12.

Sue Suter, former disability advocate and former president of the World Institute on Disabilities, addressed a conference of the Association for the Severely Handicapped in Springfield, Illinois, in September 1999. In her speech she explained and discussed the lessons disabled people must learn in life.

Lessons for the Disabled — Adapting to Change While Holding On to Values

BY SUE SUTER

Thank you for this honor, and for making this day one of the highlights of my life. In a new book called *Quotable Star Trek,* Jill Sherwin uses thousands of quotations to encourage people to think about their lives and the lessons they can learn from this popular series. Today, I want to share some of those lessons with you, as we open this conference on systems change.

The first lesson from *Star Trek* comes from one of television's first leading characters to be portrayed as having a disability—the blind chief engineer, Geordi LaForge. In a scene where LaForge is confronted by a culture that euthanizes its members with disabilities, he asks: "Who gave them the right to decide whether or not I should be here? Whether or not I might have something to contribute?"

Who has the right to judge whether people with disabilities belong? People have been raising their hands for centuries. From Greek philosophers who endorsed the "humane" disposal of disabled infants over cliffs, to 1940s German purification policies, to declarations by today's elites.

It's a condition that psychologists call the Lake Wobegon Effect. Lake Wobegon, a place where "all the women are strong, all the men are handsome, and all the children are above average." There's no such place. There never will be. More than anything else, the world needs to rediscover what's normal. Disability is a normal part of being human.

Yet women with disabilities, especially, are often devalued by the in-stitutions they should be able to count on most—their families and the women's movement. One feminist activist said, "Why study women with disabilities? They reinforce traditional stereotypes of women being de-pendent, passive and needy." To that I ask, who is an accomplice to that image? Who is abandoning the universal ideals of freedom and dignity in exchange for the easy path of appeasement? Appeasement has been defined as feeding your friends to the alligator in hopes that he'll eat you last. Everyone loses with that strategy. We must be flexible in our strategies, but we must stay honest to our cause.

The next lesson comes from Captain Picard, who said that "one of the most important things in a person's life is to feel useful." This kind of usefulness implies more than identity. It's the source of pleasure for so much of life. As the character Alexis in *Deep Space Nine* once said, "We all work for our supper. You'll be surprised how much sweeter it tastes when you do."

Unfortunately, a majority of people with disabilities don't have the chance to taste the sweet rewards of work. Unfortunately, it's usually stereotypes, not physical barriers, that stand in the way. And these prej-udices can come from the most troubling of sources. I contracted polio when I was two years old. I don't remember it. But I do remember my parents telling me about the advice the doctor gave when it was time for me to leave the hospital. He told them, "Just put her in bed; she's going to be staying there the rest of her life." I had a college counselor who advised me that going after more education might hurt me. He warned that it was hard enough for a woman with a disability to get married; a master's degree would only intimidate a man more.

And I remember when I went after my first job as a secretary. The boss nearly didn't hire me because he worried that I couldn't carry cof-fee to him every morning. Talk about a double-barrel insult—being doubted whether you could do something that you really shouldn't have to do in the first place! I should have been more assertive. But I was newly married, and getting that first job was important to me. I did get the job. I'm embarrassed to admit that I actually practiced carrying the coffee. And I never spilled coffee on the boss's lap, although the temp-tation was real. These were all well-meaning professionals who believed that they knew what was best for me. But my life would be much dif-ferent, and I probably wouldn't be with you today, if I had stayed within the boundaries of their expectations.

We are all unique. Each one of us has special gifts to add to the tap-estry we call community. But I have been among those rehabilitation counselors and administrators who have shortchanged client dreams in the name of risk management.

If a person with a severe disability says they want to become a doc-tor, should I dismiss their dreams as fantasy? Dreams are important. They reflect deeply held values. Even if the dreams seem far beyond reach, they deserve to be explored. And with a little work, they can show the path to a person's giftedness, and how they can make a difference in the world. But too often, people in our business are afraid to risk client fail-ures. We want to shelter them from defeat. And we're afraid that their failure at a job or an educational goal will be seen as a black mark against the system that tried to help. Yet as Rabbi Harold Kushner once said, pain is an unavoidable part of a normal life. Risk-taking and failures are normal for both individuals and organizations.

The next lesson comes from the powerful Klingon, Lt. Commander Worf, who, after tasting prune juice for the first time, declared it "a warrior's drink." Sometimes we need a new perspective to see familiar things as they really are. That's why this conference is so important. It brings together people with disabilities and families and professionals and advocates under one roof.

There's another reason why this conference is so important. And it can be summed up in Captain Picard's admonition that "things are only impossible, until they're not."

I remember what my father said to me when I was in the second grade. He loved me very much. He wanted me to be prepared for the future. So he warned me that I would probably never get married. He told me that I should become a clinical psychologist. I eventually did. Then he said that I should work to be the best, so that I could be independent, because some day there might not be anybody around to take care of me. Hard words for a seven-year-old girl to hear. But my father loved me. And he wanted me to be prepared. What a difference it would have made, for myself and my parents, if there was a family next door where the mother also wore braces. A role model. A person with a disability who was married, who raised children, who was nurturing and independent in her own right. Maybe even a corporate leader.

Professionals aren't the only ones who need to know that those labels can also belong to a person with disability. People with disabilities need that affirmation, as well. The truth is, most boundary-breaking work has been done by people with disabilities who had the courage to challenge the status quo.

That brings us to the final lesson from *Star Trek.* I'd like to leave you with two quotations from Captain Picard that define what it means to be human.

In *The Next Generation,* Picard confronts discrimination by agreeing that, yes, we may be different in appearance. Then he adds, "But we are both living beings. We are born, we grow, we live, and we die. In all the ways that matter, we are alike."

Then, later in the movie *Generations,* Picard confesses that "recently, I've become very much aware that there are fewer days ahead than there are behind. But I took some comfort from the fact that the family would go on."

Much of what we do (in the next two days) will center on these fundamental beliefs: that we are alike, and that no matter who we are, we have only a short time to accomplish what we desire to do.

Will our action steps create the world we want? No. But they will bring that world closer. And the swifter we act, the more days of opportunities will be given to people with disabilities, and the fuller our own accomplishments will be. And for as long as it takes to reach our goal, there will be people like you and me, who will share that same vision.

I'm proud that you, and I, belong to that family.

● *Analyzing the Characteristics of Informative Speeches*

In classroom presentations, we often make a neat and precise distinction between speech that is informative and speech that is persuasive. Of course, to some extent, this distinction is fallacious: Informative speech may inherently, indirectly, persuade; and persuasive speech may also inform. In the real world outside your class, more often than in the classroom, you will encounter situations in which no one distinguishes informing from persuading for you. Instead, you yourself draw that distinction, and it turns largely on your intentions for your speech.

Informing and Persuading.   Sue Suter's speech is informative, although it does have the indirect purpose of encouraging her audience to adopt the attitudes she describes. We offer this speech because it shows how a professional may have to deal with informative speech in the real world. Suter's speech *is* informative, but it is fundamentally different from Meyer's or List's speeches. Suter is not explaining a concept (as Meyer does) or demonstrating a process (as List does); rather, she is explaining and describing a state of being—disability.

Detail and Imagery.   When you are describing something, it is helpful to use *detail* and *imagery.* Both can help the audience understand and visualize what you are saying.

Suter uses detail very well. Though lean on statistical evidence, she is very detailed in her use of examples of the challenges that people with disabilities face. She also uses imagery very well. When she describes her childhood, and the well-intentioned yet difficult advice from her father, you can visualize the seven-year-old girl she was, dealing with physical and social challenges. And when she describes her first job as secretary, dealing with a "double-barrel insult," her words evoke strong images of her situation, as well as the intensity and range of emotions she felt.

Main Message.   Of course, central to informing an audience in any speech is a clear main message—or *topic statement.* Suter wants to explain the challenges that people with disabilities face, and she wants to focus on the lessons that can be learned from those challenges. The latter forms the main message of her speech.

Audience Adaptation and Word Choice.   Suter's *word choice* is deliberate. Each reference to *Star Trek* is not only a device for structuring her message but also a parable. Consider the following two examples:

Suter's Words	Relevance to Main Message
"The next lesson comes from Captain Picard, who said that 'one of the most important things in a person's life is to feel useful.'"	A person with a physical disability needs to feel useful every bit as much as someone who is physically able. A disabled person can contribute in many ways to our community.

Suter's Words	Relevance to Main Message
". . . Captain Picard's admonition that 'things are only impossible, until they're not.'"	Barriers are only barriers until we (in the disabled community) decide they can be overcome and we call them something else.

Suter's use of quotations from *Star Trek* is intended for humor (life lessons from a television show!) but reflects her audience analysis. *Star Trek,* both the television series and the movies, is without question a part of contemporary popular culture. Suter assumes that her audience is familiar with it, even if not well versed on all the program's characters.

The quotations themselves also enable a structure for Suter. Each "lesson" creates a component to build her speech around. The organization is randomly topical or categorical, as opposed to linear.

For more on categorical organization, see page 187.

● *Planning Your Informative Speech*

For more on speaker credibility, see pages 38 and 199.

Suter comes to this speaking situation with *primary credibility.* In this instance, her credibility is derived from her *expertise* (as a clinical psychologist and as an advocate for people with disabilities) and from her *authority* (as president of the World Institute on Disabilities) and *experience* (her own disability). She effectively reminds us of her credentials in her speech. No one in her audience can doubt that she is in a unique position to know and present the facts. Thus listeners willingly accept and digest her presentation differently than they would if she were simply a medical researcher or a lobbyist for reform.

Suter is helped by her credibility, and you will be well served to follow her example. Think about what makes you a credible speaker on the topics you choose for your informative speeches. Maybe you have significant experience with your topic. Also consider whether your audience is likely to have prior knowledge of your background, and whether you will need to give the audience cues about it in your speech.

Suter also is extremely effective at using *reiteration,* reminding her audience of her main points, in different words, at different places in her speech. Suter uses reiteration throughout her speech—both in her main message about the lessons that can be drawn for the disabled and in her simplified presentation of the lessons drawn from *Star Trek.* When drafting your informative speech, look for opportunities to reiterate your points and remind the audience of your main ideas.

Summary: Key Features of Informative Speeches

After reviewing and evaluating the speeches of Meyer, List, and Suter, you should be aware of the special characteristics of an informative speech. Keep these in mind when you prepare this type of speech.

● *Informative speeches need well-conceived organization.*

Organization shapes the way the audience receives the message. Informative speeches usually rely on one of the following organizational strategies:

Organizational strategies are the subject of Chapter 8.

1. *Chronological or temporal organization, in which the speaker moves from the "beginning" to the "ending" by using reference points in time.* For example, a speech informing an audience about Middle Eastern cooking—a type of process—might well be organized in linear fashion by chronologically describing the cooking steps as they occur in time. Intuitively this makes sense because in cooking, steps usually must be followed in a certain order, with ingredients prepared and mixed before the next step can be taken. There are a beginning and an ending, but they are structured by events—ingredient preparation—as they occur in time.

2. *Spatial organization, in which events are explained as they occur in space.* For example, an informative speech that explains a military campaign in the Second World War might be structured spatially, dictated by the *location* of certain battles and skirmishes, one before another—looking to whatever was the resolution of this particular campaign. The locations would be points on a map—pointing to that final resolution— and the locations themselves might serve as the different parts of the speech. The same might be said of the airline safety speech mentioned at the beginning of the chapter, if the flight attendant mentioned the *location* of each piece of safety equipment.

3. *Causal organization, in which the roots of a phenomenon are explained.* Each main point might focus on one cause or on one step in a chain of causation. For example, in a report on viral infections, a speaker might pose these questions: How does the virus attack a cell? How does the cell react? The speaker might then explain how the virus infects the cell, replicates itself, and ruptures the cell before attacking other cells.

4. *Topical or categorical organization, in which separate topics are presented as main points, each of which supports the topic statement or purpose of the speech.* For example, in a speech about sharks, a speaker might describe different types of sharks, explain why people are so fearful of sharks, and present scientific facts about shark attacks. The speaker would move through three different topics related to sharks.

5. *Web pattern, in which each main point is related to a core idea but the points do not fit together in a linear manner.* For example, Suter listed many lessons that were associated, but she did not mention them in any particular order.

● *Informative speeches should clarify and simplify messages for an audience.*

In informative speeches, it is vital to take any complex messages and simplify them. For example, James, a student in a speech class, gave a presentation on a seemingly complicated and difficult-to-understand topic: what

GUIDE TO INFORMATIVE SPEAKING

treatment the medical/scientific community should employ to fight cancer. His audience was made up of students in his class—few of whom had a sufficient science background to follow his speech. His topic was complex and broad. James wisely simplified things by reducing "treatments" to "gene therapy" (itself still complex) and then further reducing the topic by describing a simple three-step process to illustrate how introducing genes to cells can prevent disease.

To simplify and clarify complex messages, you may want to use any of these techniques:

1. *Move from a general/broad topic to something that is narrower and more refined ("gene therapy" instead of "cancer treatments").* Here it will be useful to ask yourself a fundamental question: At a minimum, what do I want my audience to take away from this speech? What basic message should the audience carry away? This message is the narrowed, refined message.

For tips on narrowing a topic, see page 128.

2. *Reduce the quantity of information presented.* Remember that in informative speeches there may be a great deal for the audience to remember. An old adage still rings true: Less is more. Simplifying may be accomplished by literally reducing—or diminishing—the size of a message. Obviously, a speech about gene therapy can have many parts and components. If you are speaking to a lay audience and you want to simplify, you would do well to follow James's example and reduce the number of steps necessary to explain the process. Less is more.

3. *Make complex information more familiar.* You can simplify a complex message by helping the audience understand *how* and *why* the message is complex. To accomplish this, use *definition* to explain difficult-to-follow terms and ideas; avoid jargon—technical or in-house terminology not easily understood by people outside a certain group; and compare complex ideas to other ideas with which the audience is familiar.

For more on jargon, see page 268.

● *Informative speeches should use techniques that increase audience retention of the message.*

A good informative speech does whatever is necessary to help the audience retain and remember the informative message. The speaker can accomplish this goal by simplifying and clarifying the points being made, by the creative use of visual aids, and by using reiteration to enhance retention. Reiteration—making reference to the same basic points several times in a speech—is not necessarily the same as repetition (repeating the same message). Rather, reiteration allows you to refer to a message several times but with different words each time. For example, in a speech about the triathlon, the speaker referred to the techniques for heart-rate training in three different parts of the presentation. The more often audience members hear the message, the greater is the likelihood they will remember it.

Audiovisual aids are the subject of Chapter 12.

For more on rewording, see page 273.

● *Informative speeches should always be audience centered.*

Informative speeches should be targeted and guided by your analysis of the audience. The categories on the left side of your Speech Grid ("situational characteristics," "demographics," "common ground," "prior exposure," and "audience disposition"), as well as those on the right side of the grid ("ethos," "logos," and "pathos"), should guide your selection of the final message.

Though done in different ways, each of the three speeches presented earlier in this chapter was written for a specific audience. Chad Meyer crafted his speech for his classmates in a basic speech course. He made some assumptions about their familiarity with species translocation, and he carefully used analogies as well as the specific example of the southern sea otter.

Amanda List's speech about gender roles in sports chatrooms was also written for classmates. List took a very detailed, hands-on approach for guiding listeners through sports chatrooms. She was aware that her audience was familiar with the Internet but not necessarily familiar with the methods of misrepresenting or obfuscating gender online.

In a similar vein, Sue Suter's speech about lessons for the disabled was tailored for the Association for the Severely Handicapped. In addition to assessing her audience's familiarity with disability issues, Suter assumed that many members of her audience were familiar with *Star Trek*.

In each case, the audience drove the message. As you prepare your informative speech, you, too, need to consider the audience.

For more on audience analysis, see page 90.

Preparing Your Informative Speech

A Five-Step Process

Use your CD-ROM to build your speech using the five-step process. CD-ROM: Interactive Speech Guides/Informative Speech

Use your CD-ROM to analyze your audience. Go to "Step 1 Invention/Analyze Audience." CD-ROM: Interactive Speech Guides/Informative Speech

For a sample Speech Grid, see page 115.

Audience analysis is the subject of Chapter 5.

The Speech Assignment

Prepare an informative speech in which you *explain* an idea or concept; *describe* a state of being, a thing, or a person; or *demonstrate* a process or course of action. As you develop your speech, follow the five-step process described here to invent, organize, stylize, refine and practice, and deliver your speech.

1. Inventing Your Speech

Drafting an effective informative speech begins with careful preparation and planning. You need to analyze your audience; then you need to decide whether you want to explain an idea or concept, describe a state of being, a person, or a thing, or demonstrate a process. Next you select an issue to address, draft a topic statement, research your topic, and select the ideas that will inform your audience ethically and effectively.

Hard work and perseverance are the keys to a successful speech. When you are given a major speech assignment, it is natural to wonder how you will find the time to do all the work that needs to be done. Actually, the task is not as overwhelming as it may seem — if you get to work shortly after receiving the assignment and budget your time wisely.

● Analyze Your Audience

The audience drives the message is a maxim that we emphasize throughout this text. Begin your preparation by analyzing your audience and recording your analysis on a Speech Grid. At the outset, analyze the situational characteristics, audience demographics, and common ground.

Situational Characteristics. If you are presenting an informative speech in class, note any requirements for the topic, format, and content of the speech. If you are speaking out of class, what is the occasion for your speech? Also note where you will be speaking, the time of day you will speak, the size of your audience, and the expected length of your speech.

Audience Demographics. Consider demographic categories that are likely to indicate audience interest and disposition toward informative speech topics. These categories may include political affiliation, group membership, occupation or academic major, race, ethnicity, gender mix, sexuality, income, age, religious affiliation, and family status. For example, in a speech describing modern comic book artwork, it would be helpful to know the age level of the audience, especially when deciding whether to refer to classic or contemporary comic books.

Common Ground. Consider what you and the audience have in common. In an informative speech, you can strengthen your ethos by emphasizing shared values and experiences. Brainstorm to create a list of similarities between you and your audience.

Whether to Explain, Describe, or Demonstrate.   This decision is important because it keys several of the other steps you will take in inventing and creating your informative speech. Which approach you want to use depends on your intention and the subject or topic of the speech. Ideas and concepts lend themselves to explanation. For example, in an autobiographical speech, you may want to explain how you reached a decision about where to go to school. You may be explaining the central idea that guided your final decision (for example, the school had to have a great communication department), or you may be explaining the thought process that went into making your decision (for example, first you considered large public schools, then small private schools; then you contrasted costs, proximity to home, and overall school rankings).

Description, by contrast, lends itself to entities with physical characteristics—such as people or things—although it also can lend itself to a state of being or existence—as was the case in Sue Suter's speech. We are using the term *things* loosely—it may refer to any entity, organic or not, living or not, with physical properties capable of description. For example, in your informative speech you may wish to describe something—such as a bicycle. You might describe all its parts—frame, seat stem, type of seat, wheels, gears, and so on. Or you might want to describe a former cyclist—perhaps the last winner of the Tour de France. You might describe him personally, his characteristics, or even his racing background.

Demonstration, by contrast to explanation or description, lends itself better to a process or a course of action. By *process,* we refer to some kind of systematic series of actions leading to an end. For example, in a demonstration speech, you may want to demonstrate how to bake your favorite chocolate chip cookies. What ingredients are called for? What steps are involved? What is the end product?

Any course of action can be demonstrated—within the limitations of time and space for your speech.

● Select and Refine Your Topic

For classroom informative speech assignments, you usually have some choice in topic selection. When you have a choice, use brainstorming and research to generate a list of potential subjects.

In some speech contexts, your topic will be a given. But even when your subject is given, you will still need to narrow it to fit the available time, and you will need to plan an appropriate topic statement.

Use your CD-ROM to select and refine your topic. Go to "Step 1 Invention/Select Topic." CD-ROM: Interactive Speech Guides/Informative Speech

Selecting and refining a topic are the subject of Chapter 6.

Brainstorm Topic Areas.   In an informative speech assignment, you share information and ideas with your audience. You will always sound more credible and enthusiastic if you speak about topics you care about. Brainstorm informative topics that are of interest and concern to you. Also consider topics and subjects likely to be of interest to audience members on campus and in your class. Remember to write down every idea that comes to mind when

For a description of mind mapping, see page 120.

brainstorming, without rejecting anything. Use word association or mind mapping to add to your list. Here is an example of one student's list of issues, developed through brainstorming and word association:

family	How to make Dad's recipe for chocolate chip cookies.
	How to follow my grandmother's tips for conflict resolution.
living on campus	How to organize a dorm room.
	How to prepare nutritious foods on a student budget.
as a student	Step-by-step techniques for time management.
	How to build a dark room to develop plates for photography class.
as a person	How to taste and tell the difference between different kinds of cheese.

For more on researching your topic, see page 150.

Research for Potential Topics.   Look at sources that are likely to provide topic ideas for an informative speech. These include Internet news sites, newspapers, and recent art, travel, and science magazines. Check the tables of contents in recent periodicals, if they are easily available in your library. Write down any potential topics. Do not begin reading books or articles until you select a topic.

Select the Best Topic Area.   Once you have developed a list of possibilities, select the best topic for your informative speech. The three main criteria you should use to evaluate each potential topic are

1. *Your audience's interests.* Is the topic likely to concern the audience? Can you relate the subject to the audience? Can the audience be directly involved with the issue?
2. *Your interests and expertise.* Do you know enough about the topic to be a credible speaker? Will you be able to speak with knowledge about your topic?
3. *The context of the speech.* Will the topic be appropriate, given the location, audience size, time, and occasion of the speech? Is the topic appropriate for an informative speech? For a classroom speech, is the topic acceptable to your instructor?

Exclude any topics that would be inappropriate for your audience or the speech context. On the list of remaining topics, highlight the one(s) you are most knowledgeable about and interested in. If there is more than one that you are interested in addressing, select the one that seems best, given your audience and speech context.

Narrow Your Topic.   Select a portion of your topic that you can cover in the time available for your speech. Focus your informative speech by considering which aspects of the topic will be of the greatest interest and concern to the audience and can directly involve the audience. Possibly, some aspect of the topic fits your interest and expertise. If that aspect would also be appropriate for your audience, it would be a good choice for the focus of your speech.

For more on narrowing your topic, see page 128.

Draft a Working Topic Statement and Specific Purpose.   Create a working topic and specific purpose statement for use in preparing your speech. The topic statement should express the main *idea* of your informative speech in one sentence. The specific purpose statement should address the *objective* of your speech: do you intend to explain, describe, or demonstrate? In one sentence, the specific purpose statement expresses what you want the audience to take away from your speech. You can use the software in your CD-ROM to evaluate your topic statement and specific purpose to ensure they are appropriate for an informative speech.

Keep in mind that both your topic statement and your specific purpose are *working* statements. You may revise them after learning more about audience members' perspectives on your topic or gaining insights from your research.

● *Generate Ideas to Support Your Topic Statement*

Use both brainstorming and research to develop a list of potential supporting ideas. Record these ideas on your Speech Grid. Later, you will choose the best of these ideas for inclusion in your speech outline.

Use your CD-ROM to generate and select ideas to support your topic statement. Go to "Step 1 Invention/Generate Supporting Ideas" and "Select Supporting Ideas."
CD-ROM: Interactive Speech Guides/Informative Speech

Brainstorm Supporting Ideas.   Initially list on your grid every point or idea that could develop your topic statement. Later, you will select the best points for your speech, but now your goal is to create a diverse list of ideas. Use the "Speech Message" side of the grid. In that column are three broad categories: messages that use *ethos* (credibility from authority, expertise, experience, and so on); messages that use *pathos* (ideas that succeed with an audience because they appeal to listeners on an emotional level); and messages that use *logos* (complex or difficult-to-understand ideas, made easy for the audience). Sort your supporting points according to the category in which they best fit.

For more on audience analysis and the creation of the speech message, see pages 41 and 90.

To some extent, the job of generating supporting points is guided by your intentions for your speech, whether it is to *explain* an idea or concept; to *describe* a state of being, a person, or a thing; or to *demonstrate* a process or course of action. If your informative speech is one that *explains* an idea or concept, consider these questions as you brainstorm supporting points:

- What reasons support using this idea or concept?
- What examples demonstrate this idea or concept?
- What experience do you have with this idea or concept that could be explained in a speech?
- Can your idea or concept be explained in simple terms? If it requires complex terms, how can you help the audience understand them?

For more on using simple or complex examples in your informative speech, see page 143.

If you are preparing an informative speech that *describes* a state of being, a person, or a thing, consider these questions:

- How might you use detail to describe your subject?
- Are there examples you could use to describe your subject?
- What kind of imagery would you use to help describe this thing or person? Can you form a mental image of it or this person? What words or phrases would you use to describe this mental image?
- Are there statistics that would help the audience understand your subject?
- Do you have special experience with or connection to this topic?

For a discussion of using your experience in an informative speech, see page 123.

If you are preparing an informative speech that *demonstrates* a process or course of action, consider these questions:

- What are the steps or parts (if any) to this process? How would you break them down individually to explain them?
- Can these steps or parts be easily understood and later followed by your audience?
- Can members of the audience do what you are demonstrating *while* you are demonstrating?
- Are there ideas or parts or steps to your speech that you must prepare ahead of time?
- Do you have special experience, authority, or expertise with this topic?

For more on the research process, see Chapter 7.

Research Your Topic.   In Chapter 7 we noted the necessity of research and discussed the steps to take when you research a speech. Here, we briefly review those steps and provide specific advice for researching informative speeches.

Inventory Your Research Needs.   Determine where to focus your research. Do you need to learn more about your topic? Are there ideas you plan to explain, describe, or demonstrate that will not be informative for your audience without more research? For classroom speeches, how many references to research are required?

TIP

Know what format your instructor requires for citing research, so that you can record the required information as you consult various sources.

Have a System for Organizing Your Information.   If you have an organized plan, you will not lose information, and you will be able to find the sources for the points you researched when you need them.

Discover Sources of Information on Your Topic.   Consult a wide variety of research sources, including library and online directories. Also, determine whether there are any experts you could interview in person or correspond with through e-mail. As you begin this process, bear the following in mind:

- An informative speech that *explains* an idea or concept will benefit from your research of credible sources such as experts familiar with the idea or concept.
- An informative speech that *describes* a person or thing will benefit from your research—your personal interview of the individual or your personal observation of the thing you are describing.
- An informative speech that *demonstrates* a process or course of action or *describes* a state of being will benefit from careful reflection of your

experience with the process or action or state of being. You may best accomplish this by revisiting the process or action or state of being and taking careful notes.

Read and Prioritize Your Sources.   Once you have gathered your sources, carefully read them, looking for those that are most likely to make points that explain, describe, or demonstrate your topic statement. Record these points on the "Speech Message" side of your Speech Grid as appropriate under the categories of "ethos," "pathos," and "logos." Keep complete citations for any points that you may decide to use in your speech.

For more on recording your ideas on a Speech Grid, see page 175.

Identify Gaps in Your Research, and Find Needed Information.   If you cannot find information to develop some points you hoped to make, target your research to fill in those gaps. If you continue to have difficulty, consider these options:

- *Narrow the scope of your topic.* If your topic can't be developed with the available evidence, narrow your topic or revise it into one that you can discuss with the available research.

- *Expand the scope of your topic.* If you find few credible sources because your topic is too limited, you may wish to broaden the topic. In a speech about ideas or concepts, this may mean explaining more aspects of an idea or concept—perhaps those you had intended to ignore. Or it may mean bringing in connected or ancillary ideas and concepts that relate to the original topic. For example, if your speech concerns the theory of evolution as it applies to whales, you might want to consider the same theory as it applies to other marine life. If your speech describes a person or thing, you should expand your description or expand your topic to consider related people or things. The same technique applies to a speech of demonstration. You should expand the number of steps or consider related topics. For example, in a speech demonstrating steps for baking a dessert, you might expand the topic to include steps for other courses.

- *Ask for help.* If you are having difficulty finding appropriate sources, ask your instructor or a librarian for recommendations of sources to research. Also, talk to people on campus or in your community with experience or expertise in your topic. They can advise you about the soundness of your approach and provide ideas for further research.

When you are confident that you have thoroughly researched your topic, evaluate your working topic statement. If you can support it with the ideas you have generated, keep it in that form. If you need to revise your topic statement, now is the time to do so.

● *Select the Best Ideas to Support Your Topic Statement*

Evaluate the supporting ideas in the "Speech Message" column of your Speech Grid. Base your evaluation on ethical considerations and your audience analysis. On your grid, highlight particularly promising ideas, and cross out those that are inappropriate.

For more on the principles of ethical communication, see Chapter 3.

Ethical Concerns in Issue Selection.

Review the points listed on your grid. Omit any that seem questionable from an ethical perspective. Here are some important ethical considerations for informative speakers:

1. Have you disclosed your personal knowledge and connection (if any) to the topic? Do you have any bias about the topic?

2. Have you done sufficient research to be well informed about your topic, main points, and subpoints? Do you need to do more research before you can discuss them credibly with the audience?

3. Are you making only those factual claims that you know to be true? Now that you have researched the topic, are there any points you should omit because they are inconsistent with what you learned?

4. Do any of the points you make seem exaggerated? Should you rewrite any of them to more accurately reflect the claims you can prove?

Audience Analysis and Issue Selection.

Whether you are attempting to explain or describe or demonstrate for audience members, you need to understand their orientation to your topic and the reasons for their beliefs. You can use this information to decide which points on your grid will be most effective with your audience.

Audience analysis is the subject of Chapter 5.

Expand Your Audience Analysis. After selecting a speech topic, you can expand on your audience analysis. The left side of your grid should already contain information about the speech situation, as well as information you have already learned about common ground and the demographics of the audience. To expand your audience analysis, determine audience members' *prior exposure* to your topic through surveys or interviews. If surveying or interviewing audience members isn't feasible, try indirect methods to find clues about what your audience already knows about your topic. Then make the best assumptions possible about the type of audience you will be addressing.

For more on indirect audience analysis, see page 110.

Use Your Audience Analysis to Select Points for Your Speech. You may want to make changes in the points on your grid in light of your audience analysis—for example, elaborating on an idea or substituting evidence that will be more credible. When you are using audience analysis to select points to include in your speech, here are some questions you might consider:

1. Which points will be most informative to the audience?

2. What does the audience already know about my topic?

3. How complicated is this topic? Will the audience understand everything?

4. Do any of my points relate directly to audience members' lives?

5. Does my situational audience analysis indicate that some ideas would be more effective than others? How long does the audience expect my speech to be? At what time of day am I speaking? Where is the speech taking place?

For more on situational audience analysis, see page 92.

The answers to those questions will influence your choice of points to include.

2. Organizing Your Speech

The second step in preparing your informative speech is to draft an outline of the points you have selected to support your topic statement. You will take the ideas that you highlighted on your grid and arrange them in an effective sequence. Start by considering the body of your speech, and then add the introduction, conclusion, and connecting words.

● *Outline the Body of Your Informative Speech*

Organize Your Ideas into Main Points.   Go back to your grid, and organize the highlighted ideas into a limited number of main points. These will form the body of your speech. For an informative speech, there are several ways in which you can organize ideas into main points.

Linear Organization.   If most or all of your points are in some way sequential (if they flow in a certain sequence), consider organizing them in a linear fashion. Use a *temporal* pattern to describe a sequence of events as they occur in time. This organization works well in demonstration speeches (such as a cooking demonstration) and in descriptive speeches (such as a speech organized around the events of a person's life, from childhood to adulthood). Use a *spatial* pattern if each main point covers a physical or geographic part of the topic.

If most or all of your main points suggest a cause-and-effect relationship, you may want to use a *causal* pattern. Consider a simple two-part organization, highlighting first the cause and then the effect or consequence. This pattern works well in informative speeches that explain concepts or ideas.

If most or all of your main points involve ideas or things set in opposition to one another (for example, a speech about innovations in phone technology, featuring different types of cell phones), you may want to use a *comparison* pattern. Compare or contrast the features of your topic. One phone offers voice mail; another, Internet access; another, longer battery life. Phones and features would be the main points to compare and contrast. This type of organization can work in speeches that explain concepts, describe things, or demonstrate processes.

Nonlinear Patterns.   Some speech assignments require all students to use a standard linear format (such as temporal) to organize the main points of informative speeches. But if you are not required to use a standard format, and your audience analysis indicates that a nonlinear format will be effective for your audience, consider a deferred-thesis, web, or narrative pattern. For example, a web pattern (several main points arranged in no particular order but all linking back to one core idea) can work well in speeches that explain an idea or concept or describe a state of being, a person, or a thing.

Word the Main Points.   After deciding what your main points will be and how they will be ordered, insert them in your speech outline. Remember to number each main point with a Roman numeral and to word your main points so that they accurately reflect the supporting material and generate audience interest.

Use your CD-ROM to select the best organizational pattern for your speech. Go to "Step 2 Organization/Body."
CD-ROM: Interactive Speech Guides/Informative Speech

For more on temporal organization, see page 185.

For more on spatial organization, see page 185.

For more on causal patterns, see page 186.

For more on comparison organization, see page 186.

For more on nonlinear formats, see page 208.

For a discussion of culture and organization preferences, see page 212.

For more on the web format, see page 210.

Develop and Outline Subpoints. Once your main points are determined, select from your grid the ideas that best support those main points. Both the content and the format of your supporting materials are important.

Selecting Supporting Materials. As we said earlier, audiences are affected by ethos, logos, and pathos. The materials that you select from your Speech Grid to support your main points should incorporate all three of these concepts.

To develop your *ethos,* select points that show concern for your audience's best interests. Points that demonstrate your common ground with the audience will build your credibility. Regular citation of research and good organization will show the audience that you are well prepared to speak on your topic.

To use *logos* in your informative speech, be sure to base your topic ideas on sound reasoning, credible evidence, or both. If your analysis indicates that audience members have reservations about a point you are making or believe the point is false, incorporate additional supporting explanations of that point.

To appeal to *pathos,* develop points that genuinely touch the audience's emotions. A well-reasoned informative point can be important, but effective appeals to pathos can do even more with your audience.

Creating Speech Structure. Now you are ready to insert the supporting points for the body of your informative speech into your outline. Here are three principles to follow as you do so:

1. Use proper outline format. Indent subpoints, and use capital letters to identify them. Double-indent sub-subpoints, and number each one.

2. Subpoints and sub-subpoints must be subordinate to the point they develop. Ensure that all supporting materials are relevant to the claim you place them under.

3. Research material must be properly cited in your outline. Each time you use quoted or paraphrased information in your speech, be sure to attribute it to the author. We recommend citing the author, author's qualifications, source, date, and page number on your outline. A citation is required *every time* evidence is used.

● Outline the Introduction and Conclusion

The introduction and conclusion of an informative speech consist of the same components as the introduction and conclusion of other speeches. As you draft your introduction and conclusion, be sure to include each component. Pay attention to the length of these parts of your speech. For a typical five- to ten-minute informative speech, your introduction should not exceed one minute and your conclusion should last between thirty and forty-five seconds. Your teacher is likely to provide specific time limits (reflecting the size of the class and the number of speakers).

Draft the Introduction. The introduction should set the tone for your informative speech. When drafting the introduction, consider the following advice:

For more on audience analysis and selection of the message, see pages 45 and 90.

For more on sound reasoning and credible evidence, see pages 64 and 235.

For more on pathos appeals, see page 39.

For more on outlining a speech, see page 181.

For more on proper citation form in your speeches, see Appendix B.

For more on the components of a speech outline, see page 46.

For more on the speech introduction, see page 193.

1. *Relate the attention-getter to the topic of your speech.* Most informative speech topics benefit from a strong attention-getter that dramatizes the topic for the audience. A poignant anecdote or startling statistic can pull the audience into your speech at the outset. If your audience is hostile, you may want to use an attention-getter that demonstrates respect or common ground to build rapport, or you may want to defuse tension with a humorous beginning.

For more on attention-getters, see page 193.

2. *Connect with audience members by highlighting one way in which the topic relates to them.* Summarize this connection in one or two sentences. At this point you are whetting their appetites by promising relevant information. In the body of your speech, you will explain the claim you are making.

3. *Establish credibility to build your ethos.* Your audience needs to understand why and how you have expertise, knowledge, or personal experience with your topic. Provide that information early in your speech. If you communicate your competence to discuss a topic, the audience will be inclined to believe you and follow your conclusions.

For more on speech previews, see page 200.

4. *Preview your main points to indicate the structure of your speech.* In an informative speech, a preview can set the stage for the main message. If you word your main points so as to express your main idea in the preview, they will function like a **sound bite** for your informative message.

Draft the Conclusion. Your conclusion ties together the components of your speech in an informative manner. Conclusions include two components: a summary of your main points and a clincher.

For more on the speech conclusion, see page 201.

The *summary* briefly reviews the main ideas that you developed in the body of your speech. Mention each main point in a sentence or phrase. If you use vivid language to express these points, your audience is more likely to remember your speech.

The *clincher* should leave a lasting impression on the audience. This is vital if you want audience members to retain what they heard in your informative presentation. You may want to consider one of these options for the clincher of an informative speech:

- *An appeal to the audience's emotions.* Use a dramatic example or an anecdote involving a person who benefited (or would benefit) from the topic of your speech.

- *A relevant quotation from a person the audience respects.* The audience will be more supportive of your ideas if you link your topic with the beliefs of a person whom the audience holds in high esteem.

After you draft the introduction, body, and conclusion, the next step is to insert organizing language—transitions and signposts—to ensure that the structure of your speech is clear and easy to follow.

● *Incorporate Transitions and Signposts*

Add Transitions. Transitions serve as bridges between the major parts of your speech. On your outline, insert them at the following places:

sound bite: a brief, memorable phrase that gains the audience's attention.

1. Between the introduction and the first main point
2. Between each main point
3. Between the final main point and the conclusion (Alternatively, instead of inserting a full transition, you may use a signpost here to indicate that your speech is concluding.)

For more on wording transitions, see page 190.

Word each transition to show clearly that you are moving from one idea to the next.

For more on signposts, see page 191.

Add Signposts. Properly placed signposts enhance the organization of your speech. In an informative speech, use signposts to

1. Highlight each aspect or cause of the idea or concept that you are discussing in an explanatory speech
2. Highlight each feature that you are discussing in a descriptive speech
3. Emphasize each provision or step in a demonstrative speech

Your instructor may require a bibliography at the end of your outline. Follow his or her guidelines for proper citation format.

Signposts also can help audience members realize that you are presenting a two-sided analysis of a particular point.

3. Using Effective Style

The third step in developing your informative speech is to focus on style, to ensure that the wording of your ideas on your outline is appropriate and informative. Review the outline and evaluate your word choice. If necessary, make revisions to improve your wording. When reflecting on style in an informative speech, consider the following advice:

For pointers on effective style, see Chapter 10.

For more on word choice, see page 272.

- *Use words that pull the audience into your speech.* Compelling language can play a powerful role in making a speech informative. Use striking and vivid language to help the audience appreciate and visualize your points. Include metaphors and similes to capture the audience's attention and bring your ideas to life.

- *Be sure your words are understandable.* Many informative speeches use technical terminology specific to the topic. If you must use technical terms, explain them carefully so that the audience understands what you are saying. Avoid using jargon, acronyms, and shorthand references to concepts, ideas, things, people, or processes that may be unfamiliar to your audience.

TIP

Language revisions are easy to make if you draft your outline on a word processor.

- *Simplify long and difficult sentences.* If you have lengthy sentences that contain several ideas, break them down into shorter sentences containing a single idea each. Substitute simple terms for complex phrases unless you are confident that the complex language will be more effective with your audience.

- *Avoid bias in your language.* Avoid negative stereotypes, unnecessary gender-specific references, and outdated references to ethnic groups. When describing people, or topics that refer to specific groups of people, keep your language as professional as possible.

For more on language that may not be politically correct, see page 276.

4. Refining and Practicing Your Informative Speech

Students often assume that their speeches are complete when the outline is written. But that assumption is false. The important fourth step in the speech-writing process is refining and practicing your speech. Your informative speech will be stronger if you review and revise your outline after it is written. If possible, arrange your schedule so that you have time to set your outline aside for one or two days before you review it.

● Review the Outline from a Critical Perspective

When reviewing your speech, keep in mind that audience analysis is an ongoing process and should be done again as you refine your speech. In addition, this is the time to seek critical feedback from other people and to continue to revise your outline as needed.

Analyze Your Informative Speech.   When you reread your outline, consider the speech from the audience's perspective. You may want to make an extra copy of your outline and write on it notes about possible changes to the content and structure that occur to you as you are reading.

Review the Content.   Here are some questions to ask about the content of your informative speech outline:

- Does the speech clearly indicate what you would like the audience to learn and remember?
- Is the language you have chosen appropriate for your audience? Is the tone reasonable and professional? Will the audience understand what you are trying to say?
- Do your visual aids clearly demonstrate the ideas they are intended to convey?

For more on visual aids and message clarity, see page 325.

Review the Structure.   Review the structure of your speech. Here are some questions to ask to avoid common organizational problems:

- Does the introduction have all the correct components: attention-getter, topic statement, credibility, and preview?
- Does the conclusion include a summary of main points and end with a clincher?
- Does the speech have transitions and signposts at each place where they are needed?
- Is research properly cited at each place where you refer to it in your outline? If required, is the bibliography in the proper form?

Review the Assignment (If Applicable). If the speech is for a class assignment, review the assignment description. Be certain that you are fulfilling all requirements. For example, your instructor may require a certain number of research sources, a specific kind of informative speech (such as a speech to demonstrate), or the use of visual aids.

Review the Speech Length. Make sure you know how long it will take you to deliver your informative speech. Read your outline aloud, and time yourself. For a classroom informative speech, your instructor probably will give you a maximum (and possibly a minimum) speech time. If you are delivering a speech outside of class, it is important for the length of your speech to meet the audience's expectations. If you need to make cuts or additions, use your Speech Grid as a starting place, and make sure that these changes do not affect your main informative message.

Get Feedback from Other People. Ask any willing friends, relatives, or classmates to read your outline. Here are several issues that such reviewers can address:

- Reviewers can tell you whether any of your points seem difficult to understand. Ideas that make sense to you may be unclear to another person. Do your main points suffice for the topic? Do you need to add detail? an extra step? more explanation?
- Reviewers can offer feedback about your visual aids. Are they accomplishing their purpose? Ask a reviewer to sit as far away from your visual aid as your audience will be, and check to see whether the aid is the right size.
- Reviewers can help you check for cultural understanding. If you will be speaking to a culturally diverse audience, you might benefit from asking people representing those cultures to review your outline.

As you get feedback from other people, try not to be defensive. Their constructive feedback and advice will help make your speech as strong as possible when the time comes to deliver it.

Revise Your Outline. After you and others have reviewed the content, structure, and length of your informative speech, revise your outline as needed:

1. Enhance the content of your speech by adding points, research, or visual aids.
2. Improve your word choice if parts of the speech are difficult to understand.
3. Revise the structure of your speech by adding transitions or signposts, and provide any elements missing from your introduction and conclusion.
4. Fit your speech into the allotted time for delivery by adding, deleting, or changing segments as necessary.

● *Prepare for Extemporaneous Delivery*

Practice with Your Outline. After you revise your outline, it is time to practice and polish your delivery. Begin by reading your outline orally several times, until your speech becomes so familiar that you can reduce your dependence on the outline. As you practice, try to explain subpoints in your own words, looking at your outline only if you are quoting sources directly or are losing your train of thought. Do not try to memorize your speech word-for-word. Your goal is to become comfortable delivering your speech from limited notes.

Prepare a Condensed Outline for Speaking.   After you practice your informative speech several times and are feeling confident that you can remember the order and content of your main points, begin preparing briefer notes (on note cards or on a limited number of pages) that you will use when you actually deliver the speech. Your condensed speech outline should include your main points and major subpoints. In this outline, the subpoints do not need to be expressed in complete sentences. Write just enough to help you remember the ideas you want to cover. Trust yourself to explain each subpoint without reading the words from your notes. Include direct quotations word-for-word so you will quote the source accurately.

For more on speaking from an outline, see page 289.

Besides putting the main points and subpoints into your notes, you may want to write delivery reminders on the cards as well. If you had difficulty with some aspect of delivery (such as eye contact or rate of delivery) in previous speeches, or if you had a problem while practicing, you want to be certain to avoid that problem during your speech. At the top of your note cards, you might write "slow down" or "don't block visual aid!" Print such reminders in large letters and in a color different from the color of your speech notes.

Practice the speech, using only the condensed notes. If possible, practice with a friend who can tell you whether aspects of your delivery need improvement. Are you making any ineffective gestures? Are you speaking too fast? Are you making eye contact with the audience? You will become increasingly comfortable speaking with the brief outline, and soon you will be able to speak extemporaneously to your audience.

5. Delivering Your Speech

The final step in preparing your informative speech is to present it to your audience. Before doing that, however, you can do a number of things to ensure that your delivery is effective.

Use your CD-ROM to view examples of delivery in an informative speech. Go to the "Example" button in "Step 5 Delivery/Deliver Your Speech." CD-ROM: Interactive Speech Guides/Informative Speech

● Minimize Speech Anxiety

Don't be discouraged if you are feeling apprehensive about actually presenting your informative speech. Many speakers must deliver more than a few speeches before they begin to gain confidence about public speaking.

If you experience high communication apprehension generally (*trait* anxiety) and have not sought help, look into assistance before delivering your informative speech. If you are uncomfortable about asking for help, recall that you may be able to find out about programs through a school or department Web site. You can e-mail or leave a note for your instructor if you feel more comfortable asking in writing.

To review state and trait anxiety, see page 20.

Anticipating an informative speech may cause you considerable *state* anxiety if your topic is controversial or you fear that your audience may not be interested. Remember that your anxiety will always be highest at the outset of your informative speech. During the introduction, look for friendly faces and begin your eye contact with them. Try to smile at your audience and incorporate humor if it is appropriate to the topic and you feel comfortable with it. When you establish credibility, emphasize common ground. Make clear your respect for all audience members.

Careful preparation is one way to reduce your anxiety. Use the checklist at the end of this chapter to be sure that you have taken the necessary steps. Show your outline to your instructor to reassure yourself that you are on the right track or to learn whether there are any changes that would strengthen your speech. Review the techniques for reducing anxiety that we described in Chapter 1, such as relaxation, visualization, and taking good care of yourself. Use the ones that are most helpful to you.

Remember that it is normal to experience some nervousness about delivering a speech. Also, some anxiety is positive. If you are overconfident, you may not manage or deliver the speech to the best of your ability. Never assume that a lack of nervousness means you need not carefully prepare.

For more on reducing speech anxiety, see page 21.

● *Deliver Your Informative Speech*

To review delivery skills, see Chapter 11.

Here are some reminders for effective delivery of an informative speech:

- *Begin your speech with confidence.* When it is time for you to speak, walk to the front of the room with confidence. Do not say anything that would convey a lack of conviction or preparation.

- *Use vocal variety to emphasize points.* When you come to a key point, vocal variety makes the point stand out to the audience. You can achieve variety by increasing your volume. You also can achieve it by slowing your rate of delivery slightly, reducing the volume, or altering your tone to use inflection in your voice.

- *Maintain eye contact with the audience.* Look up from your notes and at audience members as you deliver your speech. Your audience may perceive a lack of eye contact as a sign that you are not credible. A speech read from a manuscript will sound "canned" or packaged and become less engaging for the audience.

> **TIP**
>
> *Remember to make extended eye contact with individual members and to shift your gaze around the room.*

- *Use effective body language.* If you fail to gesture, or if you display distracting mannerisms, you will appear nervous. This nervousness may be interpreted as a lack of confidence in your message, undermining your credibility. Use natural gestures and controlled movement to reinforce your message.

Audiovisual aids are the subject of Chapter 12.

- *Return to your seat confidently.* When you are finished with your informative speech, gather your audiovisual aids (if any) and return to your seat in a calm, professional manner. Never assume that you gave a poor speech. If you think this about your informative speech, you will project this negative assessment nonverbally to your audience.

● *Learn from Your Informative Speech*

Use each speech you present as an opportunity to develop your public speaking ability. In the classroom, there is usually an opportunity for audience members to give you feedback and ask questions. Use interactive listening to understand your classmates' comments. Jot down their ideas for later reference. You are also likely to receive oral and written comments from your instructor. When it is appropriate (*not* during other people's speeches), write down your own thoughts about your speech and ideas for self-improvement.

For more on interactive listening, see page 77.

Set your ideas and your feedback aside for a day or two. Then look at your own reaction to your speech as well as the feedback you received. Make notes about changes you would like to make in the preparation or delivery of future speeches, and review them before you begin to plan your next speech.

For speech evaluation forms you can use to evaluate your speech, see pages 82–84.

Summary

Informative speaking is an important part of everyone's daily life. Explaining, describing, and demonstrating will often be required of you in classes on campus or later in your career and in your community. Effective informative speaking is the result of a speaker's willingness to work hard and be open-minded. It takes carefully constructed organization that is appropriate for the audience and consistent with the principles of ethical communication.

This Speech Guide presented a five-step process to follow when you are writing an informative speech. The steps are summarized in the checklist (include any additional steps that your instructor advises or assigns). If you follow these guidelines, you will become a capable informative speaker who earns respect and has influence with any audience.

Checklist

INVENTING YOUR INFORMATIVE SPEECH

Analyze Your Audience

____ Analyze your audience, and record the analysis on a Speech Grid (p. 388)

____ Decide whether to explain, describe, or demonstrate (p. 389)

Select and Refine Your Topic

____ Select your topic (p. 389)

____ Draft a working topic statement and specific purpose (p. 391)

Generate Ideas to Support Your Topic Statement

____ Brainstorm supporting ideas (p. 391)

____ Research your topic (p. 392)

Select the Best Ideas to Support Your Topic Statement

____ Ethical concerns (p. 394)

____ Audience analysis (p. 394)

ORGANIZING YOUR INFORMATIVE SPEECH

Outline the Body

____ Select and organize main points (p. 395)

____ Develop and outline subpoints, using ethos, logos, and pathos (p. 396)

Outline the Introduction and Conclusion

____ Draft an introduction containing attention-getter, topic statement, connection with the audience, credibility, and preview (p. 396)

____ Draft a conclusion containing a summary and clincher (p. 397)

Incorporate Transitions and Signposts

____ Use transitions to connect main points and major sections of the speech (p. 397)

____ Use signposts to highlight the organization of your speech (p. 398)

USING EFFECTIVE STYLE IN YOUR INFORMATIVE SPEECH

____ Review and revise the language used in your outline to ensure you are presenting ideas in an interesting manner, using understandable words, avoiding long and difficult sentences, accurately stating points, and avoiding biased language (p. 398)

REFINING AND PRACTICING YOUR INFORMATIVE SPEECH

____ Review and revise your outline from a critical perspective (p. 399)

____ Plan and practice extemporaneous delivery (p. 400)

DELIVERING YOUR INFORMATIVE SPEECH

____ Minimize speech anxiety (p. 401)

____ Follow delivery tips: Speak with conviction. Use vocal variety. Maintain eye contact. Use effective body language along with other appropriate delivery practices (p. 402)

____ Learn for your next speech by actively listening to feedback and analyzing your own speech (p. 403)

15 Guide to Persuasive Speaking

The ability to persuade your audience is an important talent to acquire. If you want to get a new policy adopted on campus, to advance in your career, or to influence members of your community, you must be able to convince other people to agree with you. Sometimes, you can obtain your goals only by motivating individuals who do not see an issue as you do to change their minds.

In Chapter 15 we examine the process of persuasive speaking and give you the opportunity to read three persuasive speeches, two delivered in the classroom and one in the community. We analyze key features of each speech and provide suggestions you can use to develop persuasive speeches. We also review the key features of persuasive speeches in general. Then we take you through a five-step process for preparing your own persuasive speech, incorporating the principles of public speaking that have been developed in Part One of this text. The five steps are the same for any prepared speech, but the decisions you make during each step are influenced by the fact that your rhetorical purpose is persuasive.

In a persuasive speech, your objective is to influence audience members' attitudes or actions. You want to encourage listeners to adopt a favorable attitude toward your position on an issue, or you want to strengthen their already favorable attitude. You also may ask them to take action in support of that position.

How do you persuade an audience? Consider a time when someone you knew convinced you to change your mind. Chances are good that the person who convinced you possessed many of these qualities:

- The person was likable and seemed trustworthy. You believed that he or she was knowledgeable about the subject under consideration.

- The person seemed sensitive to your concerns. He or she showed respect for you and did not make you feel as if you were being manipulated.

- The person gave you good reasons to change your mind. If you were uncertain about whether a statement was true, acceptable proof was provided.

- The person left a favorable impression. You came to appreciate a different perspective on the issue, and, your emotions were touched.

What is the content of a speech when a communicator is attempting to persuade an audience? In the next section are three persuasive speeches. As you read each one, determine what the speaker's thesis is, and list the main points that each speaker develops to support his or her thesis. How convincing are these reasons to you? Which speaker do you find most convincing?

For sample persuasive speeches, see pages 408, 414, and 420.

For more on the thesis of a persuasive speech, see page 134.

Speeches

Anna Martinez selected student credit card debt as the topic of her persuasive speech. At first she planned to take the position that students should not use credit cards because the costs outweigh the benefits. However, her audience analysis

View "'Extra Credit' You Can Live Without" by Anna Martinez. CD-ROM: Video Theater, Full Speeches

Anna Martinez's speech is available in outline format on page 513. Her completed Speech Grid is on page 522.

indicated that many of her listeners enjoy the flexibility that credit cards provide and a majority carry balances on their credit card accounts. To adapt her topic to this audience, which might be hostile to a proposal to stop using credit cards altogether, Martinez considered solutions that she hoped would fall within the audience's latitude of acceptance—the range of positions on an issue that the target audience could be persuaded to accept.

As you read Anna Martinez's speech, consider whether she adapted her speech message well to an audience of committed credit card users. Also reflect on other important principles of public speaking, such as the organization of the speech and use of evidence.

"Extra Credit" You Can Live Without

BY ANNA MARTINEZ

There is a dangerous product on our campus. It is marketed on tables outside the student union and advertised on the bulletin board in this classroom. Based on my audience survey, it is likely that most of you have this product in your possession right now. By the end of my speech, this product may be costing you more than it is right now. The dangerous product is credit cards.

Today, I would like to discuss the problems created by college students' credit cards and hopefully persuade you to be a careful credit card consumer. If your credit card situation is anything like mine—and over two-thirds of this class indicated that they are currently carrying a balance on one or more cards—take note: you *can* save money!

My husband and I paid for our own wedding last summer. More accurately, we used our credit cards to charge many of our wedding expenses. And thanks to Visa, we are still paying for our wedding every month! We have saved money with some of the suggestions I will present today, and you can do the same.

To that end, let's cover some of the problems created by students' credit card debt, then analyze causes of the problem, and finally consider steps you can take to be a careful credit card consumer.

We'll start with a look at the problems created by these "hazardous products."

Credit card debt on campus is a significant and growing problem.

Many students have credit card debts. This claim is supported by the analysis of Alan Blair, director of credit management for the New England Educational Loan Marketing Corporation, whose 1998 report on the corporation's Web site stated that "67% of undergraduates who have applied for their student loans have credit cards. 14% have balances between $3,000 and $7,000 and 10% have balances over $7,000." Visa must not be the only card they will ever need because Mr. Blair reported that 27 percent of undergraduates have four or more cards.

There must be plenty of businesses that "do take American Express" (and any other card). Sharon Gerrie, staff writer for the *Las Vegas Business Press,* September 4, 1998, reported a National Center for Financial Education survey indicating an average undergraduate credit card debt of $2,226 in 1997. If you are not sure how your balances compare, you are not alone. This study found that 20 percent did not know how much credit card debt they were accumulating each month.

High credit card debt can change your life for the worse. *Business Week,* March 15, 1999 (author unavailable), provided an example of how high debt can change a college student's life for the worse. Jason Britton, a senior at Georgetown University, accumulated $21,000 in debt over four years on sixteen cards! Jason reports that "when I first started, my attitude was 'I'll get a job after college to pay off all my debt.'" Then he realized that he was in a hole because he could not meet minimum monthly payments. He had to obtain financial assistance from his parents and now works three part-time jobs.

You probably do not owe $20,000 on your credit cards, but even smaller balances take their toll. Robert Frick, associate editor for *Kiplinger's Personal Finance Magazine,* March 1997, states that if you make the minimum payments on a $500 balance at an 18 percent interest rate, it will take over seven years to pay off the loan and cost $365 in interest.

High credit card debt can also haunt your finances after you graduate. Most of you carry student loans. Dr. Sandy Blum, professor of economics at Skidmore, in a February 1998 report on the New England Educational Loan Corporation Web site, notes that the average percentage of borrowers' monthly income that goes to student loan payment is 12 percent.

When you put credit card debt on top of loan debt, rent, utilities, food, the payment on that new car you want to buy, family expenses, etc., the toll can be heavy. Alan Blair's previously cited 1998 report notes serious consequences for students who cannot balance monthy expenses and debts, including "poor credit ratings, inability to apply for car loans or a mortgage, collection activity, and at worst, a bankruptcy filing."

Don't let this happen to you. After all that hard work earning a degree and finally landing a job where you don't have to wear a plastic name tag and induce people to get "fries with that order," the last thing any of us needs is to be spending our hard-earned money paying off debt, being turned down for loans, or, worse yet, being harassed by collection agencies.

Credit card debt is hazardous to students' financial health, so why are these debts piling up? Let's move on to the causes of this problem.

The reality is that credit card issuers want and aggressively seek the business of students like ourselves.

Card issuers hope to build a long-term relationship with new customers. According to the previously cited March 1997 article by Robert Frick, "It may seem foolhardy to [give] a $500 credit line to someone who has no income or credit history. But on college campuses the practice has proved to be profitable for credit card issuers eager to get their cards into the hands of young consumers before their competitors do. It's well worth their effort: three in four students keep their first credit card for 15 years or longer."

Card issuers actually troll for customers on campus because student business is profitable. Daniel Eisenberg, writer of the column "Your Money" for *Time* magazine, September 28, 1998, notes that "college students are suckers for free stuff, and many are collecting extra credit cards and heavier debts as a result." Eisenberg goes on to note that "according to a U.S. Public Interest Research Group survey out last week, students who sign up for cards at campus tables in return for 'gifts' typically carry higher unpaid balances than do other students. Visa says students generally pay bills faster than [other] cardholders."

Companies use "sucker rates" to induce students to apply for credit. *Business Week,* March 15, 1999, wrote "credit card marketers may advertise a low annual percentage rate but it often jumps substantially after three to nine months. First USA's student Visa has a 9.9% introductory rate that soars to 17.99% after five months. Teaser rates aren't unique to student cards, but a 1998 study by the Washington based U.S. Public Interest Research Group found that 26% of college students found them misleading."

So it appears that credit card companies will not stop demanding student business any time soon. What can we do about it?

My proposed solution is to be a careful credit card consumer. Why not get rid of your credit cards before it's too late? Here is my Master-Card and a good pair of scissors. I am going to cut this card in half. [Speaker cuts the card in half.] I have brought a bag of scissors; why don't you get out your cards and do the same? All right, maybe you won't go for that solution. My survey indicated that most of you enjoy the flexibility in spending that credit cards provide. I have a confession to make—that was an expired card that I just cut. I am not cutting my new MasterCard either.

So here are some other ways you should be credit card smart. One practice is to shop carefully for the best credit card rate. The companies that are not spending their money giving away pizzas and T-shirts on campus may be able to offer you a better deal.

A second solution is to read the fine print on credit card applications to learn what your actual interest rate will be. Alison Barros, a staff writer for the Lane Community College *Torch,* October 29, 1998, quoted Jonathan Woolworth, consumer protection director for the Oregon Public Interest Research Group, who wrote that "students need to read the fine print and find out how long those low interest rates last. Rates that are as low as 3% can jump to 18% within three months, and the credit card company doesn't want the student to know that."

Here is an example of the fine print on an ad that begins at 1.9 percent and soon rises. [Display the visual aid on p. 411.] If you read the fine print, you note that the rate can rise to more than 20 percent.

Third, even if you can only make the minimum payment on your cards, pay your bills on time. Robert Frick's previously cited 1997 *Kiplinger's Personal Finance Magazine* advises "a strong credit history can mean lower rates on loans and brownie points with employers, landlords, and insurance companies. The best way to build good credit is to use the card, ideally making several small transactions each month and then paying the bill on time or even early." Take responsibility to find out when your bills are due. Credit card companies are even less tolerant of excuses for lateness than speech instructors! *Business Week,* March 15, 1999, cautions that "because students move often and may

1.9% A.P.R.*

**Fill out the application below and say NO
to high interest rates forever!**

*Credit card approval contingent on verification of income, employment, and good credit standing. 1.9% offer is an introductory rate. After three months, the A.P.R. will change to 21.9%. If you fail to meet a payment deadline, or your total indebtedness on all credit cards increases by more than $5,000, your A.P.R. will become 26.9%.

not get their mail forwarded quickly, bills can get lost. Then the students fall prey to late payment fees."

Finally, you can keep money in your pocket and out of the credit card company's by paying attention to your credit report. If any agencies are "talking trash" about you with inaccurate information, be sure to have it corrected. Tess Van Duvall, a debt management consultant at Emory University, advised in the September 1997 *USA Today* magazine, "If there are errors on your credit report, they need to be corrected, because it can affect your credit rating and even keep you from getting lower interest rate loans." She goes on to note that "one 30-day late payment can make a difference in your loan interest rate."

To sum up these solutions, even if you do not want to stop using credit cards, there are many ways to be a careful credit card consumer. Shop for a good rate and be careful to read the fine print so you know what the rate really is. Know what you owe and take the responsibility to make payments on time.

This morning, we have learned about a hazardous product on campus—credit cards. We have noted the problem of high student credit card debt, analyzed some of the causes of this problem, and considered several methods for being a careful credit card consumer.

If an instructor offers you a chance for extra credit in his or her class, take advantage of the opportunity. But when a credit card issuer offers you a free T-shirt or phone card if you will sign up for their extra credit, just say no. When you pay off a credit card with a 19.9 percent interest rate, that "free T-shirt" could turn out to be the most expensive clothing you will ever buy.

● *Analyzing the Characteristics of Persuasive Speeches*

For more on persuasive strategies, see page 243.

Persuasive Strategies. Anna Martinez uses several means of persuasion discussed in this text. She uses an appeal to pathos by presenting the example of a student at Georgetown University who is working three part-time jobs to pay off credit card debt. This anecdote, showing what happened to a real student, is likely to be more compelling to a student audience than would a story about a person who graduated years ago. Martinez combines this example with logos by presenting statistics about the cost of debt to students in general. This combination of statistics with a specific example is likely to make her argument more persuasive than either one standing alone.

Another appeal to pathos occurs when Martinez asks audience members to imagine how they would feel if "after all that hard work earning a degree," they had to spend their hard-earned money paying back debts, were turned down for credit, or suffered harassment from collection agencies. Do you think this appeal to fear is likely to seem realistic to her audience?

Audience Adaptation. Audience analysis and adaptation are central to effective persuasion. One way Martinez adapted was by tailoring her speech to a potentially hostile audience—an audience in which many members would be opposed to her thesis. Her audience analysis indicated that most listeners regularly use credit cards and enjoy the flexibility that they provide. Originally, she had planned to argue that listeners should take aggressive actions such as ending their reliance on credit cards. If she had faced a more friendly audience—an audience in which most members would agree with her thesis and already were looking for ways to cut back on card use—this message could have been effective. However, her analysis suggested that not using credit cards probably fell outside the range of options that most members of her audience would consider. Therefore, she proposed a more effective use of credit cards rather than ending card use. How well do you think these solutions were adapted to the attitudes of her audience?

A second use of audience adaptation was to include the audience in the solution. There have been many proposals for government action to solve the problems of credit cards, and Martinez listed several on her Speech Grid. She made her speech relevant for audience members by focusing on actions that they themselves could take, rather than on broad solutions that the government could adopt.

Ethical Principles. Martinez faced an ethical decision when selecting arguments to use in her speech. One of her research sources noted that large credit card debts were forcing college graduates to delay purchasing a home or having children. This finding appeared to be a very persuasive argument, and she recorded it on her grid. However, a different research source made a more careful analysis of the same data and concluded that few students really delayed those decisions because of credit card debt. The audience's ability to make a good decision would have been undermined had Martinez used the argument that credit cards were delaying home buying and childbearing. To make that argument persuasively, she would have needed to omit important facts, so she crossed that claim off her grid.

An ethical persuader contributes to the audience's ability to make a good decision (see p. 58).

The first proposed solution in Anna Martinez's speech was to "get rid of your credit cards before it is too late." She accompanied that suggestion with a visual aid, a credit card that she cut in half. This is an example of the door-in-the-face strategy, because the speaker began with an action the audience was unlikely to accept and followed it up with steps that the audience would be more willing to take. Do you think that it was wrong to create the impression that the speaker was cutting a valid credit card, when in fact, it had expired? Would this strategy be more problematic if the speaker did not disclose that the card she had cut had expired?

For more on the door-in-the-face strategy, see page 247.

Organization.   Anna Martinez structured the body of her speech into a problem-cause-solution format, one of the typical patterns for persuasive speeches on a policy issue. She included a transition from the introduction to the body of her speech (*"We'll start with* a look at" on p. 408), and she provided transitions between each main point.

Notice her use of an internal summary after she discusses her four solutions. This device helps the audience to remember the actions she wants them to take.

For more on formats of persuasive speeches, see pages 186 and 248; for internal summaries, see page 191.

Evidence.   Speakers need to use evidence to back up the claims they are making, particularly when they are attempting to persuade an audience. Anna Martinez used thirteen references to evidence, taken from eight different sources, to support the points she was making. Which of her evidence sources do you find most credible? Which do you find least credible? Do you think she needed more evidence to prove any of the points she wanted to make?

Martinez consistently cited the author, his or her qualifications, the research source, and the date of her evidence. She cited this information immediately *before* presenting the evidence, as every speaker should.

● *Planning Your Persuasive Speech*

Anna Martinez made an appropriate ethical decision when planning her speech. She could have made a persuasive argument that high credit card debt will force students to postpone important decisions after graduation, and she could have supported that argument with evidence. But, instead, she rejected that claim. She took seriously the ethical duty to research carefully, and after surveying all of her research, she was not confident that this argument was true. When you prepare your persuasive speech, remember the importance of checking the arguments on your Speech Grid to ensure that they are ethically sound.

Martinez's speech also highlighted the use of audience adaptation. Her analysis indicated that the recommendation to pay off credit card debt and curtail card use in the future would be outside the latitude of acceptance of many audience members. Therefore, she revised her thesis and advocated more careful use of credit cards, without asking listeners to give up their cards. To be effective in persuasive speaking, you need to analyze your audience. Draft a thesis that represents a point of view you believe in—but one that is realistic given the attitudes of the people you are addressing.

Finally, when drafting a persuasive speech, be certain that your word choice is appropriate for your audience. Because of the context of her

For more on appropriate style, see page 276.

speech, Martinez's style was relatively informal. Martinez was speaking to an audience of her peers. She included jokes that college students would understand, along with contemporary expressions such as "talking trash" and creative wording such as "troll." Speaking to an audience of her equals, she did not want to create the impression that she felt superior to them. Her word choice would need to change if she were speaking in a different context. For example, if she were the youngest person in the room, discussing credit card debt at a financial planning seminar, her language would need to be more formal: she would need to build ethos by demonstrating a highly professional demeanor.

View "Without Liberty and Justice for All" by Enrique Morales. CD-ROM: Video Theater, Full Speeches

Enrique Morales's speech is available in key-word outline format on page 517.

Enrique Morales presented this speech to his speech class during the fall 1999 semester. He selected the topic of racially biased police traffic stops because he had been in this situation and deeply resented the way he was treated. Morales knew that several classmates had been stopped by the police without being issued a warning or citation for any offense. Only four out of twenty-two students answered "yes" to the question "Do the police need more power to enforce traffic laws?" whereas seventeen students agreed that "more needed to be done to reduce discrimination by law enforcement officers." Therefore he prepared a speech for a friendly audience.

Without Liberty and Justice for All

BY ENRIQUE MORALES

My friend received a brand new BMW from his parents as a gift for his nineteenth birthday. Like any teenager, he wanted to show off his car. So he called myself and two other friends to take out his new car and we went to a local mall. Later, we left the mall, got into the car, and started to leave. The next thing you know, we were surrounded by cops and forced out of the car by gunpoint. Now you may be asking, "Did we steal something from the mall?" No. Did we cause trouble in the mall? No. Apparently what happened was that the mall was having a problem with cars being stolen and the description they had was that it was being done by four Hispanic males. Seeing that we were four Hispanics in a brand new BMW, they made the connection that it was us. We became victims of a common police practice known as racial profiling, or driving while black or brown. Once they checked my friend's paperwork and saw that the car belonged to him, they apologized several times. But if they were truly sorry, they would not let it happen again.

We should not let these violations happen again . . . and again and again. Today, I would like to discuss steps that need to be taken to promote color-blind policing.

Twice, I have been pulled over and dismissed without any explanation after the police checked my license and registration. And my research has indicated that the incidents I am discussing are not atypical for America's minorities.

Eleven members of this class are members of minority groups. And minorities are not the only victims. Our classmate, David, who has long hair and drives an old Volkswagen van, indicated that he has been pulled over without explanation, just like me. Any starving student driving an old car is at risk for experiencing the joy of being treated guilty until proven innocent.

My analysis of this topic will begin with evidence that racial profiling is a nationwide problem. Next, I will propose remedies for this evil and show how reforms can be effective. Finally, I will challenge you to take an active role in solving this problem.

To begin, the problem of racial profiling needs fixing.

Racial profiling is a nationwide problem. Temple University professor of psychology John Lanbreth found that in New Jersey, blacks are almost five times more likely to be stopped on the New Jersey Turnpike than others. In Maryland, 71.3 percent of those searched by state police on Interstate 95 were black.

This pattern is corroborated by Joseph McNamara, former police chief in San Jose, who notes on the Intellectual Capital.com *Issue of the Week,* June 3, 1999, "unfortunately, police are more suspicious of people of color. . . . Police are under pressure to produce good arrest statistics, thus they are tempted to cut corners by employing racial profiling."

Randy Dotinga, an *APBnews.com* West Coast correspondent, November 15, 2000, reports that Gary Kaufman, a psychologist with the Michigan State Police who interviewed 131 police officers from around the country, concluded that "racial profiling does exist. It is clearly a public perception and a reality."

Racial profiling is unconscionable. One harm of racial profiling is the discriminatory treatment it inflicts on innocent citizens. White House aides Bob Nash and Janice Kearney, who were breaking no laws when they were stopped by police looking for a black man in a stolen sport utility vehicle, explained in *Jet Magazine,* October 16, 2000, that "until that moment, we had an intellectual understanding of the bogus crime of 'Driving While Black.' But, in a few terrifying moments, we felt it more deeply and more personally than any words could ever convey."

My experience with racial profiling is similar. After checking my registration, one of the officers who pulled me over last May said, "We thought you were someone else. Sorry about that." I wanted to vent my anger at the police officer, but he had the handcuffs and weapons so I kept my thoughts to myself. Whatever happened to "liberty and justice for all"?

A second problem is that racial profiling undermines confidence in the police. From the Statistical Assessment Service, a nonpartisan, nonprofit research organization, in *VitalSTATS,* April 1999, we find that "most blacks who are stopped on suspicion (like most males) will be innocent people. And the more innocent people within a given group who are treated as suspect, the more all members of the group will suspect discriminatory motives on the part of the police." David Cole, professor of law at Georgetown, indicated in *seattletimes.com,* May 22, 1999, that "if you start using race as a proxy for suspicion . . . you also create a great deal of enmity, and it undermines law enforcement when people see the police as their enemy." Many parents teach their children that "police officers are your friend." But with friends like these, who needs enemies?

Now that we have seen the need to curtail racial profiling, let's turn our attention to some solutions.

There are several treatments for reducing this ill. One remedy is that the police should keep accurate records of those they stop, enabling community members to act where needed. In Houston, they are trying not to have a problem because, according to Chris Fletcher of the Associated Press, in the *Seattle Times,* August 12, 1999, officers must enter information on the race, age, and gender of all people they stop or arrest into their patrol car computers. The reports will be placed in a database for review. Confirmed racial profiling can result in dismissal or criminal charges. Fletcher notes that "several patrolmen's associations and civil rights groups applauded the new policies."

The records can then provide a basis for action. In an Amnesty International Report on *Race, Rights, and Police Brutality,* September 1999, Attorney General Janet Reno's proposal to establish early warning systems to identify officers who engage in misconduct and provide for independent review of each department's performance is recognized as an important step.

Another step to curing the disease is greater hiring of minority officers. A study by John Donohue III of Stanford Law School and Steven Levitt of the University of Chicago, reported in *Business Week,* May 3, 1999, found that "the higher the share of police officers of a particular race in a neighborhood dominated by the same race, the lower the number of arrests [of people of that race] in the neighborhood." The article concludes that "own race policing appears to pay off by reducing both arrests and property crime—presumably because it leads to fewer false arrests and greater deterrence."

A third remedy, diversity training, is a way to promote unbiased policing across all ethnic groups. George Rice, a ten-year Drug Enforcement Agency agent now working on community policing in the nonprofit sector, noted in *Horizon Magazine,* December 1999: "for law enforcement personnel, training and experience are critical. . . . Like everyone else, police must unlearn this bias and judge people based on their actions alone." Sergeant Neal Griffin of the Escondido, California, Police Department wrote in *Police Chief Magazine,* 1997, that "when properly structured, with an eye towards applicability and relevance, diversity training can provide officers with information that makes them more effective in cross-cultural contacts, and better prepared as public servants in a pluralistic society."

What would it be like if racial profiling was alleviated? Compare this tale of two Americas and imagine where you would want to live.

The first America tolerates racial profiling. If you have ever been stopped for driving while black or brown or having a Grateful Dead sticker on your car, remember how it felt. If you have never been a victim of racial profiling, consider how you would feel about visiting a country where Americans are routinely stopped by the police more often than native citizens are. Such practices in a foreign land would be outrageous, so how can any of us accept an America where innocent citizens are treated like criminals by the police who are sworn to protect them?

Now imagine if you will, a second America, where race plays no role in determining traffic stops. According to North Carolina senator Frank Ballance Jr., in *State Legislatures,* September 1999, "no person in this state or this country should ever have to worry about being pulled over by the police because of the color of their skin." I know I would prefer this second America, wouldn't you?

This more just America will not happen overnight. In the meantime, let's consider what steps you can take in a racial profiling situation.

If you are a driver or passenger in a car that is stopped, and you suspect racial profiling, there are several actions you should take. George Rice, the ten-year Drug Enforcement Agency agent whom I previously cited, advises:

1. You do not have to answer an officer's questions, but you must show your driver's license, registration, and proof of insurance.

2. What you say to police can be used against you, and it can give officers an excuse to arrest you, especially if you are disrespectful to an officer.

3. Ask for a lawyer immediately if you're arrested.

4. Do not complain on the scene or tell the police they're wrong or that you're going to file a complaint. Instead, remember officers' badge and patrol car numbers, and immediately afterward write down everything you remember. If any witnesses are available, get their names and telephone numbers. If you feel your rights have been violated, file a written complaint with the police department's internal affairs board or civilian complaint board.

Hopefully, none of you will need to follow these steps, because you will never be victimized by the problem I have discussed today, racial profiling.

We have seen that the problem is widespread and that actions such as better records of traffic stops and diversity training can be taken to promote an America where driving while black or brown is no longer a crime. Finally, you can make a difference if you are a victim of racial profiling if you do the right thing.

The International Association of Police Chiefs 1999 resolution "Condemning Racial and Ethnic Profiling in Traffic Stops" calls on all law enforcement agencies to ensure that racial- or ethnic-based traffic stops are not being employed and that all citizens are treated with the utmost courtesy and respect when they encounter police officers. This principle would erase the crime of driving while black or brown from American criminal law.

Analyzing the Characteristics of Persuasive Speeches

Audience Adaptation. Enrique Morales surveyed his classmates and learned that he had a friendly audience. When addressing a supportive audience, a speaker can have ambitious goals, and Morales advocated government policies and individual action to reduce racial profiling. How would you have advised him to adapt his message if the audience were hostile? What if many members were apathetic—that is, having no strong position on the speaker's thesis and being not very interested in the subject of the speech?

Evidence and Reasoning. Morales used various types of evidence to support his claim that racial profiling is occurring. In the introduction, he used a vivid example detailing his own experience. Such an example can be persuasive. However, a single example does not prove a nationwide trend. This type of reasoning gives rise to a hasty generalization fallacy. A speaker should not base a general conclusion on a limited number of examples. Therefore, Morales also used evidence from three different sources to back up his claim. One of his sources was a former police chief, and another was a police psychologist. Why do you think he used these sources?

Morales used signposts well to indicate that he was about to cite research, such as "reports that" (p. 415) and "indicated in" (p. 415). These signposts cue the reader that evidence is to follow. Note also that he used quotation marks when he directly quoted from one of his sources.

Style. Enrique Morales's speech contains several examples of creative word choice. This colorful language helps to make his presentation memorable and persuasive. Compare the following examples of his word choice to ordinary language describing the same concept:

For more on the effective use of language, see page 272.

Morales's Speech	Ordinary Language
"We should not let these violations happen again…and again and again."	Let's stop these violations from happening.
"I wanted to vent my anger at the police officer, but he had the handcuffs and weapons so I kept my thoughts to myself."	I was unhappy with the police officer, but he had all the power so I remained quiet.
"Whatever happened to 'liberty and justice for all'?"	This is inconsistent with the wording of the Pledge of Allegiance.
"How can any of us accept an America where innocent citizens are treated like criminals by the police who are sworn to protect them?"	In the United States, the police are sworn to protect the rights of law-abiding citizens.

For more on the motivated-sequence pattern, see page 249.

Organization. Morales used a motivated-sequence format. Notice how he gained the audience's *attention* at the outset with the narrative about his experience with the police. He followed that account with the *need* for racial profiling to end, in main point one, and in main point two he provided three solutions for *satisfaction* of that need. Main point three called for audience *visualization,* by contrasting an America that tolerates racial profiling with an America where race plays no role in traffic stops. Morales also asked audience members who had been stopped to remember the experience, and he asked those who had not been stopped to imagine how they would feel if they were victims of police discrimination in a foreign land merely because they were Americans. Finally, he advocated *action,* providing evidence of how audience members should respond if they are in a racial profiling situation.

● *Planning Your Persuasive Speech*

Racial profiling is a very important issue for Enrique Morales. Having been stopped by the police for no apparent reason, he had direct personal involvement with the topic. He wanted to make classmates more aware of racial profiling and provide them with reasoned action that they could take if they were the victims of it. When you select your speech topics, look for issues that you feel strongly about. If you have little enthusiasm for a subject, it will be difficult to build audience interest in your speech.

Morales used audience analysis to decide to approach the racial profiling issue. Because audience members were friendly, he could assume that they would agree with him about the significance of this problem and the need for action to reduce it. He could emphasize action that society and individual audience members should take. If his research had revealed that many classmates believed that racial profiling was rare, and that the police needed more latitude to arrest suspicious persons, he might have reconsidered his specific purpose. He might simply have asked classmates to carefully consider the evidence that racial profiling exists and then advocated limited action. When you plan your persuasive speech, determine where the audience stands on your issue. Then you can determine the most appropriate objective for your speech.

Morales's thesis addressed a policy issue. He structured his speech in a motivated-sequence pattern because he wanted to focus on the need for action to solve the problem he addressed. When you prepare your persuasive speech, understand whether your thesis addresses a fact, a value, or a policy question. Be certain that the organizational pattern you choose is appropriate for the thesis you are advocating and that it is the best one for presenting your viewpoint to the audience.

This address provides an example of a persuasive speech delivered outside the classroom environment by an experienced speaker in the community. Deval Patrick addressed the Organization of Chinese Americans in Los Angeles on July 8, 1994. At the time of this speech, he was serving as an assistant attorney general in the Civil Rights Division of the U.S. Justice Department. In his speech he discussed hate crimes, including those directed at Asian Americans, and he explained the role of his office in combating acts of prejudice.

As you read this speech, compare Deval Patrick's approach to persuasive speaking to the approaches of Anna Martinez and Enrique Morales in their classroom speeches.

The Rise in Hate Crime: Anti-Immigration Policy

BY DEVAL PATRICK

Thank you so much, Daphne Kwok, for that extravagant introduction. One of the few "perks" of public service is that when one is asked to speak somewhere, one gets to have one's accomplishments exaggerated. I take it warmly, but with a grain of salt. I say to you, as I do to many audiences, that I only hope someday to be worthy of the many compliments you have given me.

My thanks go out to the Organization of Chinese Americans for inviting me to join you today. I have so much to learn about the concerns and the practical problems of the various different groups in whose interest we work in the Civil Rights Division, and being able to attend even a small part of the conferences like yours is always helpful and informative. . . .

In the division right now, in a way, everything is up for grabs—by design. Last month, we embarked on a strategic planning process by which we will, frankly, define the civil rights enforcement priorities of the Department of Justice, consulting broadly both within the department and among many distinguished advocates outside of the department as well. Our aim is to have a set of specific enforcement goals, practical problems to help solve and on which to concentrate our resources and attention. But I can tell you—with or without a strategic plan—that some serious problems already cry out for our attention.

Like you, I'm sure, I have been troubled by the rise in hate crime over the past several years, including anti-Asian violence. The latest figures from the FBI, under the Hate Crimes Statistics Act, showed 236 incidents of anti-Asian violence in 1993, against 293 victims. The National Asian Pacific Legal Consortium reported 335 incidents in 1993. According to the consortium, at least 30 of these incidents resulted in death. Imagine: 30 homicides just last year in which Asian Pacific Americans were killed simply because they were Asian Pacific Americans.

And that's 30 *reported* homicides, 335 *reported* incidents. No doubt these statistics represent only a fraction of the incidents of anti-Asian violence in this country. Language barriers, mistrust of police by recent immigrants, ignorance of hate crimes protections and civil rights laws, a reluctance of law enforcement to identify hate crimes as such—all can and often do suppress the figures reported.

The Civil Rights Division has prosecuted a number of anti-Asian violence cases in the past, most notably the Vincent Chin case in Detroit. But we can do better. . . . Our objective is to identify particular problem areas and patterns of violence—including those involving the growing numbers of organized hate groups—and to pounce on problems as we learn of them. We will need your help to get the information, to find the cases appropriate for federal prosecution. And we will vigorously pursue these cases where we have the information and the evidence. Personal safety, freedom from violence based on status, is a central concern. . . . In the Civil Rights Division, we will do our part by bringing the federal prosecutions that demonstrate that such violence has no place in this society today. . . .

In the Civil Rights Division we have targeted jurisdictions with minority language populations to provide more effective assistance. For example, in New York City recently, we objected when the jurisdiction refused to translate the names of candidates into Chinese. That produced a change. Now, New Yorkers more comfortable in Chinese than in English can join in the political process. There is much more we can do, and we are working to develop an aggressive enforcement plan for minority language issues. . . .

I have to note a personal concern, too, perhaps a bit outside of my official role and duties. I have been very troubled by the rash of anti-immigrant politics sweeping certain parts of the nation. . . . [M]ore troubling than anything we have seen in Washington is the so-called "Save Our State" (SOS) initiative on the ballot here in California this November. If passed, among other things, SOS would:

- Limit public education to children who can prove citizenship or legal residency;
- Require school districts to verify the legal residency of *all* students, as well as the status of their parent or guardian, under threat of expulsion;
- Deny publicly funded health services to noncitizens; and
- Require government officials to report "suspected" undocumented persons to the INS, nullifying any sanctuary ordinance already passed by local governments in the states. . . .

There are chilling incidents we can envision for Hispanic Americans and Asian Americans in particular who will get reported to and hassled by immigration officials because they "look" like undocumented aliens, whatever that means. As a response to immigration problems, "SOS" is like swatting a flea with a sledgehammer. As a symbolic matter, this initiative will simply permit the narrow-minded to deny that we are a multicultural society—as we have always been. It is wrong for politicians to stir up and exploit anti-immigration sentiment, passing it off as comprehensive immigration and border control policy rather than the rank, political maneuver it is.

This and other initiatives and incidents point toward a larger challenge before the Civil Rights Division: indeed before the whole nation. Forty years after *Brown v. Board of Education* and thirty years after enactment of the landmark Civil Rights Act of 1964, the civil rights of African Americans have not been fully achieved. Meanwhile, the civil rights landscape has changed dramatically. Today, issues are no longer just black and white. America has evolved and matured over the last forty years and now must learn to embrace a significantly multiethnic and multicultural society. Fear—felt by some, stirred up by a few—causes us sometimes to recoil from each other's struggles to see one group's gains as another's losses, reducing the civil rights debate to some abstract discussion about entitlements and quotas and like nonsense.

I believe that we must be bigger than that: because the real and ultimate agenda of our work is to reclaim the American conscience. Our true mission is to restore the great moral imperative that civil rights is finally all about; to re-create the shared national consensus that discrimination is wrong; and to return the language of civil rights to its essence, back to concepts of equality, opportunity, and fair play.

We must explain to the nation that civil rights is not just of concern to African Americans or disabled Americans or to those whose religion is in the minority; it is of concern to each and every one of us. Because each citizen is diminished when anyone—on account of a happenstance of birth—experiences anything less than the full measure of his or her dignity and privilege as a human being and an American citizen.

. . . [T]his effort will only succeed and it will only last if we all learn to invest in one another's civil rights—not just as a matter of political coalition building, but also as a matter of conscience.

Within broad-based groups, learning to invest in each other's struggle and to appreciate each other's perspectives is happening, with marked results. In the disabilities community, for example, people who use wheelchairs, or are blind or deaf, or have HIV or a mental illness found their way to each other and—together—enabled enactment of the Americans with Disabilities Act. The ADA became law because a wide variety of disability rights groups invested in each other's struggle and explained to Congress and the nation in a strong *collective* voice that discrimination is an experience that all people with disabilities share. . . .

There is, of course, a parallel in this audience. On many issues the Chinese-American community has joined with Japanese Americans, Korean Americans, Vietnamese Americans, Cambodian Americans, and Filipino Americans—and found strength. But we must learn to cross even these broad group boundaries and invest in our *common* struggle. The struggle that your community wages against anti-immigrant sentiment, hate crimes, unfairness in employment, and language discrimination is a struggle shared by Hispanic Americans and Jewish Americans and African Americans as well. Of course there are differences—large and small. And there are differences in histories, which we must learn to appreciate and respect. But we must keep in our minds and our hearts that the indignity of discrimination is just as profound whether it comes because you speak accented English, or have dark skin, or worship a different God than your neighbor does. Discrimination is wrong. And there is both comfort and strength that comes when we commit to each other's struggle.

At the most basic level, I think Americans understand this. Summoned to think about what makes us proud of this country, Americans understand at some level that we have a national creed, one deeply rooted in the concepts of equality, opportunity, and fair play. At some level we understand that civil rights progress—however sometimes wrenching or resisted—is ultimately the measure of the progress of our civilization. And it is up to us as members of the civil rights community to remind our fellow citizens of that creed and to help them see that the American community as a whole is ultimately the real civil rights community.

We are a great nation, it seems to me, not just because of what we have accomplished, but because of what we have committed ourselves to become. And it is that sense of hope, that sense of looking forward, that I believe has made not only our civil rights movement, but ourselves as a nation, an inspiration to the world.

Now, it's up to us. Neither this administration as a whole nor its Civil Rights Division may have all the answers. God knows, I don't. And it would be absurd to believe that we will always be beyond your criticism or someone else's. But we are here with you, looking forward, committed to earning the hope that so many place in us. Thank you very much.

● *Analyzing the Characteristics of Persuasive Speeches*

Persuasive Strategies.   Did you notice any differences in the persuasive strategies that Deval Patrick used, in comparison with those used by Anna Martinez and Enrique Morales? How would you compare the use of ethos, pathos, and logos in his message with the use in theirs?

Patrick supports his call for a consensus that all discrimination is wrong by appealing to values that his audience will find appealing. He invokes "equality, opportunity, and fair play" as justifications for his position. The audience will agree that these values justify actions against hate crime directed toward Asian Americans, and they are equally strong reasons to oppose hatred directed at any other group of people. Can you identify other appeals to values in Patrick's speech?

Audience Adaptation.   Deval Patrick's speech exemplifies several important aspects of audience adaptation. Patrick is addressing an organization of Asian Americans and has done his homework. The hate crime statistics he quotes document anti-Asian violence. He also shows sensitivity to the particular reasons why recent immigrants from Asia might not report a hate crime. He simultaneously addresses concerns of *Chinese* Americans and respects the audience as Chinese *Americans*. Rather than referring to the audience as "you" and to himself as "I," he talks about the national creed that "we" have, and he implores the audience to remind "our fellow citizens" of that creed.

Style.   Patrick's speech contains several instances of eloquent word choice. He argues that "each citizen is diminished when anyone—on account of a happenstance of birth—experiences anything less than the full measure of his or her dignity and privilege as a human being and an American citizen." These carefully chosen words have more emotional appeal than a simple claim that "racial discrimination is wrong." He reinforces his point articulately later in the speech by saying "we must keep in our minds and our hearts that the indignity of discrimination is just as profound whether it comes because you speak accented English, or have dark skin, or worship a different God than your neighbor does."

Evidence.   Patrick has expertise on his topic by virtue of his position in the Justice Department, but he nevertheless bolsters his credibility with references to evidence sources. He cites the FBI and the National Asian Pacific Legal Consortium to support his claims. His reference to sources makes him more credible by demonstrating that he is relying on the knowledge of other authorities in addition to his own knowledge.

Patrick's credibility would be less apparent to a hostile audience. For example, if Patrick (a member of Democratic president Bill Clinton's Department of Justice at the time of the speech) were speaking about the need for gun control to a predominantly Republican audience of gun owners, his audience would be disinclined to accept his assertions as fact. He would need to cite more evidence than he did in this speech and ensure that the audience would find his sources credible.

● *Planning Your Persuasive Speech*

> **TIP**
>
> *When you write your persuasive speech, try to think of how the problem you are considering impacts on the values your audience finds most important.*

If you are having difficulty thinking of a topic to address in your persuasive speech, you may want to consider a question of fairness, as Deval Patrick did. People are very amenable to persuasion when they agree that an injustice needs to be righted. Can you think of any situations or policies on your campus that seem unfair? Such a topic will relate directly to your audience, and there are probably more actions that audience members can take to address a campus problem than to address a problem that is broader in scope. Patrick identified values that were likely to be important to his audience, the Organization of Chinese Americans. What values are important to your classmates?

Summary: Key Features of Persuasive Speeches

After studying the persuasive speeches of Martinez, Morales, and Patrick, you may have noted several important characteristics of a persuasive speech. Keep these in mind when you prepare this type of speech.

● *Persuasive speeches advocate that the audience adopt a specific point of view or take a specific action.*

When delivering a persuasive speech, the speaker takes a position on the issue in question, and the message is directed toward gaining or strengthening the audience's agreement with that position. Martinez advocated specific actions that audience members should take in order to be more careful users of credit cards. Morales wanted audience members to support governmental action and take individual action against racial profiling. Patrick implored his listeners to actively support civil rights for any victims of discrimination.

● *Persuasive speeches attempt to influence the audience through evidence, reasoning, and persuasive language.*

A strong persuasive speech provides the audience with logos to support the speaker's point of view, but it also persuades by appeals to pathos. The writers of the three speeches you just read incorporated reasoning and evidence to support their claims, while at the same time employing carefully chosen words and phrases to make the presentation memorable and touch the audience's emotions. For example, Martinez referred to credit cards as "'extra credit' you can live without"; Morales reiterated the maxim "If you're really sorry, you won't let it happen again"; and Patrick characterized racism as an affront to one's "dignity and privilege as a human being and an American citizen" on account of "a happenstance of birth." It is important for you to use sound logic and credible evidence in your persuasive speech, and it also is important for you to word your ideas in an emotionally convincing manner as those speakers did.

● *Persuasive speeches can be developed through different combinations of main points.*

The choice of main points depends on the specific purpose of the speech and on the speaker's audience analysis. Martinez wanted to highlight problems caused by students' use of credit cards and then present steps the audience could take to reduce those problems. For this purpose, a problem-cause-solution format was ideal. Morales's goal was audience action against racial profiling, so he relied on a motivated-sequence pattern. Patrick used an implicit problem-solution structure: reviewing examples of prejudice and then advocating remedies for hate crimes and discrimination. Even more so than the other speakers, Patrick could assume that his audience would agree that a serious problem existed. Therefore, he focused on the personal involvement of his *audience* in the fight against discrimination.

When you decide on the main points of a persuasive speech, determine whether your speech is emphasizing a policy question or focusing on a factual or value question, and use an appropriate organizational format. You also need to decide where a two-sided strategy would be most persuasive. The Speech Guide will help you to select the optimal main points for your speech once you have decided the type of thesis you will defend.

● *Persuasive speeches should be developed with the audience in mind.*

Anna Martinez knew that her audience would not be receptive to a radical cutback in credit card use. Therefore, she had to modify her thesis to advocate moderate action. Because she was speaking to college students, she chose examples and language that would be appropriate for that audience.

Enrique Morales was speaking to a friendly audience. Therefore, he could encourage listeners to take substantial action in support of his thesis. To further strengthen audience attitudes against racial profiling, he used visualization to focus thinking on the differences between a society with and a society without racial profiling.

Deval Patrick wanted his audience to become advocates for the civil rights of all discrimination victims. Because he knew that his audience would be friendly, he implored them to become even more involved in an issue that they already were concerned with. He appealed to the audience's values and employed powerful language because he knew his audience would be most likely to take action if they were genuinely touched by his speech.

In each case, the speaker tailored the message to the particular audience he or she would be addressing. When you plan your persuasive speech, analyze your audience, and use that analysis to craft an effective message.

The Speech Assignment

Prepare a persuasive speech in which you take a position on a significant issue. Your speech should attempt to influence the audience to adopt a more favorable attitude toward your position or take action that supports your position. As you develop your speech, follow the five-step process described here to invent, organize, stylize, refine and practice, and deliver your speech.

Preparing Your Persuasive Speech
A Five-Step Process

1. Inventing Your Speech

Drafting an effective persuasive speech begins with careful preparation and planning. You need to analyze your audience, select an issue to address and draft a thesis, brainstorm arguments supporting your position, research your issue, and select the supporting arguments that will persuade your audience ethically and effectively.

When you are given a major speech assignment, it is natural to wonder how you will find the time to do all the work that needs to be done. Actually, the task is not as overwhelming as it may seem—if you get to work shortly after receiving the assignment and budget your time wisely. The five stages of preparation in this guide are the same as the ones for any other prepared speech: inventing, organizing, using style effectively, practicing, and delivering. Remember that **hard work and perseverance are the keys to a successful speech.** Review what each step entails, and plan your schedule so that you have enough time to complete each one successfully.

● *Analyze Your Audience*

The audience drives the message is a maxim that we emphasize throughout this text. Begin your preparation by analyzing your audience and recording your analysis on a Speech Grid. Sample grids can be found in the Speech Grid Application sections near the ends of Chapters 5 through 12. At the outset, analyze situational characteristics, audience demographics, and common ground.

Situational Characteristics. If you are presenting a persuasive speech in class, note any requirements for the topic, format, and content of the speech. If you are speaking out of class, what is the occasion for your speech? Will the audience be expecting a persuasive speech or a speech on a particular topic? Also note where you will be speaking, the time of day you will speak, the size of your audience, and the expected length of your speech.

Audience Demographics. Consider demographic categories that are likely to indicate audience interest and disposition toward persuasive speech topics. These categories may include political affiliation, group membership, occupation or academic major, ethnicity, gender mix, income, age, religious affiliation, and family status.

Use your CD-ROM to build your speech using the five-step process. CD-ROM: Interactive Speech Guides/Persuasive Speech

Use your CD-ROM to analyze your audience. Go to "Step 1 Invention/Analyze Audience." CD-ROM: Interactive Speech Guides/Persuasive Speech

For more on audience analysis questions, see Chapter 5.

Common Ground.   Consider what you and the audience have in common. In a persuasive speech, you can strengthen your ethos by emphasizing shared values and experiences. Brainstorm to create a list of similarities between you and your audience.

● Select and Refine Your Topic

Use your CD-ROM to select and refine your topic. Go to "Step 1 Invention/Select Topic." CD-ROM: Interactive Speech Guides/Persuasive Speech

For tips on generating potential topics, see page 118.

For out-of-class speeches, your topic may be a given. For example, your employer may ask you to develop a sales presentation for a new product, or you may want to ask your city council to allow a controversial musician to perform in the civic auditorium. For classroom persuasive speech assignments, you usually have some choice in topic selection. When you have a choice, begin by creating a list of potential subjects. Use brainstorming, word association, concept mapping, and research to develop this list.

Brainstorm Topic Areas.   In a persuasive speech assignment, you are taking a position on a *debatable* issue (one on which two or more viewpoints are reasonable). Brainstorm issues that are of interest and concern to you. Consider diverse categories such as world, national, community, and (for classroom speeches) student and campus issues. Remember to write down every idea that comes to mind when brainstorming, without rejecting any. Use word association and cognitive mapping to add to your list. Here is an example of one student's list of issues, developed through brainstorming and word association:

1. Food	dieting	diet drugs
fast food	campus food services	
2. Dreams	getting more sleep	reducing life stress
3. College	education	failing schools
	volunteer to tutor	
4. Agriculture	pesticides	protecting workers from pesticides
	César Chávez	renaming local school for César Chávez
5. Gays in the military	gay rights	health benefits for same-sex partners
6. Computers	Internet pornography	pornography degrades women

Each instructor has topic selection requirements for classroom speeches. Be sure that your topic fits the assignment.

Research for Potential Topics.   Look at sources that are likely to provide topic ideas for a persuasive speech. These include Internet news sites, newspapers, and recent news magazines. Check the table of contents in recent periodicals, if they are easily available in your library. As you discover potential topics, write them down. You may want to keep a record of sources for later research, but do not begin reading books or articles until you select a topic.

Select the Best Topic Area.   Once you have developed a list of issues, select the best topic. The three main criteria you should use to evaluate each potential topic are

1. *Your audience's interests.* Is the issue likely to concern the audience? Can you relate the subject to the audience? Can the audience be directly involved with the issue?
2. *Your interests and expertise.* Do you know enough about the topic to be a credible speaker? Will you be able to speak with conviction on that issue?
3. *The context of the speech.* Will the topic be appropriate, given the location, audience size, time, and occasion of the speech? Is the topic appropriate for persuasion? For a classroom speech, is the topic acceptable to your instructor?

Exclude any topic that would be inappropriate for your audience or the speech context. On the list of remaining topics, highlight the one(s) you are most knowledgeable about and interested in. If there is more than one that you are interested in addressing, select the one that would be best, given your audience and speech context.

Narrow Your Topic.   Select a portion of your topic that can be covered in the time available for your speech. Focus your persuasive speech by considering which aspects of the topic will be of the greatest interest and concern to the audience and can directly involve the audience. There may be an angle on the topic that best fits your interest and expertise. If that angle would also be appropriate for your audience, it would be a good choice for the focus of your speech.

Draft a Working Thesis and Specific Purpose.   Create a working thesis and specific purpose statement for use in preparing your speech. The thesis should express the main *idea* of your speech in one sentence. The specific purpose statement should express the *objective* of your speech. You can use the software in your CD-ROM to critically evaluate your working thesis and specific purpose to ensure they are appropriate for a persuasive speech.

Keep in mind that both your thesis and your specific purpose are *working* statements. You may revise them after learning more about audience members' perspectives on your topic or gaining insights from your research.

● *Generate Ideas to Support Your Thesis*

Use both brainstorming and research to develop a list of potential supporting ideas. Record these ideas on your Speech Grid. Later, you will choose the best of these ideas for inclusion in your speech outline.

Use your CD-ROM to generate and select ideas to support your thesis. Go to "Step 1 Invention/ Generate Supporting Ideas" and "Select Supporting Ideas." CD-ROM: Interactive Speech Guides/Persuasive Speech

Brainstorm Supporting Ideas.   Initially list on your grid every point that could support your thesis. Later, you will select the best points for your speech, but now your goal is to create a diverse list of ideas. To generate ideas for using each of these concepts, here are some questions to ask when brainstorming.

To Develop Your Ethos

1. Why are you knowledgeable on your topic? What experience and education can you highlight to strengthen your credibility with the audience?

2. What is your motive for selecting this topic? Do you have any bias that should be disclosed to the audience?

3. What do you and your audience have in common? Do you share common values or experiences that are relevant to your topic?

4. What are the audience's needs and concerns? What points would address the audience's needs or show sensitivity to their concerns?

To Create Arguments Relying on Logos.   In Chapter 8 we noted that there are different points that should be proved in a persuasive speech, depending on whether you are advocating action or supporting a value judgment. As you brainstorm ideas for your speech, consider ideas that could help you establish each of these points. List these ideas in the logos section of your grid.

If you are addressing a value question, here are key issues to consider:

1. What reasons could you give to support the value judgment you are making?

2. What reasons could reasonable people give against the value judgment you are making?

3. What criteria could be used to evaluate your value judgment?

If you are advocating action by audience members or by the government (in other words, if you are defending a policy thesis), consider these questions:

1. What are some of the problems that create a need for your proposed policy or action? Are there any reasons why reasonable people might deny that these problems are real and serious?

2. What are the main causes of these problems?

3. What are some possible solutions? Are there solutions that the audience can participate in?

4. How can the solutions you listed reduce the problems?

5. What are possible disadvantages of these solutions? How would you respond to such disadvantages?

To Consider Appeals to Pathos

1. What aspects of your topic may appeal to the audience's emotions?

2. Are there any examples or anecdotes that would support your position and touch the audience's emotions?

For more on issues to be addressed with policy or value questions, see pages 186–87.

TIP

You may want to subdivide the logos portion of the grid into sections for each point you must prove.

For more on the importance of addressing arguments against your thesis, see page 248.

3. What are the values of your audience? What could you say about your topic that would be consistent with their values?

Research Your Topic.   In Chapter 7 we noted the necessity of research and discussed the steps to take when you research a speech. Here, we briefly review those steps and provide advice that is specific to researching persuasive speeches.

Inventory Your Research Needs.   Determine where to focus your research. Do you need to learn more about your topic? Do you plan to make any claims that you know will not be persuasive to your audience without supporting evidence? For classroom speeches, how many references to research are required?

Have a System for Organizing Your Information.   If you have an organized plan, you will not lose information, and you will be able to find the evidence you researched when you need it.

Discover Sources of Information on Your Topic.   Consult a wide variety of research sources, including library and online directories. Also, determine whether there are any experts you could interview in person or correspond with through e-mail.

Read and Prioritize Your Sources.   Once you have gathered your sources, carefully read them, looking for those that are most likely to provide helpful information. Research priorities should include highly credible sources who support the claims you must prove in your speech (the key issues for value or policy questions). You also will need evidence to counter any arguments against your position that are likely to influence the audience.

As you discover useful evidence, record it on the "Speech Message" side of your Speech Grid. Keep complete citations for any evidence sources that you may decide to use in your speech.

Identify Gaps in Your Research, and Find Needed Information.   If you cannot find evidence to support arguments you hoped to make or to establish key issues you need to prove, target your research to fill in those gaps. If you continue to have difficulty, consider these options:

- *Focus on your strongest claims.* If the points you can prove are strong enough to justify your position, focus your research and preparation on the stronger claims that you will be able to justify.

- *Narrow the scope of your thesis.* If the position you are taking cannot be supported with the available evidence, narrow your thesis or revise it into one that you can prove with the available research.

- *Ask for help.* If you are running into a brick wall in trying to find the supporting information you need, ask your instructor or a librarian for recommendations of sources to research. Talk to people on campus or in your community who are knowledgeable about your topic. They can advise you about the soundness of your approach and provide ideas for further research.

For more on the research process, see page 148.

TIP

Know what format your instructor requires for citing research, so that you can record the required information as you consult various sources.

For more on recording evidence on your grid, see page 175.

Once you are confident that you have thoroughly researched your topic, evaluate your working thesis. If you can support it with the ideas you have generated, keep it in that form. If you need to revise your thesis, now is the time to do so. You want to know exactly what you are trying to persuade your audience to believe or do when you select the best arguments from your grid.

● Select the Best Ideas to Support Your Thesis

Evaluate the potential ideas in the "Speech Message" column of your Speech Grid, and make strategic choices about which ideas to incorporate into your speech and which to reject. Base your choices on ethical considerations, audience analysis, and the type of thesis you are advancing. On your grid, highlight particularly promising arguments, and cross out those that are inappropriate.

For more on principles of ethical persuasion, see pages 58 and 242.

Ethical Concerns in Issue Selection.   Review the arguments listed on your grid. Omit any that seem questionable from an ethical perspective. Here are some important ethical considerations for persuasive speakers:

- *Have you noted any bias that you have about your topic?* If you do have a bias, note it in the "ethos" section of your grid.
- *Have you done sufficient research to know your topic well?* The arguments on your grid should be supported by evidence from a variety of sources.
- *Is each argument on your grid likely to contribute to the audience's ability to make a good decision?* Exclude any argument that seems unlikely to be true, based on your research. If you have omitted any key facts that would be important to audience decision making, add them to your grid. You can discuss facts that are contrary to your thesis in a two-sided argument.

For more on two-sided arguments, see page 248.

- *Have you omitted arguments based on fallacious reasoning?* It is not ethical to persuade an audience with faulty logic. Reject arguments based on fallacies such as hasty generalization, post hoc, or ad hominem. Highlight arguments that are based on sound reasoning.
- *Is the research on your grid accurately attributed, quoted, or paraphrased?* Be certain that all ideas derived from your research are attributed to a source. Also, check to be certain that all quotations and paraphrases are accurate and represent the original author's point of view.

Audience Analysis and Issue Selection.   Whether you are attempting to convince audience members to change their minds on an issue or to take action, you need to understand their position on your topic and the reasons for their beliefs. You can use this information to decide which arguments on your grid will be most persuasive.

Expand Your Audience Analysis.   After selecting a speech topic, you can expand on your audience analysis. The left side of your grid should already contain information about the speech situation, in addition to information you have already learned about your common ground and audience demographics. To expand your analysis, determine audience members' *prior exposure* to your topic through surveys or interviews. Determine their attitudes, the reasons for their viewpoints, and the arguments they have already heard. If surveying or interviewing audience members is not feasible, try indirect methods to find clues about your audience's position on your topic. Then make the best assumptions possible about the type of audience you will be addressing.

For more on indirect audience analysis, see page 110.

Use Your Audience Analysis to Select Arguments.   On your Speech Grid highlight arguments that are likely to be convincing, and cross out those that you think will be less effective, given your audience analysis. You also may want to revise the arguments on your grid in light of your audience analysis—for example, elaborating on an idea or substituting evidence that will be more credible. When you are using audience analysis to select points to include in your speech, there are some questions you might consider:

- Which arguments are most likely to persuade the audience?
- Are any arguments likely to succeed or fail, given the audience's prior exposure?
- Does the audience have reservations or questions about the position you are taking? If the audience has significant concerns, you need arguments that address those concerns.
- Which arguments will relate directly to audience members' lives?
- Does your situational audience analysis indicate that some arguments would be more effective than others? How long is the speech expected to be? What time of day are you speaking? Where is the speech taking place?

For more on adapting to the speech situation, see page 92.

Your Thesis and Issue Selection.   You need to select ideas that will establish each of the essential points that must be proved in your speech. The content of these points will differ, depending on whether your thesis advocates a value or a policy. If you have few supporting ideas for one or more issues, you will need to research or brainstorm more ideas to include in your speech.

If your thesis addresses a *value* question, there are two fundamental considerations in issue selection:

1. You need criteria that are to be used to make the value judgment you are advocating.
2. You need to select ideas that enable you to apply your criteria to the person, object, or idea that you are evaluating. You typically will advance from two to five main reasons why your value judgment is true. Each reason must satisfy your criteria.

If your thesis addresses a *policy* question, there are three major issues to address:

1. *The need for the policy you are advancing.* Select significant problems that affect individual audience members or society in general.

2. *The causes of the problems you have chosen.* Highlight points that establish causation.

3. *A solution to the problem.* Choose ideas that describe the provisions of your plan (including action that audience members can take themselves), and show that your plan will mitigate the needs that you are focusing on in your speech.

After selecting ideas that support each of these major issues, you should be ready to progress from invention to organization. Your Speech Grid should be complete, with the best ideas for your speech highlighted and ideas that raise ethical concerns or appear unlikely to persuade your audience omitted.

2. Organizing Your Speech

The second step in preparing your persuasive speech is to draft an outline of the points you have selected to support your thesis. You will take the ideas that you highlighted on your grid and arrange them in an effective sequence. Start by considering the body of your speech, and then add the introduction, conclusion, and connecting words.

● *Outline the Body of Your Persuasive Speech*

Organize Your Ideas into Main Points. Go back to your grid, and organize the highlighted ideas into a limited number of main points. These will form the body of your speech. For a persuasive speech, there are several ways in which you can organize ideas into main points.

Value Patterns. If your thesis advocates a value judgment, you have three basic options for organizing your main points:

Option 1: One main point advocates criteria for the value judgment you are making, and the second main point applies those criteria to your subject. This is the typical format for organizing main points on nonpolicy questions.

Option 2: Each main point constitutes a reason why your thesis is true. Use this option only if your audience analysis indicates that the link between your main points and thesis will be obvious to the audience.

Option 3: Main points are presented as described in option 1 or option 2, and a main point that addresses audience reservations to your thesis in a two-sided argument is added. Use this format when your audience analysis indicates that members have significant reservations about your thesis and their concerns do not relate to the main points that you plan to develop.

Policy Patterns. If your thesis advocates a policy, you have several options for organizing your main points. Which one you select depends on the nature of the ideas you intend to advance. The organizational patterns, and the circumstances under which they can best be used, are as follows:

Use your CD-ROM to select the best organizational pattern for your speech. Go to "Step 2 Organization/Body."
CD-ROM: Interactive Speech Guides/Persuasive Speech

For more on main points for value questions, see page 187. For policy questions, see page 186.

Option 1: Problem-solution format or problem-cause-solution format. Use the problem-solution format if you have proof of a serious harm, a solution that will curtail the harm, and a cause that will be apparent to the audience without a detailed explanation. If the cause is not apparent, use the problem-cause-solution format so you can prove the cause of the problem to the audience and then show how your solution mitigates that cause. Anna Martinez used this format in her speech on credit card use.

Option 2: Comparative advantages. If you have a plan for action that seems worthwhile, but the problems you have isolated are not monumental, use this format. Each main point should demonstrate a benefit of your proposal over the present situation or policy.

Option 3: Motivated sequence. If your proposed solution centers on action you want the audience to take (rather than on action by an institution such as the government), a motivated sequence can be very persuasive. Structure the main points to create within the audience a desire to take personal action to solve a problem. Enrique Morales used this format in his speech on racial profiling.

Nonlinear Formats.   The formats for value and policy propositions that we just described are *linear* formats. Recall that there are also *nonlinear* formats for organizing main points. Some speech assignments require all students to use a standard linear format (such as problem-cause-solution). But if you are not required to use a standard format, and your audience analysis indicates that a nonlinear format will be effective, consider a deferred-thesis, web, or narrative pattern.

To review nonlinear formats, see page 208.

For more on culture and organization preferences, see page 212.

Word the Main Points.   After deciding what your main points will be and how they will be ordered, insert them in your speech outline. Remember to number each main point with a Roman numeral and to word your main points so that they accurately reflect the supporting material and generate audience interest.

For more on wording main points, see page 184.

Develop and Outline Subpoints.   Once your main points are determined, select from your grid the ideas that best support those main points. Both the content and the format of your supporting materials are important.

Selecting Supporting Materials.   Audiences are persuaded by ethos, logos, and pathos. The materials that you select from your Speech Grid to support your main points should incorporate all three of these concepts.

To develop your *ethos,* include points that show concern for your audience's best interests. Points that demonstrate your common ground with the audience will build your credibility. Regular citation of research and good organization will show the audience that you are well prepared to speak on your topic.

To use *logos* to persuade your audience, be sure to include ideas that provide a good basis for the claims they support. Each idea needs to be supported with sound reasoning, credible evidence, or both. If your analysis indicates that audience members have reservations about a point you are making or believe the point is false, incorporate additional supporting

For more on the effective use of evidence and reasoning, see page 232. For more on persuasive strategies, see page 243.

arguments on that point. You also might devote a subpoint to addressing that reservation in a two-sided argument.

To appeal to *pathos,* develop arguments that genuinely touch the audience's emotions. In Chapter 9 we discussed the effective use of persuasive strategies, such as an emotional appeal, a cost-benefit argument, an appeal to fear, foot-in-the-door, and door-in-the face. If you incorporate subpoints that use these strategies, along with effective use of evidence and reasoning, you enhance the probability that you will motivate the audience to accept your thesis.

Outlining Supporting Materials. Remember three principles as you insert supporting ideas into your outline:

- Use proper outline format. Indent subpoints, and use capital letters to identify them. Double-indent sub-subpoints, and number each one.
- Subpoints and sub-subpoints must be subordinate to the point they develop.
- Evidence must be properly cited in your outline. Each time you use quoted or paraphrased information in your speech, be sure to attribute it to the author. We recommend citing the author, author's qualifications, source, date, and page number on your outline. A citation is required *every time* evidence is used.

● *Outline the Introduction and Conclusion*

To review the components of introductions, see page 193. To review conclusions, see page 201.

The introduction and conclusion of a persuasive speech consist of the same components as the introduction and conclusion of other speeches. As you draft your introduction and conclusion, be sure to include each component. Pay attention to the length of these parts of your speech. For a typical five-to-ten-minute speech, your introduction should not exceed one minute and your conclusion should last between thirty and forty-five seconds.

Draft the Introduction. The introduction should set the tone for your persuasive speech. When drafting the introduction, consider the following advice:

1. *Relate the attention-getter to the topic of your speech.* Your attention-getter can dramatize the problem to your audience. A poignant anecdote or startling statistic can pull the audience into your speech at the outset. If your audience is hostile, you may want to use an attention-getter that demonstrates respect or common ground to build rapport, or you may want to defuse tension with a humorous beginning.

2. *Indicate in your thesis statement what you expect the audience to do or believe.* In a classroom speech, an explicit thesis is often a requirement. In some persuasive speaking contexts, however, a nonlinear or indirect approach may be more effective. In such cases, your thesis could be implicit or deferred.

To review deferred theses, see page 208.

3. *Connect with audience members by highlighting one way in which the topic relates to them.* Summarize this connection in one or two sentences. At this point you are whetting their appetites by promising relevant infor-

mation. In the body of your speech, you will use evidence and reasoning to provide support for the claim you are making.

4. *Establish credibility to build your ethos.* Credibility is essential in persuasive speeches. You must demonstrate your competence and gain the audience's trust before you will be believed. The audience needs to understand why you have expertise on the subject you have chosen. Keep in mind, though, that the audience will be less receptive to your message if you demonstrate your credibility with arrogance instead of professionalism. To build audience trust, it is essential to disclose any biases you have and to show respect for persons who disagree with you.

5. *Preview your main points to indicate the structure of your speech.* In a persuasive speech, the preview can set the stage for the main message. If you word your main points so as to express your main idea in a persuasive manner in the preview, they will function like a sound bite for your persuasive message.

Draft the Conclusion.   Your conclusion should wrap up your speech in a persuasive manner. Conclusions include two components: a summary of your main points and a clincher.

The *summary* briefly reviews the main ideas that you developed in the body of your speech. If you express these ideas in vivid language, they are more likely to be remembered by your audience.

The *clincher* should leave the audience motivated to act or believe in the manner you have advocated. You may want to consider one of these options for this component of your persuasive speech:

- *Appeal to the audience's emotions.* Use a dramatic example or an anecdote involving a person who benefited (or would benefit) from the proposition you advocate.

- *Call for audience action.* Persuasively remind the audience of the action you are advocating. Reiterate how important the resolution of the issue is, and review how audience members are empowered to take the necessary steps.

- *Help the audience visualize the results you seek.* End your speech with audience members imagining how their lives and the lives of others would be better if they agreed with your proposition.

- *Use a relevant quotation from a person the audience respects.* The audience will be more supportive of your ideas if you link the position you are taking with the beliefs of a person whom the audience holds in high esteem.

After you draft the introduction, body, and conclusion, the next step is to insert organizing language—transitions and signposts—to ensure that the structure of your speech is clear and easy to follow.

● *Incorporate Transitions and Signposts*

Add Transitions.   Transitions serve as bridges between the major parts of your speech. In your outline, insert them at the following places:

1. Between the introduction and the first main point

2. Between each main point

3. Between the final main point and the conclusion (Alternatively, instead of inserting a full transition, you may use a signpost here to indicate that your speech is concluding.)

For more on wording transitions, see page 190.

Word each transition to show clearly that you are moving from one idea to the next.

For more on signposts, see page 191.

Add Signposts.   You can strengthen the organization of your speech by inserting signposts. In a persuasive speech, use signposts to

1. Highlight each aspect or cause of the problem you are discussing

2. Highlight each provision or step in the solution you are advocating

3. Highlight each issue you are addressing when presenting a solution, such as the mechanics of your proposal, the reasons the proposal will reduce the problem, and the feasibility of your proposal

A bibliography is often required at the end of an outline. Check with your instructor for proper format.

Signposts also can help audience members realize that you are presenting a two-sided analysis of a particular point.

3. Using Effective Style

For pointers on effective style, see Chapter 10.

The third step in developing your persuasive speech is to focus on style, to ensure that the wording of your ideas on your outline is appropriate and persuasive. Review the outline and evaluate your word choice. If necessary, make revisions to improve your wording. When reflecting on style in a persuasive speech, consider the following advice:

- *Present your ideas in an interesting manner.*   Compelling language can play a powerful role in making a speech persuasive. Use striking and vivid language to help the audience appreciate and visualize your concerns. Include metaphors and similes to capture the audience's attention and bring your ideas to life.

- *Be sure your words are understandable.* Explain any technical jargon that you use to discuss your topic. In a persuasive speech, it is common to refer to government agencies and legislation. Avoid using abbreviations (such as "GAO") and shorthand references to policies that may be unfamiliar to your audience (such as "10-20-Life" to refer to a law that imprisons defendants who used a gun during a crime for ten years, then for twenty years, and finally for life for, respectively, their first, second, and third offenses). If you are proposing a solution in your speech, be specific. Terms such as *gun control* and *affirmative action* will have different meanings for different audience members.

- *Simplify long and difficult sentences.* If you have lengthy sentences that contain several ideas, break them down into shorter sentences containing a single idea each. For complex phrases substitute simpler terms,

TIP

Language revisions are easy to make if you draft your outline on a word processor.

unless you are confident that the complex language will be persuasive to your audience.

- *Do not overstate your claims.* The claims you make should be supported by the evidence you present. Be certain that the wording of your main points and subpoints does not exaggerate what you can prove.

- *Avoid bias in your language.* Avoid negative stereotypes, unnecessary gender-specific references, and outdated references to ethnic groups. If you are discussing a controversial issue that could offend audience members, emphasize factual statements that you can support and avoid highly opinionated language.

- *Keep your tone professional.* An audience can tell much about a speaker's character by the way the speaker treats people with whom she or he disagrees. Disagree with the ideas without attacking the person expressing them. Show that you respect people who hold a viewpoint different from yours.

For more on presenting viewpoints that may not be politically correct, see page 276.

4. Refining and Practicing Your Persuasive Speech

Students often assume that their speeches are complete when the outline is written. But that assumption is false. The important fourth step in the speech-writing process is refining and practicing your speech. Your persuasive speech will be stronger if you review and revise your outline after it is written. If possible, arrange your schedule so that you have time to set your outline aside for one or two days before you review it.

● Review the Outline from a Critical Perspective

When reviewing your speech, keep in mind that audience analysis is an ongoing process and should be done again as you refine your speech. In addition, this is the time to seek critical feedback from other people and to continue to revise your outline as needed.

Analyze Your Persuasive Speech.   When you reread your outline, consider the speech from the audience's perspective. You may want to make an extra copy of your outline and write on it notes about possible changes to the content and structure that occur to you as you are reading.

Review the Content.   Here are some questions to ask about the content of your persuasive speech outline:

- Does the speech clearly indicate what you would like the audience to do or believe?

- Are the reasons that you advance to support your proposition likely to be convincing to the audience?

- Will the audience accept the factual claims you are making? Do you need additional evidence or more credible evidence to prove any of your points?

- Is the language you have chosen appropriate for your audience? Is the tone reasonable and professional? Will the audience understand what you are trying to say?
- If you are proposing a solution, is your plan of action explained clearly? Do you show the audience a feasible way to be personally involved in the solution?

Review the Structure. Review the structure of your speech. Here are some questions to ask to avoid common organizational problems:

- Is the body of the speech in an appropriate format for a persuasive speech (for example, motivated sequence or problem-cause-solution)?
- Do the introduction and conclusion have the proper components?
- Does the speech have transitions and signposts at each place where they are needed?
- Is research properly cited at each place where you refer to it in your outline? If required, is the bibliography in the proper form?

Review the Assignment (If Applicable). If the speech is for a class assignment, review the assignment description. Be certain that you are fulfilling all requirements. For example, your instructor may require a certain number of research sources, a particular organizational pattern, or the use of visual aids.

Review the Speech Length. Read your outline aloud to see approximately how long it will take you to deliver the speech. For a classroom speaking assignment, your instructor probably will give you a maximum (and possibly a minimum) speech time. If you are delivering a speech out of class, it is important for the length of your speech to meet the audience's expectations. If your speech is too long, you will need to cut out some of your points. Refer back to your Speech Grid, and decide which arguments are least important for your particular audience. If your speech is too short, you will need to add points or develop the ones you have in greater detail. You may want to include some additional examples or use a two-sided argument to address opposing arguments that concern your audience.

Get Feedback from Other People. If you have friends, relatives, or classmates who are willing to help you prepare, have them read your outline. Here are several important issues that such reviewers can address:

- Reviewers can tell you whether any of your arguments seem unclear. Ideas that make sense to you as you are writing may be unclear to another person.
- Reviewers can tell you whether the arguments you are making seem convincing. You can ask them whether any arguments should be revised because they are not persuasive or are not adequately proved.
- Reviewers can make suggestions for additional arguments. A person who is taking a fresh look at your topic may think of an argument that you never considered. He or she can double-check your Speech Grid to see whether any of the ideas you did not select should be reconsidered.

- Reviewers can check for cultural understanding. If members of your audience are from cultures other than your own, have people from those cultures look at your outline. You may have unwittingly phrased an idea in a way that could be offensive to others, or you may have selected examples that would not be persuasive to persons from diverse backgrounds.

As you get feedback from other people, try not to be defensive. Their constructive suggestions will help make your speech as strong as possible when the time comes to deliver it.

Revise Your Outline.   After reviewing the content, structure, and length of your persuasive speech, and after receiving feedback from other people, revise your outline as needed:

1. Strengthen the content of your speech by changing the arguments, language, or evidence to make your speech more persuasive.
2. Improve your word choice to make the speech more clear or appropriate for your audience.
3. Revise the structure of your speech by adding transitions or signposts, and provide any elements missing from your introduction and conclusion.
4. Fit your speech into the allotted time for delivery by adding, deleting, or changing arguments as necessary.

● *Prepare for Extemporaneous Delivery*

Practice with Your Outline.   After you revise your outline, it is time to practice and polish your delivery. Begin practice by reading your outline orally several times, until your speech becomes so familiar that you can reduce your dependence on the outline. As you practice, try to explain subpoints in your own words, looking at your outline only if you are quoting sources directly or are losing your train of thought. Do not try to memorize your speech word-for-word. Your goal is to become comfortable delivering your speech from limited notes.

Prepare a Condensed Outline for Speaking.   After you practice your persuasive speech several times and are feeling confident that you can remember the order and content of your main points, begin preparing briefer notes (on note cards or on a limited number of pages) that you will use when you actually deliver the speech. Your condensed speech outline should include your main points and major subpoints. In this outline, the subpoints do not need to be expressed in complete sentences. Write just enough to help you remember the ideas you want to cover. Trust yourself to explain each subpoint without reading the words from your notes. Offer these explanations as you would if you were talking to a person in everyday conversation, avoiding a presentation that sounds canned or memorized. Include direct quotations word-for-word so you will quote the source accurately.

For more on speaking from an outline, see page 289.

Besides putting the main points and subpoints into your notes, you may want to write delivery reminders on the cards as well. If you had difficulty with some aspect of delivery (such as eye contact or rate of delivery) in previous speeches, or if you had a problem while practicing, you want to be certain to avoid that problem during your speech. At the top of your note cards, you might write "look up!" or "slow down!" Print such reminders in large letters and in a color different from the color of your speech notes.

Once your condensed notes are completed, continue practicing your speech using only these notes. If possible, practice with a friend who can tell you whether aspects of your delivery need improvement. Do you have any distracting mannerisms? Are you speaking in a monotone? Are you forgetting to look up from your notes? With practice, you will be more comfortable speaking with this brief outline, and you will be able to speak extemporaneously to your audience.

5. Delivering Your Speech

The final step in preparing your persuasive speech is to present it to your audience. Before doing that, however, you can do a number of things to ensure that your delivery is effective.

● *Minimize Speech Anxiety*

If you are feeling apprehensive about your persuasive speech, do not lose heart. It takes more than a couple of speeches before many speakers begin gaining confidence about public speaking.

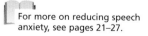
To review state and trait anxiety, see page 20.

If you experience high communication apprehension generally (*trait* anxiety) and have not sought help, look into assistance before delivering your persuasive speech. If you are uncomfortable about asking for help, recall that you may be able to find out about programs through a school or department Web site. You can e-mail or leave a note for your instructor if you feel more comfortable asking in writing.

Anticipating a persuasive speech may cause you considerable *state* anxiety if your audience is hostile or your topic is controversial. When presenting your speech, recall that anxiety is highest at the outset. During the introduction, look for friendly faces and begin your eye contact with them. Try to smile at your audience and incorporate humor if it is appropriate to the topic and you feel comfortable with it. When you establish credibility, emphasize common ground. Make clear your respect for all audience members, whether they agree with you or not. If you follow the principles of ethical communication, you are treating your audience fairly and should not fear the prospect of giving a speech.

For more on reducing speech anxiety, see pages 21–27.

Careful preparation is one way to reduce your anxiety. Use the checklist at the end of this chapter to be sure that you have taken the necessary steps. Show your outline to your instructor to reassure yourself that you are on the right track or to learn whether there are any changes that would strengthen your speech. Review the techniques for reducing anxiety that we described in Chapter 1, such as relaxation, visualization, and taking good care of yourself. Use the ones that are most helpful to you.

Remember that it is normal to experience some nervousness about delivering a speech. Also, some anxiety is positive. If you are overconfident, you may not manage or deliver the speech to the best of your ability. Never assume that a lack of nervousness means you need not carefully prepare.

Deliver Your Persuasive Speech

Here are some reminders for effective delivery of a persuasive speech:

- *Begin your speech with confidence.* When it is time for you to speak, walk to the front of the room with confidence. Do not say anything that would convey a lack of conviction or preparation.

- *Speak with conviction on key points.* When you present an argument that is very important or compelling, your delivery should show that determination. Show your determination as you would show determination in an ordinary conversation.

- *Use vocal variety to emphasize points.* When you come to a key point, vocal variety makes the point stand out to the audience. You can achieve variety by increasing your volume. You also can achieve it by slowing your rate of delivery or slightly reducing the volume.

- *Maintain eye contact with the audience.* Look up from your notes and at audience members as you deliver your speech. If you do not look at the audience, listeners may perceive that you are not trustworthy even if you are being honest. A speech read from a manuscript will sound canned or packaged.

- *Use effective body language.* If you fail to gesture, or if you display distracting mannerisms, you will appear nervous. This nervousness may be interpreted as a lack of confidence in your message, undermining your credibility. Use natural gestures and controlled movement to reinforce your message.

- *Return to your seat confidently.* When you are finished speaking, return to your seat in a calm, professional manner. Never assume that you gave a poor speech. Students often are more pessimistic about how well they have done than is warranted. Do not make disparaging comments about your speech—you are likely to be pleasantly surprised.

Learn from Your Persuasive Speech

Use each speech you present as an opportunity to develop your public speaking ability. In the classroom, there is usually an opportunity for audience members to give you feedback and ask questions. Use interactive listening to understand your classmates' comments. Jot down their ideas for later reference. You are also likely to receive oral and written comments from your instructor. When it is appropriate (*not* during other people's speeches), write down your own thoughts about your speech and ideas for self-improvement.

Set your ideas and your feedback aside for a day or two. Then look at your own reaction to your speech as well as the feedback you received. Make

---

Use your CD-ROM to view examples of delivery in a persuasive speech. Go to the "Example" button in "Step 5 Delivery/Deliver Your Speech." **CD-ROM: Interactive Speech Guides/Persuasive Speech**

Review delivery skills in Chapter 11. If you are using visual aids, review presentation tips in Chapter 12.

TIP

Remember to make extended eye contact with individual members and to shift your gaze around the room.

For more on interactive listening, see page 77.

notes about changes you would like to make in the preparation or delivery of future speeches, and review them before you begin to plan your next speech.

Summary

Persuasive speaking is an important part of everyone's daily life. Often you will need to be able to convince others to agree with you—on campus, in your career, and in your community. Successful persuasion is not an accident; it is the result of a speaker's willingness to work hard and be open-minded. It takes carefully constructed arguments that are appropriate for the audience and consistent with the principles of ethical communication.

This Speech Guide presented a five-step process to follow when you are drafting a persuasive speech. The steps are summarized in the checklist (include any additional steps that your instructor advises or assigns). If you follow these guidelines, you will become a capable persuasive speaker who can earn the respect of an audience and have an influence.

Checklist

INVENTING YOUR PERSUASIVE SPEECH

Analyze Your Audience

____ Analyze your audience, and record the analysis on a Speech Grid (p. 427)

Select and Refine Your Topic

____ Select your topic (p. 429)

____ Draft a working thesis and specific purpose (p. 429)

Generate Ideas to Support Your Thesis

____ Brainstorm supporting ideas (p. 429)

____ Research your topic (p. 431)

Select the Best Ideas to Support Your Thesis

____ Ethical concerns (p. 432)

____ Audience analysis (p. 432)

____ Ideas for value or policy thesis (p. 433)

ORGANIZING YOUR PERSUASIVE SPEECH

Outline the Body

____ Select and outline main points appropriate for policy or value proposition (p. 434)

____ Develop and outline subpoints using ethos, logos, and pathos (p. 435)

Outline the Introduction and Conclusion

____ Draft an introduction containing attention-getter, thesis, connection with the audience, credibility, and preview (p. 436)

____ Draft a conclusion containing summary and clincher (p. 437)

Incorporate Transitions and Signposts

____ Use transitions to connect main points and major sections of the speech (p. 437)

____ Use signposts to highlight each part of a set of arguments and indicate a two-sided argument (p. 438)

USING EFFECTIVE STYLE IN YOUR PERSUASIVE SPEECH

____ Review and revise the language used in your outline to ensure you are using effective style, including presenting ideas in an interesting manner, using understandable words, avoiding difficult sentences, accurately stating claims, and avoiding biased language (p. 438)

REFINING AND PRACTICING YOUR PERSUASIVE SPEECH

____ Review and revise your outline from a critical perspective (p. 439)

____ Plan and practice extemporaneous delivery (p. 441)

DELIVERING YOUR PERSUASIVE SPEECH

____ Minimize speech anxiety (p. 442)

____ Follow delivery tips: speak with conviction, use vocal variety, maintain eye contact, and use effective body language, along with other appropriate delivery practices (p. 443)

____ Learn for your next speech by actively listening to feedback and analyzing your own speech (p. 443)

16 Guide to Special Occasion Speaking

Speeches that praise, celebrate, memorialize, or otherwise commemorate special occasions have a long history. A Sumerian tablet dating back to about 2000 B.C.E. records the funeral utterances of Ludingirra lamenting the loss of his father and wife. Eulogies describe "deeds and virtues of the deceased" and express the "grief and suffering of those left behind." They are composed in lofty phrases, "an understandable feature of funeral orations the world over and at all times."[1] *Epideictic* rhetoric, a speech that praises or blames, was one of the three genres of rhetoric identified by Aristotle (trans. 1991).[2] This form of address was typically delivered on ceremonial occasions such as funerals or holidays and often celebrated timeless virtues.[3] Speeches continue to be a hallmark of special occasions in modern times. Speakers celebrate the Fourth of July, wish a newly married couple a life of happiness, or offer advice to a graduating class. A speech that entertains a club or organization after a meal is as traditional as the "rubber chicken" main course.

In Chapter 16 we examine the process of special occasion speaking and present three special occasion speeches, one delivered in the classroom and two in the community. We analyze key features of each speech and provide suggestions you can use to develop a special occasion speech. We also review the key features of special occasion speeches in general. Then we take you through a five-step process for preparing your own special occasion speech, incorporating the principles of public speaking developed in Part One of this text. The five steps are the same for any prepared speech, but the decisions you make during each step are influenced by the audience and by the occasion.

You are likely to be asked to speak on some special occasion sometime, and you will face the problem of deciding what to say. Consider the speeches you have heard at graduations, weddings, funerals or memorial services, awards ceremonies, and other events. Regardless of the occasion, chances are good that the best of these speeches had these qualities:

- The speech appealed to pathos. You laughed, cried, felt proud, or felt angry, or you experienced a range of emotions.

- The speech suited the mood of the occasion, whether joyous or solemn, lighthearted or serious.

- The speech content was appropriate for the occasion. Whether the occasion was a wedding, graduation, national holiday, or some other event, the speaker addressed a fitting subject.

- The speech was adapted to the audience. The speaker related the subject area to the audience's expectations for a speech on that occasion and related the topic to the audience's interests and values.

What makes a special occasion speech effective? As you read each speech, identify the main ideas that each speaker presents and the ways that the speakers develop their points. Does each speaker present a message that is appropriate for the occasion and the audience?

Speeches

View "My Hero, Marilyn
Hamilton" by Lillian Gentz.
CD-ROM: Video Theater, Full
Speeches

Lillian Gentz presented this speech in her public speaking class at Fresno City College. The assignment was a "heroes speech." Each student was to select a hero in his or her community or culture and tell the class why this person is a hero.[4] This speech is an example of an epideictic speech—a speech in praise (as in this case) or blame. As you read, notice how Gentz uses the principles of effective public speaking to tell the audience why Marilyn Hamilton is a hero to her.

My Hero, Marilyn Hamilton

BY LILLIAN GENTZ

Did you ever wonder how you would react if you had an accident and suddenly became paralyzed? It is not something we care to daydream about, is it? But accidents can and do happen. One occurred on a beautiful summer day in 1979. Marilyn Hamilton was hang gliding, one of her favorite passions. But on this particular day, she forgot to hook herself to her hang glider. As she plunged off the mountain, she desperately held on to her perch, which immediately sent her aircraft into a nosedive. She crashed and broke her back, becoming paralyzed from the waist down. Did this accident turn Marilyn Hamilton into a bitter person? Did she lose her zest for life? Did she quit?

The answer is no. That is why I am pleased to have the chance to tell you about my hero, Marilyn Hamilton.

You might wonder how an adventurer and athlete such as Marilyn was able to overcome paralysis, resuming her athletic career and building a very successful business.

I learned about Marilyn while working for Sunrise Medical, a company you will hear more about soon.

Today, I will focus on two of her most impressive accomplishments, Marilyn Hamilton's wheelchair manufacturing company and her successful athletic career.

I am going to begin by telling you how Marilyn achieved great success in the business world.

Starting a wheelchair manufacturing company was the last thing on Marilyn's mind when she asked her friends, Don Helman and Jim Okamoto, to create a lightweight wheelchair for her. The truth is, she hated the conventional wheelchairs because they were bulky, confining, and heavy. But most of all, the color didn't match any of her outfits. That was when the first hot purple Quickies with gold rims came to be.

In 1980, Motion Designs emerged from Don Helman's backyard shed. Sam Maddox, in *Marilyn Hamilton: A Play in Three Acts,* Web site visited August 31, 2001, reported that the company "revised the passive image of a wheelchair to one of fun and pride" and that "the chairs began to sell like crazy."

In 1985, the Quickie II was created. It was the first high-performance, folding chair to be marketed. Sam Maddox reported that "all of a sudden, Quickie was the industry standard and Marilyn Hamilton was the California businessperson of the year." Motion Designs earned $21 million from sales in 1986.

Motion Designs merged with Sunrise Medical, a larger medical equipment business in December 1986. Marilyn first served as vice president for corporate responsibility and later she became vice president for consumer development. In this position, Marilyn notes that her goal is to "preserve freedom of choice, encourage self-sufficiency, and ensure that consumers have a voice."

Now that we have seen how Marilyn Hamilton was the cofounder of a company that revolutionized the wheelchair industry, let's consider a second reason that she is my hero—her athletic accomplishments.

Marilyn refused to let paralysis hold her back from the sports that she loved.

One of her top sports is tennis. Marilyn was a two-time champion at the U.S. Women's Open Wheelchair Tournament. In 1999, her tennis wheelchair was displayed at the Smithsonian Institution.

Another sport is snow skiing. Marilyn is a six-time National Disabled Ski Champion. On the world level, the *Fresno Bee,* February 18, 1988, reported that Marilyn won the silver medal at the World Winter Disabled Games in Innsbruck, Austria.

Last but not least, Marilyn continued hang gliding after her injury, only retiring from that activity two years ago.

Now we have seen how Marilyn became paralyzed, how she created a highly successful business, and continued to experience extraordinary accomplishments as an athlete.

In closing, I would like to share with you the favorite saying of my hero, Marilyn Hamilton. "I am not made or unmade by the things that happen to me, but rather, by how I react to them." I ask you again—if you had an accident and became paralyzed, how would you react?

● *Analyzing the Characteristics of Special Occasion Speeches*

The content of Lillian Gentz's speech is appropriate for the occasion. Her speech is an example of an epideictic speech, or a speech of praise (or blame). In this case, she is praising the hero she selected, Marilyn Hamilton. As an epideictic speaker should, Lillian focuses on specific examples of Marilyn Hamilton's achievements in sports and in the business world, rather than offering unsupported generalizations. She provides concrete evidence of what her hero accomplished, including the $21 million business that she cofounded and her awards in tennis and skiing.

Gentz used implicit criteria for what constitutes a hero. Her audience was likely to support her viewpoint that Marilyn Hamilton was an appropriate choice. After all, Marilyn's response to a tragedy that would devastate most people was to create a successful business that revolutionized the wheelchair industry and to excel in sports. Had Gentz chosen a controversial or an unpopular person, she would have needed to put more emphasis on the appropriate criteria for hero status. For example, if she had selected a local official who made an unpopular decision or a labor leader who led a

To review criteria for value judgments, see page 187.

bitter strike, it would have been helpful to develop the point that heroes follow their conscience even when their actions are difficult or controversial.

Gentz incorporated pathos into her hero speech. Marilyn Hamilton responded to her paralysis by working to make life better for adults and children who use wheelchairs. At the same time, she was a champion athlete in two sports. Gentz's narratives of Marilyn Hamilton's accomplishments are positive and upbeat, and they cannot help but leave the audience touched and impressed.

Special occasion speeches should follow the same principles of organization that are appropriate for any other speech. Notice how Lillian Gentz began her speech with an introduction that included an attention-getter, topic statement, credibility statement, and preview. She also connected the speech to the audience by asking listeners to consider how any person could respond successfully to such a serious accident.

The speech is clearly divided into an introduction, body, and conclusion. Gentz uses transitions to bridge from one main idea to the next. For example, on page 449 she uses the transition statement "Now that we have seen how Marilyn Hamilton was the cofounder of a company that revolutionized the wheelchair industry, let's consider a second reason that she is my hero. . . ." Gentz also uses signposts to make the structure of her speech clear to the audience. Signposts signal the beginning of her discussion of each sport that Marilyn Hamilton is active in: "One of her top sports is tennis" (p. 449); "Another sport is snow skiing" (p. 449).

Gentz also includes evidence in her presentation. Local research sources support her claims. The use of evidence from a local newspaper allowed her to relate the speech directly to her audience.

You can use LEXIS/NEXIS to research many newspapers. See page 152 for information.

● *Planning Your Special Occasion Speech*

When your assignment is to present an epideictic speech about a person, one of the greatest challenges is selecting an appropriate individual to praise (or blame). For classroom speeches, be aware of the requirements for the assignment. In Lillian Gentz's class, the expectation was that students would select a hero from their culture or community. Your teacher may not want a speech about a celebrity whom you do not know, such as a professional athlete or entertainer. View epideictic speeches as an opportunity to tell audience members about a person you are familiar with whom they may not know. When you brainstorm possible persons for your speech, consider people who have made a difference in your life, your community, and your culture.

Lillian Gentz focused on two achievements of her hero—Marilyn Hamilton's business accomplishments and sports successes. Your epideictic speech should also be focused. A long list of a person's desirable qualities and achievements will overload the audience. You may decide that your main points will emphasize one major activity, or you may decide to use a limited number of main points to focus on a few significant characteristics or accomplishments. Use audience analysis to decide which approach is likely to give the audience the best picture of the person you are commending.

Lillian Gentz was well informed about the activities of her hero and thus able to provide many specific examples of Marilyn Hamilton's successes. You should have similar information about the subject of your speech. In addition to library and Internet research, you can obtain this information by interviewing the person you have selected or other people who know your person well. Being chosen is an honor, and you have a good chance of getting an interview, unless your person is famous or very busy.

For tips on interview research, see page 167.

Graduations are a customary time for special occasion speeches. Author Naomi Wolf (author of The Beauty Myth*) delivered this speech at Scripps College in Claremont, California, in 1992.[5] Scripps is a women's college, and Wolf's objective was to give the graduating class some advice that had been missing from the commencement speech at her own graduation from Yale in 1984.*

A Woman's Place

BY NAOMI WOLF

Even the best of revolutions can go awry when we internalize the attitudes we are fighting. The class of 1992 is graduating into a violent backlash against the advances women have made over the last 20 years. This backlash ranges from a senator using *The Exorcist* against Anita Hill, to beer commercials with the "Swedish bikini team." Today I want to give you a backlash survival kit, a four-step manual to keep the dragons from taking up residence inside your own heads.

My own commencement, at Yale, eight years ago, was the Graduation from Hell. The speaker was Dick Cavett, rumored to have been our president's brother in an all-male secret society. [*Authors' note:* Dick Cavett has been a talk show host for various networks since 1969.]

Mr. Cavett took the microphone and paled at the sight of hundreds of female about-to-be Yale graduates. "When I was an undergraduate," I recall he said, "there were no women. The women went to Vassar. At Vassar, they had nude photographs taken of the women in gym class to check their posture. One year the photos were stolen, and turned up for sale in New Haven's red light district." His punchline? "The photos found no buyers."

I'll never forget that moment. There we were, silent in our black gowns, our tassels, our brand-new shoes. We dared not break the silence with hisses or boos, out of respect for our families who'd come so far; and they kept still out of concern for us. Consciously or not, Mr. Cavett was using the beauty myth aspect of the backlash: when women come too close to masculine power, someone will draw critical attention to their bodies. We might be Elis, but we still wouldn't make pornography worth buying.

That afternoon, several hundred men were confirmed in the power of a powerful institution. But many of the women felt the shame of the powerless: the choking on silence, the complicity, the helplessness. We were orphaned from the institution.

I want to give you the commencement talk that was denied to me.

Message No. 1 in your survival kit: Redefine "becoming a woman." Today you have "become women." But that sounds odd in ordinary usage. What is usually meant by "You're a real woman now"? You "become a woman" when you menstruate for the first time, or when you lose your virginity, or when you have a child.

These biological definitions are very different from how we say boys become men. One "becomes a man" when he undertakes responsibility, or completes a quest. But you, too, in some ways more than your male friends graduating today, have moved into maturity through a solitary quest for the adult self. We lack archetypes for the questing young woman, her trials by fire; for how one "becomes a woman" through the chrysalis of education, the difficult passage from one book, one idea to the next. Let's refuse to have our scholarship and our gender pitted against each other. In our definition, the scholar learns womanhood and the woman learns scholarship; Plato and Djuna Barnes, mediated to their own enrichment through the eyes of the female body with its wisdoms and its gifts.

I say that you have already shown courage: Many of you graduate today in spite of the post traumatic syndrome of acquaintance rape, which one-fourth of female students undergo. Many of you were so weakened by anorexia and bulimia that it took every ounce of your will to get your work in. You negotiated private lives through a mine field of new strains of VD and the ascending shadow of AIDS. Triumphant survivors, you have already "become women."

Message No. 2 breaks the ultimate taboo for women. Ask for money in your lives. Expect it. Own it. Learn to use it. Little girls learn a debilitating fear of money—that it's not feminine to ensure we are fairly paid for honest work. Meanwhile, women make 68 cents for every male dollar and half of marriages end in divorce, after which women's income drops precipitously.

Never choose a profession for material reasons. But whatever field your heart decides on, for god's sake get the most specialized training in it you can and hold out hard for just compensation, parental leave, and child care. Resist your assignment to the class of highly competent, grossly underpaid women who run the show while others get the case—and the credit. Claim money not out of greed, but so you can tithe to women's political organizations, shelters, and educational institutions. Sexist institutions won't yield power if we are just patient long enough. The only language the status quo understands is money, votes, and public embarrassment.

When you have equity, you have influence—as sponsors, shareholders, and alumnae. Use it to open opportunities to women who deserve the chances you've had. Your B.A. does not belong to you alone, just as the earth does not belong to its present tenants alone. Your education was lent to you by women of the past, and you will give some back to living women, and to your daughters seven generations from now.

Message No. 3: Never cook for or sleep with anyone who routinely puts you down.

Message No. 4: Become goddesses of disobedience. Virginia Woolf once wrote that we must slay the Angel of the House, the censor within. Young women tell me of injustices, from campus rape coverups to classroom sexism. But at the thought of confrontation, they freeze into niceness. We are told that the worst thing we can do is cause conflict, even in the service of doing right. Antigone is imprisoned. Joan of Arc burns at the stake. And someone might call us unfeminine.

When I wrote a book that caused controversy, I saw how big a dragon was this paralysis by niceness. "The Beauty Myth" argues that newly rigid ideals of beauty are instruments of a backlash against feminism, designed to lower women's self-esteem for a political purpose. Many positive changes followed the debate. But all that would dwindle away when someone yelled at me—as, for instance, cosmetic surgeons did on TV, when I raised questions about silicone implants. Oh, no, I'd quail, people are mad at me!

Then I read something by the poet Audre Lorde. She'd been diagnosed with breast cancer. "I was going to die," she wrote, "sooner or later, whether or not I had even spoken myself. My silences had not protected me. Your silences will not protect you. . . . What are the words you do not yet have? What are the tyrannies you swallow day by day and attempt to make your own, until you will sicken and die of them, still in silence? We have been socialized to respect fear more than our own need for language."

I began to ask each time: "What's the worst that could happen to me if I tell this truth?" Unlike women in other countries, our breaking silence is unlikely to have us jailed, "disappeared" or run off the road at night. Our speaking out will irritate some people, get us called bitchy or hypersensitive and disrupt some dinner parties. And our speaking out will permit other women to speak, until laws are changed and lives are saved and the world is altered forever.

Next time, ask: What's the worst that will happen? Then push yourself a little further than you dare. Once you start to speak, people *will* yell at you. They *will* interrupt you, put you down and suggest it's personal. And the world won't end.

And speaking will get easier and easier. And you will find that you have fallen in love with your own vision, which you may never have realized you had. And you will lose some friends and lovers, and realize you don't miss them. And new ones will find you and cherish you.

And you will still flirt and paint your nails, dress up and party, because, as I think Emma Goldman said, "If I can't dance, I don't want to be part of your revolution." And at last you'll know with surpassing certainty that only one thing is more frightening than speaking your truth. And that is not speaking.

● *Analyzing the Characteristics of Special Occasion Speeches*

The content of special occasion speeches often includes customary themes for the occasion. One traditional theme at graduation is advice for the future, and such advice is the focus of Naomi Wolf's speech. She begins with an argument that sexism is a reality in the world the graduates will be entering, particularly when women get too close to power. Then she presents the graduates with four pieces of advice for negotiating that world.

Naomi Wolf's advice was adapted to her target audience, the graduating seniors of a women's college. Her message centered on advice for women making the transition from a college with a goal of nurturing women to a "real world" that she believed offered much less support to women. A speaker addressing a graduating class of both men and women would need to offer advice to both male and female graduates. For example, a persuasive message to encourage males in the graduating class to act against sexism in the workplace could be included.

Special occasion speeches make greater use of narratives and anecdotes to support claims than is typical in a persuasive or informative speech. Wolf supported her contention that women are critiqued when they get too close to positions of power with a narrative: at her own graduation, the speaker put down college women with an insulting joke about their appearance.

You can see in Naomi Wolf's speech several of the principles of effective organization that you have been studying. Her introduction gained the audience's attention with a striking statement: "The class of 1992 is graduating into a violent backlash against the advances women have made over the last 20 years." She oriented the audience with a clear topic statement, saying that she was giving the audience a four-step "backlash survival kit." The body of the speech is well organized. She had four main points, each a recommendation for the graduates, and she used signposting ("Message No. 1," "Message No. 2," and so on) to make it clear when she was moving from one main point to the next.

To review creative wording of main points, see page 272.

Naomi Wolf also used effective style to present her message. Her main points were creatively worded. Instead of simply saying, "I have four pieces of advice," she characterized her advice as a "survival kit." She used the metaphor of a chrysalis to describe the education process. (A *chrysalis* is a protected stage of development experienced by, for example, a butterfly, before it emerges from its cocoon.) She characterized women who speak out and speak up even though their speech upsets other people as "goddesses of disobedience."

● *Planning Your Special Occasion Speech*

Naomi Wolf is an accomplished author, and she uses her own credibility to support her contentions. In your special occasion speech, you will need evidence to support the facts that you are presenting. It is also important to be aware of the proof required to convince your audience. Wolf assumed that the graduating class at a women's college (where she was an invited speaker) would agree with her statistics and arguments about date rape, classroom sexism, and inequalities in the workplace. You need to know which facts your audience is likely to accept. If a different graduation speaker were to tell the same audience that classroom sexism was a greater problem for males than for females, he or she would need to support that claim with evidence from sources that would be credible to the Scripps College audience.

Be aware of your instructor's evidence requirements when you plan your classroom special occasion speeches.

Wolf emphasized one traditional theme of commencement speeches: advice for the graduates. Other traditional commencement topics, such as complimenting the graduates for their hard work and reflecting on the school's special qualities, were not included in this speech. Wolf was a well-known author and invited speaker, so it was reasonable to assume that the graduates would appreciate a speech presenting advice based on her expertise and experiences. When you plan a special occasion speech, be aware of the themes that are traditionally addressed on that occasion. Be certain that your message focuses on appropriate themes and generally includes topics that your audience expects to have addressed.

Yitzhak Rabin, the prime minister of Israel, was assassinated on November 4, 1995, while addressing over 100,000 persons at a peace rally in Tel Aviv. Many world leaders attended his funeral, and eulogists including King Hussein of Jordan and U.S. president Bill Clinton spoke of his leadership and his contributions to Middle East peace. One of the most memorable eulogies was presented by Noa Ben Artzi-Pelossof, Rabin's granddaughter.[6] She told mourners of the loss her family felt, and she shared her special memories of Rabin as a grandfather, breaking "into tears as she delivered the funeral's most moving eulogy."[7] As you read her eulogy, notice how she eloquently expresses her family's sorrow and provides insight into Rabin as a family person.

Eulogy at the Funeral of Yitzhak Rabin

BY NOA BEN ARTZI-PELOSSOF

Please excuse me for not wanting to talk about the peace. I want to talk about my grandfather.

You always awake from a nightmare, but since yesterday I have been continually awakening to a nightmare. It is not possible to get used to the nightmare of life without you. The television never ceases to broadcast pictures of you, and you are so alive that I can almost touch you — but only almost, and I won't be able to anymore.

Grandfather, you were the pillar of fire in front of the camp and now we are left in the camp alone, in the dark; and we are so cold and so sad. I know that people talk in terms of a national tragedy, and of comforting an entire nation, but we feel the huge void that remains in your absence when grandmother doesn't stop crying. Few people really knew you. Now they will talk about you for quite some time, but I feel that they really don't know just how great the pain is, how great the tragedy is; something has been destroyed.

Grandfather, you were and still are our hero. I want you to know that every time I did anything, I saw you in front of me. Your appreciation and your love accompanied us every step down the road, and our lives were always shaped by your values. You, who never abandoned anything, are now abandoned. And here you are, my ever-present hero, cold, alone, and I cannot do anything to save you. You are missed so much.

Others greater than I have already eulogized you, but none of them ever had the pleasure I had to feel the caresses of your arms, your soft hands, to merit your warm embrace that was reserved only for us, to see your half-smile that always told me so much, that same smile which is no longer, frozen in the grave with you.

I have no feelings of revenge because my pain and feelings of loss are so large, too large. The ground has been swept out from below us, and we are groping now, trying to wander about in this empty void, without any success so far.

I am not able to finish this; left with no alternative, I say good-bye to you, hero, and ask you to rest in peace and think about us, and miss us, as down here we love you so very much. I imagine angels are accompanying you now, and I ask them to take care of you because you deserve their protection.

We love you, Saba, forever.

● *Analyzing the Characteristics of Special Occasion Speeches*

In special occasion speeches, the content of the message is determined by the occasion itself and the audience's expectations for a speech on that occasion. Jill Werman Harris wrote that "a great eulogist honors the dead uniquely, speaking not only about what everyone treasured most but about what captivated him [or her] personally."[8]

Noa Ben Artzi-Pelossof's speech exemplifies the use of pathos in a special occasion speech. She moved her audience because she shared personal memories of her grandfather, Yitzhak Rabin. The world leaders who spoke at the funeral honored Rabin's accomplishments as a soldier, leader, and advocate for Arab-Israeli peace. Ben Artzi-Pelossof captivated the audience by sharing her feelings about Rabin as a grandfather. She recalled his soft hands, his warm embrace reserved for the family, his half-smile that told her so much. She presented him as a family hero whose appreciation and love accompanied family members at every step.

The eulogist shares his or her grief at the loss of a loved one. Noa Ben Artzi-Pelossof expressed her family's grief eloquently. She described life without her grandfather as "continually awakening to a nightmare," a "void that remains . . . when grandmother doesn't stop crying." It is also customary to offer hope in eulogies, and Ben Artzi-Pelossof said she imagined that angels were with her grandfather now and asked the angels to care for him.

The style in Noa Ben Artzi-Pelossof's eulogy is exceptional. She uses the metaphor "the pillar of fire in front of the camp" to describe her grandfather, noting that his death has left her family "in the camp alone, in the dark; . . . so cold and so sad." She expresses the tragic irony that Rabin, a person who "never abandoned anything, [is] now abandoned." She describes life without her grandfather as "groping now, trying to wander about in this empty void." Her language dramatically conveys the depth of her feelings.

Although a speaker at a funeral is not held to the same requirements for organization that would be expected in a classroom speech, Noa Ben Artzi-Pelossof's speech does have an introduction, body, and conclusion. In the introduction, she indicates that she will not be talking about Middle East peace; instead, she will tell the audience about Yitzhak Rabin, her grandfather. She then offers several thoughts about her family's grief and her special memories. We can list these thoughts, which constitute the body of her speech, in outline form:

I. Life without grandfather is a nightmare.
II. The loss of Yitzhak Rabin is an even greater family tragedy than a national tragedy.
III. Yitzhak Rabin was a hero to his family.
IV. No other eulogist could know what a warm and caring grandfather Yitzhak Rabin was.
V. Noa herself has no desire for revenge because her feelings of loss are too great.

Finally, Noa concludes by saying good-bye to her grandfather and asking the angels to care for him. She ends with a brief but effective clincher: "We love you, Saba, forever."

● *Planning Your Special Occasion Speech*

A eulogy should capture memories that are special to you. When developing a list of the thoughts that you might express about someone who has died, write down special times you had together, lessons you learned from the person you are honoring, and his or her traits that you admired. Noa Ben Artzi-Pelossof did not need to discuss Yitzhak Rabin, the world leader, because other eulogists covered this subject. If there are highlights of a person's life that the audience would expect to see covered and no other speaker is likely to mention them, you can include them in your eulogy along with your special memories.

Delivery of a eulogy can present a special challenge. The loss of a loved one or some other special person is very difficult, and you may choke up or be overcome by emotion during your speech. Remember that audience members are also grieving. If you need to pause, cry, or collect your thoughts, do so. If your emotions overwhelm you when you express an idea, you may try to express it in another way or move on to a new thought. The audience will understand your sincerity and the depth of your feelings.

You may have only a short time to prepare and practice a eulogy. You may not be able to prepare a full sentence outline, but extemporaneous delivery from limited notes will be very effective. If you write down the basic thoughts you want to express and speak from the heart, your audience will appreciate the message. If you have limited time to prepare, try to practice your speech at least once. This will help you to identify any thoughts that are likely to be too difficult to express in words.

Summary: Key Features of Special Occasion Speeches

After reading the speeches of Gentz, Wolf, and Ben Artzi-Pelossof, you may have noted several important characteristics of a special occasion speech, regardless of whether it is a hero speech, a graduation speech, or a eulogy. Although the messages vary greatly, they have several characteristics in common.

● *The content of a special occasion speech is appropriate for the occasion.*

The appropriate content for any special occasion speech is determined by social norms and traditions, although in a diverse society there is not likely to be only one tradition for any given occasion. Explaining the achievements of a hero, giving advice to a graduating class, and sharing memories of a deceased loved one are very different purposes. In each of the speeches presented in this chapter the content fits the occasion. Highlighting the virtues of a person who has died (as Noa Ben Artzi-Pelossof did) is customary in nearly any eulogy. Naomi Wolf's advice for women when they encounter sexism was specifically tailored for the women in the graduating class. When you must deliver a special occasion speech, keep in mind the type of message your audience will be expecting.

● *Appeals to pathos are a hallmark of special occasion speeches.*

A good speaker incorporates ethos, pathos, and logos in any speech. In special occasion speeches, however, there is often a greater emphasis on appeals to pathos. Lillian Gentz wanted her audience to admire her hero, Marilyn Hamilton. Naomi Wolf hoped to arouse indignation with the narrative of her own graduation and by presenting issues such as disparities in pay received by men and women. Noa Ben Artzi-Pelossof wanted her audience to empathize with her family's sense of personal loss and feel even greater admiration for Yitzhak Rabin.

Eloquent style heightens the emotional appeal of special occasion speeches. Noa Ben Artzi-Pelossof described her grandfather as "the pillar of fire" that lighted the camp. Naomi Wolf asked members of the graduating class to speak out for their beliefs and become "goddesses of disobedience."

● *Special occasion speeches place greater reliance on narratives and anecdotes as supporting materials, although evidence remains important.*

Lillian Gentz used a narrative style to highlight Marilyn Hamilton's remarkable entry into the business world. Naomi Wolf used the example of her own graduation to illustrate sexist attitudes in society. Noa Ben Artzi-Pelossof used anecdotes and examples to give the audience insight into her grandfather's humanity.

Although narratives and anecdotes are used more frequently as supporting materials in special occasion speeches, the speakers also offer evidence to support their points. Gentz included research to show Marilyn Hamilton's accomplishments in business and sports. Professional speakers often rely more on their own credibility to support claims than is common in classroom speeches. Nevertheless, Naomi Wolf used quotations from Audre Lorde and Emma Goldman to reinforce points she was making.

● *Special occasion speeches retain organization and structure.*

Regardless of a speaker's rhetorical purpose, good organization helps the audience to understand a speech. Lillian Gentz organized her main points by topic. She presented the subpoints for main point one in chronological order and for main point two in a topical order. Naomi Wolf and Noa Ben Artzi-Pelossof also carefully organized their messages. Ben Artzi-Pelossof oriented her audience at the outset, telling listeners that she wanted to talk about Yitzhak Rabin as a grandfather. She then developed five distinct ideas about her grandfather. Wolf began with an attention-getter and oriented the audience by telling listeners that she would provide a four-step survival manual. The four-step division was an effective technique for splitting her advice into distinct main points and for creating signposts to signal her movement from one element of advice to the next.

For an outline of these main ideas, see page 457.

Preparing Your Special Occasion Speech

A Five-Step Process

Use your CD-ROM to build your speech using a five-step process.
CD-ROM: Interactive Speech Guides/Special Occasion Speech

Use your CD-ROM to analyze your audience. Go to "Step 1 Invention/Analyze Audience."
CD-ROM: Interactive Speech Guides/Special Occasion Speech

Selecting and refining a topic is the subject of Chapter 6.

To review the steps in topic selection, see page 122.

The Speech Assignment

Prepare a speech to be delivered on a special occasion. Your speech content should be appropriate for the occasion and the audience you will be addressing. As you develop your speech, follow the five-step process described here to invent, organize, stylize, refine and practice, and deliver your speech.

1. Inventing Your Speech

Drafting an effective special occasion speech begins with careful preparation and planning. You need to analyze your audience, select a topic, draft a topic statement, brainstorm ideas for developing your topic, research your subject, and select the ideas that will help you achieve your purpose ethically and effectively. The occasion that creates the opportunity for you to speak should have an important influence on your speech content.

● Analyze Your Audience

The audience drives the message should be a familiar principle by now. For special occasion speeches, you need to know what type of speech your audience will be expecting. Begin your preparation by analyzing your audience and recording your analysis on a Speech Grid.

Situational Characteristics. In a special occasion speech, the situation is particularly important. What is the occasion? Why is the audience in attendance?

Audience Demographics. Analyze factors such as age, group membership, and religious and political affiliation. In a special occasion speech, you often develop ideas with narratives, anecdotes, and appeals to pathos. Audience demographics can help you decide which of these will be most effective. Many special occasions call for humor, and demographic information will assist you in choosing appropriate jokes and other entertaining material.

Common Ground. Consider what you and the audience have in common. You often deliver special occasion speeches to groups such as family and friends, a cultural group, or an organization. Pay special interest to the characteristics of these groups as you search for common ground.

● Select and Refine Your Topic

Select Your Topic. Initially, consider whether the occasion calls for a particular topic. A speech at a memorial service must focus on the person being commemorated, and the presentation of an award to the teacher of the year will focus on the honoree. If your audience will expect a particular topic, that topic should ordinarily be your selection.

If you have flexibility in choosing a topic, brainstorm subjects that would fit the occasion. Different sets of topics should come to mind for a speech on the Fourth of July, the dedication of a new school building, or an after-dinner speech for a civic organization. Here are some questions that you can ask to focus your brainstorming:

- What do you think of when you consider the occasion? Different events, such as Veterans Day, a retirement dinner, or a graduation should bring different ideas to mind.

- Have you had previous experiences that are relevant to the occasion?

- What have you learned about the occasion at school? from your family? from other members of your culture?

- Who is going to be in your audience? What subjects might listeners expect to be addressed on this occasion? Do they have particular interests or beliefs that may suggest potential topics?

You can add to your list of potential topics by researching. If you are unsure what topics are customary on a particular occasion, research that occasion. Use publications such as *Vital Speeches* or Internet resources to learn what topics others have addressed at that type of event. Remember, however, that you are just researching possible topics. It would be unethical to use another person's speech without attribution. When searching on the Internet, consider speech sites, and also search for Web sites pertaining to the event or holiday itself.

After developing a list of potential topics, select the best one for your speech. Consider how well each topic fits the audience's expectations. Your final selection should be a subject on which you will be a credible speaker. Special occasions are often emotional events, so it is important for you to be able to speak sincerely. Be sure your topic is appropriate, given the location and time of your speech and the number of people in the audience. If you are presenting a classroom speech, be certain that the topic fits the requirements of the assignment.

Sometimes a speaker feels compelled to deliver a special occasion speech that is not traditional for the occasion. For example, a graduation speaker wants to critique the school rather than congratulate the senior class and offer advice for the future, or a person speaking on a national holiday feels compelled to speak out on a social issue that has little to do with the occasion. In these situations, there may be a conflict between two important principles of public speaking: (1) messages should be adapted to the audience, and (2) ethical speakers do not present a message they do not support.

If you are a "conscientious objector" and sincerely do not believe in the traditional message for a special occasion, what should you do? One possibility is to consider whether your nontraditional message will be accepted. Kim Phuc spoke at the Vietnam War Memorial on Veterans Day in 1996. A photograph of her when she was a child in Vietnam, running away from a napalm fire during the war, had gained national prominence. She did not deliver a traditional speech honoring and thanking U.S. veterans; instead she asked the audience to stop fighting and killing around the world. She established ethos with a message of forgiveness rather than bitterness, noting that if she could talk to the pilot who dropped the bombs, she would tell

Use your CD-ROM to select and refine your topic. Go to "Step 1 Invention/Select Topic."
CD-ROM: Interactive Speech Guides/Special Occasion Speech

him "we cannot change history but we should try to do good things for the present and for the future to promote peace."[9] Kim Phuc also appealed to pathos, relating that she had feared that because of her burns she would never marry or have children, yet now she had a husband and son. Her Veterans Day message was nontraditional, but her own ethos and experience made the speech appropriate.

Mumia Abu-Jamal was invited to present a taped commencement speech at Evergreen College in Olympia, Washington, in 1999. Abu-Jamal had been found guilty of murdering a police officer in 1981 and sentenced to death. In December 2001, a federal judge reduced this sentence to life imprisonment unless Pennsylvania conducts a new sentencing hearing. He denies the charges and continues to appeal. Like Kim Phuc, Abu-Jamal did not give a traditional speech, instead arguing for the rights of repressed people in the United States. However, the reason the student committee at Evergreen College selected him was that he was a "powerful voice against the death penalty."[10] By *not* presenting a typical commencement address, he was meeting audience expectations.

Another possibility when you prefer not to give a traditional speech is to consider whether you can adapt to the audience without compromising your beliefs. When U.S. First Lady Barbara Bush addressed the graduating class at Wellesley College in 1990, she faced an audience adaptation challenge. She was the second-choice speaker. Students' first choice, author Alice Walker, was unable to attend. One hundred fifty students had signed a petition expressing outrage that the college was honoring this woman who had gained recognition through her husband's achievements, contradicting what they had been taught at Wellesley.[11] Mrs. Bush related her speech to the audience without contradicting her own beliefs. Rather than taking a position on the question of choosing a career or a family, she advised members of the graduating class to follow their dreams, whatever they might be. When she talked about the importance of making time for family life, she made clear her belief that this responsibility falls equally on fathers and mothers.[12]

The most drastic possibility when a traditional speech seems out of the question is to consider whether to decline the invitation to speak. If you cannot in good conscience present a message that satisfies audience expectations, one of your options is not to speak. A critical message at a funeral would be likely to cause emotional pain. A controversial speech might put a damper on a graduation or holiday celebration. In these circumstances, your speech would do more harm than good. Moreover, your ethos would be low because you violated audience expectations, so such a speech would be unlikely to be persuasive. If you have an important point to make, it may be best to present it in a different forum.

Instead of turning down an invitation, however, you could ask the person who invites you for feedback on the message that you would like to deliver. People who know the audience well can tell you whether your proposed speech would violate the audience's expectations, and you could discuss speech possibilities that would meet those expectations without compromising your beliefs.

In the classroom, you need to complete an assignment to receive credit, so declining to speak is not a viable option. If there is a message that you are uncomfortable delivering, talk to your instructor well in advance of the speech date.

Refine Your Topic.   To refine your topic, you need to determine your rhetorical purpose and narrow your topic so that you can cover it in the available time. Rhetorical purposes are more diverse for special occasion speeches than for informative or persuasive speeches, where the primary purpose is a given. A major part of Lillian Gentz's speech *informed* the audience about the accomplishments of her hero. Naomi Wolf delivered a *persuasive* message.

Depending on the context and audience, you may decide that your primary purpose is to inspire, entertain, inform, or persuade, or you may select a combination of purposes. Whatever rhetorical purpose you select should be consistent with audience members' expectations for the occasion. A persuasive sales message would be inappropriate on a patriotic holiday, but advocacy of national service would be reasonable. Listeners expect to be entertained at a roast, but a memorial ceremony should be more serious.

To review rhetorical purpose, see page 42.

You need to narrow the topic so that your message will fit the available time. Noa Ben Artzi-Pelossof did this by focusing on her grandfather as a family person, not as a statesman. Lillian Gentz emphasized Marilyn Hamilton's achievements in business and sports. The occasion may dictate the segment of your topic that you select. You could cover different aspects of a retiring person's life at an informal gathering at a pub than you would at a formal retirement dinner. Because several speakers are often asked to share the podium on special occasions, it is particularly important to select a message that you can present in a limited amount of time.

After you narrow your topic and identify your rhetorical purpose, draft your topic and specific purpose statements. Here are a few examples of special occasions and of topic and specific purpose statements that would be appropriate for those occasions:

Occasion: Martin Luther King Jr.'s Birthday

Topic statement: The pioneers of the civil rights movement made countless sacrifices to promote equal rights for all Americans.

Specific purpose: To inspire my audience never to forget the sacrifices made by the pioneers of the civil rights movement.

Occasion: An End-of-Summer-Camp Dinner

Topic statement: My summer as a volunteer camp counselor was filled with humorous experiences and inspiring stories.

Specific purpose: To provide the audience with an entertaining and inspiring look at my summer as a volunteer camp counselor.

Occasion: A Reception Following a Baby's Blessing or Naming Ceremony (a speech by a good friend of the family)

Topic statement: Newborn baby Amanda can count on the love and support of her parents, her extended family, and myself.

Specific purpose: To provide listeners with an informative and inspiring look at the love and support that the parents, extended family, and I will provide for newborn baby Amanda.

After creating topic and specific purpose statements, you are ready to begin planning the content of your speech. Remember that your proposed topic is a *working* idea. You can modify it after gaining insights from your research or learning more from your audience analysis about audience members' perspectives.

Generate Ideas to Develop Your Topic

Use both brainstorming and research to create a list of ideas you may want to use to develop your topic. Record each idea in the appropriate section of your Speech Grid.

Use your CD-ROM to generate and select ideas to support your topic statement. Go to "Step 1 Invention/Generate Supporting Ideas" and "Select Supporting Ideas."
CD-ROM: Interactive Speech Guides/Special Occasion Speech

To review ethos, logos, and pathos, see page 38.

For brainstorming for informative messages, see page 391. For brainstorming for persuasive messages, see page 429.

Brainstorm Supporting Ideas.   Brainstorm ideas that will enable you to use ethos, pathos, and logos to develop your special occasion speech. When brainstorming, write down each idea that comes to mind. You can eliminate less promising ideas after completing your grid.

Develop Your Ethos.   Consider your connections to the person, occasion, or topic that will be the focus of your speech. What common ground between you and the audience is relevant to the special occasion: memories, love or respect for the person being honored? fond recollections of how an occasion is celebrated in your community or culture? shared experiences such as military or community service? Also consider how your connections to the occasion show that you are a knowledgeable and trustworthy source of information about your topic.

Develop Ideas Based on Logos.   Brainstorm ideas for your special occasion speech by considering your rhetorical purpose. If one of your objectives is to inform or persuade, ask the same type of questions that you would ask when brainstorming an informative or persuasive speech. If your purpose is to entertain, try to remember humorous or lighthearted stories and examples that fit the subject of your speech. If your goal is to inspire, consider facts about your topic that would be inspiring. Such facts include stories of making sacrifices, refusing to quit despite defeat, overcoming obstacles, placing the needs of others above personal desires, and standing up for principles.

Another brainstorming objective is to think of specific examples to back up generalizations you might make in your speech. Lillian Gentz did this well when she indicated Marilyn Hamilton's specific athletic successes. Special occasion speeches often include broad, general claims such as "Organized labor has long stood for the rights of the ordinary worker," "Yuka will be a great addition to our department," or "Christine was the backbone of our volunteer organization." Generalizations will be better understood and believed if backed up by specific examples.

Consider Appeals to Pathos.   Special occasions are often times when your audience will experience strong feelings. To create appeals to pathos, here are some questions to ask:

- What sentiments are appropriate for the occasion of the speech? How can you invoke these sentiments when speaking about your topic?

- If you are speaking about a person, what endearing qualities can you bring up? (Noa Ben Artzi-Pelossof's eulogy highlighted her grandfather's human qualities quite effectively.) Are there any compelling anecdotes that give insight on the person's character?

- What lessons have you learned (for example, from your family or culture) about why this occasion is special? Why is this occasion special for you?

Research Your Topic.   You need research to learn more about the topic of your special occasion speech and to find evidence to support the claims you will be making. We discussed the research process in detail in Chapter 7. Here we summarize those steps and provide specific advice for researching special occasion speeches.

To review the research process, see Chapter 7.

Inventory Your Research Needs. There are unique research needs for a special occasion speech, along with typical research requirements such as finding evidence to support the claims you make. Some areas of research are particularly important for special occasion speaking:

- *Consider customs and traditions for speeches on your occasion.* Learn what type of message is common on this occasion. Will the cultures represented in your audience have particular expectations?

- *Look for information about the occasion or person you are speaking about.* Be sure you are more informed about the topic or person than the typical audience member.

- *Find supporting evidence for facts you need to prove in your speech.* Lillian Gentz used evidence to show that Marilyn Hamilton was given an award as the California businessperson of the year. You will need evidence to support claims that are central to your speech, particularly claims that you lack the credibility to make without proof.

- *Discover narratives and anecdotes that explain or develop points you are making.* Such stories are often used to support claims and to add human interest to a special occasion speech. Barbara Bush used narrative to make a point in her 1990 graduation speech at Wellesley College. She advised graduates to follow their dreams. She supported her advice to be true to yourself with an anecdote about a little girl who was told to choose the role of a giant, wizard, or dwarf in a game that was being played. The child asked the adult leading the game where the mermaids were supposed to stand. When the adult stated that there were no mermaids in the game, the child replied, "Oh yes there are. I am a mermaid." She knew what she was and refused to give up her identity or the game.[13]

- *Locate humorous material when it is appropriate.* Many special occasions call for jokes or amusing anecdotes. You may need to research humorous material that fits the topic and occasion of your speech.

Have a System for Organizing Your Information.   A plan for organizing the research you do will make it easy to find evidence when you prepare your speech.

To review interview techniques, see page 167.

For more on recording evidence on a Speech Grid, see page 175.

For more on researching hard-to-find evidence, see page 150.

To review ethical principles, see Chapter 3.

Discover Sources of Information on Your Topic. Research a wide variety of sources. In special occasion speeches, you are often speaking about a person. Interviews with people who know (knew) that person are particularly good sources of information. If your purpose is entertainment, you can find jokes on a wide variety of subjects using Internet sources. There are also Web sites for holidays, and any organization you are addressing is likely to maintain a Web site, facilitating audience analysis.

Read and Prioritize Your Sources. Set your priorities for the research sources you will emphasize. In a special occasion speech, knowing as much as possible about the person or occasion being commemorated is particularly important. If you are making any claims that the audience may not accept as fact, you will need supporting evidence. As you find information that may be useful in your speech, record it on the "Speech Message" side of your Speech Grid. Be certain that you keep full citations on all evidence sources that you might use in your speech.

Identify Gaps in your Research, and Find Needed Information. Decide whether you know enough about the person or occasion being celebrated to prepare an effective speech. Review your Speech Grid to see whether there are any points you still lack evidence to support. If you are missing research on essential points, do targeted research to find that information.

Once you have researched your topic well, determine whether you are likely to accomplish your specific purpose with the ideas you have researched or recorded while brainstorming. If modifications in your specific purpose or topic statement are needed, make them now. Your objective should be determined so that you can make the best choices when selecting ideas from your grid.

● Select the Best Ideas to Develop Your Topic

Evaluate the supporting ideas on your grid. Base your evaluation on ethical considerations, your audience analysis, and the extent to which the ideas support your topic statement.

Ethical Questions in Content Selection. Ethics is an important issue in every speech context. Remember basic principles such as contributing to the audience's ability to make an informed decision and proper attribution of research sources. Eliminate from your grid any ideas that do not meet the criteria for ethical communication.

The Duty to Research. The ethical obligation to research your topic thoroughly is very important in a special occasion speech. You will not honor a person well if you get his or her alma mater, career, or group membership wrong. Many audience members will be aware of facts about the person or occasion being celebrated. Your ethos will suffer if you make statements that are untrue, even if they are favorable. If you are not certain whether a claim is true, seek confirmation or omit it from your grid.

"Stretching" the Facts and the Ethical Duty to Be Truthful. A different ethical problem occurs when there is a conflict between the speaker's ethical duty to be truthful and the audience's expectations and traditions for special

occasion speeches. In some special occasion contexts, lavish praise or positive thoughts are expected. At an awards presentation, it is anticipated that the recipient will be complimented. Favorable comments about a graduating class or a retiring coworker are expected. Aristotle noted that *amplification* is traditional in epideictic speeches: the speaker aims to show the superiority of the subject's accomplishments and to "cloth the actions with greatness and beauty."[14] Despite such traditions, however, extravagant praise may not be warranted by the facts. The person to be honored may have a checkered past, or members of the graduating class may have had more difficulties than their predecessors. Can a speaker be ethical but also consistent with the expectations of the occasion? Yes—here are some suggestions.

The speaker can emphasize good qualities that can be supported by the facts. A special occasion speech is not a comprehensive historical or critical review of a person or event. An appropriate rhetorical purpose may be to point out the best in a person's or group's accomplishments. For example, Richard Nixon resigned from the presidency in disgrace over the Watergate scandal in 1974. When he died in 1994, eulogists focused on his foreign policy accomplishments and said little about Watergate.[15]

Another possibility is to turn a negative into a positive. The tragic shootings at Columbine High School on April 20, 1999, provided a challenging context for a graduation speech. Graduating senior Sara Martin offered a message of hope. She used an analogy to the stained-glass windows at Kings College Chapel in Cambridge, England, which were taken apart and numbered to save them from World War II bombings and then rebuilt after the war. She offered this vision:

> [Although] our window may appear to have been shattered, we can
> achieve a greater beauty as we put the pieces back together again....
> Like the people of Cambridge, let us recognize what is worthy to be
> saved, to be restored, and in unity rebuild the Columbine window from
> which others may draw their inspiration.[16]

One more way in which the speaker can be both ethical and truthful is by reserving amplification for the best characteristics of the person or occasion. If extravagant praise is customary or expected, it need not be used throughout the speech or on a point where it is not warranted. Instead, it will be most effective if used to highlight the best qualities. Noa Ben Artzi-Pelossof used amplification at several key places in her eulogy—for example when she referred to her grandfather as the "pillar of fire" and when she said, "Your appreciation and your love accompanied us every step down the road, and our lives were always shaped by your values." Her judicious use of amplification made Yitzhak Rabin's special attributes stand out.

Audience Analysis and Content Selection.

Which ideas are best for accomplishing your rhetorical purpose depends on who your audience members are. To ensure that your speech is adapted well to the audience, expand your audience analysis and select the best ideas based on this analysis.

Audience analysis is the subject of Chapter 5.

The left side of your grid should already contain information about the speech situation, audience demographics, and common ground. Now that you have selected a topic and determined your specific purpose, you can add to your audience analysis. If you have the opportunity to survey or interview audience members, try to learn more about them. If you are addressing a group, you may be able to talk to one of its leaders to learn more about the group. If you cannot directly obtain information about your audience, use indirect methods. If you are speaking to an organization, take a look at any literature put out by the organization (such as a newsletter) or the organization's Web page.

For more on indirect audience analysis, see page 110.

It is important to take audience members' prior exposure to, and level of interest in, your topic into account when selecting ideas from your grid. On a religious holiday, a devout group of followers would expect you to focus on sacred aspects of the occasion, but for audience members who do not actively participate in their religion, an emphasis on secular topics may be more appropriate. If listeners have diverse religious affiliations, an *informative* message (not a *persuasive,* proselytizing one) about the history of the holiday could be best.

Also determine whether audience members are expecting you to take a particular approach. You want to know whether to emphasize serious, light-hearted, or humorous information. If you will be using humor, select material that will be considered amusing and in good taste.

To review audience worldview, see page 15.

Highlight ideas that will best relate your speech to audience members' values and emotions. If you hope to inspire members of your audience, the ideas you present should be consistent with their worldview. Anecdotes and narratives should be emotionally appealing to them. A story about a child's successful first deer hunt could appeal to pathos very effectively in an audience of hunters but not in an audience of animal rights activists.

Finally, choose ideas that best fit the speech situation. Do not select an anecdote or extended joke that would consume two or three minutes of a five-minute speech. Eliminate ideas that would not be appropriate given the time of day or location of your speech.

The Occasion, Your Purpose, and Content Selection.

From the ideas that meet ethical standards and are appropriate for your audience, select those that will be best for the occasion and purpose of your speech. Use a check mark, star, or highlighter to identify the ideas you would like to include in your speech.

Consider the Occasion.   Select ideas that best fit the mood of your occasion. An after-dinner speaker would use more funny material than Naomi Wolf or Lillian Gentz did, because she or he would be speaking in a forum that demanded entertainment.

The theme of the occasion should influence the ideas you select. Who or what is being commemorated on the occasion of your speech: patriotic sacrifices? a determined struggle against difficult odds? a special person? Be sure to develop your topic with ideas that fit the occasion.

Consider Your Rhetorical Purpose.   The emphasis that you give different ideas depends on whether your purpose is to inform, persuade, inspire, or entertain your audience. If you intend to persuade or inform your audience, then you should choose points that are similar to those you would use in a persuasive or informative speech. If your purpose is to entertain, you need to look for amusing ideas and select points that you could build into a main

For developing informative points, see page 227. For developing persuasive points, see page 248.

idea with social significance. If your goal is to inspire, choose material from your grid that will touch your audience's feelings. Often you can accomplish this with examples, narratives, or anecdotes, rather than studies or expert testimony.

After selecting ideas suitable for the occasion and your purpose, you should be ready to move from invention to organization. You should have identified the points you want to include in your speech, based on ethics, audience analysis, the occasion of your speech, and your rhetorical purpose.

2. Organizing Your Speech

The second step in preparing your special occasion speech is to draft an outline of the points you have selected to support your topic statement. You will take the ideas that you highlighted on your grid and arrange them in an effective sequence. Start by considering the body of your speech, and then add the introduction, conclusion, and connecting words.

● *Outline the Body of Your Special Occasion Speech*

Organize Your Ideas into Main Points.   Go back to your grid, and organize the highlighted ideas into a limited number of main points. These will form the body of your speech. For a special occasion speech, there are many possibilities for organizing ideas into main points. Your goal is to select the pattern that best gets your ideas across to the audience.

Use your CD-ROM to select the best organizational pattern for your speech. Go to "Step 2 Organization/Body." CD-ROM: Interactive Speech Guides/Special Occasion Speech

Linear Organization.   Here are some options for the linear organization of main points in a special occasion speech:

- *Temporal pattern.* If you are highlighting events in a person's life or discussing historical events, a temporal (time sequence) pattern offers one logical way to present the information. In a 1997 Memorial Day speech, Deborah Parker used this format, highlighting the valor of "Buffalo Soldiers" in the nineteenth century and giving examples of military courage in World War II, in Vietnam, and during the 1991 operation in Somalia.[17]

For more on temporal organization, see page 185.

- *Causal pattern.* If you are presenting an award, each main point could be a reason why the person received the award. This format would also work in a nomination speech: each main point would present a reason why you support a certain candidate.

For more on causal patterns, see page 186.

- *Criteria-application pattern.* In an epideictic speech such as a hero speech, one main point could discuss the criteria for the judgment (what makes a person a hero), and a second main point could apply the criteria to the person you selected.

For more on the criteria-application pattern, see page 186.

- *Two-sided argument.* A two-sided argument is effective when your audience has reservations about some of the points you are making. For example, if the audience has doubts about the person you choose as a hero (perhaps he or she has a history of drug use or a criminal record), this format allows you to address those doubts.

For more on two-sided arguments, see page 248.

For more on the motivated-sequence format, see page 249.

For more on the categorical pattern, see page 187.

For more on the web pattern, see page 210.

For more on the use of narrative, see page 211.

For more on deferring the thesis, see page 208.

For more on wording main points, see page 184.

- *Motivated-sequence format.* If you are attempting to inspire the audience to take action on a special occasion, a motivated-sequence format would be effective. For example, a speaker on Martin Luther King Jr.'s birthday could attempt to convince the audience to vote against a ballot proposition that reduced civil rights.

- *Categorical pattern.* If your main points do not lend themselves to any of the preceding patterns, try a categorical format. With this pattern, each main point explains a different aspect (or category) of the topic. Organize ideas into categories by writing each idea highlighted on your grid on a separate note card. Then group ideas that fit together into potential main points. Using cards makes it easy to experiment with different sets of ideas until you have main points that will convey your thoughts to the audience well.

Nonlinear Organization. If you are not required to use a standard linear format, and your audience analysis indicates that a nonlinear format will be effective for your audience, consider a web, narrative, or deferred-thesis pattern:

- *Web pattern.* With a web, several main points relate to a core idea. After developing each main point, you show how it relates to the core idea. For instance, in a roast, the core idea could be that the guest of honor has always been available for her friends. To demonstrate that core idea, you could present four amusing anecdotes and at the end of each one reiterate its relevance to the core idea.

- *Narrative.* A narrative is essentially a story. From the story, the audience should be able to perceive your message. For example, in a Fourth of July speech, each main point could be a narrative describing a contribution made by a person of color to the American Revolution. From these narratives, the audience would infer your message: people of color played important roles in the revolution.

- *Deferred-thesis pattern.* When you defer your thesis, your main points relate to your thesis, but the thesis is not revealed until near the end of your speech. An Earth Day speaker could use this format to encourage members of the audience to use natural resources more carefully. The speaker might begin with four examples of companies that wasted natural resources and explain how easily the waste could have been prevented. Then after presenting these examples, the speaker's final main point would be the thesis: audience members should act to reduce their own wasteful use of resources.

Word the Main Points. After deciding what your main points will be and how they will be ordered, insert them in your outline. Remember to number each main point with a Roman numeral and to word your points so that they accurately reflect the supporting material and generate audience interest. In special occasion speeches, your wording should suit the mood of the occasion. Humorous main points would be appropriate in an after-dinner speech. In a speech at a memorial service, main points would be much more serious and restrained.

Develop and Outline Subpoints.   Once your main points are determined, select from your grid the ideas that best support those main points. Organize the supporting material into subpoints that develop each main point, and add the subpoints to your outline. When you insert supporting materials in your outline, remember these principles:

- Use proper outline format. Indent subpoints, and use capital letters to identify them. Double-indent sub-subpoints, and number each one.

- Subpoints and sub-subpoints must be subordinate to the point they develop.

- Evidence must be properly cited in your outline. Each time you use quoted or paraphrased information in your speech, be sure to attribute it to the author.

For more on outlining supporting material, see page 187.

● *Outline the Introduction and Conclusion*

The introduction and conclusion of a special occasion speech consist of the same components as the introduction and conclusion of other speeches. As you draft your introduction and conclusion, be sure to include each component. Pay attention to the length of these parts of your speech. For a typical five- to ten-minute special occasion speech, your introduction should not exceed one minute and your conclusion should last between thirty and forty-five seconds.

To review the components of introductions, see page 193. To review conclusions, see page 201.

Draft the Introduction.   The introduction should set the tone for your special occasion speech. When drafting the introduction, consider the following advice:

1. *The attention-getter should relate to the occasion of your speech.* Lillian Gentz began with a narrative and a rhetorical question, asking the audience to imagine how one would respond to a serious accident. Noa Ben Artzi-Pelossof simply noted that she was not going to emphasize Middle East peace in her eulogy and instead would speak about her grandfather. When the subject of your speech is a person, you might begin with a phrase that exemplifies his or her character. A rhetorical question asking audience members to consider their thoughts about a person or event can also be an effective attention-getter.

2. *The topic statement should indicate the main message of your speech.* In one sentence, indicate the topic and purpose of your speech.

3. *Connect with audience members by relating the topic to them.* You may note that you and the audience share a common purpose, such as honoring a person or celebrating a joyous event. If your topic is not a person or an event, you should briefly show how there is a connection between the topic and the audience.

4. *Establish credibility to build your ethos.* Briefly explain your connection to the person or event being commemorated to indicate your credibility. If the connection is well known (for example, if you are a close friend or relative of the honoree), you can mention it in a single sentence. If

To review goodwill and other dimensions of ethos, see page 39.

your message is likely to be controversial, it is important to establish common ground and build goodwill with your audience.

5. *Preview your main points to indicate the structure of your speech if you are using a linear organization.* If you do not have main points because your organization is nonlinear, you should still include a sentence to orient the audience to the direction of your speech.

Draft the Conclusion. Your conclusion should wrap up your speech and reinforce the sentiments you hope the audience will experience. Include a summary and clincher in your conclusion.

The *summary* briefly reviews the main ideas that you developed in the body of your speech. Lillian Gentz reminded the audience of why Marilyn Hamilton was her hero, using language that reflected her admiration. Summarize your main ideas with sincere words and phrases that indicate your feelings and, you hope, the audience's feelings as well.

The *clincher* should reinforce the tone of your speech and leave a lasting impression on the audience. Naomi Wolf's purpose was to offer some advice to the graduating seniors, and she ended with the striking statement that "only one thing is more frightening than speaking your truth. And that is not speaking." An after-dinner speech might end with a joke because its major rhetorical purpose is to entertain. Whatever your purpose, be certain that the tone of your clincher matches the tone of your message.

● *Incorporate Transitions and Signposts*

Add Transitions. Transitions serve as bridges between the major parts of your speech. On your outline, insert them at the following places:

1. Between the introduction and the first main point
2. Between each main point
3. Between the final main point and the conclusion (Alternatively, instead of inserting a full transition, you may use a signpost here to indicate that your speech is concluding.)

For more on wording transitions, see page 190.

Word each transition to show clearly that you are moving from one idea to the next. Lillian Gentz, for example, used a transition to move from main point one (business success) to main point two (athletic achievements).

For more on signposts, see page 191.

Add Signposts. You can strengthen the organization of your speech by inserting signposts. If you are presenting a connected set of ideas, such as a person's accomplishments or your memories of an occasion, use signposts to make each idea stand out. Signposts can also help the audience to understand different purposes of your speech. For example, commencement speakers might indicate that they are *informing* the audience of some of the graduating class's accomplishments and later indicate that they are *challenging* the graduates to take certain actions in the future.

3. Using Effective Style

The third step in developing your special occasion speech is to focus on style, to ensure that the wording of your ideas on your outline is appropriate. Attention to style is important in any speech, but it is essential in any special occasion speech if you hope to touch or inspire the audience. Review and evaluate your word choice. If necessary, make revisions to improve your wording. When reflecting on style in a special occasion speech, consider the following advice:

For pointers on effective style, see Chapter 10.

- *Use language that is sensitive to audience expectations.* Propriety is essential in special occasion speaking. Know your audience's expectations for the occasion, and ensure that your word choice is appropriate. In a serious speech, the audience should perceive your respect for the person or event. In an entertaining speech, your humor should fit audience expectations of good taste.

- *Use language that clearly conveys your praise.* When you are speaking highly of people or events, your language should clearly convey positive feelings. Be certain that your words could not be misinterpreted as a backhanded compliment, such as a statement that a coworker "did quality work *most of the time.*"

- *Use culturally appropriate phrases effectively.* When you are speaking to an audience that represents a different culture from your own, show respect for audience members by using words or expressions from their language that are traditional for the occasion. For example, during a Latina's *quinceanera,* "Felicidades" would be more appropriate than "Congratulations." If you are using phrases from a language you do not know well, be sure to verify that you are using the correct term. If you are not sure whether it would be appropriate on a Tuesday to begin a speech to a predominantly Jewish audience with "Shabbat Shalom," ask someone who is familiar with Jewish customs.

- *Present your examples, anecdotes, and narratives in an interesting manner.* Examples and anecdotes offer an effective way of touching the audience's emotions and relating your ideas. Use vivid language to make them come to life. Be sure that the details you emphasize are relevant to your message. Naomi Wolf did this well when presenting the narrative of her "graduation from hell." She focused on the sexist connotations of the speaker's remarks and omitted facts such as the weather or location of the ceremony that had no bearing on her message. If you provide a lot of irrelevant detail, you will lose the audience.

- *Avoid hyperbole and exaggeration.* In a speech praising a person or celebrating an event, avoid overusing superlatives. Your tone and word choice should be positive, but the descriptive words you use should be consistent with the facts you present.

- *Avoid bias in your language.* Avoid negative stereotypes, unnecessary gender-specific references, and outdated references to ethnic groups. For example, if gay men or lesbians are getting married, the terms *bride* and *groom* should not be used; *companions* or *spouses* would be more appropriate. Also, be aware that perspectives on events may differ from culture to culture. In a Flag Day speech, the statement "Our ancestors came to the United States to find freedom" might resonate with individuals whose ancestors voluntarily immigrated here but would not ring true with many African Americans.

4. Refining and Practicing Your Special Occasion Speech

Students often assume that their speeches are complete when the outline is written. But that assumption is false. The important fourth step in the speech-writing process is refining and practicing your speech. Your special occasion speech will be stronger if you review and revise your outline after it is written. If possible, arrange your schedule so that you have time to set your outline aside for one or two days before you review it.

● *Review the Outline from a Critical Perspective*

When reviewing your speech, keep in mind that audience analysis is an ongoing process and should be done again as you refine your speech. In addition, this is the time to seek critical feedback from other people and to continue to revise your outline as needed.

Analyze Your Special Occasion Speech. When you reread your outline, consider the speech from the audience's perspective. You may want to make an extra copy of your outline and write on it notes about possible changes to the content and structure that occur to you as you are reading.

Review the Content. Here are some questions to ask about the content of your special occasion speech:

For special occasion speeches countering audience expectations, see pages 461–62.

- Is the message consistent with the audience's expectations for the occasion? If you have made a choice to diverge from audience expectations, does your speech nevertheless show respect for the audience?

- Have you chosen examples, anecdotes, and illustrations that the audience will find appealing and inspiring? Are your ideas consistent with the audience's values?

- Is the tone of the speech appropriate for the occasion? Is your word choice appropriate for the audience and occasion?

- Will the audience accept the factual claims you are making? Do you need additional evidence or more credible evidence to prove any of your points?

Review the Structure. Review the structure of your speech. Here are some questions to ask to avoid common organizational problems:

- Is the body of the speech in an appropriate format given your rhetorical purpose? Are the main points clear?

- Do the introduction and conclusion include the proper components?
- Does the speech have transitions and signposts at each place where they are needed?
- Is research properly cited at each place where you refer to it in your outline?

Review the Assignment (If Applicable) and the Context.   If your speech is for a class assignment, review the assignment description. Be certain that you are fulfilling all requirements. Are there any expectations for the content of your speech? For example, if your speech is supposed to celebrate a hero *from your culture,* is the connection between your culture and the hero clear?

Whether you are speaking in or out of class, know your speech situation: the type of speech that is expected, where you will be speaking, and the size of your audience. Be certain that your speech is appropriate for the situation.

Review the Speech Length.   Read your outline aloud to see approximately how long it will take you to deliver the speech. For a classroom speaking assignment, your instructor probably will give you a maximum (and possibly a minimum) speech time. If you are delivering your speech out of class, it is important for the length of your speech to meet the audience's expectations.

If your speech is too long, streamline the content to fit the available time by omitting the points that are least important for the occasion or your audience. You may be able to condense some points by using only the details that are most relevant to the idea you are trying to get across. If your speech is too short, you will need to add points or develop the ones you have in greater detail. Check your Speech Grid for additional information, or conduct additional research.

Get Feedback from Other People.
   If you have friends, relatives, or classmates who are willing to help you prepare, ask them to read your outline. They can offer their perspectives on several important issues:

- Reviewers can tell you whether your ideas seem appropriate for the occasion of your speech.
- Reviewers can tell you whether your appeals to pathos are effective with them. They can evaluate the logos of your argument and tell you whether your evidence and reasoning are sound and whether any point needs additional support.
- Reviewers can check for cultural understanding. If members of your audience are from cultures other than your own, have people from those cultures look at your outline. These reviewers can tell you whether your ideas reflect the occasion from their cultural perspective.

As you get feedback from other people, try not to be defensive. Their constructive suggestions will help you strengthen your speech.

Revise Your Outline.
   After you and others have reviewed the content, structure, and length of your special occasion speech, revise your outline as necessary. You may need to make points more appropriate for the occasion,

add supporting materials that will make your speech more emotionally compelling or logically sound, or improve the organization. If your speech is not the right length, make revisions to fit it into the allotted time.

● *Prepare for Extemporaneous Delivery*

Practice with Your Outline. After you revise your outline, it is time to practice your delivery with the goal of reducing your dependence on the outline. Begin practice by reading your outline orally several times, until your speech becomes familiar. As you practice, try to explain subpoints in your own words, looking at your outline only if you are quoting sources directly or are losing your train of thought. Do not try to memorize your speech word-for-word. Your goal is to become comfortable delivering your speech from limited notes.

Some special occasion speeches must be delivered after limited preparation. For example, a memorial service may occur shortly after the death of a friend or loved one, giving a speaker little time to prepare during a period of high stress. In this circumstance, the audience will understand if you need to refer to your notes frequently. Nevertheless, the more chances you have to practice, the easier it will be to deliver your speech.

Prepare a Condensed Outline for Speaking. After you practice your special occasion speech several times and are feeling confident that you can remember the order and content of your main points, begin preparing the briefer notes (on note cards or on a limited number of pages) that you will use when you actually deliver the speech. Your condensed outline should include your main points and major subpoints. In this outline, subpoints should contain just enough information to remind you what the idea is, so you can explain it extemporaneously. Only quoted evidence should be used word for word. You may want to write delivery reminders on the cards as well. If you had difficulty with some aspect of delivery (such as eye contact or rate of delivery) in previous speeches, or if you had a problem while practicing, you want to be certain to avoid that problem during your speech. At the top of your note cards, print a reminder in bold letters, using a different color so that the reminders stand out. After your notes are consolidated, use these briefer notes when practicing.

For more on speaking from an outline, see page 289.

5. Delivering Your Speech

The final step in preparing your special occasion speech is to present it to your audience. Before doing that, however, you can do a number of things to ensure that your delivery is effective.

Use your CD-ROM to view examples of delivery in an informative speech. Go to the "Example" button in "Step 5 Delivery/Deliver Your Speech." CD-ROM: Interactive Speech Guides/Special Occasion Speech

● *Minimize Speech Anxiety*

If you are feeling anxious about your special occasion speech, do not lose heart. It is normal to have feelings of uncertainty and tension before presenting a speech, and the emotional nature of many special occasions can present a special challenge.

To review state and trait anxiety, see page 20.

Special occasion speeches can easily be a cause of *state* anxiety—apprehension caused by the specific situation. When contemplating a speech at an emotional event such as a memorial service for a friend or loved one or a life passage such as graduation, it is very reasonable to worry about breaking down while delivering your speech. Remember that the audience will have strong emotional feelings in these contexts also. They will not expect you to be stoic in the face of sadness or sentimental memories, and you will not be viewed as an inadequate speaker if the occasion brings tears to your eyes or you need to pause and get your bearings.

Use visualization and relaxation techniques to reduce your anxiety before delivering your special occasion speech. Careful preparation can also reduce anxiety. Use the checklist at the end of this chapter to be sure you have taken all the necessary steps in preparation.

Remember that it is normal to experience some nervousness about delivering a speech. Also, some anxiety is positive. If you are overconfident, you may not manage or deliver the speech to the best of your ability. Never assume that a lack of nervousness means you need not carefully prepare.

For tips for coping with speech anxiety, see page 21.

● *Deliver Your Special Occasion Speech*

When delivering a special occasion speech, pay special attention to the tone of your delivery and your pronunciation.

Your delivery needs to fit the mood of your message. When you are making solemn or serious points, your delivery should indicate respect for the occasion or person. When you have a point that is humorous or light-hearted, deliver it with energy and enthusiasm. Your facial expressions are also important and should convey your feelings. Remember that different cultures celebrate occasions such as weddings or funerals with different degrees of seriousness. Keep your delivery appropriate for the occasion.

Review delivery skills in Chapter 11. If you are using visual aids, review presentation tips in Chapter 12.

Be certain to use correct pronunciation. It is particularly important that you know how the person who is the subject of the speech pronounces his or her name. If you are using terms from an unfamiliar language, check your pronunciation with a person who knows the language well. Write out words phonetically on your notes if you need a reminder during your speech.

President John F. Kennedy followed this strategy when he prepared what turned out to be one of his most inspirational speeches. After World War II, control of the city of Berlin was divided. The western part was under the jurisdiction of the United States, Britain, and France; the eastern part was controlled by the Soviet Union. The entire city was surrounded by communist East Germany. In August 1961, the Soviets encircled West Berlin with a wall, a mass of concrete and barbed wire designed to prevent the exodus of people from east to west.[18] On June 26, 1963, Kennedy addressed a huge crowd of West Germans assembled in the shadow of the Berlin Wall. In his speech, he expressed his solidarity with his audience, using both Latin and German:

> Two thousand years ago, the proudest boast was "civis Romanus sum."
> [I am a Roman citizen.] Today, in the world of freedom, the proudest boast
> is "Ich bin ein Berliner."[19]

It has sometimes been contended that Kennedy's German was in error and that his pronunciation of "Ich bin ein Berliner" meant "I am a jelly doughnut" (*Berliner* being the name of a German bakery deli). In reality, his statement was translated by a native German speaker and was the correct way of communicating his idea in German.[20] Rather than expressing amusement at a mispronunciation, the crowd roared its approval upon hearing President Kennedy's words.[21] To ensure that he pronounced the German and Latin words in his speech correctly, Kennedy used a note card with the words written phonetically.

● *Learn from Your Special Occasion Speech*

For more on interactive listening, see page 77.

Use each speech you present as an opportunity to develop your public speaking ability. In the classroom, there is usually an opportunity for audience members to give you feedback and ask questions. Use interactive listening to understand your classmates' comments. Your instructor is likely to give you both oral and written feedback. Jot down their ideas and keep any written comments you receive, so that you can consider them when planning your next speech. When it is appropriate (*not* during other people's speeches), write down your own thoughts about your speech and ideas for self-improvement.

Summary

At some point in your life, you can expect to be called on to deliver a special occasion speech. There are many occasions at which the presentation of speeches is customary, including holidays, religious and cultural celebrations, graduations, weddings, and memorial services. If you are asked to deliver a speech on such an occasion, be aware of the type of speech your audience will be expecting. Your speech may have a variety of purposes—to inform, inspire, entertain, or persuade, depending on your audience and the event.

This Speech Guide presented a five-step process to follow when you are writing a special occasion speech. The steps are summarized in the checklist (include any additional steps that your instructor advises or assigns). If you follow these guidelines, you will be able to provide the audience with a compelling message well suited to the occasion.

Checklist

INVENTING YOUR SPECIAL OCCASION SPEECH

Analyze Your Audience

____ Analyze your audience, and record the analysis on a Speech Grid (p. 460)

Select and Refine Your Topic

____ Select your topic, keeping the occasion of your speech in mind (p. 460)

____ Refine your topic, and create topic and specific purpose statements (p. 463)

Generate Ideas to Develop Your Topic

____ Brainstorm supporting ideas (p. 464)

____ Research your topic and the occasion (p. 465)

Select the Best Ideas to Develop Your Topic

____ Review for ethical considerations (p. 466)

____ Choose ideas based on audience analysis, with consideration for the audience's expectations on the occasion (p. 467)

____ Choose ideas that are appropriate for the occasion and your purpose (p. 468)

ORGANIZING YOUR SPECIAL OCCASION SPEECH

Outline the Body

____ Organize the best ideas on your grid into main points, and select a pattern that is appropriate for your rhetorical purpose (p. 469)

____ Word the main points (p. 470)

____ Develop and outline subpoints (p. 471)

Outline the Introduction and Conclusion

____ Draft an introduction containing attention-getter, topic statement, connection with the audience, credibility, and preview (p. 471)

____ Draft a conclusion containing a summary and clincher (p. 472)

Incorporate Transitions and Signposts

____ Use transitions to connect main points and major sections of the speech (p. 472)

____ Use signposts to highlight sets of ideas that are connected and help the audience visualize speech structure (p. 472)

USING EFFECTIVE STYLE IN YOUR SPECIAL OCCASION SPEECH

____ Review and revise the language used in your outline to ensure your words show sensitivity to audience expectations, clearly convey your praise, express culturally appropriate phrases effectively, present your ideas in an interesting manner, avoid hyperbole and exaggeration, and are not biased (p. 473)

REFINING AND PRACTICING YOUR SPECIAL OCCASION SPEECH

____ Review and revise your outline from a critical perspective (p. 474)

____ Plan and practice extemporaneous delivery (p. 476)

DELIVERING YOUR SPECIAL OCCASION SPEECH

____ Minimize speech anxiety (p. 476)

____ Deliver your speech (p. 477)

____ Learn for your next speech by actively listening to feedback and analyzing your own speech (p. 478)

Source Notes

1. Kramer, S. N. (1981). *History begins at Sumer* (p. 337). Philadelphia: University of Pennsylvania Press.
2. Aristotle. (trans. 1991). *On rhetoric* (p. 1358a–b). (G. A. Kennedy, Trans.). New York: Oxford University Press.
3. Kennedy, G. A. (1991). *Aristotle on rhetoric: A theory of civic discourse* (pp. 7, 47). New York: Oxford University Press.
4. Hefner, C. M. (1996, February 18). Finding a hero: a different approach to the epideictic speech. Paper presented at the Western States Communication Association Convention, Pasadena, California.
5. Wolf, N. (1992). A woman's place. *Gifts of Speech.* Retrieved June 11, 1999 from the World Wide Web: <http://gos.sbc.edu/w/wolf.html>.
6. Ben Artzi-Pelossof, N. (1999). Yitzhak Rabin. In J. W. Harris (Ed.), *Remembrances and celebrations: A book of eulogies, elegies, letters, and epitaphs* (pp. 64–65). New York: Pantheon Books.
7. Grandfather, you were the pillar of fire. (1995, November 20). *Newsweek, 126,* 54.
8. Harris, J. W. (1999). *Remembrances and celebrations: A book of eulogies, elegies, letters, and epitaphs* (p. xvii). New York: Pantheon Books.
9. Phuc, K. (1996, November). Address at the U.S. Vietnam War Memorial. *Gifts of Speech.* Retrieved May 13, 1999 from the World Wide Web: <http://.gos.sbc.edu/p/phuc.html>.
10. Mumia commencement speech draws fire. (1999, June 14). *United Press International,* p. 1008163.
11. Wellesley students protest invitation. (1990, April 16). *St. Louis Post-Dispatch,* p. 7A.
12. Bush, B. (1990, June 1). Remarks at Wellesley College commencement. *Gifts of Speech.* Retrieved May 13, 1999 from the World Wide Web: <http://gos.sbc.edu/b/bush.html>.
13. Bush (1990, June 1).
14. Aristotle (trans. 1991, p. 1368a).
15. Richard Nixon funeral and other items of national interest. (1994, May 9). *Time, 143,* 13.
16. Martin S. (1999, May 23). Commencement address. *The Denver Post Online.* Retrieved June 27, 1999 from the World Wide Web: <www.denverpost.com/news/shot0523a.htm>.
17. Parker, D. Y. (1997, May 26). Memorial Day speech. *Gifts of Speech.* Retrieved May 13, 1999 from the World Wide Web: <http://gos.sbc.edu/p/parker.html>.
18. National Archives and Records Administration. (1996, June 12). *Exhibit Hall.* Retrieved August 9, 2000 from the World Wide Web: <www.nara.gov/exhall/originals/kennedy.html>.
19. Kennedy, J. F. (1963, June 26). "Ich bin ein Berliner." *The History Place.* Retrieved August 9, 2000 from the World Wide Web: <www.historyplace.com/speeches/berliner.htm>.
20. Lutterkort, D. (2000, May 30). Urban legends: "I am a jelly doughnut." *Information on Germany.* Retrieved August 9, 2000 from the World Wide Web: <www.watzmann.net/scg/faq-25.html>.
21. National Archives and Records Administration (1996).

17 Guide to Impromptu Speaking

SAVE FREEDOM OF SPEECH

BUY WAR BONDS

Speaking without preparation—impromptu speaking—is an important and valuable skill to learn. Because of the different ways you can apply it in your everyday life, unprepared speech is one type of speech you will be able to use immediately in other classes. Any situation that puts you in the position of having to make a speech *when you are not prepared* is an impromptu speaking situation—a surprise request for a speech in class, in the workplace, or even in a social situation, such as being asked to "say a few words" after a formal dinner. It is common to become extremely nervous in such situations. Worse, it is common for nervousness to overwhelm delivery skills as well as the ability to think and speak about the topic simultaneously.

To review delivery skills and speech anxiety, see page 21.

In an impromptu speech, you speak spontaneously about the topic you have been assigned. Your goal is to give the best analysis possible or to answer whatever question has been posed—and to do so in a way that clearly and concisely explains your position to the audience. Of course, the catch is that you make up the speech as you go along. In a truly impromptu speech, you are not giving a speech you previously planned, practiced, and delivered; instead, you are expressing ideas and words as they occur to you.

How do you give an impromptu speech for an audience? Consider any impromptu speaking situation that you have observed. If the speech was well received, the speaker and the speech probably exhibited many of these qualities:

- The speaker did not spend a lot of time thinking about what to say. The speaker began to speak quickly—and made perfect sense.

- The presentation was spontaneous and fresh; it did not sound rehearsed. Nevertheless, the speaker's points were clear and his or her reasoning and examples were easy to follow.

- The speech itself was well structured.

- The speaker may have touched on ancillary or related topics but still made it sound as if he or she was addressing the main topic.

In this chapter we explore some strategies for creating an impromptu speech. We present three impromptu speeches, briefly analyze their features, and provide suggestions you can use to develop your own impromptu speeches. We also review the key features of impromptu speeches in general. Then we take you through a three-step process you can use to prepare an impromptu speech, incorporating the principles of public speaking developed in Part One of this text. As you read each speech, note what the speaker is saying and what the topic is or is supposed to be. Each speaker began within less than a minute of being asked to speak. How convincing do you find each speech?

Speeches

Amy, a student at Santa Rosa Junior College, was asked to speak about the statement "Wait until your father gets home." Her audience consisted of other student speakers at an impromptu speech competition, as well as instructors who were evaluating the speeches.

Wait until Your Father Gets Home!

BY AMY KATE O'BRIEN

My mother and I have always fought like cats and dogs. We never seem to agree on anything. When I was younger and my mom and I were home alone arguing, and I came up with that one argument, that clincher which she could not respond to, she would always stop, look at me, and say: "Wait until your father gets home!" What a copout. The only reason she said that was because she couldn't think of anything else. That phrase has been said to children across the United States for many years...my mother heard it herself. But children are not hearing it as much anymore. This is due to changes in the family unit and society, and we have to learn to live with the changes in these fundamental aspects of our daily lives.

Everyone is a part of some type of family unit. Traditionally in America, this unit consisted of a father who worked a nine-to-five job, a mother with an apron and chocolate chip cookies in the oven, and a couple of swell kids. But, as we look at the family today, we might well find ourselves asking: "Whatever happened to Donna Reed?" She certainly isn't living at my house! Things such as the increasing cost of living mean that more and more it takes two incomes just to survive. The role of provider is being shared, and this means other roles are shared as well. Household chores are no longer an exclusively feminine domain, and men do not have the monopoly on discipline. The increased divorce rates also mean in many cases that single parents have to take care of all roles. A mother can't always say "Wait until your father gets home" if she's the only adult in the household. There is no denying a dramatic change is taking place in the American family of today.

Because society is a collection of family units, society is changing as well. Women are entering the workforce in ever-greater numbers. This means issues such as child care in the workplace are receiving greater and greater concern. These concerns are changing the shape of businesses, which are becoming more and more attuned to family issues.

The loss of the highly structured family unit also means that society has to do more parenting. This is shown to be true in our own public school system. Teachers in public schools are increasingly caught in the dilemma of whether to teach morality. With sex education, for example, many feel that the family is no longer teaching kids what they need to know about sex. They feel that this issue must be addressed in school, to protect our children. Yet some parents feel that educators are usurping their role.

In addition, single parents also have a hard time surviving. Many times they must turn to the government for financial help. Society is becoming more involved in all aspects of family units; things that used to be private matters now seem to be public domain. The changing family is changing the society we live in.

No one can deny the changes in the family of society. But how do these changes affect us? First of all, we must deal with the personal changes in our lives. Now we must cope with our parents, and our brothers and sisters (and our parents with us) in a completely different way. New roles will develop, putting more responsibility on children and more pressure on parents. We have to be adaptable and not bemoan lost days. We can't go back, so we each have to accept the present and try to make the future better. On a national level, we will have to adapt our way of thinking. Now more than ever, we must rely upon each other for support—not necessarily financial, but emotional support. Many children are no longer growing up with Donna Reed, and we still have to look out for those who perhaps do not have anyone looking out for them. Currently society has a great responsibility to take care of, at least watch over, its individual members.

When we look at the changes in the family unit and society today, it is no surprise that we do not hear "Wait until your father gets home" anymore. The structures, roles, and attitudes of both are in common flux. If we remain flexible and work to improve the structure of family and society, we can perhaps have something better. How we deal with the changes in family and society will determine our future. Hopefully, we will not have to use threats to deal with our children...we will find a better way. And hopefully, I won't fight as much with my daughter as my mother did with hers.

● *Analyzing the Characteristics of Impromptu Speeches*

Amy O'Brien's speech is an example of a spontaneous, impromptu speech, but it does not read like an unprepared speech. The way the ideas and words flow together suggests a very skilled and practiced approach, although this speech was not prepared ahead of time. O'Brien was a successful and accomplished impromptu speaker, both in class and on her community college forensics team. With less than a minute's preparation, she delivered this speech on the assigned topic.

The speech succeeds for the same reasons that all good impromptu speeches succeed: creative analysis of the topic or question, clear organization and smooth transition between ideas, and effective situational audience analysis.

Interpretation and Analysis of the Topic.   O'Brien's analysis revolves around the definition of *family* and what it means for society as well as for the individual. When she transitions between ideas (for example, at the end of the fifth paragraph, as she finishes with how the "changing family is changing the society we live in"), she is certain to give the listener a quick internal summary of the preceding paragraph's main idea before connecting it to the new topic. In this case, she opens the sixth paragraph with a special nod to the main point of the previous paragraph, then branches out to the broader question.

Equally important, O'Brien is clear from the outset about her position regarding this topic. When she states, "This is due to changes in the family unit and society, and we have to learn to live with the changes in these fundamental aspects of our daily lives," she begins the process of interpreting the topic "Wait until your father gets home," to make it applicable for modern times and the changing definition of the family structure. In the rest of her speech she explains these changes, mostly as they apply to the family and society. She takes a topic that is a quotation and proceeds to both explain and analyze it before articulating her own position.

Organization. O'Brien's structure takes its cue from the topical quotation and then divides up into a discussion of society, the family unit, and the changing roles of parents and children. Resisting the temptation to follow rather typical organizational schemes such as looking to the past, the present, and the future, she takes a more subtle and sophisticated approach. She does begin with the past, discussing stereotypical male roles as father/ provider but then quickly branches into a discussion of how roles have shifted and changed because of divorce and, by inference, single-parent homes as well as the entry of more women into the traditional workforce. Instead of discussing the present and future, O'Brien asks, "But how do these changes affect us?" She then spends the balance of her speech looking to cause and effect and answering her own question.

How to create an organized speech is the subject of Chapter 8.

Audience Adaptation. As a speaker in an impromptu situation, O'Brien has little time for in-depth audience analysis. Nevertheless, she does make some attempt to reach her audience of college students and a few teachers with examples of changes in family structure that most people in her audience will be able to identify with. Regardless of whether anyone in the audience is a parent, all have in common with O'Brien the experience of being a child. Moreover, in her passage about public school teachers and morality, she reaches out to the teachers in her audience, describing the dilemma they face when they are compelled to teach moral lessons that are better learned from parents. What teacher hasn't faced that dilemma at one time or another?

Audience analysis is the subject of Chapter 5.

● *Planning Your Impromptu Speech*

O'Brien is eloquent and fluid in her approach to her topic. She enhances her personal credibility with the audience by making personal references to family, most particularly to her relationship with her own mother. O'Brien uses this both to show some expertise with the subject matter and as part of a structural device, to make her impromptu speech more audience friendly.

She derives expertise from the personal reference because it allows her to comment on the subject of family with the knowledge and wisdom of someone with personal experience. This makes her discussion of the changing nature of families in America come across as informed and likely to be accurate. If O'Brien had hailed from another culture, or had raised herself from the time she was young, she might have had to address the topic from knowledge or awareness acquired through study or observation of the experience of others. She might still have been credible, but credible in a different way than someone with personal and intimate experience. Is one kind of credibility better than another? Not necessarily—but sometimes personal reference can be helpful because it is so deeply embedded in the speaker's memory that it is easily recalled in a spontaneous speaking situation. Under the pressure and demands of a spontaneous speech, you are likely to find it easy to recall and articulate past experiences.

Personal reference also allows O'Brien to create a nice structural device for the audience. If you reread her speech, you will notice that she both opens and closes with a reference to her mother, giving the speech symmetry and balance—a beginning and ending that meet up. The audience benefits from this balance because it means that she emphasizes the personal relationship more than once—and the more listeners hear this, the more likely they are to remember what she said.

Although O'Brien's speech is well structured, it would benefit from the inclusion of a preview, which would verbalize what she intends to do in the speech. Remember, she is making this up as she speaks; saying the preview out loud is like announcing what direction you intend to travel on a trip. If you hear yourself say it, you might actually remember what direction you want to go. In an impromptu speech, this can be vitally important.

For more on previews, see page 200.

In evaluating O'Brien's analysis of the topic, you may be struck by the fact that she chose to interpret the saying by focusing on the word *family*. There is nothing wrong with that. O'Brien is the creator of her own message, and she is free to interpret the topic in any reasonable manner. Moreover, given the immediate demands of an impromptu speech, she is pushed for time and must move and interpret as quickly as possible.

In the topic there are other words that O'Brien could have focused on. Of possible interest is the word *home*. What does *home* mean in this context? Does a family have to share a home? Given a high rate of divorce and single/shared parenting responsibilities, might the definition of *home* have changed? For families with parents who are married and living together, has the concept of working couples (as O'Brien suggests) changed our concept of what a "home" is? We mention this not to nitpick her analysis but to suggest that you have many options when addressing a topic in an impromptu fashion, which include looking at more parts or aspects or terms of the topic itself.

Frederick Garvin was a college junior when he gave this impromptu presentation in his speech class. Unlike Amy O'Brien, Garvin had no previous experience as an impromptu speaker. His topic is stated as a question and is policy oriented. He spoke to a mixed-gender audience of students, ages 18 to 23, as well as his course instructor (she officially listed herself as "over 30"). From his past interactions with some of these audience members in class, Garvin knew or deduced that some people in his audience had experimented with marijuana.

View "Should Possession of Marijuana Be Decriminalized?" by Frederick Garvin.
CD-ROM: Video Theater, Full Speeches

Should Possession of Marijuana Be Decriminalized?

BY FREDERICK GARVIN

Everybody remembers President Clinton's claim . . . if you can believe it, that he tried marijuana—but he never inhaled. As if that somehow makes it different from really smoking marijuana. Actually . . . it doesn't—but his admission did help remind us of a question our society has continued to ask for many years: Should possession of marijuana be decriminalized? I mean, the president would never have had to bother explaining his history with marijuana in this ridiculous way if the stuff weren't illegal in the first place.

So, should possession of pot be decriminalized? Should possession ever be illegal?

I'll answer this question—but first, I'd like to challenge the wording of my topic. I don't really think possession of something—unless it's a gun or a bomb, or something like that—should be illegal. I don't like the word "possession" in this topic. I don't think that's ever been the real issue. The real question is usage. Should using—or *smoking* marijuana be decriminalized? That's the real question.

And of course, as we all know from long debates with our parents—or high school counselors, or whomever . . . there's a lot of controversy about this. There's definitely two sides to this story.

In my impromptu speech today, I will argue that you will never convince people that smoking marijuana should be illegal if you start from an inconsisent premise.

To help you follow my answer, I'll analyze this by looking first to the arguments in favor of keeping things as they are—punishing people for smoking marijuana. Then I will look at the arguments against this, and in favor of decriminalizing this. Finally, I will explain why I believe a blanket prohibition on smoking marijuana is hypocritical.

So what are the arguments for keeping things as they are? For making it a crime to smoke marijuana? How many of you can remember what your teachers or parents might have said about this? Anybody remember things like this: *Marijuana leads to harder drugs.* That was always a big argument. But I never found it to be true. People I knew who experimented with harder drugs didn't start because they had been smoking marijuana.

Then there are some people who say: *Smoking marijuana is bad for you—because smoking anything is bad for you.* That might be true—although it hasn't caused our government to outlaw tobacco cigarettes.

Probably the best argument in favor of keeping things as they are is that people who abuse marijuana . . . and we all know somebody like this . . . tend to mess up in their lives. Whether it's getting homework turned in on time, or doing your best at your job or something, or worse if you have a job driving a large vehicle like a bus or a forklift. Being stoned all the time is not helpful—and can even be dangerous in these situations.

Okay, but what is the argument against this and in favor of decriminalizing smoking marijuana? It all comes down to the problem of hypocrisy. As I mentioned before, our government hasn't outlawed cigarettes—but we know they can kill people. And they're addictive. And what about alcohol? It can affect your judgment—just like marijuana. Maybe worse. But nobody is outlawing drinking. There are lots of things in our society like this—that are bad for you. But they aren't illegal. So why single out marijuana?

Don't get me wrong. I am not advocating that anyone should use or abuse marijuana. But I am saying to all in positions of authority—our government, our clergy, our parents and teachers: If you want to convince young people like me—like us—that using marijuana is wrong and should be illegal, don't sart with a premise of hypocrisy and inconsistency. If you want us to follow your lead, be consistent!

● *Analyzing the Characteristics of Impromptu Speeches*

Garvin's speech is an impromptu response to a topic phrased as a question—in this case asking for his position on decriminalizing possession of marijuana. Garvin's speech is noteworthy because of his initial shift in the emphasis and wording of the topic, along with his organization (including a very clear thesis statement and preview) and his audience analysis.

Interpretation and Analysis of the Topic.   Shifting the wording of the topic (or question) is a technique that you can use as long as you are careful not to alter the original topic radically and not to insult the source of the question (by labeling the original wording "stupid" or "misguided," for example). Garvin attempts to address the original wording of the topic and then announces his intention to shift the focus to, as he says, get to "the real question." This strategy is best used in situations where the original question or topic is a subset of something greater and speaking to the original topic might not allow you to give your audience a complete answer.

Organization.   Once Garvin makes that shift, he follows O'Brien's example in making a very clear thesis statement (he believes smoking of marijuana should be decriminalized). Unlike O'Brien, he provides a clear preview of the organization of his speech. Keep in mind that the preview is even more important in an impromptu speech than in most other types of speeches because it not only tells the audience what will follow but also helps the speaker to remember what structure or verbal path to follow in the speech.

Once Garvin has reworded the topic to address "smoking" as opposed to "possession" of marijuana, he takes a simple but straightforward structural approach, using arguments for and against his position. This comparison of pros and cons enables Garvin to look at both sides of the issue before reaching some kind of resolution and answering the topical question. This is a popular and effective way to organize impromptu responses to controversial topics. It fosters a balanced and well-thought-out answer, and the act of verbalizing pros and cons can help a nervous speaker remember what is to be said, because the speech is a series of paired opposites. If you are discussing the pros early in the speech, it is simple to remember that what comes later is the cons.

For discussion of the comparison structure, see page 186.

For more on speech anxiety, see page 19.

Also, notice that Garvin creates main points that relate to the main question he has posed (regarding decriminalization). He does not veer off into extraneous subjects (such as whether William Randolph Hearst manipulated public opinion to change marijuana laws).

Audience Adaptation.   As Frederick Garvin progresses into his speech, he attempts to make use of his audience analysis. Like Amy O'Brien, he knew in advance who his audience would be, but he did not know (until a minute before his speech) what his topic would be. Nevertheless, his audience analysis is evident in the speech, especially near the beginning when he mentions "long debates with *our* parents—or high school counselors" (emphasis added). Here he is suggesting common ground with his listeners. You can almost see members of Garvin's audience nodding at the memory— even if not everyone agrees with his conclusion. The reference establishes common ground and bolsters Garvin's credibility.

The same occurs again when Garvin argues that the best argument against the status quo is "hypocrisy." Here he is making an argument that he assumes many in his audience have heard before. Why outlaw the use of marijuana but not cigarettes or alcohol? This is a typical plea for consistency that young people make about a great many things their parents or other authority figures instruct them on. Given Garvin's use of common ground before, this kind of argument has a special appeal. It is not hard to see the picture Garvin is painting—parents who smoke and drink telling their high-school-age kids not to smoke marijuana. Garvin is assuming that this argument resonated with his audience as teenagers and thus will work here.

For more on audience demographics, see page 97.

Garvin uses this audience analysis without compromisng his own opinion. This point is worth emphasizing: engaging in audience analysis does not mean that Garvin has to adopt whatever position he believes his audience will take about marijuana decriminalization; rather, he uses the analysis to help him decide how to explain his position in a manner that will be acceptable to the audience.

● *Planning Your Impromptu Speech*

One of the things that Garvin does quite well is using repetition and reiteration to remind the audience—and himself—where he is and what he wants to say. He does this by providing a preview, a body that follows through on the preview, and a conclusion that almost follows through on the preview. In addition, he gives internal summaries of whatever the central point was. For example, in several places he reminds listeners that he is addressing the central arguments in favor of outlawing the smoking of marijuana.

This is an example that you, too, should follow. Using repetition and re-iteration does not mean that you simply repeat verbatim whatever you already said; rather, it means that you continue to emphasize your main points and remind the audience about them throughout the speech. If your speech was supposed to be approximately five minutes in length but you say everything you need to say in three minutes, do not repeat the body of the speech. When your analysis is finished, conclude the speech.

Note that Garvin's conclusion does not quite match his original thesis position. If you reread the speech, you will see that Garvin begins by saying that he will conclude that a blanket prohibition on smoking marijuana is hypocritical. This is not quite the way he concludes his speech. By the end he is really advocating that people who want to criminalize the use of marijuana shouldn't use inconsistent arguments. The conclusion sounds close to what he offered in the preview, but it is subtly different. Early on he seemed to imply that he was in favor of decriminalizing the use of marijuana. By the conclusion he was arguing that authority figures in favor of criminalization should lead by consistency.

As we discuss shortly, it is important to be sure that your thesis and your conclusion marry up. Otherwise, you may confuse the audience or, worse, communicate that you have not yet made up your mind. We explain how to avoid this problem later in the chapter.

Joe Thomas is a lawyer and a parent. Recently he helped author an argument presented before the United States Supreme Court in opposition to federal regulation of the Internet. The proposed federal law, called the Communication Decency Act, or CDA, would criminalize any indecent, offensive, or obscene message that could reach minors. Thomas and others successfully argued that restricting the Internet would undoubtedly also harm legitimate free speech and the exchange of otherwise protected ideas.

This impromptu exchange occurred at a PTA meeting. Thomas was asked to respond to questions from other parents about what will happen now that the CDA has been declared unconstitutional. His audience is made up of parents of elementary school children. Thomas himself has two children—ages seven and ten.

Protecting Your Children on the Internet

IMPROMPTU ANSWER BY JOSEPH THOMAS

Question from the Audience

Mr. Thomas, while I appreciate what you said about free speech . . . I've got to tell you: I have two daughters. Both of them use the Internet all the time. For fun—to communicate with friends. And for school projects. I know what kind of stuff there is online—but I can't always be there to supervise my kids. What are parents like me supposed to do now that the CDA won't be used anymore to protect my kids?

Mr. Thomas Responds

Actually, that's a very good question. And I know how you must feel. I have two kids, too. And they use the 'net a great deal as well. But to answer your question truthfully, I would have to say *you* have to be the one who supervises your kids. And the reason for that has less to do with you—and more to do with how inappropriate it is for the government to be involved with this. So let me answer you by speaking to that latter point. Why was it inappropriate for the government to regulate here?

The CDA was a well-intentioned piece of law, aimed at protecting kids from adult . . . predators, for lack of a better term. The thinking was—if these predators use the Internet to pander to our children, corrupting them or compelling them to buy things or see things they aren't ready for—well, then we should step in and stop this. It was a nice idea. And in an election year—it was an idea you could sell back in your home district or state.

But that wasn't the reality.

Because, you see, the CDA not only went after people who used "obscene" expression—exposing minors to that risk; it also penalized people who used "indecent" speech if any minor might come across it on the Internet. Obscene expression—like hard-core sexual images—I don't think many of us have too hard a time understanding that. We have many laws which protect minors from exposure to that right now.

But what about "indecent" speech?

What exactly is expression that is considered "indecent"? All we really know is that it is something less than obscene—but a little more than your garden-variety offensive speech. That can mean a lot of things—and depending upon where you live, can potentially get you into trouble with the federal government. And remember: We aren't talking about a simple system of fines and penalties here; there was serious jail time associated with violation of this law.

The problem is that pretty innocent and otherwise legitimate expression might get punished if the government was allowed to use the CDA. Say, for example, that you wanted to communicate with other people—parents or kids, perhaps—about the problem of teenage pregnancy. Or what happens to kids when they become runaways. Maybe you set up a chatroom for this purpose, and in your chatroom, when people ask you about the problem of teen pregnancy or runaways, you answer them in honest but shockingly frank and graphic terms. You aren't pulling any punches. Your goal is to educate people about what can happen—and maybe to educate people about how they can prevent problems at home, or prevent teenage pregnancy.

Now imagine that a young person has accessed your chatroom, and either reads whatever messages have been posted—or better, starts interacting and responding in the chatroom. If someone finds your frank discussion "indecent," you might be guilty under this law [the CDA] for exposing minors to indecent expression!

But wasn't this exactly the kind of expression and dialogue we need with our young people? Isn't talking about these problems the best way to prevent them?

The government can't know these things because the government tries to make laws that cover as many situations as possible. I understand that. Being comprehensive is very challenging. But when you get comprehensive—to cover as many possibilities as you can—you invariably start covering or outlawing situations you ought to be promoting and protecting!

So, if I can now return to your original question, this is why I say that the only person who can really protect your children in cyberspace—is *you*. Don't expect or ask your government to do this, because they never really do a good job when they try. More often than not, when they start regulating expression, they end up restricting the very kind of speech we ought to have promoted.

● *Analyzing the Characteristics of Impromptu Speeches*

Joseph Thomas's remarks provide an example of a short impromptu answer that becomes a longer impromptu speech after the speaker makes some strategic decisions about what to do with his topic. This evolution often occurs in impromptu situations in which a relatively straightforward but difficult question has been asked. The speaker is free to engage in the technique that we refer to as *short answer/long answer*. He or she offers up the short answer to the question at the beginning of the impromptu speech and then offers the longer explanation. In ways that we explore below, Thomas uses that technique in this presentation.

To review listening skills and public speaking objectives, see Chapter 4.

This speech also provides an example of the impromptu speech technique called *bridging*—taking the original topic (topic A) and bridging or transitioning to a discussion of a different but related topic (topic B). This is similar to rewording the topic, as Garvin does in his speech, but it is also different. When you use rewording, you announce your intention to change the original topic into something different, by adding to it or narrowing it and improving it for the purposes of your speech. In Garvin's case, possessing marijuana was merely a subset of the larger issue of smoking marijuana. When you use bridging, you announce your intention to shift to a related but altogether new and different topic. Naturally, the use of this strategy raises some questions about speech ethics.

Short Answer/Long Answer. Joseph Thomas quickly answers the question from the audience by saying that there is no substitute for parental supervision of children using the Internet. That is his short answer to the question "What are parents like me supposed to do . . . ?" His answer is that the parent must be the one to supervise—regardless of the hardship.

Bridging. Thomas then engages in the technique we call *bridging*, by shifting from topic A, what a parent should do, to topic B, why the government should not be in the business of regulating expression on the Internet:

Original topic A:
What a parent should do

New topic B:
Why the government should not regulate

He does not narrow or add to the original question; he bridges to a related but entirely different question. Doing so allows him to make a strong case against government regulation, arguing that it may limit the free expression of important ideas.

Audience Adaptation. Like Frederick Garvin (who had his status as a "student" in common with his audience), Thomas supports his position by engaging in some instant audience analysis. He is a parent—just like the members of his audience. Recognizing that his position may make this group a hostile audience, he says at the beginning of his speech that he has two children who use the Internet a great deal. He establishes common ground. He reminds listeners that he is in the same situation as they; that he, too, faces the difficulties of raising children—and supervising and protecting them; that their concerns are also his concerns. The establishing of common ground at the outset is intended to soften the audience's perception of his position—which may seem hard edged—and facilitates his bridge to the related topic.

For a discussion of audience disposition, see page 105.

To review the concept of common ground, see page 102.

● *Planning Your Impromptu Speech*

Thomas's speech provides a good example of the process of invention. When you are preparing to speak impromptu, first decide what you think the topic question is really asking you, then decide your answer, and then think through the reasoning for your answer. You must consider things in that order when speaking impromptu, because you are literally thinking out loud. Thomas does this quite effectively after he explains what the topic means and gives a clear and unequivocal answer. His answer is supported by the bridge that he makes when criticizing government regulation.

Thomas is shrewd in his choice of examples. The example he uses—a chatroom for discussion with parents and children about the problems of teenage pregnancy or runaways—is one that no parent in the audience is going to complain about. Parents are likely to identify with the subject matter (what parent wouldn't fear his child running away from home?). When speaking impromptu, by deliberately picking an example that the audience can empathize with, you can enhance both the logic of your argument and its emotional appeal.

For a discussion of emotional appeals, see page 39.

Finally, notice as well that although Thomas does bridge to the new topic of government restriction of expression, he is careful to return to the bridge at the end of his speech and to cross the bridge back to his original topic question. In a tidy conclusion, he both reasserts his previous answer and links it to his bridge at the same time. You should always use this technique when bridging: return to the bridge at the conclusion of your speech, and restate its connection to your topic.

Summary: Key Features of Impromptu Speeches

After reviewing and evaluating the speeches by O'Brien, Garvin, and Thomas, you should be familiar with special characteristics of impromptu speaking. Keep the following in mind as you prepare an impromptu speech.

● *Impromptu speaking requires audience analysis.*

Although impromptu speaking does not allow as much time for preparation as informative, persuasive, or special occasion speeches do, it is still possible and necessary to engage in as much audience analysis as possible for this type of speech. Quickly assess and analyze your audience just before you speak and while you are speaking. Obviously, this means you will not be using the Speech Grid but rather will be looking for broad and obvious characteristics as called for by situational audience analysis:

To review the components of the Speech Grid, see page 91.

1. Whom do you see in this audience? What sorts of *demographic* characteristics are readily observable?
2. What opportunities are there for *common ground* with this audience?
3. Is this audience likely to have had *prior exposure* to this message?
4. As you look at the audience, what do you think their *reaction* to your speech message might be? Would you categorize this audience as hostile? sympathetic? neutral?

O'Brien, Garvin, and Thomas all made use of audience analysis to help them develop their respective positions and select examples. When you are getting ready to start giving your impromptu speech, look at the audience. Whom do you see? Do you have anything in common with this audience? Have they heard this message before? How might they react?

● *Impromptu speaking requires clear structure.*

Clear structure is necessary for all types of speeches, but it is especially important for impromptu speeches. In an impromptu situation, the structure not only guides the audience but also serves as a verbal reminder to the speaker about what to say in the speech.

The three speeches in this Speech Guide demonstrate a strong sense of structure. O'Brien structures her speech by centering in on a key term in the topic ("Father"); then she moves on to talk about parental roles and the evolution of the American family unit. Her speech structure is categorical or topical (associated topics) and evolutionary (one topic gives rise to the next). It makes for a somewhat logical progression of ideas that is easy for the audience to follow.

To review categorical organization, see page 187.

By contrast, Garvin makes use of a comparison of pros and cons, which allows him to consider and weigh the arguments for and against the position he ultimately adopts. Because many audiences are often familiar with both sides of a question or issue, this structure is also easy to follow and to remember.

For more on the comparison structure, see page 186.

Thomas makes use of a modified problem-cause-solution format. His structure reflects the logic of his criticism of the CDA and his assessment that individual parental supervision of children using the Internet will be best.

To review the problem-cause-solution format, see page 186.

The structure of all three speeches is simple and easy for both the audience and the speaker to follow. Within this simplicity, however, are complex reasoning and analysis, invented in the course of the speech mostly because the speaker does not have to worry about structure. Likewise in your impromptu speeches, remember to aim for a clear and easy-to-follow structure —both for yourself and for your audience.

● *Impromptu speaking requires clear signposting.*

In an impromptu speech it is vital that you communicate with the audience *and with yourself* about where you are in your speech and where you are going. This is as much for the audience as for you. This means giving a preview of organization, telling the audience where you are by signposting in the speech at any given time, and summarizing your findings and repeating your main point in the conclusion.

For more on previews, see page 200.

In the speeches you read, only Garvin did a reasonably good job of previewing, signposting, and concluding. The structure of his speech was easy for him and his audience to follow. Although O'Brien and Thomas did some signposting and provided a conclusion, their speeches could have benefited from more signposting and a clearer summary in the conclusion.

To review signposting, see page 191.

For a discussion of repetition and speech structure, see page 272.

When you deliver your impromptu speech, try to remember all three ways of communicating where you are going: previewing, signposting, and summarizing (in the conclusion).

● *Impromptu speaking requires that you present a clear thesis or topic statement—one that makes sense at both the beginning and the end of the speech.*

The structure of your speech must be clear to the audience and to you, and you must be careful to continually restate that structure because the organization of ideas in your speech is really only as important as the thesis or main message they support. Good impromptu speaking requires you to devise a clear and easily understood thesis position or topic statement. You communicate it to your audience just before your preview of organization, and remind the audience about it in your conclusion. This is important in all kinds of public speaking but is especially so in an impromptu speech because of its spontaneous nature. In impromptu speaking, there is always a risk of straying from the topic because you are conceiving your ideas only moments before you say anything. Voicing your thesis helps keep you and the audience focused. The speeches by O'Brien, Garvin, and Thomas were fairly clear about the speakers' theses or main messages.

Of course, it is important for your thesis to be clear from the outset. It is also critical that you restate your thesis in the conclusion—and that whatever you say there is consistent with what you earlier previewed as your position or answer. This may sound obvious, but achieving this consistency is not easy in impromptu speaking. Sometimes, the position you take at the end of your speech is not quite what you previewed earlier.

Garvin's speech, for example, starts out rejecting arguments to outlaw the smoking of marijuana but concludes with something a bit different: He declares that he is *not* advocating use of marijuana; rather he wants consistent and nonhypocritical arguments to justify regulation. What happened?

Possibly, like many impromptu speakers, Garvin got most of the way into his analysis and began to develop his answer—seeing that there might be different possibilities. Recall that his was a pro/con analysis, which gave him an opportunity to look at some reasonable arguments against his position—such as the notion that you might not want someone operating heavy machinery while under the influence of marijuana. His openness to other points of view caused him to modify his original position.

Garvin's audience may have been confused about what his position really was, because he modified it midway through the speech. This is the reason why it is so important to make sure that your thesis is clear and that it is consistent at the beginning and end of your speech.

● *It is all right to reword and bridge in impromptu speaking.*

As demonstrated in the speeches by Garvin and Thomas, rewording the topic and bridging to a related yet different topic are acceptable in impromptu speaking. When you reword a topic (as Garvin did), you are paraphrasing the original topic, expressing it in your words, or you are narrowing or adding to what is already there. Garvin narrowed the scope of his inquiry from *possession* to *smoking*. When you use bridging (as Thomas did), you move to a brand-new topic, albeit one that is reasonably related to the original topic.

In your impromptu speech you may feel the need to reword or bridge, but there are certain ethical ramifications to consider. We examine them and the methods for rewording and bridging later in the chapter.

● *Effective impromptu speaking makes use of the technique of short answer/long answer.*

The technique of short answer/long answer works best in an impromptu situation in which the speaker is answering or addressing some question put forth by the audience at an earlier time—or perhaps in a spontaneous and interactive exchange between the audience and the speaker (as in Thomas's speech). This technique requires that you give the quick and direct answer to a question first and then ask audience members whether they would like the longer and more complete explanation. If they want the longer explanation, they'll let you know. If all they really wanted was your quick response, they'll probably move on to the next question. Either way, you've done a good job of making sure their question was answered.

Joseph Thomas does the best job of this when he states that supervision of the use of the Internet by children must be done by parents. Garvin starts to use this technique in his speech, but his short answer comes late in the speech and then changes at the end of the speech.

When you give an impromptu speech in response to a question or to some kind of audience interaction, remember to give the short answer first, and then ask listeners whether they want the longer answer.

● *Expectations for impromptu speaking are different from those for prepared speaking.*

A common mistake that most new impromptu speakers make is to harshly critique themselves after a speech. Given time to reflect on a speech after the fact, we all can think of things we should have said. And most certainly it is easy to be critical of your delivery mechanics in an impromptu speech. But because an impromptu speech is spontaneous and unprepared, audience expectations of the speaker are going to be different than they would be if the speaker had spent hours or days or weeks or months planning and practicing the speech. Nobody can reasonably expect an impromptu speech to be a polished, structured, witty, and well-delivered gem. Most people in your audience will understand that you are creating and speaking your message almost literally as thoughts occur to you. That is not to say that listeners will accept a poor speech. It is to say that your audience will be looking for creative analysis, a clear position and structure, and clear delivery of the message. These are the expectations you should strive to meet.

Preparing Your Impromptu Speech

A Three-Step Process

Use your CD-ROM to plan and deliver your speech using a three-step process.
CD-ROM: Interactive Speech Guides/Impromptu Speech

The Speech Assignment

Create an impromptu speech in which you analyze a topic given you by a friend, classmate, roommate, or family member. Because of the nature of impromptu speeches, the five-step process described in the previous Speech Guides condenses to a three-step process of inventing, determining the content of your speech, and delivering your speech.

1. Inventing Your Speech

Creating an impromptu speech is vastly different from creating a prepared speech. As noted before, impromptu speaking is largely unprepared. With impromptu speaking, you prepare as you go through the speech. The very first item of business for you, therefore, is to take careful note of the topic and understand what it really means.

● *Determine the True Meaning of the Topic or Question*

If your topic is abstract, you need to think about what it means to you. How do you interpret it? What is it saying to you? If your topic is stated as a question, you need to think about what the question really means. Does it mean only what it asks? Or is it more complex—and perhaps layered on top of deeper or inferred questions? What is the calling of the question? In both cases, you are essentially deciding what question you want to address and how you can select a reasonable interpretation of the topic.

How would you interpret an abstract topic such as Mark Twain's observation "Be good and you will be lonely"? This is a topic in the form of a quotation or saying. What does it mean to you? Many who look at a topic like this might tend to focus on key words, such as *good* and *lonely.* Many believe that Twain was being humorous, and perhaps ironic, suggesting that the pursuit of goodness is a lonely undertaking. It is, after all, much easier not to be good and likely that a person would have company in the undertaking. Do you agree? Is that what this quotation means to you?

How would you interpret this topic: "What is the value of higher education today?" This is a topic about a contemporary social issue. Some might interpret the question in a straightforward manner, suggesting that it seeks to address the monetary worth of a college education. Of course, what the question means depends on how one looks at some key terms. One is *higher education.* What is higher education? Traditionally, in the United States it has been anything above a high school education. But given the mass appeal of college undergraduate education, and the more daunting appeal of graduate-level education, is it still accurate to define *higher education* as education beyond the high school level? In addition, it is useful to consider what is meant by *value.* Does it mean simply "monetary worth"? Or is there also a moral aspect to *value?* The direction in which you take the topic depends on how you choose to define these terms. For example, you could explore value in the context of improving job possibilities with a good education or perhaps the value of broadening your base of knowledge. What do you think the question is asking? Briefly consider some possibilities.

● *Determine Your Position on the Topic or Question*

Once you have decided what the question or topic means to you, think about your position. Given the previous examples, you might take a stance in agreement with Twain, or you might argue that the value of higher education has changed but is still considerable. What is your position? How do you feel about the topic? How would you answer the question? As you determine a position, remember that you may agree, disagree, or do either only under certain conditions.

● *Decide What Reasons and/or Examples Support Your Position*

This step is a logical extension of the previous step. If you think you know how you feel about the topic, or what your position on the topic might be, or how you would answer whatever question was posed, then you need to consider a basic question of your own: Why? Why do you feel the way you do? Why do you take that position? Why do you answer the question in that particular manner? The *why* question asks you to get at the reasoning behind your decision. Are there arguments or reasons that support you? Are there examples you could draw upon to reinforce your position?

For example, if your position is that you agree with Twain—even though he wrote those words a long time ago—what reasons or examples could you offer to support your position? Why is it true that being good is lonely work? What would you say? One student who gave a speech on this topic suggested that being good is lonely work because so many people are self-interested and don't do things unless they can profit from them. To prove her claim, she offered several examples of ways in which society rewards aggressive, selfish action yet does little to promote or reward actions that benefit the public good or public welfare. Her examples and her argumentative reasoning supported her position on the Twain quote. Would you argue it in that way? There are other possibilities. What would you do?

Another student answered the question about the value of higher education by saying he felt that value was still there but was definitely limited today. He argued that the phrase *higher education* meant any education beyond high school education, and he claimed that in recent times the value of higher education derived mainly from its ability to make a young person attractive to prospective employers. In his calculus of things, higher education was valuable to the extent that it helped people to find jobs. While admitting this was a somewhat cynical view, this student supported his position by arguing that major fields with potential for employment after graduation were vastly more popular today than majors with little or no job potential. He gave examples of both. Again, this was only one way to answer the question. How else might you answer the question and support your response with reasoning or examples?

2. Determining the Content of Your Speech

After you work on the invention of your impromptu speech, it is time to determine the content of your speech. You will consider how your invention translates into the structure of your speech, whether rewording or bridging is necessary, and how audience analysis might affect what you say.

● *Structuring the Message and Invention*

For more on linear organization, see page 181.

The traditional linear structure of any speech is as follows:

I. Introduction (attention-getter, thesis or topic statement with preview)
II. Body
III. Conclusion

To review the speech outline, see page 182.

When you prepare a persuasive, informative, or special occasion speech, your audience analysis will help you determine what goes into the body of your speech. You will then most likely outline your speech, starting with the body. When you must give an impromptu speech, however, there is scant opportunity for advance preparation and consequently no outline to follow when you create the speech. Instead, what is most important for an impromptu speech is to be sure you understand the question or topic, be clear about your position, and be able to analyze and explain the reasoning or examples supporting your position.

Translating that to structure, we find the following: the first two steps for invention (determining the true meaning of the topic or question and determining your position on the topic or question) become the thesis or topic statement in your impromptu speech; and the reasoning and/or examples behind this position or answer become the body of your speech:

Determining the True Meaning of the Topic/Question ——┐ Introduction
(Attention-Getter/
Determining Your Position on ——┤ Thesis Topic Statement/Preview)
the Topic/Question ——┘

Determining What Reasons —→ Body of Speech
and/or Examples Support Your
Position

Conclusion

Quickly answering those questions of invention allows you to build the most important parts of your structure for your impromptu speech. That is not to say that the introduction and the conclusion are not important. Rather, remember a point made earlier in this chapter: audience expectations for an impromptu speech are different from audience expectations for a prepared speech. No one expects you to come up with the greatest, funniest, or most compelling introduction in the world. What listeners are expecting is excellent analysis of the topic, clear structure, and good delivery. That does not mean that you shouldn't attempt an interesting or provocative introduction; clearly, anything you can do to pique the audience's interest is a plus for your speech. However, you should not waste precious seconds of scarce preparation time worrying about how to introduce the speech or what joke or anecdote to tell. Spend the seconds you have on the invention questions listed above. When you know the main points of the body of the speech, the preview and conclusion will become self-evident. Each is simply a summary of the points made in the body and a reaffirmation of the thesis or topic statement. You don't need to think about them ahead of time. All you really need to focus on are the invention questions and how to translate them to the speech structure.

Rewording or Bridging

Sometimes a speaker is not satisfied with an assigned topic. Perhaps it is too broad or perhaps too narrow. Maybe there are good reasons to avoid directly addressing the topic or question. Or possibly the speaker doesn't know enough about the expected topic but does feel comfortable with a related subject. In any of these situations, the speaker might want to reword the topic or question or bridge to a topic that is related but different.

> View a student bridging the assigned topic of an impromptu speech.
> CD-ROM: Video Theater, Excerpt 17.1

For example, a speaker might not want to speak about being good, because she finds this topic too broad. So she rewords the topic, changing it from "Be good and you will be lonely" to "Always tell the truth and you will be lonely." She might justify this rewording by claiming that the original language was too broad or too vague and then explain her position. If she agrees with the statement, she might suggest that although we think that telling the truth is always a good idea, it sometimes leads to hurt feelings and broken relationships. She then would provide some examples supporting her opinion.

Another speaker might prefer not to answer the question "What is the value of higher education today?" Perhaps he might want to bridge to a related but different topic: "Should the government subsidize all education for any citizen desiring to be educated?" He might argue that the answer to the original question depends on who is doing the measuring of value—and, ultimately, on who pays the price. He might suggest that the original question begs the larger question of whether the government should pay for all education (including college). He might then argue that the government should do so, and give reasons for his position, such as to standardize the cost of higher education and to increase educational opportunity for all Americans.

Both examples—especially the second example—raise ethical concerns. In rewording the first topic to discuss "truthfulness," did the speaker really address the original topic? In bridging to the topic of government subsidizing education, did the second speaker connect a legitimate and related topic or reach too far? What do you think?

The ethical issue turns on the question of whether there is a relationship between the rewording or bridging and the original topic. In order for bridging or rewording to be ethical, that relationship has to be strong, and it must be obvious. If you want to reword or bridge in an impromptu speech, remember these ethical guidelines:

1. Ask yourself whether there is a reasonable relationship between what you are supposed to talk about and what you want to talk about (by either rewording or bridging). A relationship is "reasonable" if the average member of your audience can look at what you are supposed to talk about and clearly see what you want to talk about. If that connection is not readily apparent, the relationship is not reasonable, and you should avoid rewording or bridging in this way.

2. If you are going to reword or bridge, tell the audience what you are doing and why. Don't reword or bridge without notification or explanation. If you fail to tell the audience what you are doing and why, the audience will begin to feel that you are avoiding the topic or question or are being deceitful. People who use this technique in real life— for example, a politician or some other high-ranking official is asked about something but ducks the question by speaking about something else—often lose credibility with an audience.

3. After you reword or bridge and deliver the body of your speech, remember to return to the original topic in your conclusion. Explain the relevance of the rewording or bridge to your original topic once more. Doing so helps the audience to understand exactly why you made the choices you did for the content of the impromptu speech.

All three guidelines will serve you well for either rewording or bridging. However, the first of them (the reasonable relationship test) is especially useful for bridging. In fact, it speaks to the reason we refer to this as bridging in the first place. A bridge in the real world is a structure that connects land masses. The longer a real-world bridge is, the more support it requires to maintain its structural integrity. Without such support, the bridge would collapse of its own weight. Similarly, in an impromptu speech, if the relationship between what you are supposed to discuss and what you want to discuss is not clear, your rhetorical bridge lacks support and you will have to explain why the bridge is reasonable. Possibly, the more you have to explain, the longer the bridge will become, until your explanations sound too flimsy—and lack sufficient reasoning to support the bridge. It is then, to coin a phrase, "a bridge too far." In such a situation, you should not bridge.

If you do follow the guidelines, however, you may certainly reword or bridge, and the audience cannot fairly accuse you of unethically ducking the question or topic or trying to lead them somewhere else.

● *Situational Audience Analysis*

While you are speaking, look at your audience. Quickly assess the audience, and think about the implications of your assessment for your speech. Do you observe any demographic characteristics that might help you? Are there any opportunities for common ground? Have listeners been exposed to this message or position before? What do you think their reaction might be? Use any or all of these questions to refine your message as you speak.

Let us assume that our first speaker reworded her topic to "Always tell the truth and you will be lonely." She observes that many members of her audience are young and some are in couples. She mentions this to the audi-

View a student performing audience analysis in an impromptu speech.
CD-ROM: Video Theater, Excerpt 17.2

ence and then says that she, too, is in a romantic relationship. She argues against her position, saying that "truthfulness" is important in her relationship—as it is in theirs. She then asks whether there are some things people really don't want their lovers to tell them. Are there some topics people prefer not to be honest about? She offers some common examples—such as your mate's appearance (assuming he or she asks).

Let us assume that our second speaker bridges to the topic "Should the government subsidize all education for any citizen desiring to be educated?" In his audience he observes many college students who have to work, as well as apply for loans and get parental assistance, to pay for their higher education. He is in the same situation. He thinks of the stress his job causes him when he has to study, and he thinks of the strain that receiving money from his parents places on his relationship with them. So he mentions these difficulties and asks rhetorically how many people in the audience have experienced a similar situation. He knows that many in the audience are politically conservative and oppose government subsidies for anything, but he reasons that they may be open to his position if he brings the bridged topic down to their level and makes it personal to their situation.

Both speakers make use of audience analysis to polish and craft the content of their messages.

3. Delivering Your Speech

After brief preparation time, the final step is to deliver your impromptu speech. The topic is clear to you, and you have decided on your position and your reasoning or examples. If you needed to reword or bridge, you have done so. The message you are delivering is strongly influenced by your audience. At this point, there are two important relationships to remember.

● The Relationship of Structure and Retention

As you speak, continually remind the audience of your structure. This means *previewing* what you are going to say in the body of your speech, *signposting* between transitions in the body of the speech, and *summarizing* main points in your conclusion. Ostensibly, you do this so listeners can follow you through the speech. But equally important, you do this for yourself, to help you remember what you have thought about and promised to say. It is as much for your retention as for the audience's.

Use your CD-ROM to view an example of using structure to aid audience retention in an impromptu speech. Go to the "Example" button in "Step 5 Delivery/Emphasize Structure." CD-ROM: Interactive Speech Guides/Impromptu Speech

● The Relationship of Structure and Speech Symmetry

Also consider the need for symmetry or a sense of balance in your impromptu speech. As you wind down to the conclusion of this speech (described earlier as a simple summary and restatement of your thesis or topic statement), consider the possibility of returning to whatever introductory device you used (if you used one). If you began with a story, anecdote, or joke, perhaps return to it in the conclusion. If you began by quickly rewording or bridging, return to the original wording, or go back over the bridge, tying the topics together again. Doing so reminds the audience that

Use your CD-ROM to view examples of good delivery in an impromptu speech. Go to the "Example" button in "Step 5 Delivery/Structure and Symmetry." CD-ROM: Interactive Speech Guides/Impromptu Speech

you are aware of what you've discussed, and it leaves listeners with a sense of symmetry, of ending where you and they began. This can increase the audience's confidence that you know what you are doing and have been in control of (not controlled by) the topic.

Summary

Impromptu speaking is used in situations that call for spontaneous speech. You are given a topic—often in the form of a question—and are asked to give a presentation. Whether or not your speech class includes an assignment on this form of speech making, your life in the real world will definitely present you with many such situations.

This Speech Guide presented a three-step process to follow in an impromptu speaking situation. The steps are summarized in the checklist (include any additional steps that your instructor advises or assigns). If you follow these guidelines, you will be a capable speaker who can earn the respect of your audience.

Checklist

INVENTING YOUR IMPROMPTU SPEECH

Determine the True Meaning of the Topic or Question

____ If your topic is abstract, what does it mean to you? (p. 498)

____ If your topic is stated as a question or saying, what is it asking or saying? (p. 498)

Determine Your Position on the Question or Topic

____ What is your position about the topic or question? (p. 499)

Decide What Reasons or Examples Support Your Position

____ Are there arguments or reasons behind your position? (p. 499)

____ What examples could you use to support your position? (p. 499)

DETERMINING THE CONTENT OF YOUR IMPROMPTU SPEECH

Structuring the Message and Invention of Your Speech

____ The first two steps of invention become the thesis or topic statement of your speech (p. 500)

____ Reasoning and examples become the body of your speech (p. 500)

Rewording or Bridging

____ Ask whether there is a reasonable relationship between what you are supposed to talk about and what you want to talk about (p. 501)

____ Tell the audience if you are going to reword or bridge, and tell them why (p. 502)

    C. As the southern sea otter case demonstrates, however, there were and are problems with translocation.

        1. As of 1998, only nine of the original 139 sea otters moved to the island were still known to be there. Where did the majority of this translocated population go?

        2. Andrew Johnson, program manager for sea otter research and conservation at the Monterey Bay Aquarium, interviewed May 15, 2001, thinks some of the otters may have moved on to other channel islands and that a small number may have died.

        3. The larger amount of this population (over one hundred southern sea otters), he believes, have moved *back* to waters south of Point Conception — meaning, in effect, that in spite of a ten-year effort to protect and grow this population in another location — the sea otters have gone back to where they were before.

        4. And this is the problem with translocation: when an animal's instincts become superior to human desire to move these animals to accommodate a number of interests, the animal's instincts will usually win out.

Conclusion

   I. Translocation is a human concept, and as we have seen, it deals with complex environmental, political, and economic issues. The decisions and judgments made regarding competing interests will always be made by human beings.

  II. But as we have learned in the case of the southern sea otter — animals have their instincts, too.

References

Friends of the Sea Otter. (2001, May.) *Oil: The number one threat to the sea otter.* Retrieved from http://www.seaotters.org

Johnson, A. (2001, May 15). Interview at Monterey Bay Aquarium.

Public Law #99-625. (1986.) *The translocation law.* Retrieved from http://www.seaotters.org

Gender-Based Responses in Sports Chatrooms

See page 376 for the full text of this informative speech by Amanda J. List.

Introduction

   I. One of the things we learned very early in this class on human communication and technology was that a very specific kind of technology, computer-mediated communication, has changed the way we communicate with one another. Earlier this semester it was suggested that computer-mediated communication, like that of the Internet, may possibly alter or evolve the way that women and men communicate with each other, as it all but eliminates face-to-face contact.

  II. I thought that it would be interesting to test this theory, that the Internet alters the manner in which the sexes communicate with one another, in an arena (no pun intended) that interests me: professional sports. To be specific, baseball, football, and especially basketball; admittedly, hockey doesn't interest me in the slightest.

III. All of that having been said, today I want to demonstrate how I did a study to test whether or not the Internet truly does alter the way women and men communicate with each other on the topic of sports. I'm going to show you what I did, step-by-step, so that you can see how I reached my conclusion.

IV. First, we'll talk about how to create a working hypothesis that we can prove or disprove through experimentation. Next we'll talk about methodology: I am going to show you how you may set up a similar experiment that relates to you. For example, if one of the males in this class has an interest in knitting and has found that his maverick approach to purling is ridiculed or completely ignored by women he tries to discuss it with, he may wish to undertake a similar experiment in the Internet's undoubtedly boundless array of knitting chatrooms. By the same token, if one of the women in this room has an affinity for antique John Deere tractors, and yet has found that her method for mending a damaged chassis is overlooked despite the fact that it is completely with merit, she may wish to conduct a similar experiment in the virtual land of tractors. I'll present you with a methodology that you may put to use in your own studies. Finally, I'll show you what it is like to go online in this environment, and how to interpret the results we find.

Transition: The first step, then, is to create a working hypothesis.

Body

I. It has been my experience that I am treated as peculiar or odd when I discuss sports, even though I am very knowledgeable about sports.
   A. It would seem that women are not expected to know anything about a pitcher's ERA or a particular basketball player's tendency to miss the second in a one-and-one late in a game.
   B. When I make informed, relevant comments on a sports-related topic, especially in the presence of men, I am often met with the remark, "You sure do know a lot about sports, *for a woman!*"
   C. Having found this in the real world, I expected to find females treated in exactly the same manner online when discussing sports.
   D. I have drawn upon these experiences to create the following working hypothesis: *Assuming gender is obvious, the treatment that one receives online when discussing sports-related topics will be congruous to the treatment a person encounters in face-to-face situations.*

Transition: I am now going to move on to my discussion about methodology.

II. For the purpose of this study I created three online personas.
   A. One persona is obviously female, one is obviously male, and one is an androgynous person. The personas are very similar to each other in every respect except gender.
   B. In addition to simply creating gender-specific screen names, I also created profiles of all three personas: "Im90sGirl," "Johnny1208" and "JRG1243."

C. Although the screen names I chose are obviously gender specific (except for "JRG1243," which I purposely made androgynous), I also needed to create a profile for each character to support. These profiles gave information identifying me (respectively) as female, male, and unclear. For example, as my female identity, I gave my name as "Jill" in the profile, "Johnny" for the male, and "J.R." for the unclear profile.

D. Once I had my new identities, I was ready to foray into the world of cyber sports. I went online as all three characters at three different times of the day. The three time periods are early afternoon (1 P.M. to 5 P.M.), evening (5 P.M. to 7 P.M.), and late night (9 P.M. to midnight). I chose these three time periods in an effort to interact with a wide variety of people who would be in the chatrooms at varying times of the day.

E. My method for this study was to enter sports chatrooms as all three personas and make similar comments. In this manner I was able to observe the reactions of presumably the same participants in a chatroom to each of the three characters.

Transition: Next, let's find out what I experienced when going online.

III. I received different responses, depending on which persona I used.
   A. I went online in the early afternoon on several occasions during the study.
      1. At that particular time of the day I discovered that the overall mentality level of the participants in sports chatrooms was at about the junior high school level. The conversations taking place among the participants were banal, occasionally rude, and generally profane. At this time of the day the conversations had little, if anything, to do with sports.
      2. When I entered the sports chatrooms in the early afternoon as Johnny, I was almost always immediately insulted. During one particular foray into America Online's "Sports Center 5" chatroom, I was quickly asked which team I liked in the NBA playoffs. I replied that I thought L.A. would definitely win the title yet again this year. I was then bombarded with messages insulting the Lakers and my "manhood."
      3. A little later, I quickly signed on again as Jill. After many offers of cyber sex and insults (due to my rejections of those offers), I finally was asked which team I liked in the NBA playoffs. I gave the same answer as before. While I was again insulted by all the same participants who insulted me as Johnny, I was now thwarted with comments such as "Girls don't know anything about basketball" or "Dumb idiot, get out of here."
      4. When I signed on again as my androgynous persona, J.R., I was immediately questioned as to what gender I was. (I did not answer.) I gave the same answer to the question about the NBA, and while I was again insulted, none of the comments referenced my gender.

B. Gratefully, the level of discourse was much higher during the early evening hours, even in the same "Sports Center 5" chatroom.
   1. There were very few age/sex checks and also very few insults. I looked at several of the participants' profiles at this time of the day and discovered that their ages averaged between 20 and 40, and most were in school or were professionals. The conversations at this time of the day were only about sports, and the participants generally stuck to the topic at hand. The participants mostly backed them up with opinions, facts, and explanations.
   2. As Johnny, my comments and opinions were acknowledged and sometimes countered. I was invited into the conversation and began to really feel like "one of the guys." As Johnny, I did make certain to make one comment to purposely show ignorance about sports: I confused the Sacramento Kings with the Los Angeles Kings during a discussion of the NHL. I was mildly flamed for this comment, but I was not told that I didn't belong there, nor was I asked to leave.
   3. As Jill, during the evening hours, I was generally ignored, although I did receive a few Instant Messages requesting cyber sex. I was not welcomed into the conversations, and when I did interject a comment, I was either ignored or given a perfunctory response. As Jill, I was never asked for my opinion in the sports chatrooms during this time of day.
   4. As Jill, I again made an uneducated comment, calling the Cleveland Cavaliers the "Ohio" Cavaliers. I was told to leave the sports chat area and told that women shouldn't be in those rooms.
C. My late-night excursions into the AOL sports chatrooms were similar in many ways to my ventures in the same rooms in the early afternoons: the banter was again inane and often had very little to do with sports.
   1. As Johnny, I was again involved in conversations that centered around sports, but the other participants were much quicker to insult than the participants earlier in the evening.
   2. Frankly, it was almost impossible to conduct any kind of study as a female in the chatrooms late at night: I was sent Instant Messages literally constantly, most of which requested cyber sex. What comments I was able to make in the AOL sports chatrooms were, again, mostly ignored. I was not asked about my opinion even after I had established that I knew a lot about the topic being discussed. On one of these occasions when I was complimented for being a knowledgeable female, I replied, "I'm a lesbian." The man who had complimented me then responded, "That explains it," and quickly left the room.
   3. As my androgynous persona, I was asked a few times what my gender was, but I was again mostly treated like a male. I was flamed for following certain teams, but I was also asked my opinions and involved in what little conversation was going on.

Transition: From our experience today, and from the experiences I have told you about, we can draw our conclusion.

Conclusion

I. I have found my hypothesis to be accurate. Online, as in face-to-face situations, women's comments and participation in sports conversation with men are neither invited nor particularly welcomed. It would appear that no matter how much a woman knows about sports, her comments are not gladly received by her male counterparts. In fact, the treatment that I received during this study as Jill was consistent among the three different time periods.

II. On those occasions when I made willfully ignorant comments I was invariably flamed. As a male I was flamed for saying something stupid; but as a female I was flamed for saying something stupid *and* for being a female.

III. The other interesting result of my study was that when I went online as my androgynous persona, J.R., most of the participants I encountered seemed to assume that I was a male and treated me as such.

"Extra Credit" You Can Live Without

See page 408 for the full text of this persuasive speech by Anna Martinez.

Introduction

I. There is a dangerous product on our campus. It is marketed on tables outside the student union and advertised on the bulletin board in this classroom. Based on my audience survey, it is likely that most of you have this product in your possession right now. By the end of my speech, this product may be costing you more than it is right now. The dangerous product is credit cards.

II. Today, I would like to discuss the problems created by college students' credit cards, and hopefully persuade you to be a careful credit card consumer.

III. If your credit card situation is anything like mine—and over two-thirds of this class indicated that they are currently carrying a balance on one or more cards—take note: you *can* save money!

IV. My husband and I paid for our own wedding last summer. More accurately, we used our credit cards to charge many of our wedding expenses. And thanks to Visa, we are still paying for our wedding every month! We have saved some money we might otherwise have had to pay Visa by following the suggestions I will present today, and you can do the same.

V. To that end, let's cover some of the problems created by students' credit card debt, then analyze causes of the problem, and finally consider steps you can take to be a careful credit card consumer.

Transition: We'll start with a look at the problems created by these "hazardous products."

Body

I. Credit card debt on campus is a significant and growing problem.
   A. Many students have credit card debts.
      1. This claim is supported by the analysis of Alan Blair, director of credit management for the New England Educational Loan Marketing Corporation, whose 1998 report on the corporation's

Web site stated that "67% of undergraduates who have applied for their student loans have credit cards. 14% have balances between $3,000 and $7,000 and 10% have balances over $7,000."

2. Visa must not be the only card they will ever need because Mr. Blair reported that 27% of undergraduates have four or more cards.

3. There must be plenty of businesses that "do take American Express" (and any other card). Sharon Gerrie, staff writer for the *Las Vegas Business Press,* September 4, 1998, reported a National Center for Financial Education survey indicating an average undergraduate credit card debt of $2,226 in 1997. If you are not sure how your balances compare, you are not alone. The study found that 20% did not know how much credit card debt they were accumulating each month.

B. High credit card debt can change your life for the worse.

1. *Business Week,* March 15, 1999 (author unavailable), provided an example of how high debt can change a college student's life for the worse. Jason Britton, a senior at Georgetown University, accumulated $21,000 in debt over four years on sixteen cards! Jason reports that "when I first started, my attitude was 'I'll get a job after college to pay off all my debt.'" Then he realized that he was in a hole because he could not meet minimum monthly payments. He had to obtain financial assistance from his parents and now works three part-time jobs.

2. You probably do not owe $20,000 on your credit cards, but even smaller balances take their toll. Robert Frick, associate editor for *Kiplinger's Personal Finance Magazine,* March 1997, states that if you make the minimum payments on a $500 balance at an 18 percent interest rate, it will take over seven years to pay off the loan and cost $365 in interest.

3. High credit card debt can also haunt your finances after you graduate.

   a. Most of you carry student loans. Dr. Sandy Blum, professor of economics at Skidmore, in a February 1998 report on the New England Educational Loan Corporation Web site, notes that the average percentage of borrowers' monthly income that goes to student loan payment is 12 percent.

   b. When you put credit card debt on top of loan debt, rent, utilities, food, the payment on that new car you want to buy, family expenses, etc., the toll can be heavy.

   c. Don't let this happen to you. After all that hard work earning a degree and finally landing a job where you don't have to wear a plastic name tag and induce people to get "fries with that order," the last thing any of us needs is to be spending our hard-earned money paying off debt, being turned down for loans, or, worse yet, being harassed by collection agencies.

Transition: Credit card debt is hazardous to students' financial health, so why are these debts piling up? Let's move on to the causes of this problem.

II. The reality is that credit card issuers want and aggressively seek the business of students like ourselves.
   A. Card issuers hope to build a long-term relationship with new customers. According to the previously cited March 1997 article by Robert Frick, "It may seem foolhardy to [give] a $500 credit line to someone who has no income or credit history. But on college campuses the practice has proved to be profitable for credit card issuers eager to get their cards into the hands of young consumers before their competitors do."
   B. Card issuers actually troll for customers on campus because student business is profitable. Daniel Eisenberg, writer of the column "Your Money" for *Time* magazine, September 28, 1998, notes that "college students are suckers for free stuff, and many are collecting extra credit cards and heavier debts as a result." Eisenberg goes on to note that "according to a U.S. Public Interest Research Group survey out last week, students who sign up for cards at campus tables in return for 'gifts' typically carry higher unpaid balances than do other students. Visa says students generally pay bills faster than [other] cardholders."
   C. Companies use "sucker rates" to induce students to apply for credit. *Business Week,* March 15, 1999, wrote "credit card marketers may advertise a low annual percentage rate but it often jumps substantially after three to nine months. First USA's student Visa has a 9.9% introductory rate that soars to 17.99% after five months. Teaser rates aren't unique to student cards, but a 1998 study by the Washington based U.S. Public Interest Research Group found that 26% of college students found them misleading."

Transition: So it appears that credit card companies will not stop demanding student business any time soon. What can we do about it?

III. My proposed solution is to be a careful credit card consumer.
   A. Why not get rid of your credit cards before it's too late? Here is my MasterCard and a good pair of scissors. I am going to cut this card in half. [*Display visual aid:* Cut the card in half.] I have brought a bag of scissors, why don't you get out your cards and do the same?
   B. All right, maybe you won't go for that solution. My survey indicated that most of you enjoy the flexibility in spending that credit cards provide. I have a confession to make—that was an expired card that I just cut. I am not cutting my new MasterCard either.
   C. So here are some other ways you should be credit card smart.
      1. One practice is to shop carefully for the best credit card rate. The companies that are not spending their money giving away pizzas and T-shirts on campus may be able to offer you a better deal.
      2. A second solution is to read the fine print on credit card applications to learn what your actual interest rate will be.
         a. Alison Barros, staff writer for the Lane Community College *Torch,* October 29, 1998, quoted Jonathan Woolworth, consumer protection director for the Oregon Public Interest

Research Group, who wrote that "students need to read the fine print and find out how long those low interest rates last. Rates that are as low as 3% can jump to 18% within three months, and the credit card company doesn't want the student to know that."

b. Here is an example of the fine print on an ad that begins at 1.9 percent and soon rises. [*Display visual aid:* actual credit card advertisement, highlighting the teaser rate and indicating the regular rate in fine print.] If you read the fine print, you note that the rate can rise to more than 20 percent.

3. Third, even if you can only make the minimum payment on your cards, pay your bills on time.

a. Robert Frick's previously cited 1997 *Kiplinger's Personal Finance Magazine* article advises that "a strong credit history can mean lower rates on loans and brownie points with employers, landlords, and insurance companies. The best way to build good credit is to use the card, ideally making several small transactions each month and then paying the bill on time or even early."

b. Finally, take responsibility to find out when your bills are due. Credit card companies are even less tolerant of excuses for lateness than speech instructors! *Business Week,* March 15, 1999, cautions that "because students move often and may not get their mail forwarded quickly, bills can get lost. Then the students fall prey to late payment fees."

4. Finally, you can keep money in your pocket and out of the credit card company's by paying attention to your credit report.

a. Tess Van Duvall, a debt management consultant at Emory University, advised in the September 1997 *USA Today* magazine, "If there are errors on your credit report, they need to be corrected, because it can affect your credit rating and even keep you from getting lower interest rate loans."

b. She goes on to note that "one 30-day late payment can make a difference in your loan interest rate."

Internal summary: To sum up these solutions, even if you do not want to stop using credit cards, there are many ways to be a careful credit card consumer. Shop for a good rate and be careful to read the fine print so you know what the rate really is. Know what you owe and take the responsibility to make payments on time.

Conclusion

I. This morning, we have learned about a hazardous product on campus —credit cards. We have noted the problem of high student credit card debt, analyzed some of the causes of this problem, and considered several methods for being a careful credit card consumer.

II. If an instructor offers you a chance for extra credit in his or her class, take advantage of the opportunity. But when a credit card issuer offers you a free T-shirt or phone card if you will sign up for their extra credit, just say no. When you pay off a credit card with a 19.9 percent interest rate, that "free T-shirt" could turn out to be the most expensive clothing you will ever buy.

References

A hard lesson on credit cards (1999, March 15). *Business Week, 3620,* 197.

Barros, A. (1998, October 29). Free candy can lead to the cavity of student debt. *The (Lane Community College) Torch.* Retrieved from http://www.lanecc.edu/torch/102998/candy.html

Blair, A. D. (1998). A high wire act: Balancing student loan and credit card debt. *New England Educational Loan Corporation Website.* Retrieved from http://www.nelliemae.com/about/balance.htm

Blum, S. (1998, February). Life after debt: Results of the national student loan survey. *New England Educational Loan Corporation Website.* Retrieved from http://www.nelliemae.com/about/life.htm

Eisenberg, D. (1998, September 28). Too much college credit? *Time, 152,* 95.

Frick, R. (1997, March). Credit-smart college students. *Kiplinger's Personal Finance Magazine, 51,* 121.

Gerrie, S. (1998, September 4). Students graduate with credit card debt. *Las Vegas Business Press.* Retrieved from http://www.lvbusiness.com/news/columns/98090406o.html

Good financial health begins in college. (1997, September). *USA Today (Magazine), 126,* 8.

Key-Word Outlines

Without Liberty and Justice for All

See page 414 for the full text of this informative speech by Enrique Morales.

Introduction
  I. Story about being stopped by police when driving with my friend in his new BMW. Victims of racial profiling. . . . Police apologized but if truly sorry would not let it happen again.
 II. Violations should not happen again and again and again. Today, will discuss steps to be taken to promote color-blind policing.
III. Pulled over twice without explanation, my research indicates not atypical.
 IV. Eleven class members are minorities. David pulled over—long hair and VW van. Any starving student in old car at risk of being guilty until proven innocent.
  V. Nationwide problem, remedies, reforms can be effective, you should take active role

Transition

Body
  I. Racial profiling is nationwide problem.
   A. Extensive
      1. Temple prof. of psych. John Lanbreth found that in New Jersey, blacks are almost five times more likely to be stopped on the New Jersey Turnpike than others. In Maryland, 71.3 percent of those searched by state police on Interstate 95 were black.

*Notice that in a key-word outline,
information from evidence sources
is cited word-for-word.*

    2. Joseph McNamara, former police chief in San Jose, notes on the Intellectual Capital.com *Issue of the Week,* June 3, 1999, "Unfortunately, police are more suspicious of people of color. . . . Police are under pressure to produce good arrest statistics, thus they are tempted to cut corners by employing racial profiling."

  B. Racial profiling unconscionable

    1. Discriminates against innocent citizens. After checking my registration, the officer told me, "We thought you were somebody else. Sorry about that." Wanted to vent anger, but police had handcuffs and weapons. Kept thoughts to myself. Liberty and justice for all?

    2. Undermines confidence in the police. From the Statistical Assessment Service, a nonpartisan, nonprofit research organization, *VitalSTATS,* April 1999, "most blacks who are stopped on suspicion (like most males) will be innocent people. And the more innocent people within a given group who are treated as suspect, the more all members of the group will suspect discriminatory motives on the part of the police."

    3. Parents teach kids police are their friends. Who needs enemies?

Transition

  II. Treatments for reducing racial profiling

    A. Police keep accurate records of who they stop, enabling community members to act where needed. Reports = basis for action.

    B. Hire more minority officers. Study by John Donohue III of Stanford Law School and Steven Levitt of the University of Chicago, *Business Week,* May 3, 1999, "The higher the share of police officers of a particular race in a neighborhood dominated by the same race, the lower the number of arrests (of people of that race) in the neighborhood." Article concludes "own race policing appears to pay off by reducing both arrests and property crime—presumably because it leads to fewer false arrests and greater deterrence."

    C. Diversity training. George Rice, ten-year Drug Enforcement Agency agent now working on community policing in the nonprofit sector, *Horizon Magazine,* December 1999: "For law enforcement personnel, training and experience are crucial. . . . Like everyone else, police must unlearn this bias and judge people based on their actions alone."

Transition

  III. Compare two Americas. Imagine where you would want to live.

    A. First America tolerates racial profiling. If you ever were stopped because black, brown, Grateful Dead sticker, remember. If never victim, how would you feel about visiting country where Americans routinely stopped by police more than native citizens are?

    B. Imagine second America. Race no role in traffic stops. North Carolina senator Frank Balance Jr., *State Legislatures,* September 1999, "No person in this state or this country should ever have to worry about being pulled over by the police because of the color of their skin." I prefer second America, wouldn't you?

Transition

IV. If you are stopped and suspect profiling, actions to take. Advice comes from George Rice, previously cited:
  A. No need to answer questions, must show license, registration, proof of insurance.
  B. Words you say used against you, can give excuse to arrest you, especially if disrespectful.
  C. Ask for lawyer ASAP if arrested.
  D. Do not complain on the scene or say you will file complaint. Remember badge/patrol car numbers, right afterward, write down all you can remember about incident. Get witnesses' names/phone numbers.
  E. If feel rights violated, file written complaint with internal affairs or civilian complaint board.

Transition

Conclusion
  I. Problem widespread, actions needed to promote an America where driving while black or brown no longer crime. Do right thing if you are victim.
  II. International Police Chiefs 1999 resolution "Condemning Racial and Ethnic Profiling in Traffic Stops" calls on law enforcement agencies to ensure racial or ethnic based stops are not being employed and that all citizens are treated with utmost courtesy and respect when they encounter police officers. This would erase driving while black or brown from American criminal law.

My Hero, Marilyn Hamilton

See page 448 for the full text of this special occasion speech by Lillian Gentz.

Introduction
  I. The accident
  A. Summer day on Tollhouse Mountain, 1979
  B. Marilyn forgets to hook herself to hang glider.
  C. Plunges from Tollhouse Mountain, crashes, and is paralyzed from waist down
  D. Does she become bitter? lose her zest for life? quit? what would you do?
  II. My hero is Marilyn Hamilton.
  III. Worked for Sunrise Medical, where Marilyn has played a major role
  IV. Marilyn's accomplishments
  A. Wheelchair manufacturing company
  B. Tennis and snow ski champion

Transition

Body
  I. Wheelchair manufacturing company wasn't Marilyn's purpose for creating a lightweight wheelchair.
  A. Conventional chairs were bulky, confining, heavy, didn't match her outfits.

B. 1980, the company, Motion Designs, begins operation.
C. 1985, Quickie II, first high-performance folding chair created.
Marilyn named California businessperson of the year.
D. 1986, Motion Designs doing $21 million in sales, sold to Sunrise
Medical.

Transition

II. Marilyn refuses to let paralysis stop her from doing what she enjoyed.
A. Tennis
1. Two-time champion at U.S. Women's Open Wheelchair Tournament
2. 1999, tennis wheelchair displayed in the Smithsonian Institution
B. Snow skiing
1. Six-time National Disabled Ski Champion
2. Won silver medal at the World Winter Disabled Games in Innsbruck, Austria
C. Until two years ago, continued to hang glide

Transition

Conclusion
I. I have told you how Marilyn became paralyzed, how her business was
created, and her accomplishments as an athlete.
II. In closing, I would like to share with you Marilyn Hamilton's favorite
saying. "I am not made or unmade by the things that happen to me,
but rather, by how I react to them." If it were you, how would you
react?

Sample Speech Grids

Gender-Based Responses in Sports Chatrooms

See page 376 for the full text of this informative speech by Amanda J. List.

Topic: Gender and sports chatrooms

Topic statement: My study revealed that gender influences the responses of participants in online sports chatrooms.

Specific purpose: To inform my audience about the findings of my study on the influence of perceived gender on responses in online sports chatrooms.

AUDIENCE ANALYSIS	SPEECH MESSAGE
Situational Characteristics • 7–10 min. speech • 20 in audience • small classroom • no a-v equipment **Demographics** **Age:** 20 (3); 21 (4); 22 (5); 23 (3); 24 (2) **Major:** Undeclared (5); Media Studies (9); Communication Studies (6) **Ethnicity:** U.S.-born (15); Asian American (2) **Gender:** Female (13); Male (4) **Common Ground** • I am an undergraduate like everyone else in the class. • We are all students in this course on technology and human communication. • All of us are required to study online communication behavior. • Most of us in class have significant experience with e-mail and chatroom Internet communication. **Prior Exposure** • Most students were aware of gender bias in communication between men and women in the real world, especially as it relates to discussion about professional sports. • All students were aware of how people (mostly young men) can engage in more frank and sexually aggressive discourse online than in the real world. • Most students in this class were not aware of how males and females interacted online in sports chatrooms, nor were they aware of how males interacted with other males or with androgynous individuals.	**ETHOS** • I am very knowledgeable about sports. • Show audience how they can use a similar methodology on topics that interest them. (goodwill) • I have experience with Internet communication, including chatrooms. **PATHOS** • My informed comments about sports often met with sexist responses. • Many males made offers of cyber sex and insulted me when I said "no." **LOGOS** • Explain what a chatroom is. • Explain "netiquette." • Explain hypothesis: male-female online interaction in sports chatroom will mirror what is found in real world. • Describe how study is set up, including methodology and sample online sites. • Describe creation of online identities, including female, male, and androgynous. • Explain interaction between males and hypothetical male persona. Contrast with interaction between males and female persona, and males and androgynous persona. • Example: with male persona. Welcomed into chatrooms, treated as "one of the guys," flamed when people disagreed, but not asked to leave. • Example: made intentional mistakes. As male persona, flamed but not asked to leave. As female persona, told that women did not belong in those chatrooms. • Example: with androgynous persona. Mostly treated like male, asked for my opinions. • Explain and analyze results of study.

"Extra Credit" You Can Live Without

Topic: College students' credit card use
Thesis: Audience members should be careful credit card consumers.
Specific purpose: To persuade my audience to use credit cards carefully.

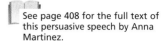

See page 408 for the full text of this persuasive speech by Anna Martinez.

AUDIENCE ANALYSIS	SPEECH MESSAGE
Situational Characteristics • 8–10 min. speech • 20–26 in audience • medium-sized classroom • PowerPoint projector may be available **Demographics** **Age:** 18–20 (7); 20–24 (10); 25–29 (6); over 30 (3) **Major:** Comm. (6), Pol. Sci. (4), Crim. (4), Teacher Ed. (3), Bus. (3), Drama, English, Econ., Pre Law, Chem., Geog. (1 each) **Ethnicity:** White (9); Latino/a (6); African American (4); Asian American (3); Indonesian (1); Swedish (1); Indian (1); did not say (1). **Common Ground** • Most classmates, myself included (20/26), have credit cards. • Most classmates, myself included (19/26), usually carry a balance on one or more cards. • Most classmates, myself included (22/26), expect to have student loans to pay back after graduation. **Prior Exposure** • Many (24 students) have seen credit card representatives on campus. All 26 students have seen advertising on campus. • How informed are you about the issue of student credit card debt? Very informed — 2 Somewhat informed — 6 Slightly informed — 8 Not informed — 10	**ETHOS** • Over ²/₃ of class carries balance on credit cards like I do. (common ground) • I did a lot of research for this speech. (credibility) • I am still paying off credit cards for my wedding bills. (credibility, common ground) • Show class what they can do to reduce credit card costs without giving up credit cards. (goodwill) • I used to work at a bank. (credibility) **PATHOS** • Example of student who was $21k in credit card debt, had to borrow from parents and work three part-time jobs. (Source 1) • Credit card companies use low "sucker rates" that rise to a high level of interest after a few months. (Source 1) • Example of starving, broke student who signed up for credit card because they were giving away free candy. (Source 2) • Students are suckers for free stuff, credit card companies give it away so that students will sign up for their cards. (Source 5) • Large credit card debts are forcing college graduates to delay purchasing a home or having children. (Source 9) • Once you graduate and get a good job where you don't have to wear a plastic name tag, you don't want to spend $$ on debt, get turned down for loans. • Visual aid idea. Create a hypothetical credit card ad that shows a low interest rate in bold and then notes (in tiny fine print) that the rate goes way up after 6 months. • Credit card companies are less tolerant of excuses for lateness than speech instructors. • Dangerous product on campus, many of you have it in your possession right now (possible attention-getter). • It's the only credit card you'll never need (possible attention-getter or joke). **LOGOS** • Solution...stop using credit cards • Solution...government ban free gifts from credit card companies on campus • Solution/visual aid idea...cut credit card in half, encourage classmates to do the same (door-in-the-face approach) • Solution...shop around for lowest possible credit card rate • Solution...join a credit union, get a low-interest loan from them • Solution...try to improve your credit score to over 700 • Solution...read the fine print when you fill out a credit card application

Sample Speech Grid, continued

AUDIENCE ANALYSIS	SPEECH MESSAGE
• Many (15/20) of students with credit cards doubt that they could estimate the balances outstanding within $100. Most (16/20) are not sure what interest rate they are paying. **Audience Disposition** • A minority of cardholders (4/20) have seriously considered canceling all their credit cards. • A minority (3/26) rarely or never expect to use credit cards in the future. • A majority of cardholders (18/20) agree with the statement "Credit cards help me manage my financial situation." • Most students (20/26) would be interested in learning how to save money when they use credit cards.	• Solution…ban credit card solicitors and advertisements from campus • A free T-shirt is not worth the money a 19.9% interest rate will cost you. • Students often move, bills get lost, must pay late fees. (Source 1) • Credit card companies mask high rates in the fine print. (Source 2) • Borrower's average income spent paying back student loans is 12%. (Source 3) • 67% of undergrads get credit cards, many carry high balances. (Source 4) • Students who sign up for credit cards on campus in return for free gifts are profitable customers, tend to carry higher balances. (Source 5) • Companies want students to take their card, want to sign them up before competitors do. (Source 6) • A strong credit history leads to lower loan rates. To get one, use credit cards and pay them off on time. (Source 6) • Average undergrad credit card debt $2,226. (Source 7) • If you can eat, wear, or listen to what you want to charge, it isn't an emergency. Don't put it on credit. (Source 8)

My Hero, Marilyn Hamilton

Topic: My Hero, Marilyn Hamilton

Topic statement: Marilyn Hamilton is my hero because she overcame paralysis by creating a successful business and excelling in athletics.

Specific purpose: To inform my audience of the reasons that Marilyn Hamilton is my hero.

See page 448 for the full text of this special occasion speech by Lillian Gentz.

AUDIENCE ANALYSIS	SPEECH MESSAGE
Situational Characteristics • 5 minute speech • 26 students in class (24 surveys returned) • small classroom • no a.v. equipment **Demographics** **Age:** Under 21 (6); 21–30 (8); 31–40 (6); 41–50 (3); 51–60 (1) **Ethnicity:** African-American (2); Hmong (5); Latino/a (8); White (7); Asian-American (2) **Gender:** Male (10); Female (14) **Educational Background:** All are community college students. Educational objective: taking class because interested, no degree plans (3); A.A. degree (9); transfer to four-year college (12) **Common Ground** • We are all community college students, living in the Central Valley of California. • Like many students (18), one of my reasons for attending college is to gain skills and knowledge that I can use in the workforce. • Like many students (17), I am working while going to school. **Prior Exposure** • Four students knew of Marilyn Hamilton's business successes. None knew of her athletic achievements. • Two students had heard of the Quickie wheelchair. • Most (20 students) were aware that there were athletic competitions for persons with disabilities. Seven students had seen a skiing event (live or on television), and four had seen tennis competition.	**ETHOS** • Living in the Central Valley of California, like Marilyn Hamilton, I have seen and heard news accounts of her successes. • I worked for Sunrise Medical, the company of which Marilyn is vice president. • I did additional research about Marilyn Hamilton for my speech. • Emphasize Marilyn's sports successes because class is interested in sports (goodwill). **PATHOS** • Ask audience members how they felt when they have needed to use a wheelchair. • Ask audience to imagine how they would feel if they suddenly became paralyzed. • Quote Marilyn Hamilton's favorite saying, "I am not made or unmade by the things that happen to me but, rather, by how I react to them." • Contrast the traditional bulky and confining wheelchairs, which did not match Marilyn's outfits, with her hot purple Quickie wheelchair with gold rims. • Narrative account of Marilyn's hang-gliding accident. • People told Marilyn her business would fail because she and her friends lacked business experience. (Source 1) • The Quickie name was based on an aircraft wing, but the other implication of "quickie" allowed for creative marketing slogans. **LOGOS** • Establish criteria to show why a person who overcame paralysis by founding a successful business and achieving athletic success is a hero. • Marilyn Hamilton did not intend to create a multimillion dollar business when she began Motion Designs in a garage with friends Don Helman and Jim Okamoto. • Motion Designs earned $21 million in sales in 1986. • Marilyn Hamilton was named California businessperson of the year (Source 1) • Motion Designs merged with Sunrise Medical, a larger medical equipment business, in December 1986. • Marilyn Hamilton served as Sunrise Medical's vice president for corporate responsibility and later vice president for consumer development.

Sample Speech Grid, continued

AUDIENCE ANALYSIS	SPEECH MESSAGE
• No student in class has needed to use a wheelchair for an extended period of time. Four have used wheelchairs in the hospital. • Few (3 students) know of any person who has received recognition at a sporting competition for disabled people. • Most (23 students) enjoy sports as a competitor or spectator. Twelve are interested in skiing and 11 are interested in tennis. None has ever tried hang gliding. **Disposition** • Most (22 students) would like to learn more about a hero in the local community. • All 24 respondents agreed that by overcoming a disabling accident or injury, a person should be considered a hero.	• Discuss my own reflections as a former employee of Sunrise Medical. • Marilyn founded "Winners on Wheels," an organization that empowers kids in wheelchairs. (Source 2) • I think Marilyn Hamilton is the greatest female athlete in history. • Display slides of Marilyn Hamilton playing tennis and skiing. • Pass pictures of Marilyn playing her sports around the audience. • Display pictures (get them blown up at Kinkos) of Marilyn playing her sports. • Marilyn was a two-time winner of the U.S. Women's Open Wheelchair Tennis Tournament. • Visual aid idea — list of Marilyn's athletic awards. • In 1999, her tennis wheelchair was on display at the Smithsonian Institution. • Marilyn spoke at the 2001 U.S. Women's Open Wheelchair Tournament Banquet. (Source 3) • Marilyn was a six-time National Disabled ski champion. • Summarize history of the World Winter Games. • Marilyn won the Silver Medal at the 1988 World Winter Disabled Games. (Source 4) • Marilyn continued hang gliding after her injury, only retiring two years ago.

APPENDIX B
A Short Guide to MLA and APA Citation Formats

When completing your speech outline or your full speech text for a researched speech, you must clearly identify all the sources you quote from, summarize, or paraphrase. To do so, you will need a style of documentation. You will use it to prepare a list called "References" or "Works Cited" for your speech. The list should be included at the end of any speech outline or full speech text that includes researched sources.

Styles of documentation have been established by academic and professional societies and journals to regularize the citing of sources. Social scientists often cite their sources with parenthetical in-text references, not numbered notes, and follow guidelines recommended by the American Psychological Association (APA). Writers in the humanities, including artists, philosophers, and literature scholars, use the style recommended by the Modern Language Association of America (MLA). Ask your instructor what style of documentation he or she prefers you to use. In this appendix we explain some conventions of both MLA and APA styles.

MLA Documentation Style: Basic Procedures

Here we explain briefly how to use MLA style to document the kinds of sources you are likely to cite in a researched speech text written for a college course. For complete information on MLA style, see Joseph Gibaldi, *MLA Handbook for Writers of Research Papers,* fifth edition (New York: Modern Language Association, 1999).

Start the MLA "Works Cited" list on a separate page at the end of your paper. All of the works you cite in your speech should be listed alphabetically by the author's last name or by the title if the work is anonymous.

● *Books*

1. A Book by One Author Citations for most books are arranged in this order:

1. Author's name (last name first)
2. Title and subtitle (underlined)
3. City of publication
4. Name of publisher, shortened as MLA recommends in Section 6.5 of the *MLA Handbook*

5. Date of publication

6. Page numbers

Wilson, Edward O. <u>The Diversity of Life</u>. New York: Norton, 1992. 94–98.

2. A Book by Two or Three Authors or Editors   Begin with the first author (or editor) listed on the title page, last name first; then list the names of the other authors (or editors), first name first. Separate the names with a comma, and insert *and* before the final name listed. Editors' names are followed by a comma and the abbreviation *eds.* If a book has only one editor, use *ed.*

Harrison, Barbara, and Gregory Maguire, eds. <u>Innocence and Experience: Essays and Conversations on Children's Literature</u>. New York: Lothrop, 1987. 173–81.

3. A Book by Four or More Authors   Begin with the first author listed on the title page, last name first, followed by a comma. Then use the abbreviation *et al.* ("and others") in place of the other authors' names.

Matsuda, Mari, et al. <u>Words That Wound: Critical Race Theory, Assaultive Speech, and the First Amendment</u>. Boulder: Westview, 1993.

4. An Anonymous Book   Begin the citation with the title, not with *Anonymous* or *Anon.* Alphabetize the entry by the title, ignoring an initial *A, An,* or *The.*

<u>The Merriam-Webster New Book of Word Histories</u>. Springfield: Merriam, 1991.

5. A Work in an Anthology   Add to your basic book entry this information: author's name, selection title, and translator (if any). Start with the author and title of the essay, short story, poem, or another work that appears in the anthology, and enclose the selection title in quotation marks.

Cheng-Ming, Wen. "Written While Sick." Trans. Jonathan Chaves. <u>The Columbia Book of Later Chinese Poetry</u>. Ed. Jonathan Chaves. New York: Columbia UP, 1980. 223.

6. An Article in a Reference Book   When citing an article in an encyclopedia or an entry in a dictionary, give the author's name first if the article is signed. Otherwise, begin with the title. If the reference work arranges articles alphabetically, omit the volume and page numbers. If you are citing a familiar reference book, such as a collegiate dictionary or the *Encyclopaedia Britannica,* do not cite the editor, and list only the edition and the year of publication. Otherwise, give full publication information.

"Noon." <u>The Oxford English Dictionary</u>. 2nd ed. 1989.

"The Fight to Mate." <u>The Encyclopedia of Mammals</u>. New York: Checkmark Books, 1984.

● *Articles and Other Items in Periodicals*

7. An Article in a Magazine   Begin with the author's name, the article title, and the title of the magazine, followed by the full date and page number(s). For MLA-style abbreviations of the names of the months (except May, June, and July), see Section 6.2 of the *MLA Handbook*.

Morrow, Barbara. "The Realms of Mackinac." Midwest Living May–June 2001: 81–88.

Roderick, Stephen. "Big Man Temporarily on Campus." The New York Times
        Magazine 25 Nov. 2001: 56–59.

8. An Article in a Scholarly Journal   Scholarly journals are usually issued no more than four times a year. Most print journals are paginated continuously throughout each annual volume. Start with the author's name—last name first—then the title of the article, then publication information. The volume number follows the journal's title. Provide the issue number only if each issue begins on page 1. Be sure to put the year of publication in parentheses.

Crenshaw, Martha. "Why America? The Globalization of Civil War." Current History
        100.650 (2001): 425–32.

9. An Article in a Newspaper   Begin with the author's name—last name first—then the title of the article. When documenting a newspaper article, give the name of the newspaper as it appears on the masthead, but omit an introductory *A, An,* or *The* (*New York Times* not *The New York Times*). If the city of publication is not part of the name of a locally published newspaper, identify the city in square brackets after the name. For nationally published newspapers, do not add the city of publication. After the name of the newspaper, give the day, month, and year of publication. Do not provide volume and issue numbers even if they are listed. If an edition is named on the masthead, add a comma after the date and specify the edition. After the publication information, give the page number(s), preceded by a colon. If the article begins on one page and ends on another, give only the first page number, followed by a plus sign.

Glader, Paul. "Rooster Breeders Lobby to Thwart Cockfight Ban." Wall Street
        Journal 28 Dec. 2001: A9+.

10. An Anonymous Article   If the author of the article you are citing is not identified, begin with the article title. Ignore an initial *A, An,* or *The* when you alphabetize the entry.

"True Believer." Newsweek 24 Dec. 2001: 38–39.

11. An Editorial in a Newspaper   Begin the citation as you would an entry for a newspaper article. If the editorial is signed, list the author's name first. If no author is identified, begin with the title. After the title, add the word *Editorial,* preceded by a period but neither underlined nor in quotation marks.

Reynolds, Glenn Hablan. "Community by the Book." Editorial. Wall Street Journal
    28 Dec. 2001: A16.

12. A Letter to the Editor   To identify a letter to the editor, add the label
Letter after the name of the author. Do not underline the word or place it in
quotation marks.

Sullivan, Ned. Letter. Wall Street Journal 28 Dec. 2001: A17.

● Government Documents

13. A Government Publication   Government publications present special
problems. If the author of the document is not identified, list the name of
the government first, followed by the name of the agency, using an abbreviation if the context makes it clear. Then give the title. End the citation
with the place and year of publication.

United States. Cong. House. Committee on the Judiciary. National Film Preservation
    Act of 1996. 104th Cong., 2nd sess. H. Rept. 104-58. Washington: GPO, 1996.

● Nonprint Sources

14. A Television or Radio Program   When citing a television or radio program, list the information in the following order:

1. Title of episode or segment (in quotation marks)
2. Title of program (underlined)
3. Title of series, if any (neither underlined nor in quotation marks)
4. Name of network
5. Call letters and city of local station (if any)
6. Broadcast date

Include any other pertinent information (e.g., performers, director, narrator,
number of episodes) between the title and the distributor.

"Frankenstein: The Making of the Monster." Great Books. Narr. Donald Sutherland.
    Writ. Eugenie Vink. Dir. Jonathan Ward. Learning Channel. 8 Sept. 1993.

15. A Sound Recording   List the title of the recording, the artist(s), the
manufacturer, and the year of issue. If the year is unknown, write *n.d.* (for "no
date"). Place a comma between the manufacturer and the date. Place periods
after the other items. If you are not using a CD, indicate the medium, neither
underlined nor enclosed in quotation marks, before the manufacturer's
name. Underline titles of recordings but do not underline or enclose in quotation marks the titles of musical compositions identified only by form, number, and key. Indicate the date of recording in addition to the year of issue.

Pontiac. Lyle Lovett. Audiocassette. MCA Records, 1987.

Mahler, Gustav. Symphony no. 7 in E minor. Perf. Leonard Bernstein et al. Sony,
    2001.

16. A Film or Video   Begin with the title, underlined, and include the director, the distributor, and the year of release. You may include other relevant information—such as the names of the writer, performers, and pro-ducer—between the title and the distributor.

It's a Wonderful Life. Dir. Frank Capra. Perf. James Stewart, Donna Reed, Lionel
Barrymore, and Thomas Mitchell. RKO, 1946.

17. An Interview   Begin with the name of the person interviewed. If the interview is part of a publication, recording, or program, enclose the title of the interview in quotation marks. If the interview is untitled, use the de-scriptive label *Interview,* and do not underline it or enclose it in quotation marks. Conclude with the relevant bibliographic information.

Blackmun, Harry. Interview with Ted Koppel and Nina Totenberg. Nightline. ABC.
WABC, New York. 5 Apr. 1994.

18. A Cartoon   Begin with the cartoonist's name. Then list the title of the cartoon (if any) in quotation marks, followed by the descriptive label *Car-toon,* neither underlined nor enclosed in quotation marks. Finally, list rele-vant publication information.

Roberts, Victoria. Cartoon. New Yorker 18 Dec. 2000: 43.

19. An Advertisement   Begin with the name of the product, company, or institution being advertised. Follow with the descriptive label *Advertisement,* neither underlined nor enclosed in quotation marks. Finally, list relevant publication information.

Eukanuba Cat Foods. Advertisement. National Geographic May 2001: 13.

● *Electronic Sources*

20. Online Scholarly Project or Reference Database   When citing a complete online scholarly project or reference database, include the following information:

1. Title of the project (underlined)
2. Name of the editor (if given)
3. Electronic publication information, including version number, date of publication or latest update, and name of any sponsoring institution
4. Date on which you accessed the site and the URL in angle brackets

Botanical.com. Vers. 7, 2001. Electric Newt. 30 Jan. 2002. <http://
www.botanical.com/>.

The Baobab Project: Sources and Studies in African Visual Culture. Ed. Suzanne
Preston Blier. 1994. Department of Fine Arts, Harvard University. 17 May 2001
<http://web-dubois.fas.harvard.edu/DuBois/baobab/baobab.html>.

21. A Commercial Web Site   Include the creator of the Web site if known, the site's name, the date of creation or latest update, the name of any organization associated with the site, the date of access, and the URL in angle brackets.

Hitchens, Richard. Holocaust Literature Research Institute. 21 Aug. 1999. U of
      Western Ontario. 14 May 2000 <http://www.arts.uwo.ca/HLRI/>.

22. *A Personal Web Site*   Follow citation guidelines for a commercial Web site. Include the name of the site (if any). If there is no name, include a description such as *Home page* (not underlined or in quotation marks). Personal sites do not have sponsors, and they often include a tilde (~) in the address to identify them as personal sites on a larger server.

An, Hume Hyung Kyu. Home page. 9 Dec. 2001. <http://home.uchicago.edu/
      ~hha1/>.

23. *An E-mail Communication*   To cite an e-mail message, give the name of the writer, the title of the message (if any) taken from the subject line and enclosed in quotation marks, a description of the message that identifies the recipient, and the date of the message.

Bederman, Jill. "Re: Top 10 Restaurants in Chicago." E-mail to Thomas J. Watson.
      20 Aug. 2000.

24. *An Online Posting*   Begin with the author's name and the title of the document in quotation marks. Follow with the description *Online posting* (not underlined and not in quotation marks), the date of the posting, the name of the forum if known, the date of access, and, in angle brackets, the online address of the list's site. If no site is known, list the e-mail address of the list's moderator.

Moore, Kate. "Oedipus Rex." Online posting. 1 Feb. 2001. NCTE-talk. 12 April 2001.
      <http://www.ncte.org/lists/ncte-talk/>.

25. *An Article in an Online Periodical*   In general, follow the guidelines for citing articles or periodicals in print sources, modifying them as appropriate for the electronic source. Be sure to include the following information:

1. Author's name (if given)
2. Title of work
3. Name of periodical (underlined)
4. Volume number, issue number, or other identifying number
5. Date of publication
6. Page numbers, paragraphs, or other sections, if numbered
7. Date of access
8. URL

If you cannot find some of this information, cite what is available.

Barnes, Michael. "Gun Records and Terror." Brady Campaign Newspage, 2, 13 Dec.
      2001, <bradycampaign.org>.

APA Documentation Style: Basic Procedures

Most disciplines in the social sciences—psychology, anthropology, sociology, political science, and economics—use the name-and-date system of documentation established by the American Psychological Association (APA). This citation style highlights publication dates in the text because the currency of published material is of primary importance in these fields. For complete information on APA style, see the *Publication Manual of the American Psychological Association,* fifth edition (Washington, DC: 2001).

● *Books*

1. A Book by One Author   Citations for most books are arranged in this order:

1. Author's name (last name first, followed by the author's first and [if available] middle initials)
2. Date of publication (in parentheses)
3. Title and subtitle (italicized; capitalize only the first word of the title and subtitle and any proper nouns)
4. City of publication
5. Name of publisher

Covey, S. (1990). *Principle centered leadership: teaching timeless principles of effectiveness.* Provo: IPCL.

2. A Book by More Than One Author or Editor

Johnson, S., & Wilson, L. (1984). *The one minute sales person.* New York: Avon Books.

Hogan, L., Metzger, D., & Peterson, B. (Eds.). (1999). *Intimate nature: The bond between women and animals.* New York: Fawcett Books.

3. A Book by a Corporate Author   List the name of the group as the author, capitalizing all major words in the name. When the author and publisher are identical, use the word *Author* after the city of publication.

Legal Assistant Management Association. (1992). *Looking back, looking forward.* Kansas City, MO: Author.

4. An Anonymous Book   When the author of a book is unknown, begin the citation with the title, italicized, followed by the date of publication in parentheses. Conclude with the place of publication and the publisher.

The American heritage dictionary of the English language (4th ed.). (2000). Boston: Houghton Mifflin.

● *Articles or Essays*

5. An Article in a Reference Book   Start with the author of the article, the publication date, and the title. Capitalize only the first word of the article title and subtitle and any proper nouns. Do not underline or italicize the article title and subtitle. Follow with the word *In*, and give the name of the editor (first initial first), followed by *Eds.* in parentheses, and then the title (italicized) of the reference work. Include the volume number (if any) and inclusive page numbers in parentheses. Conclude with the place of publication and the publisher.

Simpson, J. A. (1999). Attachment theory in modern evolutionary perspective. In
    J. Cassidy & P. R. Shaver (Eds.), *Handbook of attachment* (pp. 115–140). New
    York: Guilford Press.

6. An Article in a Scholarly Journal   Start with the author's last name and initials, followed by the date of publication in parentheses. List the title of the article and the title of the journal (italicized). Capitalize all major words in the journal title. Include the volume number. Provide the issue number only if each issue begins on page 1. Conclude with inclusive page numbers.

Cui, S. (2000). Stanley Kwan's *Center stage:* The (im)possible engagement between
    feminism and postmodernism. *Cinema Journal, 39*(4), 60–80.

7. An Article in a Magazine   Begin with the author's last name and initials, followed by the date of publication in parentheses. Next, list the title of the article. Follow with the name of the magazine and the volume number, if available. End with inclusive page numbers of the article.

Lee, T. H. (2002, January). A vertical leap for microchips. *Scientific American, 286,*
    52–59.

8. An Article in a Newspaper   Begin with the author's last name and initials, followed by the date of publication in parentheses. Next, list the title of the article and name of the newspaper. Conclude with the page number(s). If the article begins on one page and ends elsewhere, list all page numbers. Separate discontinuous pages with commas.

Boyd, R. S. (2001, December 9). World's oceans a rising threat. *The Miami Herald,*
    pp. A1, A8–A9.

9. An Editorial in a Newspaper   If the editorial is signed, begin with the author's name; otherwise, start with the title of the editorial. Follow with the publication date (year, month and day) and then the word *Editorial* in brackets. End with the name of the newspaper and the page on which the editorial appears.

Deficit politics returns. (2002, January 8). [Editorial]. *The New York Times,*
    p. A18.

● *Government Documents*

10. A Government Publication   Individuals are not usually listed as authors of government documents. Instead, use the government office as the author, followed by the publication date. Italicize the title of the document, and end with the place of publication and the publisher. When the author and publisher are the same, use the word *Author* as the name of the publisher.

United States Office of Postsecondary Education. (2001). *The incidence of crime on the campuses of U.S. postsecondary education institutions: A report to Congress.* Washington, DC: Author.

● *Nonprint Sources*

11. A Professional Web Site   When citing an entire Web site, list the name of the Web site, followed by the date of creation or last update, if available. Next write the word *Retrieved* and the date you accessed the site, followed by the URL.

American Medical Association. (2001). Retrieved August 4, 2001, from http://www.ama-assn.org/

12. A Personal Web Site   List a personal Web site as you would a professional Web site.

13. An Online Journal or Magazine Article   List an online article as you would a print article.

Gillis, M. (1995). Emerging possibilities for space propulsion [Electronic version]. *NASA Papers, 1*(1), 5. Retrieved June 3, 1996, from http://lerc.nasa.gov/www/PAO/html/wasp/pspaper.htm

14. A Newsgroup Message

Nachbur, J. (1997, June 3). Nutrient & energy metabolism in the elderly symposium. Message posted to news://bionet.molbio.ageing

15. An E-mail Communication   E-mail and other personal correspondence generally are not included in an APA-style reference list because they are not retrievable. Instead, in the text of your speech, mention the name of the correspondent and the date of the message.

16. A Personal Interview   Personal interviews that you conduct are not included in an APA-style reference list. Instead, refer to them in the text of your speech as you would refer to e-mail. For a published interview, use the format for an article.

ACKNOWLEDGMENTS

Tables and Figures

Table 1.1: "Who Do Americans Trust?" Adapted from Gallup Poll, "Level of Trust" (October 14, 2000). <www.gallup.com>. Reprinted with permission; **Figure 1.3:** "Measuring Your Level of Apprehension." Adapted material from *An Introduction to Rhetorical Communication*, 5th Edition, by J. C. McCroskey. © 1986 by J. C. McCroskey. Reprinted with permission of Prentice-Hall, Inc.; **Figure 7.1:** This material courtesy of ASCAR Online, the offical Web site of the American Society of Crows and Ravens (ASCAR). Copyright 2002. All rights reserved; **Figure 8.3:** Excerpt from "The Answer Is on the Tip of Many Tongues" by Geoffrey Numberg. From *The Washington Post National Weekly Edition*, December 17–23, 2001, p. 23. © 2001 The Washington Post. Reprinted with permission.

Illustrations

2: Erich Lessing/Art Resource, NY; **6:** Bob Daemmrich/Stock Boston; **9:** Patrick Henry before the Virginia House of Burgesses (1851) by Peter F. Rothermel. Red Hill, The Patrick Henry Memorial, Brookneal, VA.; **12:** AP Photo/Matt Anderson; **15:** AP Photo/Paul Sakuma; **16:** AP Photo/Damian Dovarganes; **20:** DILBERT reprinted by permission of United Feature Syndicate, Inc.; **26:** Reprinted with special permission of King Features Syndicate; **32:** Superstock; **34:** AP Photo; **36:** Rhoda Sidney/Stock Boston; **39:** AP Photo/Kamenko Pajic; **40:** The New Yorker Collection 1988 Donald Reilly from cartoonbank.com; **44:** Michael Newman/PhotoEdit; **52:** Michael Newman/PhotoEdit; **56:** Superstock; **60:** AP Photo/Pablo Martinez Monsivais; **62:** Bettmann/Corbis; **65:** The New Yorker Collection 2000 Peter Steiner from cartoonbank.com; **66:** David Young-Wolff/PhotoEdit; **71:** Christie's Images/CORBIS; **75:** Bob Daemmrich/Stock Boston; **78:** Bob Daemmrich/Stock Boston; **88:** Superstock; **97:** David Young-Wolff/Photo Edit; **100:** AP Photo/Herbert Knosowski; **103:** AP Photo/Ed Bailey; **106:** AP Photo/John Bazemore; **107:** The New Yorker Collection 2001 Edward Koren from cartoonbank.com; **116:** Robert Rauschenberg, "Retroactive I." The Wadsworth Atheneum Museum of Art, Hartford, CT. Gift of Susan Morse Hilles. ©Robert Rauschenberg/Licensed by VAGA, New York, NY; **122:** Eastcott/Momatiuk/Stone; **127:** Noble Stock/International Stock Photo; **131:** Stone; **140:** Superstock; **146:** Courtesy CNN; **152:** Richard Pasley/Stock Boston; **161:** David Young-Wolff/PhotoEdit; **178:** The Phillips Collection, Washington, D.C. © 2002 Milton Avery Trust/Artists Rights Society "ARS," New York; **193:** Reprinted with special permission of King Features Syndicate; **195:** Reuters/Larry Downing/Archive Photos; **198:** Bob Bowmer/The Washington Post; **202:** By permission of Johnny Hart and Creators Syndicate, Inc.; **224:** Bettmann/Corbis; **231:** James H. Davis/International Stock Photo; **239:** Stan Ries/International Stock Photo; **245:** Graeme Norways/Stone; **262:** Stuart Davis, "Premiere," Los Angeles County Museum of Art, Junior Art Council Fund Museum Purchase, Art Museum Council Fund. Photograph © 2001 Museum Associates/LACMA. © Estate of Stuart Davis/Licensed by VAGA, New York, NY; **265:** left: AP Photo/John Bazemore; right: Esbin/Anderson/Omni-Photo Communications; **275:** AP Photo/J. Scott Applewhite; **278:** Ronnie Kaufman/The Stock Market; **284:** Superstock; **287:** Will Hart/PhotoEdit; **294:** Michelle Bridwell/PhotoEdit; **301:** AP Photo/Marcy Nighswander; **302:** Mark Richards/PhotoEdit; **312:** John Still/Photonica; **315:** Patti McConville/International Stock Photo; **316:** Michael Newman/PhotoEdit; **320:** Rachel Epstein/PhotoEdit; **325:** Bob Daemmrich/Stock Boston; **332:** Derek Croucher/The Stock Market; **338:** Romare Bearden, "She-ba," 1970; paper, cloth, and paint on board, 48 in. x 35.875 in. The Wadsworth Atheneum Museum of Art, Hartford, CT. The Ella Gallup Sumner and Mary Catlin Sumner Collection Fund. © Romare Bearden Foundation/Licensed by VAGA, New York, NY; **340:** Esbin Anderson/Omni-Photo Communications; **345:** Amy C. Etra/PhotoEdit; **348:** Spencer Grant/PhotoEdit; **349:** Michelle Bridwell/PhotoEdit; **357:** Jon Feingersh/Corbisstockmarket; **370:** © Smithsonian American Art Museum, Washington, DC/Art Resource, NY; **406:** Thomas Hart Benton, "Politics, Farming, and Law in Missouri" (detail). Photo © Zeal S. Wright, Jefferson City, MO; © T.H. and R.P. Benton Testamentary Trusts/Licensed by VAGA, New York, NY; **446:** © Fine Art Photographic Library, London/Art Resource, NY; **482:** Corbis. Printed by permission of the Norman Rockwell Family Agency. © 1943 the Norman Rockwell Family Agency.

Index